Foundation ActionScript 3.0 Image Effects

Todd Yard

Foundation ActionScript 3.0 Image Effects

ISBN-13 (pbk): 978-1-4302-1871-5

ISBN-13 (electronic): 978-1-4302-1872-2

Printed and bound in the United States of America 9 8 7 6 5 4 3 2 1

Distributed to the book trade worldwide by Springer-Verlag New York, Inc., 233 Spring Street, 6th Floor, New York, NY 10013. Phone 1-800-SPRINGER, fax 201-348-4505, e-mail orders-ny@springer-sbm.com, or visit www.springeronline.com.

For information on translations, please contact Apress directly at 2855 Telegraph Avenue, Suite 600, Berkeley, CA 94705. Phone 510-549-5930, fax 510-549-5939, e-mail info@apress.com, or visit www.apress.com.

Apress and friends of ED books may be purchased in bulk for academic, corporate, or promotional use. eBook versions and licenses are also available for most titles. For more information, reference our Special Bulk Sales–eBook Licensing web page at http://www.apress.com/info/bulksales.

The source code for this book is freely available to readers at www.friendsofed.com in the Downloads section.

Credits

Lead Editor
Ben Renow-Clarke

Technical Reviewers
Brian Deitte, Chris Pelsor

Editorial Board
Clay Andres, Steve Anglin, Mark Beckner, Ewan Buckingham, Tony Campbell, Gary Cornell, Jonathan Gennick, Michelle Lowman, Matthew Moodie, Jeffrey Pepper, Frank Pohlmann, Ben Renow-Clarke, Dominic Shakeshaft, Matt Wade, Tom Welsh

Project Manager
Beth Christmas

Copy Editor
Heather Lang

Associate Production Director
Kari Brooks-Copony

Production Editor
Kelly Winquist

Compositor
Molly Sharp

Proofreader
April Eddy

Indexer
Carol Burbo

Artist
April Milne

Cover Image Designer
Corné van Dooren

Interior and Cover Designer
Kurt Krames

Manufacturing Director
Tom Debolski

For every small-town, wide-eyed pixel that ever stepped off a train in the big city with nothing but a suitcase of colors and a dream to light up the screen.

CONTENTS AT A GLANCE

CONTENTS

ABOUT THE AUTHOR

Todd Yard is software architect at Brightcove in Cambridge, Massachusetts, where he has worked since its early days in 2005 when everyone could fit into a small room. There, he is focused on the front-end rich media player framework for Brightcove's media management and distribution service. Prior to that, he was a partner with ego7 in New York and lead developer for its Flash content management system and community application suite. Sometime in the midst of all that, he developed applications, animations, and advertisements for a range of clients including GE, IBM, AT&T, and Mars.

As an author, Todd has previously contributed to 13 Flash and ActionScript books from friends of ED, including *Object-Oriented ActionScript 3.0* and *Extending Flash MX 2004*, and has served as technical editor on four others. He has also contributed a number of articles on Flash, Photoshop, and Illustrator to the *WebDesigner* and *Practical Web Projects* magazines.

When Todd is not at a computer, he might be found on a local stage somewhere singing and, on occasion, dancing. That's what he used to do before he was lured by the siren call of software development.

His personal web site can be found at `http://www.27Bobs.com`.

ABOUT THE TECHNICAL REVIEWERS

Brian Deitte is a software developer working at Brightcove, where he has helped to create a video mash-up tool built in Flex called Aftermix and various advertising solutions. Previously, he worked at Adobe on the Flex SDK team, from Flex 1.0 to Flex 2.01. He keeps a blog at `http://deitte.com`.

Chris Pelsor is an award-winning developer and manager of Tarantell's experiential technologies group, Tarantell:Hybrid. He has helped develop solutions for Adobe, Microsoft, Sony, and Jameson Whiskey. When he isn't busy sitting on a train for eight hours a week, he spends his free time perfecting his pale ale recipe and parenting two children with his partner in crime Lisa in Heidal, Norway, also known as the middle of nowhere.

ABOUT THE COVER IMAGE DESIGNER

Corné van Dooren designed the front cover image for this book. After taking a brief from friends of ED to create a new design for the Foundation series, he worked at combining technological and organic forms, with the results now appearing on this and other books' covers.

Corné spent his childhood drawing on everything at hand and then began exploring the infinite world of multimedia—and his journey of discovery hasn't stopped since. His mantra has always been "The only limit to multimedia is the imagination," a saying that keeps him moving forward constantly.

Corné works for many international clients, writes features for multimedia magazines, reviews and tests software, authors multimedia studies, and works on many other friends of ED books. You can see more of his work at and contact him through his web site, `www.cornevandooren.com`.

If you like Corné's work, be sure to check out his chapter in *New Masters of Photoshop: Volume 2* (friends of ED, 2004).

INTRODUCTION

I don't think they could have come up with a better name than "Flash." Although that name is now applicable to an entire platform that includes much more than the Flash Player and IDE, at the end of the day, whether you are developing in Flash or Flex Builder, and whether you are delivering online or through AIR, the end result is still a SWF that is rendered in the Flash Player, just as it was when Flash simply made animations. So whatever you produce—movie or application or generative art—is still "Flash." And boy, can it ever. From the very beginning, Flash movies have often evoked reactions of "Wow" and, more apropos to developers like you, "How'd they do that?"

I began working with Flash in 2000, right before the release of Flash 5. If you're an old-timer, you may recall that Flash 4 was still basically a timeline animation tool with only a handful of ActionScript commands available (I liken working in ActionScript without objects and arrays to working in Photoshop before there were layers). And yet the amount of creative and stunning Flash work that was produced in that time with those few commands was truly exciting.

That excitement, and the fact that it could be produced with little programming knowledge, attracted an amazing diversity of talent to Flash, from animators to programmers to graphic artists to musicians. What software today could do the same? This mixture of disciplines helped to create a community that explored this new technology from so many different points of view, a community that openly and happily shared its collective findings. And the end result of all this work and play and experimentation was—and still is—something to look at.

It might be an animation, a game, an application, or just something cool to ogle, but Flash produces visuals. That's what excited me when I first began nearly a decade ago and what has hooked so many others as well. The Flash platform has grown tremendously, and ActionScript, now in its third iteration, is a complex and powerful language that allows developers to create web applications to rival those built for the desktop. And with that power comes greater and finer control over the graphic elements in a Flash movie.

In this book, I will explore the myriad ways that ActionScript allows you to create and control these visuals in a SWF. Whether you produce games, applications, or cartoons, or you just want to play, this book will give you what you need to know to manipulate the pixels to your advantage.

In the first part of this book, we will step through each of the major areas of image creation and manipulation that ActionScript makes available to developers. We'll start at the drawing API, explore filters and blend modes, come to grips with BitmapData and all it provides, and then dive in depth into new features of Flash Player 10 with 3D and Pixel Bender. Once these topics are covered, we'll look at an effects library that you can use to easily create a multitude of effects through the remaining chapters of this book and beyond.

The second part of this book presents a collection of tutorials that will allow us to explore how to apply the knowledge gained in the first part. That's where we'll start to have some real fun. That's important, because it's the fun in creating with Flash that first drew so many in, myself included, and it's the fun that drives people to play, explore, and come up with some truly wonderful and creative applications. You can still build utilitarian pieces of software that have that Flash—not for general eye candy but to enhance usability, create more immersive and responsive experiences, and generally produce work that goes beyond everything else presented on the Web. This book shows you how.

Intended audience

This is not a book on object-oriented programming or ActionScript 3.0 fundamentals, nor is it a book on the Flash or Flex Builder authoring environments (in fact, in this book, I strive to have very little reliance at all on any specific IDE). You should come with familiarity of how to compile a SWF and have at least intermediate knowledge of ActionScript 3.0.

With this book, I hope to explore the fun to be had when programming graphics and share the enjoyment that I find when pushing the pixel. I was not a computer science major, nor do I come from a programming or mathematics background—I was just enamored with what Flash could do, and it pulled me in completely and hasn't let go. If you are familiar with ActionScript 3.0, are interested in all the graphic capabilities of the language, and aren't scared of some math here and there, then this book is for you.

Development environment

I'm an ActionScript developer. I go from using Flash to Flex Builder to the command-line mxmlc compiler in order to compile my SWFs nearly every day. In this book, I try to present pure ActionScript examples that can be compiled in any of the environments that do not rely on the timeline or library in Flash or on the Flex framework.

As you go through this book, you will find that examples are presented in pure ActionScript 3.0, usually with instructions to compile the SWF or to test the movie without further instructions on how to do so, since this differs in each environment. In this book's appendix, I discuss how you would work in both Flash and Flex Builder when using this book. You should only have to look at it once if you are not already familiar with how to compile with your method of choice.

If you are using Flex Builder 3, you will need to go through a few additional steps to set up the SDK that includes the new ActionScript classes available for Flash Player 10 and configure Flex Builder to compile for this version of the player. If you have not already been using these new classes, like Vector and Shader, you should have a look at the appendix now to see how to set this all up.

For the first couple of chapters, I will point to the appendix as a reminder, but if you jump through this book nonlinearly, you might take a peek at this appendix first.

Code comments

Code should contain helpful comments. I do not believe there is dispute over that. However, you may notice that the code presented within this book does not contain comments, at least in the chapter text itself. There are three reasons for this. First, it saves a heck of a lot of space not having comments, and including comments within these pages would have meant having to drop whole tutorials and present fewer examples. I wanted to present to you as much as was possible for the page limit. Second, and this is personal preference, when I am reading a book exploring new techniques, I often find a lot of code comments in the book text to be overly distracting from the code I am attempting to absorb, as the comments can double the size of code listings and make the actual code more difficult to focus on. Finally, in this book I spend a good amount of text before and after code listings, but outside of the actual code itself, detailing everything that is going on within the code. Including comments would mean either cutting these larger explanations or presenting redundant information.

But, as I said, code should contain helpful comments. You will find, in this book's support files, that all of the classes have been fully commented if you are looking at the code itself. It is only in chapters themselves that the code is presented without the comments.

Layout conventions

To keep this book as clear and easy to follow as possible, the following text conventions are used throughout:

Code is presented in `fixed-width font`.

New or changed code is normally presented in **`bold fixed-width font`**.

Menu commands are written in the form Menu ➤ Submenu ➤ Submenu.

Where I want to draw your attention to something, I've highlighted it like this:

> *Ahem, don't say I didn't warn you.*

Sometimes code won't fit on a single line in a book. Where this happens, I use an arrow like this: ➥.

```
This is a very, very long section of code that should be written all ➥
on the same line without a break.
```

Chapter 1

THE DRAWING API

Back before the earth cooled and life came crawling up from the seas, when the continents of the world were joined in a massive landmass and iPods held less than a gigabyte, Flash offered no way to dynamically create graphics. This would be a very short book if that had remained the case. Thankfully, Flash MX came out and blessed developers with its implementation of a drawing API (application programming interface), and we looked on it and saw that it was good.

A brief history of the drawing API

The original ActionScript 1.0 drawing API allowed for runtime creation of graphics using a small collection of eight simple commands to draw lines and fills. Drawing straight lines and curves and filling these with solid colors or gradients might seem a small thing in today's age of flying cars and jetpacks, but when the previous option was only to use predrawn vectors and bitmaps from the Library, a drawing API was a boon that offered countless new possibilities, from liquid interfaces to graphs and charting to complex 3D engines to dynamic visualizations.

With the introduction of ActionScript 2.0, the drawing API was given two new commands, one for drawing gradient strokes and the other for filling shapes with bitmaps. A few of the older methods were beefed up as well to offer additional functionality like defining gradient spread methods and line join and cap styles.

With ActionScript 3.0 and the new player runtime that allowed for it in Flash Player 9, all of the drawing methods were moved into their own Graphics class, as opposed to being a part of MovieClip. New methods for drawing some basic shapes, namely rectangles and ellipses, were also added. These alterations were useful but not world changing. Developers waited with bated breath.

Now, with Flash Player 10, ActionScript 3.0's drawing API gets an even more significant overhaul. Drawn graphics from one object can be easily copied into another. Whole sequences of drawing commands can be saved and rerun, even in multiple objects, at any time. Strokes, like fills, can now be filled with bitmaps. Finally, ActionScript's new shaders can be used for both strokes and fills, allowing for custom bitmap gradients and patterns.

The Graphics class and all it offers is a huge subject for a single chapter and an extremely important one. Much of the graphic manipulation we will do throughout this book relies on a firm understanding of what the methods of ActionScript's drawing API provide. So let's start at the very beginning—which is, I hear, a very good place to start—with the original eight simple commands.

What's come before

First, we will look at the methods that have been present in the drawing API from previous versions of Flash. If you are an ActionScript veteran and are familiar with the drawing API from ActionScript 2.0, feel free to skip over this section and proceed right to the new capabilities. I promise not to get offended.

If you have never used the drawing API before or would like a refresher, this section will be a quick run-through of what previous versions of ActionScript and Flash have offered. This won't be an extensive, exhaustive tutorial, since a lot of what it covers has been around for a good long while now, and I want to reserve the beef of the chapter for all the lovely new-fangled functionality. But it should get you up to speed quickly.

The drawing API works like a virtual pen that you direct, instructing it to draw lines or curves to specific coordinate positions and sometimes filling the drawn lines with color or bitmap fills. All drawing occurs through a Graphics instance and its methods, and Graphics instances are only found within a Sprite or Shape—a Graphics instance is not something you need (or, in fact, can) ever instantiate, but it can be accessed through Sprite or Shape's `graphics` property. That means if you want to draw using the API, you must first have a Sprite or a Shape, and that instance must be added to the display list. Then all drawing must occur within that Sprite or Shape through its `graphics` property.

```
var sprite:Sprite = new Sprite();
sprite.graphics.moveTo(50, 50);
```

In the case of a Sprite, which can contain other display objects, anything you draw within it using the drawing API will be rendered below any children that the Sprite may have.

Anything that should be visible in a Flash movie, game, or application must be added to the display list of the Flash Player. This is a hierarchical list of all the objects currently renderable, at the root of which is the aptly named root display object. When you create a Sprite or MovieClip document class in a Flash or an ActionScript project, the root is that same document class, and it is automatically in the display list (if you are using the Flex framework, the main application class is added to the display list automatically as well, and the root display object is accessible through its `root` *property).*

The display list can hold any object that is an instance of DisplayObject, an abstract class that is extended by concrete child classes like Bitmap, TextField, Video, Shape, and Sprite (which MovieClip extends). Once you instantiate an instance of one of these classes, it must be explicitly added to the display list or it will not be rendered. This is done by adding the instance as a child to a display object container that is already in the display list using the DisplayObjectContainer (which itself extends DisplayObject) methods `addChild()` *or* `addChildAt()`*.*

As there is a lot to cover in this book for generating and manipulating graphics, we jump right in here in Chapter 1 with the ActionScript code features for doing so. To fit as much as possible into the text, some foundation features of ActionScript and the Flash Player, like using the display list, are not covered past this little focus point. For more in-depth coverage, please see Adobe's ActionScript 3.0 documentation, or a book like Foundation ActionScript 3.0 with Flash CS3 and Flex *(ISBN: 978-1-59059-815-3) from friends of ED, which I also contributed to (and the chapter on the display list as well!).*

Once you begin drawing, the virtual pen is always at a specific coordinate position within the Sprite or Shape. It starts at (0, 0) in the display object's coordinate space and is moved around through the drawing API commands. Let's look at the basic drawing commands and explore how they can be used to manipulate that virtual pen.

Reviewing the original eight

It all began with eight little drawing commands. The following sections break them down. There won't be a quiz afterward, but it's not a bad idea to pretend there will be.

Drawing straight lines

The following moveTo() method places the virtual pen at a new coordinate position without drawing anything:

```
moveTo(x:Number,y:Number):void
```

It is as if the pen is picked up off of the piece of paper and set down at its new position by magic (or your hand, which could be magic, I guess). This is necessary when you need to draw a noncontinuous line or start at a coordinate position other than the default (0, 0).

```
lineTo(x:Number, y:Number):void
```

The lineTo() method is used to draw a line from the pen's current coordinate position to a new coordinate position specified in the parameters. This will produce a straight line from point to point.

The lineStyle() method is used to specify the various visual properties of a line, like its thickness and color.

```
lineStyle(
  thickness:Number=NaN,
  color:uint=0,
  alpha:Number=1.0,
  pixelHinting:Boolean=false,
  scaleMode:String="normal",
  caps:String=null,
  joints:String=null,
  miterLimit:Number=3
):void
```

There are lots of parameters with this method, so let's break them down:

- thickness: This specifies the thickness of the line to be drawn. A value of 0 creates a hairline stroke that doesn't scale.
- color: This parameter specifies the color for the line to be drawn.
- alpha: And this one describes the opacity for the line to be drawn.
- pixelHinting: Use the pixelHinting parameter to specify whether lines and points should be drawn at full pixel positions and at full pixel widths (true) or whether fractions of full pixels can be used, such as using a line thickness of 0.5 and placing an anchor point at (1.5, 1.5).
- scaleMode: This one specifies the way that strokes will be scaled when the display object in which they're drawn is scaled. This should be a value represented by one of the constants in the LineScaleMode class: NORMAL, NONE, VERTICAL, or HORIZONTAL.

NORMAL always scales. NONE never scales. HORIZONTAL and VERTICAL do not scale the stroke if the display object is scaled only vertically or horizontally, respectively.

- caps: The types of end caps to use on the stroke are specified with this parameter. This should be a value represented by one of the constants of CapsStyle: NONE (no cap extended off the line), ROUND (round extension of end of line), and SQUARE (square extension of end of line).
- joints: This parameter designates the type of joint to use on the stroke at any corner. This should be a value represented by one of the constants of JointStyle: MITER (creates a point only if the point's size is under the miter limit and otherwise squares it off), ROUND (rounds the corner), or BEVEL (squares off the corner). Joints and caps options are demonstrated in Figure 1-1.

Figure 1-1.
Three strokes with caps and joints set to ROUND on the left, SQUARE and BEVEL in the center, and NONE and MITER on the right

- miterLimit: This parameters works with the MITER joint style to specify how far a point at a corner of the stroke will extend before it is squared off. Figure 1-2 shows the same angle corner with three different miter limits.

Figure 1-2.
The same stroke with three different miter limits. The top has a miter limit of 5; the middle has a miter limit of 3, and the bottom has a miter limit of 0.

Before a line can be drawn, you must specify how it should look, and that is where the lineStyle() method comes in. This method needs to be called prior to any calls to lineTo() or curveTo() or else the lines drawn will have no thickness and therefore will not be visible. When the lineStyle() was introduced, only the first three parameters were available, and these controlled the pixel thickness, color, and opacity of the lines drawn. The additional parameters were added in Flash 8 and control whether lines snap to exact pixels, how they scale when a parent display object is resized, and how their end caps and joints are rendered.

```
clear():void
```

If you need to clear previously drawn graphics, the `clear()` method not only removes all drawn lines and fills but also resets the coordinate position of the virtual pen to (0, 0) and clears the line style.

To test these four methods, you will find the following code, fully commented, in the file `DrawingStraightLines.as` in this chapter's files. You can test the compiled SWF included or, to compile this class, refer to the instructions in the appendix for how to set up and compile ActionScript projects in either Flex Builder or in Flash. Run the SWF, and click and drag multiple times on the stage. You should see something like Figure 1-3. The following class, with lines to focus on in bold, produces the SWF:

```
package {

  import flash.display.Shape;
  import flash.display.Sprite;
  import flash.events.MouseEvent;
  import flash.geom.Point;

  [SWF(width=550, height=400, backgroundColor=0xFFFFFF)]

    private var _currentShape:Shape;
    private var _color:uint;
    private var _startPosition:Point;

  public class DrawingStraightLines extends Sprite {

    public function DrawingStraightLines() {
      stage.addEventListener(MouseEvent.MOUSE_DOWN, onStageMouseDown);
      stage.addEventListener(MouseEvent.MOUSE_UP, onStageMouseUp);
    }

    private function drawLine():void {
      _currentShape.graphics.clear();
      _currentShape.graphics.lineStyle(3, _color);
      _currentShape.graphics.moveTo(_startPosition.x, ➥
_startPosition.y);
      _currentShape.graphics.lineTo(stage.mouseX, stage.mouseY);
    }

    private function onStageMouseDown(event:MouseEvent):void {
      _color = Math.random()*0xFFFFFF;
      _currentShape = new Shape();
      addChild(_currentShape);
      _startPosition = new Point(stage.mouseX, stage.mouseY);
      stage.addEventListener(MouseEvent.MOUSE_MOVE, onStageMouseMove);
    }
```

```
    private function onStageMouseUp(event:MouseEvent):void {
      stage.removeEventListener(MouseEvent.MOUSE_MOVE, ➥
onStageMouseMove);
    }

    private function onStageMouseMove(event:MouseEvent):void {
      drawLine();
      event.updateAfterEvent();
    }

  }

}
```

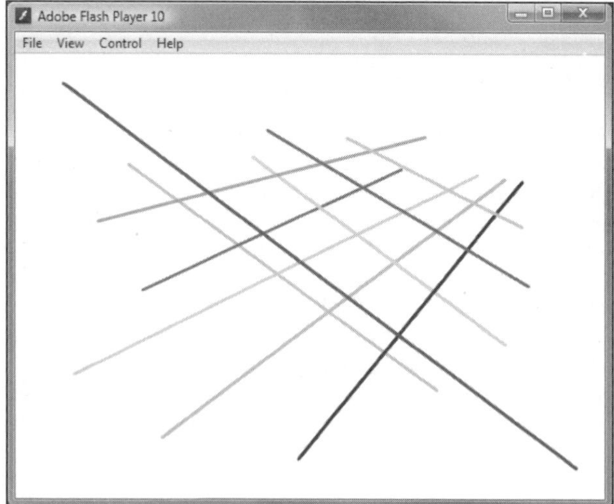

Figure 1-3. The DrawingStraightLines test that allows for dragging out randomly colored straight lines

Within this class, I set up a listener for when the stage is clicked and when the mouse is released after clicking. When the stage is clicked, the onStageMouseDown() handler is called. There, a random color is selected, and a new Shape is instantiated and added as a child to the display list. The coordinate position where the mouse is clicked is saved into the property _startPosition. Finally, a new listener is set up for when the mouse is moved, onStageMouseMove().

In onStageMouseMove(), the custom drawLine() method is invoked, and the screen is immediately updated using the updateAfterEvent() method of the MouseEvent instance. I do this so that the drawing done isn't reliant on the frame rate of the application but will instead be updated whenever the mouse is moved. That drawing is of course handled in drawLine(), where I clear any previously drawn lines in the current shape, assign a line style of 3-pixel thickness and the random color, move the virtual pen to the start position where the stage was clicked, and then draw a straight line to the current mouse position. I continue doing this every time the mouse is moved until the user releases the mouse and the `MOUSE_MOVE` listener is removed in the `onStageMouseUp()` handler.

It's a very simple drawing application done in a small amount of code. Take that, pre-rendered graphics!

Drawing curves

When you need a curve between two points, you would use the following method:

```
curveTo(
  controlX:Number,
  controlY:Number,
  anchorX:Number,
  anchorY:Number
):void
```

This draws a curved line between the current coordinates of the pen with the new coordinates specified with the `anchorX` and `anchorY` parameters. The `controlX` and `controlY` parameters are the position of the control point used to specify how the line curves using a quadratic Bezier equation.

Now, what the heck is meant by "a quadratic Bezier equation"? If you are familiar with a program like Illustrator, you will be used to Bezier curves drawn using a cubic equation, which uses two control handles to define how a curve is drawn between two anchors. The quadratic Bezier curve uses only one control point. Conceptually, you can imagine that the control point is like a magnet that is pulling at the line—a drawn line will never go directly through the control point but will be pulled in its direction.

To test and visualize this, have a look at `DrawingCurves.as` in this chapter's files. If you compile this class (remember, you can refer to the appendix for instructions) or test the SWF directly, you should see the result shown in Figure 1-4, which shows a graphic representation of the two anchor points of a curve and its control point. You can drag any of the points around to alter the curve. This is produced using the following code, with the drawing code set in bold for you:

```
package {

  import flash.display.Sprite;
  import flash.events.MouseEvent;

  [SWF(width=550, height=400, backgroundColor=0xFFFFFF)]

  public class DrawingCurves extends Sprite {

    private var _controlPoint:Sprite;
    private var _anchor0:Sprite;
    private var _anchor1:Sprite;
```

```
    public function DrawingCurves() {
      _anchor0 = addControlPoint(50, 300);
      _anchor1 = addControlPoint(500, 300);
      _controlPoint = addControlPoint(275, 100);
      drawCurve();
    }

    private function addControlPoint(x:Number, y:Number):Sprite {
      var controlPoint:Sprite = new Sprite();
      controlPoint.graphics.lineStyle(20);
      controlPoint.graphics.lineTo(1, 0);
      controlPoint.addEventListener(MouseEvent.MOUSE_DOWN, ➥
onControlDown);
      controlPoint.addEventListener(MouseEvent.MOUSE_UP, onControlUp);
      controlPoint.x = x;
      controlPoint.y = y;
      addChild(controlPoint);
      return controlPoint;
    }

    private function drawCurve():void {
      graphics.clear();
      graphics.lineStyle(3, 0xFF);
      graphics.moveTo(_anchor0.x, _anchor0.y);
      graphics.curveTo(_controlPoint.x, _controlPoint.y, ➥
_anchor1.x, _anchor1.y);
      graphics.lineStyle(1, 0, .5);
      graphics.lineTo(_controlPoint.x, _controlPoint.y);
      graphics.lineTo(_anchor0.x, _anchor0.y);
    }

    private function onControlDown(event:MouseEvent):void {
      (event.target as Sprite).startDrag();
      stage.addEventListener(MouseEvent.MOUSE_MOVE, onControlMove);
    }

    private function onControlUp(event:MouseEvent):void {
      (event.target as Sprite).stopDrag();
      stage.removeEventListener(MouseEvent.MOUSE_MOVE, onControlMove);
    }

    private function onControlMove(event:MouseEvent):void {
      drawCurve();
      event.updateAfterEvent();
    }

  }

}
```

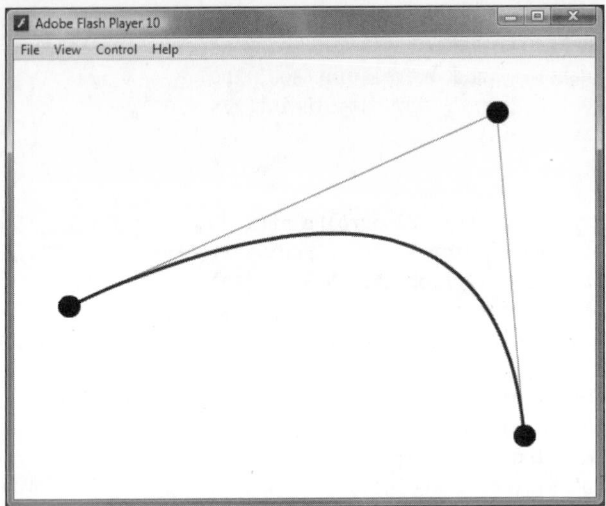

Figure 1-4. The DrawingCurves test showing how a control point acts with anchor points to make a quadratic Bezier curve

In this class, three sprites are created to represent the two anchors and control point. These are created in the addControlPoint() method, which has a simple trick of using a very thick line style (20 pixels) with a very short line in order to create a circle.

```
controlPoint.graphics.lineStyle(20);
controlPoint.graphics.lineTo(1, 0);
```

The main drawing occurs in drawCurve(), which is called whenever any of the points is dragged around the stage. Within the method, I first clear any previously drawn graphics and then create a 3-pixel thick blue line for the curve, which is drawn from _anchor0 to _anchor1 using first moveTo() and then curveTo(). I next change the line style to a thin transparent black line and draw a straight line from the current pen position at the second anchor to the control point, then another straight line to the first anchor to show how the two anchor points connect with the control point to define the curve.

Drawing solid fills

If you wish to fill a shape with a solid color, the following method is available to you:

```
beginFill(color:uint, alpha:Number=1.0):void
```

This method can be called prior to any calls to lineTo() or curveTo(), and the shape that is formed by these drawing methods will be filled with the solid color specified.

The other bookend for beginFill() is the following method:

```
endFill():void
```

This method should be called at the completion of the drawing commands that included an initial instruction to draw a fill (like beginFill() or beginGradientFill()) and instructs the Flash Player to render the fill.

Have a look at DrawingSolidFills.as to see solid fills in action. If you test this class, you will see a new background fill drawn for the entire movie whenever the stage is clicked. The following code accomplishes this, with the relevant drawing API lines in bold:

```
package {

  import flash.display.Sprite;
  import flash.events.MouseEvent;

  [SWF(width=550, height=400, backgroundColor=0xFFFFFF)]

  public class DrawingSolidFills extends Sprite {

    public function DrawingSolidFills() {
      stage.addEventListener(MouseEvent.CLICK, onStageClick);
      drawBackground();
    }

    private function drawBackground():void {
      graphics.clear();
      graphics.beginFill(Math.random()*0xFFFFFF);
      graphics.lineTo(stage.stageWidth, 0);
      graphics.lineTo(stage.stageWidth, stage.stageHeight);
      graphics.lineTo(0, stage.stageHeight);
      graphics.lineTo(0, 0);
      graphics.endFill();
    }

    private function onStageClick(event:MouseEvent):void {
      drawBackground();
    }

  }

}
```

In a later section, we will discuss drawRect(), which would simplify this drawing code (which, admittedly, is already fairly simple). In this case, I draw a rectangle covering the entire stage manually using four lineTo() commands. In the beginFill() call, I pass a random color selected from the 16 million or so available.

Drawing gradient fills

The following method allows you to fill a shape with a gradient of colors and/or alphas:

```
beginGradientFill(
  type:String,
  colors:Array,
  alphas:Array,
  ratios:Array,
```

```
    matrix:Matrix=null,
    spreadMethod:String="pad",
    interpolationMethod:String="rgb",
    focalPointRatio:Number=0
):void
```

That's a complex little method. Let's break down each of the parameters.

- type: The type of gradient to draw should be either GradientType.LINEAR or GradientType.RADIAL. Linear gradients are bands drawn in a straight line between points, while radial gradients are drawn in rings out from a central point.
- colors: This specifies an array of colors to be used in the gradient. For a linear gradient, these will be the colors from left to right (assuming you haven't rotated the gradient). For a radial gradient, the colors will be from the center out.
- alphas: An array of alpha values to be used in the gradient, with values from 0 to 1, can be specified with this parameter. There must be the same number of alpha values as there are colors, which each index in the alphas array corresponding to the alpha value of the color at the same index in the colors array.
- ratios: This holds an array of values that specify where each color in the colors array is distributed on the length of the full gradient. Each index should hold a value between 0 and 255, with 0 being the left (LINEAR) or center (RADIAL) of the gradient and 255 being the right (LINEAR) or outer radius (RADIAL) of the gradient. Just as with alphas, the length of this array must match the length of the colors and each index corresponds with the color value of the same index in the colors array.

  As an example of how ratios are used, imagine you have a rectangle that is 100 pixels wide that you fill with a linear gradient. You specify three colors, red, green, and blue, with the ratios 0, 128, and 255, respectively. This would place the full red on the left of the rectangle, the full green pretty much in the center, and the full blue on the right, with gradient values between each color. Now, if you changed the ratios to 0, 64, and 128, the full green would be at around a quarter of the width of the rectangle with the full blue at the center and extending to the right edge. Figure 1-5 shows these two scenarios.

Figure 1-5. The same gradient colors applied to the same dimensional shape with two different ratio values to control color distribution on the gradient

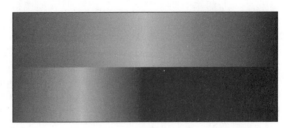

- matrix: This transformation matrix determines how the gradient will be moved, scaled, and/or rotated within its drawn shape. This must be an instance of the flash.geom.Matrix class. We'll get into matrices next chapter, but for gradients, you generally only have to create an instance and use its handy createGradientBox() method, which we'll look at in the next example.

- `spreadMethod`: This parameter determines how a gradient that is smaller than the width or height of the drawn shape will extend to fill the shape. This should be a value as represented by the constants of the SpreadMethod class: `PAD`, `REFLECT`, and `REPEAT`. `PAD` simply continues with the end color of the gradient. `REFLECT` reverses the gradient. `REPEAT`, rather unsurprisingly, repeats the gradient. Each of these spread methods is shown in Figure 1-6.

Figure 1-6.
The same gradient colors applied to the same dimensional object, with the top object using a PAD spread method, the middle using REFLECT, and the bottom using REPEAT

- `interpolationMethod`: Specify how intermediate colors in a gradient are calculated with this parameter. This should be a value represented by a constant found in InterpolationMethod: `LINEAR_RGB` or `RGB`.
- `focalPointRatio`: For radial gradients, this determines where the focal point of the gradient lies along its horizontal diameter. –1.0 and 1.0 place the focal point on the radius of the gradient, and 0 places the focal point in the center. Any intermediate value places it in between. Figure 1-7 shows several examples of the focal point adjusted for the same radial gradient.

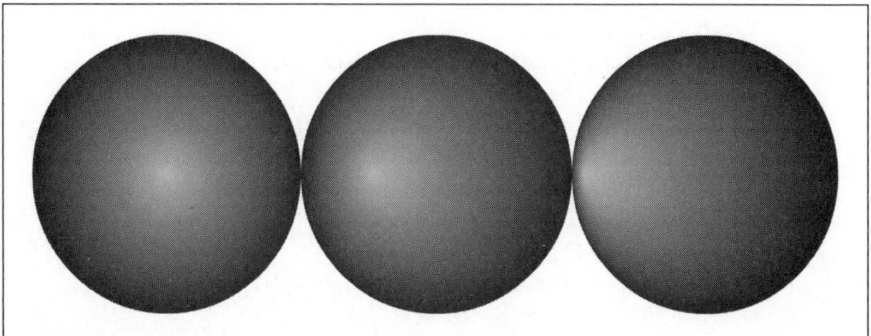

Figure 1-7. Three shapes using the same radial gradient colors and center, but with the focal point increasingly shifted to the left

If you would rather fill a drawn shape with a gradient color as opposed to a solid color, then the `beginGradientFill()` method is for you. Its type can either be linear or radial, and you must at least include an array of colors, their alphas, and their ratio positions to use. The matrix is optional (but often necessary) to rotate, reposition, or resize the gradient fill. The other parameters, which came in Flash 8 and aren't as often used, control how a gradient is extended when the shape is larger than the gradient's size, how the color gradations are calculated, and, for radial gradients, how the focal point of the gradient is offset from center.

Gradient fills offer, and require, much more configuration than solid fills. The example found as `DrawingGradientFills.as` in this chapter's files, and shown in Figure 1-8, draws a radial gradient that follows the user's mouse position. The relevant lines are in bold.

```
package {

  import flash.display.GradientType;
  import flash.display.Sprite;
  import flash.events.MouseEvent;
  import flash.geom.Matrix;

  [SWF(width=550, height=400, backgroundColor=0xFFFFFF)]

  public class DrawingGradientFills extends Sprite {

    public function DrawingGradientFills() {
      stage.addEventListener(MouseEvent.MOUSE_MOVE, onStageMouseMove);
      drawBackground();
    }

    private function drawBackground():void {
      var colors:Array = [0xFFFF00, 0xFF0000, 0x000000];
      var alphas:Array = [1, 1, 1];
      var ratios:Array = [50, 100, 255];
      var matrix:Matrix = new Matrix();
      matrix.createGradientBox(200, 200, 0, ➥
stage.mouseX-100, stage.mouseY-100);
      graphics.clear();
      graphics.beginGradientFill(GradientType.RADIAL, ➥
colors, alphas, ratios, matrix);
      graphics.lineTo(stage.stageWidth, 0);
      graphics.lineTo(stage.stageWidth, stage.stageHeight);
      graphics.lineTo(0, stage.stageHeight);
      graphics.lineTo(0, 0);
      graphics.endFill();
    }

    private function onStageMouseMove(event:MouseEvent):void {
      drawBackground();
      event.updateAfterEvent();
    }

  }

}
```

Figure 1-8. A dynamically drawn radial gradient with a center point that follows the user's mouse

Whenever the mouse is moved, the `drawBackground()` method is invoked. In this method, an array of colors from yellow to red to black is created. The `alphas` array will instruct the gradient fill to use full opacity for each color. The `ratios` array defines where each color will fall in the fill, between 0 and 255, with 0 being the center of the fill and 255 being the outer width or height for a radial gradient. This means that the first color, yellow, will be at the center of the fill. Between 50 and 100, the colors will be a gradation between yellow and red. The color will be fully red at 100. From 100 to 255, the colors will be a gradation from red to black.

Ratios are sometimes difficult to wrap your head around, but remember that all those numbers can be considered as a percentage of 255 (let's assume the term percentage didn't imply base 10). So the value of 100, where the gradient will be fully red, is 100/255, or around 39 percent, of the whole. The whole in this case is 200, which is the pixel width and height I use for the fill. 39 percent of that is 78. That means that the gradient will be fully red 78 pixels out from center.

After sorting out the ratios, a Matrix instance is used to define the transform of the gradient, including size, position, and rotation, which can be set easily using `createGradientBox()`. For this case, I make the fill 200 pixels wide and high. The rotation is set at 0 radians, or no rotation, and the position is set to be the current mouse position minus half the width and height of the fill. For this radial gradient with a width and height of 200, this will place the center of the gradient right below the mouse.

The gradient is only 200×200, but the shape I draw covers the entire stage. Because I do not define a spread method in the call to `beginGradientFill()` it uses the default, `SpreadMethod.PAD`, which continues using the last color of the gradient, in this case black, to the end of the shape. Try passing either `REPEAT` or `REFLECT` to see how these spread methods alter the gradient (for a radial gradient, these both work pretty much the same), as shown in Figure 1-9. Oooh, pretty.

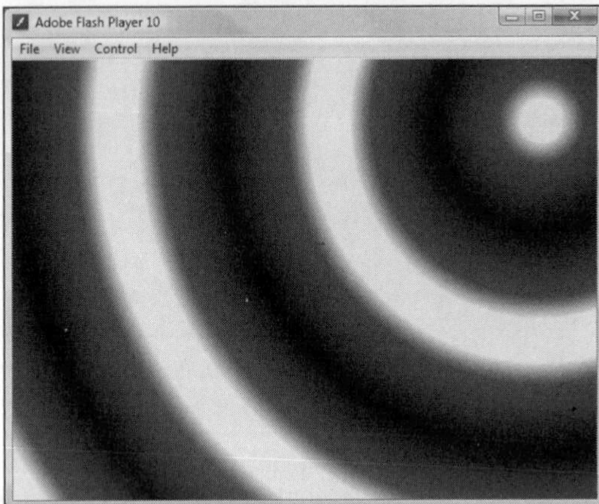

Figure 1-9. The same gradient as the previous example with the spread method set to REFLECT

Shapes made easy

Four methods are included in the drawing API to provide a simple means to draw basic rectangular and elliptical shapes.

```
drawCircle(
  x:Number,
  y:Number,
  radius:Number
):void
```

The `drawCircle()` method draws a perfect circle of the specified radius with its center at the specified x and y position.

```
drawEllipse(
  x:Number,
  y:Number,
  width:Number,
  height:Number
):void
```

The `drawEllipse()` method draws an ellipse of the specified width and height with its top left at the specified x and y position.

```
drawRect(
  x:Number,
  y:Number,
  width:Number,
  height:Number
):void
```

The drawRect() method draws a rectangle of the specified width and height with its top left corner at the specified x and y position.

```
drawRoundRect(
  x:Number,
  y:Number,
  width:Number,
  height:Number,
  ellipseWidth:Number,
  ellipseHeight:Number
):void
```

The drawRoundRect() method draws a rectangle of the specified width and height with its top left corner at the specified x and y position. The corners of the rectangle are rounded as defined by the values for ellipseWidth and ellipseHeight.

There is one more method, drawRoundRectComplex(), which allows you to use a different radius on each corner of the rectangle. Its signature is similar to drawRoundRect(), but instead of ellipseWidth and ellipseHeight, you pass in the values for four corner radii: top left, top right, bottom, bottom left, and bottom right. For example, the following would draw a rectangle with only the top two corners rounded:

```
shape.graphics.drawRoundRectComplex(0, 0, 100, 100, 5, 5, 0, 0);
```

Useful? You betcha. Undocumented? Unfortunately, yes, so use it at your own risk.

This example, with the code found in the ShapesMadeEasy.as file, draws all four of the shapes provided by these methods, as shown in Figure 1-10. The lines to look at specifically are in bold.

```
package {

  import flash.display.Sprite;

  [SWF(width=550, height=400, backgroundColor=0xFFFFFF)]

  public class ShapesMadeEasy extends Sprite {

    public function ShapesMadeEasy() {
      draw();
    }

    private function draw():void {
      var halfWidth:Number = stage.stageWidth/2;
      var halfHeight:Number = stage.stageHeight/2;
      var quarterWidth:Number = halfWidth/2;
      var quarterHeight:Number = halfHeight/2;

      graphics.beginFill(0xFF0000);
      graphics.drawCircle(quarterWidth, quarterHeight,➥
Math.min(quarterWidth, quarterHeight));
      graphics.endFill();
```

```
        graphics.beginFill(0x0000FF);
        graphics.drawEllipse(halfWidth, 0, halfWidth, halfHeight);
        graphics.endFill();

        graphics.beginFill(0x00FF00);
        graphics.drawRect(0, halfHeight, halfWidth, halfHeight);
        graphics.endFill();

        graphics.beginFill(0xFF00FF);
        graphics.drawRoundRect(halfWidth, halfHeight,➥
halfWidth, halfHeight, 70, 70);
        graphics.endFill();
      }

    }

}
```

Figure 1-10. Four shapes drawn using the built-in shape drawing methods of the drawing API

Drawing gradient lines

Gradients can be used to fill lines (or strokes), just as they can with shapes. The call is even identical, which was really nice of the Flash engineers (and have you ever once thanked them?).

```
lineGradientStyle(
  type:String,
  colors:Array,
  alphas:Array,
  ratios:Array,
  matrix:Matrix=null,
  spreadMethod:String="pad",
```

```
  interpolationMethod:String="rgb",
  focalPointRatio:Number=0
):void
```

In the following example, found in DrawingGradientLines.as, I create a dashed line using a gradient, with the gradient colors both the same but their opacities set at either 0 or 1. The file is the same as DrawingStraightLines.as except for the draw() method. Have a look at the code and test the movie, clicking and dragging to create the dashed lines, and you should see something like Figure 1-11. Once again, the important lines to note are in bold.

```
package {

  import flash.display.CapsStyle;
  import flash.display.GradientType;
  import flash.display.Shape;
  import flash.display.SpreadMethod;
  import flash.display.Sprite;
  import flash.events.MouseEvent;
  import flash.geom.Matrix;
  import flash.geom.Point;

  [SWF(width=550, height=400, backgroundColor=0xFFFFFF)]

  public class DrawingGradientLines extends Sprite {

    private var _currentShape:Shape;
    private var _color:uint;
    private var _startPosition:Point;

    public function DrawingGradientLines() {
      stage.addEventListener(MouseEvent.MOUSE_DOWN, onStageMouseDown);
      stage.addEventListener(MouseEvent.MOUSE_UP, onStageMouseUp);
    }

    private function drawLine():void {
      var thickness:Number = 40;

      var colors:Array = [_color, _color];
      var alphas:Array = [1, 0];
      var ratios:Array = [127, 127];

      var currentPosition:Point = new Point(stage.mouseX, ➥
stage.mouseY);
      var xDist:Number = (currentPosition.x - _startPosition.x);
      var yDist:Number = (currentPosition.y - _startPosition.y);
      var angle:Number = Math.atan2(yDist, xDist);
      var matrix:Matrix = new Matrix();
      matrix.createGradientBox(thickness, thickness, angle);
```

```
      _currentShape.graphics.clear();
      _currentShape.graphics.lineStyle(thickness, 0, 1, false,➥
null, CapsStyle.SQUARE);
      _currentShape.graphics.lineGradientStyle(GradientType.LINEAR,➥
colors, alphas, ratios, matrix, SpreadMethod.REPEAT);
      _currentShape.graphics.moveTo(_startPosition.x, ➥
_startPosition.y);
      _currentShape.graphics.lineTo(stage.mouseX, stage.mouseY);
    }

    private function onStageMouseDown(event:MouseEvent):void {
      _color = Math.random()*0xFFFFFF;
      _currentShape = new Shape();
      addChild(_currentShape);
      _startPosition = new Point(stage.mouseX, stage.mouseY);
      stage.addEventListener(MouseEvent.MOUSE_MOVE, onStageMouseMove);
    }

    private function onStageMouseUp(event:MouseEvent):void {
      stage.removeEventListener(MouseEvent.MOUSE_MOVE, ➥
onStageMouseMove);
    }

    private function onStageMouseMove(event:MouseEvent):void {
      drawLine();
      event.updateAfterEvent();
    }

  }

}
```

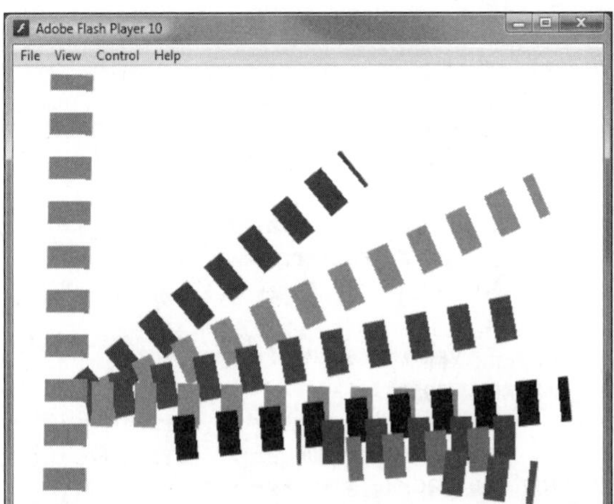

Figure 1-11. The DrawingGradientLines test with a gradient stroke using different alphas in the gradient to create dotted strokes

Now, don't panic. This is the most complex piece of code you've seen yet, so we'll take a closer look at the `draw()` method and break it down. However, the rest of the code is unchanged from the `DrawingStraightLines.as` file earlier except for the class name change and the additional imports.

First, I set several variables I will be using to draw the line, including the thickness of the line and the colors, alphas, and ratios for the gradient (note that you could make several of these constants or member properties as they do not change, but keeping them within `draw()` makes it easier to understand in this context).

```
var thickness:Number = 40;

var colors:Array = [_color, _color];
var alphas:Array = [1, 0];
var ratios:Array = [127, 127];
```

For the colors, I use the same color twice. For the alphas, I set the first color at full opacity and the second color at full transparency. The ratios for the two colors are the same and are at the approximate center of the full ratio amount, 255. Because they share the same value, 127, the gradient will be drawn with an immediate transition from the fully opaque first color to the fully transparent second color. This means everything to the left of center on the gradient will be full opacity, and everything to the right of center on the gradient will be full transparency.

The next block determines how the gradient will be rotated so that the dashes follow the direction of the line.

```
var currentPosition:Point = new Point(stage.mouseX, stage.mouseY);
var xDist:Number = (currentPosition.x - _startPosition.x);
var yDist:Number = (currentPosition.y - _startPosition.y);
var angle:Number = Math.atan2(yDist, xDist);
var matrix:Matrix = new Matrix();
matrix.createGradientBox(thickness, thickness, angle);
```

After saving the current position of the mouse, I calculate the distance from start position to the current position. The angle can be solved using the `Math.atan2()` trigonometric function, in which I plug in the x and y distances between the end points of the line. I can then create a Matrix and use the angle within its `createGradientBox()` method.

> *Determining the angle between two points is a common task in ActionScript, and so we won't dwell on the math behind it here. If you want further insight into trigonometry in ActionScript and the concepts behind it, have a look at* Foundation ActionScript 3.0 Animation: Making Things Move *from Keith Peters, also available from friends of ED (ISBN: 978-1-59059-791-0).*

Now that the gradient values are set, I can use the drawing API methods to draw the line. An important thing to notice is that before the call to `lineGradientStyle()`, there is actually a call to `lineStyle()`. This is always required, since there are certain things in `lineStyle()` that are not available in its counterpart, such as the thickness of the line.

For the other values, I pass the defaults so that I can set the sixth parameter, the style for the caps. Because I am drawing a dashed line where the dashes are square, the default rounded caps of lines look odd, so I set this to SQUARE instead.

```
        _currentShape.graphics.lineStyle(thickness, 0, 1, false,➥
null, CapsStyle.SQUARE);
        _currentShape.graphics.lineGradientStyle(GradientType.LINEAR,➥
colors, alphas, ratios, matrix, SpreadMethod.REPEAT);
```

Finally, I have the call to lineGradientStyle(), which is exactly the same as a call to beginGradientFill(). I pass in all the variables I have set up and set the spread method to REPEAT, which will continue the opaque/transparent pattern for the entire length of the line, creating dashes.

Filling shapes with bitmaps

The last feature added to the ActionScript drawing API prior to Flash Player 10 was the ability to fill shapes with bitmaps, just as it has been available for years in the Flash IDE. The process works similarly to beginFill() and beginGradientFill(), where the call to use the fill occurs before subsequent drawing commands and ends with a call to endFill(). First, let's look at the signature for this method.

```
beginBitmapFill(
  bitmap:BitmapData,
  matrix:Matrix=null,
  repeat:Boolean=true,
  smooth:Boolean=true
):void
```

Here are the relevant parameters:

- bitmap: This is the image to fill the shape with.
- matrix: This parameter is the transformation matrix to be used to move, scale, and/or rotate the bitmap in the shape.
- repeat: This parameter determines whether the bitmap should repeat if its dimensions are less than that of the shape to fill.
- smooth: Setting this parameter to true tells the Flash Player that the bitmap should have a smoothing algorithm applied when scaled up, which produces less pixelation but more blur.

The first argument, bitmap, is the important one, and is a BitmapData instance that holds the pixel data for the bitmap. All of Chapters 3 and 4 cover BitmapData, which admittedly makes me giddy with excitement, so we won't dive too much into it here. The matrix argument allows you to transform that bitmap, scaling, translating, or rotating it. By default, if the drawn shape is larger than the bitmap, the bitmap is repeated to fill the shape. This works great for tileable textures. If you don't want the repeat, you could set the third argument to false. The fourth argument, smooth, performs a smoothing algorithm on the bitmap if it is scaled up. Unless you require a pixelated image, or need faster draws, leaving this as true is generally a good thing.

Let's look at the drawing code necessary to fill shapes with bitmaps. The following class can be found as FillingShapesWithBitmaps.as in this chapter's files. An example of its output is shown in Figure 1-12.

```
package {

  import flash.display.BitmapData;
  import flash.display.Shape;
  import flash.display.Sprite;
  import flash.geom.Matrix;

  [SWF(width=550, height=400, backgroundColor=0xFFFFFF)]

  public class FillingShapesWithBitmaps extends Sprite {

    public function FillingShapesWithBitmaps() {
      draw();
    }

    private function makeBitmapData():BitmapData {
      var bitmap:BitmapData = new BitmapData(100, 100);
      bitmap.perlinNoise(40, 40, 2, Math.random(), true, false);
      return bitmap;
    }

    private function draw():void {
      var bitmap:BitmapData = makeBitmapData();

      var width:Number = stage.stageWidth/2;
      var height:Number = stage.stageHeight/2;
      var radius:Number = 70;

      var shape:Shape = new Shape();
      with (shape.graphics) {
        beginBitmapFill(bitmap);
        drawRoundRect(0, 0, width, height, radius, radius);
        endFill();
      }
      addChild(shape);

      shape = new Shape();
      var matrix:Matrix = new Matrix();
      matrix.translate((width-bitmap.width)/2, ➥
(height-bitmap.height)/2);
      with (shape.graphics) {
        beginBitmapFill(bitmap, matrix, false);
        drawRoundRect(0, 0, width, height, radius, radius);
        endFill();
      }
```

```
            shape.x = width;
            addChild(shape);

            shape = new Shape();
            matrix.rotate(Math.PI/4);
            with (shape.graphics) {
              beginBitmapFill(bitmap, matrix, false);
              drawRoundRect(0, 0, width, height, radius, radius);
              endFill();
            }
            shape.y = height;
            addChild(shape);

            shape = new Shape();
            matrix = new Matrix();
            matrix.scale(20, 20);
            with (shape.graphics) {
              beginBitmapFill(bitmap, matrix, false, false);
              drawRoundRect(0, 0, width, height, radius, radius);
              endFill();
            }
            shape.x = width;
            shape.y = height;
            addChild(shape);
          }

        }

      }
```

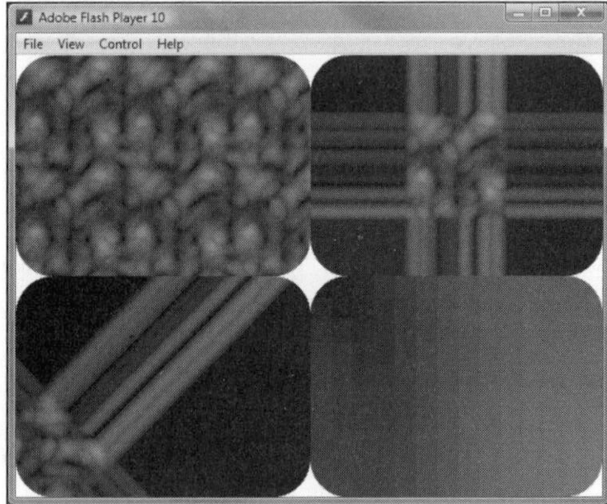

Figure 1-12. The FillingShapesWithBitmaps test with four shapes filled with the same bitmap image transformed using a matrix

The constructor of this class calls a `draw()` method where the majority of the code is kept. The first thing that method does is call out to `makeBitmapData()` to return a BitmapData instance.

```
var bitmap:BitmapData = makeBitmapData();
```

Again, we will cover BitmapData extensively both in its own chapters and throughout this book. Briefly, the BitmapData constructor accepts width and height for the bitmap as the first two parameters, so here I am creating a 100×100 bitmap. I then call its `perlinNoise()` method to create a quick and dirty, but very pretty, bitmap image. That method will be covered in depth in Chapter 4. Here, it allows me in one line to create a bitmap image without having to load something in, which is very sweet of it. This BitmapData instance is then returned from the function.

```
var bitmap:BitmapData = new BitmapData(100, 100);
bitmap.perlinNoise(40, 40, 2, Math.random(), true, false);
return bitmap;
```

Once I have a bitmap image, I can use the drawing API to fill a shape with it, which is done first in the following lines in `draw()`:

```
with (shape.graphics) {
  beginBitmapFill(bitmap);
  drawRoundRect(0, 0, width, height, radius, radius);
  endFill();
}
```

Since I am not transforming the bitmap and want the repeat by default, I only need to pass the image to the `beginBitmapFill()` method. You can see that I use the `with` statement to wrap the drawing code so that I don't have to use `shape.graphics` before each line, as it is implied because of `with`, which makes things a little more readable.

For the second shape, I use a matrix to translate the image so that it will be centered within the shape.

```
var matrix:Matrix = new Matrix();
matrix.translate((width-bitmap.width)/2, (height-bitmap.height)/2);
with (shape.graphics) {
  beginBitmapFill(bitmap, matrix, false);
```

In the `beginBitmapFill()` call, I pass the matrix in as the second parameter and set the `repeat` option to `false`. This will center the bitmap and extend its edges to the ends of the shape.

For the next shape, I basically repeat the same thing, except here I also rotate the matrix.

```
matrix.rotate(Math.PI/4);
```

This rotation will occur around the (0, 0) position of the fill. Again, because `repeat` is set to `false`, the edge of the bitmap will be stretched to the edge of the shape.

For a final shape, I scale up the bitmap by 2,000 percent and disable smoothing.

```
matrix = new Matrix();
matrix.scale(20, 20);
with (shape.graphics) {
  beginBitmapFill(bitmap, matrix, false, false);
```

In the call to `beginBitmapFill()`, I pass `false` as the final argument, which disables the smoothing that is normally applied. The result is the shape in the lower right will have large pixelated blocks.

That's really all there is to drawing with bitmap images. We'll dive into BitmapData and all the possibilities in Chapters 3 and 4, but hopefully, this has given you a little nibble to whet your appetite.

And in with the new

Here we are! Here we are! Here we are! (Can you tell I'm excited?) Each new version of Flash has introduced a number of improvements to the drawing API, but none so significant as this latest release. Through this last section we will explore the new functionality of the drawing API and what the new feature set enables.

Copying graphics

This feature is quite simple in concept but is an extremely welcome addition to the drawing API toolkit. Previously, any drawing done in a Sprite or Shape has been tied to that Sprite or Shape. There has been no way to copy the graphics from one Graphics object to another. You could either use BitmapData to copy the image, as a bitmap but not as a vector, or you could save all drawing procedures in order to re-create the image, which is not a terribly scalable solution.

Now, you can use `copyGraphics()`, which has the following beautifully simple signature:

```
copyGraphics():void
```

With `copyGraphics()`, any contents of one Graphics instance can be copied into another at any time. That's pretty darn cool. We will explore one possible use of this through this next example, which creates something akin to the old Spirograph, and was inspired by the Flash site `http://www.myoats.com`, as shown in Figure 1-13.

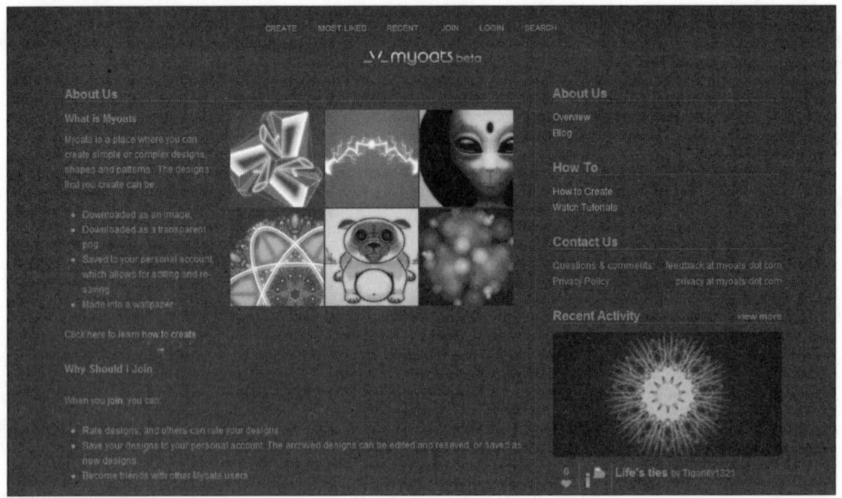

Figure 1-13. The myoats.com web site provides an innovative Flash drawing application.

The class can be found as CopyingGraphics.as in the files for this chapter. If you compile that class, or test the SWF directly, you will see a black stage where you can click and drag to draw a line, with the whole image rotating as you draw. The drawn line is duplicated nine times around the center of the stage and updated as you draw. If you use the up or down arrow, you can increase or decrease the number of duplicated segments. The result of some clicking and dragging can be seen in Figure 1-14.

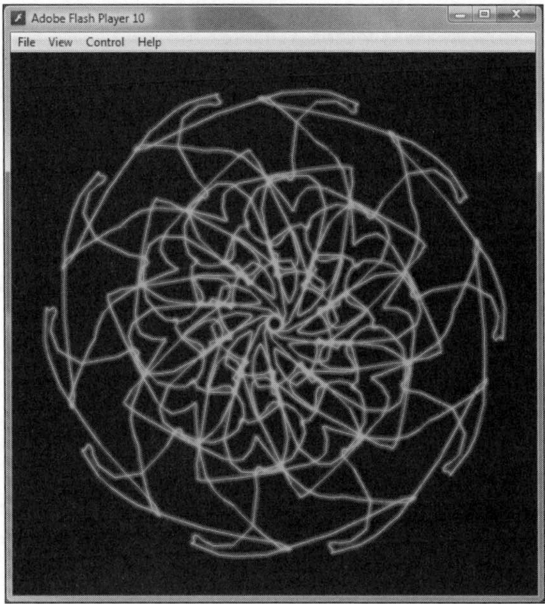

Figure 1-14. The CopyingGraphics test with duplicated graphics paths rotated around a central point

This is a pretty hefty class in comparison with some of the earlier examples, so have a perusal of the code, play with the finished application, and I'll break down the relevant pieces after the listing.

```
package {

  import flash.display.Shape;
  import flash.display.Sprite;
  import flash.events.KeyboardEvent;
  import flash.events.Event;
  import flash.events.MouseEvent;
  import flash.filters.GlowFilter;
  import flash.ui.Keyboard;

  [SWF(width=550, height=550, backgroundColor=0)]

  public class CopyingGraphics extends Sprite {
```

```
private static const INIT_SEGMENTS:uint = 10;
private static const MAX_SEGMENTS:uint = 20;
private static const MIN_SEGMENTS:uint = 3;
private static const THICKNESS:uint = 1;
private static const COLOR:uint = 0x66CCCC;
private static const ROTATION_RATE:uint = 1;

private var _shapeHolder:Sprite;
private var _shapes:Vector.<Shape>;

public function CopyingGraphics() {
  init();
}

public function init():void {
  _shapeHolder = new Sprite();
  _shapeHolder.x = stage.stageWidth/2;
  _shapeHolder.y = stage.stageHeight/2;
  addChild(_shapeHolder);
  _shapes = new Vector.<Shape>();
  for (var i:uint = 0; i < INIT_SEGMENTS; i++) {
    addSegment();
  }
  positionSegments();
  stage.addEventListener(MouseEvent.MOUSE_DOWN, onStageMouseDown);
  stage.addEventListener(MouseEvent.MOUSE_UP, onStageMouseUp);
  stage.addEventListener(KeyboardEvent.KEY_DOWN, onStageKeyDown);
  filters = [new GlowFilter(COLOR)];
}

private function draw():void {
  var shape:Shape = _shapes[0];
  shape.graphics.lineTo(shape.mouseX, shape.mouseY);
  var segments:uint = _shapeHolder.numChildren;
  for (var i:uint = 1; i < segments; i++) {
    _shapes[i].graphics.copyFrom(shape.graphics);
  }
}

private function addSegment():void {
  var shape:Shape = new Shape();
  if (_shapes.length > 0) {
    shape.graphics.copyFrom(_shapes[0].graphics);
  } else {
    shape.graphics.lineStyle(THICKNESS, COLOR);
  }
  _shapes.push(shape);
  _shapeHolder.addChild(shape);
}
```

```
    private function removeSegment():void {
      var shape:Shape = _shapes.pop();
      _shapeHolder.removeChild(shape);
    }

    private function positionSegments():void {
      var segments:uint = _shapeHolder.numChildren;
      var angle:Number = 360/segments;
      for (var i:uint = 1; i < segments; i++) {
        _shapes[i].rotation = angle*i;
      }
    }

    private function onStageMouseDown(event:MouseEvent):void {
      var shape:Shape = _shapes[0];
      shape.graphics.moveTo(shape.mouseX, shape.mouseY);
      addEventListener(Event.ENTER_FRAME, onThisEnterFrame);
    }

    private function onStageMouseUp(event:MouseEvent):void {
      removeEventListener(Event.ENTER_FRAME, onThisEnterFrame);
    }

    private function onThisEnterFrame(event:Event):void {
      _shapeHolder.rotation += ROTATION_RATE;
      draw();
    }

    private function onStageKeyDown(event:KeyboardEvent):void {
      switch (event.keyCode) {
        case Keyboard.UP:
          if (_shapeHolder.numChildren < MAX_SEGMENTS) {
            addSegment();
            positionSegments();
          }
          break;
        case Keyboard.DOWN:
          if (_shapeHolder.numChildren > MIN_SEGMENTS) {
            removeSegment();
            positionSegments();
          }
          break;
      }
    }

  }

}
```

After the package and class declarations and class imports, I declare a number of constants I will use in the application. INIT_SEGMENTS is the starting number of segments that will be rotated with the drawn lines. MAX_SEGMENTS and MIN_SEGMENTS define the upper and lower limits for the number of segments that can be drawn. THICKNESS and COLOR will be used to define the look of the line that is drawn. Finally, ROTATION_RATE will control how fast the shapes rotate as you draw.

The properties that are declared after the constants will hold references to the shapes and sprites in the application. _shapeHolder will hold a reference to the main sprite in which all the other shapes are added. It will be this instance that is rotated as you draw. The _shapes vector array will hold references to all the Shape instances that are added to _shapeHolder.

If you haven't worked much yet with the Vector class in ActionScript 3.0, available in Flash Player 10, this is a data structure very similar to Array, with the same Array methods you know and love but with a much stricter set of rules. The most apparent is that a vector requires a designated basetype when it is instantiated, and the vector will only accept objects of that specified basetype. This means that if you declare the following

```
var sprites:Vector.<Sprite> = new Vector.<Sprite>();
```

you can only put Sprite instances into this vector, unlike an array which can accept any type. The greatest benefit of this is that any value pulled from this vector is of a known type and does not need to be cast from Object, as you would have to do with an array, nor do you have to check to ensure that type:

```
var sprite:Sprite = sprites.pop();
```

If you tried to do this with an array, an exception would be thrown without casting the element removed from the array to Sprite. This cleans up the code considerably and allows for faster execution.

Within the constructor, I merely invoke the init() method. Usually, when I need more than two or three lines of code upon initialization, I will put this code into a method named init() as opposed to placing it in the constructor.

The first thing I do in the init() method is create the _shapeHolder sprite, position it at stage center, and add it to the display list.

```
_shapeHolder = new Sprite();
_shapeHolder.x = stage.stageWidth/2;
_shapeHolder.y = stage.stageHeight/2;
addChild(_shapeHolder);
```

I then instantiate the _shapes vector array, loop through the initial number of segments, and call a new method, addSegment(), which adds a single segment to _shapeHolder.

positionSegments() is called after the loop, which will rotate the segments evenly around the center.

```
_shapes = new Vector.<Shape>();
for (var i:uint = 0; i < INIT_SEGMENTS; i++) {
  addSegment();
}
positionSegments();
```

Now, let's have a look at addSegment().

```
var shape:Shape = new Shape();
if (_shapes.length > 0) {
  shape.graphics.copyFrom(_shapes[0].graphics);
} else {
  shape.graphics.lineStyle(THICKNESS, COLOR);
}
_shapes.push(shape);
_shapeHolder.addChild(shape);
```

After creating a new Shape instance, I check to see if this is the first created. If it is not the first created, which is the one I will be drawing in, I call the fancy new copyFrom() method of the drawing API. This takes whatever graphics that have been drawn in the initial shape (_shapes[0]) and copies them into the new shape. If, instead, this is the first shape being drawn, I set the lineStyle to be used for that shape. Finally, I add the new shape to the _shapes vector and as a child to _shapeHolder.

After the segments are added within the loop in init(), positionSegments() is called to rotate the segments around the registration point of _shapeHolder, which is at the center of the stage. This is done by simply dividing the number of segments by 360 degrees and setting each segment to a multiple of that angle.

```
var segments:uint = _shapeHolder.numChildren;
var angle:Number = 360/segments;
for (var i:uint = 1; i < segments; i++) {
  _shapes[i].rotation = angle*i;
}
```

The final lines of init() set up three listeners for events on the stage and apply a glow filter to the lines drawn just to add a bit of visual flare. We are in Flash, after all! (More on filters in the next chapter.)

If you look at the handlers for those events, you can see within the onStageMouseDown() handler I call moveTo() on the main (or first) shape so that its virtual pen will move to the position that the mouse is at. I then create a new listener for the ENTER_FRAME event.

```
var shape:Shape = _shapes[0];
shape.graphics.moveTo(shape.mouseX, shape.mouseY);
addEventListener(Event.ENTER_FRAME, onThisEnterFrame);
```

The onStageMouseUp() handler simply removes this listener. The onThisEnterFrame() handler rotates the _shapeHolder instance a little each frame and calls the draw() method, where all the drawing takes place.

```
_shapeHolder.rotation += ROTATION_RATE;
draw();
```

draw(), which is called from within the onThisEnterFrame() handler, first grabs a reference to the first shape where all the drawing will take place and draws a line to the mouse's new position.

```
var shape:Shape = _shapes[0];
shape.graphics.lineTo(shape.mouseX, shape.mouseY);
```

Remember this occurs every frame while the mouse is down, and even if the mouse was not moved, _shapeHolder itself is rotating, changing the position of the mouse in relation to itself. After I draw the line, I run through all the remaining segments and call the handy dandy copyFrom() method to copy the graphics from the first shape to all the others. Nice and easy!

```
var segments:uint = _shapeHolder.numChildren;
for (var i:uint = 1; i < segments; i++) {
  _shapes[i].graphics.copyFrom(shape.graphics);
}
```

The final listener set up within the init() method is for the KEY_DOWN event. The onStageKeyDown() handles this event. Within that method, I look for the up or down arrow keys. If the up key has been pressed, I make sure that I haven't exceeded the allowed maximum number of segments. If I haven't, I call addSegment() and reposition all the segments to account for the new number.

```
case Keyboard.UP:
  if (_shapeHolder.numChildren < MAX_SEGMENTS) {
    addSegment();
    positionSegments();
  }
```

If, however, the down key is pressed, I make sure I have more than the allowed minimum number of segments. If I do, I can call the new removeSegment() and reposition the remaining segments.

```
case Keyboard.DOWN:
  if (_shapeHolder.numChildren > MIN_SEGMENTS) {
    removeSegment();
    positionSegments();
  }
```

removeSegment() has the simple task of removing the last child from the _shapeHolder sprite, which is stored in the last index of the _shapes vector.

```
var shape:Shape = _shapes.pop();
_shapeHolder.removeChild(shape);
```

Go ahead and play in the final application and see what you can create with an array of rotated shapes. Be sure to use the up and down arrows to increase or decrease the number of segments to see how that affects the output. Some other humble attempts on my part are shown in Figure 1-15.

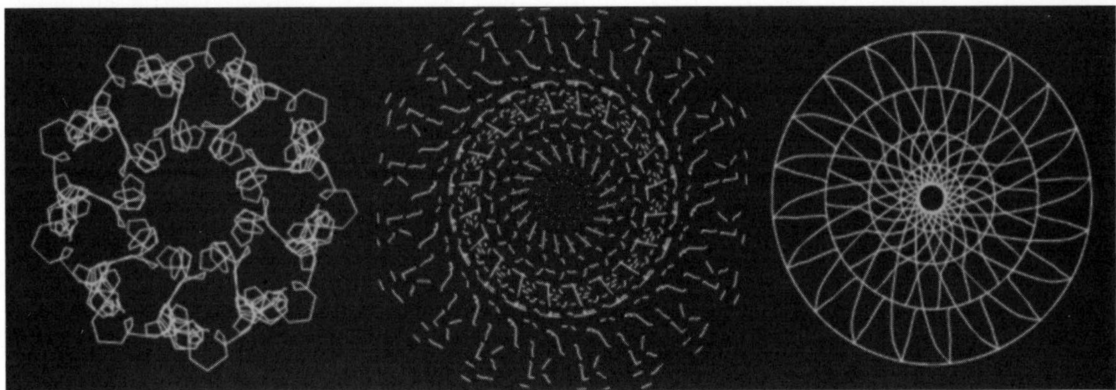

Figure 1-15. More fun attempts at duplicated graphics paths using the CopyingGraphics test

Drawing bitmap strokes

Using bitmaps for strokes has been a feature of the Flash IDE since Flash 8, but now an ActionScript implementation has finally been added with `lineBitmapStyle()`. The signature is exactly the same as `beginBitmapFill()` but is obviously applied to lines drawn, not their fills.

```
lineBitmapStyle(
  bitmap:BitmapData,
  matrix:Matrix=null,
  repeat:Boolean=true,
  smooth:Boolean=true
):void
```

Once again, Chapters 3 and 4 will dive deeply into BitmapData and all the wonders it provides, so I won't spend too much time here explaining that class. With BitmapData and its pixel information defined, though, you can call this method to fill whatever strokes are drawn with that pixel information. The `matrix` argument allows you to transform the bitmap, scaling it up, rotating it, etc. `repeat`, which will nearly always be `true` for a drawn stroke, determines whether the bitmap will be repeated over the length of the stroke if that length exceeds the size of the bitmap. Finally, the `smooth` argument determines whether any bitmap scaled up will be smoothed. Setting this to `false` will cause scaled-up bitmaps to become pixelated but will improve performance.

The following class can be found as DrawingBitmapStrokes.as in this chapter's files. If you test the SWF and click and drag several times on the stage, you should see something like Figure 1-16.

```
package {

  import flash.display.BitmapData;
  import flash.display.Shape;
  import flash.display.Sprite;
  import flash.events.MouseEvent;

  [SWF(width=550, height=400, backgroundColor=0xFFFFFF)]

  public class DrawingBitmapStrokes extends Sprite {

    public function DrawingBitmapStrokes() {
      stage.addEventListener(MouseEvent.MOUSE_DOWN, onStageMouseDown);
      stage.addEventListener(MouseEvent.MOUSE_UP, onStageMouseUp);
    }

    private function createBrushStroke():void {
      var radius:uint = Math.random()*10 + 2;
      var diameter:uint = radius*2;
      var shape:Shape = new Shape();
      shape.graphics.beginFill(Math.random()*0xFFFFFF);
      shape.graphics.drawCircle(radius, radius, radius);
      shape.graphics.endFill();
      var brushStroke:BitmapData = new BitmapData(➥
diameter, diameter, true, 0x00000000);
      brushStroke.draw(shape);
      graphics.lineStyle(diameter);
      graphics.lineBitmapStyle(brushStroke);
    }

    private function onStageMouseDown(event:MouseEvent):void {
      createBrushStroke();
      graphics.moveTo(stage.mouseX, stage.mouseY);
      stage.addEventListener(MouseEvent.MOUSE_MOVE, onStageMouseMove);
    }

    private function onStageMouseUp(event:MouseEvent):void {
      stage.removeEventListener(MouseEvent.MOUSE_MOVE, ➥
onStageMouseMove);
    }

    private function onStageMouseMove(event:MouseEvent):void {
      graphics.lineTo(stage.mouseX, stage.mouseY);
      event.updateAfterEvent();
    }

  }

}
```

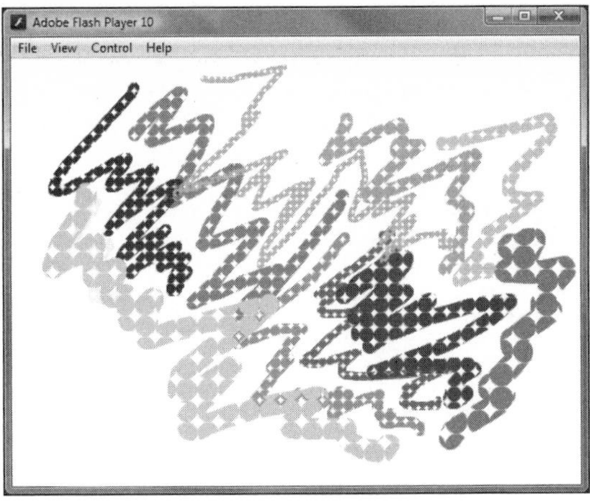

Figure 1-16.
The DrawingBitmapStrokes test with lines drawn using a generated bitmap

The majority of this code is similar to several of the examples thus far in this chapter, creating listeners for when the stage is clicked and when the mouse is released. In the handler for when the stage is clicked, `onStageMouseDown()`, I call a custom method, `createBrushStroke()`, move the virtual pen to the current mouse position, and then set up a listener for when the mouse moves. The handler for that event is `onStageMouseMove()`, which simply calls `lineTo()` to draw the line to the new position and updates the screen.

`createBrushStroke()` is where all the magic happens. The first two lines establish two variables, the radius and diameter of a circle I will use for the bitmap image. The radius will be a random value between 2 and 12, and the diameter, of course, will be twice that (why make up our own rules of geometry?).

The next several lines use drawing API code, which you should be pretty familiar with now, to draw a circle within a newly created shape. The color used in `beginFill()` is a random color within the 16 million or so available.

I then have two lines that create a new BitmapData instance and draw the circle vector into it. In the BitmapData constructor, the first two parameters are the width and height of the bitmap. The third argument, which you haven't seen yet, allows for transparent bitmaps. The fourth argument is the color that should be used as the default for the pixels in the bitmap. By default, this is solid white, so here I set it to be black with an opacity of 0.

Before ActionScript 3.0, colors used in Flash were defined as 16-bit values, which basically meant that the number only held the values for the three color channels. Represented as hexadecimal, a 16-bit number looked like 0xRRGGBB. With certain commands in ActionScript 3.0, you can now pass 32-bit numbers. The extra values are used to define the alpha channel of the color, between 0 and 0xFF. A 32-bit number in hexadecimal representing a color looks like 0xAARRGGBB. Therefore, in this example, I pass the constructor for BitmapData a value of 0x00000000, which is black (all color channels at 0) and 0 opacity. Black at full opacity would be represented as 0xFF000000. For this example, the RGB values are actually unimportant, since the pixel has no opacity applied.

We'll discuss 16-bit and 32-bit colors and hexadecimal representation in more depth in Chapter 3.

With the bitmap data defined, I can assign it as a stroke. Just like with lineGradientStyle(), I first have to call lineStyle() in order to set the thickness of the line, else the thickness will be 0 and the line will not be seen. I set the thickness to be the diameter and then call lineBitmapStyle() and pass the bitmap data. Now, all lines drawn will have a repeated image of the circle that I drew into the bitmap.

Preserving path data

One of the biggest additions to the drawing API is the ability to define drawing commands as distinct objects, not just as temporary calls to a Graphics instance. This means that, instead of calling lineStyle() and lineTo() directly, you could create a GraphicsStroke instance defining a line style and a GraphicsPath defining any number of lineTo() calls. These objects, which all implement the new IGraphicsData interface, can then be passed to the new drawGraphicsPath() method of the Graphics class.

Here's a quick snippet of code to show the syntax of some of these objects:

```
var stroke:GraphicsStroke = new GraphicsStroke(3);
stroke.fill = new GraphicsSolidFill(0xFF);
var path:GraphicsPath = new GraphicsPath();
path.lineTo(100, 0);
var commands:Vector.<IGraphicsData> = new Vector.<IGraphicsData>();
commands.push(stroke);
commands.push(path)
graphics.drawGraphicsData(commands);
```

Now, why on earth would you need to do this, you ask? Surely, we have done just fine calling drawing commands directly for numerous versions of Flash, thank you very much. Well, one great use would be for an undo feature in a drawing program. If each segment of a path was saved as a distinct object, these could be stored in a vector holding IGraphicsData objects. Removing commands from this vector and redrawing the shape would then be short work. Another use is when just a certain part of a complex routine needs to be altered, like color or transparency. That one aspect could be changed and the shape redrawn with minimal fuss, which is something we will explore in the next example.

The new classes that implement IGraphicsData all for the most part correspond to the drawing API commands you are familiar with, with a couple of exceptions:

- **GraphicsBitmapFill**: This class defines the settings for a bitmap fill of a shape. Its constructor matches the call to beginBitmapFill() exactly.
- **GraphicsEndFill**: This class corresponds to the drawing API command endFill() and does not take any arguments in its constructor.
- **GraphicsGradientFill**: This class defines the settings for a gradient fill of a shape. Its constructor matches the call to beginGradientFill() exactly.
- **GraphicsPath**: This class is an exception to the 1:1 correspondence between drawing API command and IGraphicsData implementation. A GraphicsPath instance actually holds a number of moveTo(), lineTo(), and curveTo() commands with their respective data. Basically, any drawing command that doesn't define the beginning or end of a fill or stroke should be included within a GraphicsPath instance.

- **GraphicsShaderFill**: This class defines the settings for a shader fill of a shape. Its constructor matches the call to `beginShaderFill()` exactly. We'll cover shaders and their use in the drawing API a little later in this chapter and in Chapter 5.
- **GraphicsSolidFill**: This class defines the settings for a solid color fill of a shape. Its constructor matches the call to `beginFill()` exactly.
- **GraphicsStroke**: This class defines the settings for the line style of a stroke, whether it be a solid color, gradient, bitmap, or shader. The constructor is nearly identical to `lineStyle()`, except instead of a color being an argument, an object implementing IGraphicsFill is expected as a final argument. This object could be an instance of GraphicsBitmapFill, GraphicsGradientFill, GraphicsShaderFill, or GraphicsSolidFill, so effectively any type of stroke can be defined in a single object.
- **GraphicsTriangleFill**: This class corresponds with the drawing API command `drawTriangles()`. We'll discuss this command a little later in the chapter.

Seem like a lot to digest? When first looking at the sheer number of new objects available for the drawing API, it can seem a little overwhelming—believe me, I speak from experience. However, when you consider that these objects still perform the same methods you are already familiar with, just packaged up in a different way, it's not as daunting as it initially might seem.

In this next example, we will explore a number of these commands in a simple drawing application that allows the user to alter the color or thickness of the stroke of all drawn lines at any time. Have a look at `PreservingPathData.as` to see the completed and commented class. Test `PreservingPathData.swf` to see the final application. Click and drag to draw lines, and use the up and down arrows to alter the thickness of the stroke. Press the spacebar to change the color of the stroke. The result will look similar to Figure 1-17. Want to see how it is done?

```
package {

  import flash.display.*;
  import flash.events.KeyboardEvent;
  import flash.events.MouseEvent;
  import flash.ui.Keyboard;

  [SWF(width=550, height=400, backgroundColor=0xFFFFFF)]

  public class PreservingPathData extends Sprite {

    private static const INIT_THICKNESS:uint = 5;
    private static const MAX_THICKNESS:uint = 50;
    private static const MIN_THICKNESS:uint = 1;

    private var _thickness:uint;
    private var _drawing:Boolean;
    private var _commands:Vector.<IGraphicsData>;
    private var _lineStyle:GraphicsStroke;
    private var _currentPath:GraphicsPath;
```

```
    public function PreservingPathData() {
      init();
    }

    private function init():void {
      var color:uint = Math.random()*0xFFFFFF;
      _thickness = INIT_THICKNESS;
      graphics.lineStyle(_thickness, color);
      _lineStyle = new GraphicsStroke(_thickness);
      _lineStyle.fill = new GraphicsSolidFill(color);
      _commands = new Vector.<IGraphicsData>();
      _commands.push(_lineStyle);
      stage.addEventListener(MouseEvent.MOUSE_DOWN, onStageMouseDown);
      stage.addEventListener(MouseEvent.MOUSE_UP, onStageMouseUp);
      stage.addEventListener(KeyboardEvent.KEY_DOWN, onStageKeyDown);
    }

    private function redrawPath():void {
      graphics.clear();
      graphics.drawGraphicsData(_commands);
    }

    private function onStageKeyDown(event:KeyboardEvent):void {
      if (!_drawing) {
        switch (event.keyCode) {
          case Keyboard.UP:
            if (_thickness < MAX_THICKNESS) {
              _lineStyle.thickness = ++_thickness;
              redrawPath();
            }
            break;
          case Keyboard.DOWN:
            if (_thickness > MIN_THICKNESS) {
              _lineStyle.thickness = --_thickness;
              redrawPath();
            }
            break;
          case Keyboard.SPACE:
            _lineStyle.fill = new GraphicsSolidFill(➥
Math.random()*0xFFFFFF);
            redrawPath();
            break;
        }
      }
    }

    private function onStageMouseDown(event:MouseEvent):void {
      _drawing = true;
      var x:Number = stage.mouseX;
```

```
      var y:Number = stage.mouseY;
      _currentPath = new GraphicsPath();
      _currentPath.moveTo(x, y);
      _commands.push(_currentPath);
      graphics.moveTo(x, y);
      stage.addEventListener(MouseEvent.MOUSE_MOVE, onStageMouseMove);
    }

    private function onStageMouseMove(event:MouseEvent):void {
      var x:Number = stage.mouseX;
      var y:Number = stage.mouseY;
      _currentPath.lineTo(x, y);
      graphics.lineTo(x, y);
      event.updateAfterEvent();
    }

    private function onStageMouseUp(event:MouseEvent):void {
      _drawing = false;
      stage.removeEventListener(MouseEvent.MOUSE_MOVE, ➥
onStageMouseMove);
    }

  }

}
```

Figure 1-17. The PreservingPathData test with the same path as on the left redrawn on the right with a thicker stroke

The three constants I define at the top of the class hold the values for the initial thickness setting of the drawn line and the maximum and minimum values for the thickness, respectively. For the private properties, `_thickness` will hold the value of the current thickness of the stroke on the path. The `_drawing` variable will serve as a flag for when the user is actively drawing or not.

The next three properties are the ones that make use of the new drawing API classes:

```
private var _commands:Vector.<IGraphicsData>;
private var _lineStyle:GraphicsStroke;
private var _currentPath:GraphicsPath;
```

_commands will hold the vector array of the IGraphicsData commands that will define the path. When drawGraphicsData() is called, it expects an array of this type. _lineStyle will hold a reference to the current line style of the path, including its thickness and color. Saving this as a variable will allow me at any time to change the thickness or color of the stroke. Finally, _currentPath will hold a reference to the current graphics path that is being drawn.

In the first two lines of the init() method, I find a random color for the stroke and set the initial thickness value. These are passed as parameters to lineStyle(). In addition to this, though, I also create a new GraphicsStroke instance, passing the thickness in the constructor.

```
_thickness = INIT_THICKNESS;
graphics.lineStyle(_thickness, color);
_lineStyle = new GraphicsStroke(_thickness);
```

Defining the fill is a little trickier, requiring a GraphicsSolidFill to be defined and assigned to the fill property of _lineStyle.

```
_lineStyle.fill = new GraphicsSolidFill(color);
```

Although this might seem like extra work, having the fill defined in this way makes it easy to define different stroke fills for a path and swap them out as needed. It also condenses into a single command what normally takes two for all but a solid color fill. Remember that to set a gradient line for a path directly you have to make two separate calls, one to lineStyle() to set the thickness and another to lineGradientStyle() to set the gradient properties. With GraphicsStroke, defining a gradient line can be accomplished using a single object as opposed to two, and the consistency it introduces when declaring strokes makes it much easier to work with in the end.

After _lineStyle is defined, I create a new vector array for IGraphicsData objects. The first of these will actually be _lineStyle. Any further drawing done will have its data pushed into this array, making it a snap to redraw the shape at any time since all of the commands will be saved.

```
_commands = new Vector.<IGraphicsData>();
_commands.push(_lineStyle);
```

The final two lines of init() set up two listeners, one for when the mouse clicks the stage, and another for when it is released. When the stage is clicked, onStageMouseDown() is invoked, which contains the following code.

```
_drawing = true;
var x:Number = stage.mouseX;
var y:Number = stage.mouseY;
```

```
_currentPath = new GraphicsPath();
_currentPath.moveTo(x, y);
_commands.push(_currentPath);
graphics.moveTo(x, y);
stage.addEventListener(MouseEvent.MOUSE_MOVE, onStageMouseMove);
```

The first thing done here is that the _drawing flag is set to true. I will use this to prevent keyboard events from being processed if the user is currently drawing. Next, I assign the current mouse coordinates into x and y variables. These values are passed as arguments to moveTo() in a new GraphicsPath instance I create and assign to _currentPath. This is the path that is being started by this mouse click. I push this path into the _commands vector to save it for later and then call moveTo() on this sprite's graphics instance to move the virtual pen to the new location. Finally, I set up a listener for when the mouse moves. That listener is removed and the _drawing flag is set to false in the onStageMouseup() handler.

onStageMouseMove() handles the event for when the mouse is moved. In that handler, I pass the current coordinates to the _currentPath's lineTo() method and pass the same coordinates to this sprite's graphics.lineTo() method, which draws the line. updateAfterEvent() is called to update the screen with these changes.

```
var x:Number = stage.mouseX;
var y:Number = stage.mouseY;
_currentPath.lineTo(x, y);
graphics.lineTo(x, y);
event.updateAfterEvent();
```

So let's take a step back. Why does it seem as if I am duplicating code here, calling methods not only on this sprite's graphics property but also on the _currentPath GraphicsPath instance? It isn't absolutely necessary that I have this duplication—I could simply update the _currentPath with the new moveTo() or lineTo() and call drawGraphicsData() to redraw the line. However, doing so will redraw the entirety of _currentPath, not just the most recent update, and if the user has been dragging for a while, this could be a large number of commands. I have this duplication in place so that I can not only save the data for the graphics path into _currentPath for reuse later but also draw only what is needed as the drawing is updated.

The final piece of code to look at takes advantage of all the saved drawing data and utilizes the drawGraphicsData() method that this whole section is about! It is found in the onStageKeyDown() and redrawPath() methods.

In init(), I had set up one more listener, this one for the KEY_DOWN event. The handler for that onStageKeyDown() will only run its code if the _drawing flag is false, which means the user is not currently drawing. So if the user is not drawing, I look for three separate keys. The up and down arrows will alter the thickness of the stroke if the _thickness values are within the limits, and the spacebar will change the fill color of the stroke by creating a new GraphicsSolidFill instance with a new random color (alternatively, you could just change the color property on the fill after casting it to GraphicsSolidFill). If the thickness or color changes, I call redrawPath().

```
if (!_drawing) {
  switch (event.keyCode) {
    case Keyboard.UP:
      if (_thickness < MAX_THICKNESS) {
        _lineStyle.thickness = ++_thickness;
        redrawPath();
      }
      break;
    case Keyboard.DOWN:
      if (_thickness > MIN_THICKNESS) {
        _lineStyle.thickness = --_thickness;
        redrawPath();
      }
      break;
    case Keyboard.SPACE:
      _lineStyle.fill = new GraphicsSolidFill(Math.random()*0xFFFFFF);
      redrawPath();
      break;
  }
}
```

Now, I have saved all the drawing that has occurred in the _commands vector, including the _lineStyle GraphicsStroke and any number of GraphicsPath instances, depending on how many times the user has clicked and dragged. But all of that drawing can be re-created with a single call to drawGraphicsData(), which I do in the redrawPath() method after first clearing all previous graphics.

```
graphics.clear();
graphics.drawGraphicsData(_commands);
```

Here, I have presented a simple example of altering the color or thickness of a stroke, but remember that any of the drawing commands can be saved and altered in this way. Want to swap in a new Bitmap fill for a shape? Want to change a curved path into a straight one, or smooth a curve of multiple points? There are countless possibilities that having these commands as distinct objects provides, and we will explore them as we continue through this book. Maybe you'll even see more in the next section.

Changing points on a path

A feature related to the drawGraphicsData() method presented in the last section is the new drawPath() method of the Graphics class. As opposed to the "draw everything at once" nature of drawGraphicsData(), which you've got to respect for its ambition, drawPath() draws only a single path using the current fill and stroke settings for the Graphics instance.

That single path can be any combination of moveTo(), lineTo(), and curveTo() commands. The signature of this method is as follows:

```
drawPath(
  commands:Vector,
  data:Vector,
  winding:String="evenOdd
):void
```

Let's have a look at each of those parameters.

- commands: A vector of GraphicsPathCommand values that define the lines and shapes to be drawn
- data: The anchor point coordinates (and control points, for curves) that each drawing path command requires
- winding: Defines the direction that a path will be drawn and affects how overlapping paths are filled

When you call this method, the first parameter would be a vector array of integers. Each index would be a different integer corresponding to the constants of the GraphicsPathCommand class, like CURVE_TO, LINE_TO, and MOVE_TO. The second parameter is a vector array of Numbers where parameters for a single drawing command are spread out over multiple indices.

This is a little odd conceptually, so let's take a step back and imagine we want to save drawing commands for a simple line from (10, 10) to (20, 20). This requires a moveTo() command to move to the start position and a lineTo() command to draw to the end position. This could be represented in vectors used by the drawPath() method as follows:

```
var commands:Vector.<int> = new Vector.<int>();
commands.push(GraphicsPathCommand.MOVE_TO);
commands.push(GraphicsPathCommand.LINE_TO);

var data:Vector.<Number> = new Vector.<Number>();
data.push(10, 10);
data.push(20, 20);

graphics.drawPath(commands, data);
```

Since push() allows for multiple arguments, you can pair up the coordinates in single calls as demonstrated here in order to have it make more sense visually, but the end result for data in this example is a vector with a length of 4, whereas the commands vector has only a length of 2.

The third and final argument in drawPath() is the winding option, which defines the direction of how a path is drawn, This has the most obvious effects on fills, where overlapped filled areas will appear either filled or not depending on the winding rule. The default winding rule, and the only one previously available through the Flash IDE and the drawing API, is EVEN_ODD. The alternative now is NON_ZERO. Figure 1-18 shows the difference that the winding rule can have on two overlapping fills.

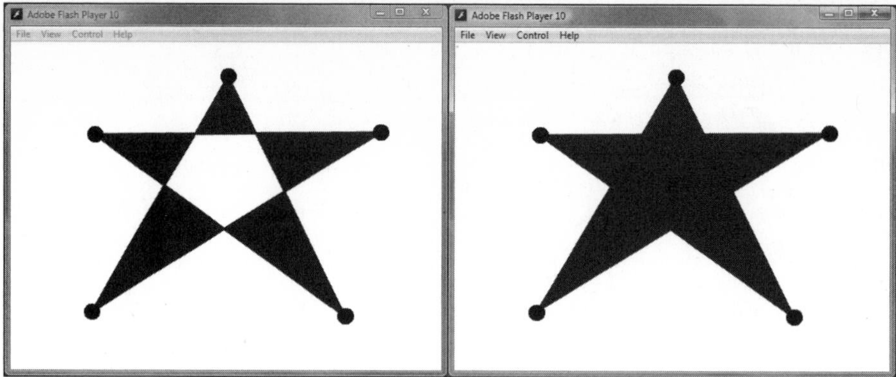

Figure 1-18. The same path drawn with a winding rule of EVEN_ODD on the left and NON_ZERO on the right

The drawPath() method is most useful if you are optimizing performance and find bottlenecks in your drawing code, as it will generally render faster than calling multiple drawing commands. As you will find in the next tutorial, it is also useful, like drawGraphicsData() proved to be, in redrawing shapes that have been saved from previous drawing actions.

Have a look at ChangingPointsOnAPath.as in this chapter's files, and test the corresponding SWF to see the finished application, which is shown in Figure 1-19. As you click the stage, anchor points are added, and lines are drawn between these points. If at any time you click an anchor, you can drag it around the stage, and the line will redraw itself. Let's look through the code to see how this is accomplished.

```
package {

  import flash.display.GraphicsPathCommand;
  import flash.display.Sprite;
  import flash.events.MouseEvent;

  [SWF(width=550, height=400, backgroundColor=0xFFFFFF)]

  public class ChangingPointsOnAPath extends Sprite {

    private const COLOR:uint = 0xFF;
    private const THICKNESS:uint = 3;

    private var _pathCommands:Vector.<int>;
    private var _pathData:Vector.<Number>;
    private var _anchors:Vector.<Sprite>;
    private var _anchor:Sprite;
    private var _anchorIndex:uint;

    public function ChangingPointsOnAPath() {
      init();
    }
```

```
    private function init():void {
      _anchors = new Vector.<Sprite>();
      _pathCommands = new Vector.<int>();
      _pathData = new Vector.<Number>();
      graphics.lineStyle(THICKNESS, COLOR);
      stage.addEventListener(MouseEvent.MOUSE_DOWN, onStageMouseDown);
    }

    private function addAnchor(x:Number, y:Number):void {
      var anchor:Sprite = new Sprite();
      anchor.graphics.lineStyle(20);
      anchor.graphics.lineTo(1, 0);
      anchor.addEventListener(MouseEvent.MOUSE_DOWN, onAnchorDown);
      anchor.addEventListener(MouseEvent.MOUSE_UP, onAnchorUp);
      anchor.x = x;
      anchor.y = y;
      addChild(anchor);
      _anchors.push(anchor);
    }

    private function redrawPath():void {
      graphics.clear();
      graphics.lineStyle(THICKNESS, COLOR);
      graphics.drawPath(_pathCommands, _pathData);
      var dataLength:uint = _pathData.length;
      graphics.moveTo(_pathData[dataLength-2], ➥
_pathData[dataLength-1]);
    }

    private function onAnchorDown(event:MouseEvent):void {
      _anchor = event.target as Sprite;
      _anchor.startDrag();
      _anchorIndex = _anchors.indexOf(_anchor);
      stage.addEventListener(MouseEvent.MOUSE_MOVE, onAnchorMove);
      event.stopPropagation();
    }

    private function onAnchorMove(event:MouseEvent):void {
      _pathData[_anchorIndex*2] = _anchor.x;
      _pathData[_anchorIndex*2+1] = _anchor.y;
      redrawPath();
      event.updateAfterEvent();
    }

    private function onAnchorUp(event:MouseEvent):void {
      if (_anchor) {
        _anchor.stopDrag();
        stage.removeEventListener(MouseEvent.MOUSE_MOVE, onAnchorMove);
      }
    }
```

```
        private function onStageMouseDown(event:MouseEvent):void {
          var x:Number = stage.mouseX;
          var y:Number = stage.mouseY;
          addAnchor(x, y);
          if (_pathCommands.length < 1) {
            _pathCommands.push(GraphicsPathCommand.MOVE_TO);
            graphics.moveTo(x, y);
          } else {
            _pathCommands.push(GraphicsPathCommand.LINE_TO);
            graphics.lineTo(x, y);
          }
          _pathData.push(x, y);
        }

      }

    }
```

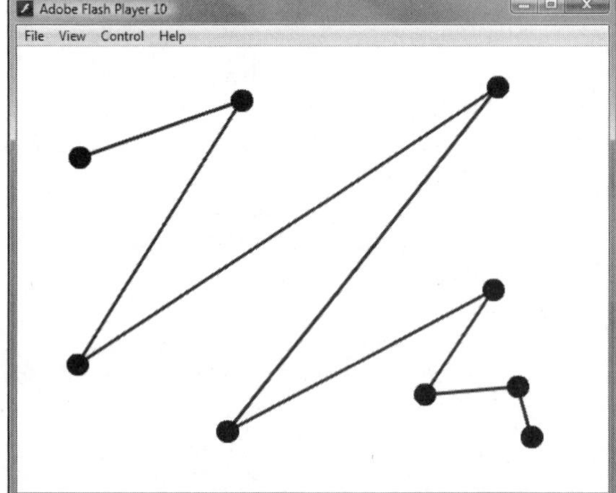

Figure 1-19. The ChangingPointsOnAPath test allowing for the path to be redrawn when an anchor point is dragged using the drawPath() command with saved path data

At the top of the class, you will see that I declare two constants, COLOR and THICKNESS, to be used for the line that will be drawn. For the properties, _pathCommands and _pathData will hold the path data that will be passed to drawPath(); _anchors will hold references to each anchor drawn; _anchor will hold a reference to an anchor being dragged; and _anchorIndex will store the index of the anchor being dragged.

The first three lines of the init() method just instantiate vectors for the properties.

```
_anchors = new Vector.<Sprite>();
_pathCommands = new Vector.<int>();
_pathData = new Vector.<Number>();
```

Aren't vectors a wonderful addition to ActionScript, ensuring that all values assigned to an array are of a specified type? Go on; show your love.

After assigning values to the properties in the init() method, I set up the line style to be used for the paths I will draw. I then set up a listener for when the stage is clicked, onStageMouseDown(), which contains the following code:

```
addAnchor(x, y);
if (_pathCommands.length < 1) {
  _pathCommands.push(GraphicsPathCommand.MOVE_TO);
  graphics.moveTo(x, y);
} else {
  _pathCommands.push(GraphicsPathCommand.LINE_TO);
  graphics.lineTo(x, y);
}
_pathData.push(x, y);
```

First, I call the addAnchor() method that takes the (x, y) coordinate of the mouse click and adds a sprite to the stage to represent an anchor point. The if conditional that follows checks to see if _pathCommands is empty, which would be the case if this was the first time the stage was clicked. If it is the first time, I call moveTo() and pass a MOVE_TO command to be stored in the _pathCommands vector. If _pathCommands is already storing some data, I know to call lineTo() and push a LINE_TO command into the _pathCommands vector. Finally, I push the coordinate into the _pathData vector, which is needed whether it is a MOVE_TO or LINE_TO call.

Like I did earlier in this chapter in the DrawingCurves class, I create a sprite to represent an anchor and use a thick line of a tiny length in order to create a quick-and-dirty circle in the addAnchor() method.

```
var anchor:Sprite = new Sprite();
anchor.graphics.lineStyle(20);
anchor.graphics.lineTo(1, 0);
```

Also, in this method, I set up listeners for both the MOUSE_DOWN and MOUSE_UP events on the sprite and position the anchor at the specified coordinates. Finally, I add the anchor to the display list and push it into the _anchors vector.

Now, when an anchor is clicked, the onAnchorDown() method will handle the event.

```
_anchor = event.target as Sprite;
_anchor.startDrag();
_anchorIndex = _anchors.indexOf(_anchor);
```

This stores a reference to the clicked anchor in the _anchor property and starts dragging the anchor. The index of the anchor is determined by finding the clicked anchor in the _anchors vector. I do this here so it doesn't need to be done constantly as the mouse is moved. You will see how that index is used in a moment.

The last two lines of onAnchorDown() set up a listener for when the mouse is moved, and stop the propagation of the MOUSE_DOWN event so that the stage doesn't get notification of it and add another anchor.

As the anchor is dragged, the onAnchorMove() handler is called. This updates the appropriate indices in _pathData with the new coordinate positions of the dragged anchor and calls the method redrawPath() to update the display.

```
_pathData[_anchorIndex*2] = _anchor.x;
_pathData[_anchorIndex*2+1] = _anchor.y;
redrawPath();
```

How exactly does this work? Since I know I am saving two coordinate positions for every anchor created, I can take the anchor's index and multiply it by 2 to find the x coordinate index, and then add 1 to find the y coordinate index (e.g., the anchor stored at index 2 of _anchors will have its coordinates stored at indices 4 and 5 in _pathData).

The last handler to discuss before looking at redrawPath() is onAnchorUp(), which stops the dragging of the anchor and removes the MOUSE_MOVE listener. This is only done if the anchor was first clicked. Since anchors are added on MOUSE_DOWN of the stage, a new anchor will be created and receive the MOUSE_UP event notification before it has been dragged. The conditional in that method prevents that.

The final piece of this class is the important redrawPath() method, which contains the following ActionScript:

```
graphics.clear();
graphics.lineStyle(THICKNESS, COLOR);
graphics.drawPath(_pathCommands, _pathData);
var dataLength:uint = _pathData.length;
graphics.moveTo(_pathData[dataLength-2], _pathData[dataLength-1]);
```

After clearing the graphics and setting up the line style again using the constants, I call drawPath() and pass in the two vectors containing the path information. I then have to explicitly call moveTo() to set the virtual pen at the last coordinate position (which would be at the end of _pathData) so that any subsequent calls will start from that last position. Otherwise, perhaps a bit counter-intuitively, the pen will start at (0, 0).

With this code, the path drawn by the user is stored and can be updated at any time with new coordinate positions for any of the anchor points. If you play around with the file, you should see how easy it is to redraw complex vectors with the data saved and simply passed back into drawPath(), another handy method in the drawing API arsenal.

Rendering triangles

One method that was included in the drawing API in the latest version of Flash, drawTriangles(), is specifically for the support of ActionScript 3D rendering by providing a means for triangular faces to have any type of fill applied with the proper transforms to scale and skew the fill within the face. This can be accomplished without the new drawTriangles() method, but it sure is a heck of a lot easier now!

Will you be using drawTriangles() in your day-to-day work? Probably not unless you are actively working on a 3D rendering engine in ActionScript. However, there could quite possibly be times that you need to do perspective distortion on an image that can't be accomplished by skewing the image or rotating the display object in three dimensions (more on that is coming in Chapter 6, which covers 3D), and in those cases, drawTriangles() would be perfect for the task.

Breaking down the drawTriangles method

First, let's take a look at the signature of drawTriangles():

```
drawTriangles(
  vertices:Vector.<Number>,
  indices:Vector.<int>=null,
  uvtData:Vector.<Number>=null,
  culling:String="none"
):void
```

Instead of defining each of these parameters here together, we will look at examples that help to do that for each parameter individually.

As you can see, the only required parameter is the first one, vertices, which is a vector array of numbers defining coordinate positions of vertices on your triangles. Each pair of indices represents the coordinate position of a vertex. It goes without saying (and yet here it is) that in order to define a triangle, you will need at least three vertices. So in its simplest form, you could use drawTriangles() as in the following example:

```
package {

  import flash.display.Sprite;

  [SWF(width=550, height=400, backgroundColor=0xFFFFFF)]

  public class DrawTrianglesVerticesTest extends Sprite {

    public function DrawTrianglesVerticesTest() {
      var vertices:Vector.<Number> = new Vector.<Number>();
      vertices.push(100, 50);
      vertices.push(150, 100);
      vertices.push(50, 100);

      graphics.beginFill(0xFF);
      graphics.drawTriangles(vertices);
      graphics.endFill();
    }

  }

}
```

Here, I have created a new vector to hold the vertices and have pushed in three pairs of coordinate pairs. We then call drawTriangles() with this vector, filling the triangle with a solid blue fill. The output of this movie is shown in Figure 1-20.

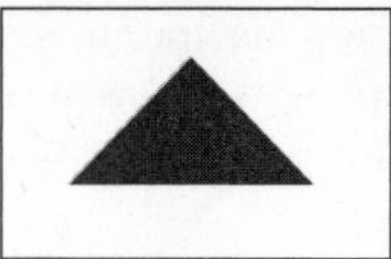

Figure 1-20.
A simple vector triangle drawn using the drawTriangles() command

So why would you use this instead of a few `lineTo()` commands? Well, you probably wouldn't. As I mentioned, the true power of this method comes in its use for rendering bitmaps on polygon meshes, which usually consist of lots of triangles. To take advantage of that, we need to look at the additional parameters of this method.

The second parameter of `drawTriangles()` is a vector array of int values that define, in groups of three, the vertices from the `vertices` vector that make up a triangle. If you don't specify indices, as I didn't in the first example, each trio of vertices will make up a triangle. This is fine if each vertex is only in one triangle, but most often, you will have vertices that are shared by triangles, as is the case when you have a connected mesh, so it is important then to use the `indices` parameter to define your triangles.

In this second example, which builds off of the first, I create a second triangle that is below the first triangle. The two triangles will actually share two of their vertices, which means in total I only need to define four vertices, and I will use the indices parameter in the `drawTriangles()` call to specify how the vertices should be used to make up the triangles. The different lines from the previous class (other than the class and constructor name) are in bold.

```
package {

  import flash.display.Sprite;

  [SWF(width=550, height=400, backgroundColor=0xFFFFFF)]

  public class DrawTrianglesIndicesTest extends Sprite {

    public function DrawTrianglesIndicesTest() {
      var vertices:Vector.<Number> = new Vector.<Number>();
      vertices.push(100, 50);
      vertices.push(150, 100);
      vertices.push(50, 100);
      vertices.push(100, 150);

      var indices:Vector.<int> = new Vector.<int>();
      indices.push(0, 1, 2);
      indices.push(1, 2, 3);

      graphics.beginFill(0xFF);
      graphics.drawTriangles(vertices, indices);
      graphics.endFill();
    }

  }

}
```

As you can see here, I add only a single new vertex to the `vertices` vector. I then create a new `indices` vector to hold the trio of indices that will make up each triangle. The first group I push in is `0, 1, 2`, meaning the first three indices (at index positions 0, 1, and 2 in the `vertices` vector) make up the first triangle. The second group is `1, 2, 3`, the index positions of the vertices that make up the second triangle. This should provide some insight into how you could define a polygon mesh consisting of vertex positions and how these vertices, when combined in groups of three, would make up triangles to fill. Testing the application shows two triangles sharing a common side, which looks suspiciously like a four-sided polygon and can be seen in Figure 1-21.

Figure 1-21.
Two triangles defined using four vertices and the indices option of the drawTriangles() command

The third parameter of `drawTriangles()` is another vector, this one holding numbers that determine the UVT texture coordinates for a bitmap fill (U, V, and T are variables representing texture coordinates). Basically, this allows you to define where on a bitmap each vertex should get its image from and is extremely useful for texture mapping. We will look at this parameter more in a moment when we move to a more complex example using a bitmap image.

Before that, though, let's talk about the fourth parameter, `culling`, a string that takes one of the constants from flash.display.TriangleCulling. Culling is a rendering determination for triangles, in which how a triangle appears in the coordinate space determines whether the fill within that triangle will be rendered. This is an optimization that usually manifests itself in 3D as backface culling, in which triangles that are facing towards the viewer are rendered and those facing away from the viewer are not, saving processes. An example of how backface culling works is shown in Figure 1-22.

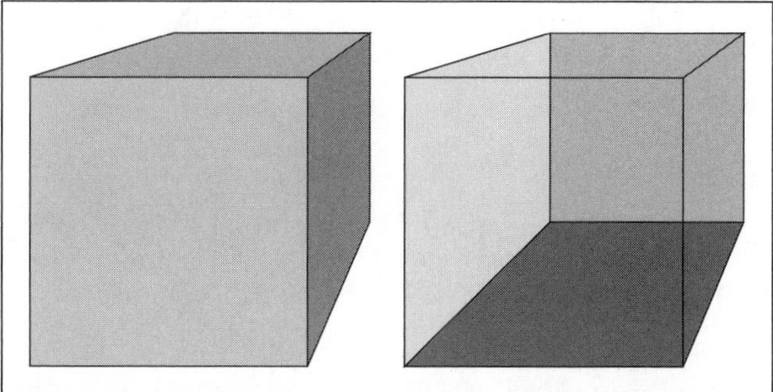

Figure 1-22. Two cubes with the same sides. The cube on the left shows the front-facing sides to the viewer. The cube on the right shows the back-facing sides with those facing the user rendered transparent so the ones behind can be seen. When backface culling is enabled, the sides that face away from the viewer, like those on the right, would not be rendered.

In this illustration, the cube on the right shows the sides on the cube facing away from the viewer. With backface culling, these would not be rendered. However, without backface culling, the back-facing faces would be drawn in addition to the ones facing the user (shown on the left). If the faces were drawn at the proper depths, the worst part is that the Flash Player would have to draw faces that are not even seen. If depths have not been properly sorted, it is possible that the back-facing sides would be drawn on top of the ones facing the viewer, as shown in the cube on the right.

So how exactly do you determine what is facing toward the user and what is facing away? Since a triangle always consists of three indices, these indices will appear to the viewer either in a clockwise or counterclockwise fashion. In the last ActionScript example, the first triangle was defined with the order of vertices being 0, 1, and 2. When this is rendered (since I am not doing anything like 3D transformation) it results in a triangle with its vertices appearing clockwise to the viewer, as shown in Figure 1-23.

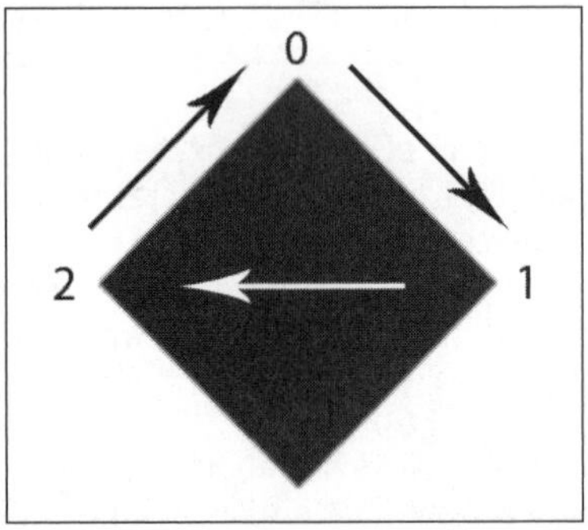

0

2 1

Figure 1-23. The first triangle from the previous example had its vertices defined in a manner that will appear clockwise to the viewer.

Alternatively, I could have defined that first triangle using the order 0, 2, 1. This would result in a counterclockwise layout when rendered, as shown in Figure 1-24. I have purposely defined the second triangle in the example code in a counterclockwise order.

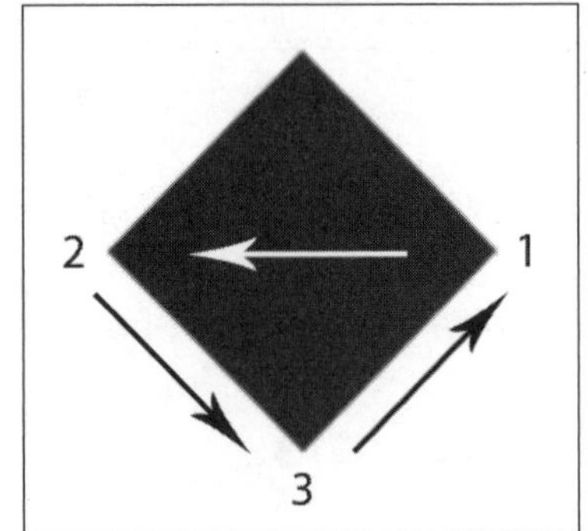

Figure 1-24. The second triangle from the previous example had its vertices defined in a manner that will appear counterclockwise to the viewer.

OK, so now you know about clockwise and counterclockwise orders, but how does that interact with the culling value? Well, by default, there is no culling, which means that it doesn't matter if a triangle's vertices are in a clockwise or counterclockwise order—the fill will always be rendered. If you have set either `POSITIVE` or `NEGATIVE` for the fourth parameter in drawTriangles(), though, fills will appear depending on whether the triangles appear clockwise or counterclockwise.

> *POSITIVE and NEGATIVE are actually referring to a polygon face's* normal *vector, which is a vector that is perpendicular to the surface of the polygon. Polygons that appear with a counterclockwise order of vertices have a* normal *that is pointing toward the viewer on a negative z axis. Polygons with a clockwise vertex ordering have a* normal *pointing away from the viewer, a positive value on the z axis. These are more heady 3D concepts that are a bit beyond the scope of this book, apart from this informative and friendly little focus point.*

In this final example, I set the culling value to show how it can affect the rendering of the triangles. All that has changed with this new class from the previous example, other than the name, are the bold lines.

```
package {

  import flash.display.Sprite;
  import flash.display.TriangleCulling;

  [SWF(width=550, height=400, backgroundColor=0xFFFFFF)]

  public class DrawTrianglesCullingTest extends Sprite {

    public function DrawTrianglesCullingTest() {
      var vertices:Vector.<Number> = new Vector.<Number>();
      vertices.push(100, 50);
      vertices.push(150, 100);
      vertices.push(50, 100);
      vertices.push(100, 150);

      var indices:Vector.<int> = new Vector.<int>();
      indices.push(0, 1, 2);
      indices.push(1, 2, 3);

      graphics.beginFill(0xFF);
      graphics.drawTriangles(vertices, indices, null, ➥
TriangleCulling.POSITIVE);
      graphics.endFill();
    }

  }

}
```

By setting the culling to POSITIVE, the top triangle disappears. You can think about its normal being positive on the z axis, or more simply, you can think about its vertices being in a clockwise order. Because of this, the triangle is not rendered. If you switch the culling in this class to NEGATIVE, you will see the top triangle rendered and the bottom hidden, for the exact opposite reasons.

Using bitmap fills

OK, we did a nice little skip and jump over the third parameter of drawTriangles(), but that is where the real power of the method can be utilized. UV coordinates are positions on a bitmap that are set for each defined vertex. These coordinates are normalized, meaning that each number is between 0 and 1, inclusive. On the x axis, 0 corresponds to the left edge of the bitmap, while 1 corresponds to the right edge. On the y axis, 0 corresponds to the top edge of the bitmap while 1 corresponds to the bottom edge. This translates into (0, 0) being the top left of the bitmap, (0, 1) being the top right, (1, 0) being the bottom left, and (1, 1) being the bottom right. The middle of the bitmap would be represented with the UV coordinate of (0.5, 0.5). These coordinates are shown in Figure 1-25.

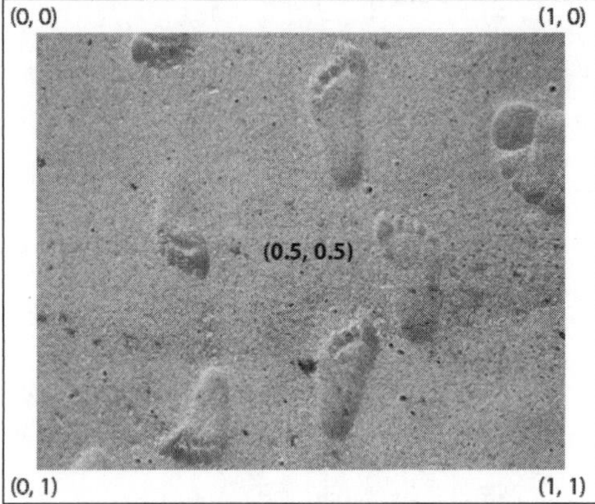

Figure 1-25. The UV coordinates of a rectangular bitmap that are used to map vertices to positions on the image

What this all means is that, for vertex 0, you can define that it gets its image data from a specific position on the bitmap. For instance, if vertex 0 gets its image data from (0, 0) on the bitmap and vertex 1 gets its data from (0, 1), then that triangle edge will be filled with all of the image data from the top edge of the bitmap across its entire width.

> *You will notice that the third parameter is actually called uvtData, not uvData. So what the heck is this "t"? If you include a third coordinate for every vertex in your triangles, then this corresponds to the t value, which is the "distance from the eye to the texture in eye space," according to the ActionScript documentation. Using this value will enable some perspective distortion correction when using drawTriangles() for texturing in 3D space. The lower the number set for t, the more the image will be scaled down at that vertex on the triangle.*
>
> *Figure 1-26 shows two rectangles consisting of two triangles each using the same bitmap fill. The triangles on the left only use UV data, and the distortion is apparent. The triangles on the right use UVT coordinates, and the distortion is greatly reduced. You can find the class that produces this SWF as DrawTrianglesUVTTest.as in this chapter's files.*

Figure 1-26. DrawTrianglesUVTTest, which shows how setting the t property for a texture coordinate can greatly reduce distortion of images when applied to triangles distorted by perspective.

This is all somewhat vague conceptually and is much easier to digest through a working example. Wouldn't you know, I can whip one of those up?

Have a gander at `RenderingTriangles.as` in this chapter's files. If you test the corresponding SWF, you should see something like what is shown in Figure 1-27. If you drag any of the numbered anchors around, the bitmap fill will skew to fill the triangle shapes, producing some interesting distortions. This is by far the most complex piece of code we've dealt with in this chapter (and in the first chapter, too!), so I will break it down piece by piece.

```
package {

  import flash.display.Bitmap;
  import flash.display.BitmapData;
  import flash.display.Loader;
  import flash.display.LoaderInfo;
  import flash.display.Sprite;
  import flash.events.Event;
  import flash.events.MouseEvent;
  import flash.net.URLRequest;
  import flash.text.TextField;

  [SWF(width=550, height=400, backgroundColor=0xFFFFFF)]

  public class RenderingTriangles extends Sprite {

    private var _anchors:Vector.<Sprite>;
    private var _anchor:Sprite;
    private var _anchorIndex:uint;
    private var _vertices:Vector.<Number>;
    private var _indices:Vector.<int>;
    private var _uvtData:Vector.<Number>;
    private var _image:BitmapData;

    public function RenderingTriangles() {
      loadImage();
    }
```

```
    private function loadImage():void {
      var loader:Loader = new Loader();
      loader.contentLoaderInfo.addEventListener(Event.COMPLETE, ➥
onImageLoaded);
      loader.load(new URLRequest("../../assets/footprints.jpg"));
    }

    private function defineTriangles():void {
      var border:Number = 50;
      var width:Number = stage.stageWidth;
      var height:Number = stage.stageHeight;

      _anchors = new Vector.<Sprite>();
      addAnchor(border, border);
      addAnchor(width-border, border);
      addAnchor(width/2, height/2);
      addAnchor(border, height-border);
      addAnchor(width-border, height-border);

      _vertices = new Vector.<Number>();
      for each (var anchor:Sprite in _anchors) {
        _vertices.push(anchor.x, anchor.y);
      }

      _indices = new Vector.<int>();
      _indices.push(1, 0, 2);
      _indices.push(0, 2, 3);
      _indices.push(1, 2, 4);
      _indices.push(2, 3, 4);

      _uvtData = new Vector.<Number>();
      _uvtData.push(0, 0);
      _uvtData.push(1, 0);
      _uvtData.push(.5, .5);
      _uvtData.push(0, 1);
      _uvtData.push(1, 1);
    }

    private function addAnchor(x:Number, y:Number):void {
      var anchor:Sprite = new Sprite();
      anchor.graphics.lineStyle(20);
      anchor.graphics.lineTo(1, 0);
      anchor.addEventListener(MouseEvent.MOUSE_DOWN, onAnchorDown);
      anchor.addEventListener(MouseEvent.MOUSE_UP, onAnchorUp);
      anchor.x = x;
      anchor.y = y;
      var label:TextField = new TextField();
      label.x = -4;
      label.y = -9;
```

```
      label.mouseEnabled = false;
      label.textColor = 0xFFFFFF;
      label.text = String(_anchors.length);
      anchor.addChild(label);
      addChild(anchor);
      _anchors.push(anchor);
    }

    private function draw():void {
      graphics.clear();
      graphics.beginBitmapFill(_image);
      graphics.drawTriangles(_vertices, _indices, _uvtData);
      graphics.endFill();
    }

    private function onAnchorDown(event:MouseEvent):void {
      _anchor = event.target as Sprite;
      _anchor.startDrag();
      _anchorIndex = _anchors.indexOf(_anchor);
      stage.addEventListener(MouseEvent.MOUSE_MOVE, onAnchorMove);
    }

    private function onAnchorMove(event:MouseEvent):void {
      _vertices[_anchorIndex*2] = _anchor.x;
      _vertices[_anchorIndex*2+1] = _anchor.y;
      draw();
      event.updateAfterEvent();
    }

    private function onAnchorUp(event:MouseEvent):void {
      if (_anchor) {
        _anchor.stopDrag();
        stage.removeEventListener(MouseEvent.MOUSE_MOVE, onAnchorMove);
      }
    }

    private function onImageLoaded(event:Event):void {
      var loaderInfo:LoaderInfo = event.target as LoaderInfo;
      var bitmap:Bitmap = loaderInfo.content as Bitmap;
      _image = bitmap.bitmapData;
      defineTriangles();
      draw();
    }

  }

}
```

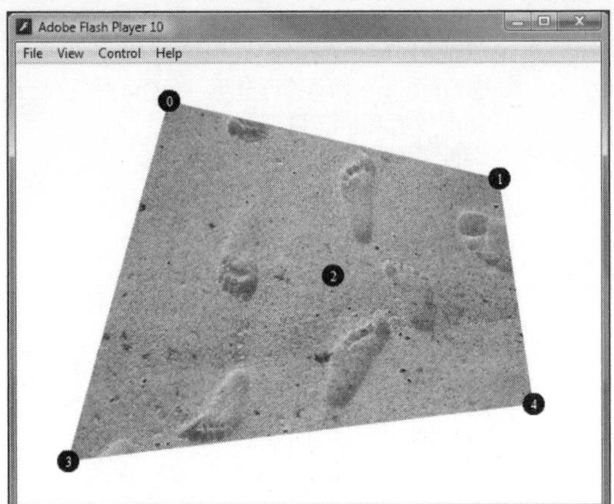

Figure 1-27.
The RenderingTriangles.swf test that uses four triangles to draw a bitmap image and allows for image distortion through dragging of the anchors

First, let's talk about what each of the properties in the class will hold.

```
private var _anchors:Vector.<Sprite>;
private var _anchor:Sprite;
private var _anchorIndex:uint;
private var _vertices:Vector.<Number>;
private var _indices:Vector.<int>;
private var _uvtData:Vector.<Number>;
private var _image:BitmapData;
```

I do something similar in this class to what I did in ChangingPointsOnAPath. If you recall from that example, I created visible anchor points that could then be clicked and dragged. In this class, `_anchors` is a vector array holding references to all those anchor points, while `_anchor` holds the reference to the current anchor point being dragged, and `_anchorIndex` stores the index position of that anchor within the `_anchors` vector, to be used to update coordinates as the anchor is dragged.

The next three properties correspond to the three arguments I will use in the `drawTriangles()` call. We looked at vertices and indices in the last example. `_uvtData` is another vector that will hold all of the UV information for the vertices.

Finally, `_image` will keep a reference to the bitmap data used for the triangle texture. Of course, I have to get that image from somewhere. That is handled by the loading of the file `footprints.jpg`, included with this chapter's files.

```
loader.load(new URLRequest("../../assets/footprints.jpg"));
```

This call occurs in `loadImage()`, which is called from within this class's constructor. In the handler for the image load completion event, I get the reference to the bitmap loaded in and save its data into the `_image` property. I then call two new methods, `defineTriangles()` and `draw()`.

```
_image = bitmap.bitmapData;
defineTriangles();
draw();
```

The first method will set up all of the triangle drawing properties, including the UV data. The second will actually draw the images using triangles. Let's look first at defineTriangles(), block by block.

```
var border:Number = 50;
var width:Number = stage.stageWidth;
var height:Number = stage.stageHeight;
```

border, arbitrarily set to 50, will be used to define the initial size of the triangular mesh. The width and height are set from the current size of the stage. Once these variables are set, I create the _anchors vector and add five anchors through the addAnchor() method.

```
_anchors = new Vector.<Sprite>();
addAnchor(border, border);
addAnchor(width-border, border);
addAnchor(width/2, height/2);
addAnchor(border, height-border);
addAnchor(width-border, height-border);
```

We will get to that addAnchor() code in a moment, but it works similarly to ChangingPointsOnAPath, where a sprite is added to the display list at the specified coordinate position and its reference is pushed into the _anchors vector.

Once the anchors are created, I can easily set up the vertices of the triangles by using the coordinates of the anchor sprites.

```
_vertices = new Vector.<Number>();
for each (var anchor:Sprite in _anchors) {
  _vertices.push(anchor.x, anchor.y);
}
```

_vertices, a vector of numbers, is instantiated in the first new line. I then run through all the anchors and push their coordinate positions into the _vertices vector. After that, I instantiate the _indices vector and push into this four separate groups of three.

```
_indices = new Vector.<int>();
_indices.push(1, 0, 2);
_indices.push(0, 2, 3);
_indices.push(1, 2, 4);
_indices.push(2, 3, 4);
```

These define the four triangles that will make up the mesh. For example, the first triangle is made up of vertices 1, 0, and 2, which are the top right, top left, and middle vertices, respectively. I do not worry too much here about clockwise or counterclockwise ordering, since no backface culling is needed in this example.

With _vertices and _indices defined, I only need to define UV data.

```
_uvtData = new Vector.<Number>();
_uvtData.push(0, 0);
_uvtData.push(1, 0);
```

```
_uvtData.push(.5, .5);
_uvtData.push(0, 1);
_uvtData.push(1, 1);
```

Here you can see five sets of coordinates being pushed into the _uvtData vector. Each one corresponds to a vertex stored in _vertices (e.g., _uvtData[0] and _uvtData[1] correspond to the vertex whose coordinates are stored in _vertices[0] and _vertices[1]). Remember, each coordinate position is normalized, which means it falls between 0 and 1, inclusive. Keeping that in mind, the first coordinate position for the first vertex is at the top left of the bitmap. The second vertex, which I defined at the top right of the triangle mesh, is at the top right of the bitmap. The third vertex, placed right in the center of the mesh, is given a UV position of (.5, .5), or right at the center of the bitmap.

That's it for the values that are passed to drawTriangles(). The remaining code in the class handles the drawing and dragging of the anchors. For the drawing, it is very similar to what was demonstrated in ChangingPointsOnAPath, so we will not step through all that code again. The new lines create a TextField instance and add it to the anchor.

```
var label:TextField = new TextField();
label.x = -4;
label.y = -9;
label.mouseEnabled = false;
label.textColor = 0xFFFFFF;
label.text = String(_anchors.length);
anchor.addChild(label);
```

The text assigned is the current length of the _anchors array (so the first anchor will have the text "0", the second will have "1", etc.). This way, you can see very clearly the index of each vertex/anchor. After the text field is added in addAnchor(), I add the anchor to the display list and push its reference into the _anchors vector.

The anchors not only show the positions of the triangles' corners but are draggable elements that allow you to reposition the triangles and therefore distort the image. I have demonstrated this dragging code previously in ChangingPointsOnAPath, so there should be nothing surprising in this code, except perhaps how easy it is to do image distortion with the new drawing API!

```
private function onAnchorDown(event:MouseEvent):void {
  _anchor = event.target as Sprite;
  _anchor.startDrag();
  _anchorIndex = _anchors.indexOf(_anchor);
  stage.addEventListener(MouseEvent.MOUSE_MOVE, onAnchorMove);
}

private function onAnchorMove(event:MouseEvent):void {
  _vertices[_anchorIndex*2] = _anchor.x;
  _vertices[_anchorIndex*2+1] = _anchor.y;
  draw();
  event.updateAfterEvent();
}
```

```
private function onAnchorUp(event:MouseEvent):void {
  if (_anchor) {
    _anchor.stopDrag();
    stage.removeEventListener(MouseEvent.MOUSE_MOVE, onAnchorMove);
  }
}
```

When an anchor is clicked, onAnchorDown() is called, and the anchor's dragging begins. I save a reference to the anchor in _anchor and save its _anchorIndex as well. The final line of the handler sets up a listener for when the mouse moves as the anchor is dragged.

The onAnchorMove() handler updates the (x, y) coordinates of the vertex that corresponds to the dragged anchor. With these values updated, draw() can be called to redraw the bitmap within the triangles based on the new vertex values.

Finally, onAnchorUp() handles when the anchor is released, stopping its drag and removing the MOUSE_MOVE listener.

The last piece of code to examine in this class is the drawTriangles() call, which is made in the draw() method. This is initially called from the onImageLoaded() handler.

```
private function draw():void {
  graphics.clear();
  graphics.beginBitmapFill(_image);
  graphics.drawTriangles(_vertices, _indices, _uvtData);
  graphics.endFill();
}
```

Pretty straightforward, no? The work came in setting up the variables, but now, with those defined, I simply need to start the bitmap fill and pass all of the values to drawTriangles(). Go ahead and test the completed application now and drag the anchors about the stage. Now, imagine doing that on a 3D model and give a sigh of anticipation for the wonderful possibilities.

Introducing shaders

Shaders, Reader. Reader, Shaders.

This is a huge topic, and as such I have reserved a whole chapter for it later in the book. I considered giving a little peek at what was to come, but think after such a mammoth first chapter, everyone deserves a time away from the keyboard. (Remember, we're doing this for the fun!)

All I shall say is that the drawing API now includes two methods, one for fills and one for strokes, that allow you to draw with the new Shader class. A Shader holds a function that interacts with each pixel of an image. You can then take that filtered image and use that for a fill or stroke.

The two methods that handle this functionality look like this:

```
beginShaderFill(shader:Shader, matrix:Matrix=null):void
lineShaderStyle(shader:Shader, matrix:Matrix=null):void
```

You will notice that both take the shader to use and an optional matrix to transform it. More to come in Chapter 5!

Summary

The drawing API is a fantastic set of tools that an entire book could be spent exploring. I have tried to touch on each aspect of the API in this chapter, diving more deeply into the new features that have been introduced with Flash Player 10, like IGraphicsData and rendering triangles. There is still more to explore, but thankfully, we are just in our first chapter! We will take advantage of the drawing API extensively in the chapters and examples to come, so it is important to have a solid foundation about what the API can do. Plus, making graphics from scratch is just plain cool.

In the next chapter, we will begin to explore the built-in filters and blend modes that ActionScript and its display objects offer. Like the drawing API, there are what look to be only a few commands, but with them in hand (or in code), the range of possibilities is staggering. Take a breath; take a break. Then I'll see you after the page turn.

Chapter 2

FILTERS AND BLEND MODES

Don't tell the last chapter if it comes around asking, but sometimes vectors are just not enough. Now, don't get me wrong—I love a good solid-colored circle that scales without pixelation just as much as the next guy. For the longest time, Flash was a program devoted to vectors and their animation. Using vectors in movies brought down file size and, when used properly, performed better than animating bitmaps. But in this broadband world populated by supercharged Flash Players, Flash movies and applications can more easily take advantage of bitmaps and bitmap effects, and we can thank our lucky pixels.

When Flash 8 was released, a whole slew of new graphics capabilities were introduced into the Flash and Flex Builder IDEs as well as the Flash Player runtime for this purpose. Two of these features, blend modes and filters, were familiar to users of other graphics software like Photoshop and Illustrator and were a welcome addition, especially when workflows required reproduction of Photoshop layouts or effects in Flash, or applications required animated bitmap effects like glowing buttons or blurred elements.

In this chapter, we will look at both filters and blend modes as they are available through ActionScript 3.0 and explore some of the uses for each. These features are most useful when combined in more complex effects, so it is important to have a firm understanding of their individual capabilities before moving on to more fully realized case studies.

Applying blend modes

I remember when I learned Photoshop some years ago that the general approach to teaching blend modes was to explain in a sentence what something like Multiply did and include a picture for demonstration. After that, you were sent off into the wild and left to experiment as you designed to determine the best blend mode to use for a certain effect. Click around in the Layers palette long enough and eventually you'd find a blend mode that worked for you, whether you truly understood it or not.

I must admit, when preparing for this chapter, it was very tempting to follow suit. Blend modes are conceptually very simple, but their practical application is sometimes difficult to communicate and really often does result only from a bit of luck and guesswork. However, blend modes can be incredibly powerful and useful in more complex effects, so it is necessary to really know what is going on under the hood, so to speak.

So what exactly is a blend mode? Simply put, a blend mode is a setting on a display object that alters the color of each individual pixel of the display object based on the color of the visible pixel below it. There is a `blendMode` property on DisplayObject itself, which can be set to any constant value of the BlendMode class. That means that items like Sprite, Shape, Bitmap, or TextField can each get their own blend mode setting.

By default, a display object has a `BlendMode.NORMAL` setting, which means that its pixels' colors are not affected by the colors of the pixels below. An opaque display object with a `BlendMode.NORMAL` setting will therefore completely obscure or cover pixels below it. But that's not exciting, is it?

When a different blend mode is chosen, though, a new pixel color is determined based on the blend mode setting and the color values of each of the display object's pixels and the pixels below it. A simple example would be the `BlendMode.ADD` setting, which simply adds the values of the two pixels and returns the result as a new pixel color, with 0xFF (255) being the upper limit. So if a display object was dark red (0x330000) and the background below it was medium gray (0x666666), adding each of the color channels separately would produce a color that was a lighter red—0x996666, which, broken down into individual color channels, would be 0x33 + 0x66 for red, 0x00 + 0x66 for green, and 0x00 + 0x66 for blue.

> *If the concept of color channels is foreign to you, you might have a quick jump ahead to the next chapter on `BitmapData`, where I discuss this topic in more depth, as it is an important component of manipulating bitmap information.*

"That's all very mathematically interesting," I hear you say, "but what does that mean to me?" The truth is, in general, use of blend modes still often comes down to what works best for each specific need. There are some generally useful and commonly understood applications of specific modes—for instance, using `SCREEN` when creating a highlight on a darker color or `MULTIPLY` when creating shadows—but for many others, it will require some experimentation when the need arises.

But that doesn't mean I'm not going to help. In this section, we will look at each of the blend modes in turn and use a helpful little application in order to better conceptualize how pixels interact when each blend mode is applied.

Working with the BlendModes application

Included with this chapter's download files are a `BlendModes.as` class file and the compiled `BlendModes.swf`. If you open the SWF, you will see the application shown in Figure 2-1, with three images across the top. The goat and stagecoach images have been duplicated and stacked on the right with the stagecoach image on top of the goat image. Since the initial blend mode for the stacked stagecoach image is set to `NORMAL`, the stagecoach image completely obscures the goat image underneath. If you hover over any of the images, you will see a readout below each with the color value of the rolled-over pixel in each image, both as a hexadecimal value and broken out into the decimal value for each channel, as well as large, colored rectangles displaying the actual pixel color. If you click the images and hold down the mouse button, a small target will appear on each image to show the pixel being evaluated. You can also click and drag the mouse off the images to leave the target drawn.

To change the blend mode being used on the top right image, simply click the name of the blend mode at the bottom of the application. This will cycle through all available blend modes for a display object. If you would like to swap either of the two source images (left or middle), double-click the image to replace, and you will get a browse dialog you can use to select a new image.

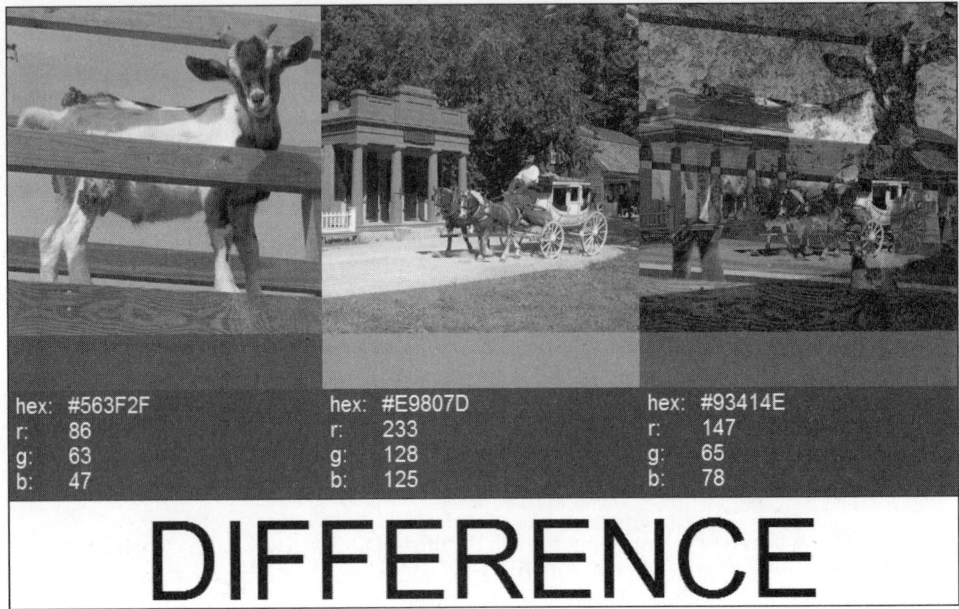

Figure 2-1. The BlendModes application that lets you compare the effects of blend modes on pixels

> *Blend modes rely on the interaction of pixel values in the individual color channels of an image. As such, black and white screenshots are not always the best representation of how blend modes affect two images. Be sure to open the `BlendModes.swf` file as you continue through this section in order to see the effects.*

Although we will not be dissecting the code used to create this application, it is not especially complex and only contains a single class with around 300 lines of code. There are several lines that deal with BitmapData, a class we will go into in depth in the next chapter, the most noteworthy being the use of `getPixel()` to retrieve the color of the pixels hovered over. There is also the loading and use of a custom shader, which is part of a big and exciting topic we will explore more fully in Chapter 5.

The line most appropriate to this discussion on blend modes is the single line where the blend mode is set for the top right image. That's right, a single line. That line is contained in the `onBlendModeClick()` handler that occurs when the text field at the bottom of the application is clicked.

```
private function onBlendModeClick(event:MouseEvent):void {
  var index:uint = _blendModes.indexOf(_blendModeLabel.text);
  if (++index >= _blendModes.length) {
    index = 0;
  }
  var blendMode:String = _blendModes[index];
  _blendModeLabel.text = blendMode;
  _blendedBitmap.blendMode = BlendMode[blendMode];
  displayColorData();
}
```

In this class, `_blendModes` is an array containing all the names of the blend modes as they are stored as constants in the BlendMode class. This means that `"normal"` is not held in the array, but rather the string `"NORMAL"`, which is the name of the constant in BlendMode, that is, `BlendMode.NORMAL`. As an interesting aside, this array is populated in the `init()` function of this class by using the little utility treasure `describeType()` to inspect the BlendMode class and some E4X operations. For those interested, this is explained in more depth in the comments in the file.

The first thing this handler does is check where the current blend mode resides in the list of blend modes. If we have reached the end of the list, which is checked in the conditional, we return to the beginning. This allows us to continually cycle through the blend modes. The new blend mode name selected from the list is assigned to the `text` property of the textfield, and the new blend mode itself is assigned to the stacked bitmap image using the array access operator on BlendMode. This means that if the `blendMode` string selected is `"DIFFERENCE"`, the value assigned to `_blendedBitmap.blendMode` will be `BlendMode["DIFFERENCE"]`, which is the same as accessing the value with `BlendMode.DIFFERENCE`.

Have a look through the rest of the file if you are curious about what is going on or if you want to take a peek at some of the BitmapData and Shader functionality we will be exploring in the coming chapters. There are also several uses of the drawing API when creating the colored rectangles (`drawColorRect()`) and when drawing the targets (`onHolderMouseDown()`), so you can see we are already using the skills from the last chapter for practical application. See? I told you it would all come in handy!

As we progress through the blend modes, I will be referring to this application in order to demonstrate how pixels interact.

Examining the modes

Let's now step through each blend mode and examine how resulting pixel values are calculated based on the images. First, in addition to the `BlendModes.swf` that you can use to test each mode with actual images and compare pixels, let's create a new file that we can use to test the equations that calculate the results for the blend modes. Create a new

ActionScript 3.0 class, and save it as BlendModeFunctions.as. Here's all the code we will need to start:

```
package {

  import flash.display.Sprite;

  public class BlendModeFunctions extends Sprite {

    public function BlendModeFunctions() {
      var topPixel:Object = {red:0xFF, green:0x33, blue:0x99};
      var bottomPixel:Object = {red:0x99, green:0xFF, blue:0x99};
      var method:String = "normal";

      var red:Number = this[method](topPixel.red, bottomPixel.red);
      var green:Number = this[method](topPixel.green, bottomPixel.green);
      var blue:Number = this[method](topPixel.blue, bottomPixel.blue);
      var resultPixel:uint = (red << 16) | (green << 8) | (blue);
      trace(resultPixel.toString(16));
    }

  }

}
```

You can compile this using your tool of choice (remember to look at the appendix if you need guidance on how to compile an ActionScript class using Flash or Flex Builder). Note that the output of this file will only be a trace statement, so if you are testing the precompiled SWF outside of an IDE you won't see anything but a white stage.

Here, the constructor creates a number of local variables. The first two lines are two colors that we will use to calculate the results of different blending modes applied. topPixel would be a pixel within the display object with the blend mode applied, while bottomPixel would be a colored pixel below it. The variable method will hold the name of the method you wish to test, which will correspond to the different blend modes you can apply.

The next three lines find a resultant red, green, and blue color based on the method called. Each line passes in the corresponding color channel value from the topPixel object and the bottomPixel object. These three channel results are then combined into a single color using some bitwise operations, and the resulting color is traced as a hexadecimal value.

As we move through this section and add methods, change the value assigned to the method variable to match the name of the method to test.

```
var method:String = "normal";
```

Play around with different color values as well to see different results. Right now, we have no methods to call, so we better start cracking.

In the constructor for BlendModeFunctions, I have used bit shifting in order to create a new color from the three constituent color channels:

```
var resultPixel:uint = (red << 16) | (green << 8) | (blue);
```

Bit shifting is a larger subject that we will not be going into in great depth in this book, but in this context, it provides an easy way to take the values from 0–255 (or 8 bits) that make up each color channel and shift them into the proper range of a larger number that holds enough data for all three color channels (0 to 16,777,215, which are the total number of colors available when stored in 24 bits).

A bitwise operator like left shift (<<) operates on binary values and moves the values over the specified number of bits. So if we have the hexadecimal value of 0xFF for the red channel, shifting this number over 16 bits will produce a hexadecimal result of 0xFF0000, which you should recognize as the actual hexadecimal value for red. The bitwise OR (|) then combines the three numbers together in a way that preserves the values in each channel.

Working in the opposite direction, we can extract an individual color component from an RGB numeric value by using the right-shift operator (>>) and the bitwise AND (&). Like the left-shift operator, the right-shift operator shifts the bits, but this time to the right. So to extract the red value from 0xFFCC00, you would use (0xFFCC00 >> 16). This would leave us with 0xFF. You can do the same to extract the other color components, but if you just use (0xFFCC00 >> 8) to extract green, you are actually left with 0xFFCC, since the red pixel values have been shifted over as well. To fix this, we use the bitwise AND, which compares two binary numbers and, in this case, drops off any values but those stored in the first 8 bits: (0xFFCC00 >> 8 & 0xFF).

The way this works is more easily understood when you look at the binary representation of these numbers. 0xFFCC is 1111111111001100 in binary and 0xFF is 11111111. The bitwise AND looks at each bit, which in base 2 can either be a 0 or 1, and returns 1 only if both values it compares are 1. Bit positions where one or both of the values are 0 will result in 0. The operation of (0xFFCC & 0xFF) therefore looks like this:

```
  1111111111001100
&         11111111
------------------
          11001100
```

11001100 in binary is 204 in decimal or CC in hexadecimal, which, of course, is the value of the green channel.

The examples of this book will use bitwise operations for extracting and combining colors in this way using these common techniques. For more information on bitwise operations and bit shifting, you should refer to Adobe's ActionScript documentation.

NORMAL

There's not much to say on this one. This is the default blend mode setting for display objects, and when applied to a display object, that object's pixels will not interact with the pixels underneath to affect the color values. Figure 2-2 shows, in the stacked image at the right, that the stagecoach image completely obscures the goat image, and the color values remain unchanged. The method added to our BlendModeFunctions class would look like this:

```
public function normal(topPixel:uint, bottomPixel:uint):uint {
  return topPixel;
}
```

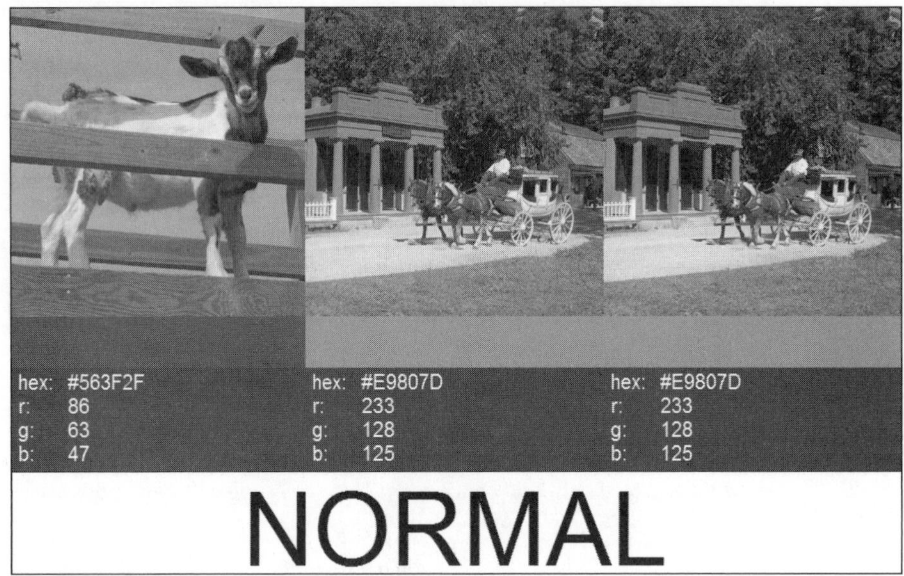

Figure 2-2. The NORMAL mode applied to the middle image over the left image with the result shown on the right.

MULTIPLY

When the blend mode is set to MULTIPLY, the pixels of the display object are multiplied with the pixels below, and the results of each color channel are normalized by dividing by 255 (0xFF). The function in our class to perform this operation would look like this:

```
public function multiply(topPixel:uint, bottomPixel:uint):uint {
  return (bottomPixel * topPixel)/255;
}
```

If you want to test this in the BlendModes.as file, be sure to change the method to multiply.

```
var method:String = "multiply";
```

As an example of how this blend mode would work, if the display object pixel is medium gray, 0x666666, and the color beneath it is light red, 0xCC9999, the resulting color would be a darker red, 0x513D3D.

Let's plug in the numbers for red to see how that works. 0x66 in decimal is 102. 0xCC is 204. If you multiply these together and divide by 255, you get 81.6 in decimal, or 0x51 in hexadecimal.

Using MULTIPLY will always result in darker colors. It's great when you need to create shadows on objects, and I often use it when I need a simple way to darken a color channel when creating bitmap effects. The result is shown in Figure 2-3.

Figure 2-3. The MULTIPLY mode applied to the middle image over the left image with the result shown on the right.

SCREEN

The SCREEN mode is a little bit more complex in equation, but conceptually, you can imagine it as simply doing the opposite of the MULTIPLY mode, lightening colors in a way that makes it extremely useful for highlight effects. It is also useful in creating the Marlene Dietrich Vaseline-on-a-camera-lens effect by screening a blurred copy of an image over the original image and setting it at a low opacity. Screen those wrinkles away!

For SCREEN, the way a resulting pixel is calculated is by taking the inverse of each color (that is, subtracting the value from 255), multiplying the results together, normalizing this value, and taking the inverse of the result once more. It is more easily digested in numbers and code than in English explanations:

```
public function screen(topPixel:uint, bottomPixel:uint):uint {
  return (255 - ((255 - topPixel) * (255 - bottomPixel))/255);
}
```

To demonstrate this, let's take red (0xFF0000) over medium gray (0x666666). The result of this using SCREEN would be 0xFF6666, or a lighter red. Plugging in numbers for the blue channel, we get the following:

```
255 - ((255 - 0x00) * (255 - 0x66))/255
255 - ((255 - 0) * (255 - 102))/255
255 - 39015/255
102 // 0x66
```

You can see the results of the SCREEN mode in Figure 2-4.

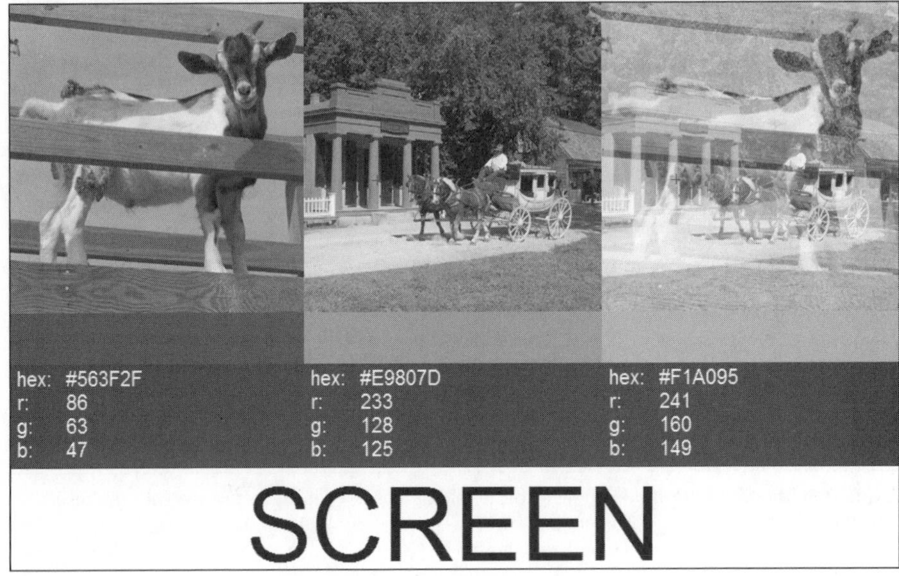

Figure 2-4. The SCREEN mode applied to the middle image over the left image with the result shown on the right.

HARDLIGHT

With HARDLIGHT, things get a little more complex. Basically, HARDLIGHT (as well as OVERLAY, as you will see) combines MULTIPLY and SCREEN together in a single blend mode. When the underlying color is greater than 50 percent gray (a value of 127.5 for a channel), the pixel is screened, and when the underlying color is less than 50 percent gray, it is multiplied. The result of this is that pixels of the display object are screened or multiplied based on the pixel values from the original display object itself—where the display object is lighter, its colors will be screened over the underlying elements, and where the display object is darker, its colors will be multiplied. An example is shown in Figure 2-5.

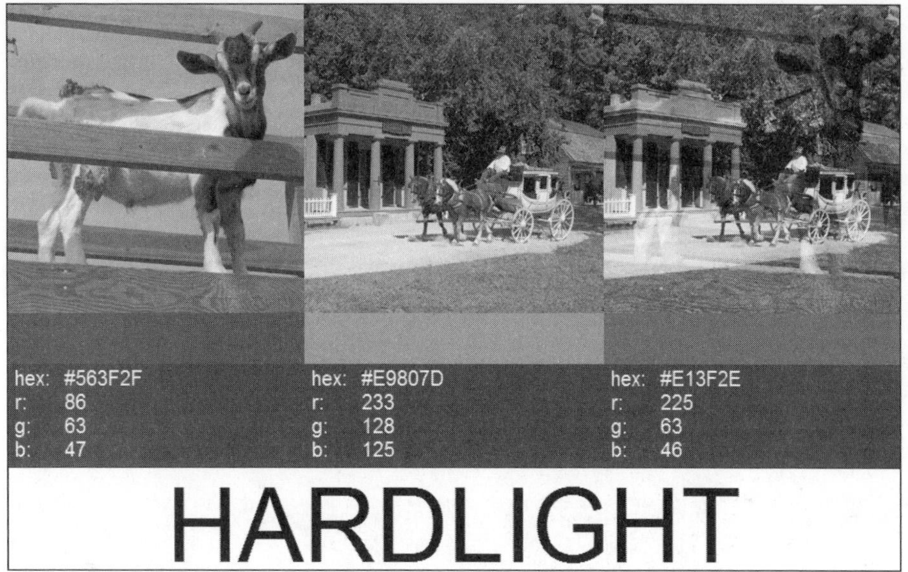

Figure 2-5. The HARDLIGHT mode applied to the middle image over the left image with the result shown on the right.

To make this concept easier to digest, we can reuse the `screen()` and `multiply()` functions we used in the examples previously. However, the values passed to the functions must be slightly altered from a straight screen or multiply operation. For a multiply operation, the pixels from the display object are first multiplied by 2 before being passed to our `multiply()` function. For a screen operation, the display object pixels are first multiplied by 2 and then 255 is subtracted from this value. The resulting method to perform a hardlight operation would therefore look like this:

```
public function hardlight(topPixel:uint, bottomPixel:uint):uint {
  var color:uint;
  if (topPixel > 127.5) {
    color = screen(bottomPixel, 2 * topPixel - 255);
  } else {
    color = multiply(bottomPixel, 2 * topPixel);
  }
  return color;
}
```

The `HARDLIGHT` blend mode works great for enhancing an image by duplicating the original image and setting the duplicate to `HARDLIGHT`. This makes the darker regions in the original image darker and the lighter regions lighter, creating more contrast and saturating the image. Add a little blur, and a nice glow is produced. `HARDLIGHT` is also useful when applying both shadows and highlights to the underlying image, since the pixel values of the display object are the ones used to determine what is multiplied or screened.

OVERLAY

The OVERLAY blend mode is very similar to HARDLIGHT, except instead of screening or multiplying based on the display object, the background pixels are used for this determination. That means that when the background pixel's color is greater than medium gray, the display object pixel is screened, and when the background pixel is less than medium gray, the display object pixel is multiplied. This can be expressed using our afore-written functions as follows:

```
public function overlay(topPixel:uint, bottomPixel:uint):uint {
  return hardlight(bottomPixel, topPixel);
}
```

Notice that all the overlay() function is required to do is to call the hardlight() function, reversing the topPixel and bottomPixel arguments. The result of applying OVERLAY is shown in Figure 2-6.

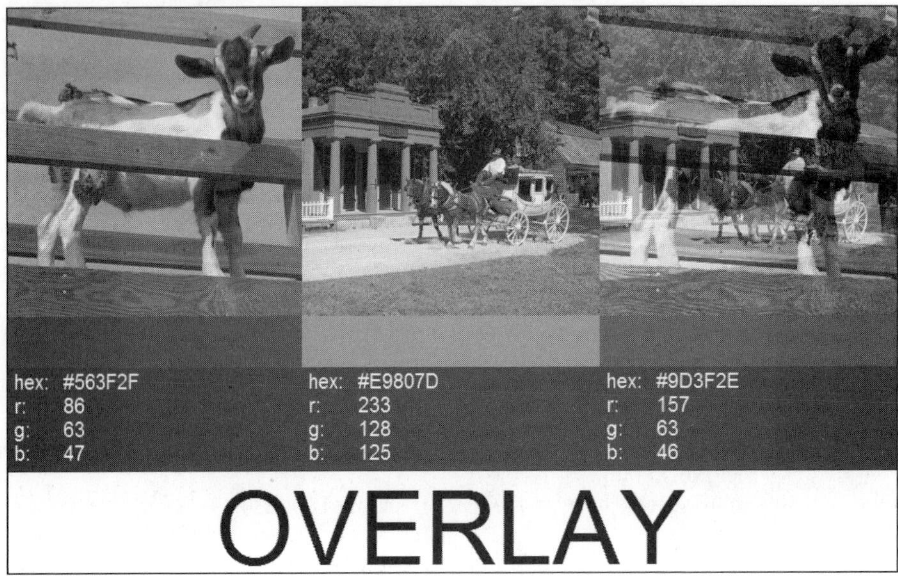

Figure 2-6. The OVERLAY mode applied to the middle image over the left image with the result shown on the right.

OVERLAY, like HARDLIGHT, can be used for enhancing an image by creating a duplicate above the original and setting its blend mode to OVERLAY. In that case, it will act exactly the same as HARDLIGHT, since the background pixels and the display object are identical. When there is a slight difference between the two images, the results of using OVERLAY will be more subtle than those of HARDLIGHT. OVERLAY is also useful for sharpening an image when used in combination with the ConvolutionFilter by setting a duplicated, sharpened image to OVERLAY and placing it over the original image.

ADD

When compared with some of the previous blend modes, the ADD blend mode is pretty simple. The pixel values of the display object and the background are added together, with a maximum of 255 applied. Continuing with our handy dandy methods, we would get the following:

```
public function add(topPixel:uint, bottomPixel:uint):uint {
  return Math.min(255, bottomPixel + topPixel);
}
```

Using this blend mode, a medium gray color (0x666666) added with green (0x00FF00) would result in a lighter green (0x66FF66).

ADD is useful when you need to blow out an image, as in an overexposure. As long as one of the colors used is not pure black, the result will always be a lighter image (black, of course, has a brightness of 0, so will not affect any color, since adding by 0 has no effect on the final brightness). You can see ADD demonstrated in Figure 2-7.

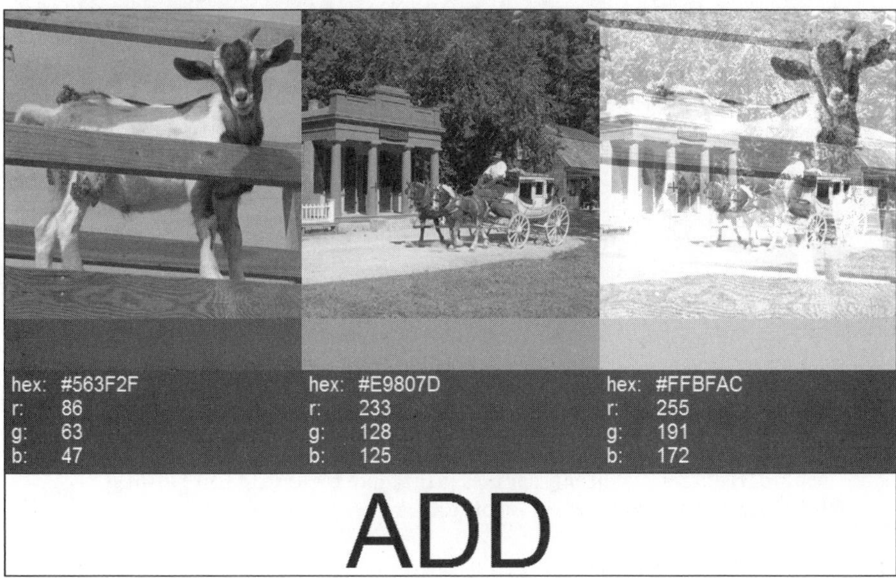

Figure 2-7. The ADD mode applied to the middle image over the left image with the result shown on the right.

SUBTRACT

Going hand in hand with ADD, the SUBTRACT blend mode causes the pixel values of the display object to be subtracted from the background color, with a minimum of 0 enforced. This would be expressed in ActionScript as follows:

```
public function subtract(topPixel:uint, bottomPixel:uint):uint {
  return Math.max(0, bottomPixel - topPixel);
}
```

Using this blend mode, a medium gray color (0x666666) subtracted from a light blue (0xCCCCFF) would result in a darker blue (0x666699).

As a counterpart to ADD, SUBTRACT is useful when you need to darken an image. Subtracting one image from itself will produce a pure black image, but subtracting a solid color like a light gray will uniformly darken all the colors of an image. The result of using SUBTRACT is shown in Figure 2-8.

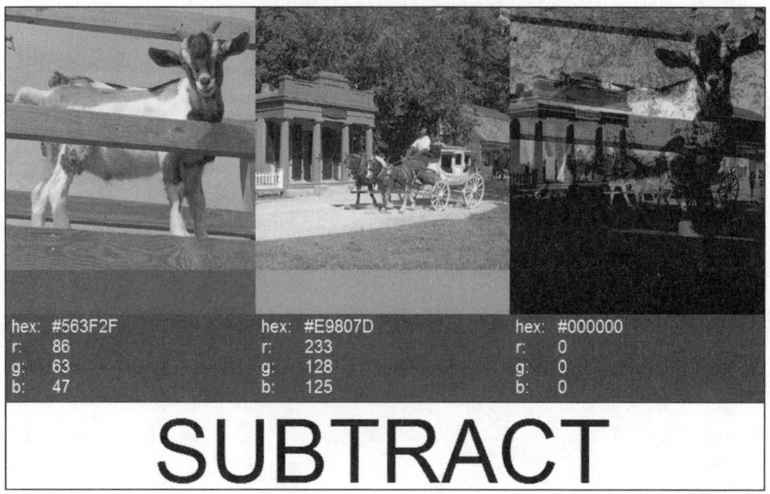

Figure 2-8. The SUBTRACT mode applied to the middle image over the left image with the result shown on the right.

LIGHTEN

With the LIGHTEN blend mode, the lighter of the display object's and background's colors is used for the resulting color. No further calculation is done on the color. As a function, it would look like this:

```
public function lighten(topPixel:uint, bottomPixel:uint):uint {
  return Math.max(topPixel, bottomPixel);
}
```

So if a display object was red (0xFF0000) and the background was blue (0x0000FF), the resulting color of the display object with the LIGHTEN blend mode applied would be a purple (0xFF00FF).

One use for this blend mode is if you have some bright object in one image, perhaps stars in the night sky, that you wish to superimpose on another image. Since only the lighter colors will be used, the stars will remain visible over a new image with the black night sky removed, as long as the background image contains pixels brighter than that black night sky, of course.

The result of using LIGHTEN is shown in Figure 2-9.

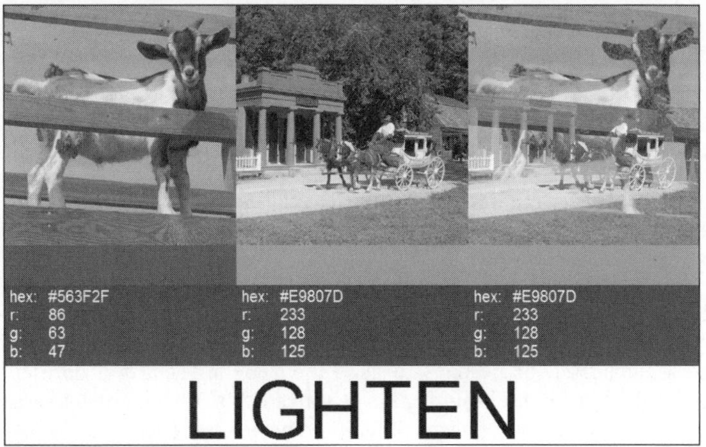

Figure 2-9. The LIGHTEN mode applied to the middle image over the left image with the result shown on the right.

DARKEN

I bet you can guess what this blend mode will get you. DARKEN is the flip side of LIGHTEN, like some evil, cooler twin, where the darker of the two colors from a display object and the background will be kept in the resulting image. The function in ActionScript would look like the following:

```
public function darken(topPixel:uint, bottomPixel:uint):uint {
  return Math.min(topPixel, bottomPixel);
}
```

A terrific use for this blend mode is if you have a black and white image, perhaps ink or line drawings on a piece of white paper, and you only want the ink to be seen. By applying the DARKEN mode, the white areas will drop out and only the black will be applied to the background image. DARKEN is demonstrated in Figure 2-10.

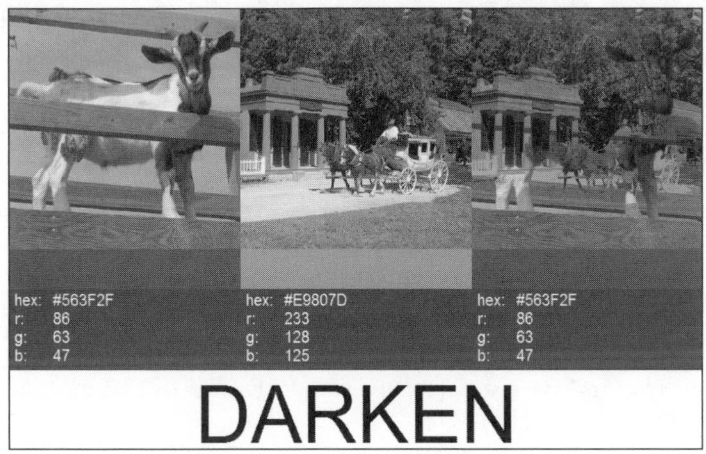

Figure 2-10. The DARKEN mode applied to the middle image over the left image with the result shown on the right.

DIFFERENCE

The DIFFERENCE blend mode takes the display object's pixel value and the background's pixel value and subtracts the lesser from the greater. This can be easily determined by finding the absolute value of the difference between the two. Translated to ActionScript, we get this:

```
public function difference(topPixel:uint, bottomPixel:uint):uint {
  return Math.abs(topPixel - bottomPixel);
}
```

Honestly, the greatest amount of use I've found for this blend mode (and a lot of use, at that) is in Photoshop itself when I need to determine the difference between two images that are nearly duplicates, or perhaps to align them. By applying the difference blend mode to two similar images, the resulting image is nearly black when the two are perfectly aligned, and any colored areas highlight differences between the two.

That's great for image compositing, but what about runtime in Flash? DIFFERENCE is a great blend mode to try out for special effects, sometimes creating solarized images depending on the inputs. You can see the funky results in Figure 2-11.

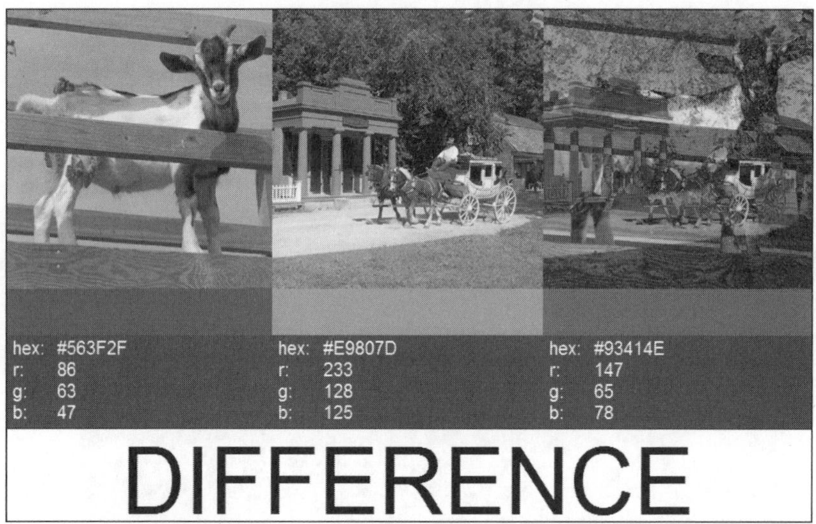

Figure 2-11. The DIFFERENCE mode applied to the middle image over the left image with the result shown on the right.

INVERT

INVERT inverts the background. The background's pixels are inverted based on the opaque pixels of the display object, with no account taken for the color of the display object. The method to do this looks like this:

```
public function difference(topPixel:uint, bottomPixel:uint):uint {
  return (255 - bottomPixel);
}
```

Inverting an image can easily be done using the ColorTransform or the ColorMatrixFilter, so `INVERT` is most useful when only portions of the underlying image need to be transformed based on the shape of the display object. `INVERT` is shown in Figure 2-12.

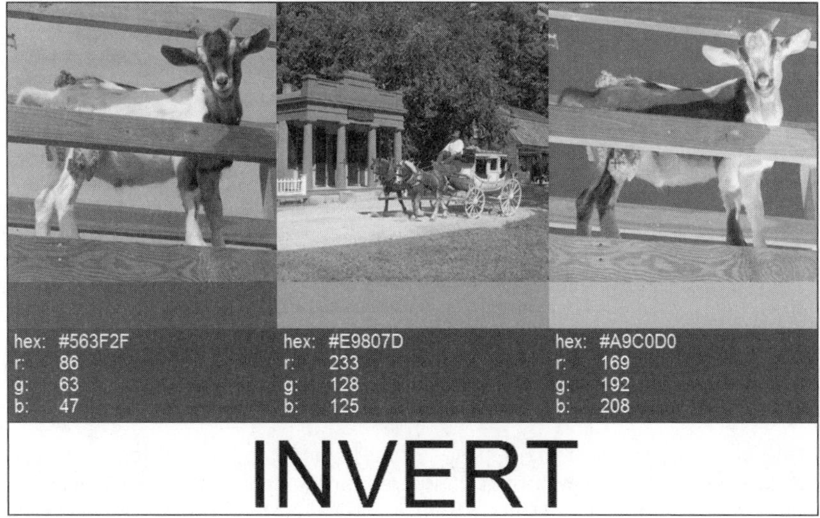

Figure 2-12. The INVERT mode applied to the middle image over the left image with the result shown on the right.

LAYER

The `LAYER` blend mode is used only in combination with other blend modes applied to child display objects, namely `ALPHA` and `ERASE`. These blend modes only work when applied to display objects contained within a display object container with the `LAYER` blend mode applied, or if the container is cached as a bitmap using the `cacheAsBitmap` setting. Generally, if I am ever called to use these other blend modes (which is admittedly rare), I simply cache my container object as a bitmap as opposed to setting this blend mode.

ALPHA

The `ALPHA` blend mode applies the display object's alpha channel to any other display object below it in the display object container. This is a unique blend mode in that it effectively punches through multiple display objects as opposed to working only on the immediately underlying colors. No colors from the display object with `ALPHA` applied will be visible in the resulting image, but its opacity values will be applied to any display object within the same container that it overlaps.

This blend mode is extremely useful for creating masks of variable transparency (basically, masks with blurred edges), as shown in Figure 2-13. The class used to create this effect can be found in this chapter's files as `AlphaModeTest.as`.

Figure 2-13. The ALPHA mode applied to a circular shape with a fill containing gradient transparency placed over another image in the same container set to LAYER. The shape used is shown on the left.

ERASE

The ERASE blend mode is just the opposite of ALPHA and can be used for the same purposes. It all depends on if you want the transparent or the opaque pixels to punch through to the underlying images. With ERASE, any opaque pixel in the original display object will cause the underlying pixels in the display objects within the same container to be transparent. Once again, the original display object that this blend mode is applied to will not be visible in the resulting image.

The effect of ERASE is shown in Figure 2-14. The class used to create this effect can be found in this chapter's files as `EraseModeTest.as`.

Figure 2-14. The ERASE mode applied to a circular shape with a fill containing gradient transparency placed over another image in the same container set to LAYER. The shape used is shown on the left.

SHADER

The SHADER blend mode is a new mode and is unique to Flash and ActionScript (sorry, Photoshop users!). This is a blend mode that you don't actually have to set—it is set for you if you apply a Shader instance to the `blendShader` property of a display object.

Shaders are custom routines that perform actions on individual pixels, and they do it incredibly fast. This is a topic we will explore in depth in Chapter 5, but one of a shader's uses is to provide new blend modes. Figure 2-15 shows an example of a shader applied to a display object that uses the brightness values of the display object and the colors of the underlying pixels, in the same way as Photoshop's Luminosity blend mode.

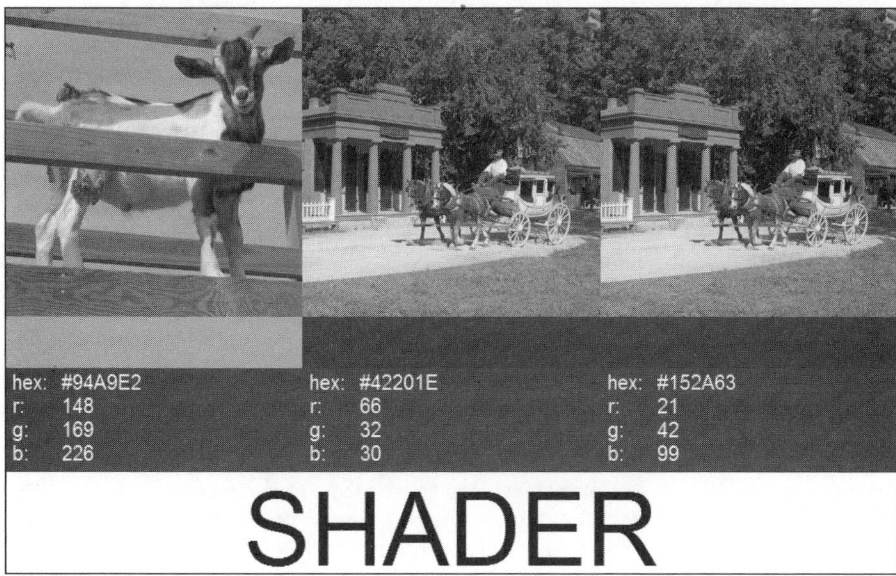

Figure 2-15. The SHADER mode with a custom shader enabling a Luminosity blend mode applied the middle image over the left image with the result shown on the right, though not noticeable in grayscale due to the nature of the blend mode.

Using filters

Admittedly, filters are very fun to play with. Those who first discover them in Flash, Photoshop, Illustrator, or other programs are a bit like Homer Simpson playfully frolicking in indulgent glee through the Land of Chocolate. But although there are some very neat out-of-the-box tricks to take advantage of, bitmap filters are a bit of a double-edged sword. On the one hand, they give you incredible power to enhance objects with cool effects in an extremely easy and intuitive way, but on the other hand, they can often result in recognizable and canned effects that immediately point to either a laziness or lack of imagination. The trick is to use them sparingly in a subtle manner when on their own and more often in combination with other filters or actions to create more complex effects.

All bitmap filters in ActionScript inherit from flash.filters.BitmapFilter, which is itself an abstract class that cannot be instantiated. All but three, ColorMatrixFilter, DisplacementMapFilter, and ConvolutionFilter, are also accessible through the Flash IDE (and in my humble opinion, these three that are not in the IDE are the best of the lot!). Creating a filter is as easy as instantiating a class and passing in the parameters that should be applied to the filter:

```
var blurFilter:BlurFilter = new BlurFilter(10, 10);
```

If you need to alter the properties applied to a filter, all of its applicable fields are surfaced through implicit getter/setters:

```
blurFilter.blurX += 2;
blurFilter.blurY += 2;
```

Of course, a filter without a display object is about as useful as Madonna performing Shakespeare—even if it's there, who's ever going to see it? To see the effects of a filter, you need to apply it in some way to a display object (I can't help with Madonna's career choices). You can do this through ActionScript in one of two ways.

The first way a filter can be applied, and the way we will explore filters in this chapter, is by assigning a BitmapFilter child class instance to a display object's `filters` property. This property actually takes an array of BitmapFilters, so you can assign multiple filters in order to compound effects.

```
var glowFilter:GlowFilter = new GlowFilter();
var blurFilter:BlurFilter = new BlurFilter();
sprite.filters = [glowFilter, blurFilter];
```

Once you assign filters to a display object, copies are made, so if you change a value in the original filter, it will not affect the display object's filters. In order to update a filter on a display object, you need to retrieve its filters through its `filters` property (which itself returns a copy of the filters), alter the filter values, and then reassign the filters to the display object through the same `filters` property. Consider the following code, which builds on the previous example:

```
var filters:Array = sprite.filters;
var blurFilter:BlurFilter = filters[1] as BlurFilter;
blurFilter.blurX += 2;
sprite.filters = filters;
```

Here, we first retrieve a copy of the `filters` array. The second filter in this array we know to be a BlurFilter instance, so we can cast to that (if you did not know this, you could cycle through the array to check where the blur was located). Once we add to the BlurFilter's `blurX` property, we reassign the array, with the altered blur value, back to the display object.

The other way to use filters is to apply them to BitmapData instances using that class's `applyFilter()` method. We will explore BitmapData and this method in the next two chapters. For the rest of this chapter, though, we will examine each of the BitmapFilter child classes that are available in ActionScript. In order to facilitate this, I will use a single class for all of the examples, which can be extended to demonstrate each filter. You will find it in this chapter's files as BitmapFilterTest.as. Here is all of its code:

```
package {

  import flash.display.Shape;
  import flash.display.Sprite;

  public class BitmapFilterTest extends Sprite {

    protected var _shape:Shape;

    public function BitmapFilterTest() {
      createShape();
      applyFilter();
    }

    private function createShape():void {
      var sideWidth:Number = 150;
      _shape = new Shape();
      _shape.graphics.beginFill(0x003333);
      _shape.graphics.drawRect(-sideWidth/2, -sideWidth/2, ➥
sideWidth, sideWidth);
      _shape.graphics.endFill();
      _shape.x = stage.stageWidth/2;
      _shape.y = stage.stageHeight/2;
      addChild(_shape);
    }

    protected function applyFilter():void {}

  }

}
```

All this class does is create a new Shape instance and add it to the stage. It then calls a protected applyFilter() method, which can be overridden for each example.

BlurFilter

The BlurFilter is perhaps the easiest filter to create, and one of the most useful in application. The constructor for this class looks like the following:

```
BlurFilter(
  blurX:Number = 4.0,
  blurY:Number = 4.0,
  quality:int = 1
)
```

The parameters, thankfully, are all of the straightforward variety:

- blurX: This sets the amount of blur on the x axis.
- blurY: This sets the amount of blur on the y axis.
- quality: This determines the number of passes that should be made when blurring the display object, with a higher number of passes resulting in a higher quality blur. A setting of BitmapFilterQuality.LOW is best if you are updating blurs constantly, especially on larger objects. If you are performing a one-time blur, a setting of BitmapFilterQuality.HIGH, though more processor intensive, will produce something like a Gaussian blur.

The BlurFilter is demonstrated by the class BitmapFilterTest, which can be found in this chapter's files and contains the following code:

```
package {

  import flash.filters.BitmapFilterQuality;
  import flash.filters.BlurFilter;

  [SWF(width=550, height=400, backgroundColor=0xEEEEEE)]

  public class BlurFilterTest extends BitmapFilterTest {

    override protected function applyFilter():void {
      var filter:BlurFilter = new BlurFilter(2, 150, ➥
BitmapFilterQuality.HIGH);
      _shape.filters = [filter];
    }

  }

}
```

If you compile this movie (please see the appendix if that phrase has no meaning for you) or test the compiled SWF, you will see the rectangle blurred mostly on the y axis, as shown in Figure 2-16. Try changing the quality setting in the class and recompiling to see how this affects the blur.

Figure 2-16. The BlurFilter applied to a rectangle shape

One thing to note about the BlurFilter, and filters in general, is that if there are directional settings (like vertical and horizontal or rotation), they do not rotate with their display objects. If you alter the class with the following, you will see the result, as shown in Figure 2-17.

```
    override protected function applyFilter():void {
      var filter:BlurFilter = new BlurFilter(2, 150, ➥
BitmapFilterQuality.HIGH);
      _shape.filters = [filter];
      _shape.rotation = 45;
    }
```

Figure 2-17.
The BlurFilter applied to a rectangle shape that has been rotated. Note that the blur does not rotate with the object.

As you can see, the blur is still applied to the screen's y axis, not the rotated display object's y axis. Although a nice effect in this instance, if you wish to rotate filters with the display objects, you will need to actually draw the filtered display object into a BitmapData instance and then rotate a Bitmap containing that data.

Blurs by themselves are nice to draw users' focus to important objects. For instance, this might be useful in an animation with a depth of field effect where the foreground is in focus but the background (and extreme foreground) might be blurred. In an application, you might blur background elements when a pop-up dialog is opened, as occurs when using the Flex framework, focusing the user on the active window.

Blurs are also extremely useful when creating more complex effects. Many of the dynamic textures I create or distress techniques I employ utilize the BlurFilter at some point or another. We will look at such applications later in the book.

DropShadowFilter

The DropShadowFilter draws a blurred, solid-colored copy of your object behind the object. It has a large number of settings that make possible a varied number of effects. The DropShadowFilter's constructor looks like this:

```
DropShadowFilter(
  distance:Number = 4.0,
  angle:Number = 45,
  color:uint = 0,
  alpha:Number = 1.0,
  blurX:Number = 4.0,
  blurY:Number = 4.0,
  strength:Number = 1.0,
  quality:int = 1,
```

```
    inner:Boolean = false,
    knockout:Boolean = false,
    hideObject:Boolean = false
)
```

Remember the simple, bygone days of BlurFilter and its three parameters? Things get a little more complex with DropShadowFilter. Let's break down all those options:

- `distance`: This parameter sets the offset, in pixels, from the original object by which the blurred duplicate will be placed.
- `angle`: The direction of the offset shadow from the object is determined with this parameter.
- `color`: This one sets the color the shadow.
- `alpha`: And this one sets the opacity of the shadow.
- `blurX`: The amount of blur on the x axis is set with `blurX`.
- `blurY`: And `blurY` specifies the amount of blur on the y axis.
- `strength`: In setting the strength of the shadow, higher numbers darken the overall shadow, which creates more contrast with the background.
- `quality`: This determines the number of passes for the blur, just as you saw with the BlurFilter (in fact, it is performing the same blur).
- `inner`: Use `inner` to say whether the shadow is drawn inside or outside the object. By setting `inner` to `true`, you can have the shadow only drawn within the confines of the display object itself. This creates the illusion that the display object is a hole cut into the background, with its colors maintained.
- `knockout`: Use `knockout` to specify whether the fill of the object should be made transparent, showing only the shadow with the shape of the object knocked out. If you don't want the display object's colors maintained, you can set `knockout` to `false`, which reveals the background colors through the display object while still drawing the shadow as if the object's colors were visible (basically, the shadow's colors are knocked out by the display object's pixels to reveal the background colors below). This is useful when a shape is to be used to punch a hole in a background, but the colors of the background should be maintained. In this case, in combination with setting `knockout` to `true`, the shadow that is drawn appears to be a hole, as shown in Figure 2-18.
- `hideObject`: When set to `true`, this parameter hides the display object entirely and draws the shadow without any knockout (if `knockout` is `false`). The result is a shadow cast without an object, which is useful when you need a shadow alone. Imagine an animation with a plane flying overhead and only its shadow is cast on the ground. In application development, I have used this technique when I needed to match one component that had drop shadows built in with another that did not. Applying drop shadows to complex components can cause performance problems, so often, it is better to draw a shadow on an object underneath the component. In this case, the object casting the shadow can be hidden while the shadow appears to be cast by the component itself.

Figure 2-18.
The DropShadowFilter applied to a rectangle shape with inner and knockout set to true

The effect as shown in Figure 2-18 is created with the class DropShadowFilterTest. The entire code of the class follows:

```
package {

  import flash.filters.BitmapFilterQuality;
  import flash.filters.DropShadowFilter;

  [SWF(width=550, height=400, backgroundColor=0xEEEEEE)]

  public class DropShadowFilterTest extends BitmapFilterTest {

    override protected function applyFilter():void {
      var filter:DropShadowFilter = new DropShadowFilter(10);
      filter.blurX = 15;
      filter.blurY = 15;
      filter.quality = BitmapFilterQuality.HIGH;
      filter.inner = true;
      filter.knockout = true;
      _shape.filters = [filter];
    }

  }

}
```

This extends BitmapFilterTest and adds a DropShadowFilter instance to the shape, setting a number of its properties. The inner shadow that knocks out the object creates an effect where the shape seems to be cutting into the background.

GlowFilter

Rather unsurprisingly, the GlowFilter creates glows. More specifically, the filter creates solid colored glows of varying opacity around display objects (but that would have been a really long name). Its properties are actually a subset of the DropShadowFilter, and its constructor looks like the following:

```
GlowFilter(
  color:uint = 0xFF0000,
  alpha:Number = 1.0,
```

```
    blurX:Number = 6.0,
    blurY:Number = 6.0,
    strength:Number = 2,
    quality:int = 1,
    inner:Boolean = false,
    knockout:Boolean = false
)
```

The parameters for GlowFilter are a subset of those that have already been covered for DropShadowFilter, so I won't break them down again here. The biggest difference between this filter and DropShadowFilter, other than the defaults, is that you cannot set a distance and angle as you can for a drop shadow. This means that the glow always originates right at the borders of the display object (this also means that you can create glows using the DropShadowFilter by settings its distance to 0, at which point its angle has no effect, and the shadow will originate at the borders of the object).

If you ever need an object's borders to glow, this filter will be your friend. Subtle rollover effects on interactive objects are a common use for this filter. Creating an inner glow on text to contrast it better with the background is also a useful technique. If you are animating and need to create a rim light for an object in silhouette, this filter can also be useful.

One of my favorite uses for a GlowFilter isn't immediately obvious from its name, and that is to create solid outlines on objects. You can do this by setting the `blurX` and `blurY` down to 2 and increasing the `strength`. The `quality` setting you give the filter will affect the thickness of the outlines you create. The effect is shown in Figure 2-19.

Figure 2-19. The GlowFilter applied to a rectangle shape and text producing an outline effect

You will find the class that creates this effect in this chapter's files as `GlowFilterTest.as`.

```
package {

  import flash.filters.BitmapFilterQuality;
  import flash.filters.GlowFilter;
  import flash.text.TextField;
  import flash.text.TextFormat;
  import flash.text.TextFormatAlign;

  [SWF(width=550, height=400, backgroundColor=0xEEEEEE)]

  public class GlowFilterTest extends BitmapFilterTest {
```

```
      override protected function applyFilter():void {
        var filter:GlowFilter = new GlowFilter(0x000000);
        filter.blurX = 2;
        filter.blurY = 2;
        filter.strength = 255;
        filter.quality = BitmapFilterQuality.MEDIUM;
        filter.knockout = true;
        _shape.filters = [filter];

        var field:TextField = new TextField();
        var textFormat:TextFormat = new TextFormat("Arial", 40);
        textFormat.align = TextFormatAlign.CENTER;
        field.multiline = true;
        field.defaultTextFormat = textFormat;
        field.text = "Glow\nFilter";
        field.x = _shape.x - field.width/2;
        field.y = _shape.y - field.height/2;
        field.filters = [filter];
        addChild(field);
      }

    }

  }
```

The class builds on the base BitmapFilterTest class by applying the filter to _shape but also creates a TextField instance to better demonstrate the filter. The filter is applied both to the shape and the field, with the low blur amount and high strength setting, along with the knockout to remove the fill color, helping to create the outline effect.

GradientGlowFilter

The GradientGlowFilter is actually more similar to the DropShadowFilter than to GlowFilter—I suppose GradientDropShadowFilter was just too unruly of a class name. Like the DropShadowFilter, the GradientGlowFilter creates a blurred copy of the object and places it at an offset and angle from the original object (recall that `distance` and `angle` are not settings available for the GlowFilter). However, instead of filling the duplicate with a solid color, the GradientGlowFilter fills the blurred copy with a gradient.

The constructor has a daunting number of parameters but is less overwhelming when you consider that the majority of these settings are already familiar from the previous filters.

```
GradientGlowFilter(
  distance:Number = 4.0,
  angle:Number = 45,
  colors:Array = null,
  alphas:Array = null,
  ratios:Array = null,
  blurX:Number = 4.0,
```

```
        blurY:Number = 4.0,
        strength:Number = 1,
        quality:int = 1,
        type:String = "inner",
        knockout:Boolean = false
    )
```

The majority of the parameters for this filter remain consistent with DropShadowFilter. The major differences between this filter's and the DropShadowFilter's settings is that, instead of color and alpha values, this GradientGlowFilter requires three separate arrays of color, alpha, and ratio values (as you are already familiar with from the previous chapter's drawing API commands using gradients, `beginGradientFill()`, and `lineGradientStyle()`). The GradientGlowFilter also does not give you the option of `hideObject`, as the DropShadowFilter does. Finally, while the DropShadowFilter has an `inner` Boolean property, the GradientGlowFilter instead has a `type` property, which offers even more control. The breakdown of these different properties follows:

- `colors`: This is an array of color values defining the colors in the gradient.
- `alphas`: This is an array of opacity values for the gradient colors with one value for each color in the gradient, meaning the lengths of both arrays will always be equal.
- `ratios`: This is an array of values defining the distribution of the color values along the full width of the gradient, with each index holding a value between 0 and 255. Once again, this array will be of an equal length to the `colors` array.
- `type`: This determines whether the gradient drawn will be inside, outside, or both inside and outside the object to which the filter is applied. This property can accept one of three values from the BitmapFilterType class. `BitmapFilterType.INNER` is the default and will draw the gradient over the pixels of the display object, just as with inner drop shadows. `BitmapFilterType.OUTER` will draw a more traditional drop shadow at an offset and angle outside of the object. The third type, `BitmapFilterType.FULL`, will draw both the inner and outer glows.

If you find that you need a little more control over the colors and alphas of glows or drop shadows than the GlowFilter or DropShadowFilter provide, you will want to explore this class to see whether it can create the effect you require. Just as in the last example, you can also use this filter to create interesting outline effects, but with multiple colors, as shown in Figure 2-20.

Figure 2-20. The GradientGlowFilter applied to a rectangle shape and text producing a gradient outline effect

This effect is created with the class GradientGlowFilterTest in this chapter's files, which contains the following code:

```
package {

  import flash.filters.BitmapFilterQuality;
  import flash.filters.BitmapFilterType;
  import flash.filters.GradientGlowFilter;
  import flash.text.TextField;
  import flash.text.TextFieldAutoSize;
  import flash.text.TextFormat;
  import flash.text.TextFormatAlign;

  [SWF(width=550, height=400, backgroundColor=0xEEEEEE)]

  public class GradientGlowFilterTest extends BitmapFilterTest {

    override protected function applyFilter():void {
      var filter:GradientGlowFilter = new GradientGlowFilter();
      filter.distance = 0;
      filter.colors = [0xCC88FF, 0xCC88FF, 0x663399, 0x006666];
      filter.alphas = [0, .6, .9, 1];
      filter.ratios = [0, 50, 100, 255];
      filter.type = BitmapFilterType.FULL;
      filter.blurX = 2;
      filter.blurY = 2;
      filter.quality = BitmapFilterQuality.MEDIUM;
      filter.knockout = true;
      _shape.filters = [filter];

      var field:TextField = new TextField();
      var textFormat:TextFormat = new TextFormat("Arial", 36);
      textFormat.align = TextFormatAlign.CENTER;
      field.autoSize = TextFieldAutoSize.CENTER;
      field.multiline = true;
      field.defaultTextFormat = textFormat;
      field.text = "Gradient\nGlow\nFilter";
      field.x = _shape.x - field.width/2;
      field.y = _shape.y - field.height/2;
      field.filters = [filter];
      addChild(field);
    }

  }

}
```

This example is just a variation of the previous example for the GlowFilter with the new filter applied. As such, most values and logic remains the same with the exception of gradient colors, alphas, and ratios being set.

BevelFilter

The BevelFilter allows you to add bevel effects to display objects by specifying two different color/alpha values that appear at opposite angles, giving the illusion of light and shadow hitting raised edges. The constructor for the BevelFilter contains many of the properties you are already familiar with from the previous filters:

```
BevelFilter(
  distance:Number = 4.0,
  angle:Number = 45,
  highlightColor:uint = 0xFFFFFF,
  highlightAlpha:Number = 1.0,
  shadowColor:uint = 0x000000,
  shadowAlpha:Number = 1.0,
  blurX:Number = 4.0,
  blurY:Number = 4.0,
  strength:Number = 1,
  quality:int = 1,
  type:String = "inner",
  knockout:Boolean = false
)
```

As you can see, many of our old favorites are here, doing the same, reliable things (thank goodness—it makes it so much easier to learn that way!). The major difference with BevelFilter is that you have both highlight and shadow colors and alphas. Besides that for color information, the properties are the same as those you saw in the GradientGlowFilter. The new parameters follow:

- `highlightColor`: The RGB color for the bevel's highlight
- `highlightAlpha`: The opacity of the bevel's highlight
- `shadowColor`: The RGB color of the bevel's shadow
- `shadowAlpha`: The opacity of the bevel's shadow

The BevelFilter is great for creating simple bevels, either soft and blurred or hard and chiseled. It is a very recognizable filter, second only to your friendly neighborhood drop shadow, so use it with caution. I find it best for very subtle effects that give just a slight look of depth to otherwise flat vectors.

The following code, found as `BevelFilterTest.as` in this chapter's files, produces the effect shown in Figure 2-21:

```
package {

  import flash.display.Shape;
  import flash.filters.BevelFilter;

  [SWF(width=550, height=400, backgroundColor=0xEEEEEE)]
```

```
    public class BevelFilterTest extends BitmapFilterTest {

      override protected function applyFilter():void {
        var filter:BevelFilter = new BevelFilter(10);
        filter.highlightAlpha = .5;
        filter.shadowAlpha = .5;
        filter.blurX = 15;
        filter.blurY = 15;
        filter.strength = 80;
        _shape.filters = [filter];

        var shape:Shape = new Shape();
        shape.graphics.beginFill(0x004444);
        shape.graphics.drawRect(-50, -50, 100, 100);
        shape.graphics.endFill();
        shape.x = stage.stageWidth/2;
        shape.y = stage.stageHeight/2;

        filter.distance = 5;
        filter.angle = 225;
        filter.strength = 1;
        shape.filters = [filter];
        addChild(shape);
      }

    }

  }
```

Figure 2-21.
The BevelFilter applied to two rectangle shapes to create a double bevel

By using a large blur and high strength, you can achieve a chiseled look as I've done here. To create an inset in the rectangle, I've added a new, smaller rectangle and applied a variation of the bevel, reversing its angle so that the illusory light appears to be striking an indented surface. Notice that you can alter the values of the same filter, and doing so does not affect the original filter applied to the larger rectangle. Remember, you can do this because, when a filter is passed to a display object, it is a copy that is actually applied.

GradientBevelFilter

Offering even finer control over the colors and alphas in a bevel, the GradientBevelFilter takes the BevelFilter a step further by allowing you to specify gradient values for the bevels drawn. So if a white highlight isn't enough for the light color of a bevel, you could use this filter to specify a highlight that moves through multiple colors to achieve the desired effect.

The GradientBevelFilter constructor is exactly the same as the GradientGlowFilter:

```
GradientBevelFilter(
  distance:Number = 4.0,
  angle:Number = 45,
  colors:Array = null,
  alphas:Array = null,
  ratios:Array = null,
  blurX:Number = 4.0,
  blurY:Number = 4.0,
  strength:Number = 1,
  quality:int = 1,
  type:String = "inner",
  knockout:Boolean = false
)
```

The parameters of this filter are exactly the same as the GradientGlowFilter. Playing a little with these properties, you can create some interesting—if not everyday—effects. The following class, found as `GradientBevelFilter.as`, in this chapter's files, reuses the additional textfield that was added for the GlowFilterTest:

```
package {

  import flash.filters.BitmapFilterQuality;
  import flash.filters.BitmapFilterType;
  import flash.filters.GradientBevelFilter;
  import flash.text.TextField;
  import flash.text.TextFieldAutoSize;
  import flash.text.TextFormat;
  import flash.text.TextFormatAlign;

  [SWF(width=550, height=400, backgroundColor=0xEEEEEE)]

  public class GradientBevelFilterTest extends BitmapFilterTest {

    override protected function applyFilter():void {
      var filter:GradientBevelFilter = new GradientBevelFilter(60);
      filter.colors = [0x0000FF, 0xFF00FF, 0x0000FF, ➥
0x00FFFF, 0x0000FF];
      filter.alphas = [0, 1, 0, 1, 0];
      filter.ratios = [0, 24, 128, 232, 255];
```

```
            filter.blurX = 15;
            filter.blurY = 15;
            filter.quality = BitmapFilterQuality.MEDIUM;
            filter.type = BitmapFilterType.FULL;
            filter.strength = 1;
            filter.knockout = true;
            _shape.filters = [filter];
            _shape.alpha = .3;

            var field:TextField = new TextField();
            var textFormat:TextFormat = new TextFormat("Arial", 36);
            textFormat.align = TextFormatAlign.CENTER;
            field.autoSize = TextFieldAutoSize.CENTER;
            field.multiline = true;
            field.defaultTextFormat = textFormat;
            field.text = "Gradient\nBevel\nFilter";
            field.x = _shape.x - field.width/2;
            field.y = _shape.y - field.height/2;

            filter.distance = 1;
            filter.angle = 225;
            filter.blurX = 2;
            filter.blurY = 2;
            field.filters = [filter];
            addChild(field);
        }

    }

}
```

The gradient applied is transparent in the middle and the outer edges, leaving an interesting band on the top left and bottom right of our shape (these positions are dictated by our 45 degree angle), which I then hide by setting `knockout` to `true`. The entire effect I reduce by setting the shape to a lower opacity.

With the textfield, I apply a variation of this filter, reducing the distance and blur and reversing the angle. The result, shown Figure 2-22, is an interesting text effect that could be worked into a chrome-like effect or a neon sign.

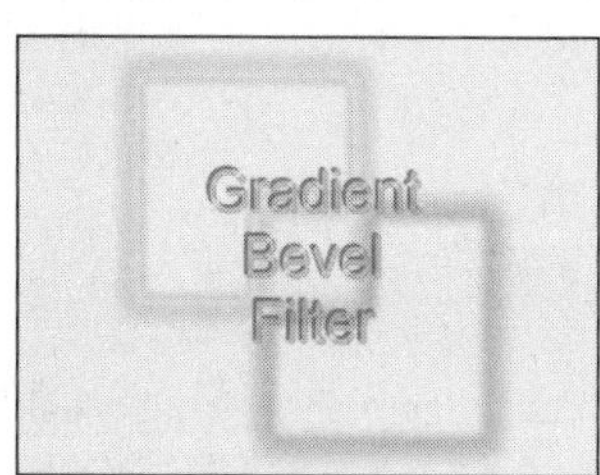

Figure 2-22.
The GradientBevelFilter applied to a single rectangle shape and textfield

ColorMatrixFilter

Up to this point, the filters we've examined have been, for the most part, straightforward. With the ColorMatrixFilter, we get into a little more advanced territory. This filter allows you to affect the colors of a display object by multiplying its color transform by a new color matrix. Those are all very nice words to read in a sentence, but what do they mean exactly?

To understand this filter, you must understand, at least in part, matrix operations and linear algebra. If you love mathematics in all of its numerical splendor, you're in luck! If you don't, I would encourage you to soldier on, since matrix operations are used not only in this but in other aspects of ActionScript as well, including the coming ConvolutionFilter.

Understanding matrices

A matrix is simply a grid of numbers. That's it. A 1×3 matrix, which consists of one row of three columns, could be represented as follows:

```
| 255  0  255 |
```

The bars on either end of the numeric values here represent the two ends of a row in the matrix. Let's imagine these numbers in the matrix represented the RGB values of a pixel, in this case purple. The beauty of matrices is that in a single entity we can include multiple related values while still keeping the values separate, and when we want to affect those values in any way, we can use matrix operations (like addition and multiplication) to alter the original matrix. These operations provide a faster way of cumulatively manipulating these multiple values, and there are already established matrices that can be used for these common operations.

Adding matrices The simplest operation one can perform on a matrix is addition. This can be performed on two matrices of the same number of rows and columns. So if we wanted to add a medium green pixel to our purple pixel, we would use the operation

```
| 255  5  255 |  +  | 0  127  0 |
```

When you add two matrices together, you simply have to use basic addition on each element position to produce a result. The formula for adding two 1×3 matrices would therefore be

```
| A1  A2  A3 |  +  | B1  B2  B3 |  =➡
  | (A1 + B1)  (A2 + B2)  (A3 + B3) |
```

If we plug in our two RGB colors, we get this:

```
| 255  0  255 |  +  | 0  127  0 |  =➡
  | (255 + 0)  (0 + 127)  (255 + 0) |  =➡
    | 255  127  255 |
```

The RGB value of 255, 127, and 255 is #FF7FFF in hexadecimal, which is a lighter purple.

Multiplying matrices Of course, with colors, we already have the ability to add two colors together easily to get a new color, since a single RGB color can be represented as a single number. But what if you wanted to darken a color by 50 percent? That would require breaking the color up into its constituent parts and performing the multiplication operation on each and then putting the color back together into a single entity. However, if your color was stored in a matrix, you could multiply the color matrix by your percentage value and get your darker color in a single operation.

When multiplying a matrix with a scalar value (scalar meaning having only a single value, as opposed to something like an array or another matrix, which holds multiple component values), all you have to do is multiply each element of the matrix by the value. Multiplying our RGB value would look like this:

```
0.5 * | 255  127  255 |  =➥
   | (255 * 0.5)  (127 * 0.5)  (255 * 0.5) |  =➥
     | 127.5  63.5  127.5 |
```

Things get even more interesting when you want to multiply each of the elements by a different number, which requires another matrix. In this case, you will actually use a matrix that represents a scale transform and multiply this with the RGB matrix. When multiplying two matrices, you must have the number of columns in one matrix match the number of rows in another. This means to multiply against a 1×3 matrix you need at least a 3×1 matrix. A matrix used to scale each element of a 1×3 matrix would be a 3×3 matrix:

```
                      | S1   0   0 |
| A1  A2  A3 |   *    |  0  S2   0 |
                      |  0   0  S3 |
```

In this case, the first matrix represents our RGB color. The second matrix is our transform matrix that we will use to scale the brightness of each of the constituent parts of our color. Notice the diagonal placement of the nonzero elements. This leverages the formula for matrix multiplication so that each of those numbers affects only a single element in the RGB matrix. That formula, which looks a lot hairier than it actually is, follows:

```
A  =  | A1  A2  A3 |

      | B11  B12  B13 |
B  =  | B21  B22  B23 |
      | B31  B32  B33 |

A * B  =  | ((A1*B11) + (A2*B21) + (A3*B31))  ➥
            ((A1*B12) + (A2*B22) + (A3*B32))  ➥
            ((A1*B13) + (A2*B23) + (A3*B33)) |
```

The limitations of print require the result to wrap onto three lines, but this is actually still just a 1×3 matrix (not a 3×3). If you look closely, you will see that each of the final elements is calculated by multiplying each element in the original matrix by the elements from a single row from the second matrix. So for the first element position in the result, the full row of matrix A is multiplied by the first column in matrix B. The second element is determined by multiplying matrix A's single row by the second column in matrix B, and then the third element is determined by the same row from matrix A multiplied by the third column in matrix B.

This is the standard matrix multiplication formula, and it works the same if you have more or fewer columns and rows. The result is that you can perform some pretty complex calculations on groups of numbers, where the resulting value of one number is dependent on a number of other values.

For a scale transform, though, each resulting value is really only dependent on another single value from the scale transform matrix, and you can see this by actually using the scale transform matrix in our formula.

```
C  =  | 255  127  255 |

      | 0.5    0    0 |
S  =  |   0  0.3    0 |
      |   0    0  0.1 |

C * S  =  | ((255*0.5) + (127*0) + (255*0))  ➥
            ((255*0) + (127*0.3) + (255*0))  ➥
            ((255*0) + (127*0) + (255*0.1)) |
```

Here, C represents our color, and S represents the scale transform. With this transform, we are looking to scale the red channel down by 50 percent, the green by 30 percent, and the blue by 10 percent. Plugging those values into our formula still appears a bit of a mess, but once we get rid of all those 0 products, we get the cleaner

```
C * S  =  | ((255*0.5)  (127*0.3)  (255*0.1)) |
```

Well, that's more inviting, isn't it? With the scale transform, the result is that each color channel is multiplied by a single value, with the final color being `| 127.5  38.1  25.5 |`, or #7F2619.

This all still seems like a lot of math and operations, though, doesn't it? Well, it would be if the matrix operations we use in ActionScript weren't all handled for us, which makes them, on the whole, much more pleasant to work with. ActionScript has a Matrix class that you can use when you need to perform matrix operations, and for colors, we have the fantastic ColorMatrixFilter, which, in the end, is what this section is all about. So now that you know the basics of what is happening with matrices (and if you would like to know more, I'd suggest a linear algebra reference you can do some light reading of—it's great for the beach!), let's look at this colorful filter and see what it provides.

Using matrices with the ColorMatrixFilter

To test your newfound matrix knowledge using the ColorMatrixFilter, I have prepared a base class that can be used with each of the remaining three filters, which all are demonstrated best with an image. For that end, the base class will load an image that can then have filters applied.

The following class, saved as ImageFilterTest.as in this chapter's files, contains the code that will be used to load an image for filter application:

```
package {

  import flash.display.Bitmap;
  import flash.display.Loader;
  import flash.display.LoaderInfo;
  import flash.display.Sprite;
  import flash.events.Event;
  import flash.net.URLRequest;

  public class ImageFilterTest extends Sprite {

    protected var _bitmap:Bitmap;

    public function ImageFilterTest(path:String=null) {
      loadImage(path || "../assets/goat.jpg");
    }

    private function loadImage(imagePath:String):void {
      var loader:Loader = new Loader();
      loader.contentLoaderInfo.addEventListener(Event.COMPLETE, ➥
onImageLoaded);
      loader.load(new URLRequest(imagePath));
    }

    private function onImageLoaded(event:Event):void {
      var loaderInfo:LoaderInfo = event.target as LoaderInfo;
      loaderInfo.removeEventListener(Event.COMPLETE, onImageLoaded);
      _bitmap = loaderInfo.content as Bitmap;
      _bitmap.x = stage.stageWidth/2 - _bitmap.width/2;
      _bitmap.y = stage.stageHeight/2 - _bitmap.height/2;
      addChild(_bitmap);
      applyFilter();
    }

    protected function applyFilter():void {}

  }

}
```

All this class does is load and center an image (if you are compiling this class, make sure your directory structure has an assets directory up a level with the goat.jpg file within it, as will be the case with the downloaded files; either that, or enter the path to a known file on your system). The applyFilter() method is waiting to be overridden by a child class. Let's take a look at such a child class.

The following can be found as ColorMatrixFilterTest.as in this chapter's files. Using it we can play and test with different matrix values:

```
package {

  import flash.filters.ColorMatrixFilter;

  [SWF(width=550, height=400, backgroundColor=0xEEEEEE)]

  public class ColorMatrixFilterTest extends ImageFilterTest {

    override protected function applyFilter():void {
      var matrix:Array = [
        1, 0, 0, 0, 0,
        0, 1, 0, 0, 0,
        0, 0, 1, 0, 0,
        0, 0, 0, 1, 0
      ];
      var filter:ColorMatrixFilter = new ColorMatrixFilter(matrix);
      _bitmap.filters = [filter];
    }

  }

}
```

Here, the applyFilter() method is overridden. I first set up a matrix, which for the ColorMatrixFilter is just a linear array of numbers. I've arranged the array so that at least the structure looks like a 4×5 matrix (we'll talk about that matrix in a moment). This matrix is passed to a new ColorMatrixFilter instance, which accepts only a single parameter—a nice change from some of the previous filters! This filter instance is then assigned to the filters array of the bitmap. If you compile the SWF with the matrix value as shown, you will see what is shown in Figure 2-23.

Figure 2-23.
The ColorMatrixFilter applied to loaded image. The matrix used is an identity matrix, resulting in no effect on the image.

Your eyes do not deceive. You'll notice that nothing seems to be happening in Figure 2-23. This is because of the values of the matrix assigned, which is known as an identity matrix. This type of matrix has ones in the main diagonal elements and zeros elsewhere, and the interesting feature of such a matrix is that, when multiplying against it, it returns the original matrix with no transforms. Imagine the scale transform we discussed in the last section with ones for all the scaling values instead of 0.5, 0.3, and 0.1. If you multiplied each value of the RGB color by 1, you would just get the original value. This is an identity matrix.

So that's why we see nothing yet in this example, but what, exactly, are all those elements in the matrix anyway, and how do they affect the colors of our image? The matrix can be explained in the following manner:

```
    R  G  B  A  offset
R | 1  0  0  0  0       |
G | 0  1  0  0  0       |
B | 0  0  1  0  0       |
A | 0  0  0  1  0       |
```

If you are a user of the Flash IDE, this matrix corresponds at least partially with the advanced color effect settings, as shown in Figure 2-24, with the 1 values from this matrix being the RGBA multipliers and the last column being the RGBA offsets. With the identity matrix shown here, you can see that the RGBA multipliers are 1 (or 100 percent of the original RGBA value) and the offsets are 0, which results in no change to the image.

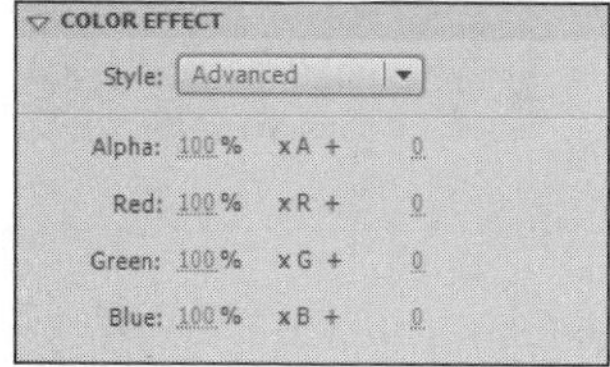

Figure 2-24.
The advanced color effect settings in Flash CS4

Conceptually, I like to think of the rows as output and the columns as input. So if you want to only see the red channel in your image, as in Figure 2-25, you can set the matrix in our ColorMatrixFilterTest class to the following:

```
var matrix:Array = [
  1, 0, 0, 0, 0,
  0, 0, 0, 0, 0,
  0, 0, 0, 0, 0,
  0, 0, 0, 1, 0
];
```

Figure 2-25.
The image is tinted red, as only the red color channel is used for both input and output. Other color channels contain all black pixels.

The matrix here is taking the red channel as input for the output red channel. The green and blue channels do not use any channel information. The result is an image tinted red. Of course, you could also achieve a red-tinted image as long as any of the color information is only used for the red channel. Here, the blue channel's information is used for the red channel, as shown in Figure 2-26:

```
var matrix:Array = [
  0, 0, 1, 0, 0,
  0, 0, 0, 0, 0,
  0, 0, 0, 0, 0,
  0, 0, 0, 1, 0
];
```

Figure 2-26.
The image is tinted red, as only the red color channel is used for output based on the original blue channel. Other color channels contain all black pixels.

If you wanted to swap the red and blue's channel information, the matrix can be changed to the following, which produces the result in Figure 2-27:

```
var matrix:Array = [
  0, 0, 1, 0, 0,
  0, 1, 0, 0, 0,
  1, 0, 0, 0, 0,
  0, 0, 0, 1, 0
];
```

Figure 2-27.
The image with its red and blue color channel information swapped, though not noticeable in grayscale

Notice that in the first row, the blue channel's input is used for the red channel's output, and vice versa in the third row for the blue channel.

Brightening an image Now, if you want to brighten the colors of an image, you have two options. First, you could simply alter the RGBA multipliers so that each channel's color information was doubled (or increased by some other percentage), as shown in Figure 2-28, using the following matrix:

```
var matrix:Array = [
  2, 0, 0, 0, 0,
  0, 2, 0, 0, 0,
  0, 0, 2, 0, 0,
  0, 0, 0, 1, 0
];
```

Figure 2-28.
The image with each pixel doubled in value

As an alternative, you could leave the multipliers at 1 and, instead, use the offsets to add value to each channel. The offsets can be anywhere between –255 and 255. The following uses the offsets to brighten an image, as shown in Figure 2-29:

```
var matrix:Array = [
  1, 0, 0, 0, 100,
  0, 1, 0, 0, 100,
  0, 0, 1, 0, 100,
  0, 0, 0, 1,   0
];
```

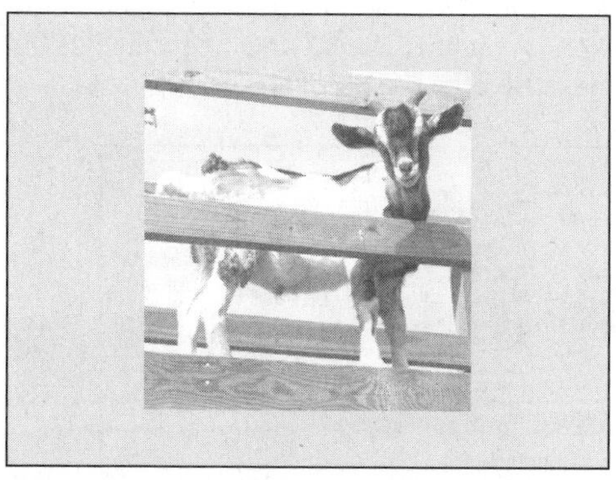

Figure 2-29.
The image with each pixel value offset by 100

Notice how this washes out the image, as opposed to the previous example, which still had heightened contrast. This is because the offsets are using addition to add to the channel value while the multipliers are using, well, multiplication. That means that a value of 0 will remain 0 with a multiplier, meaning blacks will stay black, but with an offset, the brightness will always get added to.

Desaturating an image With color matrices, you can do some pretty cool things, and since applying color matrices is an element of image processing that has been extensively explored, you can find matrices already established to achieve any number of color effects. One such matrix converts a color image to grayscale. The matrix to achieve that follows:

```
var matrix:Array = [
  0.3, 0.59, 0.11, 0, 0,
  0.3, 0.59, 0.11, 0, 0,
  0.3, 0.59, 0.11, 0, 0,
  0,   0,    0,    1, 0
];
```

This basically takes a little input from each color channel (adding up to 1) to use as the same output for each channel. Since each channel's output is the same value, you get gray colors. The reason more information is used from the green channel than the blue is to account for differences in relative screen luminosity of each channel. You could achieve grayscale images as long as the output of all three channels was identical, though. The values used here are just some accepted values for a fairly accurate grayscale image (though you can also find other equally accepted values).

Inverting to a negative image Inverting all of the colors of an image is also an easy effect to achieve, as shown in Figure 2-30. This is accomplished with the following matrix:

```
var matrix:Array = [
  -1,  0,  0, 0, 255,
   0, -1,  0, 0, 255,
   0,  0, -1, 0, 255,
   0,  0,  0, 1, 0,
];
```

Here, you can see each color channel is multiplied by –1. This negative value is then offset by 255. The result of this is that white, 255, becomes –255 after multiplication, then 0 after the offset addition. Black, 0, would become 255. A number like 50 would become 205. All the colors are thus inverted, and you get a negative effect.

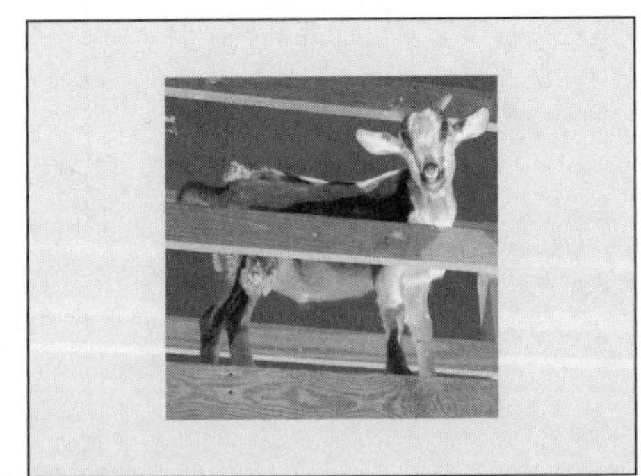

Figure 2-30.
The inverse of the image creating a photo negative effect

Tinting an image The last matrices we will look at here are for tinting an image. One well-known effect is to give an image a sepia tone. This can be achieved with the following matrix:

```
var matrix:Array = [
  0.5,  0.59, 0.11, 0, 0,
  0.4,  0.59, 0.11, 0, 0,
  0.16, 0.59, 0.11, 0, 0,
  0,    0,    0,    1, 0
];
```

That's great for that single effect, but for more general tinting, we can alter the code slightly so that any color could be used to tint an image. If you replace the applyFilter() method in the ColorMatrixFilterTest class with the following, you will produce an image with a purple tone:

```
override protected function applyFilter():void {
  var color:uint = 0xFF00CC;
  var r:uint = color >> 16 & 0xFF;
  var g:uint = color >> 8 & 0xFF;
  var b:uint = color & 0xFF;
  var matrix:Array = [
    r/255, 0.59, 0.11, 0, 0,
    g/255, 0.59, 0.11, 0, 0,
    b/255, 0.59, 0.11, 0, 0,
    0,     0,    0,    1, 0
  ];
  var filter:ColorMatrixFilter = new ColorMatrixFilter(matrix);
  _bitmap.filters = [filter];
}
```

Now, you can specify any color to be used. Here, we use right bit shifting to extract each individual color channel. This value will be between 0 and 255, so by dividing by 255 in the matrix for the red input channel, we are setting different percentage values for each output channel based on the original red channel values. Try plugging in different colors to see the results of different tints applied. And give yourself a pat on the back for wrestling matrices to the ground!

ConvolutionFilter

Maybe I shouldn't have said anything boastful about your conquering matrices in the last section, since now the ConvolutionFilter is looming over you, ready to chew up your matrices and spit them out on your pixels. But have courage! Despite its uncommon name, daunting list of parameters, and myriad possible effects, the ConvolutionFilter is as easy to tame as the ColorMatrixFilter, since it builds on your knowledge of matrix transform operations (and really, it's just a big cuddly bear of a filter anyway).

Convolving pixels

The ConvolutionFilter takes a matrix of values and calculates a new value for each pixel in an image based on the matrix, just like with the ColorMatrixFilter. With the ConvolutionFilter, though, the matrix determines how a pixel is affected by its surrounding pixels.

Let's take as a simple example this 1×3 matrix:

```
| 0  1  0 |
```

With the ConvolutionFilter, the middle element in the matrix, in this case 1, is used for the pixel being manipulated. This matrix element is multiplied by the pixel value (it performs this on each of the pixel's color channels separately). Values to the right and left of this element (and above and below if we have a two-dimensional matrix) are used for the pixels to the right and left of the main pixel being evaluated. These matrix elements are also multiplied with those pixels, and the results of all of this are added to the main pixel being manipulated. We can express this in a formula as follows:

```
M = | M11  M12  M13 |
dst(x, y) = (src(x-1, y)*M11  +  src(x, y)*M12  +  src(x+1, y)*M13)
```

As you can see, the pixel to the left of our pixel being evaluated (x-1) is multiplied by the first element in the matrix. The main pixel itself is multiplied by the second element, and the pixel to the right of the main element (x+1) is multiplied by the third matrix element. The products are then all added together. This is performed for all pixels in an image.

If you plug in our matrix in the example, `| 0  1  0 |`, you will see that this matrix will result in no change to an image, since the pixels to the left and right are multiplied by 0 and the main pixel being evaluated is multiplied by 1. We could try to plug in different numbers in this simple matrix, but to really do some cool stuff with convolution, we need to use a two-dimensional matrix. Here is a 3×3 matrix that will also result in no change to an image:

```
| 0  0  0 |
| 0  1  0 |
| 0  0  0 |
```

Just like our 1×3 example, this one multiplies all the surrounding pixels by 0 and the main pixel being evaluated (in the center) by 1. The formula to calculate this is the same as before (just with lots more numbers!):

```
    | M11  M12  M13 |
M = | M21  M22  M23 |
    | M31  M32  M33 |
dst(x, y) = (src(x-1, y-1)*M11 + src(x, y-1)*M12 + src(x+1, y-1)*M13) +
  (src(x-1, y)*M21 + src(x, y)*M22 + src(x+1, y)*M23) +
  (src(x-1, y+1)*M31 + src(x, y+1)*M32 + src(x+1, y+1)*M33)
```

With the ConvolutionFilter, you can use matrices as large and small as are necessary for your required effect. Generally, though, you can get some decent effects with simple 3×3 matrices, and that's what we'll be using mostly here.

Understanding the parameters

So now it's time to test out some fancy matrices and see how these affect an image. First, though, let's take a look at the constructor for the ConvolutionFilter:

```
ConvolutionFilter(
  matrixX:Number = 0,
  matrixY:Number = 0,
  matrix:Array = null,
  divisor:Number = 1.0,
  bias:Number = 0.0,
  preserveAlpha:Boolean = true,
  clamp:Boolean = true,
  color:uint = 0,
  alpha:Number = 0.0
)
```

Many of the parameters of ConvolutionFilter are unique to that filter because many of them apply to the matrix that is the bread and butter to the filter. Let's look at each parameter briefly in turn before diving into lengthy explanations.

- `matrixX`: The number of columns in the matrix provided
- `matrixY`: The number of rows in the matrix provided
- `matrix`: An array of numbers to use to transform the colors of an image
- `divisor`: The number by which matrix results will be divided to scale back the resulting value within a usable range
- `bias`: The amount to add to the resulting pixel value
- `preserveAlpha`: Whether the convolution effect is applied to the alpha channel as well as the color channels; default is just to affect the color channels
- `clamp`: Whether the image should be clamped, repeating pixel values when the convolution effect extends past the edge of an image
- `color`: When the `clamp` property is set to `false`, the color that should be used for pixels that extend beyond the source image
- `alpha`: When the `clamp` property is set to `false`, the opacity that should be used for pixels that extend beyond the source image

Breaking these properties down into individual line items is not the easiest way to explain or understand them, since many of them are closely tied together. We will instead look at how they relate to each other.

Let's jump to the third parameter to help explain the first two. `matrix` is, of course, the matrix you wish to pass to the filter to perform the convolution effect. Since this is just an array, there is no way to determine from that parameter alone the dimensions (number of rows and columns) of the matrix. As an example, consider the following matrix:

```
var matrix:Array = [0, 0, 0, 0, 1, 0, 0, 0, 0];
```

This could either be a 3×3 matrix or a 1×9 matrix (or even a 9×1 matrix). Therefore, we need the first two parameters of ConvolutionFilter to tell it the dimensions of the matrix, with matrixX being the number of columns and matrixY being the number of rows.

After that we have a divisor parameter. The divisor allows you to scale back the color value of the resulting pixel. The formula, if you look back, adds a lot of values together. This will often result in color values greater than 255 for each channel and simply produce a blown-out white image. The divisor provides a means to control this by allowing you to divide the result by the specified number. Generally, a divisor that is the sum of all the matrix elements will help to smooth out the color intensity of the resulting image.

The bias allows you to add or subtract from the resulting pixel color value. So if the resulting pixel should always be brightened (and if the multiplication matrix does not handle that), you could pass an additional bias of a positive number.

So the matrix, divisor, and bias all work together to produce a final pixel color. The matrix is multiplied against the pixel's and its neighbors' values, with the product divided by the divisor and the bias added to this result.

Finally, the last three parameters are also all tied closely together (and for the most part I leave these as the defaults). clamp determines how pixels at the edge of the image are calculated. For instance, if you have a 3×3 matrix, for the pixels along the right side of your image, there is no pixel at (x + 1) to use in the calculations. Having clamp set to true, as it is by default, tells the filter to extend the visible pixels when required and use these for the calculations, so when (x + 1, y) doesn't exist, then the value of (x, y) will be used.

If, however, you don't want this default behavior of extending the pixel values, you can set clamp to false, in which case the filter uses the color and alpha values that you specify in the last two parameters. So if you wanted an opaque black to be used, you would set clamp to false, color to 0x000000, and alpha to 1.

Got all that? There's a reason that this filter is so close to end of this chapter—this isn't your BlurFilter, ladies and gentlemen! Of course, the best way to clarify what these parameters can do is to plug in some numbers and see how the image is affected.

Applying the filter

To demonstrate this filter, I have created ConvolutionFilterTest.as, which is available in this chapter's files. Here is the code for the class:

```
package {

  import flash.filters.ConvolutionFilter;

  [SWF(width=550, height=400, backgroundColor=0xEEEEEE)]

  public class ConvolutionFilterTest extends ImageFilterTest {

    override protected function applyFilter():void {
      var matrix:Array = [
```

```
          0, 0, 0,
          0, 1, 0,
          0, 0, 0
        ];
        var filter:ConvolutionFilter = new ConvolutionFilter();
        filter.matrixX = 3;
        filter.matrixY = 3;
        filter.matrix = matrix;
        filter.divisor = 1;
        filter.bias = 0;
        _bitmap.filters = [filter];
      }

    }

  }
```

Once more, I extend the ImageFilterTest written for the ColorMatrixFilter example. If you compile this as shown, you will see the image unaffected since the matrix is one we've already identified as a matrix that multiplies the current pixel color value by 1 and all the surrounding pixel color values by 0.

Before playing more with the matrix, let's look at the bias in isolation. If you change its value to 100 you should see a result like Figure 2-31. Because the matrix doesn't affect the image, the bias of 100 has the effect of lightening each pixel color channel by 100. If you try –100, you will see that the image is darkened uniformly.

Figure 2-31. The ConvolutionFilter applied but with only the bias lightening the pixels

Blurring Set the bias back to 0 now, and let's plug in a new matrix value. Try the following:

```
  var matrix:Array = [
    1, 1, 1,
    1, 1, 1,
    1, 1, 1
  ];
```

```
var filter:ConvolutionFilter = new ConvolutionFilter();
filter.matrixX = 3;
filter.matrixY = 3;
filter.matrix = matrix;
filter.divisor = 9;
filter.bias = 0;
```

Here, the matrix forces the pixel being evaluated to be affected in equal parts by all of its immediately surrounding pixels. We alter the `divisor` so that it is the sum of the matrix elements (try changing it to 1 to see the image with many blown-out white pixels). The result is a blur, as shown in Figure 2-32.

Figure 2-32.
A slight blur applied to the image through convolution

The blur occurs because each pixel is altered in value to become a little closer in value to its surrounding pixels, which loses definition in the image. If you wanted a greater blur, you could increase the size of the matrix so the pixel evaluated is affected by an even wider range of surrounding pixels:

```
var matrix:Array = [
  1, 1, 1, 1, 1, 1, 1,
  1, 1, 1, 1, 1, 1, 1,
  1, 1, 1, 1, 1, 1, 1,
  1, 1, 1, 1, 1, 1, 1,
  1, 1, 1, 1, 1, 1, 1,
  1, 1, 1, 1, 1, 1, 1,
  1, 1, 1, 1, 1, 1, 1
];
var filter:ConvolutionFilter = new ConvolutionFilter();
filter.matrixX = 7;
filter.matrixY = 7;
filter.matrix = matrix;
filter.divisor = 49;
```

Note that this could be created more easily with a loop, but for instructional purposes, I write out the matrix for more clarity. With more pixels brought into the mix, the blur is greater, producing the result shown in Figure 2-33.

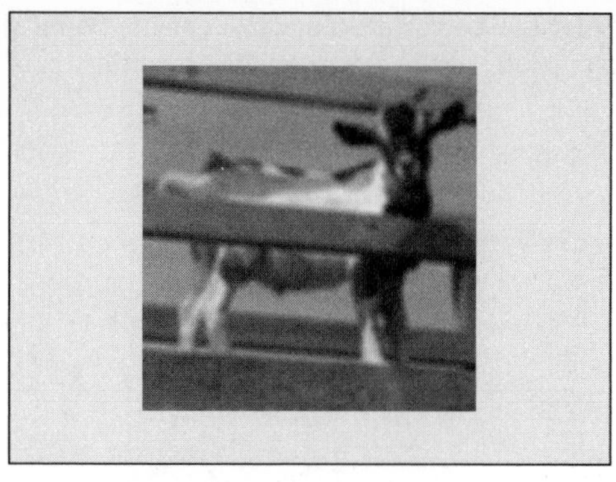

Figure 2-33.
A more intense blur applied to the image through convolution

There are a number of established matrices to perform different blurs. For instance, the following matrix will produce a Gaussian blur, as shown in Figure 2-34. This example uses a 7×7 matrix but could be expanded to a larger matrix to produce a larger blur effect.

```
var matrix:Array = [
  1, 1, 2,  2, 2, 1, 1,
  1, 1, 2,  4, 2, 1, 1,
  2, 2, 4,  8, 4, 2, 2,
  2, 4, 8, 16, 8, 4, 2,
  2, 2, 4,  8, 4, 2, 2,
  1, 1, 2,  4, 2, 1, 1,
  1, 1, 2,  2, 2, 1, 1
];
var divisor:Number = 0;
for each (var index:Number in matrix) {
  divisor += index;
}
var filter:ConvolutionFilter = new ConvolutionFilter();
filter.matrixX = 7;
filter.matrixY = 7;
filter.matrix = matrix;
filter.divisor = divisor;
```

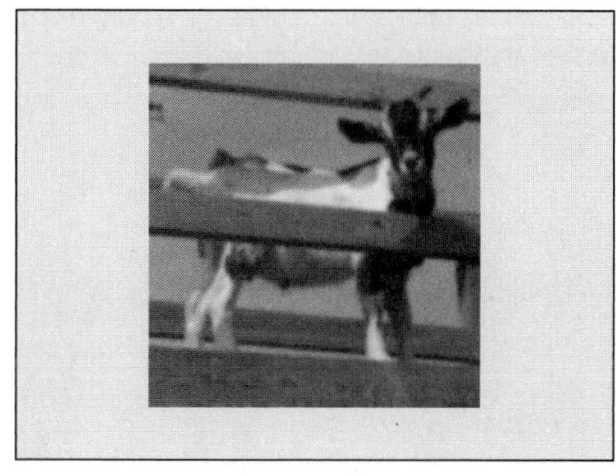

Figure 2-34.
A Gaussian blur applied to the image through convolution

Sharpening Another popular effect that can be achieved through convolution is sharpening, as shown in Figure 2-35. Let's take a look at the matrix and the result first and then discuss how it is achieved.

```
var matrix:Array = [
   0, -1,  0,
  -1,  5, -1,
   0, -1,  0
];
```

Figure 2-35.
A 3×3 matrix is applied for sharpening.

With this matrix, the main pixel evaluated has its color information multiplied by 5. This obviously can produce a large value for the result. However, the negative numbers around the central element result in the neighboring pixels getting their values subtracted from the main pixel. This means that for like brightness values, the end result will pretty much be the value of the original pixel (5n – 4n = n). But for neighboring pixels that are at a lower brightness value, the resulting pixel will be brighter since less will be subtracted. For neighboring pixels that are at a higher brightness value, the resulting pixel will be darker. This means, in a nutshell, that colors that are next to like colors will remain the same, while colors that are next to brighter colors will darken, and colors that are next to darker colors will brighten. The result is sharpening.

Just as with blurs, there are a number of different sharpening matrices you could apply. Here is a 5×5 high-pass sharpening matrix, and its result is shown in Figure 2-36. A high-pass sharpening filter keeps detailed areas of an image, like edges, generally unaffected while applying sharpening to larger, blurrier areas with less detail.

```
var matrix:Array = [
   0, -1, -1, -1,  0,
  -1,  2, -4,  2, -1,
  -1, -4, 13, -4, -1,
  -1,  2, -4,  2, -1,
   0, -1, -1, -1,  0
];
var divisor:Number = 0;
for each (var index:Number in matrix) {
  divisor += index;
}
```

```
var filter:ConvolutionFilter = new ConvolutionFilter();
filter.matrixX = 5;
filter.matrixY = 5;
filter.matrix = matrix;
filter.divisor = divisor;
```

Figure 2-36.
A 5X5 matrix is applied for sharpening.

Embossing Embossing is another technique that is possible through the ConvolutionFilter. This works by doing similar edge detection and pixel manipulation as we discussed for the sharpening matrices. However, for embossing, we want to increase or decrease brightness values based on a single direction, not in all directions, to give the illusion of light hitting the image and its raised edges.

You can enter the following matrix to see embossing in action, as shown in Figure 2-37.

```
var matrix:Array = [
  -2, -1,  0,
  -1,  0,  1,
   0,  1,  2
];
```

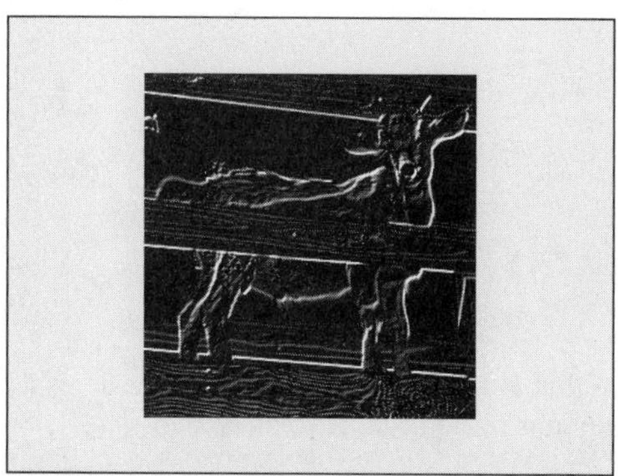

Figure 2-37.
An embossing effect can be created created through convolution.

This matrix works by detecting edges to the top left and the bottom right of the main pixel. A pixel that has a neighboring pixel to the bottom right that is of high value and that is not balanced by an equally bright pixel to the top left, then the main pixel is brightened.

In all other cases, the pixel is darkened. This explanation, I think, is more easily digested if we plug in some numbers.

Forgetting RGB colors for a moment, let's represent the pixel value being evaluated and its neighboring pixel values using the following matrix:

```
| 5  5  5 |
| 5  5  5 |
| 5  5  5 |
```

If we multiply each value by the corresponding elements in the convolution matrix, we get the following:

```
| -10  -5   0 |
|  -5   0   5 |
|   0   5  10 |
```

If you add all of those values together, you see that we get 0. Our pixel is colored black.

Now, let's try a pixel with neighboring pixels where the upper left is brighter:

```
| 5  5  5 |
| 5  5  0 |
| 5  0  0 |
```

Perform our simple multiplication again, and we get this:

```
| -10  -5   0 |
|  -5   0   0 |
|   0   0   0 |
```

We get a negative number, which will also result in a black pixel.

Finally, let's put higher values in the bottom right position:

```
| 0  0  5 |
| 0  5  5 |
| 5  5  5 |
```

This, of course, would result in the following:

```
|  0  0   0 |
|  0  0   5 |
|  0  5  10 |
```

Now, we get a positive result (20) that is four times the value of our original pixel. This would probably translate to white in our final image. *Et voilà*—embossing!

Of course, we can change the direction of the light by altering the positive and negative values in our matrix. In the following, I've changed the direction so that the light appears to be hitting the image from the left, as shown in Figure 2-38:

```
var matrix:Array = [
  1, 0, -1,
  2, 0, -2,
  1, 0, -1
];
```

Figure 2-38.
Another embossing effect with the light illusion appearing from the left

Outlining The last convolution effect we will look at is related to the sharpening effect we previously explored in that it also uses edge detection in a uniform manner to highlight the areas of high contrast in an image. The result is an outline effect where detected edges are brightened and areas of similar color are darkened, as in Figure 2-39.

Figure 2-39.
The ConvolutionFilter creating an outlining effect

This effect can be achieved with the following code. I have included the full class this time since I've added the ColorMatrixFilter to invert the image. By inverting, the edges become dark, creating more of a drawn outline mode.

```
package {

  import flash.filters.ConvolutionFilter;
  import flash.filters.ColorMatrixFilter;

  [SWF(width=550, height=400, backgroundColor=0xEEEEEE)]
```

```
public class ConvolutionFilterTest extends ImageFilterTest {

  override protected function applyFilter():void {
    var matrix:Array = [
       0, -1,  0,
      -1,  4, -1,
       0, -1,  0
    ];
    var divisor:Number = 0;
    for each (var index:Number in matrix) {
      divisor += index;
    }
    var filter:ConvolutionFilter = new ConvolutionFilter();
    filter.matrixX = 3;
    filter.matrixY = 3;
    filter.matrix = matrix;
    filter.divisor = divisor;
    filter.bias = 0;

    matrix = [
      -1,  0,  0, 0, 255,
       0, -1,  0, 0, 255,
       0,  0, -1, 0, 255,
       0,  0,  0, 1, 0
    ];
    var colorFilter:ColorMatrixFilter = ➥
new ColorMatrixFilter(matrix);

    _bitmap.filters = [filter, colorFilter];
  }

}

}
```

As you can see, the matrix is, in fact, very similar to the sharpening matrix, the main difference being that the sum of the elements works out to be 0, not 1. We can intensify this outlining effect by widening the range of pixels evaluated, which, of course, means increasing the dimensions of the matrix. Try this 5×5 matrix, which produces the result shown in Figure 2-40:

```
var matrix:Array = [
  -1, -1, -1, -1, -1,
  -1, -1, -1, -1, -1,
  -1, -1, 24, -1, -1,
  -1, -1, -1, -1, -1,
  -1, -1, -1, -1, -1
];
```

```
var divisor:Number = 0;
for each (var index:Number in matrix) {
  divisor += index;
}
var filter:ConvolutionFilter = new ConvolutionFilter();
filter.matrixX = 5;
filter.matrixY = 5;
```

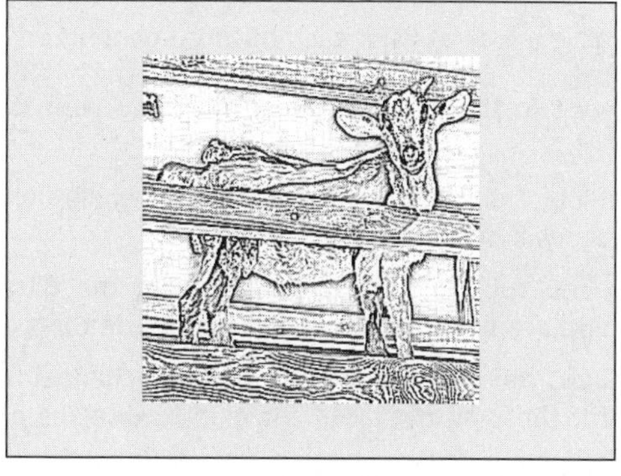

Figure 2-40.
A 5X5 matrix used to create a different outline effect, almost like a woodcut

DisplacementMapFilter

Since this filter is being presented after the mammoth that is the ConvolutionFilter, you would be forgiven for believing that this filter ups the complexity even more. However, the DisplacementMapFilter is in actuality much simpler than the ConvolutionFilter and I have placed it here more to keep it in close proximity to, and provide a segue for, the next chapter, which presents the BitmapData class.

Since so much of the DisplacementMapFilter relies on an understanding of the BitmapData class, this section won't be an in-depth exploration of the filter (we'll save that for Chapter 4). Rather, let's just briefly look at what this filter does and create a quick example to whet your appetite.

The DisplacementMapFilter takes a grayscale image (or rather one color or alpha channel from an RGB or RGBA image, which is itself an 8-bit grayscale image) and, using this as a displacement map, distorts another image based on the pixel values from the map. Pixels in the map that are brighter than medium gray will move the destination image's pixels up and to the left. Pixels that are darker in color will move the destination pixels down and to the right.

Let's break down the parameters of DisplacementMapFilter to see how each affects the filter. Remember, next chapter begins the deep dive into BitmapData, so a number of these parameters might be unfamiliar (and that's OK!). Here is the constructor:

```
DisplacementMapFilter(
  mapBitmap:BitmapData = null,
  mapPoint:Point = null,
```

```
    componentX:uint = 0,
    componentY:uint = 0,
    scaleX:Number = 0.0,
    scaleY:Number = 0.0,
    mode:String = "wrap",
    color:uint = 0,
    alpha:Number = 0.0
)
```

You know the routine by now. Let's have a look at what each of those parameters means.

- `mapBitmap`: This is the reference to the BitmapData instance you wish to use to displace your image.
- `mapPoint`: The `mapPoint` is the point on the destination image at which the top left corner of the displacement map will be aligned.
- `componentX`: Use this to set the color or alpha channel from the BitmapData instance to use for the 8-bit displacement map to displace pixels on the x axis.
- `componentY`: With this parameter, you can set the color or alpha channel from the BitmapData instance to use for the 8-bit displacement map to displace pixels on the y axis.

  Because the `componentX` and `componentY` properties are separate parameters, you can have the red channel of the BitmapData instance control the displacement on the x axis, and the green channel affect the y axis.
- `scaleX`: This parameter determines the amount of displacement to apply on the x axis: the larger the number, the bigger the visible displacement.
- `scaleY`: This one determines the amount of displacement to apply on the y axis: again, the larger the number, the bigger the visible displacement.
- `mode`: The `mode` parameter determines how pixels are handled when the effect extends beyond the edges of the image. This value should be found in the DisplacementMapFilterMode constants. `WRAP` pulls in pixels from the opposite side of the image; `CLAMP` repeats pixels at the edge, as with the ConvolutionFilter; `IGNORE` simply uses the source pixel color; and `COLOR`, again like with ConvolutionFilter, uses the color and alpha value specified for this filter.
- `color`: When the mode property is set to `COLOR`, this is the color that should be used for pixels that extend beyond the source image.
- `alpha`: When the mode property is set to `COLOR`, this is the opacity that should be used for pixels that extend beyond the source image.

In the following example, I load in a new image that will be easier to see the displacement effects on. A white circle is drawn using the drawing API and then drawn into a BitmapData instance with a black background (don't worry—that's covered in the next chapter). This image is blurred using the handy blur filter so that we get values ranging from black to white and all intermediate grays. Using this image as the map, I apply a DisplacementMapFilter to the loaded image of a colorful checkerboard, which becomes noticeably distorted, as shown in Figure 2-41.

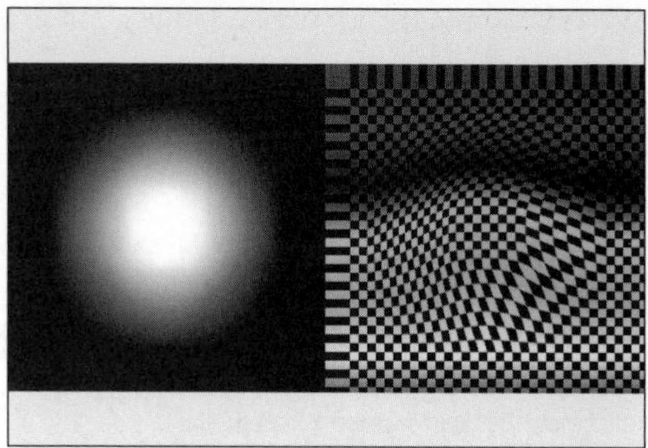

Figure 2-41. A DisplacementMapFilter applied to the image on the right using the map from the left

As you can see in the example, the places in the original image that correspond to the white areas of the map have been pushed up and to the left. The black areas have been pushed down and to the right, as is most noticeable at the top and left of the image where the pixels have just been repeated.

This is the code used to produce the result seen in Figure 2-41. I won't be breaking this down here since we will be exploring the DisplacementMapFilter in more depth in Chapter 4 after we get into BitmapData. Consider this a tantalizing glimpse of the future.

```
package {

  import flash.display.Bitmap;
  import flash.display.BitmapData;
  import flash.display.BitmapDataChannel;
  import flash.display.Shape;
  import flash.filters.BlurFilter;
  import flash.filters.DisplacementMapFilter;
  import flash.filters.DisplacementMapFilterMode;
  import flash.geom.Matrix;
  import flash.geom.Point;

  [SWF(width=600, height=400, backgroundColor=0xEEEEEE)]

  public class DisplacementMapFilterTest extends ImageFilterTest {

    public function DisplacementMapFilterTest() {
      super("../assets/checkers.jpg");
    }

    override protected function applyFilter():void {
      var shape:Shape = new Shape();
      shape.graphics.beginFill(0xFFFFFF);
      var radius:Number = (Math.min(_bitmap.width, ➥
_bitmap.height) - 150)/2;
```

```
            shape.graphics.drawCircle(radius, radius, radius);
            shape.graphics.endFill();

            var map:BitmapData = new BitmapData(_bitmap.width, ➥
_bitmap.height, false, 0xFF000000);
            var matrix:Matrix = new Matrix();
            matrix.translate((_bitmap.width - radius*2)/2, ➥
(_bitmap.height - radius*2)/2);
            map.draw(shape, matrix);
            var blurFilter:BlurFilter = new BlurFilter(80, 80);
            map.applyFilter(map, map.rect, new Point(), blurFilter);
            var mapBitmap:Bitmap = new Bitmap(map);
            mapBitmap.y = _bitmap.y;
            _bitmap.x = mapBitmap.width;
            addChild(mapBitmap);

            var filter:DisplacementMapFilter = new DisplacementMapFilter();
            filter.mapBitmap = map;
            filter.componentX = BitmapDataChannel.RED;
            filter.componentY = BitmapDataChannel.RED;
            filter.scaleX = 30;
            filter.scaleY = 30;
            filter.mode = DisplacementMapFilterMode.CLAMP;
            _bitmap.filters = [filter];
        }

    }

}
```

There are some pretty interesting effects that can be achieved through the DisplacementMapFilter, including dynamic liquefy effects, fisheye lens distortion, or wrapping textures around objects. To achieve these effects takes a greater understanding of BitmapData and some more serious math, so we'll leave discussion of that until later in the book once you have the basics down.

Summary

In this chapter alone, we have covered extensively the blend modes and filters that are a part of the ActionScript language and at your beck and call for creating some truly stunning effects through individual use as well as in some creative combinations. A lot of math has been thrown at you this chapter, and that was important, not only to help you better understand the mechanics of some of these features but also to prepare you for creating your own blend modes and filters a little later in this book as we get into Pixel Bender and the new ActionScript Shader class.

But first, next chapter, we'll be looking at quite possibly my favorite class in all of ActionScript, and that is the BitmapData class. Yes, I admit, I'm practically giddy. Its introduction a few versions of Flash ago was one of the things that prompted me to set out to write this book (sorry for the delay, but I got a little waylaid with getting married, moving to a new state and job, having a baby, and buying a home). You've already seen a bit of its use in this chapter through the image loading and the DisplacementMapFilter, but that is, as they say, just the tip of the iceberg. The BitmapData class offers a huge amount of functionality for manipulating bitmap images, and it's a class that enables many of the image effects we will spend the latter half of this book creating.

Needless to say, there's a lot to the BitmapData class. So before turning the page, take a break, go live a little, and come back when you are all set to dive head first into the pixels once more.

Chapter 3

BITMAPS AND BITMAPDATA

There's a great scene at the end of *The Matrix* (you know, the good one) where Neo is suddenly able to see the world around him as a representation of symbols, the program underneath that makes up the illusion of the world. Once he recognizes the nature of these symbols, he is able to manipulate them, and therefore his whole environment, displaying what amounts to superpowers as he pushes, pulls, and transforms the world around him.

If that's not a geek's dream, I'm not sure what is. And although you won't be mistaken for Superman any time soon while programming in ActionScript, once you begin to recognize and understand the little pieces of the code that make up the entirety of an application, an effect, or an image, you will wield more power in the little world inside the Flash Player.

I don't think this is truer anywhere than with pixel manipulation and the class that enables it in ActionScript, BitmapData. Through this class, you have access to the underlying pixels of an image, and you can create, copy, merge, transform, and manipulate to your heart's content. BitmapData is, I feel, the single most important ActionScript class when it comes to creating stunning image effects, because it gives you access to the underlying pixel information.

"Pixel," as you may well know, is short for "picture element," and control over the elemental parts of an image is a powerful thing indeed. In fact, through the creative use of BitmapData, a majority of the effects we explore throughout the rest of this book are enabled. But building effects using BitmapData requires a firm understanding of all of its capabilities. That's what this and the next chapter are all about.

Understanding bitmaps in ActionScript

Back in the days of ActionScript 2.0, including a bitmap in your application meant loading it into a MovieClip instance and dealing with it as an immutable image. You could size and rotate the MovieClip in which it was embedded, but the internal pixels of the bitmap were off limits.

With ActionScript 3.0, the way bitmaps were dealt with in the Flash Player, and thus through ActionScript, changed dramatically. Images were no longer objects that had to be embedded in other display objects in order to be rendered but were display objects in their own right with pixel information that could now be accessed and altered. We now had Bitmap and BitmapData.

Introducing Bitmap

Any visual piece in a Flash movie or application is a display object, derived from the DisplayObject class. In the first chapter using the drawing API, we took advantage of Shapes and Sprites. If you have created multiframe symbols in a Flash file's library, you are dealing with MovieClips. You can also create TextField instances to display text and Video instances to play back videos.

For bitmap images, we have the Bitmap class, and this can be used without ever even thinking about BitmapData (though that's rather rude to do). You could perhaps embed an image in your application if you are using the Flex compiler using the embed metatag:

```
[Embed(source="/assets/logo.png")]
public var LogoImage:Class;
```

Alternatively, you could export an image from the library in the Flash IDE. In either case, if you instantiate this exported class, what you have will actually be a Bitmap instance that can be added to the stage:

```
var logo:Bitmap = new LogoImage() as Bitmap;
addChild(logo);
```

If you are loading an image at runtime, as we did in the last chapter, it is a Bitmap instance within the loader's content that you can then add to the stage:

```
private function onImageLoaded(event:Event):void {
  var loaderInfo:LoaderInfo = event.target as LoaderInfo;
  var bitmap:Bitmap = loaderInfo.content as Bitmap;
  addChild(bitmap);
}
```

So if all you are doing is loading and displaying images, the Bitmap class is all you would need to worry about. It is a display object that contains bitmap information that can be added to the display list.

Accessing BitmapData

But loading and displaying alone isn't much fun, is it? If you want to get to the underlying pixels of a bitmap and perform some transformations, you need to access the Bitmap instance's pixel data. As it turns outs, this can be accessed through the `bitmapData` property of Bitmap, which holds, you guessed it, a BitmapData instance.

A BitmapData instance holds all the pixel information of a single bitmap. Through this class, per-pixel or per-channel operations can be performed. Using this class, you can push pixels around, alter their color and opacity, and replace or extract whole regions of pixel data. This is the class on which cool effects are made, and we will explore its multitude of methods that enable this manipulation throughout the rest of this and the next chapter.

The properties of BitmapData are fairly limited—most of its capabilities lie within its methods—and all are read only. The `transparent` property tells you whether the pixels in the image can be transparent or not. This does not mean the image *is* transparent, but rather whether pixels accessible through the BitmapData instance contain alpha information. All of the pixels certainly could be opaque, but a true transparent setting means the pixels are 32-bit, not 24-bit, and you are able to alter the alpha of the pixels.

If "24-bit" and "32-bit" are terms that mean nothing to you, take heart: all is explained in the next section on channel information. For now, just understand that 24-bit colors contain just color information, while 32-bit colors contain color and alpha information.

The width and height properties of BitmapData give you the pixel dimensions of the instance. Remember, since pixels can be transparent, these properties are not necessarily the width and height of the visible image. You can certainly create a BitmapData instance that is 100×100 pixels with completely transparent pixel content, in which case the width and height will remain 100×100 even though no pixels are visible.

The final property is rect, which is a Rectangle instance defining the size and position of the image. The position will actually always be (0, 0). The size will be the values of the width and height properties. So, you might be thinking, "What's the point of rect?" Well, a lot of the BitmapData methods require a Rectangle to define regions. In many cases, perhaps the majority, it is the rect of a BitmapData instance you will use, so having this as an accessible property means you don't have to keep creating new Rectangle instances every time you call on these methods. Consider the following two blocks of code, which do the exact same thing:

```
var rect:Rectangle = new Rectangle(0, 0, data.width, data.height);
data.applyFilter(data, rect, new Point(), blurFilter);

data.applyFilter(data, data.rect, new Point(), blurFilter);
```

I certainly prefer the second approach, don't you?

Understanding channel data

A carpenter should know more about nails than that you hit them with a hammer. Hopefully, a dentist wouldn't pull out a drill without a full understanding of what a tooth was (then again, how the heck did he get that diploma?). In a similar way, it is pointless for us to use the ActionScript tools to manipulate pixels without first understanding what exactly a pixel is. So before we dive into the BitmapData methods, we're going to take a step back and look at our little friend, the pixel, and discuss how its data is stored.

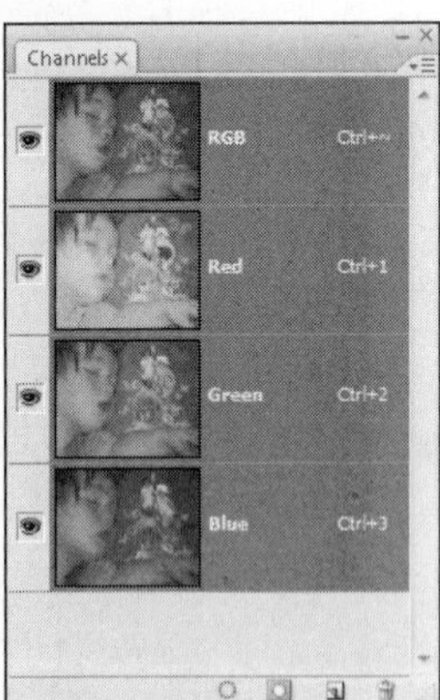

Figure 3-1. The Channels palette in Photoshop

For once, those coming from Photoshop and a design background have a little bit of an advantage over programmers who might not have dealt too much with graphics programming in the past. (This is a rare thing for the designers reading an ActionScript book, so we have to let them enjoy the moment!) Figure 3-1 shows the Channels palette in Photoshop. For Photoshop users, color channels and 24-bit and 32-bit colors are part of the everyday workflow. For others, these terms might seem alien. To better understand them, we'll first take a look at a bit.

Storing grayscale

"Bit" is short for "binary digit," and it is a way to store information that only requires one of two values, 0 and 1. If a bit is on, it holds a value of 1. If a bit is off, it holds a value of 0. And that's all it can hold. If you put two bits together, this offers you four possible permutations (and a shave and a haircut—sorry, I couldn't resist). The following is 0 to 3 in binary (the numeric system best used to represent bits), showing the four possible values that 2 bits can hold:

```
00
01
10
11
```

To understand binary representation better, let's first look at decimal representation. With decimal numbers, each digit can hold one of ten possible values, 0 to 9. Each digit is a power of 10 based on its position, so 1, is 10^0; 10 is 10^1; 100 is 10^2, and so on. As schoolchildren, we all did a good job with memorization of our mathematical tables, so 13 was always 13, but really you can think of that decimal number as $(1 * 10^1) + (3 * 10^0)$.

With the binary numeric system, it is 2, not 10, raised to a power at each position, so in the first position it is 2^0; in the second position, it is 2^1; in the third, it is 2^2, and so on. The binary number 101 can, therefore, be represented as $(1 * 2^2) + (0 * 2^1) + (1 * 2^0)$, which is 5 in decimal.

So 1 bit can hold two possible values. 2 bits can hold four. 3 bits can hold eight. If you put 8 bits together, you get a grand total of 256 possible values, from 0 to 255 in decimal. This 8 bits of data can be stored in a pixel, and it turns out that these 8 bits are a great way to store brightness values, with 0 representing black, 255 representing white, and all numbers in between representing a different value of gray. A collection of these 8-bit pixels in a two-dimensional grid can represent a photorealistic image, albeit only in black, white, and grays. Figure 3-2 shows an image that contains only 8 bits of data per pixel, resulting in a grayscale image.

Figure 3-2. A grayscale image with only 8 bits of data per pixel

Perhaps if we all had two fingers and two toes then bits and binary would come naturally. But 8 bits of data represented in binary just looks like a lot of zeros and ones to me (which, of course, is all it is):

```
10101101
```

Thankfully, there is a common shorthand for representing binary, and that is to use hexadecimal, which is a base 16 numeral system. Although we don't have 16 fingers and 16 toes, this still makes for a much more readable form for a collection of bits.

With hexadecimal, each symbol can represent one of 16 possible values. The symbols used are 0 to 9 and then A through F, with A being 10 in decimal, B being 11, C being 12, and so on. Because each symbol is one of 16 values, each hexadecimal value can effectively represent 4 bits of binary information (called a nibble).

So for the previous example, the first four binary digits, 1010, can be represented with the hexadecimal symbol A (or 10 in decimal). The second set of four binary digits, 1101, can be represented with the hexadecimal symbol D (or 13 in decimal). The decimal equivalent of these eight binary digits is actually 173 (or 10 * 16 + 13 * 1), so the following three values are three representations of the same number in three different numeral systems:

```
Base 2      Base 10     Base 16
10101101    173         AD
```

We won't be going any deeper into numeral systems and how these work, since that is a bit (pun intended) beyond the scope of this book, and in ActionScript, you rarely have to worry about converting between numeral systems. ActionScript deals with numbers, so it doesn't matter which numeral system you utilize. Generally, decimal numbers will be used in the code, and the hexadecimal system is most useful when representing color values. Converting between decimal and hexadecimal (and indeed between any of the numeral systems) is handled for you behind the scenes in the Flash Player.

What is most useful to take away from this discussion on binary, decimal, and hexadecimal systems is that all are merely different ways of representing the same numeric data.

A grayscale image, therefore, will contain an array of pixels, and each of these pixels will store one value between #00 and #FF in hexadecimal (the pound sign being common prefix notation for hexadecimal values, though in ActionScript and other programming languages the prefix 0x is used in the code), or 0 to 255 values in decimal. Put them all together and you have a pretty black-and-white image (unless the image itself is ugly, of course, in which case no pixel value will help you).

Adding color

For a true color image, we need more data per pixel. On a color monitor, a pixel is represented using a combination of three light sources placed extremely close together displaying intensities of red, green, and blue, respectively. Because of the size and relatively close proximity of these light sources, the human eye is tricked into seeing a single color for each pixel, much a like a pointillism painting done by tiny little gnomes. The intensity of each of those colored lights can be represented using the 8 bits of data, or 256 values, that you saw with a grayscale image.

A colored pixel can therefore be represented using three different sets of 8-bit data for the red, green, and blue intensities. These sets are what we refer to as the color channels. These three channels combined give you a total of 24 bits of data, which offers a total of 16,777,216 different possible permutations (256 * 256 * 256). Depending on the value for each color channel, you get a different resulting color.

For instance, let's squint our eyes together and imagine a single pixel. The numeric value of the color stored in the pixel can be anywhere from 0 to 16,777,216. This 16-million decimal value looks like this in binary:

```
11111111  11111111  11111111
```

The first 8 bits of data represent the red channel; the second 8 bits represent the green channel; and the third 8 bits represent the blue channel. All the bits right now are turned on (i.e., they hold a value of 1, not 0—it's not as if they are attracted to you, though I'm sure you are a very nice person).

The same 16-million decimal value represented in hexadecimal gives you the following:

```
FF  FF  FF
```

If you have worked at all with hexadecimal color notation, you know that this value of #FFFFFF is pure white. Each colored light will be at full intensity, and our eyes will see white for the single pixel.

However, if the values of the red and green channels are 0, this gives you the following numbers in binary, decimal, and hexadecimal:

```
                RED     GREEN      BLUE
Base 2:    00000000  00000000  11111111
Base 10:          0         0       255
Base 16:         00        00        FF
```

In this case, the hexadecimal result is #0000FF, which results in a pure blue color. Of the three colored lights used for the pixel, only the blue light will be on, and at full intensity.

In such a way, you can combine these three channels of intensity information and represent one of over 16 million colors. Each channel in itself just contains grayscale information, or rather intensity values that can be represented visually as grayscale. It is only in combining the three channels that we can represent color.

Representing transparency

In ActionScript, one additional channel can be used for a pixel, and that is its alpha channel. Like the color channels, this channel is a set of 8 bits that can hold a value anywhere from 0 to 255 in decimal. A value of 0 represents complete transparency, while a value of 255 (#FF) represents complete opacity.

If you have your basic addition down (which I hope you do since here we are talking about multiple numeral systems!), you will realize that an additional 8 bits of data means that our pixels will contain a total of 32 bits of information—24 for the color channels plus 8 more for the alpha. This alpha channel means that there are now a total of 4,294,967,296 values that can be used for a single pixel! Of course, how each channel is stored is more easily seen when using binary or hexadecimal notation:

```
               ALPHA       RED     GREEN      BLUE
Base 2:     11111111  00000000  00000000  11111111
Base 16:          FF        00        00        FF
```

In this case, the 32-bit value for our pixel is #FF0000FF, which is still blue, but also noted to be 100 percent opaque. If the pixel was 50 percent opaque, its hexadecimal value would be #7F0000FF. A fully transparent blue pixel would hold the value of #000000FF.

Since an alpha channel contains 8 bits of data just like the color channels, it also can be visually represented quite handily with a grayscale value, and the alpha channel of a full image can be represented with a grayscale image. If you are a user of Photoshop, a layer mask that you apply to a layer, as shown in Figure 3-3, is just a grayscale representation of the alpha channel you are applying to those pixels.

Figure 3-3. A layer mask applying alpha transparency to a layer in Photoshop

Of course, there are no little colored lights on your monitor that are used to render alpha values. Transparency is handled internally in the Flash Player itself, calculating how a partially transparent pixel will interact with the colors below it. It is the final, calculated, opaque RGB value that is then rendered on your screen (which is one reason why many transparent pixels can cause a slowdown of rendering in the Flash Player).

Specifying channels

As we progress through this book, and especially through this chapter, I will be referring to—and we will be consistently using—color and alpha channels in our effects. Some of the methods we will discuss in the next chapter accept a channel, or at least a signifier for a channel, as a parameter. This might be the channel to use for intensity values, or it might be the channel to which an effect is applied.

ActionScript provides a BitmapDataChannel class that contains a number of constants that can be used to specify a channel for the methods that require it. For instance, `BitmapDataChannel.ALPHA` can be passed to the `copyChannel()` method so that the alpha channel of one BitmapData instance can be copied to another:

```
bitmapData.copyChannel(
  sourceBitmapData,
  sourceBitmapData.rect,
  new Point(),
  BitmapDataChannel.ALPHA,
  BitmapDataChannel.ALPHA
);
```

Channels and how color data is stored are important aspects of image manipulation. This section, although by no means an exhaustive reference, should aid you through this book and help you master the effects it presents.

Speaking of which, now that you know the ins and outs of colors and channels, it's time we got back to our main topic, BitmapData.

Loading, creating, and displaying bitmaps

You can't have much fun with bitmap manipulation until you have a bitmap to manipulate. There are a number of ways to get access to bitmaps and display them in your application, and the best method will depend on your environment and your needs for the application. In this section, we will cover the different ways to load or create bitmaps and then how to display those bitmaps within the Flash Player.

Embedding or loading assets

The easiest way to get at a bitmap is to embed the bitmap in your SWF, which is handled in two different ways, depending on your compiler. First, if you are using Flex Builder, the mxmlc compiler through the command line, or the Flex compiler as an option in the Flash IDE, you can use the embed metatag to embed your bitmap asset, as was discussed in the "Introducing Bitmap" section earlier this chapter.

If you are using the Flash IDE, you can import the bitmap into your library and export it for ActionScript (in this case, perhaps as the class LogoImage). As these two methods are not consistent for all environments, we will not use them in the examples in this book. Please see the Flex or Flash documentation for further information on these methods.

No matter your method of choice for embedding, you can instantiate the bitmap using the class constructor and cast it as a Bitmap. Since Bitmap is a DisplayObject, you can then add it directly to the display list for rendering:

```
var logo:Bitmap = new LogoImage() as Bitmap;
addChild(logo);
```

The method we will use to access bitmaps in our examples, and the one you saw in the previous chapter, is to use the Loader class to load in a bitmap at runtime. This works the same no matter your compiler or development environment. Basically, Loader, which is a DisplayObject itself, is a wrapper that you can add to the display list and position, scale, rotate, set visibility, and so on, while it loads displayable data, like a SWF or bitmap image, asynchronously behind the scenes.

```
var loader:Loader = new Loader();
loader.contentLoaderInfo.addEventListener(
  Event.COMPLETE,
  onImageLoaded
);
loader.load(new URLRequest(imagePath));
```

The Flex Builder examples presented in this book use ActionScript projects, not Flex projects. If you are using the Flex framework, you should use the mx.controls.Image class to load in your image. This implements the IUIComponent interface, allowing it to be added to the display list in your application. If you just use Loader, you would need to create a UIComponent container in which to add the Bitmap before it could be added to the display list.

However, we won't be adding the Loader to the display list in our examples, although you certainly could (if all you are doing is loading and displaying, there is no reason why not). We will need access to the underlying bitmap in order to access its bitmap data, so it is best to grab this from the Loader instance once the bitmap fully loads and add this directly to the display list:

```
private function onImageLoaded(event:Event):void {
  var loaderInfo:LoaderInfo = event.target as LoaderInfo;
  var bitmap:Bitmap = loaderInfo.content as Bitmap;
  bitmap.x = 100;
  bitmap.y = 100;
  addChild(bitmap);
}
```

The bitmap is actually the first (and only) child of the Loader instance and can be obtained using `getChildAt()`, but if you have not saved a reference to the Loader, the easiest way to access the bitmap is to look at the LoaderInfo instance's `content` property, as we do here. This can be cast to Bitmap, positioned, sized and added to the display list.

One thing you will need to be cognizant of when loading images into the Flash Player is the player's security sandbox and how that can prevent certain interaction with pixel data. If you are loading an image delivered from the same domain as your SWF, you will be able to access its underlying pixels without issue. If, however, your SWF is loading an image from a different domain, you will get a security exception when trying to access its bitmap data, or even when trying to cast to Bitmap or set its smoothing property. In these cases, the domain hosting the image file will need a cross-domain policy file that grants access to the SWF for such operations, and you will need to explicitly set the `loadPolicyFile` *property on the LoaderContext used when loading the image. For more information on Flash's security sandbox and policy files, please refer to Adobe's ActionScript documentation. In this book, all of the examples will use image paths relative to the SWF. These images will therefore be within the same sandbox as the SWFs and will not require policy files in order for us to get access to the pixels.*

Creating bitmaps from scratch

Instead of loading in a bitmap, you can create one from scratch at runtime and fill it with whatever you need. This requires the creation of two separate objects: a BitmapData instance to define the pixel information and a Bitmap instance containing the data to add to the display list.

Instantiating BitmapData

Creating bitmap data is a breeze, with a simple constructor that takes four parameters, two of which are optional. Here is the signature for the constructor:

```
BitmapData(
  width:int,
  height:int,
  transparent:Boolean = true,
  fillColor:uint = 0xFFFFFFFF
)
```

`width` and `height` are the dimensions of the image. Once you set these, the dimensions are unalterable. To add pixels to an image would require you to create a new BitmapData instance of the larger dimensions and copy in the first instance's pixel information.

The `transparent` property specifies whether the bitmap data will hold 24-bit or 32-bit pixel values—basically, whether the pixels can be transparent or not. This is unalterable as well, so you need to specify on creation of bitmap data what type of data it will hold.

The fourth parameter, `fillColor`, is the color that will be assigned to undefined pixels (ones you don't explicitly set data for). Consider the following line of ActionScript:

```
var bitmapData:BitmapData = new BitmapData(100, 100);
```

In this case, the initial bitmap data will contain an image that is 100×100 pixels, where each pixel is pure white at full opacity, since those are the defaults. If you wanted the initial bitmap data to be fully opaque black, you could use this:

```
var bitmapData:BitmapData = new BitmapData(100, 100, true, 0xFF000000);
```

Note that, because the third parameter has been set to `true`, the pixels could be filled with transparent pixels at some point. If we know that the bitmap will never need any transparency, we can save memory by setting `transparent` to `false`:

```
var data:BitmapData = new BitmapData(100, 100, false, 0xFF000000);
```

If, as is often the case, you need the initial bitmap data to contain completely transparent pixels until you add opaque pixels to it, you would make sure the alpha channel of the `fillColor` parameter contains a value of 0:

```
var data:BitmapData = new BitmapData(100, 100, true, 0x00000000);
```

Here, it doesn't really matter what we define for the RGB color channels of the `fillColor`, since the default pixel will always be transparent anyway (unless, that is, you will be performing certain operations that use color data from a transparent pixel or merge alpha from another BitmapData instance into this one).

Once the BitmapData instance is created, you can add additional pixel data to it in any number of ways using methods we will be discussing throughout the rest of this chapter and the next. However, much like the Invisible Man when he's in the buff, without a Bitmap instance to wrap around your pixel data there is nothing much to see.

Adding data to a Bitmap instance

Bitmap is a DisplayObject child class and one of the rare children that takes any arguments at all in its constructor. This is because without additional data, a Bitmap instance doesn't hold much purpose, and this normally can be passed in the constructor.

```
Bitmap(
  bitmapData:BitmapData = null,
  pixelSnapping:String = "auto",
  smoothing:Boolean = false
)
```

The first parameter, `bitmapData`, is the data you wish to display. If this is not passed in the constructor, it can be passed in at a later time using the `bitmapData` property of Bitmap. This property is also useful for swapping the bitmap data being displayed at any time.

The `pixelSnapping` parameter accepts a string (best to use one of the constants of flash.display.PixelSnapping: `NEVER`, `ALWAYS`, and `AUTO`) and determines whether pixels for the bitmap are snapped to the nearest pixel or not. The default setting, `AUTO`, means that as long as the bitmap is not rotated, skewed, or scaled, it will snap to the nearest pixel. This setting results in the fastest rendering for bitmap images, since it takes advantage of the Flash Player's vector renderer. Alternatively, a setting of `NEVER` means that no pixel snapping will ever occur. A setting of `ALWAYS` means that pixel snapping will be used even when the image is transformed in some way. Generally, leaving this setting at the default value works in most cases.

The final parameter, `smoothing`, tells the Flash Player whether a smoothing algorithm should be applied to the image when it is scaled. No smoothing means faster renders but may produce noticeable pixelation when an image is scaled up. In Figure 3-4, you can see an image scaled up with `smoothing` turned both on and off.

Using this constructor, you can pass the bitmap data we created in the previous examples in upon instantiation and then add the bitmap directly to the display list. In this next piece of code, we create an opaque red image and add it to the stage:

```
var data:BitmapData = new BitmapData(100, 100, false, 0xFFFF0000);
var bitmap:Bitmap = new Bitmap(data);
addChild(bitmap);
```

It's not much yet, but it's a start!

Figure 3-4. An image scaled up with no smoothing on the left and smoothing on the right

Drawing existing graphics into bitmaps

One of the easiest ways to create an image at runtime, apart from loading one into the player, is to take an existing display object and draw its pixel data into a BitmapData instance. This is accomplished using the `draw()` method of BitmapData.

```
public function draw(
  source:IBitmapDrawable,
  matrix:Matrix = null,
  colorTransform:ColorTransform = null,
  blendMode:String = null,
  clipRect:Rectangle = null,
  smoothing:Boolean = false
):void
```

We'll look at each of the parameters you can pass to this constructor in the next several sections, but here is the general breakdown.

- `source`: The object to draw pixels from, either a DisplayObject or BitmapData instance, which both implement IBitmapDrawable
- `matrix`: The Matrix instance to be used to transform the size, position, or rotation of the drawn pixels
- `colorTransform`: The ColorTransform to be used to alter the colors of the drawn pixels

- blendMode: The blend mode to apply to the pixels as they are drawn onto the existing pixels in the BitmapData instance
- clipRect: The rectangular region of the source object from which to draw pixels
- smoothing: Whether smoothing should be applied to drawn pixels that are scaled up

Specifying the source

The first parameter in the constructor, source, is the object from which you wish to copy the pixel data. This can be any DisplayObject instance (Sprite, MovieClip, TextField, etc.) or another BitmapData instance, as these are the only two classes that implement the IBitmapDrawable interface.

When you call draw(), the source's pixel data is drawn into the BitmapData instance, and no connection remains with the original source object. This means that if you transform the source in any way, the BitmapData's pixel data will not change. If you call this method without any additional parameters specified (you can see that they are all optional), the original source pixels are copied with no transformations applied. We can look at a quick example to see this in action.

The following class can be found in this chapter's files as DrawTest.as. This is the entirety of the code for testing the simplest form of the draw() method, with the important lines highlighted in bold. (Remember, the appendix includes information on how to create project and compile SWFs, so please flip to that if it is unclear how to create a SWF from this class. This will be the last time it will be mentioned!)

```
package {

  import flash.display.Bitmap;
  import flash.display.BitmapData;
  import flash.display.Sprite;
  import flash.events.KeyboardEvent;
  import flash.geom.ColorTransform;
  import flash.ui.Keyboard;

  [SWF(width=600, height=250, backgroundColor=0x000000)]

  public class DrawTest extends Sprite {

    private var _circle:Sprite;
    private var _bitmapData:BitmapData;

    public function DrawTest() {
      createBitmap();
      createCircle();
      stage.addEventListener(KeyboardEvent.KEY_DOWN, onStageKeyDown);
    }
```

```
        private function createBitmap():void {
          _bitmapData = new BitmapData(
            stage.stageWidth,
            stage.stageHeight,
            true,
            0x00000000
          );
          var bitmap:Bitmap = new Bitmap(_bitmapData);
          addChild(bitmap);
        }

        private function createCircle():void {
          _circle = new Sprite();
          _circle.graphics.beginFill(0xFF0000);
          _circle.graphics.drawCircle(0, 0, 25);
          _circle.graphics.endFill();
          addChild(_circle);
          _circle.x = stage.mouseX;
          _circle.y = stage.mouseY;
          _circle.startDrag();
        }

        private function onStageKeyDown(event:KeyboardEvent):void {
          if (event.keyCode == Keyboard.SPACE) {
            _bitmapData.draw(stage);
            var transform:ColorTransform = new ColorTransform();
            transform.color = Math.random()*0xFFFFFF;
            _circle.transform.colorTransform = transform;
          }
        }

      }

    }
```

If you compile and test this movie, or run the SWF included with this chapter's files, you will see a circle that follows the mouse around the stage. That functionality is handled in the createCircle() method called from the constructor. createBitmap(), also called from the constructor, creates a Bitmap instance and places it on the stage. Although I pass it a new BitmapData instance, nothing is drawn into this object at the start of the movie. Instead, in the BitmapData constructor, I specify that the pixel data will be of the same dimensions as the stage, that the pixels can be transparent, and that any undefined pixel will be completely transparent (and black, though this is unimportant in this example). The result is that the bitmap added to the stage at the start of the movie is the same size as the stage but completely transparent.

If you press any key on the keyboard, the onStageKeyDown() handler is invoked, and if the key was the spacebar, the draw() method on the BitmapData instance is called. All I pass to it is a copy of the stage, which is a display object itself. This means the whole stage, including all of its child display objects, is drawn into the bitmap data, which then is immediately displayed within the bitmap added to the stage. What you get after moving the circle around a bit and hitting the space bar a number of times is something like Figure 3-5. We have effectively copied the pixels of the entire stage into the bitmap data.

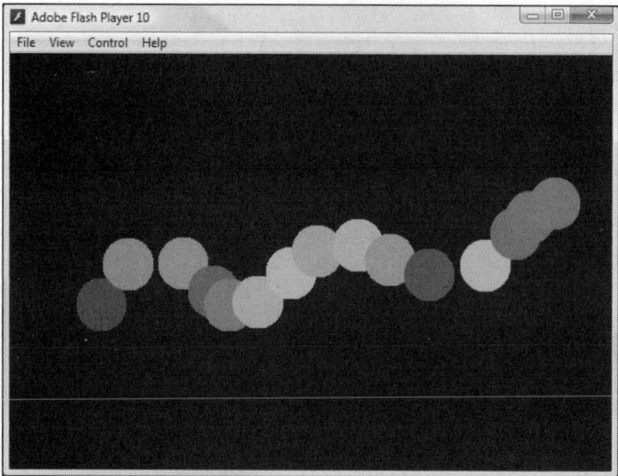

Figure 3-5. The draw() method used to copy the contents of the stage

The code in DrawTest demonstrates a couple of key features of BitmapData. First, you see how simple it is to pass a display object into the `draw()` method and effectively get a screen capture of that object. By performing this on the whole stage, we can get a screen capture of an entire application. Second, any changes to a BitmapData instance cause any Bitmap instances referencing that data to immediately update. We didn't have to call anything additionally to see our changes in the bitmap once `draw()` was invoked.

The immediate update that occurs on a Bitmap instance when the referenced BitmapData instance changes can cause performance problems if a lot of operations are being performed between screen updates. Thankfully, a couple of built-in methods of BitmapData can help with this: `lock()` and `unlock()`. `lock()` basically informs the renderer that no updates should occur based on changes in the pixel data until the `unlock()` method has been called, releasing the image, so to speak. `unlock()` takes one optional parameter that allows you to specify the rectangular region that was updated while the image was locked. If this is not specified, the entirety of the pixel data is considered changed.

Transforming source pixels

The second parameter of `draw()` is `matrix`, and this specifies any scaling, positioning, or rotation transformations you want to apply to the source object's pixels as they are drawn into the bitmap data. The object must be an instance of the Matrix class, which does all the heavy mathematical lifting of the matrix calculations for your desired transformations (so let's give a big thank you to Matrix!). This parameter is extremely useful if the source is of a different size than the bitmap, such as when you are creating a thumbnail copy of an image or display object.

You can modify the DrawTest class so that, in addition to copying the contents of the stage, a smaller thumbnail copy is drawn. To accomplish this, be sure to import flash.geom.Matrix, and then add the following lines in the onStageKeyDown() handler:

```
private function onStageKeyDown(event:KeyboardEvent):void {
  if (event.keyCode == Keyboard.SPACE) {
    _bitmapData.draw(stage);
    var matrix:Matrix = new Matrix();
    matrix.scale(.5, .5);
    _bitmapData.draw(stage, matrix);
    var transform:ColorTransform = new ColorTransform();
    transform.color = Math.random()*0xFFFFFF;
    _circle.transform.colorTransform = transform;
  }
}
```

Be sure that you do not remove the first call to draw(). We are adding a second call here, but passing a matrix that forces the image copied to be scaled down by 50 percent. The result of adding these lines, and a bit of clicking around, is shown in Figure 3-6.

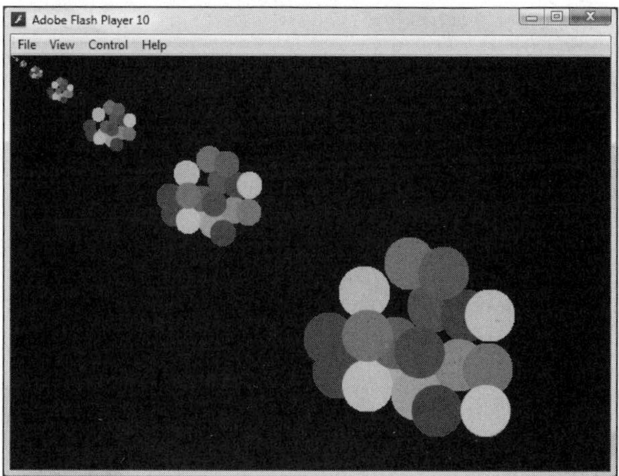

Figure 3-6. An additional copy of the stage is scaled down and drawn in the upper left.

As you can see, the full stage is copied into the smaller area at the top left. Each time the stage is copied, it also copies the smaller copy, resulting in smaller and smaller subsequent copies (if you look closely as you press the spacebar, the smaller copies are always one circle behind the next larger copy).

Why are the copies drawn at the top left? When draw() is called, pixels copied in are always drawn from the origin, (0, 0), unless a translation for the pixels is specified in the matrix. In this example, we are not passing any matrix into the first draw() command, and in the second draw(), we are not performing any translation, just a scaling. The result is both copies being drawn from the top left (which is not noticeable for the larger image since it is the same size as the stage). To translate the pixels of the smaller copy, perhaps to the bottom right corner, you could add the following bold line:

```
var matrix:Matrix = new Matrix();
matrix.scale(.5, .5);
matrix.translate(300, 200);
_bitmapData.draw(stage, matrix);
```

Another way to transform the pixels as they are drawn into the bitmap data is to alter their colors. This is accomplished using a ColorTransform instance and passing it as the third parameter to draw(). You could use this effectively to create a grayscale copy of an image or for creating ghosting effects where the alpha of the copied image is set at a lower opacity.

A ColorTransform instance has a number of properties that can affect each color channel's pixels, properties which directly correspond to the Advanced Color Effect settings in the Flash CS4 IDE, as shown in Figure 3-7.

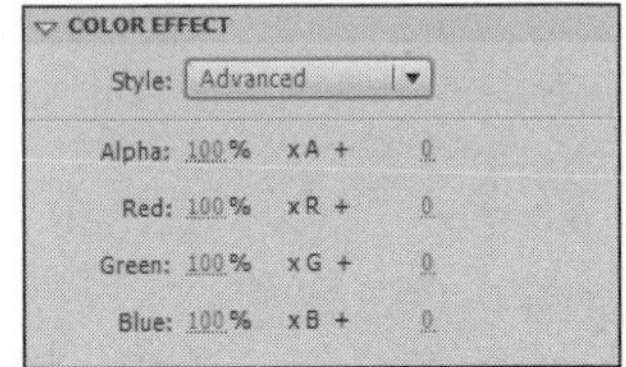

Figure 3-7.
The Advanced Color Effect settings panel in Flash CS4

The constructor for ColorTransform gives you the ability to set each of these properties.

```
ColorTransform(
  redMultiplier:Number = 1.0,
  greenMultiplier:Number = 1.0,
  blueMultiplier:Number = 1.0,
  alphaMultiplier:Number = 1.0,
  redOffset:Number = 0,
  greenOffset:Number = 0,
  blueOffset:Number = 0,
  alphaOffset:Number = 0
)
```

Each pixel in each channel is calculated using the following formula:

```
originalChannelPixel*channelMultiplier + channelOffset
```

In the case of the default value, if a pixel in a channel was 0xFF, the final pixel value would also be 0xFF, or would show no change:

```
0xFF*1 + 0
```

If you wanted to lessen the brightness of the pixels in a channel by 50 percent, you would pass 0.5 as the channel multiplier. For instance, the following transform lessens the brightness in all three color channels by 50 percent:

```
new ColorTransform(0.5, 0.5, 0.5);
```

To brighten all red pixels by a value of 20, you could use the following transform:

```
new ColorTransform(1, 1, 1, 1, 20);
```

Finally, to invert an image, just as we did with the ColorMatrixFilter, you could use the following transform:

```
new ColorTransform(-1, -1, -1, 1, 255, 255, 255);
```

Adding to the DrawTest example, you can use a color transform to invert the colors of the stage pixels as they are copied. To do so, change or add the following bold lines in DrawTest to achieve this:

```
private function onStageKeyDown(event:KeyboardEvent):void {
  if (event.keyCode == Keyboard.SPACE) {
    _bitmapData.draw(stage);
    var matrix:Matrix = new Matrix();
    matrix.scale(.5, .5);
    matrix.translate(300, 200);
    var transform:ColorTransform = ➥
new ColorTransform(-1, -1, -1, 1, 255, 255, 255);
    _bitmapData.draw(stage, matrix, transform);
    transform = new ColorTransform();
    transform.color = Math.random()*0xFFFFFF;
    _circle.transform.colorTransform = transform;
  }
}
```

The numbers passed to the ColorTransform constructor invert the colors of the pixels. This transform is then passed to the draw() method and produces the result in Figure 3-8.

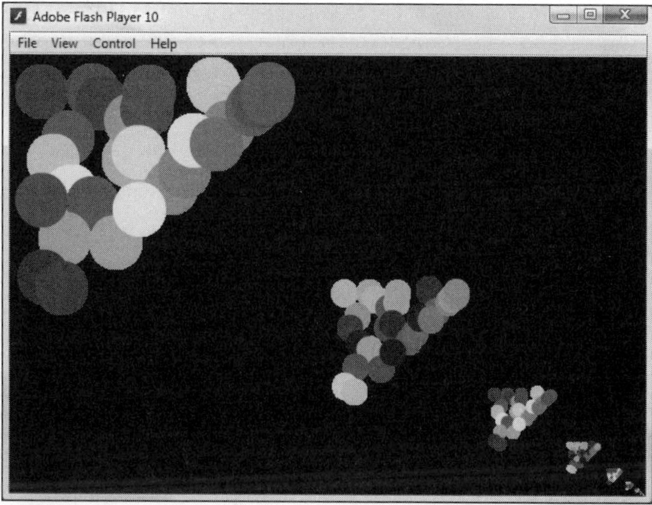

Figure 3-8. The colors of each stage duplicate are inverted using a color transform.

Wrapping up the draw() method's parameters

One additional parameter for `draw()` that enables transformation of a source object's pixels is the `blendMode` option, which allows you to specify how the copied pixels will be applied to the current pixels in the bitmap data. For instance, if you pass `BlendMode.ADD` as the fourth parameter to `draw()`, the source object's pixels will be added to the bitmap data's pixels using the formula we discussed for `ADD` in the previous chapter (the source pixel channel plus the destination pixel channel with a limit of 0xFF). One possible use for this is in creating brushes as you might find in Photoshop. These brushes have blending options that match the layer modes, like `MULTIPLY`, that can be applied as you paint. Such functionality could be replicated in ActionScript by using the `draw()` method when copying a brush's image onto the canvas and specifying a particular blend mode.

`clipRect` is the fifth possible parameter for `draw()`, and this allows you to specify which region of the source object you wish to copy. If this is not specified, as we have seen in DrawTest, the whole of the source object is copied. But if you need more control over just copying a portion of the source, you can specify this region as a rectangle that is passed as the `clipRect` parameter.

The final parameter for `draw()` is `smoothing`, and this specifies whether pixels from the source, when scaled or rotated during the copy (as determined by the matrix passed) are smoothed to reduce jaggedness that might appear. This can slow the operation down but sometimes is necessary to produce aesthetically pleasing results.

Copying existing bitmap data

Copying answers might be frowned on in school, and the moral debate around cloning rages on, but there's nothing at all wrong with resorting to duplication of pixels in ActionScript. In addition to drawing existing display objects into bitmap data, you can also create new pixel data by copying the data from other BitmapData instances. A number of methods allow you to do this, one of which is the `draw()` method we explored in the last section, which in addition to taking display objects also takes BitmapData instances. However, although `draw()` is great if you need to perform transformations (position, scale, rotation, skew, or color) as you copy, if you just need to copy exact pixel data with no transformations, there are better, faster methods to use.

Cloning

`clone()` is the first method of choice for copying bitmap data from one instance to another. This will return an exact copy of the original bitmap data—same size, same bit depth, same pixels, same everything—a duplication of its image DNA, so to speak.

```
var dupe:BitmapData = original.clone();
```

When you have cloned bitmap data, there is no reference that remains between the original and the clone, so any transformation performed on either the original or the clone will not affect the other.

Copying pixels

If you need to copy only a region of pixels from an image or to copy into a certain position in a destination image, copyPixels() will be the method to use. This is more complex than clone() but still usually fairly simple.

```
public function copyPixels(
  sourceBitmapData:BitmapData,
  sourceRect:Rectangle,
  destPoint:Point,
  alphaBitmapData:BitmapData = null,
  alphaPoint:Point = null,
  mergeAlpha:Boolean = false
):void
```

This is how the parameters for copyPixels() break down:

- sourceBitmapData: The source bitmap data from which you are copying pixels
- sourceRect: The rectangular region from the source data from which you are copying pixels
- destPoint: The point in the destination bitmap data that corresponds to the top left pixel in the region being copied
- alphaBitmapData: The bitmap data to be used for the alpha information in the copied pixels
- alphaPoint: The point in the alphaBitmapData that corresponds to the top left pixel in the region being copied
- mergeAlpha: Determines whether the alpha data from the source and destination images are merged when the pixels are copied

For copyPixels(), the first three parameters are required and the last three are optional, and generally, you won't need to set those last three, which makes working with the method much more straightforward.

As for the first three, sourceBitmapData is the BitmapData instance with the pixel data you wish to copy. sourceRect is the rectangular region from that source that should be copied. If you want to copy the whole of the source, you can use the source's rect property:

```
destination.copyPixels(source, source.rect, new Point());
```

If, however, a different region within the source should be copied, you can create a new Rectangle instance to define the desired region:

```
var rectangle:Rectangle = new Rectangle(10, 10, 100, 100);
destination.copyPixels(source, rectangle, new Point());
```

The third parameter for copyPixels() is the point in the destination bitmap where you wish to copy the source's pixel data. This point will be the top left corner for where the new region of pixel data is inserted. In the previous examples, the new region of pixel data will be drawn at (0, 0).

The alphaBitmapData and alphaPoint parameters for copyPixels() allow you to specify a different BitmapData instance to use for alpha information when copying the pixels. If the bitmap data you are copying color data from is only 24-bit, this allows you to add opacity information to the pixels copied. If the source does have alpha information, the alphaBitmapData's and the sourceBitmapData's alpha information are both used. The alphaPoint defines the top left point on the alphaBitmapData from which the alpha data will be taken.

The final parameter of copyPixels() is another alpha option, mergeAlpha. This is false by default and specifies that only the color information from the source is copied. If you wish to use the source's alpha information as well and have this merge with the alpha information of the destination bitmap data, set this to true.

To see copyPixels() in action, have a look at CopyPixelsTest.as and the corresponding CopyPixelsTest.swf in this chapter's files. This application loads in a large bitmap file and displays a scaled down version on screen. By hovering over parts of the smaller image, a zoomed in version will appear, displaying the pixel data at 100 percent. You can see the results in Figure 3-9.

Figure 3-9. A smaller version of a loaded image is displayed on the left with the actual pixel size displayed in a region on the right.

Before we walk through CopyPixels.as, let's have a quick look at the base class that it extends. This class, AbstractImageLoader, simply loads in an image so that it can be processed. We'll be using this class in other examples in this and future chapters, as loading in an image is something we'll frequently have to do in order to create image effects! Here's the code, which shouldn't contain any surprises since it is the standard bitmap loading we've previously discussed. If it does surprise you, well, you must be a wonderful person to throw a party for.

```
package {

  import flash.display.Bitmap;
  import flash.display.Loader;
  import flash.display.LoaderInfo;
  import flash.display.Sprite;
  import flash.events.Event;
  import flash.net.URLRequest;

  public class AbstractImageLoader extends Sprite {

    protected var _loadedBitmap:Bitmap;

    public function AbstractImageLoader(path:String) {
      loadImage(path);
    }

    private function loadImage(imagePath:String):void {
      var loader:Loader = new Loader();
      loader.contentLoaderInfo.addEventListener(
        Event.COMPLETE,
        onImageLoaded
      );
      loader.load(new URLRequest(imagePath));
    }

    private function onImageLoaded(event:Event):void {
      var loaderInfo:LoaderInfo = event.target as LoaderInfo;
      _loadedBitmap = loaderInfo.content as Bitmap;
      runPostImageLoad();
    }

    protected function runPostImageLoad():void {}

  }

}
```

As you can see, once the bitmap loads, it is saved into the property `_loadedBitmap` but is not actually added to the stage. The method `runPostImageLoad()` is then called, and it will be overridden by child classes.

Now, we can look at the class that extends AbstractImageLoader and creates the CopyPixelsTest.swf. The following is the entirety of that class with important lines to note in bold:

```
package {

  import flash.display.Bitmap;
  import flash.display.BitmapData;
  import flash.events.MouseEvent;
  import flash.geom.Matrix;
  import flash.geom.Point;
  import flash.geom.Rectangle;

  [SWF(width=750, height=500, backgroundColor=0x000000)]

  public class CopyPixelsTest extends AbstractImageLoader {

    private var _largeImage:BitmapData;
    private var _smallImage:BitmapData;
    private var _zoomedImage:BitmapData;
    private var _scale:Number;

    public function CopyPixelsTest() {
      super("../../assets/canyon.jpg");
    }

    override protected function runPostImageLoad():void {
      _largeImage = _loadedBitmap.bitmapData;
      createBitmaps();
      drawZoomedImage(0, 0);
      stage.addEventListener(MouseEvent.MOUSE_MOVE, onStageMouseMove);
    }

    private function createBitmaps():void {
      var matrix:Matrix = new Matrix();
      _scale = stage.stageHeight/_largeImage.height;
      matrix.scale(_scale, _scale);
      _smallImage = new BitmapData(
        _largeImage.width*_scale,
        _largeImage.height*_scale
      );
      _zoomedImage = _smallImage.clone();
      _smallImage.draw(_largeImage, matrix);
      var bitmap:Bitmap = new Bitmap(_smallImage);
      addChild(bitmap);
      bitmap = new Bitmap(_zoomedImage);
      bitmap.x = bitmap.width;
      addChild(bitmap);
    }
```

```
    private function drawZoomedImage(x:Number, y:Number):void {
      x = Math.min(x, _largeImage.width - _zoomedImage.width);
      y = Math.min(y, _largeImage.height - _zoomedImage.height);
      var rectangle:Rectangle = new Rectangle(x, y, ➥
_zoomedImage.width, _zoomedImage.height);
      _zoomedImage.copyPixels(_largeImage, rectangle, new Point());
    }

    private function onStageMouseMove(event:MouseEvent):void {
      var x:Number = event.localX;
      var y:Number = event.localY;
      if (getChildAt(0).hitTestPoint(x, y)) {
        drawZoomedImage(x/_scale, y/_scale);
      }
    }

  }

}
```

If you are compiling this yourself and are using the same directory structure and assets as the downloaded files, you should have the `canyon.jpg` *image two directories up from where the SWF is compiled and in an* `assets` *subdirectory. If you do not, simply change the string path to the asset to one on your system.*

In the overridden `runPostImageLoad()` method that is invoked by the super class, I save a reference to the bitmap data of the bitmap loaded in and call a `createBitmaps()` method and a `drawZoomedImage()` method before adding a listener for when the mouse is moved about the stage.

A large bitmap image has loaded at this point, but that is not what will be displayed on stage. Instead, in the `createBitmaps()` method a Matrix instance is used to define a scaled down transformation based on the stage height and the image height. For instance, if the stage is 500 pixels tall and the image is 1,000 pixels tall, the `_scale` variable will hold the value 0.5. This, through the matrix transformation, will scale the bitmap data down 50 percent when passed in the `draw()` method.

```
_scale = stage.stageHeight/_largeImage.height;
matrix.scale(_scale, _scale);
_smallImage = new BitmapData(
  _largeImage.width*_scale,
  _largeImage.height*_scale
);
```

`_smallImage` is instantiated with a width and height to match the scaled down pixel data. Since the zoomed in image in this example will be the exact same width and height as the small image, `clone()` can be called to quickly copy the dimensions into a new BitmapData instance. I do this before the large image is drawn into the small image so that I don't clone all that pixel data into the zoomed image unnecessarily.

With the large bitmap data drawn into the _smallImage object at a scaled down size, _smallImage can be passed to a new Bitmap instance and added to the stage. I then can do the same for _zoomedImage, although that currently has no pixel data. The bitmap referencing the _zoomedImage object is placed directly to the right of the bitmap referencing _smallImage.

drawZoomedImage() is a method that takes x and y parameters and copies pixels from the large image into the zoomed image. The region of the large image that will be copied is defined by the x and y parameters and the width and height of the zoomed image that will be drawing its pixels. Because of this, in the method's first two lines, the x and y are limited in range so that they do not exceed the width and height of the large image minus the width and height of the zoomed image.

```
x = Math.min(x, _largeImage.width - _zoomedImage.width);
y = Math.min(y, _largeImage.height - _zoomedImage.height);
```

This ensures that the copied region will always be the width and height of the zoomed image's area. The rectangle defining the region to copy is then passed to the copyPixels() method of _zoomedImage, which draws the copy of the _largeImage into itself starting at the top left pixel.

```
_zoomedImage.copyPixels(_largeImage, rectangle, new Point());
```

This drawZoomedImage() method is called immediately after the bitmaps are created so that the initial zoom will be of the top left corner of the large image. In the onStageMouseMove() handler that is invoked as the mouse is moved, I first check to see if the mouse is over the small image. If it is, I call drawZoomedImage(), but with the x and y adjusted for the scale of the large image. That means that if the _scale is 50 percent and the x is halfway across the small image, it is the x position of halfway across the large image that is sent to the drawZoomedImage() method.

Setting regions of pixels

Two additional ways of copying pixels is to use the combinations of getPixels() and setPixels() or getVector() and setVector() to copy regions of data from one BitmapData instance into another. These combinations work similarly and differ in only the type of data used by each. getVector() and setVector() work with vectors of uints, while getPixels() and setPixels() work with a ByteArray. As such, getPixels() and setPixels() are more useful when passing or retrieving binary data defining bitmap images to an external server or application.

When retrieving a region of information from one BitmapData instance, you will need to define the region using a Rectangle instance. Passing this to either getPixels() or getVector() will return the pixel data for that region.

```
public function getPixels(rect:Rectangle):ByteArray

public function getVector(rect:Rectangle):Vector.<uint>
```

This pixel data could then be passed to another BitmapData instance (or to the same instance, but perhaps moved to a different position if you're feeling playful) using the corresponding setter method, which takes the data along with the rectangular region in which to insert the data.

```
public function setPixels(
  rect:Rectangle,
  inputByteArray:ByteArray
):void

public function setVector(
  rect:Rectangle,
  inputVector:Vector.<uint>
):void
```

So copying from a region of one image to another using the `getVector()`/`setVector()` combination could be performed with the following lines:

```
var rect:Rectangle = new Rectangle(0, 0, 100, 100);
var pixels:Vector.<uint> = image0.getVector(rect);
image1.setVector(rect, pixels);
```

Using `getPixels()` and `setPixels()` is virtually the same, except for one difference due to how byte arrays are read. After extracting the pixel data as a byte array, you have to explicitly set its position to 0 so that it will start at that position when its data is read during the `setPixels()` operation. The lines would look like the following:

```
var rect:Rectangle = new Rectangle(0, 0, 100, 100);
var bytes:ByteArray = image0.getPixels(rect);
bytes.position = 0;
image1.setPixels(rect, bytes);
```

These methods are demonstrated in this chapter's SetPixelsTest files. The class used extends another handy abstract base class, this one to load in two files and display them side by side with a space to the right to display a composited image. We'll also use this base class a number of times in this and the next chapter, so let's take a quick look at its code:

```
package {

  import flash.display.Bitmap;
  import flash.display.BitmapData;
  import flash.display.Loader;
  import flash.display.LoaderInfo;
  import flash.display.Sprite;
  import flash.events.Event;
  import flash.geom.Point;
  import flash.net.URLRequest;
```

```
        public class DualImageTest extends Sprite {

          private static const IMAGE_0:String = "../../assets/hydrant.jpg";
          private static const IMAGE_1:String = "../../assets/fungus.jpg";

          protected var _bitmap0:Bitmap;
          protected var _bitmap1:Bitmap;
          protected var _bitmapData0:BitmapData;
          protected var _bitmapData1:BitmapData;

          public function DualImageTest() {
            loadImage(IMAGE_0);
          }

          private function loadImage(imagePath:String):void {
            var loader:Loader = new Loader();
            loader.contentLoaderInfo.addEventListener(
              Event.COMPLETE,
              onImageLoaded
            );
            loader.load(new URLRequest(imagePath));
          }

          protected function operateOnImages():void {}

          private function onImageLoaded(event:Event):void {
            var loaderInfo:LoaderInfo = event.target as LoaderInfo;
            var bitmap:Bitmap = loaderInfo.content as Bitmap;
            addChild(bitmap);
            if (numChildren == 1) {
              _bitmap0 = bitmap;
              _bitmapData0 = bitmap.bitmapData;
              loadImage(IMAGE_1);
            } else {
              _bitmap1 = bitmap;
              _bitmapData1 = bitmap.bitmapData;
              bitmap.x = _bitmap0.width;
              operateOnImages();
            }
          }

        }

      }
```

Notice that when both images have been loaded operateOnImages() is called from within the onImageLoaded() handler. It is this method that will be overridden in the child classes to perform the specific operations on the loaded images.

Now, we can look at the ActionScript class that extends DualImageTest in order to test and demonstrate getPixels() and setPixels(), found in the file SetPixelsTest.as. The following is all the code from this class:

```
package {

  import flash.display.Bitmap;
  import flash.display.BitmapData;
  import flash.geom.Rectangle;
  import flash.utils.ByteArray;

  [SWF(width=1200, height=600, backgroundColor=0x000000)]

  public class SetPixelsTest extends DualImageTest {

    override protected function operateOnImages():void {
      var width:uint = _bitmapData0.width;
      var height:uint = _bitmapData0.height;
      var newData:BitmapData = new BitmapData(width, height);
      var rect:Rectangle = new Rectangle(0, 0, width, 1);
      var bitmapData:BitmapData;
      var bytes:ByteArray;
      for (var row:uint = 0; row < height; row++) {
        bitmapData = (row % 2) == 0 ? _bitmapData0 : _bitmapData1;
        rect.y = row;
        bytes = bitmapData.getPixels(rect);
        bytes.position = 0;
        newData.setPixels(rect, bytes);
      }
      var bitmap:Bitmap = new Bitmap(newData);
      addChild(bitmap);
      bitmap.x = _bitmap1.x + _bitmap1.width;
    }

  }

}
```

Here, in operateOnImages(), I create a new BitmapData instance that is the same height and width as the loaded images. I then run through each row of the loaded images by using the height in pixels within a for loop. In each iteration of the loop, the modulo operator is used to determine whether data will be extracted from _bitmapData0 or _bitmapData1:

```
bitmapData = (row % 2) == 0 ? _bitmapData0 : _bitmapData1;
```

If the row is even, _bitmapData0's pixel data will be used. For odd rows, _bitmapData1's pixel data will be used.

The rectangle I use to define the region of pixels to retrieve (and set) has a constant width that is equal to the width of the loaded bitmaps and a height of 1 pixel:

```
var rect:Rectangle = new Rectangle(0, 0, width, 1);
```

However, within each loop iteration, I change the rectangle's y value so that a new row within the loaded images is referenced.

```
rect.y = row;
```

Using this rect value, I retrieve the row of pixels from one of the two loaded images and copy these to the new bitmap data. Once all rows have been copied, the data is added to a Bitmap instance, and this is added to the stage. The result of this is illustrated in Figure 3-10, which shows alternating rows of each of the images on the left copied into the final image on the right.

Figure 3-10. A new image on the right drawn row by row using alternating rows from the images on the left

Using bitmaps with the drawing API

Up to this point, we have been displaying bitmap data by passing the data into Bitmap instances and adding these instances to the stage. There is one additional way that bitmap data can be displayed within the Flash Player, and that is through the use of the drawing API commands that deal specifically with bitmap data, `beginBitmapFill()` and `lineBitmapStyle()`.

We covered these commands and how they are used to draw bitmap data back in Chapter 1. We will use them in later examples in this book as well, since they work terrifically when you need to tile a bitmap over a large area. Just to serve as a reminder for the methods, here are the signatures for each, and you will note that the parameters are the same for both.

```
public function beginBitmapFill(
  bitmap:BitmapData,
  matrix:Matrix = null,
  repeat:Boolean = true,
  smooth:Boolean = false
):void

public function lineBitmapStyle(
  bitmap:BitmapData,
  matrix:Matrix = null,
  repeat:Boolean = true,
  smooth:Boolean = false
):void
```

As is obvious from their names (isn't that handy how the engineers did that?), `beginBitmapFill()` applies to the fills of shapes while `lineBitmapStyle()` applies to the lines/strokes. In both cases, the bitmap data to be drawn is the first parameter. You can pass in some matrix transformation (the same as used with `BitmapData.draw()`) as the second parameter. The third parameter, `repeat`, determines if the bitmap data is tiled when its dimensions are less than the area needing to be filled. Finally, the `smooth` parameter determines whether a scaled up image is smoothed upon scaling. Basically, a value of `false`, which is the default, will perform a nearest-neighbor algorithm on a pixel, which can result in visible pixelation. A value of `true` will result in a bilinear algorithm being applied, which calculates new pixel values based on the average value of multiple surrounding pixels. This takes more processing, so only use it when the pixelation is noticeable and unwanted.

Cleaning up

The comedian George Carlin had a great routine in which he used to point out mankind's attachment to stuff. We live; we accumulate stuff; we move to larger spaces to allow for more stuff; and we even travel with little cases full of our stuff because we can't bear to be without our beloved stuff. We love stuff.

But it can build up tremendously and overwhelm us. In Flash, bitmap data accounts for a lot of stuff—there's a lot of data to be stored for a large image. Loading in and holding lots of that data in memory can overwhelm the player and cause memory issues, so it's best to clean up and get rid of the pixel data when it is no longer needed.

BitmapData offers a way to do this through its `dispose()` method. There's not much to say about this one other than that it frees up the memory that was being used to store the bitmap data and that the object at that point is effectively no longer usable and can be deleted. Although you could rely on garbage collection to do this if you remove all references to the bitmap data, it is better to force this operation if you know the data is no longer used. And why not? Calling the method is as simple as the following line of code:

```
bitmapData.dispose();
```

Accessing and manipulating colors

Oh, what a dull, drab, pre-Oz world we would live in without the existence of color. Fortunately, color is easy to work with in ActionScript and a cinch to use in conjunction with BitmapData. There are a number of methods provided that allow you to access colors from within the pixel data and set or alter colors for both individual pixels and regions of pixels. Let's leave Kansas behind, Toto.

Getting and setting single pixels

Sometimes it is hard to admit, but my first foray into graphics software was Microsoft Paint. I was working graveyard shift at a temporary office job doing data processing. One of the perks of working in the middle of the night was that, occasionally, there were long stretches of time where you were paid to just sit there waiting for your next assignment, and people spent this time reading, sleeping, talking, or doing whatever was allowed to fill the time. I was bored one particular night and so opened up Paint and clicked out, pixel-by-pixel, a portrait complete with manual dithering of colors and showed off the result to my manager. Next thing I knew, I was in the graphics department teaching myself Photoshop and Illustrator.

The beauty of Paint is its utter simplicity. There is no greater graphical control than setting a single pixel's color in an image. ActionScript offers similar fine control through its `setPixel()` method of BitmapData, which allows you to specify the exact pixel color at a certain point on a bitmap image. The signature of `setPixel()` takes the x and y positions of the pixel to set and the color to use.

```
public function setPixel(x:int, y:int, color:uint):void
```

Calling this method will set the RGB values for the specified pixel. If you wish to set the alpha value as well (otherwise, the original alpha value of the pixel is maintained), you would call the related method `setPixel32()`:

```
public function setPixel32(x:int, y:int, color:uint):void
```

As you can see, it has the same signature, though the color value should be 32-bit instead of 24-bit.

If you are using either of these methods, remember that any object referencing the bitmap data (like a Bitmap instance) is updated whenever the data changes. In cases where multiple calls to `setPixel()` or `setPixel32()` are being made, you can improve performance by calling the `lock()` method, discussed earlier, before the `setPixel()` or `setPixel32()` operations, then `unlock()` when the operations are complete.

Creating a pixel painting application

Creating an application that allows a user to paint individual pixels is a piece of cake using these methods. Have a look at SetPixelTest.swf in this chapter's download files to see a simple example. If you open the SWF and click around the stage, you should see something like Figure 3-11.

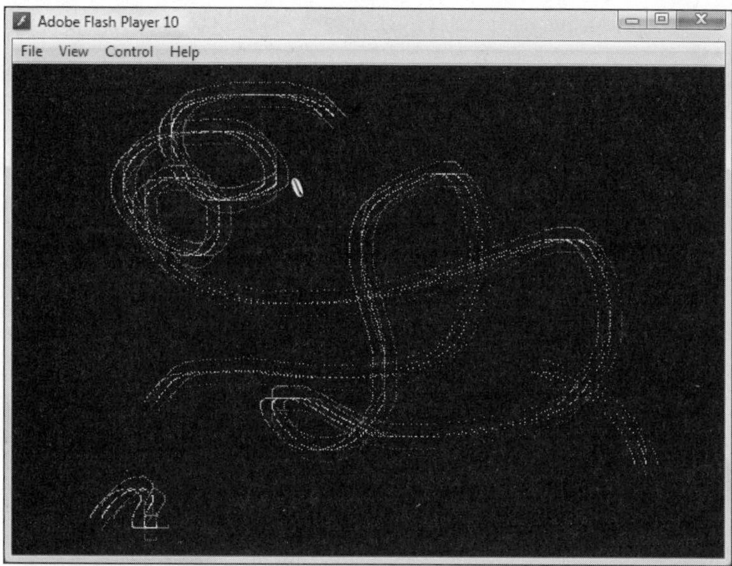

Figure 3-11. A simple drawing application demonstrating setPixel32()

The ActionScript file SetPixelTest.as in this chapter's files contains the entirety of the code needed for this application:

```
package {

  import flash.display.Bitmap;
  import flash.display.BitmapData;
  import flash.display.Sprite;
  import flash.events.MouseEvent;

  [SWF(width=600, height=400, backgroundColor=0x000000)]

  public class SetPixelTest extends Sprite {

    private var _canvas:BitmapData;

    public function SetPixelTest() {
      _canvas = new BitmapData(
        stage.stageWidth,
        stage.stageHeight,
        true,
        0x00000000
      );
```

```
      var bitmap:Bitmap = new Bitmap(_canvas);
      addChild(bitmap);
      stage.addEventListener(MouseEvent.MOUSE_DOWN, onStageMouseDown);
      stage.addEventListener(MouseEvent.MOUSE_UP, onStageMouseUp);
    }

    private function onStageMouseDown(event:MouseEvent):void {
      stage.addEventListener(MouseEvent.MOUSE_MOVE, onStageMouseMove);
    }

    private function onStageMouseUp(event:MouseEvent):void {
      stage.removeEventListener(MouseEvent.MOUSE_MOVE, ➥
onStageMouseMove);
    }

    private function onStageMouseMove(event:MouseEvent):void {
      var x:Number = event.localX;
      var y:Number = event.localY;
      var radius:uint = 10;
      _canvas.lock();
      _canvas.setPixel32(x, y, 0xFFFFFFFF);
      _canvas.setPixel32(x+radius, y, 0xFFFF0000);
      _canvas.setPixel32(x-radius, y, 0xFF00FF00);
      _canvas.setPixel32(x, y+radius, 0xFF0000FF);
      _canvas.setPixel32(x, y-radius, 0xFFFF00FF);
      _canvas.unlock();
      event.updateAfterEvent();
    }

  }

}
```

In the constructor for this class, I create a new transparent BitmapData instance the size of the stage and pass this to a Bitmap instance, which I then attach to the stage. Listeners are set up for when the user both clicks and releases the stage. The handlers for these events simply add or remove another listener for when the mouse moves, so that drawing begins when the stage is clicked and ends when it is released.

In the `onStageMouseMove()` handler, I lock _canvas so that the multiple calls to `setPixel32()` do not force the bitmap to update. I then call `setPixel32()` five times to set five different colors around the current mouse position. I use this method instead of `setPixel()`, because the original bitmap data is transparent. If you do not pass in alpha values, the pixels will remain transparent (alternatively, I could have made the original bitmap data opaque and then used `setPixel()` without issue). Once I have colored the five pixels, I release the bitmap data so that the bitmap itself can update.

Voilà! A simple drawing application in less than 50 lines of code. Sure, the UI won't win any awards (except perhaps for minimalism), but you can't fault the success of `setPixel()`!

Determining pixel values

Of course, with setter methods usually come corresponding getter methods, and such is the case with setPixel() and setPixel32(). To retrieve pixel values, we can use getPixel() and getPixel32(). These both take a point within bitmap data and return the pixel value at that location, with getPixel32() returning a 32-bit number containing alpha information.

```
public function getPixel(x:int, y:int):uint
public function getPixel32(x:int, y:int):uint
```

The most obvious use for these functions is to enable color picker functionality as is found in pretty much any graphics software. The sample file GetPixelTest.swf shows how this could work with the class found in GetPixelTest.as. The following is the entirety of the class, which once again extends DualImageTest:

```
package {

  import flash.display.Bitmap;
  import flash.display.BitmapData;
  import flash.events.MouseEvent;

  [SWF(width=1200, height=600, backgroundColor=0x000000)]

  public class GetPixelTest extends DualImageTest {

    private var _screenshot:BitmapData;

    override protected function operateOnImages():void {
      _screenshot = new BitmapData(
        stage.stageWidth,
        stage.stageHeight
      );
      _screenshot.draw(stage);
      stage.addEventListener(MouseEvent.MOUSE_MOVE, onStageMouseMove);
    }

    private function onStageMouseMove(event:MouseEvent):void {
      var x:Number = event.localX;
      var y:Number = event.localY;
      var color:uint = _screenshot.getPixel(x, y);
      graphics.clear();
      graphics.beginFill(color);
      graphics.drawRect(0, 0, stage.stageWidth, stage.stageHeight);
      graphics.endFill();
    }

  }

}
```

Remember, when the images are finished loading, the operateOnImages() method will be called from the super class. Within this method, I create a new BitmapData instance and copy into this all of the pixels currently displayed on the stage. Note that I keep this in memory but do not actually add this to the display list. I then set up a listener for when the mouse moves about the stage.

When onStageMouseMove() is invoked, I use getPixel() to determine the color of the pixel stored in the screen capture data. I then recolor the whole stage background to match this color.

Although for this quick example I keep the screen capture in memory, if you were building an actual color picker, you would only capture the pixels of the stage when you needed to sample them (such as when a standard color picker pop-up is opened). And then, of course, it goes without saying that once you are done with the data, dispose() should be called to clean things up. Let's be tidy coders.

Filling regions of color

There are a number of methods of BitmapData that you can use to either discover or fill regions of color. The first we will discuss is getColorBoundsRect(), which returns the smallest rectangular region in which a specified color can be found.

```
public function getColorBoundsRect(
  mask:uint,
  color:uint,
  findColor:Boolean = true
):Rectangle
```

Skipping the initial parameter for a moment, the method takes as its second parameter the color to find. The third parameter, findColor, determines whether the rectangle returned will define the region that fully encloses pixels of the specified color (true, the default), or whether the rectangle returned will define the region that fully encloses all pixels that do not contain the specified color.

The first parameter, mask, allows you to confine searches to a channel or channels. Basically, when a pixel value is looked at, a bitwise AND operation is performed with the mask and only results that equal the specified color value are seen as matches.

Yeah, that made as little sense to me the first time I read it as well. So let's break it down a bit how masks are used.

As an example, if we are looking for a pure blue pixel, we would specify the color as 0x0000FF. Remember that this in binary is

```
00000000  00000000  11111111
```

If all we want is pure blue, the mask we would pass to the getColorBoundsRect() method would use 0xFF for all three color channels. This would be represented by the following binary number:

```
11111111  11111111  11111111
```

Now, consider the following purple pixel as one we are examining to see if it matches the pure blue color we wish to find:

```
11111111  00000000  11111111
```

If we use the bitwise AND operation, which will return 1 only if both bits are 1 and 0 in all other cases, with this purple pixel value and the mask, we get the following result:

```
  11111111  00000000  11111111  (pixel)
+ 11111111  11111111  11111111  (mask)
------------------------------
  11111111  00000000  11111111  (result)
```

Since the result of the bitwise AND with our purple pixel does not equal the specified blue color, this pixel is not determined as a match. If we perform this same operation on a pure blue pixel, the result is a pure blue numeric value that matches our specified color:

```
  00000000  00000000  11111111  (pixel)
+ 11111111  11111111  11111111  (mask)
------------------------------
  00000000  00000000  11111111  (result)
```

If you are looking to match an exact color, you will want to pass 0xFFFFFF (24-bit) or 0xFFFFFFFF (32-bit) as your mask. If you are more interested in finding a value in a certain channel, you will pass a mask that contains the full value (0xFF) in the desired channel and a 0 value in the other channels. For example, if we were just interested in finding full values in the blue channel, the mask would be 0x0000FF. Consider then what would happen when we looked for our blue color (0x0000FF) and were examining the same purple pixel:

```
  11111111  00000000  11111111  (pixel)
+ 00000000  00000000  11111111  (mask)
------------------------------
  00000000  00000000  11111111  (result)
```

In this case, since all we are interested in is the blue channel, the purple pixel passes our test since its blue channel is 0xFF and would be considered a match.

This mask technique is something we will encounter again when we discuss the `threshold()` method of BitmapData in the next chapter.

We will create a test for this method in a moment, but first, we will look at another method dealing with regions of color that we'll also use in the example, `fillRect()`. This method simply fills a specified region in an image with a specified color.

```
public function fillRect(rect:Rectangle, color:uint):void
```

Now, isn't that a breath of fresh air after `getColorBoundsRect()`? If you ever need to create a solid block of a specified color, this is the quickest way to do it.

Testing getColorBoundsRect

To see an example of both getColorBoundsRect() and fillRect() in action, have a look at ColorRegionTest.swf in this chapter's files; it's shown in Figure 3-12. As you hover over the image on the left, the pixel color is shown on the right (using similar code to GetPixelTest). The color hovered over is passed as the color argument for getColorBoundsRect(), and the region returned is drawn into the middle image using fillRect().

Figure 3-12. Hovering over a pixel in the left image shows its color on the right and draws a rectangle over the center image based on the region containing that color.

Let's take a look at the code, found in ColorRegionTest.as:

```
package {

  import flash.display.Bitmap;
  import flash.display.BitmapData;
  import flash.events.MouseEvent;
  import flash.geom.Rectangle;

  [SWF(width=1200, height=600, backgroundColor=0x000000)]

  public class ColorRegionTest extends DualImageTest {

    override protected function operateOnImages():void {
      _bitmap1.bitmapData = _bitmapData0.clone();
      _bitmapData1.dispose();
      stage.addEventListener(MouseEvent.MOUSE_MOVE, onStageMouseMove);
    }

    private function drawBackground(color:uint):void {
      graphics.clear();
```

```
      graphics.beginFill(color);
      graphics.drawRect(0, 0, stage.stageWidth, stage.stageHeight);
      graphics.endFill();
    }

    private function drawColorBoundsRect(color:uint):void {
      var rect:Rectangle = ➥
_bitmapData0.getColorBoundsRect(0xFFFFFFFF, color);
      _bitmap1.bitmapData.fillRect(rect, color);
    }

    private function onStageMouseMove(event:MouseEvent):void {
      var x:Number = event.localX;
      var y:Number = event.localY;
      if (_bitmap0.hitTestPoint(x, y)) {
        var color:uint = _bitmapData0.getPixel32(x, y);
        drawBackground(color);
        drawColorBoundsRect(color);
      }
    }

  }

}
```

In the operateOnImages() method, I clone() the left image's bitmap data and pass this to the second image. I am free to dispose of the original bitmap data for the second image, since it is not used in this example. A listener is then set up for when the mouse moves.

onStageMouseMove() will be called as the mouse moves, and if it is determined that the mouse is over the first image, I use getPixel32() to find the value of the pixel below the mouse. This is passed to drawBackground(), which simply draws a colored rectangle over the whole stage background, as well as to drawColorBoundsRect().

```
if (_bitmap0.hitTestPoint(x, y)) {
  var color:uint = _bitmapData0.getPixel32(x, y);
  drawBackground(color);
  drawColorBoundsRect(color);
}
```

In drawColorBoundsRect(), I call getColorBoundsRect() on the left bitmap, passing in the color hovered over as well as a mask that will only return the specified pixel (if it matches in all channels). With the region of the bitmap containing the specified pixel determined, I pass the color and the region to the second bitmap data's fillRect() method, which draws the region of the specified color.

```
      var rect:Rectangle = ➥
_bitmapData0.getColorBoundsRect(0xFFFFFFFF, color);
      _bitmap1.bitmapData.fillRect(rect, color);
```

Flooding with color

The final method I will discuss this section dealing with coloring regions of data is `floodFill()`. This method basically works like the magic wand tool in Photoshop with a Tolerance setting of 0, filling in all contiguous regions of the same pixel color with another specified color.

```
public function floodFill(x:int, y:int, color:uint):void
```

One obvious use for such a method, other than replicating the magic wand tool, is creating a coloring book application where whole enclosed regions can be colored in easily with a single click.

As an example, have a look at `FloodFillTest.swf` in this chapter's download files. You are presented with a black-and-white line drawing and a palette of colors across the bottom of the screen. If you click any of the palette swatches, the rectangle at the lower left is updated to show you your selection. Clicking anywhere within the line drawing fills the clicked region with the selected color. The result of some creative clicking is shown in Figure 3-13.

Figure 3-13. A coloring book application using floodFill() to insert a single color into a contiguous region

With the image loading handled in AbstractImageLoader once again, the class that creates this application, found as `FloodFillTest.as` in this chapter's files, only requires the following code:

```
package {

  import flash.display.Bitmap;
  import flash.display.BitmapData;
  import flash.events.MouseEvent;
  import flash.geom.Rectangle;

  [SWF(width=600, height=800, backgroundColor=0xFFFFFF)]

  public class FloodFillTest extends AbstractImageLoader {
```

```
    private static const SWATCH_SIZE:uint = 50;

    private var _image:BitmapData;
    private var _palette:BitmapData;
    private var _currentColor:uint;

    public function FloodFillTest() {
      super("../../assets/castle.gif");
    }

    private function createPalette():void {
      _palette = new BitmapData(stage.stageWidth, SWATCH_SIZE);
      var rect:Rectangle = ➥
new Rectangle(0, 0, SWATCH_SIZE, SWATCH_SIZE);
      var lastSwatch:uint = _palette.width - SWATCH_SIZE;
      for (var x:uint = SWATCH_SIZE*2; x<=lastSwatch; x+=SWATCH_SIZE) {
        rect.x = x;
        var color:uint = Math.random()*0xFFFFFF;
        color = 0xFF << 24 | color;
        _palette.fillRect(rect, color);
      }
      var bitmap:Bitmap = new Bitmap(_palette);
      bitmap.y = stage.stageHeight-bitmap.height;
      addChild(bitmap);
    }

    override protected function runPostImageLoad():void {
      addChild(_loadedBitmap);
      _image = _loadedBitmap.bitmapData;
      createPalette();
      _currentColor = 0xFFFFFF;
      stage.addEventListener(MouseEvent.MOUSE_DOWN, onStageMouseDown);
    }

    private function onStageMouseDown(event:MouseEvent):void {
      var x:uint = event.localX;
      var y:uint = event.localY;
      if (y > _image.height) {
        var rect:Rectangle = ➥
new Rectangle(0, 0, SWATCH_SIZE*2, SWATCH_SIZE);
        _currentColor = _palette.getPixel32(x, y-_image.height);
        _palette.fillRect(rect, _currentColor);
      } else {
        _image.floodFill(x, y, _currentColor);
      }
    }

  }

}
```

When the runPostImageLoad() is called from the super class, I add the loaded bitmap to the stage and save a reference to its bitmap data in the _image property. I then call createPalette(), a method that will create the swatches across the bottom of the application. Of course, if you were building a polished application, you would probably include a color picker component or at least define color values to be used, but for a simple demonstration of floodFill(), this quick-and-easy color swatch palette does the trick just fine.

In the createPalette() method, I first create a new BitmapData instance that is the width of the stage and height of the swatches (which has been set as a constant at the top of the class). A rectangle is then created that will determine the dimensions and position of each swatch. The for loop that follows runs through the number of swatches that the width of the stage dictates, minus 100 pixels at the left that will be used for the selected color. Notice that in each iteration of the loop I change the rectangle's x property, since each new swatch drawn starts at a new x position in the _palette bitmap data.

```
for (var x:uint = SWATCH_SIZE*2; x <= lastSwatch; x+=SWATCH_SIZE) {
  rect.x = x;
```

For a swatch's color, I select a random value between 0 and 0xFFFFFF. One interesting line to note is the following:

```
color = 0xFF << 24 | color;
```

Since the color I select is only 24-bit (I don't want the alpha to be variable, or I could have selected a random number between 0 and 0xFFFFFFFF) and fillRect() requires a 32-bit number, I have to insert the alpha value using a bitwise left-shift operator. This takes a full channel value of 0xFF and pushes it to the bit positions in the color value that hold the alpha information. The rectangle and color are then passed to _palette's fillRect() method in order to color the swatch.

Once the for loop completes and all the swatches are drawn, I add the palette bitmap to the stage. All that's left is the code to enable user interaction, which is found in the onStageMouseDown() handler. In this method, I use a simple if conditional to determine whether the click happened in the palette or on the image. If it was in the palette, I call getPixel32() to find the color clicked and draw this into the current color swatch using fillRect() once more.

```
_currentColor = _palette.getPixel32(x, y-_image.height);
_palette.fillRect(rect, _currentColor);
```

If, on the other hand, the image was clicked, I call floodFill() with the click coordinates and the currently selected color.

```
_image.floodFill(x, y, _currentColor);
```

BitmapData handles the rest and colors in the enclosed region with the new color.

Transforming color

We've explored how to access and set a single pixel's color and how to find and fill regions with a single color. How would you go about altering color hue, brightness, or saturation across a region or the entirety of an image? The answer is to use the colorTransform() method of BitmapData.

We examined how a color transform matrix works last chapter with ColorMatrixFilter and how the ColorTransform class works earlier this chapter. Well, BitmapData instances actually have a colorTransform() method that you can pass a rectangular region and a ColorTransform instance in order to alter the region's pixel colors in a similar way to the ColorMatrixFilter.

```
public function colorTransform(
  rect:Rectangle,
  colorTransform:ColorTransform
):void
```

As a final example this chapter, we are going to look at using BitmapData's colorTransform() in an application that offers the ability to alter a single image's hue and brightness in a similar way to Photoshop's Variations dialog, which is shown in Figure 3-14. A quick ActionScript variant (a variation on Variations!) is shown in Figure 3-15.

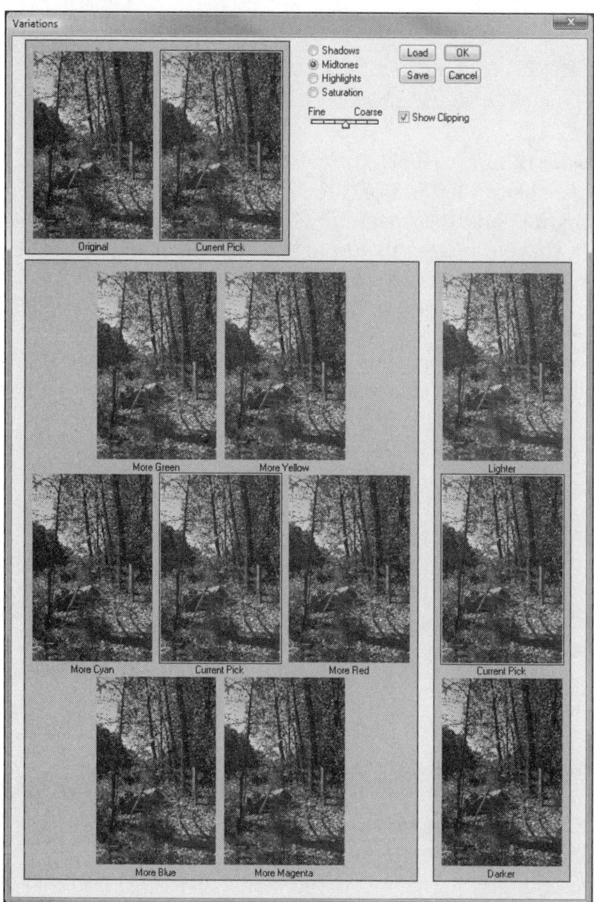

Figure 3-14.
Photoshop's Variations dialog, which lets you select a color variation from an original image

Figure 3-15. An ActionScript version of Variations using ColorTransform

If you test out the `ColorTransformTest.swf` included with this chapter's files, you will see six variants of the same image. The top left image is the current original. The image to its immediate right is slightly brighter, and the image to its right, in the top right corner, is slightly darker. In the bottom row are images that brighten the red, green, or blue channels, respectively. If you click any image, the clicked image becomes the new original in the top left and the other five images are updated to become variants of this new original.

Creating such an application is actually very easy with BitmapData and ColorTransform doing all the work. The following class, `ColorTransformTest.as`, shows you what you would need:

```
package {

  import flash.display.Bitmap;
  import flash.display.BitmapData;
  import flash.events.MouseEvent;
  import flash.geom.ColorTransform;
  import flash.geom.Matrix;

  [SWF(width=800, height=500, backgroundColor=0x000000)]

  public class ColorTransformTest extends AbstractImageLoader {

    private var _bitmaps:Vector.<Bitmap>;
```

```
    public function ColorTransformTest() {
      super("../../assets/harbor.jpg");
    }

    override protected function runPostImageLoad():void {
      _bitmaps = new Vector.<Bitmap>();
      var imageSize:Number = stage.stageWidth/3;
      for (var row:uint = 0; row < 2; row++) {
        for (var column:uint = 0; column < 3; column++) {
          createBitmap(column*imageSize, row*imageSize);
        }
      }
      var sourceData:BitmapData = _loadedBitmap.bitmapData;
      var matrix:Matrix = new Matrix();
      var scale:Number = imageSize/sourceData.width;
      matrix.scale(scale, scale);
      var copiedData:BitmapData = new BitmapData(
        sourceData.width*scale,
        sourceData.height*scale
      );
      copiedData.draw(sourceData, matrix);
      createVariations(copiedData);
      stage.addEventListener(MouseEvent.CLICK, onMouseClick);
    }

    private function createBitmap(x:Number, y:Number):void {
      var bitmap:Bitmap = new Bitmap();
      bitmap.x = x;
      bitmap.y = y;
      addChild(bitmap);
      _bitmaps.push(bitmap);
    }

    private function createVariations(original:BitmapData):void {
      var brighten:Number = 1.3;
      var darken:Number = 0.7;
      _bitmaps[0].bitmapData = original;
      _bitmaps[1].bitmapData = makeVariation(original, ➥
new ColorTransform(brighten, brighten, brighten));
      _bitmaps[2].bitmapData = makeVariation(original, ➥
new ColorTransform(darken, darken, darken));
      _bitmaps[3].bitmapData = makeVariation(original, ➥
new ColorTransform(brighten));
      _bitmaps[4].bitmapData = makeVariation(original, ➥
new ColorTransform(1, brighten));
      _bitmaps[5].bitmapData = makeVariation(original, ➥
new ColorTransform(1, 1, brighten));
    }
```

```
    private function makeVariation(
      original:BitmapData,
      transform:ColorTransform
    ):BitmapData {
      var variation:BitmapData = original.clone();
      variation.colorTransform(variation.rect, transform);
      return variation;
    }

    private function onMouseClick(event:MouseEvent):void {
      for each (var bitmap:Bitmap in _bitmaps) {
        if (bitmap.hitTestPoint(event.localX, event.localY)) {
          createVariations(bitmap.bitmapData);
          break;
        }
      }
    }

  }

}
```

Once again, just as in the last example, this class extends AbstractImageLoader, which handles the loading of an external image. When runPostImageLoad() is called, the first thing I do is create a vector to hold the bitmaps I will create. I then divide the stage into thirds and use a nested for loop to run through the three columns and two rows in order to fill the stage with six bitmaps.

```
for (var row:uint = 0; row < 2; row++) {
  for (var column:uint = 0; column < 3; column++) {
    createBitmap(column*imageSize, row*imageSize);
  }
}
```

The creation of the Bitmap instances (with no BitmapData at this time) is all handled in the createBitmap() method, which simply instantiates and positions a Bitmap instance and adds it to the stage.

Once the bitmaps have been created, I grab a reference to the loaded bitmap's bitmap data and store this in sourceData. A matrix is used to set a scale transform for the bitmap data so that it is scaled down to fit within the size of the bitmaps. copiedData is created to hold this scaled down bitmap, with a call to draw() used to copy the source data into copiedData at the scaled down size.

```
var sourceData:BitmapData = _loadedBitmap.bitmapData;
var matrix:Matrix = new Matrix();
var scale:Number = imageSize/sourceData.width;
matrix.scale(scale, scale);
```

```
var copiedData:BitmapData = new BitmapData(
  sourceData.width*scale,
  sourceData.height*scale
);
copiedData.draw(sourceData, matrix);
```

The next step is to alter the colors on the variant images using `colorTransform()`. This is handled in `createVariations()`, which takes a BitmapData source and passes this to the top left bitmap.

```
_bitmaps[0].bitmapData = original;
```

For the remaining bitmaps, I call a `makeVariation()` method and pass to it the original's data as well as a ColorTransform instance defining the desired color transform. In `makeVariation()`, I first `clone()` the original's data so that any transform applied does not affect the original and then call `colorTransform()` on the copy, passing the rectangular region (in this case, the whole image) and the ColorTransform to apply.

```
var variation:BitmapData = original.clone();
variation.colorTransform(variation.rect, transform);
```

This altered copy is returned to `createVariations()`, where it is passed to a bitmap for display.

The only remaining piece is the code that allows the user to click a variant to be used as a new original image from which more variants are made. This is handled in the `onMouseClick()` handler, which runs through all of the bitmaps to see which was clicked. This bitmap's data is then sent to the `createVariations()` method, resulting in all the bitmaps being refreshed with new data.

Summary

Who knew that there would be so much to know about a little collection of colored rectangles? A massive amount of functionality for image manipulation is made available through BitmapData, and in this chapter, we've covered the basic operations needed to load, create, and display bitmap data in the Flash Player. We looked at operations that give control over the smallest graphical unit, the pixel, and how to affect the color of entire regions of pixels. Lots of features were covered over the course of lots of pages, and yet we have just scratched the surface of BitmapData.

In the next chapter, we will continue our exploration of this class and investigate more advanced methods that it provides, like generating Perlin noise, distorting through displacement maps, and mapping to custom color palettes. Now that you have the basic operations down, we can pull out the big guns. Time to really push those pixels around!

Chapter 4

ADVANCED BITMAP MANIPULATION

Back in the '80s on the television show *Cheers*, the character of Dr. Frasier Crane once spouted a great line I've always remembered, "Oh, now you're saying I'm redundant, that I repeat myself, that I say things over and over?" Well, I find something a bit humorously redundant about the title of this chapter. There really is nothing basic about bitmap manipulation, but we can look at those topics covered in the last chapter as, if not basic, at least the foundation knowledge that is required in order to perform more advanced bitmap manipulation through ActionScript.

The last chapter contained a lot of information on bitmaps in Flash, from loading and creating images to adding them to the display list, to manipulation of individual pixel colors and regions of colors. There were a lot of basics to cover on pixels and channels and how color and alpha information is represented. Like most topics, covering the basics and understanding them is necessary before you can get to the more advanced, and, let's face it, cool stuff.

This chapter gets into the cool stuff. You have learned to crawl and now in this chapter will walk, run, and sprint through the more complex methods that BitmapData offers, and we will explore what image effects such methods will help us to achieve.

Adding Pixel Randomization

The human mind is quick to recognize patterns. Without this ability, we could not learn languages, logically deduce results from actions, or most importantly, wear plaid. Patterns can be pleasing to the eye and mind, but sometimes the existence of patterns can produce a visual or mental conformity that is undesired. A face that is perfectly symmetrical looks unnatural to the human eye. It is boring to eat the same food at every meal. And why do Scooby and Shaggy walk past the same painting three times when going down the hall?

Thankfully, we don't live in an interminable *Groundhog Day* where there is no variation and all outcomes are predetermined. There is a random quality to our lives and to what we experience around us. When creating visual effects, especially those that attempt to re-create aspects of the world around us, a quality of randomization is necessary in order to break out of the visual patterns inherent in computer graphics, if that is your desire (hey, some people like their timepieces synchronized and perfectly folded outfits laid out for each day of the week!). In this section, we will look at several ways to introduce a random factor in bitmap effects you create.

Dissolving Pixels

`pixelDissolve()` is an interesting effect you can apply to a bitmap that offers a way to create a transition from one image into another or between an image and a solid color. In either case, random pixels in the destination image are replaced by the corresponding pixels in the source image. When animated, one image appears to dissolve in groups of pixels from the destination image into the source image.

The effect, if I may be blunt, reminds me of a PowerPoint transition from the 1990s or a Star Trek beam effect on a shoestring budget (or is that redundant?). So unless you are purposely attempting to re-create these effects, getting real use out of this method requires some creativity. However, I have found that it can be useful for introducing a slight grain or irregularity to images by performing a single dissolve with a small number of pixels between the source image and a random destination image or even a solid color.

The following is the method signature for `pixelDissolve()`:

```
public function pixelDissolve(
  sourceBitmapData:BitmapData,
  sourceRect:Rectangle,
  destPoint:Point,
```

```
    randomSeed:int = 0,
    numPixels:int = 0,
    fillColor:uint = 0
):int
```

Let's break down the parameters to see what control this method offers:

- sourceBitmapData: This is the image into which you wish to dissolve your destination image.
- sourceRect: This is the region of the source image you wish to use for the dissolve. If you want to use the entirety of the source image, you could simply reference the rect property of the source BitmapData object.
- destPoint: This is the point of the top left pixel from where the rectangle specified by sourceRect will be drawn. Again, if you wish to use the entirety of the source image, you can pass a Point instance with (0, 0) as the x and y values.
- randomSeed: This number will be used as the base for the pseudorandom calculations of this method. We'll look at this more in depth in a moment.
- numPixels: This specifies the number of pixels that should be used from the source image to replace pixels in the destination image. If the number of pixels is the total number of pixels in the source image (sourceBitmapData.width * sourceBitmapData.height), all the pixels will be replaced. If the number of pixels is half of that, only half of the pixels will be replaced. By changing the value of numPixels over time from 0 to the total number of pixels in the image, you can create an animated effect of one pixel slowly dissolving into another image.
- fillColor: This color will be used to replace pixels in the destination image. This is only used when the source and destination images are the same. In that case, dissolving from one to the other really wouldn't do anything, since all of the pixels are the same, so in this case, the pixelDissolve() method can be used to dissolve from the destination image to the color specified by the fillColor parameter, or vice versa. We'll look at this in the coming example.

Now, let's take a step back and look at that fourth parameter, randomSeed. This value is required to create the animated effect where pixels dissolve from one image to another over time. If we call the pixelDissolve() method multiple times over a number of timed intervals, which is necessary to create animation, we want to have the same pixels that had already dissolved in previous frames to remain dissolved in subsequent frames as we dissolve more pixels, but the random nature of the pixels selected by this method would prevent this. However, the random nature of the pixels selected isn't truly random; it's a calculated value that only appears to be random to our eyes. That value is calculated from an initial seed value, the integer value passed as the randomSeed parameter. To enable you to pass the correct seed value in a subsequent call in order to maintain the same dissolved pixels, the pixelDissolve() method returns an integer value that you can use for the randomSeed parameter when that next call is made.

Basically, you can start by passing 0 the first time the method is called, or some randomly generated number—passing Number(new Date()) is always a simple way to create a fairly random integer—then use the integer value returned by the method for the subsequent call's `randomSeed` value. Each time you make the call, you would save the value returned and pass this as the `randomSeed` value for the subsequent call. This allows the dissolved pixels to build up over the course of the animated transition as opposed to getting randomly replaced anew each interval.

Let's take a look at one particular application of this effect that doesn't involve an animated transition and might not be an obvious use for the method. This section of the chapter is on adding a random factor to images, and this can be accomplished with `pixelDissolve()` by introducing a small amount of a color in a random pattern about an image. The result, with a little saturation and blur applied, reminds me a bit of a pointillism painting like those of Georges Seurat. You can see the effect applied in Figure 4-1.

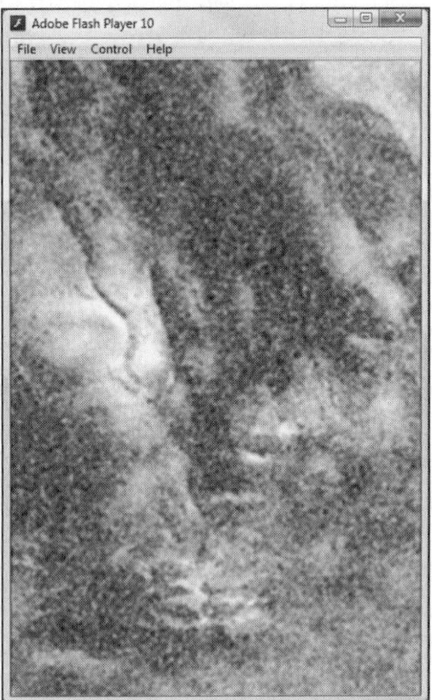

Figure 4-1.
The pixelDissolve() method applied to an image to create a pointillism effect

This example uses the same AbstractImageLoader base class that was used in the previous chapter. It is also included with this chapter's files. The class is extended once again to load in an image, after which a pixel dissolve is applied. The following is the entirety of the code for the example, which you can find in this chapter's files as `PixelDissolveTest.as`:

```
package {

  import flash.display.BitmapData;
  import flash.filters.BlurFilter;
  import flash.filters.ColorMatrixFilter;
  import flash.geom.Point;
```

```
    [SWF(width=400, height=600, backgroundColor=0x000000)]

    public class PixelDissolveTest extends AbstractImageLoader {

      public function PixelDissolveTest() {
        super("../../assets/fungus.jpg");
      }

      override protected function runPostImageLoad():void {
        var bitmapData:BitmapData = _loadedBitmap.bitmapData;
        var numPixels:uint = (bitmapData.width*bitmapData.height)/3;
        bitmapData.pixelDissolve(
          bitmapData,
          bitmapData.rect,
          new Point(),
          0,
          numPixels,
          0xFFFFFFFA
        );
        _loadedBitmap.filters = [
          getSaturationFilter(),
          new BlurFilter()
        ];
        addChild(_loadedBitmap);
      }

      private function getSaturationFilter():ColorMatrixFilter {
        var r:Number = 0.3;
        var g:Number = 0.59;
        var b:Number = 0.11;
        var amount:Number = 2.2;
        var inverse:Number = 1-amount;
        var matrix:Array=[
          inverse*r+amount, inverse*g,        inverse*b,        0, 0,
          inverse*r,        inverse*g+amount, inverse*b,        0, 0,
          inverse*r,        inverse*g,        inverse*b+amount, 0, 0,
          0,                0,                0,                1, 0
        ];
        return new ColorMatrixFilter(matrix);
      }

    }

  }
  }
```

The relevant pixelDissolve() lines are in bold. You can see that the number of pixels affected is a third of the pixels in the entire image. Because I am using the same image as the source and destination, I can introduce a color as the final parameter to be used for that third of the pixels (I chose a slight off-white). Since I am not creating an animated effect, I can simply pass 0 as the random seed, though if you wanted a different image each time the application was run you could set this value using some random calculation.

To get the effect to really work, I find a blur is absolutely necessary, so this is added to the Bitmap instance's list of filters (remove this to see how a nonblurred dissolve looks, but I'll warn you that it's ugly). Depending on the image, you might wish to saturate the colors, and I do this here by applying a ColorMatrixFilter that uses a matrix that will result in saturation. If you look at how the matrix is calculated, you will see that if the amount is 0, the resulting matrix would be one to make an image grayscale:

```
| 0.3  0.59  0.11  0  0 |
| 0.3  0.59  0.11  0  0 |
| 0.3  0.59  0.11  0  0 |
| 0.0  0.00  0.00  1  0 |
```

An amount of 1 would result in an identity matrix, which would have no affect on the image:

```
| 1  0  0  0  0 |
| 0  1  0  0  0 |
| 0  0  1  0  0 |
| 0  0  0  1  0 |
```

The value of 2.2 results in a matrix that looks (roughly) like this:

```
|  1.84  -0.71  -0.13  0  0 |
| -0.36   1.49  -0.13  0  0 |
| -0.36  -0.71   2.07  0  0 |
|  0.00   0.00   0.00  1  0 |
```

You can see that the pixel values of each channel are increased using the brightness values from that channel, while also being reduced (using those negative multipliers) by the brightness values of the other channels. The result is a more saturated image. And a pretty effect to boot.

Making some noise

Digital noise is the pixel imperfections, variations of brightness or color, introduced to an image usually during initial capture. This noise can have a number of causes, but the result is usually unwanted, and we strive to produce images without these imperfections.

So why on earth would we ever want to add noise to an image? Well, sometimes pristine, perfect images can appear too perfect, since we are used to at least small imperfections in images that might not be immediately noticeable. A little noise goes a long way in turning an obviously computer-generated image into something a bit more realistic. Also, when you are attempting to create an effect reminiscent of something that occurs in the real world, like film grain in an older movie, noise is a handy way to achieve this. It can also be used for generating random speckled images that can be turned into star fields or the night sky, as will be demonstrated in Chapter 7.

Calling noise() on a BitmapData instance is not the same as applying noise in Photoshop, where you can control the amount of noise that is added and still retain the features from the original image. BitmapData's noise() replaces all pixels in an image. So if you wish to apply a small amount of noise to an image, you must first create the noise in a new BitmapData instance, then copy the noise into your destination image (using something like draw(), copyPixels(), or copyChannel()) at your desired amount. We will be applying noise in a number of effects throughout this book so we will examine this further in later examples.

The noise() method of BitmapData has the following signature:

```
public function noise(
  randomSeed:int,
  low:uint = 0,
  high:uint = 255,
  channelOptions:uint = 7,
  grayScale:Boolean = false
):void
```

And here is what each of those parameters represents:

- randomSeed: This is the number to be used as the base for the pseudorandom calculations of this method. This parameter serves the same purpose as it did with pixelDissolve(), providing a number from which the random calculations can begin.
- low: This specifies the minimum brightness value for a pixel that should be used in the noise generation.
- high: This specifies the maximum brightness value for a pixel that should be used in the noise generation. For instance, the default values for low and high will create pixels with brightness values from 0 to 255. If you wanted less of a range, perhaps more midrange numbers, you could set the low to 100 and the high to 150. Figure 4-2 shows noise generated using the default values on the left and using 100 for low and 150 for high on the right.

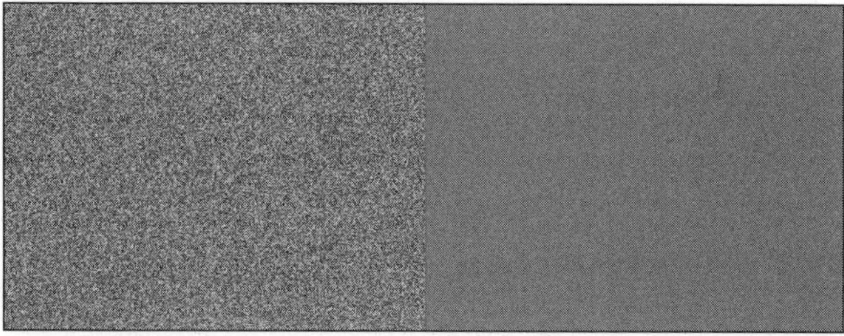

Figure 4-2. The noise() method with the default settings for low (0) and high (255) on the left, and with low=100 and high=150 on the right, reducing the noise contrast

- channelOptions: This determines in which channels the noise will be generated. We'll look at this more in depth in a moment.
- grayScale: This parameter determines whether the noise will be rendered in grayscale (true) or full color (false).

Let's take a closer look now at the fourth parameter, channelOptions. This integer value can be any combination of the constants found in the BitmapDataChannel class. If you wanted noise that was only in the red channel, you could pass BitmapDataChannel.RED (or 1) for the channelOptions. For green, you would pass BitmapDataChannel.GREEN (or 2). You can combine channels by using the bitwise OR (|). So combining red and green channels, which would result in red, green, and yellow pixels, you would pass this:

```
BitmapDataChannel.RED | BitmapDataChannel.GREEN
```

The decimal equivalent of this operation is 3, as demonstrated when we look at RED (1) and GREEN (2) represented in binary and combine them using bitwise OR, which results in 1 if either component is 1:

```
  01
| 10
----
  11
```

11 in binary is 3 in decimal. The default value of 7 that noise() uses is a combination of all three color channels, resulting in a full range of colored pixels in the noise.

One simple effect that can be achieved using noise() is the animated white noise from older television sets when dials were set to frequencies that had no data, as you might recall from the classic "They're here!" scene in the movie *Poltergeist*. A screenshot of the animated effect isn't a good representation (and not nearly as evocatively scary), but Figure 4-3 shows a single frame from the animation.

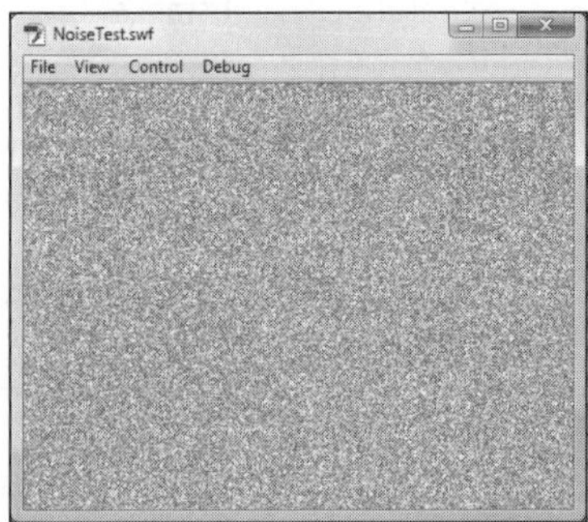

Figure 4-3. A single frame from animated noise re-creating television white noise

The full code for the effect follows, and you can find it as NoiseTest.as in this chapter's files:

```
package {

  import flash.display.Bitmap;
  import flash.display.BitmapData;
  import flash.display.Sprite;
  import flash.events.Event;
  import flash.utils.getTimer;

  [SWF(width=400, height=300, backgroundColor=0x000000)]

  public class NoiseTest extends Sprite {

    private var _bitmapData:BitmapData;

    public function NoiseTest() {
      _bitmapData = new BitmapData(
        stage.stageWidth,
        stage.stageHeight
      );
      makeNoise();
      addChild(new Bitmap(_bitmapData));
      addEventListener(Event.ENTER_FRAME, onSpriteEnterFrame);
    }

    private function makeNoise():void {
      _bitmapData.noise(getTimer(), 100, 255, 7, true);
    }

    private function onSpriteEnterFrame(event:Event):void {
      makeNoise();
    }

  }

}
```

This simple class creates a new BitmapData instance the size of the stage. Noise is added to the image within the makeNoise() method, and the image is added to the stage. Finally, within the constructor, an event listener is set up to be called every frame. Within the handler for the ENTER_FRAME event, makeNoise() is called, so each frame the noise is generated anew.

The makeNoise() method itself contains a single line that invokes the noise() method of BitmapData. I use getTimer() for the randomSeed parameter so that each time noise() is called it is with a different number. The low value is set to 100, which means we won't get very dark pixels, and the high value is left at 255, or full brightness. For channelOptions, I use the default 7 (or all channels), but this isn't too important since I pass true as the final parameter, which converts the image to grayscale.

If you open NoiseTest.swf from this chapter's download files, you will see the result. Ah, I can almost see the rabbit ears and needle-nose pliers used in place of a missing channel knob. Old technology is so quaint.

Applying Perlin noise

The movie *Tron*, in addition to inspiring my friends and me when we were younger to transform our Frisbees into painful projectiles as we tried to turn our bicycles at impossible 90 degree angles, was a pioneering effort for computer-generated graphics in film. As those who have seen the movie will attest, there is an unreal, pristine appearance to this early CGI (which lent itself well to the video game setting). The textures of objects are smooth and plastic. The people (or programs) stand out against their backdrops because of the random visual quality to skin and cloth that is not quite matched by their surroundings.

Ken Perlin, who worked on *Tron* while at Mathematical Application Group, Inc., was frustrated by what he called the "machine-like" appearance of the models in *Tron*, and after the movie's completion, he developed a method of creating procedural textures (textures created with a mathematical algorithm) that could be applied to images to introduce that random quality we recognize in the world around us, enabling more realistic, less perfect computer-generated imagery. These procedural textures can be used to scuff up a surface, generate smoke or fire, create stone or marble—the applications of his work are numerous, and his developments on noise and procedural textures are used everywhere today in 3D, visual effects, and image manipulation or enhancement.

Perlin's work is surfaced in ActionScript through BitmapData's perlinNoise() method (a shame the convention is not to capitalize the first letter of a method—Professor Perlin surely deserves it!). This method generates a pseudorandom—like all procedural textures, it only has the appearance of being random—noise image that replaces all pixels in the BitmapData instance. The beauty of this Perlin algorithm is that it creates noise over multiple layers, each called an octave, which, like a musical octave, is twice the frequency of the octave below it, and these octaves when combined create an apparently more-random texture.

Like the old adage goes, a picture is worth a thousand verbose explanations of a mathematical formula. Figure 4-4 shows several examples of Perlin noise that can be generated using BitmapData's perlinNoise() method.

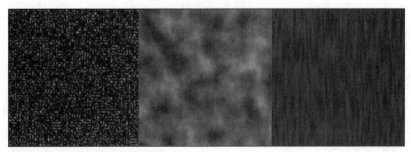

Figure 4-4. Different results from using the perlinNoise() method

So how do you create images like this? The following is the signature of `perlinNoise()`:

```
public function perlinNoise(
  baseX:Number,
  baseY:Number,
  numOctaves:uint,
  randomSeed:int,
  stitch:Boolean,
  fractalNoise:Boolean,
  channelOptions:uint = 7,
  grayScale:Boolean = false,
  offsets:Array = null
):void
```

Yes, it's trying to show off with lots of parameters. Let's look at each in turn:

- `baseX`: This is the frequency of the noise on the x axis. The lower the value (which results in a higher frequency), the more detailed the noise will appear. Generally, you can match the frequency to the number of pixels, so for an image that is 256 pixels wide, you could set the frequency to 256. To increase the detail, you could reduce the value to 128. Reducing the value to just a few pixels will produce noise that appears to be tiny speckles, an extremely high frequency.
- `baseY`: This is the frequency of the noise on the y axis. Figure 4-5 shows a 512×512 image with the `baseX` and `baseY` values set as 512, 256, and 64, respectively, from left to right.

Figure 4-5. Perlin noise with the baseX and baseY settings at 512, 256, and 64, respectively, for a 512×512 image

- `numOctaves`: This specifies the number of different noise functions to run and combine into the final image. If you use only one octave, you will get one layer of noise at the specified `baseX` and `baseY` frequencies. For each additional octave, a new layer will be added with the frequencies twice that of the previous layer. For instance, if you have set `baseX` and `baseY` to 256 and set the `numOctaves` to 3, the second noise function will use a `baseX` and `baseY` value of 128 (which is a higher frequency), and the third noise function will use a `baseX` and `baseY` of 64. Increasing the number of octaves will produce more-detailed random noise but does require more processing and can slow down an animated effect.

Figure 4-6 shows a 512×512 image with the baseX and baseY values set as 256 and the numOctaves set to 1, 3, and 6, respectively.

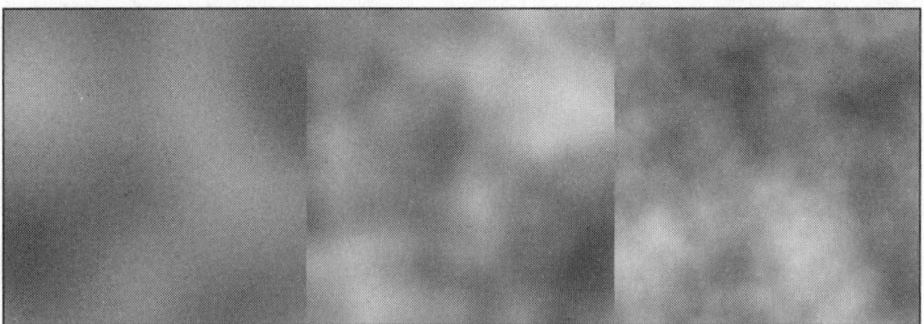

Figure 4-6. Perlin noise with the numOctaves set at 1, 3, and 6, respectively, for a 512×512 image with a baseX and baseY of 256

- randomSeed: This number is used as the base for pseudorandom calculations to generate the noise, just as with noise() and pixelDissolve().
- stitch: This determines whether the edges of the generated noise are smoothed to enable better tiling of the noise when applied to a larger shape or image.
- fractalNoise: This parameter determines whether the noise generated will be fractal noise (true) or turbulence (false). With turbulence, the gradient produced contains visible discontinuities where there are sharp contrasts in the colors of the gradient. These edges can be useful when producing certain effects like ocean ripples or fire.

  Figure 4-7 shows an image with fractalNoise set to true and false, respectively.

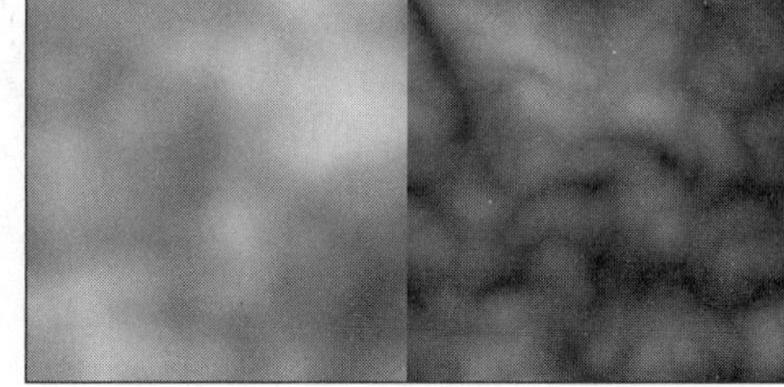

Figure 4-7. Perlin noise with the fractal noise on the left and turbulence on the right

- channelOptions: This parameter determines in which channels the noise will be generated, just as with the noise() method.
- grayScale: This one determines whether the noise generated will be grayscale (true) or will use the color channels specified in the channelOptions parameter.
- offsets: This array of Points is used to offset the noise in each octave. Each Point in the array affects a singular octave where the Point in the first index affects the first octave; the second Point affects the second octave, and so on. By altering these values over time, you can animate the noise in an image, which is the basis for many effects like smoke and fire. Note that, since each Point controls a different octave, you can animate different octaves at different rates or in different directions.

There is a lot to the perlinNoise() method and a lot that can be accomplished using this method within a larger effect, such as creating animated effects like ocean waves, flame, and smoke, or creating textures like wood grain, rust, and marble. We will be exploring some of these effects in the later chapters of this book, but in the meantime, we can create a simple file that allows us to play with the parameters to see their effect.

If you open the file PerlinNoiseTest.as provided with this chapter's files, you will find the following code:

```
package {

  import flash.display.Bitmap;
  import flash.display.BitmapData;
  import flash.display.BitmapDataChannel;
  import flash.display.Sprite;
  import flash.events.Event;
  import flash.geom.Point;

  [SWF(width=500, height=500, backgroundColor=0x000000)]

  public class PerlinNoiseTest extends Sprite {

    private static const BASE_X:Number = 200;
    private static const BASE_Y:Number = 200;
    private static const NUM_OCTAVES:Number = 2;
    private static const RANDOM_SEED:Number = Number(new Date());
    private static const STITCH:Boolean = false;
    private static const FRACTAL:Boolean = true;
    private static const CHANNELS:uint = BitmapDataChannel.RED;
    private static const GRAYSCALE:Boolean = false;
    private static const OFFSET_X_RATE:Number = 2;
    private static const OFFSET_Y_RATE:Number = 5;

    private var _bitmapData:BitmapData;
    private var _offsets:Array;

    public function PerlinNoiseTest() {
      _bitmapData = new BitmapData(
        stage.stageWidth,
        stage.stageHeight
      );
      _offsets = [];
      for (var i:uint = 0; i < NUM_OCTAVES; i++) {
        _offsets.push(new Point());
      }
      makePerlinNoise();
      addChild(new Bitmap(_bitmapData));
      addEventListener(Event.ENTER_FRAME, onSpriteEnterFrame);
    }

    private function makePerlinNoise():void {
      _bitmapData.perlinNoise(
```

```
                BASE_X,
                BASE_Y,
                NUM_OCTAVES,
                RANDOM_SEED,
                STITCH,
                FRACTAL,
                CHANNELS,
                GRAYSCALE,
                _offsets
                );
            }

            private function onSpriteEnterFrame(event:Event):void {
              var point:Point;
              var direction:int;
              for (var i:uint = 0; i < NUM_OCTAVES; i++) {
                point = _offsets[i] as Point;
                direction = (i%2==0) ? -1 : 1;
                point.x += OFFSET_X_RATE/(NUM_OCTAVES-i)*direction;
                point.y += OFFSET_Y_RATE/(NUM_OCTAVES-i)*direction;
              }
              makePerlinNoise();
            }

          }

        }
```

If you test this file, you will see that by default you get an animation of the image, as shown in Figure 4-8.

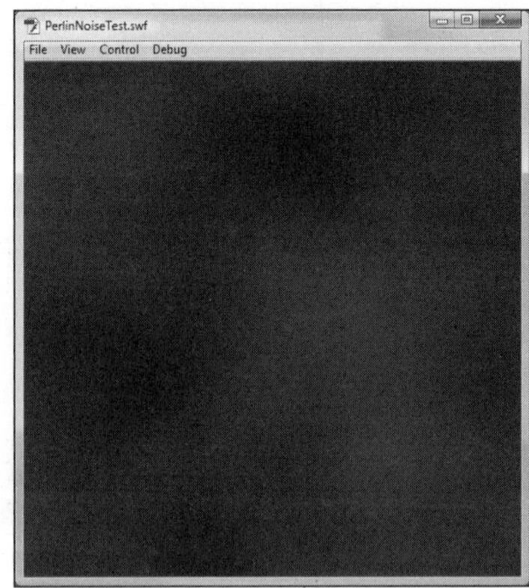

Figure 4-8. One frame from animated Perlin noise with two octaves moving in different directions at different rates

The animation moves two different octaves in the noise in different directions at different rates. If you look at the code in the class, you can see that in the constructor a new BitmapData instance is created where all of the noise will be applied. I then create a new _offsets array that can be populated with points to match the number of octaves specified in the NUM_OCTAVES constant. Finally, makePerlinNoise() is called to generate the noise, a Bitmap with the BitmapData is added to the stage, and a listener is set up for the ENTER_FRAME event.

The makePerlinNoise() method merely calls perlinNoise() on the bitmap data, using the constants specified at the top of the class and the _offsets array. This array is updated each frame in the onSpriteEnterFrame handler. The for loop that alters the Point values contains some code that first determines a direction to animate an octave based on whether the iterator for that loop iteration is even or odd:

```
direction = (i%2==0) ? -1 : 1;
```

If i%2 does not have a remainder, it is an even number and will use the direction –1. For odd numbers, a direction of 1 is used.

The rate of the animation is determined by the number of the octave as well. The highest octave will use the OFFSET_X_RATE and OFFSET_Y_RATE values as they are, since when i is equal to (NUM_OCTAVES-1), which it would be in the last iteration of the loop, NUM_OCTAVES-(NUM_OCTAVES-1) would result in 1 as the denominator for each offset. The lower the octave, the more the offset number will decrease, which will slow the animation for those octaves.

As an example, consider if three octaves are used with an OFFSET_X_RATE of 2 and an OFFSET_Y_RATE of 5. In the first loop iteration, the direction would be –1. point.x and point.y would be calculated with the following:

```
point.x += 2/(3-0)*-1; // evaluates to approximately -.667
point.y += 5/(3-0)*-1; // evaluates to approximately 1.667
```

When i=1, direction would be 1, and point.x and point.y would become the following:

```
point.x += 2/(3-1)*1; // evaluates to approximately 1
point.y += 5/(3-1)*1; // evaluates to approximately 2.5
```

In the final iteration of the loop for the last octave, when i=2, direction would once again be –1. point.x and point.y would then be as follows:

```
point.x += 2/(3-2)*-1; // evaluates to approximately -2
point.y += 5/(3-2)*-1; // evaluates to approximately -5
```

This produces the effect of having the higher frequencies animate more quickly than the lower frequencies.

Since this file has all the perlinNoise() parameters stored as constants at the top, it is easy to play with the numbers in order to see differences. Let's first reduce the parameters to a simple set of values to build from:

```
private static const BASE_X:Number = 500;
private static const BASE_Y:Number = 500;
private static const NUM_OCTAVES:Number = 1;
private static const RANDOM_SEED:Number = Number(new Date());
private static const STITCH:Boolean = false;
private static const FRACTAL:Boolean = true;
private static const CHANNELS:uint = BitmapDataChannel.RED;
private static const GRAYSCALE:Boolean = false;
private static const OFFSET_X_RATE:Number = 0;
private static const OFFSET_Y_RATE:Number = 0;
```

These new values produce the image as shown in Figure 4-9.

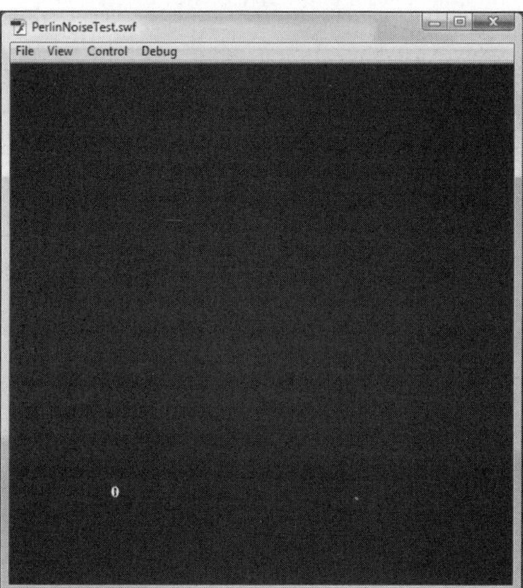

Figure 4-9.
The number of octaves in the previous example is reduced to 1, and baseX and baseY are set to 500.

To see more detail in the noise by increasing its frequency, we can lower the values of its BASE_X and BASE_Y. Try lowering just one to see the effect of increasing the frequency on a single axis.

```
private static const BASE_X:Number = 100;
```

Figure 4-10 shows the result of increasing the frequency on the x axis.

Figure 4-10.
The previous example with the baseX reduced to 100, creating a more vertical pattern

If you increase it even more, you can begin to see how textures like fabrics and wood might be created, as shown in Figure 4-11:

```
private static const BASE_X:Number = 5;
private static const BASE_Y:Number = 200;
```

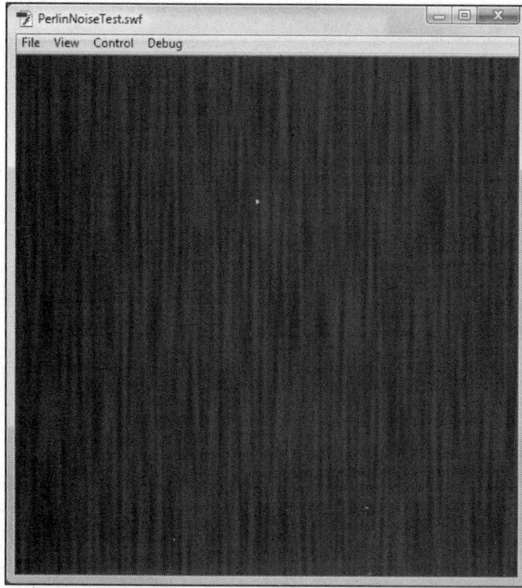

Figure 4-11.
The previous example with the baseX reduced to 5 and the baseY reduced to 100, producing almost a textile pattern

Now, let's explore adjusting the octaves. We'll start by setting the BASE_X and BASE_Y to 200 using a single octave, which results in Figure 4-12:

```
private static const BASE_X:Number = 200;
private static const BASE_Y:Number = 200;
```

Figure 4-12.
The previous example with the baseX and baseY set to 200 with a single octave

Now, increase the NUM_OCTAVES to 3 to see all the extra detail that is added, as shown in Figure 4-13:

```
private static const NUM_OCTAVES:Number = 3;
```

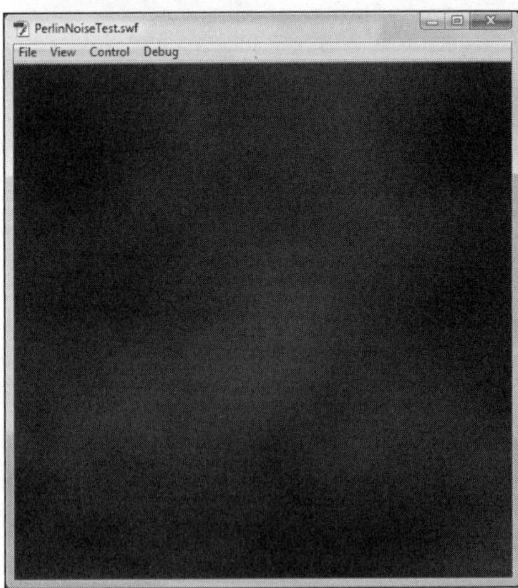

Figure 4-13.
The previous example with the numOctaves increased to 3

Again, what this does is layer three separate noise images where each image uses twice the frequency of the previous image. These images are using the fractal noise option currently. We can switch it to turbulence to get a very different result, as shown in Figure 4-14:

```
private static const FRACTAL:Boolean = false;
```

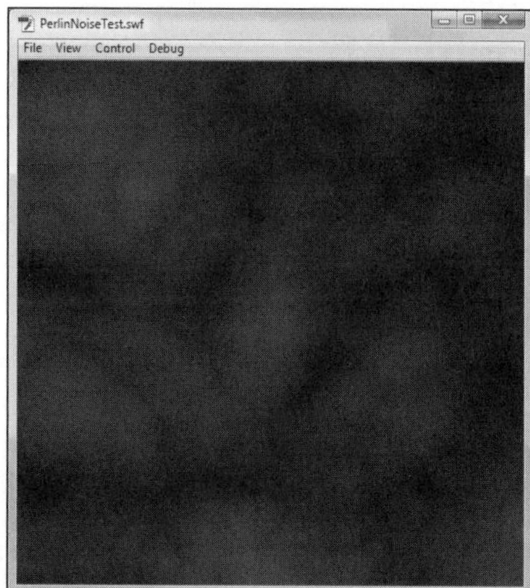

Figure 4-14.
The previous example with the fractalNoise set to false, producing turbulence

Finally, let's create a multicolor noise image by passing in two color channels. Remember, this works the same as passing channels to the noise() method, which we discussed earlier this chapter. You can use the bitwise OR operator to pass in multiple channels using the constants of the BitmapDataChannel class. This results in an image like Figure 4-15, where red, blue, and purple are visible in the noise:

```
private static const CHANNELS:uint = ➥
BitmapDataChannel.RED | BitmapDataChannel.BLUE;
```

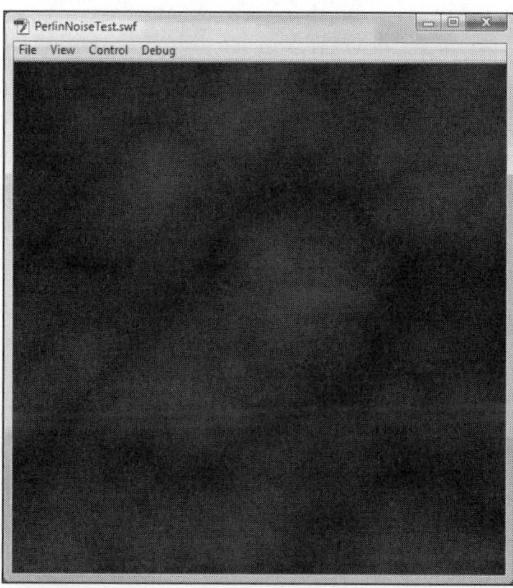

Figure 4-15.
The previous example with the red and blue color channels used, though not apparent when rendered in a grayscale screenshot

There are lots of permutations to play with, including the offset values. Tweak the numbers and settings to see what you can create. We'll be using Perlin noise in a lot of practical applications as we move forward in this book, so a strong familiarity with what the `perlinNoise()` method can produce is important.

Applying filters to BitmapData

In Chapter 2, we walked through the bitmap filters that are available in ActionScript, filters such as BlurFilter and ColorMatrixFilter. A lot of capabilities are bundled up in those filters that help tremendously in creating complex composite effects. If you recall, these filters could be applied to display objects using the `filters` property of DisplayObject. However, we can also apply these filters directly to images through BitmapData's `applyFilter()` method.

Using filters

Unlike applying a filter through DisplayObject's `filters` array, using `applyFilter()` permanently alters the pixels of an image, so its effects are said to be destructive, which means you can't undo the effect once it is applied. However, the benefits of this are that the filters do not need to be recalculated and reapplied if there is a transformation on the Bitmap or its data; plus, you can extract pixel data from and process further the actual filtered image, not on the underlying unfiltered image, as would happen if you only applied filters through the `filters` array on the Bitmap holding the bitmap data.

`applyFilter()` is a relatively (at least relative to some of the other methods we explore this chapter!) simple method with the following signature:

```
public function applyFilter(
  sourceBitmapData:BitmapData,
  sourceRect:Rectangle,
  destPoint:Point,
  filter:BitmapFilter
):void
```

And here are its parameters:

- `sourceBitmapData`: This is the image to which you wish to apply the filter, with the result shown in the destination image. Often, this is the same as the destination image, but you can specify a different image as the source.
- `sourceRect`: This is the region of the source image to which to apply the filter.
- `destPoint`: This specifies the top left pixel in the destination image that corresponds to the top left pixel from the sourceRect.
- `filter`: This is the BitmapFilter instance to apply to the source image.

We will explore a concrete application of this in the next section on the DisplacementMapFilter (and in some later examples this chapter), but an example of applying a blur to an image would look like the following:

```
bitmapData.applyFilter(
  bitmapData,
  bitmapData.rect,
  new Point(),
  new BlurFilter(10, 10)
);
```

Displacing pixels

At the end of Chapter 2, we briefly looked at the DisplacementMapFilter and how it could be used to distort pixels in an image, as shown in Figure 4-16.

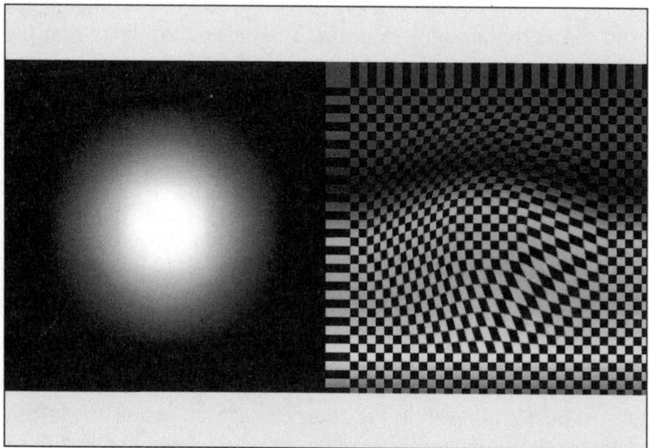

Figure 4-16. The example from Chapter 2 using the DisplacementMapFilter to distort a checkerboard using the map on the left

At the time, we put off a deep discussion of the filter since so much relied on knowledge of BitmapData, which we had yet to cover. Well, now it's covered. So let's get cracking on some displacing!

The signature of the DisplacementMapFilter's constructor is as follows:

```
DisplacementMapFilter(
  mapBitmap:BitmapData = null,
  mapPoint:Point = null,
  componentX:uint = 0,
  componentY:uint = 0,
  scaleX:Number = 0.0,
  scaleY:Number = 0.0,
  mode:String = "wrap",
  color:uint = 0,
  alpha:Number = 0.0
)
```

Take a breath. Here are its parameters:

- mapBitmap: This specifies the BitmapData instance to use to distort the pixels in the destination image.
- mapPoint: This is the top left pixel in the destination image that will correspond with the top left pixel of the displacement map.
- componentX: Use the brightness values from this color channel to distort the destination image on the x axis.
- componentY: Use the brightness values from this color channel to distort the destination image on the y axis.
- scaleX: This specifies the amount to distort the destination image on the x axis. We will look at how this is used shortly.
- scaleY: And this is the amount to distort the destination image on the y axis. We will look at how this is used shortly.
- mode: This filter mode determines how pixels out of range of the map will be rendered. This should be one of the constants of DisplacementMapFilterMode: WRAP will pull in pixels from the opposite side of the region. CLAMP will repeat pixels on the edge of the region. IGNORE will use the source pixel value. COLOR will use the color and alpha specified for the filter.
- color: Assign this color to out-of-range pixels if the mode has been set to COLOR.
- alpha: Assign this alpha value to out-of-range pixels if the mode has been set to COLOR.

You may recall from Chapter 2 that any pixels in the displacement map that are brighter than medium gray will push the pixels in the source image up and to the left. Any pixels in the map that are darker than medium gray will push pixels down and to the right. So how exactly are pixels pushed around based on these values of the displacement map? It all is handled by the following formula, as presented in the ActionScript 3.0 documentation:

```
dstPixel[x, y] = srcPixel[
  x + ((componentX(x, y) - 128) * scaleX) / 256,
  y + ((componentY(x, y) - 128) * scaleY) / 256
]
```

Crystal clear, isn't it? Let's break it down into its component parts to better understand it.

```
dstPixel[x, y]
```

This represents the final pixel at coordinate (x, y). For a pixel at coordinate (0, 0), we will use the formula to determine which pixel from the source image is moved into that position.

```
x + ((componentX(x, y) - 128) * scaleX) / 256
```

This is what will be used to determine the x position of the source pixel that will be used for the destination pixel. The 128 and 256 numbers are constants and the scaleX variable we will pass to the filter to control the amount of distortion, but where exactly does componentX(x, y) come from? This is the brightness value that is found at the (x, y) position of the specified color channel in the displacement map bitmap data, adjusting for the mapPoint offset. Remember that componentX (the parameter passed to the filter) is one of the four channels. If the mapPoint value we also passed is (0, 0), componentX(x, y) will return the brightness value of the specified channel at the (x, y) coordinate in the displacement map.

Let's imagine a displacement map that has a brightness value of 0x80 (128 in decimal) in the red channel at coordinate position (0, 0). If we pass a scaleX amount of 10 and the componentX value of BitmapDataChannel.RED, plugging these numbers into our formula gives us the following:

```
0 + ((componentX(0, 0) - 128) * 10) / 256
0 + ((128 - 128) * 10) / 256
0
```

If we were using the red channel for componentY as well, this would also result in 0. So in this case, since the value in that position in the map was medium gray, the destination pixel will be the same as the source pixel at the same position—there is no pushing around of this pixel.

If, however, the brightness value at (0, 0) is 0xFF, or 255 in decimal, the formula will give us something different:

```
0 + ((componentX(0, 0) - 128) * 5) / 256
0 + ((255 - 128) * 10) / 256
0 + (127 * 10) / 256
5
```

Again, if we also use the red channel for componentY, this will yield a value of 5 as well. This means that when we have a brightness value of full white and have set the scaleX and scaleY to be 10, the pixel that is drawn in the destination's (0, 0) position will be the pixel found at (5, 5) in the source.

What happens when the brightness value is 0x00, or black? Plugging into the formula shows us what we will get:

```
0 + ((componentX(0, 0) - 128) * 5) / 256
0 + ((0 - 128) * 10) / 256
0 + (-128 * 10) / 256
-5
```

In this case, the source coordinate that would be used is (–5, –5). Depending on the mode passed in, this will result in pixels from the opposite side wrapping over (WRAP), pixels at the edge repeated (CLAMP), the source pixel at the coordinate position with no distortion (IGNORE), or a specific color (COLOR). Of course, if the coordinate we were looking at happened to be in the middle of the image, say, at (100, 100), the source pixel that will be drawn into the destination would be the pixel found at (95, 95).

A lot can be achieved with displacement maps, though many times, a hefty amount of math is required in order to determine how a map should be drawn to displace pixels into the proper positions. There are several effects that can be achieved without heavy mathematical computation (by us anyway; I don't speak on behalf of the Flash Player), such as using Perlin noise to displace an image to create rippling water or crackling fire, an effect we will produce in Chapter 8. You can also create a displacement of pixels for glass distortion or for wrapping textures over objects, as I will demonstrate in the next example, with a map generated through the use of other filters.

Adding textures to objects

One simple application of a displacement map is to distort images to produce a pseudo-3D effect where it appears as if the displaced pixels are wrapped around an object. This works best for objects that contain small bevels and that have a flat surface, such as textfields, and with textures that are irregular where the distortion will not produce odd artifacts that are easily noticeable. One example of this effect is shown in Figure 4-17.

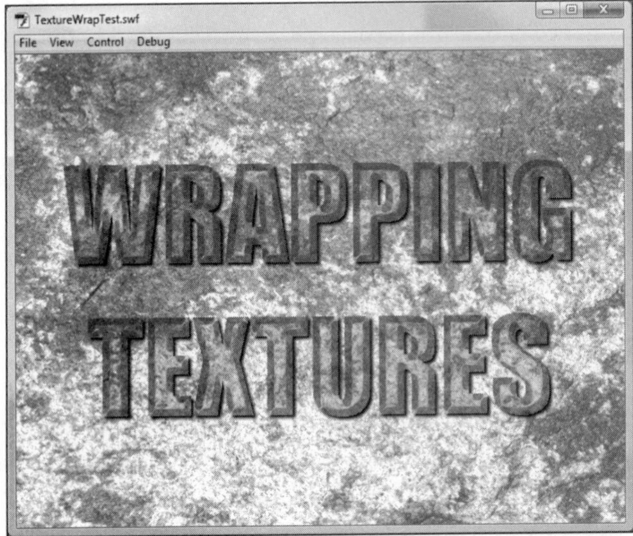

Figure 4-17. A stone texture applied to text with it distorted to match the bevel using a displacement map

The following class, found as `TextureWrapTest.as` in this chapter's files, produces this result. In this class I create a textfield and apply a bevel filter to it that will become the basis of the displacement map.

```
package {

  import flash.display.Bitmap;
  import flash.display.BitmapData;
  import flash.display.BitmapDataChannel;
  import flash.display.BlendMode;
  import flash.filters.BitmapFilterQuality;
  import flash.filters.BevelFilter;
  import flash.filters.DisplacementMapFilter;
  import flash.filters.DropShadowFilter;
```

```
  import flash.geom.ColorTransform;
  import flash.geom.Matrix;
  import flash.geom.Point;
  import flash.text.TextField;
  import flash.text.TextFieldAutoSize;
  import flash.text.TextFormat;
  import flash.text.TextFormatAlign;

  [SWF(width=640, height=480, backgroundColor=0x202020)]

  public class TextureWrapTest extends AbstractImageLoader {

    public function TextureWrapTest() {
      super("../../assets/stone.jpg");
    }

    override protected function runPostImageLoad():void {
      var width:Number = stage.stageWidth;
      var height:Number = stage.stageHeight;
      var map:BitmapData = new BitmapData(
        width,
        height,
        true,
        0x00000000
      );
      var texturedText:BitmapData = map.clone();
      var textfield:TextField = createTextField(0x808080, 0xFFFFFF);
      var matrix:Matrix = new Matrix();
      matrix.translate((width-textfield.width)/2, ➥
(height-textfield.height)/2);
      map.draw(textfield, matrix);
      var displacementMapFilter:DisplacementMapFilter =
        new DisplacementMapFilter(
          map,
          new Point(),
          BitmapDataChannel.RED,
          BitmapDataChannel.RED,
          10,
          10
        );
      var bitmapData:BitmapData = _loadedBitmap.bitmapData;
      texturedText.applyFilter(bitmapData, texturedText.rect,➥
new Point(), displacementMapFilter);
      var alphaChannel:uint = BitmapDataChannel.ALPHA;
      texturedText.copyChannel(
        map,
        map.rect,
        new Point(),
        alphaChannel,
```

```
          alphaChannel
        );
        textfield = createTextField(0xFFFFFF, 0x000000);
        map.draw(textfield, matrix);
        var colorTransform:ColorTransform = ➥
  new ColorTransform(1, 1, 1, .4);
        texturedText.draw(map, null, colorTransform, BlendMode.MULTIPLY);
        texturedText.applyFilter(texturedText, texturedText.rect,➥
  new Point(), new DropShadowFilter());
        bitmapData.colorTransform(
          bitmapData.rect,
          new ColorTransform(1.2, 1.2, 1.2)
        );
        addChild(_loadedBitmap);
        addChild(new Bitmap(texturedText));
      }

      private function createTextField(
        textColor:uint,
        highlightColor:uint
      ):TextField {
        var textfield:TextField = new TextField();
        textfield.autoSize = TextFieldAutoSize.LEFT;
        textfield.multiline = true;
        var textFormat:TextFormat = ➥
  new TextFormat("Impact", 130, textColor);
        textFormat.align = TextFormatAlign.CENTER;
        textfield.defaultTextFormat = textFormat;
        textfield.text = "WRAPPING\nTEXTURES";
        var bevelFilter:BevelFilter = new BevelFilter(8, 225);
        bevelFilter.highlightColor = highlightColor;
        bevelFilter.strength = 4;
        bevelFilter.blurX = bevelFilter.blurY = 2;
        bevelFilter.quality = BitmapFilterQuality.HIGH;
        textfield.filters = [bevelFilter];
        return textfield;
      }

    }

  }
```

To better understand what's going on, first have a look at `createTextField()`, in which I create a new TextField instance with the following lines:

```
var textfield:TextField = new TextField();
textfield.autoSize = TextFieldAutoSize.LEFT;
textfield.multiline = true;
var textFormat:TextFormat = new TextFormat("Impact", 130, textColor);
```

```
textFormat.align = TextFormatAlign.CENTER;
textfield.defaultTextFormat = textFormat;
textfield.text = "WRAPPING\nTEXTURES";
```

If you do not have the font Impact installed on your system, replace this font name with any font containing wide characters that you have available.

The text color is controlled through a parameter since, in the initial call to `createTextField()`, I wish to have the face of the text appear middle gray so that there will be no distortion to that part of the image when the text is used as a displacement map. A subsequent call to `createTextField()` specifies a color of white so that I may overlay the text with a brighter face.

The lines that follow the TextField creation apply a bevel filter to the field.

```
var bevelFilter:BevelFilter = new BevelFilter(8, 225);
bevelFilter.highlightColor = highlightColor;
bevelFilter.strength = 4;
bevelFilter.blurX = bevelFilter.blurY = 2;
bevelFilter.quality = BitmapFilterQuality.HIGH;
textfield.filters = [bevelFilter];
```

Here, `highlightColor` is specified in the parameters for the method so that when the first textfield is created as a displacement map, the color might be white. Then when the method is called a second time to create a textfield to overlay the distorted image, the highlight color can be made black. The other settings create a nice hard chiseled look for the text. Note that the rotation is set to 225. This results in the initial displacement map with white (the highlight color) being on the lower right of the text, which we know will result in pixels being pushed up and to the left, and black being on the upper left, which results in pixels being pulled down and to the right. Since the face of the text is medium gray (0x808080), this combination of shadow and highlight will effectively pull the texture around the beveling of the text.

Back in `runPostImageLoad()`, two BitmapData instances are created, one for the displacement map and one to draw the distorted texture into using the map. Both are transparent by default.

```
var map:BitmapData = new BitmapData(width, height, true, 0x00000000);
var texturedText:BitmapData = map.clone();
```

I next call `createTextField()` to create the textfield with the bevel applied to it that will act as the displacement map for the stone texture. I draw this textfield into the map BitmapData instance, scaling it up to fill the stage (and to match the size of the loaded stone texture).

```
      var textfield:TextField = createTextField(0x808080, 0xFFFFFF);
      var matrix:Matrix = new Matrix();
      matrix.translate((width-textfield.width)/2, ➥
(height-textfield.height)/2);
      map.draw(textfield, matrix);
```

With the map ready, I can create the DisplacementMapFilter and apply it to the loaded stone texture, drawing the results into the texturedText BitmapData instance.

```
      var displacementMapFilter:DisplacementMapFilter =
        new DisplacementMapFilter(
          map,
          new Point(),
          BitmapDataChannel.RED,
          BitmapDataChannel.RED,
          10,
          10
        );
        var bitmapData:BitmapData = _loadedBitmap.bitmapData;
        texturedText.applyFilter(bitmapData, texturedText.rect,➥
new Point(), displacementMapFilter);
```

This will result in the texture becoming distorted by the text displacement map. To remove all of the pixels that do not correspond to the text, I copy the alpha channel from the map into the distorted image, which will leave only the pixels where the text was drawn opaque. All other pixels will become transparent. We will be looking more closely at the copyChannel() method in a later section.

```
var alphaChannel:uint = BitmapDataChannel.ALPHA;
texturedText.copyChannel(
  map,
  map.rect,
  new Point(),
  alphaChannel,
  alphaChannel
);
```

The final steps are just some aesthetic tweaks. A new textfield is created with a white face and a dark beveling all around. This is drawn into the map BitmapData instance so that it can be applied as an overlay, using a blend mode of MULTIPLY, to the distorted text to produce some 3D lighting.

```
textfield = createTextField(0xFFFFFF, 0x000000);
map.draw(textfield, matrix);
var colorTransform:ColorTransform = new ColorTransform(1, 1, 1, .4);
texturedText.draw(map, null, colorTransform, BlendMode.MULTIPLY);
```

Finally, a drop shadow is added the distorted text to also help pop it out from the background. That background is also brightened slightly for this same purpose using a ColorTransform, then the loaded texture is added to the stage and the distorted text is added above it.

```
      texturedText.applyFilter(texturedText, texturedText.rect,➥
new Point(), new DropShadowFilter());
      bitmapData.colorTransform(
```

```
    bitmapData.rect,
    new ColorTransform(1.2, 1.2, 1.2)
  );
  addChild(_loadedBitmap);
  addChild(new Bitmap(texturedText));
```

This same technique, with some minor tweaks depending on the application, could be reused in a number of situations, from texturing a whole interface to creating effects like glass distortion, as is demonstrated in the file `GlassEffect.as` included with this chapter's files.

Creating a fisheye lens

More complex effects can be achieved using the DisplacementMapFilter with some more intense math applied. Instead of walking through that intense math, I will point you to a great collection of displacement methods that do some of that for you, found at `http://code.google.com/p/as3filters/`. Rakuto Furutani has provided an as3.Filter class under an MIT license that includes a number of methods to create displacement maps for twirling, pinching, and bulging an image. It is worth taking a quick look here to see just what can be achieved with the built-in displacement map.

The following class, FisheyeLensTest, uses a modified version of Rakuto's code to distort the underlying image based on the current mouse position. If you open and test this class, or run the accompanying SWF, you will see something like Figure 4-18.

Figure 4-18. A checkerboard dynamically displaced with a fisheye lens that follows the mouse position

Here's the code for Figure 4-18:

```
package {

  import flash.display.Bitmap;
  import flash.display.BitmapData;
  import flash.display.BitmapDataChannel;
  import flash.events.MouseEvent;
  import flash.filters.DisplacementMapFilter;
  import flash.filters.DisplacementMapFilterMode;
  import flash.geom.Point;

  [SWF(width=640, height=480, backgroundColor=0x202020)]

  public class FisheyeLensTest extends AbstractImageLoader {

    private static const DIAMETER:uint = 200;

    private var _bitmapData:BitmapData;
    private var _lens:BitmapData;
    private var _lensBitmap:Bitmap;

    public function FisheyeLensTest() {
      super("../../assets/checkers.jpg");
    }

    override protected function runPostImageLoad():void {
      _bitmapData = _loadedBitmap.bitmapData.clone();
      _lens = createLens(DIAMETER);
      _lensBitmap = new Bitmap(_lens);
      _lensBitmap.visible = false;
      applyLens();
      addChild(_loadedBitmap);
      addChild(_lensBitmap);
      stage.addEventListener(MouseEvent.MOUSE_MOVE, onStageMouseMove);
      stage.addEventListener(MouseEvent.MOUSE_DOWN, onStageMouseDown);
      stage.addEventListener(MouseEvent.MOUSE_UP, onStageMouseUp);
    }

    private function createLens(
      diameter:uint,
      amount:Number=0.8
    ):BitmapData {
      var lens:BitmapData = new BitmapData(
        diameter,
        diameter,
        false,
        0xFF808080
      );
```

```
      var center:Number = diameter/2;
      var radius:Number = center;
      for (var y:uint=0; y < diameter; ++y) {
        var ycoord:int = y - center;
        for (var x:uint = 0; x < diameter; ++x) {
          var xcoord:int = x - center;
          var distance:Number = ➥
Math.sqrt(xcoord*xcoord + ycoord*ycoord);
          if (distance < radius) {
            var t:Number = ➥
Math.pow(Math.sin(Math.PI/2 * distance/radius), amount);
            var dx:Number = xcoord * (t - 1)/diameter;
            var dy:Number = ycoord * (t - 1)/diameter;
            var blue:uint = 0x80 + dx * 0xFF;
            var green:uint = 0x80 + dy * 0xFF;
            lens.setPixel(x, y, green << 8 | blue);
          }
        }
      }
      return lens;
    }

    private function applyLens():void {
      var displacementMapFilter:DisplacementMapFilter =
        new DisplacementMapFilter(
          _lens,
          new Point(stage.mouseX-DIAMETER/2, stage.mouseY-DIAMETER/2),
          BitmapDataChannel.BLUE,
          BitmapDataChannel.GREEN,
          DIAMETER,
          DIAMETER,
          DisplacementMapFilterMode.CLAMP
        );
      _loadedBitmap.bitmapData.applyFilter(
        _bitmapData,
        _bitmapData.rect,
        new Point(),
        displacementMapFilter
      );
    }

    private function onStageMouseMove(event:MouseEvent):void {
      _lensBitmap.x = stage.mouseX - DIAMETER/2;
      _lensBitmap.y = stage.mouseY - DIAMETER/2;
      applyLens();
      event.updateAfterEvent();
    }
```

```
        private function onStageMouseDown(event:MouseEvent):void {
          _lensBitmap.visible = true;
        }

        private function onStageMouseUp(event:MouseEvent):void {
          _lensBitmap.visible = false;
        }

      }

    }
```

In the runPostImageImage() method, I save a clone of the loaded bitmap into the _lensBitmap property. createLens() is called to create a new BitmapData instance drawn to provide the distortion of a fisheye lens. This bitmap data is added through a Bitmap to the display list, but hidden. This is done so that at any time the user may toggle its visibility by clicking the stage to see what the map looks like that is creating the distortion.

applyLens() is called to apply the lens distortion the first time, and the loaded bitmap and the lens are both added to the display list. Three listeners are set up for when the mouse moves, the stage is clicked, and the mouse is released. The MOUSE_DOWN and MOUSE_UP handlers simply toggle the visibility of the lens. The MOUSE_MOVE handler calls applyLens() to update the image based on the current mouse position.

Within applyLens(), a new DisplacementMapFilter is created with the lens bitmap data. You can see the BLUE channel is used for distorting the x axis, while the GREEN channel is used to distort the y. This filter is applied to the data in _loadedBitmap, but you will notice that the source is actually our saved _bitmapData. This is so each time the image is distorted it uses the original loaded data, not the data that has been distorted in previous calls.

Finally, let's take a little tour of the createLens() method that creates the lens in the first place. Within this method a new BitmapData instance is created with the desired diameter and a default color of medium gray, which we know will result in no distortion.

```
var lens:BitmapData = new BitmapData(
  diameter,
  diameter,
  false,
  0xFF808080
);
```

Then, after assigning values to center and radius (which are equal but kept as separate to make some of the equations more understandable), I set up an outer for loop to run through all the rows of the bitmap data. ycoord holds the distance from center of the current row each iteration of the outer loop. The inner loop runs through all columns in the bitmap data. xcoord holds the distance from center of the current column.

```
var center:Number = diameter/2;
var radius:Number = center;
```

```
for (var y:uint=0; y < diameter; ++y) {
  var ycoord:int = y - center;
  for (var x:uint = 0; x < diameter; ++x) {
    var xcoord:int = x - center;
```

Now comes the work. First, the distance from the center of the current coordinates is calculated using the good old Pythagorean theorem. Only if this distance is within the radius will any color need to be drawn, since those outside of the sphere of distortion will have the default medium gray.

```
var distance:Number = Math.sqrt(xcoord*xcoord + ycoord*ycoord);
if (distance < radius) {
```

The next several steps use that intense math I mentioned previously to determine what color to draw at each coordinate. `t` will be a percentage between 0 and 1 based on the distance from `center` and the amount of distortion. The `Math.sin()` calculation is what creates the distortion using standard trigonometry to determine a number between 0 (at the center of the circle) and 1 (at the radius of the circle). When the amount is set to 1, `t` will equal the number returned in the `Math.sin()` call, since that is simply raising the result to the power of 1. If the amount was 0, `t` would equal 1, since raising the result to the power of 0 will always give us 1. With `t=1`, you can see that the `dx` and `dy` variables would be 0 and the blue and green colors used in `setPixel()` would be medium gray.

```
var t:Number = Math.pow(Math.sin(Math.PI/2 * distance/radius), amount);
var dx:Number = xcoord * (t - 1)/diameter;
var dy:Number = ycoord * (t - 1)/diameter;
var blue:uint = 0x80 + dx * 0xFF;
var green:uint = 0x80 + dy * 0xFF;
lens.setPixel(x, y, green << 8 | blue);
```

When the amount is greater than 0, though, as with the default 0.8, `t` will adhere closely to the results of the `Math.sin()` calculation. In that case, dx and dy will hold small positive or negative values (depending on the coordinate position relative to center) that will tint the blue and green colors passed to the `setPixel()` method, and so will result in pushing the pixels at those coordinate positions.

A lot can be accomplished with the DisplacementMapFilter by rolling up your sleeves and dusting off your old trigonometry and geometry books. Similar math will also serve you well as you experiment with Pixel Bender, which we get into next chapter. As the last example showed, though, math isn't always necessary to achieve some pretty cool effects with displacement maps, and we'll prove that more in later examples in this book. But first, we have plenty of exciting aspects of BitmapData left to explore.

Performing channel operations

Directing a movie would be an extremely difficult task if a director could not communicate with actors independently and could only give direction to the cast as a whole. Mixing down a song without access to independent tracks would be unthinkable in a modern music studio. With BitmapData in ActionScript, thankfully we aren't limited to only being able to affect composite image data but instead have access to each individual color channel that makes up the image.

Most of the methods we've explored thus far have been applied to all channels of an image or use the data from all channels as a single composite. There are several methods, though, that deal more specifically with individual channels within an image, and the ability to affect these channels independently will aid us tremendously as we create effects.

Copying channels

You saw last chapter how pixels can be copied from one image into another using copyPixels(). A similar function, copyChannel(), provides this ability for channels so that a single channel can be copied from one BitmapData instance into another, or one channel of a BitmapData instance can be copied into another channel in the same instance.

```
public function copyChannel(
  sourceBitmapData:BitmapData,
  sourceRect:Rectangle,
  destPoint:Point,
  sourceChannel:uint,
  destChannel:uint
):void
```

Here is how the parameters break down:

- sourceBitmapData: The source image from which to copy the channel can be the same as the destination image if you wish to copy one channel of an image into another channel of the same image.
- sourceRect: This is the region of the image's channel to copy. To copy the entire image, you could use the source bitmap data's rect property.
- destPoint: These coordinates of the top left pixel in the destination image map to the top left pixel of the source image's copied region. If the dimensions of the two images match and you are copying over the entire channel, you would pass a Point instance with (0, 0) as the x and y coordinates.
- sourceChannel: This channel to copy from the source bitmap data should be a constant of the BitmapDataChannel class, such as BitmapDataChannel.RED.
- destChannel: This is the channel in which to copy the source bitmap data's channel.

Copying channels within an instance

As we discussed in the previous chapter, a single channel in an image is composed of 8-bit pixels containing values from 0 to 255. If rendered to the screen, this would appear as a grayscale image. It is only when multiple channels are combined that 24-bit (or 32-bit) pixels produce a color image. In Photoshop, you can see these grayscale representations of an image in the Channels palette, as shown in Figure 4-19.

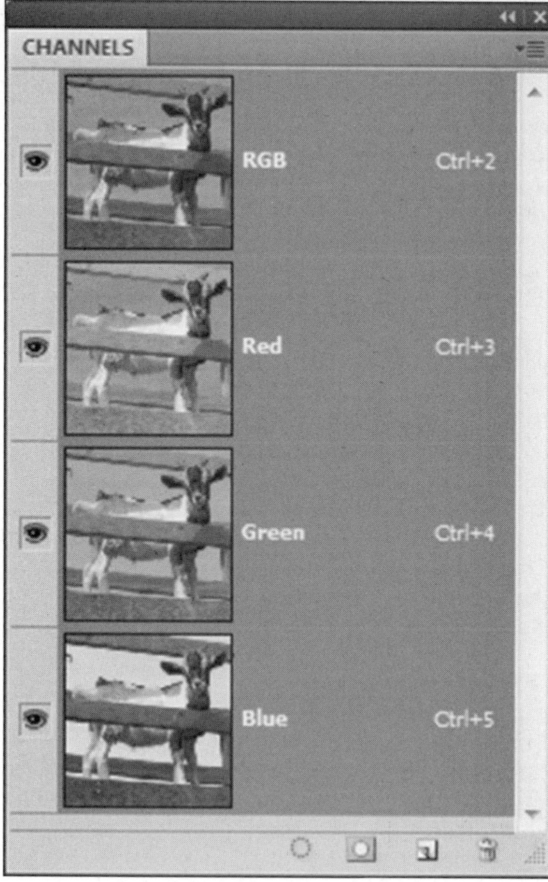

Figure 4-19.
The Channels palette in Photoshop showing the grayscale representations of the color channels

You can create your own version of the channels 8-bit visualization by copying a single channel, like red, into the other two color channels of an image. With the same brightness values used in all three channels, you will get a grayscale image that shows the value of the single channel copied from the composite image. The following code, found as `CopyChannelTest.as` in this chapter's files, does just that:

```
package {

  import flash.display.Bitmap;
  import flash.display.BitmapData;
  import flash.display.BitmapDataChannel;
  import flash.geom.Point;

  [SWF(width=900, height=300, backgroundColor=0x000000)]
```

```
public class CopyChannelTest extends AbstractImageLoader {

  private var _channels:Vector.<uint>;

  public function CopyChannelTest() {
    super("../../assets/goat.jpg");
    _channels = new Vector.<uint>();
    _channels.push(BitmapDataChannel.RED);
    _channels.push(BitmapDataChannel.GREEN);
    _channels.push(BitmapDataChannel.BLUE);
  }

  override protected function runPostImageLoad():void {
    var bitmapData:BitmapData = _loadedBitmap.bitmapData;
    var red:BitmapData = bitmapData.clone();
    var green:BitmapData = bitmapData.clone();
    var blue:BitmapData = bitmapData.clone();
    createChannelBitmap(red, BitmapDataChannel.RED, 0);
    createChannelBitmap(green, BitmapDataChannel.GREEN, red.width);
    createChannelBitmap(blue, BitmapDataChannel.BLUE, red.width*2);
    bitmapData.dispose();
  }

  private function createChannelBitmap(
    bitmapData:BitmapData,
    channelToCopy:uint,
    x:Number
  ):void {
    for each (var channel:uint in _channels) {
      if (channel != channelToCopy) {
        bitmapData.copyChannel(
          bitmapData,
          bitmapData.rect,
          new Point(),
          channelToCopy,
          channel
        );
      }
    }
    var bitmap:Bitmap = new Bitmap(bitmapData);
    bitmap.x = x;
    addChild(bitmap);
  }

 }

}
```

I have reused the handy AbstractImageLoader base class once again to load in an image. In the constructor for the class, I set up a new vector containing all three BitmapDataChannel color channel values so that I can iterate over them later. The `runPostImageLoad()` method clones the loaded bitmap data three times, once for each channel, and passes each to the `createChannelBitmap()` method along with the single channel to copy into the other two channels and the x position on the stage of the final bitmap. Finally, within that method, I dispose of the original bitmap data since it is no longer needed.

The `createChannelBitmap()` is where BitmapData's `copyChannel()` method is called. This is done within a loop that iterates over each channel, skipping the one from which I am copying. For the other two channels, I copy in the `channelToCopy` data. This means that, for the red bitmap data, I will copy the `RED` channel into the `BLUE` and `GREEN` channels. With the channel data copied, I create a new Bitmap instance, pass in the new bitmap data, and then add this to the display list at the specified x position.

The result of this is shown in Figure 4-20, with the left image showing the red channel's data, the center image showing the green channel's data, and the right image showing the blue channel's data.

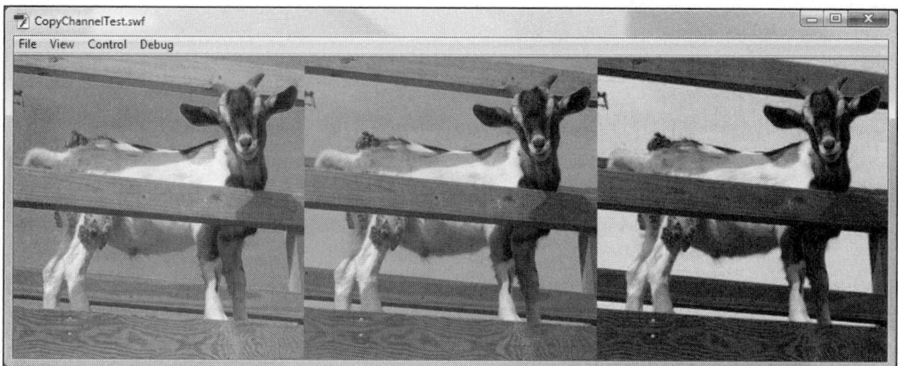

Figure 4-20. The three channels of the image represented in their own BitmapData instances, with red on the left, green in the middle, and blue on the right

Copying channels between instances

You can also copy channels from one image into another. One useful application of this is to copy alpha information from one image into another, as we did in the TextureWrapTest example. As another example, consider that you have loaded an image into your application that does not contain alpha information and you want to create a border effect. You can, of course, apply a mask to a Bitmap instance containing the image, but if you need to further manipulate the bitmap data going forward and you need the manipulations to also apply to the alpha, the better option is to bake the alpha mask into the bitmap data itself. `copyChannel()` will do this for you.

Have a look at Figure 4-21. On the left is a shape that is drawn through the drawing API, and on the right is a loaded image with the alpha from the shape used as a mask.

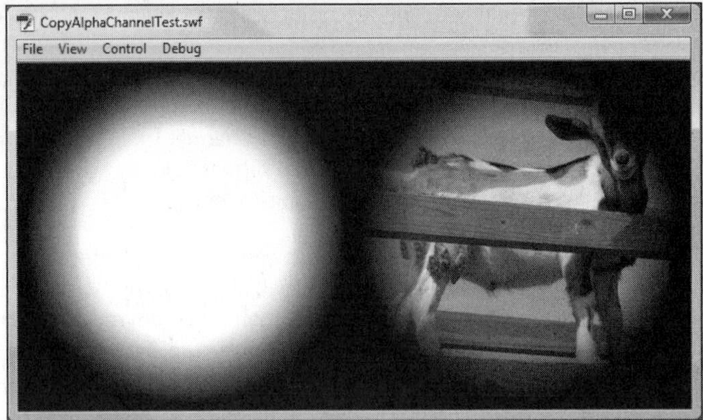

Figure 4-21. An alpha channel copied from the image on the left, created with the drawing API, applied to the image on the right

The following class, CopyAlphaChannelTest, which can be found in this chapter's files, shows how this is accomplished:

```
package {

  import flash.display.Bitmap;
  import flash.display.BitmapData;
  import flash.display.BitmapDataChannel;
  import flash.display.Shape;
  import flash.filters.BlurFilter;
  import flash.geom.Point;

  [SWF(width=600, height=300, backgroundColor=0x000000)]

  public class CopyAlphaChannelTest extends AbstractImageLoader {

    public function CopyAlphaChannelTest() {
      super("../../assets/goat.jpg");
    }

    override protected function runPostImageLoad():void {
      var bitmapData:BitmapData = _loadedBitmap.bitmapData;
      var width:Number = bitmapData.width;
      var height:Number = bitmapData.height;
      var bitmapCopy:BitmapData = new BitmapData(
        width,
        height,
        true,
        0x00000000
      );
```

```
            bitmapCopy.copyPixels(bitmapData, bitmapData.rect, new Point());
            bitmapData.dispose();
            var shape:Shape = createMask(width, height);
            var shapeBitmapData:BitmapData = new BitmapData(
              width,
              height,
              true,
              0x00000000
            );
            shapeBitmapData.draw(shape);
            bitmapCopy.copyChannel(
              shapeBitmapData,
              shapeBitmapData.rect,
              new Point(),
              BitmapDataChannel.ALPHA,
              BitmapDataChannel.ALPHA
            );
            _loadedBitmap.bitmapData = bitmapCopy;
            _loadedBitmap.x = width;
            addChild(_loadedBitmap);
          }

          private function createMask(width:Number, height:Number):Shape {
            var shape:Shape = new Shape();
            shape.graphics.beginFill(0xFFFFFF);
            shape.graphics.drawEllipse(30, 30, width-60, height-60);
            shape.graphics.endFill();
            shape.filters = [new BlurFilter(50, 50)];
            addChild(shape);
            return shape;
          }

        }

      }
```

Yet again, the AbstractImageLoader base class steps up like a good sport and handles the underlying loading of the image. Once the image is loaded, `runPostImageLoad()` is invoked. After storing some property values in variables at the top of the method, I create a new BitmapData instance that is the same size as the loaded image but that can contain 32-bit pixel values. I copy the pixels from the loaded image into this copy. This is necessary in this instance, since the loaded image is a JPG without any alpha information. If I just copied an alpha channel into the image, it would still not render the opacity. Creating a new BitmapData instance and copying the original data into it solves this problem. Once the original is copied, I can dispose of it to save memory.

The next step is to create the mask, which is done in the aptly named `createMask()` method. There, I draw an ellipse in a new Shape instance and blur it. This is added to the display list so we can see the mask.

Back in `runPostImageLoad()`, I create one more BitmapData instance in which I draw the new mask. Since `copyChannel()` only works with BitmapData instances, I can't just use the shape as is but must draw its pixel information into a BitmapData instance. With that done, I can call `copyChannel()` and copy the alpha information from the mask into the alpha channel of the loaded image. I position this composited image to the right of the mask shape on the stage, and the work is complete.

Extracting channel information

In the CopyChannelTest example, you saw how we can visualize channel values as a grayscale version of the image. Another way of visualizing this data is through a histogram, which is basically a column chart that shows the frequency of each brightness value for all pixels in an image. Photoshop has a Histogram palette, shown in Figure 4-22, specifically for the purpose of displaying histograms of each channel and the composite image. In these charts, the x axis represents the brightness value, from 0 to 255, with the y axis showing the number of pixels that hold each brightness value. By reading histograms, you can easily see how brightness values are distributed throughout an image and then use this information for setting levels to better redistribute the values.

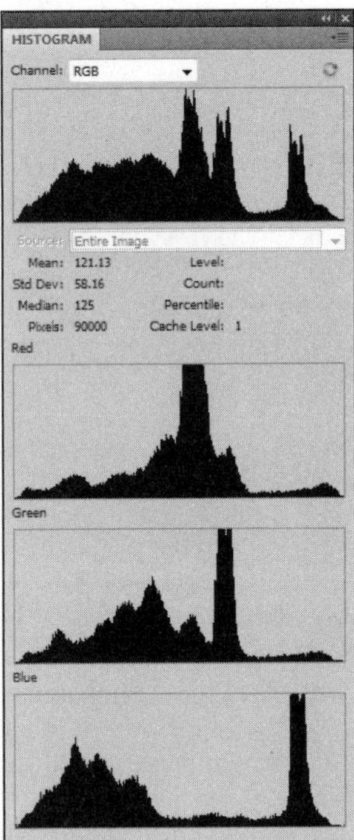

Figure 4-22. The Photoshop Histogram palette, showing the distribution of pixels in each channel

We can access the pixel brightness values and create histograms from this data in ActionScript as well using BitmapData's `histogram()` method, which contains the following signature:

```
public function histogram(
  hRect:Rectangle = null
):Vector.<Vector.<Number>>
```

A single parameter—how refreshing! Here's what this parameter signifies:

- hRect: This is the region of the image from which you want to read the brightness values. If no rectangle is passed in, the whole image is assessed.

And you're not reading that return data type incorrectly. It really is as odd looking as that. What the histogram() method returns is a vector of four vectors. Each of these four vectors holds data for a single channel: red, green, blue, and alpha. This data for a channel is stored as a vector of numbers, 256 values to be precise, with each index holding the number of pixels in that channel that contain the corresponding brightness value. For instance, the red vector will have 256 values stored in it. The value at the index position 0 will hold the number of pixels that have no brightness in the red channel, while the value at the index position 255 will hold the number of pixels that have full brightness.

Using this histogram information you can create your own visualization of the channel data, as shown in Figure 4-23.

Figure 4-23. The histogram of the image on the left represented as overlapping columns on the right

This is accomplished in the following class, HistogramTest, in this chapter's files:

```
package {

  import flash.display.Bitmap;
  import flash.display.BitmapData;
  import flash.display.BitmapDataChannel;
  import flash.geom.Point;
  import flash.geom.Rectangle;

  [SWF(width=600, height=300, backgroundColor=0x000000)]
```

```
public class HistogramTest extends AbstractImageLoader {

  public function HistogramTest() {
    super("../../assets/goat.jpg");
  }

  override protected function runPostImageLoad():void {
    var bitmapData:BitmapData = _loadedBitmap.bitmapData;
    addChild(_loadedBitmap);
    var histogram:Vector.<Vector.<Number>> = bitmapData.histogram();
    var maxPixels:uint = getMaxPixels(histogram);
    var histogramData:BitmapData = new BitmapData(
      256,
      256,
      false,
      0xFF000000
    );
    drawChannelData(
      maxPixels,
      histogramData,
      histogram[0],
      BitmapDataChannel.RED
    );
    drawChannelData(
      maxPixels,
      histogramData,
      histogram[1],
      BitmapDataChannel.GREEN
    );
    drawChannelData(
      maxPixels,
      histogramData,
      histogram[2],
      BitmapDataChannel.BLUE
    );
    var histogramBitmap:Bitmap = new Bitmap(histogramData);
    histogramBitmap.x = bitmapData.width + (bitmapData.width-256)/2;
    histogramBitmap.y = (bitmapData.height-256)/2;
    addChild(histogramBitmap);
  }

  private function getMaxPixels(
    histogram:Vector.<Vector.<Number>>
  ):uint {
    var maxPixels:uint = 0;
    var x:uint;
    var channel:Vector.<Number>;
```

```
      for (var i:uint = 0; i < 3; i++) {
        channel = histogram[i];
        for (x = 0; x < 256; x++) {
          maxPixels = Math.max(channel[x], maxPixels);
        }
      }
      return maxPixels;
    }

    private function drawChannelData(
      maxPixels:uint,
      bitmapData:BitmapData,
      channelData:Vector.<Number>,
      channel:uint
    ):void {
      var channelBitmapData:BitmapData = bitmapData.clone();
      var y:Number;
      for (var x:uint = 0; x < 256; x++) {
        y = channelData[x]/maxPixels*256;
        channelBitmapData.fillRect(
          new Rectangle(x, 256-y, 1, y),
          0xFFFFFFFF
        );
      }
      bitmapData.copyChannel(
        channelBitmapData,
        channelBitmapData.rect,
        new Point(),
        channel,
        channel
      );
    }

  }

}
```

After the bitmap is loaded, which of course is handled in the base class, I add it to the stage as is. Then, in the third line of runPostImageLoad(), I call histogram() on the BitmapData instance. The vector returned by this method is immediately passed to a custom getMaxPixels() method, which runs through the three color channels (skipping the alpha channel, which is not represented in this example) and determines the maximum number of pixels that appears for all of the brightness values across all channels. This maximum value will be used as the top of the histogram chart.

With the maxPixels value assigned, I make three calls to drawChannelData(), passing in the maxPixels, a 256×256 BitmapData instance I will use to show the brightness values, the channel vector from the histogram vector that I wish to draw, and the color channel

I want to draw the data into for the chart. The last several lines of runPostImageLoad() simply add the histogram image to the display list.

Now, let's take a closer look at drawChannelData(), which is called once for each color channel. The first thing I do in this method is clone the image I will be drawing into. This is done to make it easier to draw into a single channel in the final image. By creating a new image to first draw into, I can simply draw white columns using fillRect() and use copyChannel() to copy over just a single channel into the final composite image. Using this method, I can create a histogram chart with overlapping data (alternatively, you could do as Photoshop does and create three separate histogram charts, one for each color channel).

The for loop that follows runs through all 256 values in the channel. The height of the column is calculated using the brightness value divided by the maximum pixels in order to determine a percentage between 0 and 1. This percentage is then multiplied by the height of the chart, which is 256 pixels.

```
y = channelData[x]/maxPixels*256;
```

Because I will be drawing the columns from the bottom of the chart, the Rectangle instance passed to fillRect() has its y position set to the height of the chart minus the height of the column. This is given a color of full white so that when I copy over just a single channel into the final chart, the channel will have a full brightness value for the column as well, no matter which channel is being copied over.

```
channelBitmapData.fillRect(new Rectangle(x, 256-y, 1, y), 0xFFFFFFFF);
```

Finally, once the chart for a single channel is drawn in drawChannelData(), I use copyChannel() to copy the single channel into the composite chart image. Doing this for each of three channels produces the overlap of data that allows us to see all the channel data in a single, readable histogram image. Rainbows are pretty.

Beyond making pretty rainbow pictures, histogram data could be used to perform an automatic adjustment of an image's levels. The technique would involve generating the histogram data and analyzing the output to determine where the majority of the pixels lay in the full brightness range to set new black-and-white points of a level adjustment.

Setting thresholds

threshold() is probably one of the most complex methods that BitmapData has to offer. This method tests pixels in an image against a color value specified in the parameters and colors the pixels that pass the test with a specific color. The test depends on the mathematical operation passed to the method. For instance, you can test for a color value in an image that is equal to a specified color and recolor all pixels that have that color. Alternatively, you can recolor all pixels that are not equal to a specified color. You can also find pixels that have a greater or lesser brightness value than the specified color. And, for all these tests, you can test against all channels of a pixel or a combination of channels.

Using this method and testing an image's pixels for specific color values, you can recolor a certain color or color range in an image. Another common use is chroma keying using a blue screen or green screen, where you remove a certain color from an image and replace it with another image.

The signature of threshold is an insight into the method's complexity:

```
public function threshold(
  sourceBitmapData:BitmapData,
  sourceRect:Rectangle,
  destPoint:Point,
  operation:String,
  threshold:uint,
  color:uint = 0,
  mask:uint = 0xFFFFFFFF,
  copySource:Boolean = false
):uint
```

The key to understanding `threshold()` is getting a firm grasp on each of its parameters. Here they are explained:

- `sourceBitmapData`: This is the source image that you wish to test for pixel values, and does not have to be the image that you wish to apply a threshold to (and from which you are calling the `threshold()` method). This allows you to copy source pixels from another image if they meet a certain criteria. For instance, if you had a bitmap containing red text that you wished to apply to another image, you could call `threshold()` on that image and pass in the text bitmap as the source, specifying that any red pixels should be copied over.
- `sourceRect`: This is the region of the source image to test against. To test the entirety of the source, you would pass the source's `rect` property.
- `destPoint`: The top left pixel in the destination image that maps to the top left pixel in the region specified by the `sourceRect` parameter.
- `operation`: This operation should be performed during the test against pixels and can be any one of the strings `"<"`, `"<="`, `">"`, `">="`, `"=="`, or `"!="`. For instance, if you were only interested in pixels being exactly equal to a certain color passing the threshold test, you would pass in `"=="`. We will discuss how this value is used in the equations for a test after we cover the parameters.
- `threshold`: This is the 32-bit color value that pixels are tested against. We will discuss how this value is used in the equations for a test after we cover the parameters.
- `color`: This is the 32-bit color to assign to pixels that pass the threshold test. For instance, if you are doing chroma keying, you can set this color to be fully transparent, 0x00000000. Your image with the specified color removed can then be overlaid on top of another image with the desired background.

- `mask`: This value can be used as a mask to isolate the threshold test to certain color channels. Basically, for the channels you wish to test against, you would use a value of FF, and for those you wish to ignore, you would use 00. For instance, to look at only the red channel in the threshold test, you would pass 0x00FF0000. We will discuss how this value is used in the equations for a test after we cover the parameters.
- copySource: Use this to specify whether pixels that fail the threshold test are copied from the source image to the destination image. If this value is `false`, no pixels are copied from the source to the destination, and the destination's pixels that fail the threshold test remain unchanged.

Several of the parameters passed to `threshold()`—`operation`, `threshold`, `color`, and `mask`—are used together in the test for pixels in the source image. The logic of the test, as is listed in the Adobe documentation, follows:

1. If `((pixelValue & mask) operation (threshold & mask))`, set the pixel to `color`.
2. Otherwise, if copySource `== true`, set the pixel to the corresponding pixel value from sourceBitmap.

What we have here are our bitwise operations like we explored in previous chapters, and just as in previous chapters, they are much more easily understood with numbers and examples than they are with English explanations.

Imagine we have an image with a green screen background, and this green color, by some fluke of nature and photo technology, is a pure 0xFF00FF00 (remember, that's 32-bit with full opacity) with no variation. In this case, we would want to isolate this single color and set all pixels in the image that were this color to be fully transparent. This gives us three of our desired values.

```
var operation:String = "==";
var threshold:uint = 0xFF00FF00;
var color:uint = 0x00000000;
```

For the mask, at this point, all we care about are the green and alpha channels, so we will set the mask value to isolate just these channels.

```
var mask:uint = 0xFF00FF00;
```

If we pass these four parameters to `threshold()`, the method will run through each pixel in an image and compare the pixel value in an equation with our parameters. Let's take a look at when a red pixel is assessed. `(pixelValue & mask)` looks like the following when represented (and calculated) in binary:

```
  11111111 11111111 00000000 00000000 (red)
& 11111111 00000000 11111111 00000000 (mask)
-------------------------------------
  11111111 00000000 00000000 00000000 (result, 0xFF000000 in hex)
```

`(threshold & mask)` represented in binary would give us the following:

```
  11111111 00000000 11111111 00000000 (threshold)
& 11111111 00000000 11111111 00000000 (mask)
-------------------------------------
  11111111 00000000 11111111 00000000 (result, 0xFF00FF00 in hex)
```

The two results are then compared using the operator we specified:

```
0xFF000000 == 0xFF00FF00
```

Since this evaluation returns false, the red pixel fails the threshold test and is not recolored. For a green pixel, though, (`pixelValue & mask`) gives us this:

```
  11111111 00000000 11111111 00000000 (green)
& 11111111 00000000 11111111 00000000 (mask)
-------------------------------------
  11111111 00000000 11111111 00000000 (result, 0xFF00FF00 in hex)
```

This, of course, results in

```
0xFF00FF00 == 0xFF00FF00
```

Since this is a true statement, the pixel is recolored to be 0x00000000, or fully transparent. We have effectively knocked that color out of our image.

Creating 1-bit bitmaps

Photoshop has a Threshold adjustment that will turn a bitmap into an image with exactly two colors, black and white, reminiscent of when bitmaps were exactly that—a collection of single bits, with a pixel either being on or off, that is, black or white. The threshold value determines which pixels are black and which are white based on their original brightness. For instance, the default value of 128 that is applied when the Threshold dialog is opened, as shown in Figure 4-24, will set any pixels that have a brightness greater than or equal to 128 (after the image is made grayscale) to white. All darker pixels will be black. The result of applying a threshold can be seen in many of the filters, like Note Paper, Stamp, Plaster, or Torn Edges, as shown in Figure 4-25.

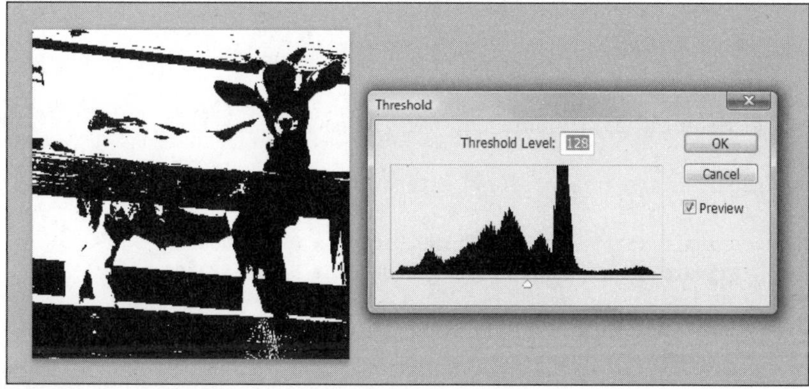

Figure 4-24. The Threshold dialog in Photoshop, reducing the image to two colors

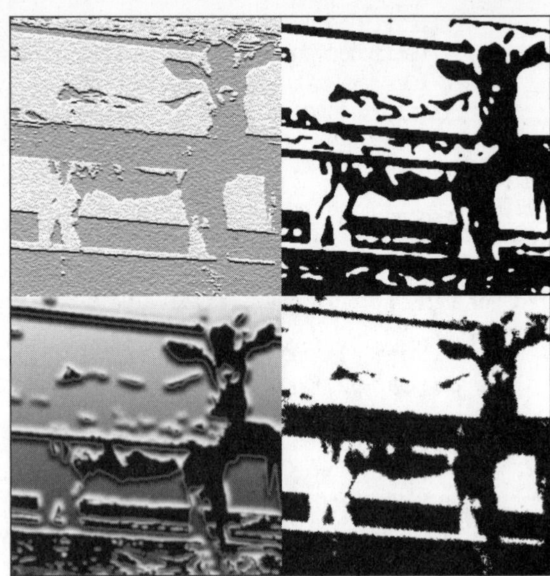

Figure 4-25.
Filters in Photoshop that use threshold as the basis of the effect

We can use the threshold() method in ActionScript to do the same thing. This is accomplished by first converting an image to grayscale and then applying a threshold that sets any pixels under a certain brightness to one color and any pixels greater than the specified brightness to another color (or vice versa).

The following class, ThresholdTest, does just that. In addition to applying a threshold, to create more of an effect, the result is slightly blurred and a bevel is applied. The end effect is almost like pools of paint defining the darker regions of the image, as shown in Figure 4-26.

```
package {

  import flash.display.BitmapData;
  import flash.filters.BevelFilter;
  import flash.filters.BitmapFilter;
  import flash.filters.BlurFilter;
  import flash.filters.ColorMatrixFilter;
  import flash.geom.Point;

  [SWF(width=300, height=300, backgroundColor=0xFFEFEE)]

  public class ThresholdTest extends AbstractImageLoader {

    private static const THRESHOLD:uint = 0xFF660000;
    private static const PAINT_COLOR:uint = 0xFF883300;

    public function ThresholdTest() {
      super("../../assets/goat.jpg");
    }
```

```
    override protected function runPostImageLoad():void {
      var bitmapData:BitmapData = _loadedBitmap.bitmapData;
      var copiedData:BitmapData = new BitmapData(
        bitmapData.width,
        bitmapData.height,
        true,
        0x00000000
      );
      desaturate(bitmapData);
      copiedData.threshold(
        bitmapData,
        bitmapData.rect,
        new Point(),
        "<",
        THRESHOLD,
        PAINT_COLOR,
        0xFFFF0000,
        false
      );
      applyFilter(copiedData, new BlurFilter(1.2, 1.2));
      applyFilter(copiedData, new BevelFilter());
      _loadedBitmap.bitmapData = copiedData;
      addChild(_loadedBitmap);
      bitmapData.dispose();
    }

    private function applyFilter(
      bitmapData:BitmapData,
      filter:BitmapFilter
    ):void {
      bitmapData.applyFilter(
        bitmapData,
        bitmapData.rect,
        new Point(),
        filter
      );
    }

    private function desaturate(bitmapData:BitmapData):void {
      var matrix:Array = [
        0.3, 0.59, 0.11, 0, 0,
        0.3, 0.59, 0.11, 0, 0,
        0.3, 0.59, 0.11, 0, 0,
        0,   0,    0,    1, 0
      ];
      applyFilter(bitmapData, new ColorMatrixFilter(matrix));
    }

  }

}
```

Figure 4-26. threshold() applied to the image, with a blur and bevel added to create a pooling paint effect

In the runPostImageLoad() method, the first thing that is done after saving a reference to the loaded bitmap data is to create a new BitmapData instance. The instance is the same width and height of the loaded data but it contains pixels that are fully transparent by default. The loaded bitmap data is then passed to a desaturate() method that uses the ColorMatrixFilter and the handy BitmapData.applyFilter() method covered earlier this chapter (see how it's all coming together?) to transform the image into a grayscale representation.

This grayscale image is passed as the source to the threshold() method, with the THRESHOLD to test against defined as a constant at the top of the class along with the color to use for pixels that pass the test. The operation is "<" and the mask is isolating the red channel (since I now have a grayscale image to test, I could have passed any of the color channels since they are all now equal). The logic for the test basically then is that any pixels that are less than the THRESHOLD value will be assigned the PAINT_COLOR value. All other pixels will remain unaffected, which means that since I have set the copySource as false these pixels will remain completely transparent. The final image then will have just the darker pixels of the image filled in with the PAINT_COLOR and the lighter pixels completely transparent.

Because using threshold() in this way produces the jagged results inherent in a 1-bit image, I apply a slight blur to the result and a bevel filter to make the "paint" appear more three dimensional.

Chroma keying

As I mentioned at the start of this section, one common use of threshold is for chroma keying, or removing a color of a specified value in an image to be replaced by another image. Unfortunately, this is not as easy as the last example where we were testing for a specific color. Because it is virtually impossible to have a single color that can be keyed out, chroma keying involves removing a specified range from an image. threshold() itself does not work with ranges, but by applying the method a number of times, we can accomplish this.

Isolating a range with threshold() is done by setting a tolerance (or the cuter term "fuzziness," as is used in the Color Range selection in Photoshop) for the threshold color so that colors that fall within a range will be removed. This needs to be done for each color channel separately and the tolerance ideally would be for values both greater and less than the threshold. This adds up to a lot of calls to threshold().

In the following example, found as ColorReplaceTest.as with this chapter's files, the loaded image has its sky replaced with a Perlin noise-generated image of clouds. The result is shown in Figure 4-27.

```
package {

  import flash.display.BitmapData;
  import flash.display.BitmapDataChannel;
  import flash.filters.BlurFilter;
  import flash.geom.ColorTransform;
  import flash.geom.Point;
```

```
  [SWF(width=300, height=300, backgroundColor=0xFFFFFF)]

  public class ColorReplaceTest extends AbstractImageLoader {

    private static const COLOR_TO_REPLACE:uint = 0x819AD3;
    private static const TOLERANCE:uint = 32;

    private var _originalData:BitmapData;
    private var _isolatedData:BitmapData;

    public function ColorReplaceTest() {
      super("../../assets/goat.jpg");
    }

    override protected function runPostImageLoad():void {
      _originalData = _loadedBitmap.bitmapData;
      _isolatedData = createCloudImage(_originalData.width,➥
_originalData.height);
      var red:uint = COLOR_TO_REPLACE>>16 & 0xFF;
      var green:uint = COLOR_TO_REPLACE>>8 & 0xFF;
      var blue:uint = COLOR_TO_REPLACE & 0xFF;
      applyThreshold("<", Math.max(0, red-TOLERANCE)<<16,➥
0x00FF0000);
      applyThreshold(">", Math.min(255, red+TOLERANCE)<<16,➥
0x00FF0000);
      applyThreshold("<", Math.max(0, green-TOLERANCE)<<8,➥
0x0000FF00);
      applyThreshold(">", Math.min(255, green+TOLERANCE)<<8,➥
0x0000FF00);
      applyThreshold("<", Math.max(0, blue-TOLERANCE),➥
0x000000FF);
      applyThreshold(">", Math.min(255, blue+TOLERANCE),➥
0x000000FF);
      _isolatedData.applyFilter(_isolatedData, _isolatedData.rect,➥
new Point(), new BlurFilter(2, 2));
      _originalData.copyPixels(
        _isolatedData,
        _isolatedData.rect,
        new Point()
      );
      _isolatedData.dispose();
      addChild(_loadedBitmap);
    }

    private function createCloudImage(
      width:Number,
      height:Number
    ):BitmapData {
      var bitmapData:BitmapData = new BitmapData(
```

```
        width,
        height,
        true,
        0x00000000
      );
      bitmapData.perlinNoise(100, 100, 3, 0, false, true,➥
BitmapDataChannel.RED, true);
      var colorTransform:ColorTransform = ➥
new ColorTransform(1.5, 1.4, 1.2, 1, 20, 20, 20);
      bitmapData.colorTransform(bitmapData.rect, colorTransform);
      return bitmapData;
    }

    private function applyThreshold(
      operation:String,
      threshold:uint,
      mask:uint
    ):void {
      _isolatedData.threshold(
        _originalData,
        _originalData.rect,
        new Point(),
        operation,
        threshold,
        0x00000000,
        mask,
        false
      );
    }

  }

}
```

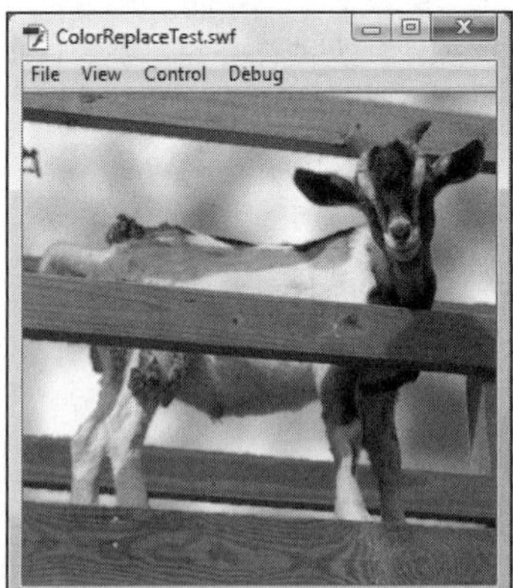

Figure 4-27. The sky removed from the image using threshold with a new image of the sky inserted in its place

createCloudImage() creates a new BitmapData instance with some Perlin noise that is yellowed using a ColorTransform. It is this new image that is used in the calls to threshold() (found within the applyThreshold() method). In the threshold() call, the original loaded image is tested, with pixels that pass each test being set to transparent. This method is called six times, twice for each channel. For instance, the first two calls to applyThreshold() test the red channel.

```
applyThreshold("<", Math.max(0, red-TOLERANCE)<<16, 0x00FF0000);
applyThreshold(">", Math.min(255, red+TOLERANCE)<<16, 0x00FF0000);
```

Any pixels with brightness values in the red channel that are less than the COLOR_TO_REPLACE's red channel minus the TOLERANCE of 32 are set to transparent. Any pixels with brightness values in the red channel that are greater than the COLOR_TO_REPLACE's red channel plus the TOLERANCE are also set to transparent. This set of two tests is run for each of the three channels. The end result is an image of clouds where the pixels are only opaque (and therefore visible) in the tolerance range around the specified COLOR_TO_REPLACE (which is the blue of the sky).

This cloud image with transparent pixels is slightly blurred using applyFilter() so that the edges aren't too jagged. Finally, it is copied into the original image. Only the opaque pixels are copied over, which means only the clouds are applied to the original image.

Mapping palettes

The final method of BitmapData that we will look at is perhaps my favorite, paletteMap(). In fact, while initially exploring this method when it was first introduced in Flash 8, I conceived of writing this book (I wished at the time for a similar book to which I could refer; there wasn't one, so I decided to write it).

paletteMap() remaps the pixels of an image to a custom palette passed as parameters. Using this method, you can perform tasks like applying a gradient map to an image, where different brightness values are mapped to different colors on a gradient, setting levels or curves or for creating posterization effects.

The following is the signature for paletteMap():

```
public function paletteMap(
  sourceBitmapData:BitmapData,
  sourceRect:Rectangle,
  destPoint:Point,
  redArray:Array = null,
  greenArray:Array = null,
  blueArray:Array = null,
  alphaArray:Array = null
):void
```

The first few parameters for paletteMap() are old standards followed by a number of arrays. Here's how they all break down:

- sourceBitmapData: This is the image to use as the source for the pixel remapping. Often, the BitmapData instance on which paletteMap() is invoked is also the source, but this parameter allows you to specify another image.
- sourceRect: This specifies the region in the sourceBitmapData to be used. To use the entirety of the image, you would use the rect property of the sourceBitmapData.
- destPoint: This is the top left pixel in the destination image, which corresponds to the top left pixel in the sourceRect.
- redArray: In this array of 256 values, each index corresponds to a color for a certain brightness level. This is where the remapping is specified. For instance, if you want all red channel values that have a brightness of less than 50 to instead have a color value of 0x000000, the first 50 indices in this array would be set to 0x000000. If no array is passed in, the channel values will remain unchanged.

  It is important to note that the final pixel color is determined by combining all color array values, so if the 0 index of the redArray was 0xFF0000, the greenArray was 0x00FF00, and the blueArray was 0x0000FF, the final pixel will be white. If, however, the blueArray index 0 was set to be 0x000000, the final pixel will be yellow, since the red and green channels would still be at full brightness according to their array values at index 0. But, lest you think that the channels are isolated at all in their arrays, if the redArray index 0 was 0xFFFFFF and the other two arrays have 0x000000 in their first index, the final pixel will still be white, since the three color array values are added together for the final pixel color.
- greenArray: This works the same as the redArray, but for the green channel.
- blueArray: This works the same as the redArray, but for the blue channel.
- alphaArray: This works the same as the redArray, but for the alpha channel.

Despite the number of parameters, the method itself is not that complex. The first three parameters are common to many of the BitmapData methods. The last four parameters are four arrays, which specify how each brightness value will be mapped per channel. The complexity is in determining how to populate those arrays. We will look at ways in the next several sections.

Assigning custom color palettes

The first thing I used paletteMap() for a few years ago was a gradient mapping application, as shown in Figure 4-28 and viewable at www.27bobs.com/applications/GradientMapper.html. In this application, you can create a custom gradient and apply this as a gradient map to a loaded image, where the brightness value of each pixel is mapped to a color on the gradient, just as with the Gradient Map adjustment layer that can be applied in Photoshop.

Figure 4-28. The GradientMapper application that allows you to remap an image's color palette to a custom gradient

The process of creating a gradient map is to first convert the image to grayscale so that there is a single brightness value per pixel to evaluate. You then must create an array of 256 values that maps each brightness value to a color on the gradient. This can be populated, as I originally did it when I was oh so young and naïve, by calculating the color value of each channel based on its position between two ratio stops in the gradient and their corresponding color stops. The easier way to do it is to simply draw your gradient into a shape and use `getPixel()` to grab each color value at each x coordinate.

The following class, GradientMapTest, demonstrates this technique. The class, shown in its entirety here, is included with this chapter's files:

```
package {

  import flash.display.BitmapData;
  import flash.display.GradientType;
  import flash.display.Shape;
  import flash.filters.ColorMatrixFilter;
  import flash.geom.Matrix;
  import flash.geom.Point;
```

```
[SWF(width=300, height=330, backgroundColor=0x000000)]

public class GradientMapTest extends AbstractImageLoader {

  public function GradientMapTest() {
    super("../../assets/goat.jpg");
  }

  override protected function runPostImageLoad():void {
    var bitmapData:BitmapData = _loadedBitmap.bitmapData;
    var width:uint = stage.stageWidth;
    var height:uint = stage.stageHeight;
    var colors:Array = [0x0066FD, 0xFFFFFF, 0xFFFFFF,➥
0x996600, 0xFFCC00, 0xFFFFFF];
    var ratios:Array = [0, 95, 124, 130, 165, 255];
    var alphas:Array = [1, 1, 1, 1, 1, 1];
    var matrix:Matrix = new Matrix();
    matrix.createGradientBox(256, height);
    var shape:Shape = new Shape();
    shape.graphics.beginGradientFill(
      GradientType.LINEAR,
      colors,
      alphas,
      ratios,
      matrix
    );
    shape.graphics.drawRect(0, 0, 256, height);
    shape.graphics.endFill();
    var gradient:BitmapData = new BitmapData(256, height);
    gradient.draw(shape);
    var red:Array = [];
    var zeros:Array = [];
    var color:uint;
    for (var i:uint = 0; i < 256; i++) {
      color = gradient.getPixel(i, 0);
      red.push(color);
      zeros.push(0);
    }
    gradient.dispose();
    shape.scaleX = width/256;
    addChild(shape)
    desaturate(bitmapData);
    bitmapData.paletteMap(
      bitmapData,
      bitmapData.rect,
      new Point(),
      red,
      zeros,
      zeros
```

```
      );
      addChild(_loadedBitmap);
    }

    private function desaturate(bitmapData:BitmapData):void {
      var matrix:Array = [
        0.3, 0.59, 0.11, 0, 0,
        0.3, 0.59, 0.11, 0, 0,
        0.3, 0.59, 0.11, 0, 0,
        0,   0,    0,    1, 0
      ];
      bitmapData.applyFilter(
        bitmapData,
        bitmapData.rect,
        new Point(),
        new ColorMatrixFilter(matrix)
      );
    }

  }

}
```

Near the top of the `runPostImageLoad()` method, I set up the values that will control the gradient:

```
      var colors:Array = [0x0066FD, 0xFFFFFF, 0xFFFFFF,➥
0x996600, 0xFFCC00, 0xFFFFFF];
      var ratios:Array = [0, 95, 124, 130, 165, 255];
      var alphas:Array = [1, 1, 1, 1, 1, 1];
```

This gradient is the classic chrome gradient you see in nearly every application that supports gradients, but few people actually use it, so I'm giving it some love. This gradient is then drawn into a shape that is 256 pixels wide and the height of the stage. The height is not that important to determine gradient colors, but as I will be adding the gradient to the stage for display once I have grabbed its colors, giving it a height to match the stage means I don't have to do any resizing of its height later.

```
var matrix:Matrix = new Matrix();
matrix.createGradientBox(256, height);
var shape:Shape = new Shape();
shape.graphics.beginGradientFill(
  GradientType.LINEAR,
  colors,
  alphas,
  ratios,
  matrix
);
shape.graphics.drawRect(0, 0, 256, height);
shape.graphics.endFill();
```

Of course, to use `getPixel()`, I need the gradient to be in a BitmapData instance, so I draw it into one in the next two lines.

```
var gradient:BitmapData = new BitmapData(256, height);
gradient.draw(shape);
```

I can now run through the 256 pixels that make up the width of the gradient and populate the color arrays with the colors found. I actually only need to do this for a single array, since all brightness values for each color channel will be the same with a grayscale image. For the other color channels, I can pass an array of zeros. Remember that a final pixel color is determined by adding all three channel values together, so having two color channels full of zero values will mean that the colors from the other color channel array will be used exactly.

```
var red:Array = [];
var zeros:Array = [];
var color:uint;
for (var i:uint = 0; i < 256; i++) {
  color = gradient.getPixel(i, 0);
  red.push(color);
  zeros.push(0);
}
```

Just to make sure this last point is clear, if the color on the gradient at pixel 0 is 0x0066FD, this is the color that will be pushed into the red array. The zeros array will obviously have a 0. If I then pass the zeros array for the `greenArray` and `blueArray` parameters in `paletteMap()`, the following operation will be performed when determining a pixel color for a pixel that has a brightness of 0 in the red channel:

```
  11111111 00000000 01100110 11111101 (red)
| 11111111 00000000 00000000 00000000 (green)
| 11111111 00000000 00000000 00000000 (blue)
-------------------------------------
  11111111 00000000 01100110 11111101 (result)
```

If conceptually this seems odd, you can adjust the code in the GradientMapTest so that each channel array is populated by the brightness value just for that channel, but that involves bit shifting both right and left:

```
var red:Array = [];
var green:Array = [];
var blue:Array = [];
var color:uint;
for (var i:uint = 0; i < 256; i++) {
  color = gradient.getPixel(i, 0);
  red.push((color >> 16 & 0xFF) << 16);
  green.push((color >> 8 & 0xFF) << 8);
  blue.push(color & 0xFF);
}
```

This will push 0x000000 into the red array, 0x006600 into the green array, and 0x0000FD into the blue array. Our binary operation then would look like the following:

```
  11111111 00000000 00000000 00000000 (red)
| 11111111 00000000 01100110 00000000 (green)
| 11111111 00000000 00000000 11111101 (blue)
-------------------------------------
  11111111 00000000 01100110 11111101 (result)
```

As you can see, though, the resulting color is the same. I'll take the simpler way, any day.

Back in the class, once I have populated the red and zeros arrays with values, I dispose of the gradient image and add the shape to the display list after scaling its width to match the stage. I then desaturate the image using the ColorMatrixFilter as in previous examples. Finally, I call `paletteMap()` on the desaturated image using the `red` array and pass the `zeros` array for both the green and blue channels.

```
desaturate(bitmapData);
bitmapData.paletteMap(
  bitmapData,
  bitmapData.rect,
  new Point(),
  red,
  zeros,
  zeros
);
```

The result is chrome goat, as shown in Figure 4-29. That poor goat.

Figure 4-29.
A gradient mapped to the brightness values of the image using paletteMap()

Applying levels

In Photoshop, the Levels dialog, shown in Figure 4-30, allows you to set the black, medium gray, and white points of an image. Adjusting these values can brighten or darken an image, adjust contrast, and redistribute brightness values to stretch the tonal range of an image. This is done through a remapping of the color palette as you saw in the last example.

Figure 4-30. The Levels dialog in Photoshop, which allows for redistribution of an image's pixel brighness values

The black point represents the brightness value below which all pixels will be black. The default setting of 0 shows that only pixels with a brightness of 0 will be black. However, if the black point is moved to 50, all pixels with a composite brightness value of 50 will be remapped to black, with pixels with a brightness value greater than 50 being redistributed across the full range of 256 values.

This is perhaps more easily understood with numbers than with sentences. Consider five values (we will use 8-bit values for easier demonstration): 0x00, 0x22 (34 in decimal), 0x7F (127 in decimal), 0xAA (170 in decimal), and 0xFF (255 in decimal, but you knew that).

```
0  34  127  170  255 (colors)
0      127       255 (levels)
```

The default levels for an image's black, medium gray, and white points will be 0, 127, and 255. If we adjust the levels so that the black point is 50 and the medium gray is 150, our color values get redistributed and remapped between these new points. Any brightness value less than 50 would get remapped to 0, which would include 0x00 (already 0) and 0x22. With 50 as the new black point and 150 as the new medium gray, any brightness values between these points would get redistributed between this new range. This would occur for the 0x7F value. The redistribution is handled by finding the difference between the brightness value and the new black point (in this case, 127 – 50 = 77) and dividing this by the new range between the black point and medium gray point (77 / 100 = .77) to get a percentage. This is then multiplied by the constant midpoint in the full range of 256 brightness values (127, or 128, depending on how you round) to determine the new brightness value.

```
blackPoint = 50
midPoint = 150
newRange = midPoint - blackPoint
previousValue = 127
newValue = ((previousValue - blackPoint)/newRange)*127
newValue = 97
```

The same would be done for redistributing brightness values between the new medium gray and white points, as can be demonstrated with the 0xAA brightness value.

```
midPoint = 150
whitePoint = 255
newRange = whitePoint - midPoint
previousValue = 170
newValue = ((previousValue - midPoint)/newRange)*128 + 127
newValue = 151
```

Notice that the equation is the same except for two things: we multiply by 128, since we used 127 in the previous equation for half of the full range (and we need to account for 0–255, and half of this leaves us a remainder of 1), and the final value needs to be added to the constant midpoint since the value returned by the preceding equation will be between 0 and 128.

A final step in the remapping would be to set values above the white point to be 0xFF, just as values below the black point were set to be 0x00. Since, in this example, we have not altered the white point, this step is unnecessary.

Running our calculations on our initial five brightness values then yields the following results:

```
0  34  127  170  255 (before)
   50     150    255  (levels)
0   0   97  151  255 (remapped)
```

The end effect would be a darker image with the initial brightness values (except for values of 0xFF) all lowered based on the new levels.

The following class, LevelsTest, which of course you can find in this chapter's files, puts these equations to use by applying two different levels of operations on our favorite goat (whom we really should name since he's doing all this work for us). The result is shown in Figure 4-31.

```
package {

  import flash.display.Bitmap;
  import flash.display.BitmapData;
  import flash.geom.Point;

  [SWF(width=900, height=300, backgroundColor=0x000000)]

  public class LevelsTest extends AbstractImageLoader {

    public function LevelsTest() {
      super("../../assets/goat.jpg");
    }

    override protected function runPostImageLoad():void {
      var bitmapData:BitmapData = _loadedBitmap.bitmapData;
```

```
    addChild(_loadedBitmap);
    var clone:BitmapData = bitmapData.clone();
    setLevels(clone, 0, 100, 200);
    var bitmap:Bitmap = new Bitmap(clone);
    bitmap.x = bitmapData.width;
    addChild(bitmap);
    clone = bitmapData.clone();
    setLevels(clone, 100, 127, 155);
    bitmap = new Bitmap(clone);
    bitmap.x = bitmapData.width*2;
    addChild(bitmap);
  }

  protected function setLevels(
    bitmapData:BitmapData,
    blackPoint:uint,
    midPoint:uint,
    whitePoint:uint
  ):void {
    var r:Array = [];
    var g:Array = [];
    var b:Array = [];
    for (var i:uint = 0; i <= blackPoint; i++){
      r.push(0);
      g.push(0);
      b.push(0);
    }
    var value:uint = 0;
    var range:uint = midPoint - blackPoint;
    for (i = blackPoint + 1; i <= midPoint; i++){
      value = ((i - blackPoint)/range) * 127;
      r.push(value << 16);
      g.push(value << 8);
      b.push(value);
    }
    range = whitePoint - midPoint;
    for (i = midPoint + 1; i <= whitePoint; i++){
      value = ((i - midPoint)/range) * 128 + 127;
      r.push(value << 16);
      g.push(value << 8);
      b.push(value);
    }
    for (i = whitePoint + 1; i < 256; i++){
      r.push(0xFF << 16);
      g.push(0xFF << 8);
      b.push(0xFF);
    }
    bitmapData.paletteMap(
      bitmapData,
```

```
            bitmapData.rect,
            new Point(),
            r,
            g,
            b
          );
        }

      }

    }
```

Figure 4-31. Levels set on the image shown on the left using paletteMap(), with the middle image being brightened and the right image receiving increased contrast

In this class, the `runPostImageLoad()` method clones the loaded bitmap data twice and passes the clones to the `setLevels()` method with the desired black, medium gray, and white point settings. The altered bitmap data of each clone is then added to the display list through a Bitmap.

The meat of the class lies in the `setLevels()` method, which looks daunting but just contains the logic and formulas discussed previously. First, I create three arrays that will hold the mapped values.

```
var r:Array = [];
var g:Array = [];
var b:Array = [];
```

Then I run through all brightness values that will be black based on the position of the black point, which is any value at an index position less than or equal to the black point.

```
for (var i:uint = 0; i <= blackPoint; i++){
  r.push(0);
  g.push(0);
  b.push(0);
}
```

The next for loop remaps brightness values between the new black and medium gray points, using the formula discussed previously. The newly calculated value needs some left bit shifting to put it at the proper bit position for each specific channel.

```
var range:uint = midPoint - blackPoint;
for (i = blackPoint + 1; i <= midPoint; i++){
  value = ((i - blackPoint)/range) * 127;
  r.push(value << 16);
  g.push(value << 8);
  b.push(value);
}
```

This is done for the brightness values between the medium gray and white points as well.

```
range = whitePoint - midPoint;
for (i = midPoint + 1; i <= whitePoint; i++){
  value = ((i - midPoint)/range) * 128 + 127;
  r.push(value << 16);
  g.push(value << 8);
  b.push(value);
}
```

Finally, the brightness values that are greater than the white point are set to be 0xFF, or 255, shifted into the appropriate bit positions for each channel.

```
for (i = whitePoint + 1; i < 256; i++){
  r.push(0xFF << 16);
  g.push(0xFF << 8);
  b.push(0xFF);
}
```

With the values for the arrays all calculated, `paletteMap()` can be called to remap the images with the new palettes.

Posterizing

Posterization, or quantization, is a technique where the number of colors in an image is limited to a certain finite set. We can achieve this effect, with a little work, using `paletteMap()` and the `setLevels()` method we used in the previous example. The trick is that the levels need to be applied to each channel individually with the results combined into the final composite image.

The process requires the following steps:

1. Create a separate BitmapData instance for each channel containing the grayscale representation of the channel, as shown in Figure 4-32.
2. For each grayscale channel image, run through a loop for the number of desired `levels` minus one. We use `levels` minus one, since we will be making two-color images and combining them, so a `levels` setting of 2 only needs a single iteration in our loop since each iteration results in a two-color channel image.

Figure 4-32. Three different images must first be produced, one for each channel holding its grayscale representation.

3. During each iteration of the `levels` loop, clone each channel image and set the threshold for each clone so that it consists of two colors. The position of the threshold depends on the level. The first iteration of the loop, for instance, will produce a black-and-white image where more of the image is black than white. A second iteration will produce a black-and-white image where there is less black and more white. The last iteration of the loop will produce an image that is mostly white with a little black. Figure 4-33 shows the channels of the goat with the three images each that would be produced with a `levels` setting of 4.

Figure 4-33. Each channel (red on the top row, green in the middle, and blue on the bottom) with threshold applied three different times

4. For each of the black-and-white channel images, adjust the colors so that each black-and-white image is made up of white and a gray. The images that were mostly black due to a high threshold will be lighter grays than those that had lower thresholds. Figure 4-34 shows the images from Figure 4-33 with these brightness adjustments applied.

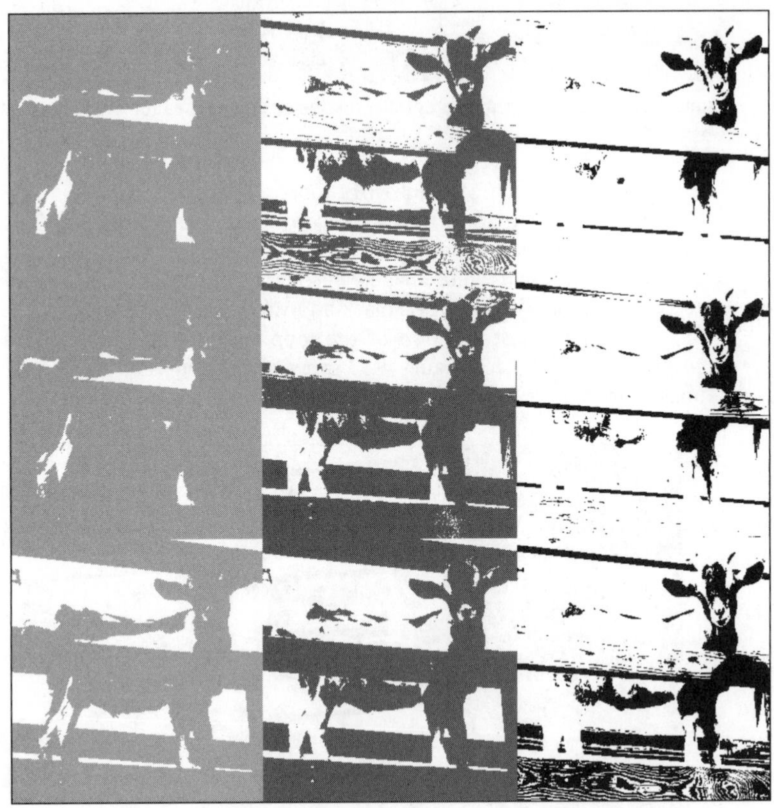

Figure 4-34. The higher threshold images have their brightness increased so that the multiple images can be layered using MULTIPLY resulting in multiple levels of gray.

5. Combine the multiple channel images (based on the number of levels) for each channel using the `MULTIPLY` blend mode so that each channel has a limited number of colors in a grayscale image. Using `MULTIPLY` with the darker images applied to the lighter images means that each of the levels of gray will be visible in the final composite channel, as shown in Figure 4-35.

6. With the final individual channel images composited, copy each channel into the final full-color image so that the grayscale values of each channel will combine to produce the limited set of colors in the final composite, as shown in Figure 4-36.

Figure 4-35. The multiple images for each channel are combined using MULTIPLY to create multiple levels of gray in a single image, with the red channel image on the left, the green channel in the center, and the blue channel on the right.

Figure 4-36.
The three channel images recombined into a single image, with the limited brightness colors in each channel limiting the colors in the final composite image

Simple, right? OK, there's a reason this is the last example of the chapter on advanced bitmap manipulation. But after all that we've covered, you're ready to tackle this example's complexity. The following class, PosterizeTest, demonstrates how to apply this technique to an image, and its results are shown in Figure 4-37.

```
package {

  import flash.display.Bitmap;
  import flash.display.BitmapData;
  import flash.display.BitmapDataChannel;
  import flash.display.BlendMode;
  import flash.geom.ColorTransform;
  import flash.geom.Point;
  import flash.geom.Rectangle;

  [SWF(width=900, height=300, backgroundColor=0x000000)]

  public class PosterizeTest extends LevelsTest {

    override protected function runPostImageLoad():void {
      var bitmapData:BitmapData = _loadedBitmap.bitmapData;
      addChild(_loadedBitmap);
```

```
      var clone:BitmapData = bitmapData.clone();
      posterize(clone, 4);
      var bitmap:Bitmap = new Bitmap(clone);
      bitmap.x = bitmapData.width;
      addChild(bitmap);
      clone = bitmapData.clone();
      posterize(clone, 2);
      bitmap = new Bitmap(clone);
      bitmap.x = bitmapData.width*2;
      addChild(bitmap);
    }

    private function posterize(
      bitmapData:BitmapData,
      levels:uint
    ):void {
      var red:BitmapData = makeImageFromChannel(bitmapData,➥
BitmapDataChannel.RED);
      var green:BitmapData = makeImageFromChannel(bitmapData,➥
BitmapDataChannel.GREEN);
      var blue:BitmapData = makeImageFromChannel(bitmapData,➥
BitmapDataChannel.BLUE);
      var sourceChannels:Vector.<BitmapData> =➥
new Vector.<BitmapData>();
      sourceChannels.push(red);
      sourceChannels.push(green);
      sourceChannels.push(blue);

      red = new BitmapData(bitmapData.width, bitmapData.height);
      green = red.clone();
      blue = red.clone();
      var adjustedChannels:Vector.<BitmapData> =➥
new Vector.<BitmapData>();
      adjustedChannels.push(red);
      adjustedChannels.push(green);
      adjustedChannels.push(blue);

      var channelData:BitmapData;
      var threshold:uint;
      var colorTransform:ColorTransform;
      var brightness:uint;
      var j:uint;
      levels--;
      for (var i:uint = 0; i < levels; i++) {
        threshold = 255*((levels-i)/(levels+1));
        brightness = 255*((levels-i-1)/levels);
        colorTransform =➥
new ColorTransform(1, 1, 1, 1, brightness, brightness, brightness);
        for (j = 0; j < 3; j++) {
```

```
          channelData = sourceChannels[j].clone();
          setLevels(channelData, threshold, threshold, threshold);
          adjustedChannels[j].draw(
            channelData,
            null,
            colorTransform,
            BlendMode.MULTIPLY
          );
        }
      }

      copyChannel(red, bitmapData, BitmapDataChannel.RED);
      copyChannel(green, bitmapData, BitmapDataChannel.GREEN);
      copyChannel(blue, bitmapData, BitmapDataChannel.BLUE);
    }

    private function makeImageFromChannel(
      bitmapData:BitmapData,
      channel:uint
    ):BitmapData {
      var clone:BitmapData = bitmapData.clone();
      var rect:Rectangle = clone.rect;
      var pt:Point = new Point();
      clone.copyChannel(bitmapData, rect, pt, channel,➥
BitmapDataChannel.RED);
      clone.copyChannel(bitmapData, rect, pt, channel,➥
BitmapDataChannel.GREEN);
      clone.copyChannel(bitmapData, rect, pt, channel,➥
BitmapDataChannel.BLUE);
      return clone;
    }

    private function copyChannel(
      source:BitmapData,
      destination:BitmapData,
      channel:uint
    ):void {
      destination.copyChannel(
        source,
        source.rect,
        new Point(),
        channel,
        channel
      );
    }

  }

}
```

Figure 4-37. Two examples of posterization applied to the image on the left, with the middle image showing four levels and the right image showing two levels

This class takes advantage of inheritance by extending the previous example's LevelsTest class. I use the `setLevels()` method that was set up there (separating this method out into a utilities class would be a good idea so it could be used anywhere, and we will discuss just that in Chapter 7).

The `runPostImageLoad()` method here is purposely kept simple with all of the heavy processing going on in the `posterize()` method. You can see that I simply clone the loaded bitmap data, pass the clone to the `posterize()` method, and then add the clone to the display list through a Bitmap instance. This is done twice with the first clone being posterized to four levels and the second clone being posterized to two levels.

```
var clone:BitmapData = bitmapData.clone();
posterize(clone, 4);
var bitmap:Bitmap = new Bitmap(clone);
bitmap.x = bitmapData.width;
addChild(bitmap);
```

The first thing that I do in the `posterize()` method is make three new images, each being a grayscale representation of one of the three color channels. These are pushed into a vector array for easy reference.

```
      var red:BitmapData = makeImageFromChannel(bitmapData,➥
BitmapDataChannel.RED);
      var green:BitmapData = makeImageFromChannel(bitmapData,➥
BitmapDataChannel.GREEN);
      var blue:BitmapData = makeImageFromChannel(bitmapData,➥
BitmapDataChannel.BLUE);
      var sourceChannels:Vector.<BitmapData> =➥
new Vector.<BitmapData>();
      sourceChannels.push(red);
      sourceChannels.push(green);
      sourceChannels.push(blue);
```

The makeImageFromChannel() method that is called in these lines copies the specified channel into the other two channels. Doing so produces a grayscale image, since a pixel will then have the same brightness value in all three color channels. Creating these three separate grayscale images is necessary so that I can perform operations on a single channel using methods that can only be applied to all channels in a single BitmapData instance.

The next thing that happens in the posterize() method is that I create three new BitmapData instances the same width and height as the image, but with white pixels by default. These three images will be used to copy the processed images into for each level. Each image copied in will contain darker pixels, and the MULTIPLY blend mode will be used when copying, so the white base means that the copied in images will always darken the pixels of the base image. I push these images into a vector as well for easy access later.

```
      red = new BitmapData(bitmapData.width, bitmapData.height);
      green = red.clone();
      blue = red.clone();
      var adjustedChannels:Vector.<BitmapData> =➥
new Vector.<BitmapData>();
      adjustedChannels.push(red);
      adjustedChannels.push(green);
      adjustedChannels.push(blue);
```

Now, I can run through the desired levels and create different two-color images using a threshold. Since a single iteration in the loop will produce a two-color image, I first reduce the levels passed in by one since a levels setting of 2 will only require a single run through the loop.

Perhaps an easier way to think about it is that we have a pure white image for each channel (saved into the adjustedChannels vector) that we are applying a black-and-white or gray-and-white image to within each loop. That means with no iterations of the loop we will have a single level, white, while a single iteration will produce two levels, black and white. A third iteration will produce a three-color image, with black, gray, and white. Each additional iteration will apply a different shade of gray. All this means that I need to run through the loop one less than the total desired levels.

```
levels--;
for (var i:uint = 0; i < levels; i++) {
```

Inside the loop, I determine a threshold to set the image to based on the current level.

```
threshold = 255*((levels-i)/(levels+1));
```

If we plug in some numbers, you will perhaps more easily see how this works. Let's consider the call made to posterize() with a levels setting of 4. Since this is reduced to 3 before the loop, the first iteration when i=0 will result in the following (remember that threshold is a uint, so it will automatically be rounded down):

```
threshold = 255*((3-0)/(3+1));
threshold = 255*(3/4);
threshold = 191;
```

So the threshold of the first image will be 191, resulting in an image where there is more black than white (depending on the image, of course, but generally speaking this will be the case). The second iteration of the loop when `i=1` results in the following:

```
threshold = 255*((3-1)/(3+1));
threshold = 255*(2/4);
threshold = 127;
```

This will produce an image where the medium gray brightness value of 127 is used as the threshold for the resulting black-and-white image. The final iteration of the loop where `i=2` will produce the following:

```
threshold = 255*((3-2)/(3+1));
threshold = 255*(1/4);
threshold = 63;
```

Setting the threshold to 63 will result in an image where most of the pixels will be white with a smaller percentage made black.

Of course, if I apply these two-color images as is to the `adjustedChannels` image, I will get a mostly black image in the first iteration, and no further iterations through the loop will matter, since any lower threshold will result in less black, and that black will be in the same areas as the first iteration. Using `MULTIPLY` to blend the images from these latter iterations will have no effect. What needs to be done is to lighten the results of the higher thresholds so that each iteration of the loop produces a slightly darker image that can be applied using `MULTIPLY`. That means that I start with a pure white image before the first loop. The second loop will give me a light-gray-and-white image that can be blended using `MULTIPLY` to the white image. The next iteration will produce a darker-gray-and-white image. The final loop should produce a black-and-white image. Since each iteration produces a slightly darker gray than the previous iteration, I can blend all the images together and create a composite grayscale image with a limited number of grayscale values. Determining how to brighten the image is handled in the following lines:

```
        brightness = 255*((levels-i-1)/levels);
        colorTransform =➥
new ColorTransform(1, 1, 1, 1, brightness, brightness, brightness);
```

The ColorTransform instance will be applied to the image created in the loop, and it will be brightened by the amount specified in the `brightness` variable. The formula for `brightness` will result in a number that is progressively lower each iteration of the loop. If we plug in numbers as we did with `threshold`, we will see how this works. Consider the first iteration when `i=0` and `threshold`, as we determined, will be 191.

```
brightness = 255*((3-0-1)/3);
brightness = 255*(2/3);
brightness = 170;
```

In this case, the resulting image will be brightened by 170 in each channel. Since the image will initially be black and white once a threshold is applied, the calculation is easy here, with the final gray being 0xAAAAAA (or 170 in each channel). This gray-and-white image will then be applied to the white base image stored in the `adjustedChannels` vector.

The second iteration of the loop when i=1 results in the following:

```
brightness = 255*((3-1-1)/3);
brightness = 255*(1/3);
brightness = 85;
```

This image will then have white and gray of 0x555555 (85 in each channel). Finally, the iteration where i=2 gives us the following:

```
brightness = 255*((3-2-1)/3);
brightness = 255*(0/3);
brightness = 0;
```

There will be no brightness adjustment here, which means the image will remain black and white.

The last piece within the for loop, now that the threshold and brightness values have been calculated, is to apply these settings to the channel images and apply the adjusted images to the final composite channel images. This is handled in the nested for loop.

```
for (j = 0; j < 3; j++) {
  channelData = sourceChannels[j].clone();
  setLevels(channelData, threshold, threshold, threshold);
  adjustedChannels[j].draw(
    channelData,
    null,
    colorTransform,
    BlendMode.MULTIPLY
  );
}
```

I first clone a fresh copy of the channel image and then call setLevels() (presented in the last example and present in the super class's code), using the threshold value to create a two-color image. This is one way to apply a threshold. Of course, you learned earlier this chapter that the same can be accomplished with the appropriately named threshold() method of BitmapData. The code to use threshold() instead of setLevels() would be

```
for (j = 0; j < 3; j++) {
  channelData = sourceChannels[j].clone();
  channelData.fillRect(channelData.rect, 0xFFFFFFFF);
  channelData.threshold(
    sourceChannels[j],
    channelData.rect,
    new Point(),
    "<",
    threshold<<16,
    0xFF000000,
    0x00FF0000
  );
```

```
        adjustedChannels[j].draw(
          channelData,
          null,
          colorTransform,
          BlendMode.MULTIPLY
        );
      }
```

The final line in this nested `for` loop draws the adjusted two-color image into the composite channel image, applying the ColorTransform to brighten the gray and using the `MULTIPLY` blend mode so that darker colors will overlay the lighter colors, but white itself will be ignored.

With the outer `for` loop completed for all the desired levels, I am left with three composite channel images each with a limited number of grayscale colors. These are copied into the final image into their appropriate channels in these final lines of the `posterize()` method.

```
      copyChannel(red, bitmapData, BitmapDataChannel.RED);
      copyChannel(green, bitmapData, BitmapDataChannel.GREEN);
      copyChannel(blue, bitmapData, BitmapDataChannel.BLUE);
```

Whew! The final posterize effect demonstrates a number of techniques from this and the last several chapters including copying full images and individual channels, working with channel data, applying ColorTransforms and blend modes, and of course, setting thresholds through the `paletteMap()` or `threshold()` methods. If it hadn't earlier, I think this chapter has certainly earned its title of "Advanced Bitmap Manipulation" now!

Two methods that are not presented in depth in this chapter are BitmapData's `merge()` and `compare()`. Each combines the pixel data from two images with `merge()` blending the pixels of each image based on a multiplier and `compare()` showing the difference between each image's pixels. If I personally used these more and hadn't already filled two full chapters with BitmapData, there might be more than this single focus point, but I rarely, if ever, use them, and here we are at the end of two full chapters. However, for an example of the output of each method, have a look at `MergeTest.swf` and `CompareTest.swf` in this chapter's files. You should refer to Adobe's ActionScript documentation for further explanation of these methods.

Summary

In two chapters, we have stepped through nearly all the properties and methods of BitmapData, from loading or creating, to copying, recoloring, applying filters to, and manipulating channel data, regions, and individual pixels. Tremendous power is contained within this single ActionScript class, and its functionality has innumerable practical applications. Although these two chapters have been more of an introduction to the methods and simple examples of their capabilities, in most cases, effects will be created through combinations of these methods, as you saw a little bit in the last example on posterization.

It is the combination of BitmapData's methods, in addition to the capabilities of the drawing API, graphic filters, and blend modes, that we will be exploring through the latter part of this book in order to create more complex effects.

Before we get to those effects, there are a couple of remaining aspects of graphic manipulation in ActionScript that must be covered. In the next chapter, we briefly leave our little ActionScript editors of choice and enter the world of the Pixel Bender Toolkit where ActionScript shaders are created. If the capabilities of the built-in filters, blend modes, and BitmapData methods haven't been enough to impress you, then shaders might just do it for you, since they allow you to create your very own custom effects. Turn the page, and I will show you how.

Chapter 5

PIXEL BENDER AND SHADERS

There's an old saying that goes, "Give a man a fish, you have fed him for today. Teach a man to fish, and you have fed him for a lifetime." That's all very good if you like fish, or fishing analogies in general (and hey, who doesn't?), but what has that to do with Flash, you may well ask? Well, ActionScript comes with a lot of great tools that have been provided for us by the programmers behind the player and the language, but even they conceded they couldn't fulfill all the graphical needs for all the developers going forward. Even if that was feasible, given the rampant creativity that exists in the constantly evolving Flash community, having dozens of filters and blend modes to cover all possible graphical situations would greatly increase the size of the Flash Player. So instead of giving us the fish, they have handed us a rod. Welcome to Pixel Bender.

Pixel Bender is not a part of the Flash IDE or of the Flex framework, and it is not an aspect of the ActionScript language. Pixel Bender is a completely separate programming language that allows you to define algorithms to perform per-pixel manipulation of images, and it does so incredibly quickly. ActionScript provides access to the Pixel Bender kernels, or shaders, so at runtime in the Flash Player you can process images using these algorithms and perform some fantastic visual effects not possible with other aspects of the ActionScript language at the same speed.

In this chapter, we will explore how to create these Pixel Bender shaders and how these may be used at runtime through ActionScript. Pixel Bender provides a whole new sea of possibilities to explore, so I hope you like to fish.

Pixel Bender is not just for Flash and can be used with other Adobe products like After Effects and Photoshop and, in fact, offers a lot of additional functionality in these environments that is not available in the Flash Player, as I will discuss in the "Knowing Flash's limitations" section. Obviously, for the context of this book, we will be discussing how Pixel Bender works with Flash and ActionScript. It is also worth noting that another potential use of Pixel Bender beyond image processing is to process nonimage data as a background job in a separate thread that will not affect your application's responsiveness. This is a subject that is not directly related to image processing and is beyond the scope of this chapter, though we will discuss how to run a background job to process image data at the end of this chapter.

Understanding shaders

Pixel Bender is referred to in parts of the Adobe documentation as a "programming language," but in others, this language is referred to as the "Pixel Bender language," because a number of pieces make up the Pixel Bender technology, of which the language is only one. To understand Pixel Bender as an umbrella term for a collection of functionality, we must define each of the component parts.

- *Kernel*: When you write your image-processing algorithms, you are creating a Pixel Bender kernel, which will be saved with the extension `.pbk`.
- *Pixel Bender language*: This is the language you will use to write your kernels. It is based on GLSL, which is itself based on C. If you know C, you're in for a smooth ride. If you don't, but have a firm grasp of at least ActionScript, the Pixel Bender language really is not hard to pick up owing to the limited set of functions that it actually provides. I speak from experience: I do not know C and had no issues writing Pixel Bender kernels, so none should feel daunted.
- *Pixel Bender Toolkit*: This is the application that you will use to write your kernels, as shown in Figure 5-1. This separate IDE ships with Flash CS4 but can also be downloaded from Adobe Labs at `http://labs.adobe.com/technologies/pixelbender/`. Using this application, you can compile your kernel into bytecode that can be loaded into the Flash Player and used to manipulate image data.

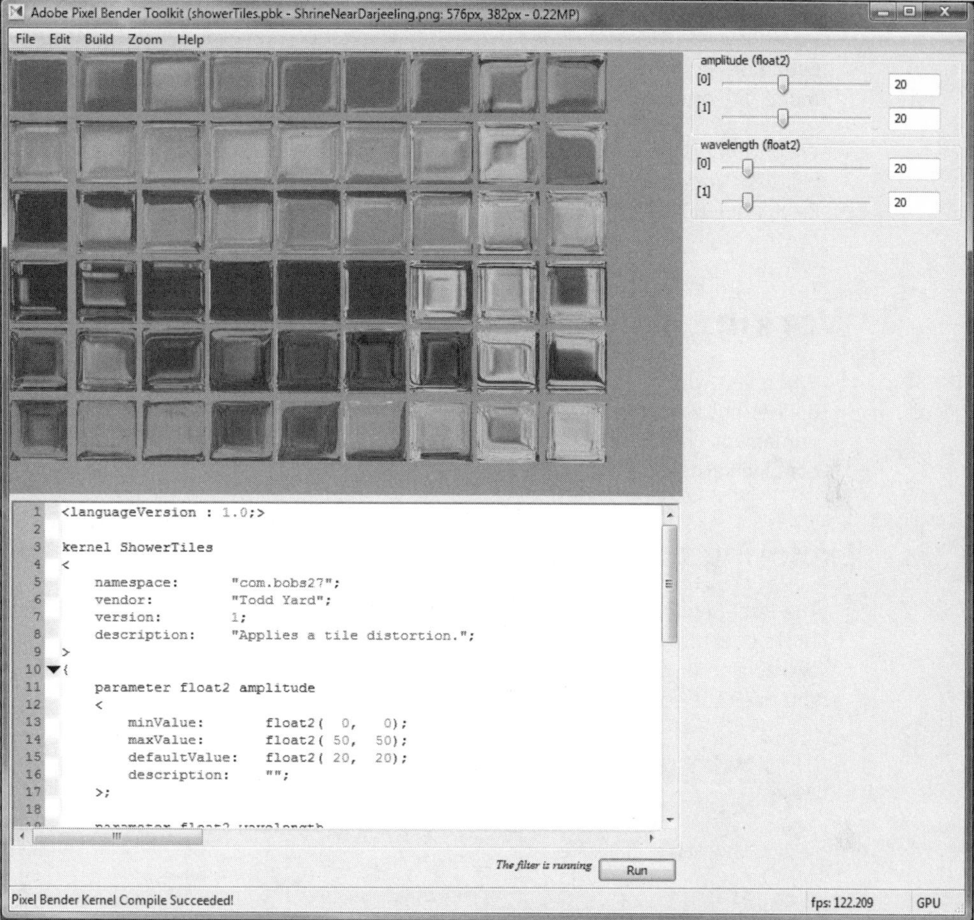

Figure 5-1. The Adobe Pixel Bender Toolkit, the birthplace of shaders

- *Pixel Bender bytecode*: The Flash Player cannot read the kernels directly, but can read the bytecode generated from compiling the kernels through the Pixel Bender Toolkit. These will have an extension of `.pbj` and can be embedded into a SWF using the `Embed` metatag (if you are using the Flex compiler) or loaded at runtime using the ActionScript URLLoader class.
- *Shader*: In ActionScript, Pixel Bender bytecode is wrapped in a shader. A shader accepts input, performs calculations on that input as defined in the original kernel using optional parameters, and then outputs the processed data for use in the Flash Player. Shaders are used to create visual effects when applied as filters, blend modes, or custom fills and strokes.

The workflow for creating what will be an image effect using Pixel Bender in ActionScript is to first write a kernel using the Pixel Bender language in the Pixel Bender Toolkit. This kernel is compiled into bytecode through the toolkit, and this bytecode is loaded into the Flash Player (either embedded in the SWF when it is compiled, or loaded at runtime). The bytecode is stored in an ActionScript Shader instance that can be applied as a filter, blend mode, fill, or stroke.

We'll look more closely at how shaders are accessed and applied in ActionScript shortly, but first, you need to know how to create them in the first place. For that, we have the Pixel Bender Toolkit.

Working with the Pixel Bender Toolkit

When you write a shader for ActionScript, you will be writing it not within Flash or Flex Builder but within the Adobe Pixel Bender Toolkit, an application dedicated to the development of Pixel Bender kernels. Within this simple application you can create, test, and compile kernels for use within the Flash Player.

Exploring the interface

The Pixel Bender Toolkit is installed with Flash CS4 and can be found in your `Adobe/Adobe Tools` directory within your program files (assuming a default installation). The Toolkit is also available through Adobe Labs at `http://labs.adobe.com/technologies/pixelbender/`. If you open the application you will see something like Figure 5-2.

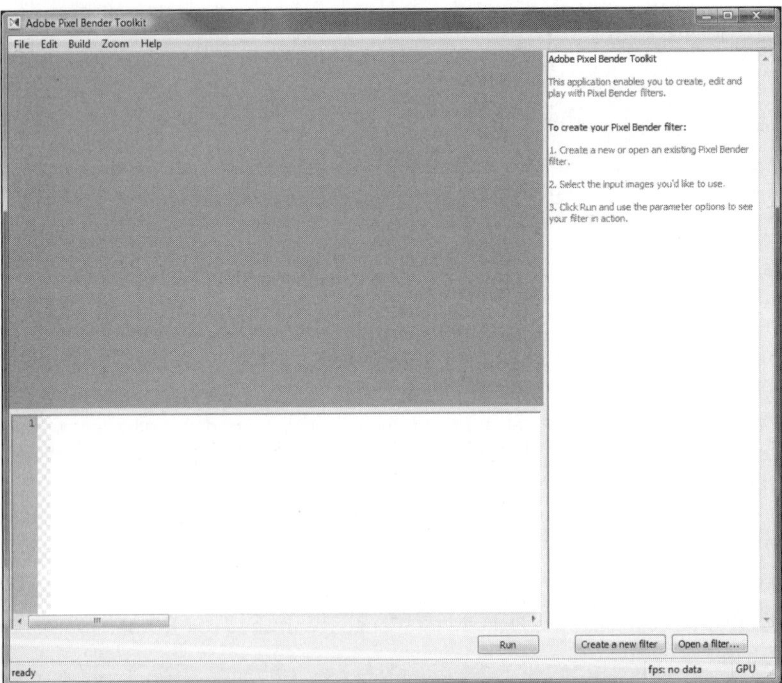

Figure 5-2. The Pixel Bender Toolkit upon opening

Let's open a kernel and load an image to see how to work within the interface:

1. Select File ➤ Load Image 1 to open a file browse dialog. By default, this should show the contents of the `sample images` directory under the Pixel Bender Toolkit installation. Select `YellowFlowers.png`. The image should open and display in the top left of the interface, as shown in Figure 5-3. This is the Image View section of the application where you will see the results of the kernel run against the pixels in the image.

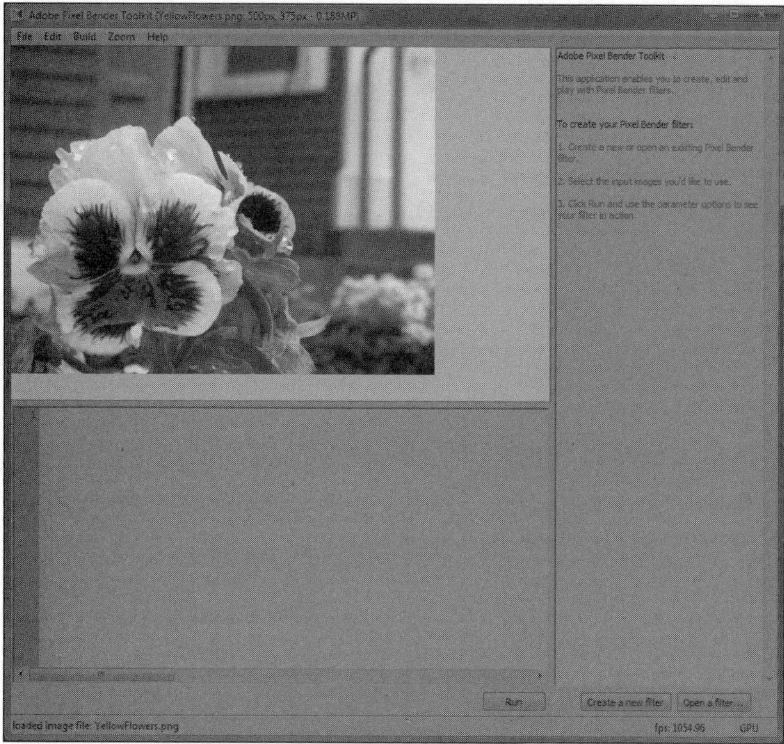

Figure 5-3. The Image View of the Pixel Bender Toolkit with an image loaded

2. Select File ➤ Open Filter to open a kernel. Kernel files will have a `.pbk` extension, and by default you should see the kernels that shipped with Pixel Bender in the `pixel bender files` directory. Select `twirl.pbk`. At this point, the bottom left of the interface should be populated with the script that creates the kernel, as in Figure 5-4. This is the Source Editor where you will program the kernels using the Pixel Bender programming language.

Figure 5-4. The Source Editor of the Pixel Bender Toolkit where the kernel code is entered

3. With a kernel opened, you will oftentimes have parameters that can be set. You will not see these automatically upon opening a kernel, though, but must first run the kernel. Click the Run button in the bottom right of the interface. A very slight twirl will be applied to the image using the default parameter settings, and the right side of the interface will populate with controls for setting a number of parameters, as shown in Figure 5-5. This is the Filter Parameter User Interface, with its controls defined from within the kernel script.
4. To see the effect more clearly, set the center parameter sliders to 250 for [0] and 187 for [1], which is the approximate center of the image. Set the radius slider to 60 and twirlAngle to 360. The image should be automatically updated after each change, and the end result will look like Figure 5-6.

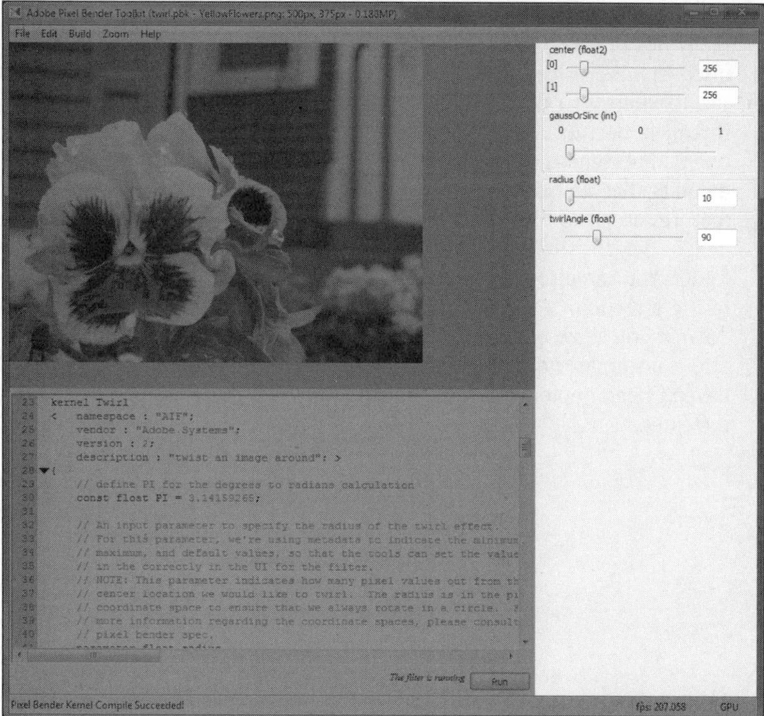

Figure 5-5.
The Filter Parameter User Interface of the Pixel Bender Toolkit where parameter controls are surfaced

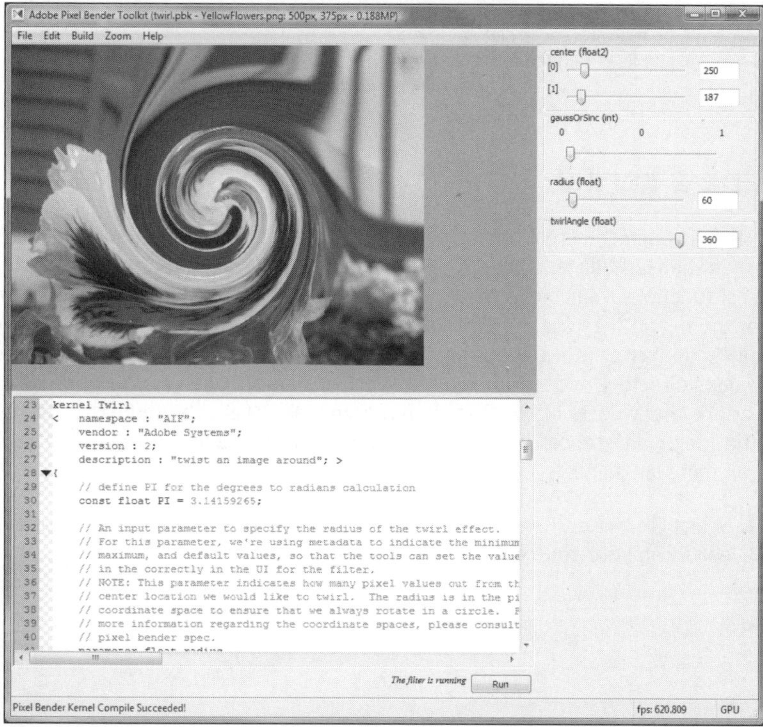

Figure 5-6.
The twirl kernel distorting the loaded image

5. Open the menus at the top of the interface to see what options are offered. There's really not much to the application that requires a lot of in-depth exploration and discovery. We will look at the File menu more closely as we create examples, but this is where you open and save kernels, open images to test upon, save images that have been processed, and compile the bytecode for Flash. The Edit menu can open a Preferences dialog, as shown in Figure 5-7, which for the most part contains defaults that do not need to be changed, like enabling warnings when non-Flash features are used. However, you can change the default directories for kernels and images, which is handy if you do not save your work into the default installation folder. You can also set the background color to something other than black (I like to use a medium gray) and can set defaults for your kernel definitions. Finally, the Zoom menu allows you to set different zoom levels, which you may use on occasion after cursing at the screen when trying to use the standard Ctrl+/- shortcuts that haven't been implemented (or maybe that's just me and I need to cut back on my caffeine).

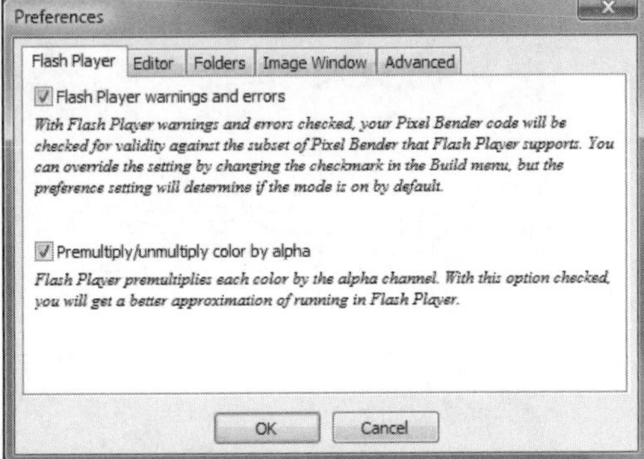

Figure 5-7. The Edit ➤ Preferences dialog in the Pixel Bender Toolkit

Creating a kernel

Let's step through the creation and testing of a kernel and compile the bytecode needed for use in the Flash Player. This will not be a lesson in C, nor will we cover all of the mathematical functions available in the Pixel Bender programming language—there are quite a few of them, and they are mostly fairly standard operations, many of which have equivalents in ActionScript (it's a good idea to have the language reference, which you can find in the docs directory under your Pixel Bender installation, open as you work). What we will look at are the aspects of the Pixel Bender language that are unique to that technology and the major differences between writing ActionScript and writing in the Pixel Bender programming language.

1. Select File ➤ New Kernel Filter from the menu at the top. The following script should appear in your source editor:

```
<languageVersion : 1.0;>

kernel NewFilter
<   namespace : "Your Namespace";
    vendor : "Your Vendor";
    version : 1;
    description : "your description";
>
{
    input image4 src;
    output pixel4 dst;

    void
    evaluatePixel()
    {
        dst = sampleNearest(src,outCoord());
    }
}
```

The namespace and vendor properties will read "Your Namespace" and "Your Vendor", respectively, if you have not changed these defaults in your Preferences. These attributes are useful documentation of a kernel and are required for compiling. Also important is the languageVersion at the top, defining the version of Pixel Bender that the kernel was written for, so leave this as is. The name of your kernel is defined after the kernel keyword, and the kernel code is then enclosed within curly braces.

2. Change the name of the kernel to Desaturate, and enter a description, as in the following example. Feel free to change the vendor and namespace to your own.

```
kernel Desaturate
<   namespace : "com.bobs27";
    vendor : "Todd Yard";
    version : 1;
    description : "Desaturates an image by a specified amount.";
>
```

3. The next two lines of the kernel define the input and output for the kernel, src, and dst:

```
input image4 src;
output pixel4 dst;
```

The names of these (src and dst) can be whatever you set them to be, but every kernel should have an input and output defined using the keywords. The data type of the input or output immediately follows the keywords, and these are usually image4 for input and pixel4 for output. image4 means there are four elements per pixel (the color and alpha channels), and similarly, pixel4 will hold a pixel with four components (once again, the color and alpha channels).

These lines basically say that the input for the kernel will be a 32-bit image and the output for each run of the algorithm will be a single 32-bit pixel. The algorithm is called once per pixel (these calls are all done in parallel), so when we write our script, it will look to process a single pixel in the image.

As I am not a fan of too many abbreviations in my code, I generally change the name of these parameters to something more explicit. For this example, alter yours as well to the following:

```
input image4 source;
output pixel4 result;
```

4. The last block within the kernel is the evaluatePixel() function. When developing kernels for ActionScript, this is the only function that can be defined (though Pixel Bender supports other function definitions when exporting to other applications). The return type of evaluatePixel() is always void, and the function will never accept any parameters itself, so its signature will never change. It is just the contents of the function that you will update to alter the resulting pixel based on your algorithm.

   The default evaluatePixel() function has a single line of code that uses two built-in functions in the Pixel Bender programming language, outCoord() and sampleNearest(). Let's first update the lines to use our new parameter names, and then we'll discuss what each of these does.

   ```
   void
   evaluatePixel()
   {
       result = sampleNearest(source, outCoord());
   }
   ```

   Whatever you assign to your output variable (in this case, remember, we called it result) will be assigned to the current pixel being evaluated. sampleNearest() is a built-in function that you will use in nearly all of your kernels. It takes two parameters, an image (it could be one of the image1, image2, image3, or image4 types, depending on the color depth, though most usually it will be of the image4 type and will be one of the input parameters) and a coordinate that is a float2 type. float2 is a vector of two floating point numbers (there is also the scalar type float, which is a single floating point number, and the vectors float3 and float4, which contain three or four floating point numbers, respectively). To get the float2 coordinate of the current pixel being evaluated, we use outCoord(), which returns its x and y position. You will nearly always use this in your code, unless you are creating an image effect independent of the actual pixels in the image.

   sampleNearest() is one of three functions that returns a pixel value in an image based on a coordinate position. This function uses nearest neighbor sampling to return a pixel color. The other two sampling options, sample() and sampleLinear(), are actually identical and perform a bilinear interpolation of the adjacent pixels. The difference in these interpolation methods is only noticeable when the coordinates passed to the functions are not at pixel centers. All three of these functions are overloaded and accept any of the four image data types. In each case, the function will return a pixel type with the same number of channels as the image type (pixel4 will be returned if image4 was passed in, pixel3 for image3, etc.).

5. If you do not have the WildFlowers.png image currently loaded, use File ➤ Load Image 1 to select it. Once this loads, click the Run button in the lower right corner. No parameters should appear on the right of the interface, since we have yet to

define any, and the image of the flowers should remain unchanged, since right now, our evaluatePixel() function simply returns the pixel evaluated without any processing.

6. The first thing we will do is look at how channel information can be accessed and altered. A variable of the pixel4 data type has r, g, b, and a properties that can be accessed. (r can also be accessed as x or s; g can be accessed as y or t; b can be accessed as z or p; and a can be accessed as w or q. I find this confusing myself, though I'm sure there is good reason for it. For our purposes, r, g, b, and a will do nicely, and we will quietly sweep those other names under the rug.) Each of these properties holds a value between 0 and 1, which corresponds to 0–255 in ActionScript for a channel brightness value. You can directly alter the brightness of a specific channel by accessing its corresponding property. For instance, to reduce the red channel by 50 percent, you can change the code in evaluatePixel() to the following:

```
void
evaluatePixel()
{
    pixel4 px = sampleNearest(source, outCoord());
    px.r *= 0.5;
    result = px;
}
```

If you run this, you will see a resulting image like Figure 5-8.

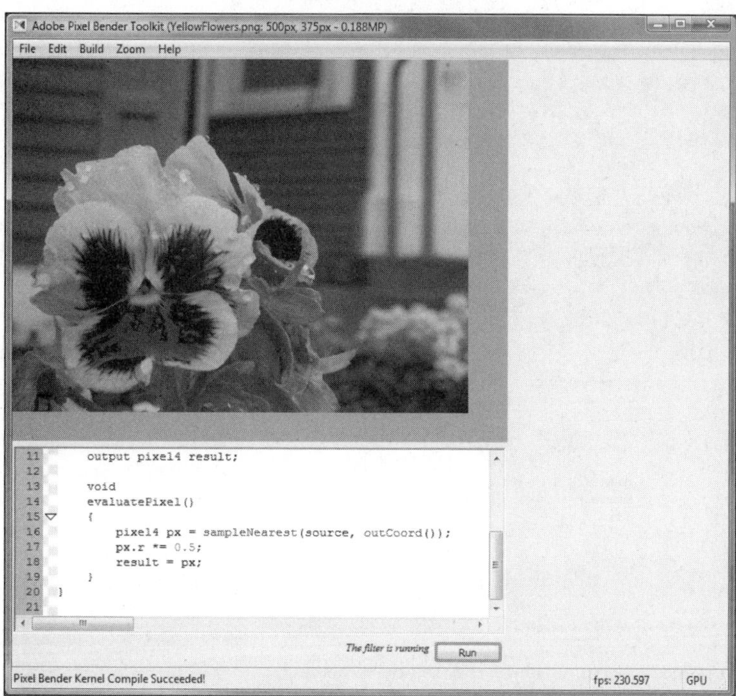

Figure 5-8. The red channel reduced by 50 percent

7. One of the cool abilities of these pixel vectors is that you can access channels simultaneously to manipulate their values, called swizzling. So if you wanted to reduce brightness of an image in all channels by 50 percent, instead of calling the following:

```
px.r *= 0.5;
px.g *= 0.5;
px.b *= 0.5;
```

you can tackle all three channels at the same time by changing your code to the following:

```
void
evaluatePixel()
{
    pixel4 px = sampleNearest(source, outCoord());
    px.rgb *= 0.5;
    result = px;
}
```

You can see the result in Figure 5-9. Personally, I think swizzling is pretty fantastic.

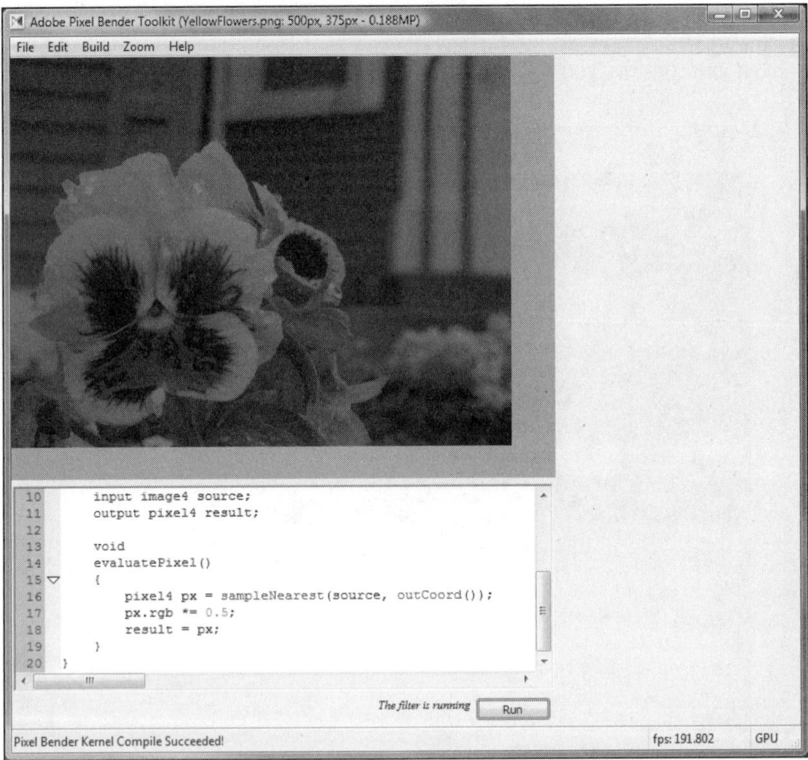

Figure 5-9. All color channels reduced by 50 percent

8. Using swizzling, you can easily do some swift manipulation of channels, like replacing all channels with the red channel (as we did last chapter through several copyChannel() calls of BitmapData), with the result shown in Figure 5-10:

```
pixel4 px = sampleNearest(source, outCoord());
px.rgb = px.rrr;
result = px;
```

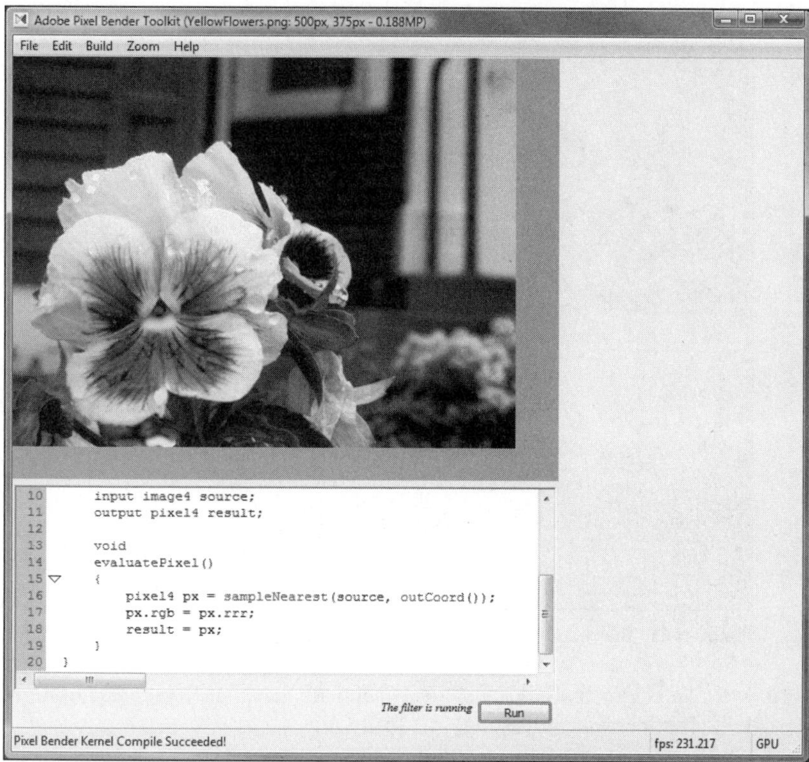

Figure 5-10. The red channel data used for all three channels, though difficult to recognize in a grayscale image

Or swapping the brightness data between two channels, like the following example, which swaps the red and blue channels with the result shown in Figure 5-11:

```
pixel4 px = sampleNearest(source, outCoord());
px.rb = px.br;
result = px;
```

9. To create a kernel that will desaturate an image by a certain amount, we will first declare a constant value outside of our evaluatePixel() function using the const keyword. This value can then be reused in all calls to the evaluatePixel() function.

```
const float3 grayValues = float3(0.3, 0.59, 0.11);

input image4 source;
output pixel4 result;
```

Here, a constant named grayValues contains a vector of three float values. These values you may recognize as the numbers we used with ColorMatrixFilter to create a grayscale image.

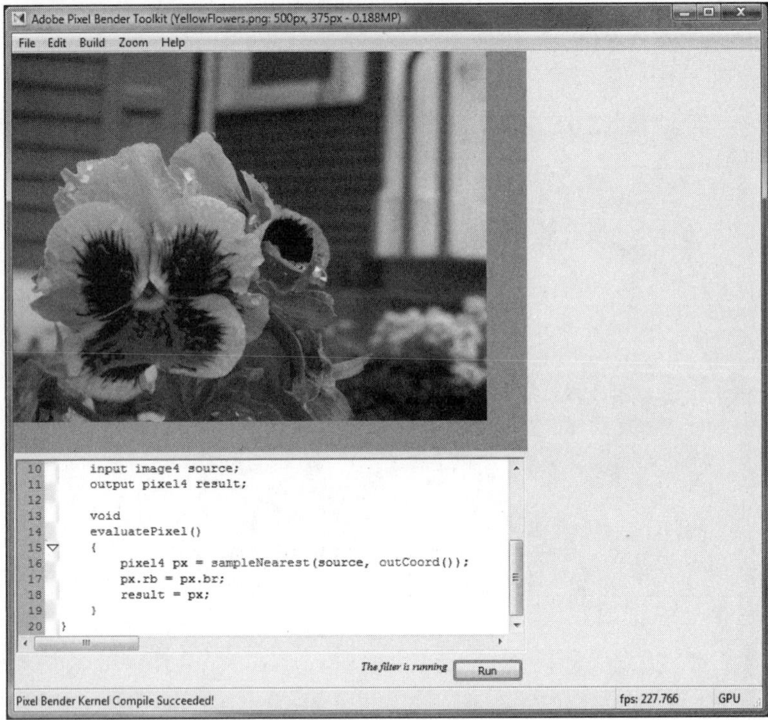

Figure 5-11. The red and blue channels' data swapped

10. Now, let's alter the evaluatePixel() function so that it will desaturate an image fully. The following code does just that:

```
void
evaluatePixel()
{
    pixel4 px = sampleNearest(source, outCoord());
    float distanceToDesaturatedValues = dot(px.rgb, grayValues);
    float3 fullDesaturate = float3(distanceToDesaturatedValues);
    px.rgb = fullDesaturate;
    result = px;
}
```

distanceToDesaturatedValues is a float value we populate by using the dot() function, which returns the dot product of two vectors. The dot product, also known as a scalar product, is the distance between two vectors, so what we are finding out here is how far our current pixel colors are from the desaturated values.

In the next line, we assign a float3 vector to the fullDesaturate variable. All we do to accomplish this is wrap our single float value in the float3 type, which gets automatically converted to be a vector of three floating point numbers, all of the same value.

In the final new line, we assign this new float3 vector of desaturated values to the `rgb` properties of our pixel and return this as a result. The processed image is shown in Figure 5-12.

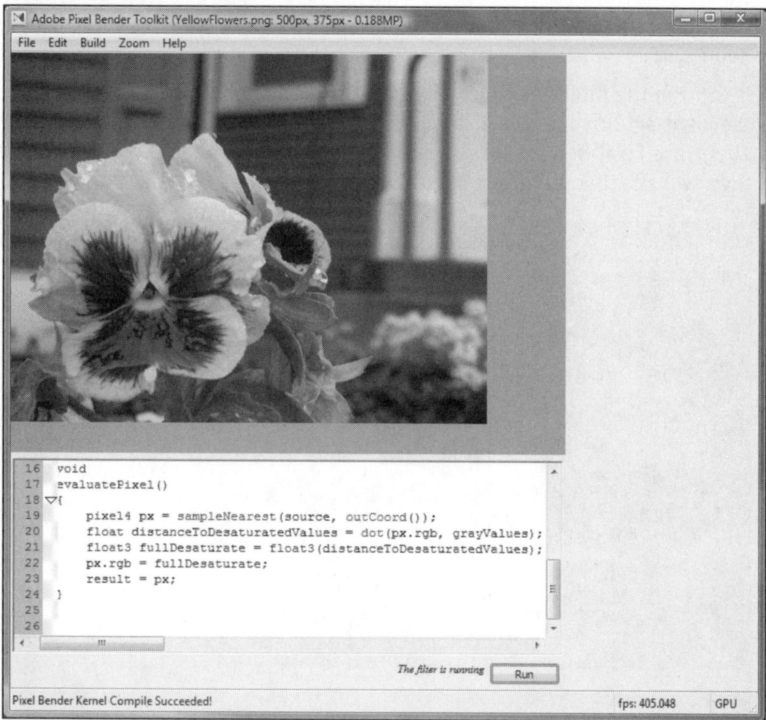

Figure 5-12. Full desaturation applied to the image though no difference can be seen here in a grayscale image

11. This kernel would be better if the level of desaturation was configurable. You can add any number of parameters to a kernel that can then have values passed in, in our case through an ActionScript shader. A parameter is defined outside of your `evaluatePixel()` function, where you define the input, output, and any constants. We will add a `percent` parameter that will take a value between 0 and 1, with 0 being no desaturation and 1 being full desaturation.

```
parameter float percent
<
    minValue:       0.0;
    maxValue:       1.0;
    defaultValue:   1.0;
    description:    "Percent image should be desaturated.";
>;

const float3 grayValues = float3(0.3, 0.59, 0.11);

input image4 source;
output pixel4 result;
```

The `parameter` keyword is used to define the parameter, followed by the data type (float works for us since we require a number between 0 and 1) and the name of the parameter. Within the parameter definition, you want to at least set the `minValue` and `maxValue` attributes, though it is a good idea to also provide a `defaultValue`. The description is great for documentation of the class and can be read through the debugger.

If you run the filter again, you will find that you now have a UI element pop up on the right side of the application, as in Figure 5-13. That's one of the nice things about the Pixel Bender Toolkit: it allows you to very easily see how different settings will affect your images by giving you UI controls for your parameters.

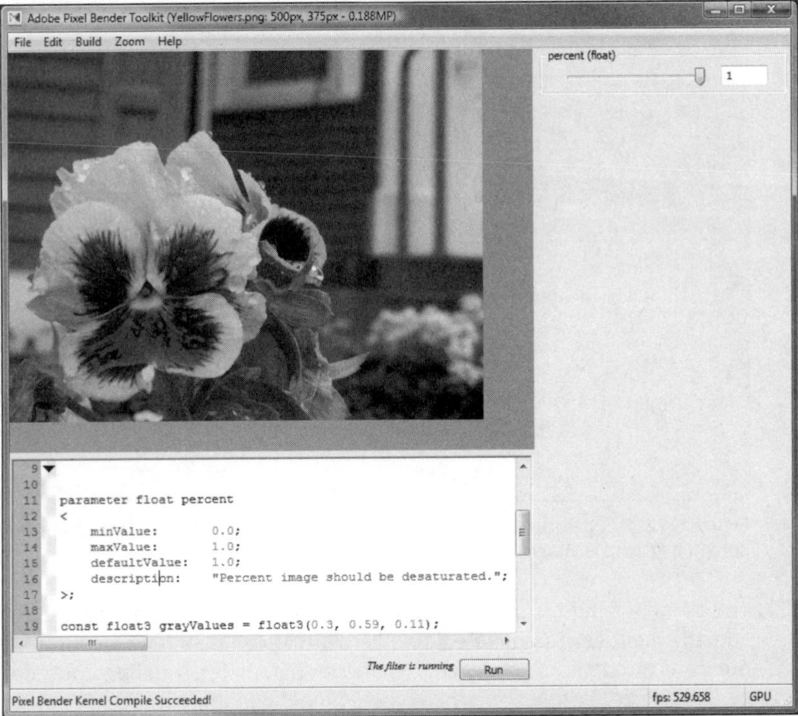

Figure 5-13. A percent parameter is defined, surfacing a UI control.

Adjusting the percent slider won't do anything at this time, since we have not used it in our `evaluatePixel()` code. We'll do that now.

12. To take advantage of the `percent` parameter we added in the last step, change the `evaluatePixel()` code to the following:

```
void
evaluatePixel()
{
    float4 px = sampleNearest(source, outCoord());
    float distanceToDesaturatedValues = dot(px.rgb, grayValues);
    float3 fullDesaturate = float3(distanceToDesaturatedValues);
    float3 noDesaturate = px.rgb;
```

```
    px.rgb = mix(noDesaturate, fullDesaturate, percent);
    result = px;
}
```

The first new line grabs the RGB values of our unprocessed pixel. The next line uses the built-in `mix()` function to interpolate between the unprocessed pixel and the fully desaturated pixel by a specified percentage. Basically, if `percent` was 0, the `noDesaturate` pixel value would be used fully. If `percent` was 1, `fullDesaturate` would be used fully. Any amount in between these values would mix the two at the specified percentage.

If you run your filter now, you will see that dragging the percent slider will adjust the amount of desaturation that is applied to the image, as shown in Figure 5-14. The full kernel code, which can be found in this chapter's files as `desaturate.pbk`, follows:

```
<languageVersion: 1.0;>

kernel Desaturate
<
    namespace:      "com.bobs27";
    vendor:         "Todd Yard";
    version:        1;
    description:    "Desaturates an image by a specified amount.";
>
{
    parameter float percent
    <
        minValue:       0.0;
        maxValue:       1.0;
        defaultValue:   1.0;
        description:    "Percent image should be desaturated.";
    >;

    const float3 grayValues = float3(0.3, 0.59, 0.11);

    input image4 source;
    output pixel4 result;

    void
    evaluatePixel()
    {
        float4 px = sampleNearest(source, outCoord());
        float distanceToDesaturatedValues = dot(px.rgb, grayValues);
        float3 fullDesaturate = float3(distanceToDesaturatedValues);
        float3 noDesaturate = px.rgb;
        px.rgb = mix(noDesaturate, fullDesaturate, percent);
        result = px;
    }

}
```

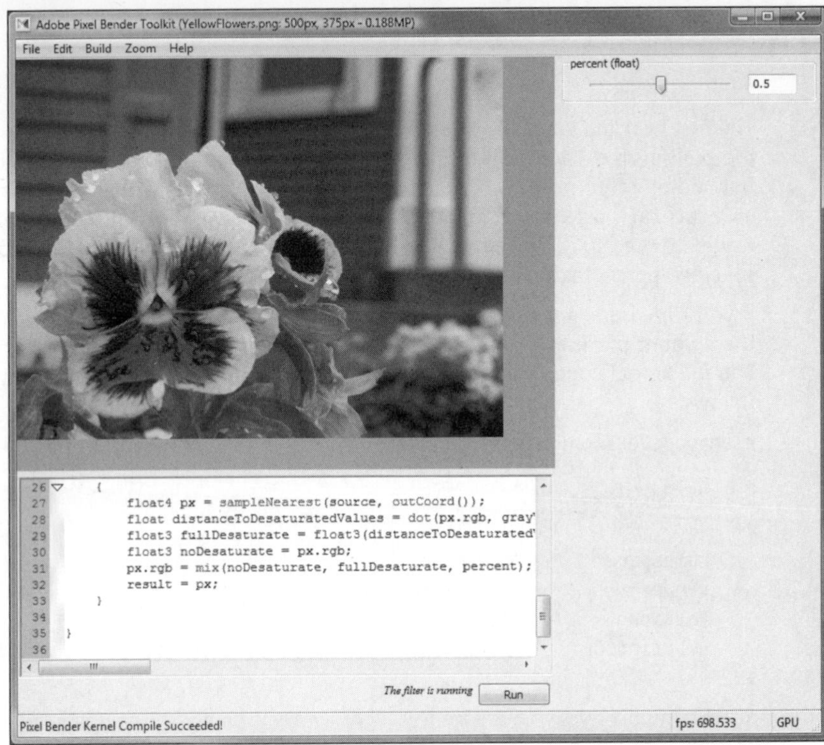

Figure 5-14. A desaturation of 50 percent is applied to the image using the configurable percent parameter.

13. Once you are satisfied with a filter, you can compile it as bytecode for use with ActionScript. This is handled through the File ➤ Export Filter for Flash Player menu command. There are no options here, just a browse dialog to let you choose where to save the file and what it should be named. Go ahead and save the kernel as `desaturate.pbk` if you haven't done so already, and compile the bytecode as `desaturate.pbj`.

That's it for the Pixel Bender Toolkit. In just a few pages, you learned an entirely new application and have scratched the surface of a new language, so that's not too shabby. We will be working within the toolkit to explore some shader possibilities throughout this chapter, but for now, we will return to our ActionScript editor to see how this bytecode can be used in the Flash Player.

Knowing Flash's limitations

There are several caveats to working with Pixel Bender in the Flash Player, especially if you are referring to the documentation that includes functionality that is available to other applications but not to Flash.

- There is no support for arrays. This really hurts, but what can you do? If you require array-like functionality, you will need to define multiple variables that you can treat as an array in your code (e.g., `color0`, `color1`, and `color2` could represent three entries that would more easily be defined as an array of three values). Pixel Bender does support a matrix type or the vectors (like float2, float3, and float4), so these are ways to get a collection of related variables into the kernel (they are even typed as Array in ActionScript, though of fixed length).
- Loops are not supported. This is more of a hurdle than the lack of support of arrays. For instance, if you need to determine pixel values that radiate out from the current pixel, perhaps to create a blur, you cannot use a looping structure to do this but must explicitly test against each pixel, which makes enabling this to be configurable difficult at the very least.
- No Boolean type is supported. This isn't a huge deal, since you can simply use an int and assign either 0 or 1.
- Regions, which make up a large part of the documentation for Pixel Bender, are not supported in the Flash Player. You cannot access or act on regions of pixel data and cannot use any of the built-in region functions.
- You cannot create additional functions for subroutines, as is demonstrated in the documentation. This is annoying but simply means your `evaluatePixel()` function must contain all of the logic.
- You cannot import libraries to use within a kernel. Like any type of modular development, this would ease the burden of performing repetitive tasks and speed development but is not supported at this time. Be ready for lots of copying and pasting.
- The Pixel Bender documentation presents an `evaluateDependents()` function that allows you to compute values once that can then be used for all pixels. Forget about it. Walk away, and forget you ever saw it.
- Shaders in the Flash Player are run not on the GPU but on the CPU. This software implementation of Pixel Bender makes things more consistent cross-platform and on different machines, especially when certain graphics capabilities are not supported and the Flash Player would have to fall back on a software implementation anyway. But it does make it slower than running effects in the toolkit or with After Effects or Photoshop. When using shaders, test on different machines and different operating systems to determine whether the results are satisfactory.

That might seem like a lot of limitations, and, well, it is; let's be honest. However, a lot is still possible with the Flash Player implementation of Pixel Bender, as you will discover in the coming pages. When ActionScript was first rolled out, there were something like eight commands, but the stuff people produced was incredible. I've no doubt similar surprises will come with Pixel Bender. Be sure to keep your eye on the Pixel Bender Exchange on Adobe's web site to see the latest contributions.

Using shaders in the Flash Player

Playing around in the Pixel Bender Toolkit is all well and good, but to take advantage of the Pixel Bender kernels in the Flash Player, we need to get their compiled bytecode into a SWF and then apply it to display objects through ActionScript. Compared with writing the kernels (which, as you just saw, isn't even a difficult task), using them in your applications is a snap. Here's how.

Embedding bytecode

If you are using the Flex compiler, you can simply embed the bytecode at compile time just as you would embed images or fonts (to use the Flex compiler within the Flash IDE, see the appendix). This will embed the Pixel Bender bytecode into your application at compile time, allowing you to immediately access the data. Since this is not compatible with those users not using the Flex compiler, we won't be using this method in our examples, but the code needed to embed the bytecode and instantiate a shader would look like the following, which you can find as `DesaturateWithEmbedTest.as` in this chapter's files. The result is shown in Figure 5-15.

```
package {

  import flash.display.Bitmap;
  import flash.display.Shader;
  import flash.display.Sprite;
  import flash.filters.ShaderFilter;
  import flash.utils.ByteArray;

  [SWF(width=500, height=500, backgroundColor=0x000000)]

  public class DesaturateWithEmbedTest extends Sprite {

    [Embed(source='/source/desaturate.pbj',➥
mimeType='application/octet-stream')]
    private static const DesaturateKernel:Class;

    [Embed(source='/source/butterflies.jpg')]
    private static const BitmapClass:Class;

    public function DesaturateWithEmbedTest() {
      var bitmap:Bitmap = new BitmapClass() as Bitmap;
      var byteArray:ByteArray = new DesaturateKernel() as ByteArray;
      var shader:Shader = new Shader(byteArray);
      var filter:ShaderFilter = new ShaderFilter(shader);
      bitmap.filters = [filter];
      addChild(bitmap);
    }

  }

}
```

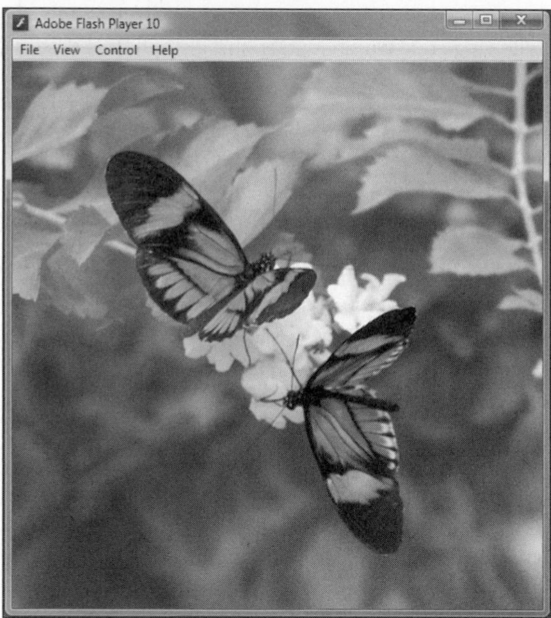

Figure 5-15. The desaturate shader embedded in the SWF and applied to an image, though not apparent in a grayscale screenshot

The bytecode is embedded using the `Embed` metatag with the `mimeType` attribute set as `"application/octet-stream"`. Like all embeds, it is included as a class that can be instantiated at runtime. When it is instantiated, you can see that it is actually a ByteArray instance. It is this ByteArray that can be passed in the constructor to Shader, and through this Shader instance, you can set parameters.

One way to apply a shader to an image is through a filter. To do this, you pass the Shader instance to the ShaderFilter constructor. ShaderFilter is another BitmapFilter, like BlurFilter or DropShadowFilter, but its job is to wrap Pixel Bender shaders. Since it is just another BitmapFilter, it can be applied in the same way as the filters we've previously explored, either through DisplayObject's `filters` array (as we do here) or through BitmapData's `applyFilter()` method.

This process of embedding the bytecode is great if you are using the Flex compiler and will always be applying the shader, as long as you don't mind that the SWF contains the extra bytes and increased file size because of it. If, however, you are not using the Flex compiler, need the shaders to load only if applied, or want to keep the size of the initial SWF down, you will need to load in the bytecode at runtime. We look at how in the next section.

Loading kernels at runtime

A process that will work in both Flash and Flex Builder to use shaders, no matter the compiler, is to load the bytecode for the kernels in at runtime. This is similar to loading any type of data in at runtime using the URLLoader class, except the data you are loading in is the bytecode. The following code would load in and instantiate a shader, which could then be applied as a filter:

```
private function loadShader(path:String):void {
  var loader:URLLoader = new URLLoader();
  loader.dataFormat = URLLoaderDataFormat.BINARY;
  loader.addEventListener(Event.COMPLETE, onShaderLoaded);
  loader.load(new URLRequest(path));
}

private function onShaderLoaded(event:Event):void {
  var loader:URLLoader = event.target as URLLoader;
  _shader = new Shader(loader.data as ByteArray);
}
```

You can see that other than setting the dataFormat for the URLLoader to BINARY, there is nothing out of the ordinary about the loading of the data. Once the data has loaded, you can cast it as a ByteArray and pass it to the Shader constructor—piece of cake. We'll create a concrete example for loading the bytecode in the next section.

Allowing for loading or embedding

To make it easier to work with the shaders throughout the rest of this chapter, we'll create a wrapper class that will allow you to either embed or load the bytecode depending on your compiler of choice. Basically, the ShaderWrapper class, as we will call it, will take either a path to a file or the embedded class in its constructor. It will then load the bytecode if it needs to, or simply instantiate the ByteArray class, and create a Shader instance which can then be accessed outside of the class. The following code, found as ShaderWrapper.as in this chapter's files, accomplishes this:

```
package {

  import flash.display.Shader;
  import flash.events.Event;
  import flash.events.EventDispatcher;
  import flash.net.URLLoader;
  import flash.net.URLLoaderDataFormat;
  import flash.net.URLRequest;
  import flash.utils.ByteArray;

  public class ShaderWrapper extends EventDispatcher {

    private var _shader:Shader;

    public function ShaderWrapper(pathOrClass:Object) {
      var shaderClass:Class = pathOrClass as Class;
      if (shaderClass != null) {
```

```
        createShader(ByteArray(new shaderClass()));
      } else if ((pathOrClass as String) != null) {
        load(pathOrClass as String);
      } else {
        throw new Error("Invalid object passed to constructor.");
      }
    }

    private function createShader(data:ByteArray):void {
      _shader = new Shader(data);
      dispatchEvent(new Event(Event.COMPLETE));
    }

    private function load(path:String):void {
      var loader:URLLoader = new URLLoader();
      loader.dataFormat = URLLoaderDataFormat.BINARY;
      loader.addEventListener(Event.COMPLETE, onShaderLoaded);
      loader.load(new URLRequest(path));
    }

    private function onShaderLoaded(event:Event):void {
      var loader:URLLoader = event.target as URLLoader;
      createShader(loader.data as ByteArray);
    }

    public function get shader():Shader {
      return _shader;
    }

  }

}
```

The constructor of the class takes an object, which should either be the embedded bytecode class or a path to the `.pbj` file. If it is the class, then `createShader()` is called immediately, and the Shader instance is created. If it is a path to a file, `load()` is called, which makes a request for the bytecode. The handler for the `COMPLETE` event then passes the loaded bytecode to `createShader()`, at which time a new `COMPLETE` event is dispatched to any listeners to inform them that the shader is ready. The shader itself can be accessed through the implicit `shader` getter method.

To demonstrate this class, let's take a look at `DesaturateTest.as`, included with this chapter's files as well. This class extends the AbstractImageLoader that we've used in previous chapters to load in an image to process and then applies our desaturate shader to the loaded image. The actual class file includes lines both to embed the bytecode (which is commented out by default in the file) as well as to load it at runtime. The results would be the same as those shown in Figure 5-15. The following code is the class with the commented out lines to embed the bytecode removed for readability. I will show how you can use these lines in the next section:

```
package {

  import flash.display.Shader;
  import flash.filters.ShaderFilter;
  import flash.events.Event;

  [SWF(width=500, height=500, backgroundColor=0x000000)]

  public class DesaturateTest extends AbstractImageLoader {

    private var _shaderWrapper:ShaderWrapper;

    public function DesaturateTest() {
      super("../../assets/butterflies.jpg");
    }

    override protected function runPostImageLoad():void {
      _shaderWrapper = ➥
new ShaderWrapper("../../assets/desaturate.pbj");
      if (_shaderWrapper.shader == null) {
        _shaderWrapper.addEventListener(Event.COMPLETE,➥
onShaderLoaded);
      } else {
        applyShader();
      }
    }

    private function applyShader():void {
      var shader:Shader = _shaderWrapper.shader;
      var filter:ShaderFilter = new ShaderFilter(shader);
      _loadedBitmap.filters = [filter];
      addChild(_loadedBitmap);
    }

    private function onShaderLoaded(event:Event):void {
      applyShader();
    }

  }

}
```

In the `runPostImageLoad()` method, which you may recall is invoked after the image is loaded and ready for processing, we create a new ShaderWrapper instance and pass in the path to the `.pbj` file (if you are testing this file, make sure the path is correct according to your file system and how you've laid out the documents). Since this will require loading, the shader property will initially be null, so we set up a listener for when the COMPLETE event is fired. Within that event handler, onShaderLoaded(), we call applyShader(), which grabs a reference to the shader and passes this into a new ShaderFilter instance. This filter is then applied to the loaded bitmap.

If you want to embed the bytecode instead, add the embed tag at the top of the class:

```
[Embed(source='/source/desaturate.pbj',➥
mimeType='application/octet-stream')]
private static const DesaturateKernel:Class;
```

Then you can use the constructor that passes the class to the ShaderWrapper instance:

```
_shaderWrapper = new ShaderWrapper(DesaturateKernel);
```

The result will look the same.

Deconstructing shaders

A number of different classes are related to or incorporated into the Shader class in ActionScript. Before we create more complex examples, let's look at these classes to see how they work together.

Shader

This, of course, is the class that you pass the bytecode to and then interact through to process image data. You've already seen how the loaded bytecode may be passed to the Shader constructor.

```
var shader:Shader = new Shader(byteArray);
```

As an alternative to this method, you can pass the bytecode to the Shader instance after instantiation through its write-only byteCode property.

```
var shader:Shader = new Shader();
shader.byteCode = byteArray;
```

Shader includes two more properties, data and precisionHint. precisionHint determines the precision of mathematical operations, basically how far to carry out to the right of the decimal before rounding occurs. The default is ShaderPrecision.FULL, which tells the shader to use the IEEE 32-bit floating point standard. Generally, this is what you want unless you are seeing a slowdown, which can occur with some operations. In that case, you can use ShaderPrecision.FAST, which is less precise but can speed up calculations. Be warned that it can also produce different results on different machines.

The data property of Shader holds an instance of the ShaderData class, through which you can access information about the shader and can read and set parameters. We'll look at that more closely next.

ShaderData

A ShaderData instance can be found in any Shader instance's `data` property that has loaded bytecode. ShaderData contains a number of properties that allow you to inspect the shader and set parameters:

- `version`: The version of Pixel Bender the kernel was written for
- `name`: The name of the shader, as was set through the `name` attribute in the kernel
- `namespace`: The namespace that was defined for the shader, as was set through the `namespace` attribute in the kernel
- `description`: The description of the shader's purpose, as was set through the `description` attribute in the kernel
- `vendor`: The vendor for the shader, as was set in the `vendor` attribute in the kernel

In addition to these properties, there will be input properties of the ShaderInput type, which will take their names from how they were named in the kernel (for instance, `src` or `source`). Blend mode shaders will take two inputs, which we will look at in a later section, though you do not actively have to set these properties.

Also present in a ShaderData instance may be configurable parameters that will be instances of ShaderParameter. These will only appear if they were defined in the kernel, and their names as well will be dependent on how they were named in the kernel.

ShaderInput

Shaders can have zero or more inputs, which will be a BitmapData or ByteArray instance, or a vector of numbers. The ShaderInput instances that may be present in a shader (depending on if they have been defined in the kernel) allow you to set these inputs.

The name of the property through which the ShaderInput is accessed is dependent on how it was defined in the kernel. For instance, we defined the input in our desaturate kernel as `source`, so that is how it can be accessed in the ActionScript shader. Note that we didn't have to do that when applying the shader in our example, though. This is because in some cases the input is implied, as when a filter is applied to a DisplayObject or BitmapData instance. Only when there are additional inputs (imagine you have created a filter that requires a second image in order to process the first image) or when there is no specific image the shader is applied to do you need to worry about setting the input for the shader. You would set this through the `input` property of the ShaderInput instance:

```
shader.source.input = bitmapData;
```

Remember that the name of the property, in this case `source`, is dependent on how the shader was defined.

ShaderParameter

When parameters have been defined in the kernel, as we did with the `percent` parameter for the desaturate kernel, these are surfaced in ActionScript as ShaderParameter instances through a ShaderData instance.

```
parameter float percent
<
    minValue:       0.0;
    maxValue:       1.0;
    defaultValue:   1.0;
    description:    "percent image should be desaturated";
>;
```

Just as with the ShaderInput instances, a ShaderParameter is accessed through a ShaderData instance using the name that was given to it in the kernel (in our example, percent). A ShaderParameter instance will have the following properties:

- `name`: The name of the parameter, as defined in the kernel
- `description`: The description of the parameter's purpose, as defined in the kernel
- `type`: The name of the data type for the parameter, as defined in the kernel (Note that this will be the Pixel Bender type, like float, not the ActionScript equivalent, like Number.)
- `index`: The index of the parameter in the kernel definition
- `minValue`: An array containing the minimum value setting as defined in the kernel
- `maxValue`: An array containing the maximum value setting as defined in the kernel
- `defaultValue`: An array containing the default value as defined in the kernel
- `value`: An array containing the current value assigned to the parameter

It is important to note that all of the value properties (`minValue`, `maxValue`, `defaultValue`, and `value`) contain arrays, even if the data type for the parameter is scalar (float, int). This means that when assigning values, as we will do in the next section, you will always need to use an array.

Also, although the ShaderParameter contains the `min` and `max` values, that does not mean that you must adhere to them, and there is nothing that enforces them or throws an error if you ignore them (though you could certainly modify the ShaderWrapper class to take and handle invalid parameters).

ShaderJob

You would use a ShaderJob if you are running a shader behind the scenes as a background process. You would basically create a ShaderJob instance, pass it a shader to use, pass in an object to process, and then call `start()` to begin the job. You can subscribe to an event to know when the job is complete. We will explore this in more detail at the end of this chapter.

ShaderEvent

When using ShaderJob, you need to be informed of when a job is complete. For that, you use the `ShaderEvent.COMPLETE` event. When we look at ShaderJob at the end of this chapter, we will also look at how ShaderEvent ties in to the process.

Passing parameters to shaders

Earlier this section, we loaded in our desaturate kernel into the Flash Player and applied it to an image. What we did not do was set the percent parameter on our shader, so the default of 1.0 was applied. Now that you've had a look at what makes up a shader on the ActionScript side, you can apply your knowledge to the example and dynamically set the percent property.

To set the value of a parameter, you need to access the corresponding ShaderParameter instance through the ShaderData instance of the shader. You then assign a value to the shader parameter's value property. This will always be an array, even if the parameter is for a scalar value (in which case it will be an array of length 1).

We will alter the DesaturateTest class so that the percentage of desaturation is dependent on the position of the mouse on the x axis. Full desaturation will occur when the mouse is at the right of the stage, and no desaturation will occur when the mouse is on the left of the stage. The following changes to the code handle this:

```
private function applyShader():void {
  addChild(_loadedBitmap);
  setDesaturationFilter();
  stage.addEventListener(MouseEvent.MOUSE_MOVE, onStageMouseMove);
}

private function setDesaturationFilter():void {
  var percent:Number = stage.mouseX/stage.stageWidth;
  var shader:Shader = _shaderWrapper.shader;
  shader.data.percent.value = [percent];
  var filter:ShaderFilter = new ShaderFilter(shader);
  _loadedBitmap.filters = [filter];
}

private function onStageMouseMove(event:MouseEvent):void {
  setDesaturationFilter();
}

private function onShaderLoaded(event:Event):void {
  applyShader();
}
```

In addition to these changes, you will also need to import the flash.events.MouseEvent class at the top of the class.

In the applyShader() method, we are now adding the loaded bitmap, calling a new setDesaturationFilter() method, and setting up an event listener for when the mouse moves. You will notice that, within that onStageMouseMove() handler, we are simply calling the same setDesaturationFilter() method to update the filter.

The setDesaturationFilter() determines the desired percent of desaturation based on the position of the mouse as a percent of the width of the stage. It then sets the value of the percent parameter of the shader. The remaining lines existed in our original implementation, with a new ShaderFilter being instantiated for our shader, which is then applied to the loaded bitmap.

Providing accessors

This code works and is a fine implementation, but I'm a bit bothered by the perceived (by me, at least) clunkiness of the following line:

```
shader.data.percent.value = [percent];
```

First, having to go through the data property is something I always forget (thank heavens for code hints and compile-time errors), and setting the value of the parameter also seems to be counterintuitive to how I want to work with a parameter. I understand that there may be times when you need to do runtime introspection of parameters to determine the min and max settings and data type, but generally, you won't be doing this and just want to set the property. Finally, having to wrap a scalar value in an array seems sloppy to me, and is something that I do forget (and you don't get a nice compile-time error for that).

Ideally, I would want to set a property with something as simple as this:

```
shaderWrapper.percent = percent;
```

There is a way to do exactly this using the Proxy class, but first, let's do a simple modification to the ShaderWrapper class to at least give us something close. You can then leverage those changes in creating a new proxy class, if that is more your cup of tea. You can add the following bold lines to create an explicit getter and setter for shader parameters:

```
private function onShaderLoaded(event:Event):void {
  var loader:URLLoader = event.target as URLLoader;
  createShader(loader.data as ByteArray);
}

public function getParameter(name:String):Object {
  if (_shader.data.hasOwnProperty(name)) {
    var value:Object = _shader.data[name].value;
    var type:String = _shader.data[name].type;
    if (type == "float" || type == "int") {
      value = (value as Array)[0];
    }
    return value;
  }
  return null;
}

public function setParameter(name:String, value:Object):Boolean {
  if (_shader.data.hasOwnProperty(name)) {
    if (!(value is Array)) {
      value = [value];
    }
```

```
      _shader.data[name].value = value;
      return true;
    }
    return false;
  }

  public function get shader():Shader {
    return _shader;
  }
```

As you can see, in getParameter(), we take all the fuss out of accessing the parameter by digging into the shader.data and grabbing the value from within the ShaderParameter instance. If the value is scalar, we take it out of the array's first index. In setParameter(), we reverse this by wrapping single scalar values in an array so that this doesn't have to be handled outside of the function. With these changes, you can then alter the DesaturateTest class to set the percent parameter (with some extra code to check whether the parameter has even changed) with the following code:

```
private function setDesaturationFilter():void {
  var percent:Number = stage.mouseX/stage.stageWidth;
  if (_shaderWrapper.getParameter("percent") != percent) {
    _shaderWrapper.setParameter("percent", percent);
    var shader:Shader = _shaderWrapper.shader;
    var filter:ShaderFilter = new ShaderFilter(shader);
    _loadedBitmap.filters = [filter];
  }
}
```

This makes the code much more readable to me, but we can go even further to make shaders easier to work with.

Creating a proxy

The setParameter() method works and is simple with no fuss, but if you want to enable setting a shader parameter with something as simple as an implicit setter, as in the following line of code, you need to look to the Proxy class:

```
shaderWrapper.percent = percent;
```

The flash.utils.Proxy class allows you to create dynamic classes that redirect calls for undefined methods and properties to a set of methods that allow you to determine what actions to perform with those calls. It is an ideal class for wrapping objects like Shader that could contain any number of inputs and parameters that are not known beforehand.

The way it works is that Proxy contains a number of methods that are called when a method or property is accessed on an instance and that property or method is not defined in the class. This book is not a general ActionScript reference, so we won't deep dive into the whole class and all the possibilities, but we will look at how you can use a Proxy subclass to help wrap Shader.

Have a look at the following code, and we'll break it down to discuss its important aspects. Don't be daunted by its length. More than half of the code is the same as ShaderWrapper, and the remaining new code is mostly to enable event dispatching.

```
package {

  import flash.display.Shader;
  import flash.events.Event;
  import flash.events.EventDispatcher;
  import flash.events.IEventDispatcher;
  import flash.net.URLLoader;
  import flash.net.URLLoaderDataFormat;
  import flash.net.URLRequest;
  import flash.utils.ByteArray;
  import flash.utils.Proxy;
  import flash.utils.flash_proxy;

  dynamic public class ShaderProxy extends Proxy➥
implements IEventDispatcher {

    private var _shader:Shader;
    private var _eventDispatcher:EventDispatcher;

    public function ShaderProxy(pathOrClass:Object) {
      _eventDispatcher = new EventDispatcher();
      var shaderClass:Class = pathOrClass as Class;
      if (shaderClass != null) {
        createShader(ByteArray(new shaderClass()));
      } else if ((pathOrClass as String) != null) {
        load(pathOrClass as String);
      } else {
        throw new Error("Invalid object passed to constructor.");
      }
    }

    private function createShader(data:ByteArray):void {
      _shader = new Shader(data);
      dispatchEvent(new Event(Event.COMPLETE));
    }

    private function load(path:String):void {
      var loader:URLLoader = new URLLoader();
      loader.dataFormat = URLLoaderDataFormat.BINARY;
      loader.addEventListener(Event.COMPLETE, onShaderLoaded);
      loader.load(new URLRequest(path));
    }

    private function onShaderLoaded(event:Event):void {
      var loader:URLLoader = event.target as URLLoader;
```

```
    createShader(loader.data as ByteArray);
  }

  override flash_proxy function getProperty(name:*):* {
    if (_shader) {
      return getParameter(name);
    }
    return null;
  }

  override flash_proxy function setProperty(name:*, value:*):void {
    if (_shader) {
      setParameter(name, value);
    }
  }

  public function getParameter(name:String):Object {
    if (_shader.data.hasOwnProperty(name)) {
      var value:Object = _shader.data[name].value;
      var type:String = _shader.data[name].type;
      if (type == "float" || type == "int") {
        value = (value as Array)[0];
      }
      return value;
    }
    return null;
  }

  public function setParameter(name:String, value:Object):Boolean {
    if (_shader.data.hasOwnProperty(name)) {
      if (!(value is Array)) {
        value = [value];
      }
      _shader.data[name].value = value;
      return true;
    }
    return false;
  }

  public function addEventListener(
    type:String,
    listener:Function,
    useCapture:Boolean=false,
    priority:int=0,
    useWeakReference:Boolean=true
  ):void {
    _eventDispatcher.addEventListener(type, listener,➥
useCapture, priority, useWeakReference);
  }
```

```
        public function removeEventListener(
          type:String,
          listener:Function,
          useCapture:Boolean=false
        ):void {
          _eventDispatcher.removeEventListener(type, listener, useCapture);
        }

        public function dispatchEvent(event:Event):Boolean {
          return _eventDispatcher.dispatchEvent(event);
        }

        public function willTrigger(type:String):Boolean {
          return _eventDispatcher.willTrigger(type);
        }

        public function hasEventListener(type:String):Boolean {
          return _eventDispatcher.hasEventListener(type);
        }

        public function get shader():Shader {
          return _shader;
        }

      }

    }
```

Since a Proxy instance is not an event dispatcher, we have to include one to be able to dispatch the COMPLETE event. The class implements the IEventDispatcher interface, so there are a number of required methods for this, but you can see that all of them simply pass the call directly to the EventDispatcher instance.

The more interesting code is that featuring the getProperty() and setProperty() methods. These are the methods that are invoked when a property is either accessed, getProperty(), or set, setProperty(), and that property is not defined in the class (there is also a callProperty() that does the same thing for methods, but we don't need that for this example). All that we have these methods do, after checking whether the shader exists or not, is to call the corresponding getParameter() or setParameter()—not much more to it than that. But what that allows is for the DesaturateTest, if the code was changed to use ShaderProxy instead of ShaderWrapper, to use the following lines in its setDesaturationFilter() method:

```
private function setDesaturationFilter():void {
  var percent:Number = stage.mouseX/stage.stageWidth;
  if (_shaderProxy.percent != percent) {
    _shaderProxy.percent = percent;
    var shader:Shader = _shaderProxy.shader;
    var filter:ShaderFilter = new ShaderFilter(shader);
    _loadedBitmap.filters = [filter];
  }
}
```

This is demonstrated in the DesaturateWithProxyTest.as file that is included with this chapter's files. You can decide yourself if this extra functionality is worth it, since the drawback is that, with the dynamic nature of ShaderProxy, you don't get the compile-time checking of your interaction with this class.

Bending pixels

A wise man on the magic moving picture box once offered in his hand a pebble to his student and informed him that once the pebble could be snatched up the student would be ready. Well, for quite a few pages, I have been taunting with a pebble, and it's time for you to snatch it up, young Grasshopper. There has been a lot of exploration of how to create a kernel, compile it for Flash, load it at runtime, and set its parameters, but there hasn't been too much shader production up until now. At this point, we have covered nearly all you need to know about using shaders, we just haven't applied that knowledge beyond simple desaturation through a filter, and that we could do three chapters ago with the built-in filters.

You got the pebble? Great. Let's do some kung fu.

Creating a custom filter

This first effect shows how to apply posterization and a threshold to an image as we did last chapter using both the threshold() and paletteMap() methods of BitmapData. It then goes further and shows how to act on that threshold data. In this example, we render horizontal lines over the darker pixels of the image based on the threshold, but you could apply this technique to any effect that required separation of your image into brighter and darker areas. Images with the shader applied are shown in Figure 5-16.

Figure 5-16. Three images with the horizontalLines shader applied

The full code of the Pixel Bender kernel follows. We'll take a closer look at the bold lines so you can understand exactly what is going on. The file can be found as horizontalLines.pbk with this chapter's files.

```
<languageVersion : 1.0;>

kernel HorizontalLines
<
    namespace:      "com.bobs27";
    vendor:         "Todd Yard";
    version:        1;
    description:    "Draws horizontal lines➥
over darker areas of image.";
>
{
    parameter float levelsThreshold
    <
        minValue:       0.0;
        maxValue:       1.0;
        defaultValue:   0.4;
        description:    "The threshold used➥
to determine the light and dark areas.";
    >;

    parameter float4 foregroundColor
    <
        minValue:       float4(0.0, 0.0, 0.0, 0.0);
        maxValue:       float4(1.0, 1.0, 1.0, 1.0);
        defaultValue:   float4(1.0, 1.0, 1.0, 1.0);
        description:    "The color to use➥
for the lighter areas of the image.";
    >;

    parameter float4 backgroundColor
    <
        minValue:       float4(0.0, 0.0, 0.0, 0.0);
        maxValue:       float4(1.0, 1.0, 1.0, 1.0);
        defaultValue:   float4(0.0, 0.0, 0.0, 1.0);
        description:    "The color to use➥
for the darker areas of the image.";
    >;

    input image4 source;
    output pixel4 result;

    void
    evaluatePixel()
    {
```

```
            float2 coord = outCoord();
            pixel4 px = sampleNearest(source, coord);
            if (mod(coord.y, 2.0) >= 1.0) {
                float numLevels = 4.0;
                px = floor(px*numLevels)/numLevels;

                float luminance = px.r * 0.3 +
                                  px.g * 0.59 +
                                  px.b * 0.11;

                if (luminance <= levelsThreshold) {
                    px = backgroundColor;
                } else {
                    px = foregroundColor;
                }
            } else {
                px = foregroundColor;
            }
            result = px;

        }

    }
```

If you load this kernel into the Pixel Bender Toolkit and load `YellowFlowers.png`, you will see something like Figure 5-17. Play around with the colors and the threshold value to see how the parameters affect the processed image.

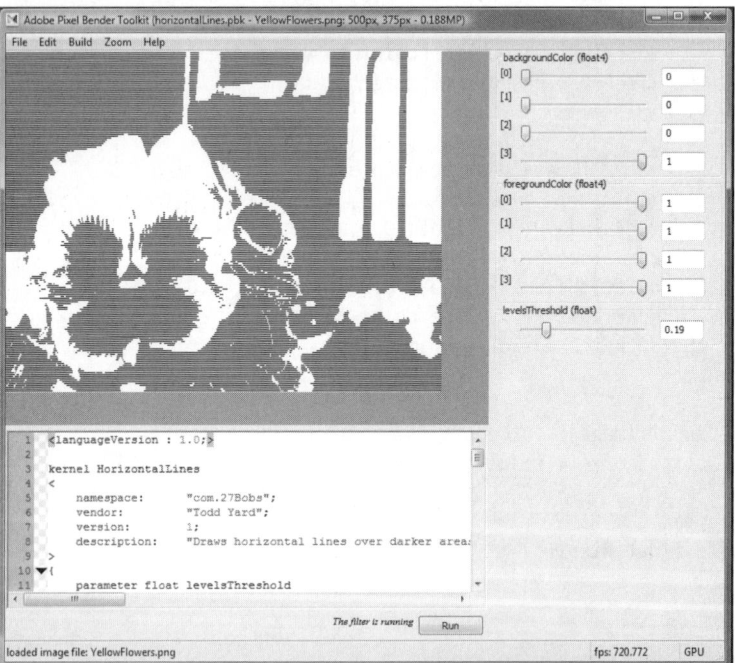

Figure 5-17. The horizontalLines shader applied to the YellowFlowers image in the toolkit

This kernel defines three parameters at the top. The first is the threshold that should be applied to the image, between 0 and 1 (oftentimes, since it is easier to work with floats in the code, and since this is how colors are represented in the Pixel Bender language, 0 and 1 are used where in ActionScript we are used to working with 0–255 for channel values). The other two parameters hold the values for the foreground and background colors that will be applied to the processed image. The foreground will apply to the lighter pixels with the background applying to the darker pixels. These, you will note, also use 0 to 1 in each channel to hold the brightness value, not 0–255.

The first two lines of the evaluatePixel() function grab the current coordinate being evaluated and the color value of the pixel at that coordinate. We used these in our earlier desaturate example, and you will see these used nearly always, at least in this book, so they will probably not be mentioned again. It is the next lines that are the most interesting.

First, we use the mod() function to determine whether the row of our current pixel is even or odd. This is the same as using the modulo operator in ActionScript.

```
if (coord.y % 2 == 1) {
```

If we are currently evaluating a pixel on an odd row, we perform some posterization or quantization on our image. This is handled with these two lines:

```
float numLevels = 4.0;
px = floor(px*numLevels)/numLevels;
```

With these lines, we reduce the number of colors in our image, which I find works better for the effect. It does this by multiplying the brightness level in each channel by the number of levels, flooring this, and then dividing the result by the same number of levels. If you plug in numbers, you can better understand how this works. Values between 0.0 and 0.25 will produce 0.0. Values between of 0.25 and 0.5 will produce 0.25. Values between 0.5 and 0.75 will produce 0.5, and values from 0.75 to 1.0 will produce 0.75. A value of 1.0 will remained unchanged. Thus each channel is reduced to one of five brightness values and the overall palette is reduced.

How is each channel affected individually if the operation is performed against the single variable holding all channels? This might not be immediately obvious from the lines, but since px holds a vector of four numbers (one for each channel), multiplying a scalar value against it will perform the operation on each component of the vector individually. The same applies to the flooring and division. The second line could be written equivalently as follows:

```
px.r = floor(px.r*numLevels)/numLevels;
px.g = floor(px.g*numLevels)/numLevels;
px.b = floor(px.b*numLevels)/numLevels;
px.a = floor(px.a*numLevels)/numLevels;
```

Yes, the alpha channel is affected as well, but if the alpha is 1.0, no change occurs. Alternatively, you could assign the RGB values to a new float3, perform the operations, and then put these back into the pixel4 variable.

```
float3 colors = px.rgb;
colors = floor(colors*numLevels)/numLevels;
px.rgb = colors;
```

Continuing on in evaluatePixel(), the lines after the quantization determine the luminance of the current pixel using a standard equation for calculating luminance and numbers that you've seen previously, including in the desaturation filter earlier this chapter. Using this luminance value, we check to see on which side of the threshold the pixel brightness falls. For the brighter values, we draw the foreground color. Darker colors get the background color. For pixels on even rows, we also assign the foreground color.

You can compile this kernel as horizontalLines.pbj, or use the file included with this chapter's files. To apply the shader to an image in ActionScript, we can adapt the DesaturateTest (or DesaturateWithProxyTest, as I do here) to configure and apply the shader as a filter. The following code can be found as HorizontalLinesTest.as:

```
package {

  import flash.display.Shader;
  import flash.filters.ShaderFilter;
  import flash.events.Event;

  [SWF(width=400, height=500, backgroundColor=0x000000)]

  public class HorizontalLinesTest extends AbstractImageLoader {

    private var _shaderProxy:ShaderProxy;

    public function HorizontalLinesTest() {
      super("../../assets/cadillac.jpg");
    }

    override protected function runPostImageLoad():void {
      _shaderProxy =➥
new ShaderProxy("../../assets/horizontalLines.pbj");
      if (_shaderProxy.shader == null) {
        _shaderProxy.addEventListener(Event.COMPLETE, onShaderLoaded);
      } else {
        applyShader();
      }
    }

    private function applyShader():void {
      _shaderProxy.foregroundColor = [0.68, 0.7, 0.75, 1.0];
      _shaderProxy.backgroundColor = [0.1, 0.25, 0.3, 1.0];
      _shaderProxy.levelsThreshold = 0.25;
      var shader:Shader = _shaderProxy.shader;
      var filter:ShaderFilter = new ShaderFilter(shader);
      _loadedBitmap.filters = [filter];
      addChild(_loadedBitmap);
    }
```

```
    private function onShaderLoaded(event:Event):void {
      applyShader();
    }

  }

}
```

Just as with DesaturateTest, we load in the Pixel Bender bytecode and apply this as a filter to the loaded bitmap. Because this class takes advantage of the ShaderProxy presented previously, we can set the properties directly on the proxy, and these get passed in the correct form to the wrapped Shader instance. The rest of the code to apply the filter remains unchanged.

The SWF produced by this class should look like Figure 5-18. Although on the surface this is a seemingly simple effect, the kernel itself introduced how to apply a threshold and how to posterize an image, techniques that will come in useful for many effects as we continue.

Figure 5-18.
The horizontalLines shader loaded at runtime and applied to a half-buried Cadillac

Enabling new blend modes

Up until this point, we have been applying the shaders as filters (and remember, you can also use `applyFilter()` to accomplish the same thing with BitmapData objects). Another common use for shaders is to introduce new blend modes that can be applied to images, which take into account the image the blend is being applied to and the pixels beneath the image.

To build a shader that can be applied as a blend mode, we need to define a kernel that has at least two inputs. Other than that, construction of a kernel does not change much, as you can see in the following code, colorBurn.pbk, which recreates a common Photoshop blend mode that is not a part of ActionScript.

```
<languageVersion : 1.0;>

kernel ColorBurn
<   namespace:       "com.bobs27";
    vendor:          "Todd Yard";
    version:         1;
    description:     "Darkens the background color➥
to reflect the source color.";
>
{

    parameter float percent
    <
        minValue:       0.0;
        maxValue:       1.0;
        defaultValue:   1.0;
        description:    "The amount of blend to apply.";
    >;

    input image4 source;
    input image4 background;
    output pixel4 result;

    void
    evaluatePixel()
    {
        float2 coord = outCoord();
        pixel4 px = sampleNearest(source, coord);
        pixel4 bg = sampleNearest(background, coord);
        pixel4 fullBlend = px;
        if (px.r > 0.0) {
            fullBlend.r = 1.0 - min(1.0, (1.0-px.r)/bg.r);
        }
        if (px.g > 0.0) {
            fullBlend.g = 1.0 - min(1.0, (1.0-px.g)/bg.g);
        }
        if (px.b > 0.0) {
            fullBlend.b = 1.0 - min(1.0, (1.0-px.b)/bg.b);
        }
        result = mix(px, fullBlend, percent);
    }

}
```

As you can see, for a blend mode, we need to define two inputs, here named `source` and `background`. One of the great things about using a shader as a blend mode is that we can allow for percentages of the blend, as you find in Photoshop. With that, instead of having to use the full blend always, we can specify an amount to apply, and that can be dynamic. Included in the previous kernel is a `percent` parameter that serves this purpose.

For the `evaluatePixel()` function, we first grab the current pixel coordinate and then get the pixel values for the source and background images. In the next line, we copy the values of our source pixel into a new variable, `fullBlend` (it is important to note that this does create a copy, not a reference). We then use an equation I dug up online that Photoshop uses to calculate its `Color Burn` blend mode.

To apply the blend by the specified percent, we once again use the `mix()` function (we used it with desaturate as well), mixing between the original source pixel and the fully blended pixel, assigning the result to the `result` variable. You can see the effect if you load in two images using File ➤ Load Image 1 and File ➤ Load Image 2, which should give you something like Figure 5-19.

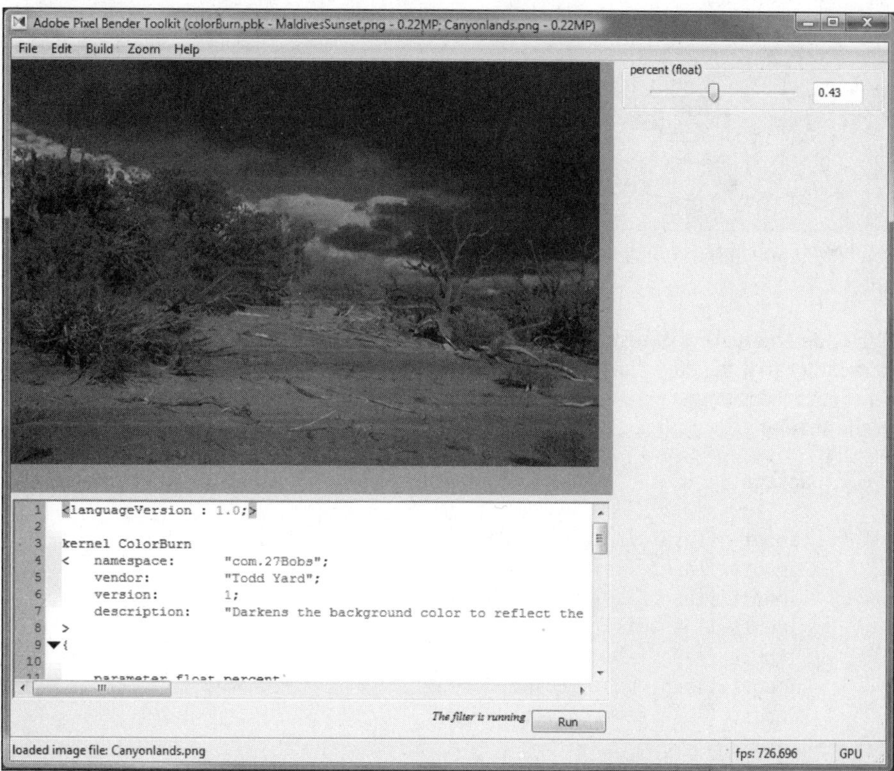

Figure 5-19. Two images loaded into the toolkit to test the Color Burn blend mode

Now, to apply this blend mode in ActionScript requires nearly the same steps as applying a shader as a filter, except instead of using the ShaderFilter and the `filters` property of DisplayObject, you use the `blendShader` property. The following class, which extends the

DualImageTest example I first introduced in Chapter 2 when we explored blend modes, applies the compiled colorBurn.pbj, which you can find in this chapter's files, as a blend mode to the stacked image. You can see the result in Figure 5-20.

Figure 5-20. ColorBurnTest showing two images with the custom Color Burn blend mode applied

The code to create this result can be found as ColorBurnTest.as in this chapter's files. Remember that the base class, DualImageTest, loads in the two images and positions them. The operateOnImages() method is called after that, which the child class overrides to load in the shader.

```
package {

  import flash.display.Bitmap;
  import flash.display.BitmapData;
  import flash.display.BlendMode;
  import flash.display.Shader;
  import flash.filters.ShaderFilter;
  import flash.events.Event;
  import flash.geom.Point;

  [SWF(width=1200, height=600, backgroundColor=0x000000)]

  public class ColorBurnTest extends DualImageTest {

    private var _shaderProxy:ShaderProxy;
```

```
    override protected function operateOnImages():void {
      _shaderProxy = new ShaderProxy("../../assets/colorBurn.pbj");
      if (_shaderProxy.shader == null) {
        _shaderProxy.addEventListener(Event.COMPLETE, onShaderLoaded);
      } else {
        applyShader();
      }
    }

    private function applyShader():void {
      var bitmap0:Bitmap = getChildAt(0) as Bitmap;
      var bitmap1:Bitmap = getChildAt(1) as Bitmap;
      var bottomBitmap:Bitmap = new Bitmap(bitmap0.bitmapData);
      var topBitmap:Bitmap = new Bitmap(bitmap1.bitmapData);
      addChild(bottomBitmap);
      addChild(topBitmap);
      topBitmap.x = bottomBitmap.x = bitmap1.x + bitmap1.width;
      _shaderProxy.percent = 0.6;
      topBitmap.blendShader = _shaderProxy.shader;
    }

    private function onShaderLoaded(event:Event):void {
      applyShader();
    }

  }

}
```

At this point in this book, the only code that should be new to you is where the blendShader property is set on the display object. The rest of the applyShader() code creates two new bitmaps using the data from the loaded images and stacks them on the right. Just as you saw in the last example, we can use the ShaderProxy instance to set the percent parameter for the shader. The shader itself can then be set as the blendShader for the Bitmap instance. Note that you do not have to set the blendMode to BlendMode.SHADER, since that is done automatically when the blendShader property is set. Isn't that considerate?

That's it! We do not need to set either of the input parameters when we use a shader as a blend mode. The Flash Player handles that for us with no fuss. It will also update the shader every time the screen updates and forces a refresh of that region.

The code for the kernel to create a blend mode wasn't too complex (and admittedly, the equation came from Adobe's own documentation). The addition of the percent parameter offers functionality beyond what is offered in the built-in Flash blend modes but is common in something like Photoshop. Now, if you would like the same sort of functionality for the built-in blend modes, you merely need to create shaders that follow the same structure as our example here. There was a reason that Chapter 2 contained formulas for all the blend modes, and that was to make it easy for you to adapt these as shaders, if you wished. For instance, the following code is what you would use to create a shader for a Multiply blend mode that accepted percent for the blend. It can be found as multiply.pbk (with its compiled bytecode as multiply.pbj) in this chapter's files.

```
<languageVersion : 1.0;>

kernel Multiply
<   namespace:      "com.bobs27";
    vendor:         "Todd Yard";
    version:        1;
    description:    "Multiplies the background color➥
and source color.";
>
{

    parameter float percent
    <
        minValue:       0.0;
        maxValue:       1.0;
        defaultValue:   1.0;
        description:    "The amount of blend to apply.";
    >;

    input image4 source;
    input image4 background;
    output pixel4 result;

    void
    evaluatePixel()
    {
        float2 coord = outCoord();
        pixel4 px = sampleNearest(source, coord);
        pixel4 bg = sampleNearest(background, coord);
        pixel4 fullBlend = px*bg;
        result = mix(px, fullBlend, percent);
    }

}
```

Drawing with shaders

The final method for rendering shaders in the Flash Player is to use the built-in methods of the drawing API, lineShaderStyle() and beginShaderFill(), which work very similarly to how lineBitmapStyle() and beginBitmapFill() work, except you pass in a shader instead of bitmap data. You might use this to draw with generated patterns or to create custom gradients, as you will see in this next example.

Creating custom gradients

The following kernel can be found as `squareGradient.pbk` in this chapter's files. It allows you to draw a fill using the square gradient type that can be found in Illustrator or Photoshop but is not available in ActionScript. Once again, you should see the setup of a kernel, despite its desired end use, does not change greatly.

```
<languageVersion : 1.0;>

kernel SquareGradient
<
    namespace:      "com.bobs27";
    vendor:         "Todd Yard";
    version:        1;
    description:    "Creates a square gradient.";
>
{
    parameter int rotation
    <
        minValue:       int(0);
        maxValue:       int(360);
        defaultValue:   int(0);
        description:    "The rotation of the gradient.";
    >;

    parameter float2 center
    <
        minValue:       float2(0.0,0.0);
        maxValue:       float2(1024.0,1024.0);
        defaultValue:   float2(256.0,256.0);
        description:    "The center of the gradient.";
    >;

    input image4 gradient;
    output pixel4 result;

    void
    evaluatePixel()
    {

        float2 coord = outCoord();
        float2 relativePos = coord - center;
        float theta = atan(relativePos.y, relativePos.x);
        theta = degrees(theta) - float(rotation);
        if (theta < -360.0) {
            theta += 720.0;
        } else if (theta < 0.0) {
            theta += 360.0;
        } else if (theta > 360.0) {
```

```
                theta -= 360.0;
            }
            theta = clamp(theta, 1.0, 359.0);
            result = sampleNearest(gradient, float2(floor(theta), 1));
        }

    }
```

One problem with drawing gradients using Pixel Bender is that it is difficult to get desired gradient values in as parameters unless the number of color stops is predefined. I've found one way to work around this is to pass in an image of the desired gradient and use this to determine the pixel colors. As you can see, this kernel takes one input, which I've named `gradient`. This would be an image that is 360 pixels wide (the height is unimportant as long as it is at least one pixel high). The code in `evaluatePixel()` determines the angle of the current pixel in relation to the specified gradient center and finds the corresponding pixel value on the gradient image, from 1 to 359.

To run this example in Pixel Bender, you will need to load in some image as Image 2 to dictate pixel dimension and a gradient image for Image 1. A gradient image is provided as `gradient.jpg` with this chapter's files. The results should look like Figure 5-21.

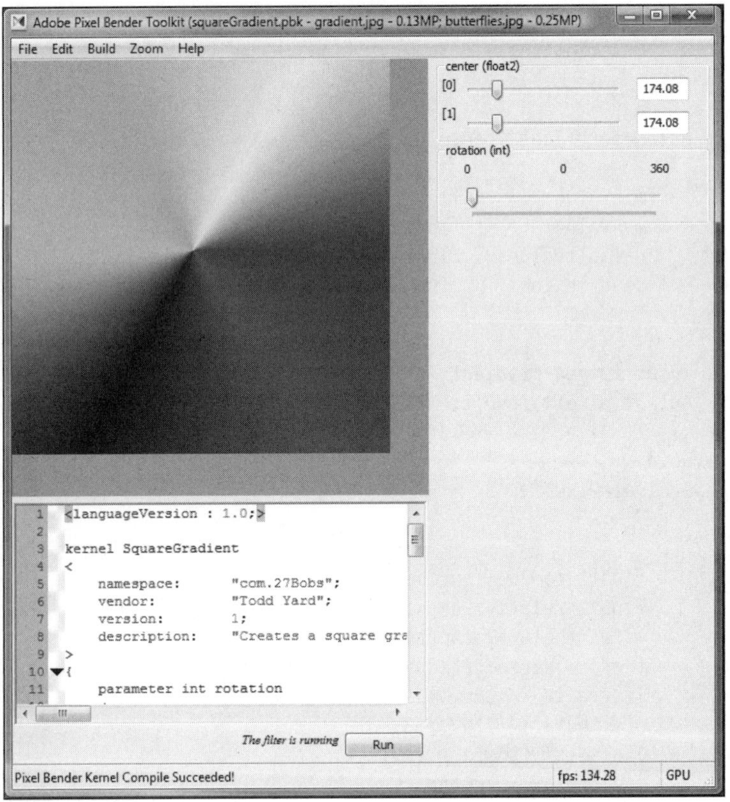

Figure 5-21. The squareGradient kernel at work in the toolkit

To draw with this gradient in ActionScript, we need to load the bytecode, pass the center position and a gradient image to the shader, and then use the drawing API. The following class, SquareGradientTest, found in this chapter's files as well, does just that:

```
package {

  import flash.display.BitmapData;
  import flash.display.GradientType;
  import flash.display.Shader;
  import flash.display.Shape;
  import flash.display.Sprite;
  import flash.events.Event;
  import flash.geom.Matrix;

  [SWF(width=300, height=300, backgroundColor=0x000000)]

  public class SquareGradientTest extends Sprite {

    protected var _shaderProxy:ShaderProxy;

    public function SquareGradientTest() {
      _shaderProxy =➥
new ShaderProxy("../../assets/squareGradient.pbj");
      if (_shaderProxy.shader == null) {
        _shaderProxy.addEventListener(Event.COMPLETE, onShaderLoaded);
      } else {
        drawShader();
      }
    }

    protected function drawShader():void {
      var width:Number = stage.stageWidth;
      var height:Number = stage.stageHeight;
      _shaderProxy.center = [width/2, height/2];
      _shaderProxy.gradient = getGradient();
      graphics.beginShaderFill(_shaderProxy.shader);
      graphics.drawRect(0, 0, width, height);
      graphics.endFill();
    }

    protected function getGradient():BitmapData {
      var colors:Array = [0xFF0000, 0xFF00FF, 0x0000FF,➥
0x00FFFF, 0x00FF00, 0xFFFF00, 0xFF0000];
      var alphas:Array = [1, 1, 1, 1, 1, 1, 1];
      var ratios:Array = [0, 38, 84, 125, 171, 214, 255];
      var matrix:Matrix = new Matrix();
      matrix.createGradientBox(360, 1);
      var shape:Shape = new Shape();
```

```
      shape.graphics.beginGradientFill(GradientType.LINEAR,➥
colors, alphas, ratios, matrix);
      shape.graphics.drawRect(0, 0, 360, 1);
      shape.graphics.endFill();
      var bitmapData:BitmapData = new BitmapData(360, 1);
      bitmapData.draw(shape);
      return bitmapData;
    }

    private function onShaderLoaded(event:Event):void {
      drawShader();
    }

  }

}
```

There really is not much new with this code, which shows just how far you've come in several chapters. The constructor sets up the ShaderProxy instance. When the shader is ready, `drawShader()` will be called. This passes the `center` parameter to the shader as well as the `gradient` input, which is generated in the `getGradient()` method. `beginShaderFill()` is then called, with the shader passed as the parameter. Normal drawing can proceed with the shader now acting as the fill.

Some changes will need to be made to the ShaderProxy class to allow for the input to be set in this way. We only coded it to get and set parameters using the implicit getter/setter functionality of Proxy. So with no further changes to ShaderProxy, you would have to set the gradient input with the following code:

```
_shaderProxy.shader.data.gradient.input = getGradient();
```

Yuck. I'd rather ShaderProxy was finessed to allow for setting of inputs in the same way it allows for setting of parameters. The following changes to the ShaderProxy class accomplish this:

```
override flash_proxy function getProperty(name:*):* {
  if (_shader) {
    var result:Object = getParameter(name);
    if (result == null) {
      result = getInput(name);
    }
    return result;
  }
  return null;
}

override flash_proxy function setProperty(name:*, value:*):void {
  if (_shader) {
    if (!setParameter(name, value)) {
      setInput(name, value);
```

```
        }
      }
    }

    public function getInput(name:String):Object {
      if (_shader.data.hasOwnProperty(name) && ➥
    _shader.data[name] is ShaderInput) {
        return _shader.data[name].input;
      }
      return null;
    }

    public function setInput(name:String, value:Object):Boolean {
      if (_shader.data.hasOwnProperty(name) && ➥
    _shader.data[name] is ShaderInput) {
        _shader.data[name].input = value;
        return true;
      }
      return false;
    }

    public function getParameter(name:String):Object {
      if (_shader.data.hasOwnProperty(name) && ➥
    _shader.data[name] is ShaderParameter) {
        var value:Object = _shader.data[name].value;
        var type:String = _shader.data[name].type;
        if (type == "float" || type == "int") {
          value = (value as Array)[0];
        }
        return value;
      }
      return null;
    }

    public function setParameter(name:String, value:Object):Boolean {
      if (_shader.data.hasOwnProperty(name) && ➥
    _shader.data[name] is ShaderParameter) {
        if (!(value is Array)) {
          value = [value];
        }
        _shader.data[name].value = value;
        return true;
      }
      return false;
    }
```

In addition to these changes, the ShaderParameter and ShaderInput classes must be imported at the top of the class. The new methods setInput() and getInput() can be used to set or retrieve the input values, but if the names of the inputs are invoked directly, the getProperty() and setProperty() methods will be called. These first check to see if the specified name is a parameter. If it isn't, then the setInput() or getInput() methods are attempted.

The result of these changes is shown in Figure 5-22.

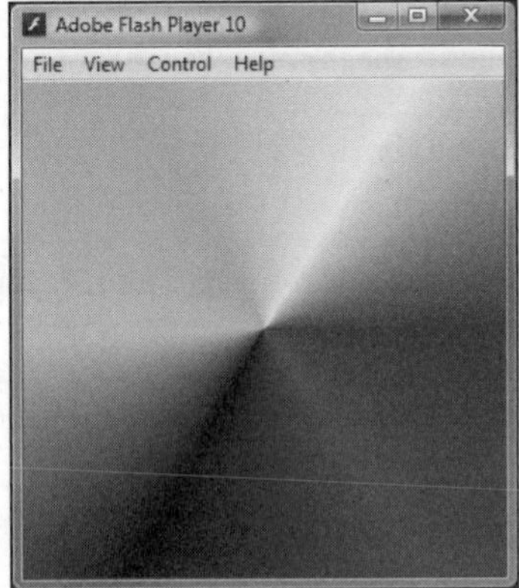

Figure 5-22. The squareGradient shader loaded into the Flash Player

Animating fills

We can take this example a step further by animating the shader. The process of animating a shader is no different than animating any other element through code: you update properties over time. For a shader, this simply means updating the parameter or parameters of the shader and then reapplying the shader through the drawing API, a blend mode, or a filter.

The following code, found as AnimatedSquareGradientTest.as in this chapter's files, extends the class from the last example. In every frame, the shader is updated with a new rotation, and the center is derived from the current position of the mouse.

```
package {

  import flash.events.Event;

  [SWF(width=300, height=300, backgroundColor=0x000000)]

  public class AnimatedSquareGradientTest extends SquareGradientTest {

    private static const ROTATION_RATE:Number = 5;

    private var _rotation:Number;

    public function AnimatedSquareGradientTest() {
      _rotation = 0;
    }
```

```
        private function updateShader():void {
          _rotation += ROTATION_RATE;
          if (_rotation >= 360) {
            _rotation = 0;
          }
          _shaderProxy.rotation = _rotation;
          _shaderProxy.center = [stage.mouseX, stage.mouseY];
          graphics.clear();
          graphics.beginShaderFill(_shaderProxy.shader);
          graphics.drawRect(0, 0, stage.stageWidth, stage.stageHeight);
          graphics.endFill();
        }

        override protected function drawShader():void {
          super.drawShader();
          addEventListener(Event.ENTER_FRAME, onSpriteEnterFrame);
        }

        private function onSpriteEnterFrame(event:Event):void {
          updateShader();
        }

      }

    }
```

The rotation and center parameters get updated every frame, and then the graphics are simply redrawn using the shader fill. It's really that easy.

Performing heavy processing

We've all been frustrated by it at different times. You are working in an application and are performing some procedure when the interface seizes up and is unresponsive. You have either encountered a bug and are in the process of crashing, or the application is being taxed with the request and is pooling all of its resources to tackle it. In either case, it's almost as if you are dangling off the edge of a cliff, waiting to see if gravity and friction will be your friend and plop you back to safety or whether you need to hold up your Wile E. Coyote "Uh-oh!" sign as you plunge.

You don't want to leave your users hanging (or teetering, if we follow the simile through). In all the previous examples, we have applied shaders to display objects and seen their results immediately. Not too much processing needed to occur, so there wasn't a concern about the responsiveness of the application. With some procedures, though, you may wish to crunch the numbers and process the images behind the scenes and update for the user only when the work is complete. This can be accomplished in ActionScript with the ShaderJob class.

Setting up and using a ShaderJob instance is fairly straightforward. The process is made up of several steps:

1. Create a ShaderJob instance, and pass it the shader that will perform the operation and the target object that will receive the output. This target will be a BitmapData instance, a ByteArray, or a vector of numbers.
2. Set up an event listener for when the shader's operation is complete.
3. Tell the ShaderJob instance to begin its operation.
4. In the handler for the completion event, access the target of the ShaderJob instance to get the shader's output and do whatever needs to be done with the output (e.g., drawing with bitmap data, applying a filter, etc.).

We won't be creating a new kernel for this next example but will reuse the square gradient from the last one. There is no reason why this shader should need to be run as a background process, as it produces a simple effect, but it allows you to see very clearly what is needed to run a shader job. You can apply the same technique if you have a more processor-intensive filter or are crunching numbers with the shader.

The following class extends SquareGradientTest and can be found in this chapter's files as `ShaderJobTest.as`:

```
package {

  import flash.display.BitmapData;
  import flash.display.ShaderJob;
  import flash.events.ShaderEvent;

  [SWF(width=300, height=300, backgroundColor=0x000000)]

  public class ShaderJobTest extends SquareGradientTest {

    private var _shaderJob:ShaderJob;

    override protected function drawShader():void {
      var width:Number = stage.stageWidth;
      var height:Number = stage.stageHeight;
      var bitmapData:BitmapData = new BitmapData(width, height, true);
      _shaderProxy.center = [width/2, height/2];
      _shaderProxy.gradient = getGradient();
      _shaderJob = new ShaderJob(_shaderProxy.shader, bitmapData);
      _shaderJob.addEventListener(ShaderEvent.COMPLETE,➥
onShaderComplete);
      _shaderJob.start();
    }

    private function onShaderComplete(event:ShaderEvent):void {
      graphics.beginBitmapFill(event.bitmapData);
      graphics.drawRect(0, 0, stage.stageWidth, stage.stageHeight);
      graphics.endFill();
```

```
      }

    }

  }
```

The result of this would be the same as Figure 5-22.

You can see that you set up the shader parameters in the same way as with any other shader (after all, it is the same shader we used before, the only difference is in how the shader operation is run). The ShaderJob constructor takes the shader that will be performing the operation, and the target that will receive the output. In our case, we pass in a BitmapData instance, since we know the shader is set up to return image data. The constructor can take two more parameters, and they all are actually optional. The signature of the constructor looks like the following:

```
ShaderJob(
  shader:Shader = null,
  target:Object = null,
  width:int = 0,
  height:int = 0
)
```

The following are the parameters for the constructor:

- `shader`: The shader performing the operation
- `target`: The BitmapData, ByteArray, or Vector.<Number> instance that will be receiving the shader output
- `width`: The width of the result data, in the case of a ByteArray or Vector.<Number> (Since these objects do not contain dimensions like BitmapData, the width must be specified.)
- `height`: The height of the result data, in the case of a ByteArray or Vector.<Number> (Since these objects do not contain dimensions like BitmapData, the height must be specified.)

In our example, after the constructor is called, we set up an event listener for when the job is complete. A call to ShaderJob's `start()` method follows to kick off the job.

The handler for the completion event receives a ShaderEvent instance. This instance will contain a `bitmapData`, `byteArray`, or `vector` property holding the shader's output. This is how we access the bitmap data in this example and set it as the bitmap fill for a drawing routine.

See? I told you there was nothing to it. The only other things that should be mentioned about ShaderJob are one additional property and one more method. The `progress` property returns the percent of the operation that is completed, between 0 and 1. This is not returned in any event, so you must set up polling of this data through a Timer or frame loop. You could use this information for a progress bar, as you find in Photoshop when a processor-intensive filter is being run. Finally, ShaderJob offers a `cancel()` method that will halt an operation that has been previously started through the `start()` method. As for that `start()` method, it takes one optional parameter, the Boolean `waitForCompletion`, which is `false` by default. This value determines whether the job is run in the background (`false`) or synchronously in the main thread (`true`).

Summary

Pixel Bender offers a whole new world to explore for creating image effects in ActionScript. There are limitations, sure, but there are so many more possibilities. In this chapter, we have stepped through how to create and test a kernel in the Pixel Bender Toolkit, how to compile the bytecode for use in the Flash Player, how to embed or load the bytecode for use through ActionScript, and the different methods for applying loaded shaders to display objects through filters, blend modes, and the drawing API. In the last section, we also took a brief look at how to use ShaderJob to run shader operations in the background to keep your interface responsive during heavy operations.

That's a lot of info for a single chapter, but why should this chapter be any different than the previous ones? This book is all about providing you with as much relevant information as possible, so you can go out and create some fantastic and useful image effects. Pixel Bender and all that it offers can now be added to your arsenal. Need a new blend mode, or require the ability to lessen the effects of the built-in blend modes? Is there a filter that BitmapData cannot be wrangled into providing or is too slow in producing? Are there patterns and textures that you wish to use with the drawing API that need to be dynamically generated? Pixel Bender can be your answer to these and many more questions.

There is just one more aspect of ActionScript we will look at before tackling some more fully realized effects and applications, and it is a subject that can equally excite and terrify developers because of its perceived complexity, 3D. In the next chapter, we will look at what ActionScript offers for the realm of the third dimension on your two-dimensional computer screen. No 3D specs required!

Chapter 6

ACTIONSCRIPT IN THE THIRD DIMENSION

We live in a 3D world, and yet for the most part, our information is still stored and delivered in a 2D form. So although we walk through a world existing visually on all sides of us, collecting data that we can reach out and touch, walk around, explore, and occasionally bump into, when we present this data to others, it is most often in the form of the written word on a page or screen, a flat picture, or a moving two-dimensional image. No wonder we try so hard to introduce the third dimension to these forms of communication.

It's interesting to me that Flash, an animation tool, from the very beginning offered the ability to manipulate the fourth dimension of time, skipping over the third dimension entirely. For the longest time, Flash developers have been all but begging for Adobe to include 3D capabilities in the player like were present in the Shockwave Player or other Web3D technologies (alright, I lie; at times, I believe actual begging was involved). Of course, the argument against 3D functionality was always the large size of the player that would be needed for it and the higher requirements of the end user's system.

How that fourth dimension flies, though. With Flash Player 10, Adobe has introduced a limited feature set that enables developers to more easily implement 3D into their movies and applications without requiring hard-core gamers' systems or massive downloads. Remember the fishing analogy from the beginning of the last chapter? Consider this functionality to be more tackle. Developers have not been given a fully fledged 3D rendering engine in the player, but they have been given the tools to create 3D more easily than ever before in Flash. In this chapter, we will look at how.

> *Although the process for adding 3D to your Flash applications has been simplified in the latest version of the player and methods to enable this are built into the core ActionScript language, the topic is still a relatively complex one. I strive in this chapter to present the ideas as simply and straightforward as possible but consider some of the concepts herein to be a step up in complexity from the previous chapters.*

Displaying objects with depth

Much like General Zod and his cohorts from *Superman II*, display objects for the longest time have been trapped on a two-dimensional plane. They could be moved or scaled on the x and y axes and rotated on a flat plane. Any 3D code that was present in Flash applications was managing 3D coordinates in memory and translating them to the two-dimensional coordinate system in the player. Now, obviously there is always translation of 3D coordinates to a 2D space for rendering, since we are dealing with flat monitors and not three-dimensional holographic projections (I only hope this book remains in print long enough for that statement to become obsolete), but wouldn't it be nice to move the calculations for the translation of these coordinates from our own code to the native code in the Flash Player?

Well, say hello to "z." ActionScript 3.0 has added a number of new properties to DisplayObject that allow movement, scaling, and rotation of instances in all three dimensions. Welcome native 3D to the Flash Player.

Translating in three dimensions

In addition to the standard x and y properties that we all know and love, DisplayObject now sports a new z property that allows the placement of the instance on the z axis. For those not familiar at all with 3D, the z axis is most often represented as being perpendicular to the screen, and this is the way that it is represented in Flash. The x axis, as you will be familiar, runs horizontally across the screen. The y axis runs vertically. The z axis points directly out from the screen and controls how near or far objects appear in relation to the viewer, as shown in Figure 6-1.

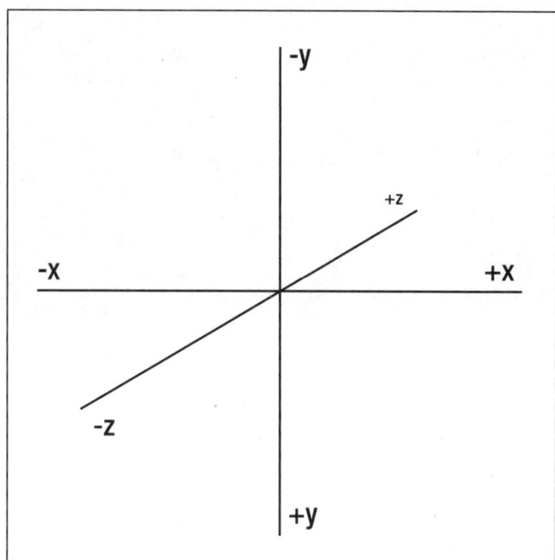

Figure 6-1. The x, y, and z axes as represented in the Flash Player

In Flash, the positive z axis points away from the viewer. That means that as an object's position on the z axis is increased, it will appear farther and farther away from the viewer. As an object's z position is decreased, it will move closer to the viewer.

There is not much more to basic 3D placement of objects in ActionScript beyond setting the z property, just as we are used to setting the x and y properties of display objects. Isn't that fantastic? There are some additional features that we will explore in the next section that affect exactly how the 3D-to-2D transforms are calculated, but for quick and dirty 3D depth, all you need to do is set the z.

In this next class example, I create a number of circles to represent possible navigation menu items. The circles are all placed at a fixed radius about a common center. However, the z of each circle is set to be 150 higher than the previous circle, which means as more circles are added, they will be rendered farther away, as shown in Figure 6-2.

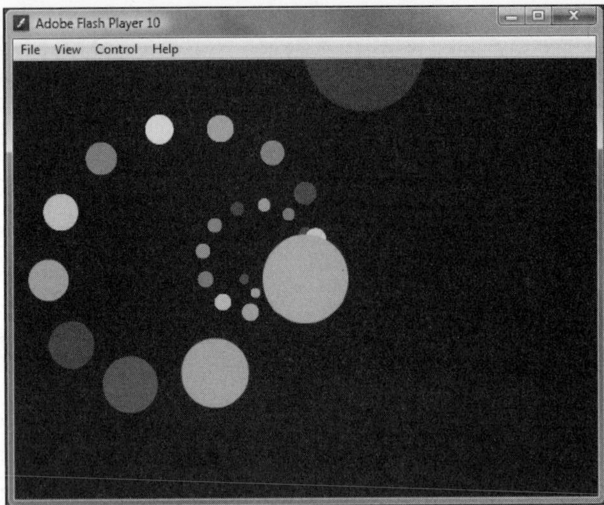

Figure 6-2. Circles placed around a common x and y center but at different z depths

Have a look at the code, which can be found in this chapter's files as AxisTranslationTest.as, and we will break down the relevant lines:

```
package {

  import flash.display.Sprite;
  import flash.events.MouseEvent;

  [SWF(width=550, height=400, backgroundColor=0x111111)]

  public class AxisTranslationTest extends Sprite {

    private static const NUM_ITEMS:uint = 30;
    private static const ITEM_RADIUS:uint = 40;
    private static const Z_DIST_BETWEEN_ITEMS:uint = 150;
    private static const ITEM_DIST_FROM_CENTER:uint = 300;
    private static const ANGLE_BETWEEN_ITEMS:Number = 30*(Math.PI/180);

    private var _menu:Sprite;
    private var _menuItems:Vector.<Sprite>;

    public function AxisTranslationTest() {
      _menu = new Sprite();
      _menuItems = new Vector.<Sprite>();
      for (var i:uint = 0; i < NUM_ITEMS; i++) {
        createMenuItem(i);
      }
```

```
        addChild(_menu);
        navigateToItem(_menuItems[0]);
        stage.addEventListener(MouseEvent.CLICK, onStageClick);
      }

      private function createMenuItem(index:uint):void {
        var menuItem:Sprite = new Sprite();
        menuItem.graphics.beginFill(Math.random()*0xFFFFFF);
        menuItem.graphics.drawCircle(0, 0, ITEM_RADIUS);
        menuItem.graphics.endFill();
        menuItem.x = Math.cos(ANGLE_BETWEEN_ITEMS*index)➥
*ITEM_DIST_FROM_CENTER;
        menuItem.y = Math.sin(ANGLE_BETWEEN_ITEMS*index)➥
*ITEM_DIST_FROM_CENTER;;
        menuItem.z = index*Z_DIST_BETWEEN_ITEMS;
        menuItem.addEventListener(MouseEvent.CLICK, onMenuItemClick);
        _menuItems.push(menuItem);
        _menu.addChildAt(menuItem, 0);
      }

      private function navigateToItem(menuItem:Sprite):void {
        _menu.x = stage.stageWidth/2-menuItem.x;
        _menu.y = stage.stageHeight/2-menuItem.y;
        _menu.z = -menuItem.z;
      }

      private function onMenuItemClick(event:MouseEvent):void {
        navigateToItem(event.target as Sprite);
        event.stopPropagation();
      }

      private function onStageClick(event:MouseEvent):void {
        navigateToItem(_menuItems[0]);
      }

    }

  }
```

In the constructor for this class, a new Sprite instance is created to hold all of the menu items (remember, the circles here represent these menu items). The depth of the menu itself will change as a new item is selected, as opposed to the depths of each individual item. I also create a vector to hold references to all of the menu item sprites. The loop that follows adds each item using the createMenuItem() method. Once all of the items are added, the menu sprite is added to the stage; the first menu item is navigated to using the navigateToItem() method, and an event listener for when the stage is clicked is set up.

The createMenuItem() method creates a new sprite and draws a circle within it using a random color. The x and y properties of the item are determined using standard trigonometry to find the position based on the current angle and the distance of the item from the center of the navigation, which is the radius of the circular navigation.

```
menuItem.x = Math.cos(ANGLE_BETWEEN_ITEMS*index)*ITEM_DIST_FROM_CENTER;
menuItem.y = Math.sin(ANGLE_BETWEEN_ITEMS*index)*ITEM_DIST_FROM_CENTER;
```

The z property is populated using the current item index of the menu multiplied by the distance between each item. That means that the first item will have a z value of 0; the second will have a z value of 150; the third a value of 300; and so on. The higher the z value, the farther away the item will appear.

```
menuItem.z = index*Z_DIST_BETWEEN_ITEMS;
```

After the circle is drawn and the axes coordinates are set, an event listener is added for when the item is clicked, and the item is pushed into the `_menuItems` vector. The following line is an important one to call further attention to:

```
_menu.addChildAt(menuItem, 0);
```

The display list in the Flash Player is what controls the depth of all of the display objects in the list. This is irrespective of whatever z value each display object has. This means that even though one item is set at a z position of –100 and another is set at a z position of 200, the item at the farther z position (200) can still appear above the "closer" item at the z position of –100, depending on how the items were added to the display list. For instance, consider the following code:

```
var sprite0:Sprite = new Sprite();
sprite0.z = -100;
sprite0.graphics.beginFill(0x0000FF);
sprite0.graphics.drawRect(0, 0, 100, 100);
sprite0.graphics.endFill();

var sprite1:Sprite = new Sprite();
sprite1.z =- 200;
sprite0.graphics.beginFill(0xFF0000);
sprite0.graphics.drawRect(0, 0, 100, 100);
sprite0.graphics.endFill();

addChild(sprite0);
addChild(sprite1);
```

In this case, the blue rectangle, `sprite0`, is set at a depth of –100, which is closer to the viewer than the red rectangle, `sprite1`, which is given a z position of 200. However, the red rectangle will appear on top in the Flash Player, completely obscuring the blue rectangle, since it was added at a higher depth in the display list.

> *Setting the z property of a display object will control how its 3D coordinates are translated into 2D coordinates on the screen and how the object will be scaled based on its position in 3D space. Depths, however, are not controlled by the z positions of relative objects, but rather on their index positions in the display list. To have z positions translate into display list depth positions, you must add logic to your application to swap depths of objects based on these values. We explore this technique later in this chapter.*

Now, let's consider again the last line of code in the `createMenuItem()` method.

```
_menu.addChildAt(menuItem, 0);
```

Because the positions on the display list, not the z positions, determine the depths of objects, I use the `addChildAt()` method to add each additional menu item *below* all other items by inserting it at index 0. Since each time the `createMenuItem()` method is called the index of the menu item is higher, the z position will be greater as well, and the object should appear farther away. By placing the item at the bottom of the display list stack in the menu sprite, the depth of each item in relation to the other items is consistent with its z position.

The final logic in AxisTranslationTest is what occurs when an item is clicked. Both the `onMenuItemClick()` and the `onStageClick()` call the `navigateToItem()` method, with the latter simply calling the method with the first menu item as the parameter. This will capture any clicks that are not directly on an item and return the navigation to the top menu item, allowing the user to navigate back. Because of this capture of the stage click, I have to stop the propagation of the click event within the `onMenuItemClick()` handler so that the stage click handler is not invoked as well when an item is clicked.

```
navigateToItem(event.target as Sprite);
event.stopPropagation();
```

The `navigateToItem()` method centers the menu on the screen based on the clicked item. It does this by offsetting the menu coordinates based on the coordinate positions of the menu item. That means that when the z position of the menu item is 300, the menu will be given a z position of –300 (the same applies for the x and y axes as well, except the center of the stage is taken into account). The end result is that the clicked menu item appears centered on the screen at a z position of 0.

```
_menu.x = stage.stageWidth/2-menuItem.x;
_menu.y = stage.stageHeight/2-menuItem.y;
_menu.z = -menuItem.z;
```

This example could certainly benefit from some animation to transition between one item and the next, but for simplicity's sake, this was left out so that we could more easily focus on the 3D coordinate position setting (in the next chapter, we will look at some classes we can use throughout the rest of this book to handle tasks like animating our effects). We have with a tiny amount of code—and no 3D math at all—created a 3D navigation. And it just gets better as we delve deeper.

Changing perspective

You have already seen how easy it is to place and render objects in 3D space within the Flash Player without any 3D or complex mathematics (at least by us!). Obviously, calculations occur behind the scenes that take the 3D coordinates of our display objects and transform these values for rendering on the 2D screen. Through ActionScript, we can alter how these transformations are performed by altering the variables used in the calculations.

Exploring perspective projection

When display objects are moved in the 3D space of the Flash Player, the player uses a perspective projection to determine how the 3D coordinates are translated to 2D coordinates on the screen. 3D projection in general is a way to map three-dimensional objects to a two-dimensional plane. A simple diagram of how these properties apply to a perspective projection is shown in Figure 6-3.

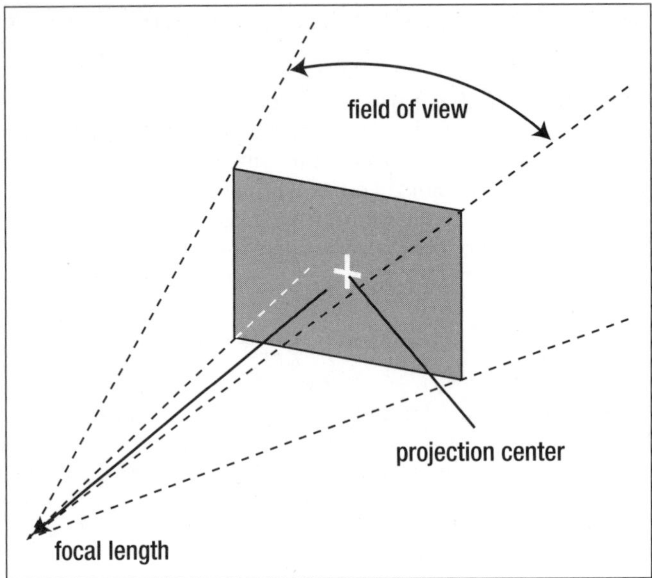

Figure 6-3. How properties of a perspective projection apply to a 3D view

Perspective projection in ActionScript uses three different variables to determine how each point in a 3D space is represented on the 2D plane: `fieldOfView`, `focalLength`, and `projectionCenter`.

- `fieldOfView`: The `fieldOfView` is the angular extent of the 3D space that is visible in the 2D projection. This is an angle between 0 and 180 (values of exactly 0 and 180 will surface runtime warnings). The higher the value, which means the larger the angle of the visible view, the more distortion that will be applied to the objects as they are mapped to the 2D plane. As the value approaches 0, there will be little distortion and the object's x and y properties in 2D will closely match the x and y properties in the 3D space with the z plane appearing almost flattened so that little depth is represented. As the value of the field of view increases, more distortion is applied as more of an angle of the 3D space is mapped to the 2D plane. A fisheye lens effect is a common result of a large field of view. Figure 6-4 shows how several rotated planes would appear with a small field of view and with a large field of view.

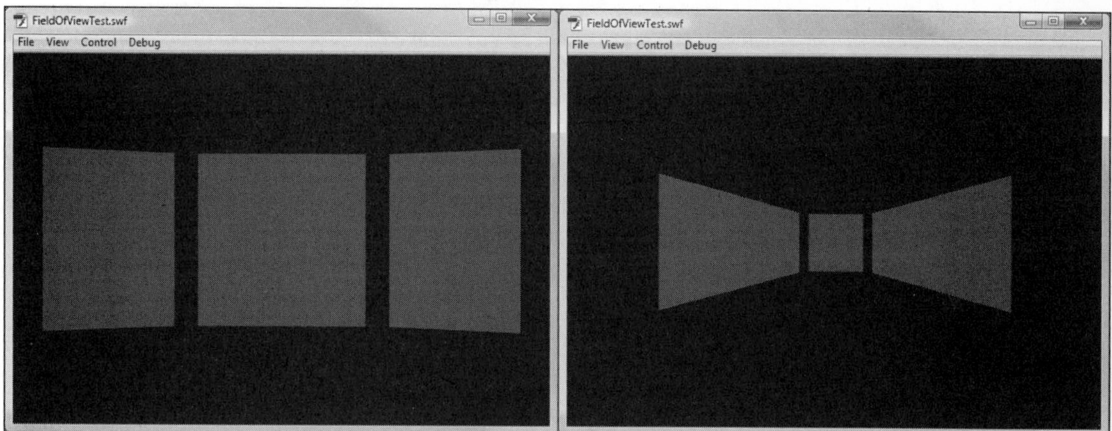

Figure 6-4. The effects of a small field of view on the left and the same planes rendered with a large field of view on the right

- `focalLength`: This value, the distance on the z axis from the viewer to the display object, works hand in hand with the field of view to determine the amount of distortion that is applied to the display objects when mapping from 3D to 2D. A high value produces an effect similar to a telephoto lens, whereas a low value produces an effect similar to a wide-angle lens. Generally, you do not have to worry about setting this property, since it is automatically calculated based on the field of view the view width using the following formula:

  ```
  focalLength = stageWidth/2 * (cos(fieldOfView/2) / sin(fieldOfView/2)
  ```

- `projectionCenter`: This is the vanishing point on the 2D plane to which 3D display objects recede as they increase their position on the positive z axis. As objects move farther back in 3D space, they are skewed toward the 2D vanishing point and, at a certain point, will become so small they will not be rendered.

The PerspectiveProjection instance that holds these properties for a display object container can be found in the display object's `transform` property, demonstrated in the following line of code:

```
sprite.transform.perspectiveProjection.fieldOfView = 100;
```

By default, the `perspectiveProjection` for a `transform` will be null. You must first assign a new instance to the property if you wish to alter values on that container.

```
sprite.transform.perspectiveProjection = new PerspectiveProjection();
```

If you do not set a PerspectiveProjection for a display object container that holds children moved in 3D space, the projection will be taken from its parent container. If this parent does not contain a PerspectiveProjection instance, it will look to its parent, and so on until the root is reached. The root always has a default PerspectiveProjection instance with a `fieldOfView` of 55 and a `perspectiveCenter` set at the center of the stage. You can alter the properties at any time and it will affect any 3D display objects.

> *If you have assigned a PerspectiveProjection instance to a display object container and then change the PerspectiveProjection properties of the root, these will (somewhat unintuitively to me) override the properties of the child display object container.*

The easiest way to see how these properties of PerspectiveProjection affect the rendering of display objects is through a quick example. The file `PerspectiveProjectionTest.as` in this chapter's files draws 80 rectangular borders and places them on 20 planes in 3D space. The center of the projection follows the mouse about the screen and the field of view can be altered by holding down the up and down arrow keys. The output of this class is shown in Figure 6-5. The code for the class follows:

```
package {

  import flash.display.Shape;
  import flash.display.Sprite;
  import flash.events.KeyboardEvent;
  import flash.events.MouseEvent;
  import flash.geom.PerspectiveProjection;
  import flash.geom.Point;
  import flash.ui.Keyboard;

  [SWF(width=600, height=600, backgroundColor=0x000000)]

  public class PerspectiveProjectionTest extends Sprite {

    public function PerspectiveProjectionTest() {
      transform.perspectiveProjection = new PerspectiveProjection();
      for (var i:uint = 0; i < 20; i++) {
        var color:uint = Math.random()*0xFFFF;
        for (var j:uint = 0; j < 4; j++) {
          var x:uint = (j == 0 || j == 1) ? 400 : 0;
          var y:uint = (j == 1 || j == 2) ? 400 : 0;
          createPlane(color, x, y, (20-i)*500);
        }
      }
      setVanishingPoint(stage.mouseX, stage.mouseY);
      stage.addEventListener(MouseEvent.MOUSE_MOVE, onStageMouseMove);
      stage.addEventListener(KeyboardEvent.KEY_DOWN, onStageKeyDown);
    }
```

```
    private function createPlane(
      color:uint,
      x:Number,
      y:Number,
      z:Number
    ):void {
      var plane:Shape = new Shape();
      plane.graphics.beginFill(color);
      plane.graphics.drawRect(0, 0, 200, 200);
      plane.graphics.drawRect(20, 20, 160, 160);
      plane.graphics.endFill();
      plane.x = x;
      plane.y = y;
      plane.z = z;
      addChild(plane);
    }

    private function setVanishingPoint(x:Number, y:Number):void {
      transform.perspectiveProjection.projectionCenter =➥
new Point(x, y);
      graphics.clear();
      graphics.lineStyle(0, 0x666666);
      graphics.lineTo(x, y);
      graphics.moveTo(stage.stageWidth, 0);
      graphics.lineTo(x, y);
      graphics.moveTo(stage.stageWidth, stage.stageHeight);
      graphics.lineTo(x, y);
      graphics.moveTo(0, stage.stageHeight);
      graphics.lineTo(x, y);
    }

    private function onStageMouseMove(event:MouseEvent):void {
      setVanishingPoint(stage.mouseX, stage.mouseY);
      event.updateAfterEvent();
    }

    private function onStageKeyDown(event:KeyboardEvent):void {
      var projection:PerspectiveProjection =➥
transform.perspectiveProjection;
      var fieldOfView:Number = projection.fieldOfView;
      switch (event.keyCode) {
        case Keyboard.UP:
          fieldOfView += 2;
          break;
        case Keyboard.DOWN:
          fieldOfView -= 2;
          break;
      }
```

```
            projection.fieldOfView = Math.max(0.1,➥
Math.min(fieldOfView, 179.9));
            event.updateAfterEvent();
        }

    }

}
```

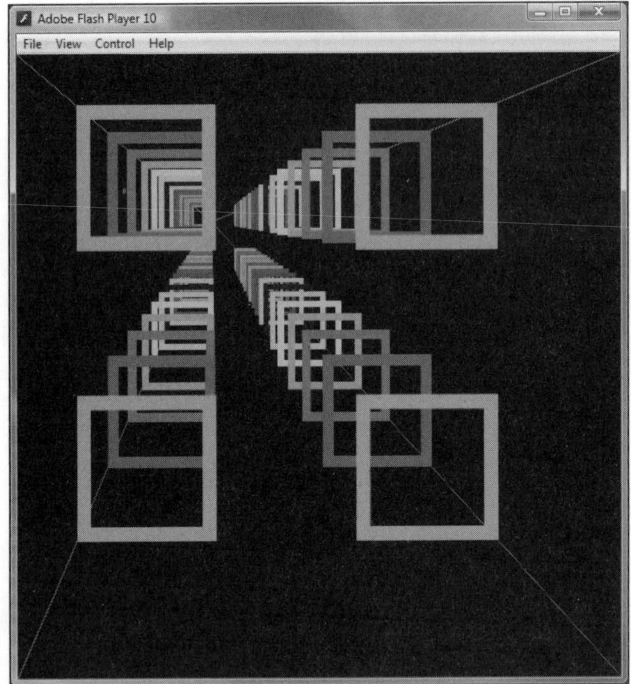

Figure 6-5. Multiple rectangular borders are drawn on multiple planes to demonstrate changes in field of view and center of projection.

The two for loops in the constructor run through 20 planes and 4 corners on each plane to create a total of 80 rectangles in the createPlane() method. The x and y values of each rectangle are determined based on the current iteration of the nested loop, ensuring that all four corners are created for each depth.

```
for (var i:uint = 0; i < 20; i++) {
  var color:uint = Math.random()*0xFFFF;
  for (var j:uint = 0; j < 4; j++) {
    var x:uint = (j == 0 || j == 1) ? 400 : 0;
    var y:uint = (j == 1 || j == 2) ? 400 : 0;
    createPlane(color, x, y, (20-i)*500);
  }
}
```

The projection center is set at the current mouse position in the setVanishingPoint() method, which is called not only in the constructor but also whenever the mouse is moved and the onStageMouseMove() handler is invoked.

```
transform.perspectiveProjection.projectionCenter = new Point(x, y);
```

In addition to setting the projection center, setVanishingPoint() also draws four lines from the corners of the stage to the vanishing point to make it clear where this point lies.

When a key is pressed and onStageKeyDown() is invoked, the current field of view is grabbed from this sprite's perspective projection.

```
var projection:PerspectiveProjection = transform.perspectiveProjection;
var fieldOfView:Number = projection.fieldOfView;
```

If the up or down arrow is being pressed, the field of view is increased or decreased, respectively. When the new value is assigned back to the projection, Math.min() and Math.max() are used to clamp the value between 0.1 and 179.9, since 0 and 180 will cause warnings.

```
projection.fieldOfView = Math.max(0.1, Math.min(fieldOfView, 179.9));
```

Play around with the SWF produced by this class to see how different settings for the field of view change how the objects are rendered on the 2D screen and how altering the center for the projection affects where objects are placed and how they recede to the vanishing point.

Extruding text

As cool as 3D display objects are, the biggest limitation is that in the end you are simply placing 2D planes in 3D space. Not to insult those friendly little sprites, but display objects have no depth, and this can limit the number of applications where they are useful unless a little creativity applied.

You might have noticed in the last example that, when the field of view is set to a low value and planes of display objects are placed close together, you can actually create an illusion of depth for a single object. In this next class, with an example of its output shown in Figure 6-6, I create a number of textfields and place these close together on the z axis. Once again, I make the placement of the projection center dependent on the mouse position and the field of view controlled by the up and down arrows (if you do not have Impact installed on your system, be sure to change the font name to one you have available).

```
package {

  import flash.display.Sprite;
  import flash.events.KeyboardEvent;
  import flash.events.MouseEvent;
  import flash.filters.BlurFilter;
  import flash.filters.GlowFilter;
```

```
import flash.geom.PerspectiveProjection;
import flash.geom.Point;
import flash.geom.ColorTransform;
import flash.ui.Keyboard;
import flash.text.TextField;
import flash.text.TextFieldAutoSize;
import flash.text.TextFormat;

[SWF(width=800, height=600, backgroundColor=0x000000)]

public class ExtrudeText extends Sprite {

  private static const EXTRUDE_DEPTH:uint = 30;
  private static const Z_DIST_BETWEEN_ITEMS:uint = 5;

  public function ExtrudeText() {
    transform.perspectiveProjection = new PerspectiveProjection();
    for (var i:uint = 0; i < EXTRUDE_DEPTH; i++) {
      createField(i);
    }
    stage.addEventListener(MouseEvent.MOUSE_MOVE, onStageMouseMove);
    stage.addEventListener(KeyboardEvent.KEY_DOWN, onStageKeyDown);
  }

  private function createField(index:uint):void {
    var field:TextField = new TextField();
    field.selectable = false;
    field.autoSize = TextFieldAutoSize.LEFT;
    field.defaultTextFormat = new TextFormat("Impact", 80, 0x66AAFF);
    field.text = "EXTRUDE TEST";
    field.x = stage.stageWidth/2 - field.width/2;
    field.y = stage.stageHeight/2 - field.height/2;
    field.z = index*Z_DIST_BETWEEN_ITEMS;
    if (index == 0) {
      field.filters = [
        new GlowFilter(0xFFFFFF, .5, 6, 6, 2, 1, true)
      ];
    } else {
      field.filters = [new BlurFilter(0, 0)];
      var darken:Number =➥
.1 + (EXTRUDE_DEPTH-index)/EXTRUDE_DEPTH*.8;
      field.transform.colorTransform =➥
new ColorTransform(darken, darken, darken);
    }
    addChildAt(field, 0);
  }

  private function onStageMouseMove(event:MouseEvent):void {
    var x:Number = stage.mouseX;
    var y:Number = stage.mouseY;
```

```
      transform.perspectiveProjection.projectionCenter =➥
new Point(x, y);
      event.updateAfterEvent();
    }

    private function onStageKeyDown(event:KeyboardEvent):void {
      var projection:PerspectiveProjection =➥
transform.perspectiveProjection;
      var fieldOfView:Number = projection.fieldOfView;
      switch (event.keyCode) {
        case Keyboard.UP:
          fieldOfView += 2;
          break;
        case Keyboard.DOWN:
          fieldOfView -= 2;
          break;
      }
      projection.fieldOfView =➥
Math.max(.1, Math.min(fieldOfView, 179.9));
      event.updateAfterEvent();
    }

  }

}
```

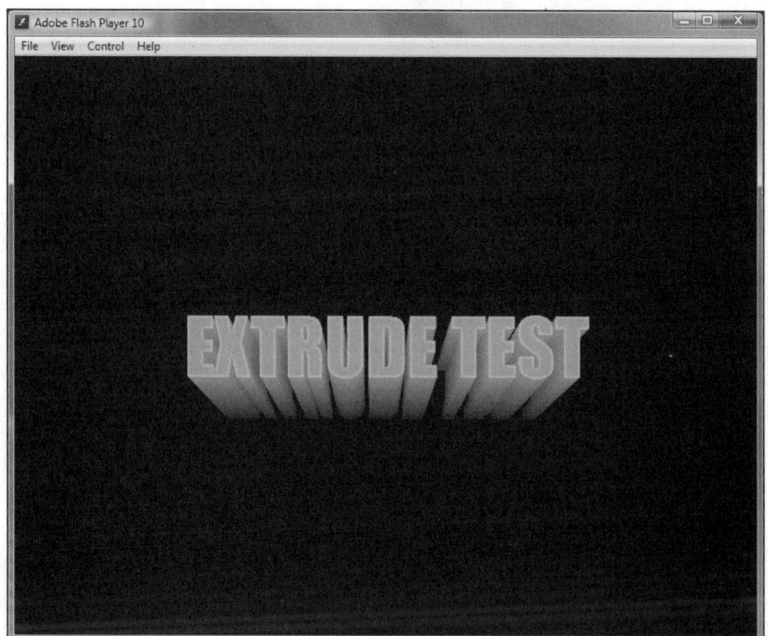

Figure 6-6. Text extruded by creating multiple copies at close depths and manipulating the perspective

The code that controls the perspective projection remains the same as the previous example, so instead, I have called attention to the two constants that control the number of copies of the textfield that are made (EXTRUDE_DEPTH) and the distance between each textfield on the z axis (Z_DIST_BETWEEN_ITEMS).

```
private static const EXTRUDE_DEPTH:uint = 30;
private static const Z_DIST_BETWEEN_ITEMS:uint = 5;
```

In the createField() method that instantiates and adds the textfield, I check the index of the textfield being created. For the first instance, a GlowFilter is applied to darken the textfield's edges to make it more legible. For every other textfield, a BlurFilter with no blurX and blurY is applied. Now why the heck is this done? In order to apply the ColorTransform as I do in the next two lines, the textfields need to be rasterized (turned into bitmaps); otherwise, the transform will not affect the textfield displaying a system font. The easiest way to turn a textfield into a bitmap is to apply a bitmap filter to it. I use the BlurFilter, since it is the easiest to construct with no settings, but any of the filters could be used. Once this filter is applied, the color can be darkened, which results in the extruded text darkening in color the further back it is on the z axis, giving a further illusion of depth.

```
      if (index == 0) {
        field.filters = [
          new GlowFilter(0xFFFFFF, .5, 6, 6, 2, 1, true)
        ];
      } else {
        field.filters = [new BlurFilter(0, 0)];
        var darken:Number =➥
.1 + (EXTRUDE_DEPTH-index)/EXTRUDE_DEPTH*.8;
        field.transform.colorTransform =➥
new ColorTransform(darken, darken, darken);
      }
```

You could almost be fooled into thinking we have a 3D extrusion, and, may I say, once again we've done it without any 3D math.

Rotating around axes

In addition to moving display objects through 3D space, Flash Player 10 offers the ability to rotate those display objects on three axes as well so that the 3D planes do not always have to be pointed directly at the viewer. Previously, we have only had the ability to rotate a display object on the axis perpendicular to the viewer or screen, which is actually the z axis in a 3D space. The x axis, as we've already discussed, runs horizontally across the view while the y axis runs vertically. How an object rotates about each of these axes is demonstrated in Figure 6-7.

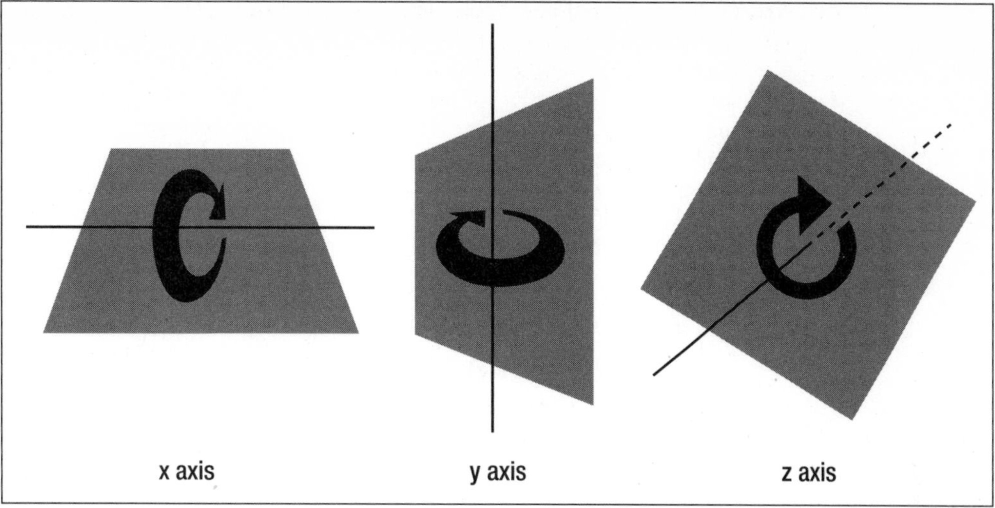

Figure 6-7. Rotation along each of three axes

To set the rotation on each of these axes, DisplayObject has been given three new and straightforward properties: `rotationX`, `rotationY`, and `rotationZ` (`rotation` on its own still exists and is equivalent to `rotationZ`). Rotating a display object in 3D space is as easy as altering one of these properties.

Flipping an image

To demonstrate how simple it is to rotate display objects in 3D, I've turned once more to the class AbstractImageLoader to load in an image. In the child class, found in this chapter's files as `ImageFlip.as`, the overridden `runPostImageLoad()` method adds the loaded bitmap to a sprite that is positioned at the center of the stage. The bitmap itself is centered within the parent sprite so that when the parent sprite rotates, the bitmap will rotate in the center, not on its top-left registration point. The rotation is handled in an `ENTER_FRAME` event handler that adds 1 to the `rotationY` property of the parent sprite each frame. The static result is shown in Figure 6-8.

```
package {

  import flash.display.Sprite;
  import flash.events.Event;

  [SWF(width=800, height=800, backgroundColor=0x000000)]

  public class ImageFlip extends AbstractImageLoader {

    private var _imageHolder:Sprite;

    public function ImageFlip() {
      super("../../assets/butterflies.jpg");
    }
```

```
override protected function runPostImageLoad():void {
  _imageHolder = new Sprite();
  _imageHolder.x = stage.stageWidth/2;
  _imageHolder.y = stage.stageHeight/2;
  _loadedBitmap.x = -_loadedBitmap.width/2;
  _loadedBitmap.y = -_loadedBitmap.height/2;
  _imageHolder.addChild(_loadedBitmap);
  addChild(_imageHolder);
  addEventListener(Event.ENTER_FRAME, onSpriteEnterFrame);
}

private function onSpriteEnterFrame(event:Event):void {
  _imageHolder.rotationY += 1;
}

  }

}
```

Figure 6-8. An image rotating about its y axis

It's difficult to get much simpler than that! Such an image flip effect could be used for an image transition, a card game like Memory where cards are flipped over, or an image carousel navigation. You will notice if you run the SWF, though, that the plane is made up of two sides with the image reversed when the plane is reversed. There is no backface culling with rotated display objects, just as there is no depth swapping, so you must keep this in mind as you construct effects. We'll cover backface culling, what exactly that means and how you get it, later in the chapter.

Scrolling text

So we've rotated a sprite, but it's good to remember that these 3D capabilities are a part of DisplayObject, not just Sprite, which means we can perform similar effects on other display objects like textfields. A simple example to demonstrate is shown in Figure 6-9, which features the familiar *Star Wars*–like scrolling title sequence. This is easily accomplished with the following class, found as ScrollingText.as in this chapter's files:

```
package {

  import flash.display.Sprite;
  import flash.events.Event;
  import flash.text.TextField;
  import flash.text.TextFieldAutoSize;
  import flash.text.TextFormat;
  import flash.text.TextFormatAlign;

  [SWF(width=800, height=600, backgroundColor=0x000000)]

  public class ScrollingText extends Sprite {

    private var _textfield:TextField;

    public function ScrollingText() {
      _textfield = new TextField();
      _textfield.width = stage.stageWidth/2;
      _textfield.selectable = false;
      _textfield.autoSize = TextFieldAutoSize.LEFT;
      _textfield.multiline = true;
      _textfield.wordWrap = true;
      var format:TextFormat = new TextFormat("Impact", 40, 0xFFFFFF);
      format.align = TextFormatAlign.JUSTIFY;
      _textfield.defaultTextFormat = format;
      _textfield.text = "This is a simple example of scrolling text ➥
like you might find at the beginning of a movie that came out ➥
a long time ago in a galaxy exactly like this one...";
      _textfield.y = stage.stageHeight/3;

      var textHolder:Sprite = new Sprite();
      textHolder.x = stage.stageWidth/2 - _textfield.width/2;
      textHolder.y = stage.stageHeight/2;
      textHolder.z = -200;
```

```
      textHolder.rotationX = -60;
      textHolder.addChild(_textfield);
      addChild(textHolder);

      addEventListener(Event.ENTER_FRAME, onSpriteEnterFrame);
    }

    private function onSpriteEnterFrame(event:Event):void {
      _textfield.y -= 1;
    }

  }

}
```

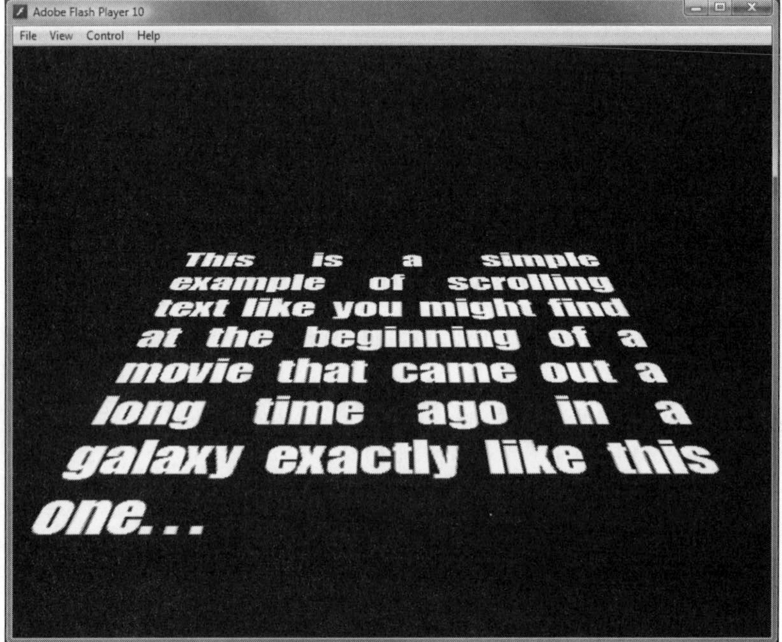

Figure 6-9. A field of text scrolling in perpsective into the distance

In the constructor for this class, I create a textfield with multiline text and nest this within a Sprite instance. The textfield itself is simply positioned at a higher y position but is not itself moved in 3D space. The container sprite, though, is centered on the stage and rotated on the x axes by –60 degrees (I could have accomplished the same by rotating 300 degrees, but –60 seems more intuitive to me). This rotation is what places the nested text at the familiar perspective distortion. Each frame that follows the textfield is moved up the y axis of its rotated parent sprite, which results in the text scrolling into the distance without it drawing too close to the vanishing point. The text remains legible long enough to read, after which point the movie can start. Now, where's my popcorn?

Constructing models out of planes

Even though we only have planes to work with, that does not mean you cannot construct simple 3D models out of those planes. If you manage the depths of your planes (which we will discuss in a later section), you can create objects with multiple planar sides, like picture cubes and 3D image galleries.

In this next example, I rotate a number of planes around a central y axis in order to create a tree model. Using this method, I can create a number of trees and place these within a container sprite that can then be rotated and positioned, which in turn rotates and positions all of its child elements. The result is shown in Figure 6-10.

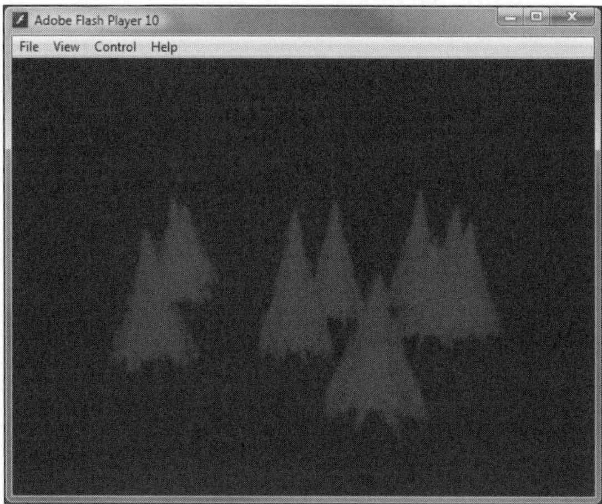

Figure 6-10. A collection of trees made up of rotated planes with their images created using bitmap data methods and filters

This class takes advantage of a number of the features we have covered up to this point in this book, including creating a bitmap image from scratch, applying noise and filters, copying channels, drawing the image using the drawing API, and placing and rotating objects in 3D space (of course, that also means the class is a little larger than our previous examples). Have a look over the code, and I will step through the more interesting and relevant lines:

```
package {

  import flash.display.Bitmap;
  import flash.display.BitmapData;
  import flash.display.BitmapDataChannel;
  import flash.display.Sprite;
  import flash.filters.BlurFilter;
  import flash.filters.DisplacementMapFilter;
  import flash.filters.DisplacementMapFilterMode;
  import flash.events.Event;
  import flash.geom.Point;
```

```
[SWF(width=550, height=400, backgroundColor=0x111911)]

public class Forest extends Sprite {

  private static const TOTAL_TREES:uint = 10;
  private static const TREE_DISPERSAL:uint = 400;
  private static const TREE_SIZE:uint = 100;
  private static const PLANES_IN_TREE:uint = 4;

  private var _forest:Sprite;

  public function Forest() {
    createForest();
    rotationX = 15;
    addEventListener(Event.ENTER_FRAME, onSpriteEnterFrame);
  }

  private function createForest():void {
    _forest = new Sprite();
    _forest.x = stage.stageWidth/2;
    _forest.y = stage.stageHeight/2;
    var treeImage:BitmapData = createTreeImage();
    for (var i:uint = 0; i < TOTAL_TREES; i++) {
      _forest.addChild(createTree(treeImage));
    }
    addChild(_forest);
  }

  private function createTreeImage():BitmapData {
    var point:Point = new Point();
    var treeImage:BitmapData = new BitmapData(
      TREE_SIZE,
      TREE_SIZE,
      true,
      0x00000000
    );
    var leaves:BitmapData = treeImage.clone();
    var noise:BitmapData = treeImage.clone();
    leaves.fillRect(leaves.rect, 0xFF005500);
    noise.perlinNoise(TREE_SIZE/10, TREE_SIZE/8, 2, 0, false, true);
    leaves.copyChannel(
      noise,
      noise.rect,
      point,
      BitmapDataChannel.RED,
      BitmapDataChannel.ALPHA
    );
```

```
      var sprite:Sprite = new Sprite();
      sprite.graphics.beginBitmapFill(leaves);
      sprite.graphics.lineTo(TREE_SIZE/2, 10);
      sprite.graphics.lineTo(TREE_SIZE-10, TREE_SIZE-10);
      sprite.graphics.lineTo(10, TREE_SIZE-10);
      sprite.graphics.lineTo(TREE_SIZE/2, 10);
      sprite.graphics.endFill();
      treeImage.draw(sprite);

      var displaceFilter:DisplacementMapFilter =➥
new DisplacementMapFilter(
        noise,
        new Point(),
        BitmapDataChannel.RED,
        BitmapDataChannel.RED,
        0,
        -TREE_SIZE/4
      );
      var blurFilter:BlurFilter = new BlurFilter(4, 4);
      treeImage.applyFilter(treeImage, treeImage.rect,➥
point, displaceFilter);
      treeImage.applyFilter(treeImage, treeImage.rect,➥
point, blurFilter);

      noise.dispose();
      leaves.dispose();

      return treeImage;
    }

    private function createTree(treeImage:BitmapData):Sprite {
      var tree:Sprite = new Sprite();
      for (var i:uint = 0; i < PLANES_IN_TREE; i++) {
        tree.addChild(createTreePlane(treeImage, i));
      }
      tree.scaleY = 1+Math.random()*.8;
      tree.x = Math.random()*TREE_DISPERSAL-TREE_DISPERSAL/2;
      tree.z = Math.random()*TREE_DISPERSAL-TREE_DISPERSAL/2;
      return tree;
    }

    private function createTreePlane(
      treeImage:BitmapData,
      index:uint
    ):Sprite {
      var bitmap:Bitmap = new Bitmap(treeImage);
      bitmap.x = -TREE_SIZE/2;
      bitmap.y = -TREE_SIZE/2;
      var treePlane:Sprite = new Sprite();
```

```
      treePlane.rotationY = index*(180/PLANES_IN_TREE);
      treePlane.addChild(bitmap);
      return treePlane;
    }

    private function onSpriteEnterFrame(event:Event):void {
      _forest.rotationY += 1;
    }

  }

}
```

First, let's take a look at the four constants at the top of the class and what they modify:

- TOTAL_TREES: The total number of trees you want created
- TREE_DISPERSAL: The minimum distance apart on the x and z axes trees can be randomly placed
- TREE_SIZE: The pixel size of the trees, width and height, when they are created
- PLANES_IN_TREE: The number of 2D planes that are rotated about the y axis to create a 3D tree model

In the constructor of this class, the createForest() method is called, which we will step into next and which basically creates all of the trees and the container sprite. After the forest is created, this document class sprite is rotated on the x axis by 15 degrees to create an overhead view of the trees. This rotation needs to occur in this parent class, as opposed to on the forest itself, since the forest will be rotating on the y axis and that rotation would conflict with this x axis rotation and the overhead angle would not be maintained.

createForest() creates and centers the forest sprite. It then calls createTreeImage() to create the bitmap data image that will be used for all rotated planes in a tree. This is passed to all the calls to createTree(), which occurs within a for loop that adds the required number of trees to the forest.

```
var treeImage:BitmapData = createTreeImage();
for (var i:uint = 0; i < TOTAL_TREES; i++) {
  _forest.addChild(createTree(treeImage));
}
```

createTreeImage() is our hefty exercise of the BitmapData knowledge explored in Chapters 3 and 4. First, I create three transparent bitmap data objects of the same size.

```
var treeImage:BitmapData = new BitmapData(
  TREE_SIZE,
  TREE_SIZE,
  true,
  0x00000000
);
var leaves:BitmapData = treeImage.clone();
var noise:BitmapData = treeImage.clone();
```

Next, I fill the leaves bitmap data with a darker green and fill the noise bitmap data with grayscale Perlin noise. This noise is used as the alpha transparency for the green leaves by copying the black-and-white red channel from the noise into the alpha channel for the leaves.

```
leaves.fillRect(leaves.rect, 0xFF005500);
noise.perlinNoise(TREE_SIZE/10, TREE_SIZE/8, 2, 0, false, true);
leaves.copyChannel(
  noise,
  noise.rect,
  point,
  BitmapDataChannel.RED,
  BitmapDataChannel.ALPHA
);
```

The drawing API lines that follow draw this leaves bitmap data into a shape that is triangular (and slightly smaller than the bitmap so that rougher edges caused by the alpha transparency might be more apparent). This shape is then drawn into the treeImage bitmap data so that additional manipulation can be easily applied.

```
var sprite:Sprite = new Sprite();
sprite.graphics.beginBitmapFill(leaves);
sprite.graphics.lineTo(TREE_SIZE/2, 10);
sprite.graphics.lineTo(TREE_SIZE-10, TREE_SIZE-10);
sprite.graphics.lineTo(10, TREE_SIZE-10);
sprite.graphics.lineTo(TREE_SIZE/2, 10);
sprite.graphics.endFill();
treeImage.draw(sprite);
```

The last bit of createTreeImage() applies two filters to the treeImage bitmap data. First, a displacement map using the Perlin noise is applied to distort the leaves on the y axis. Then a slight blur is applied.

```
      var displaceFilter:DisplacementMapFilter =➥
new DisplacementMapFilter(
        noise,
        new Point(),
        BitmapDataChannel.RED,
        BitmapDataChannel.RED,
        0,
        -TREE_SIZE/4
      );
      var blurFilter:BlurFilter = new BlurFilter(4, 4);
      treeImage.applyFilter(treeImage, treeImage.rect,➥
point, displaceFilter);
      treeImage.applyFilter(treeImage, treeImage.rect,➥
point, blurFilter);
```

The last few lines simply dispose of the data no longer needed and return the treeImage bitmap data out of the function. How's that for an application of our BitmapData kung fu skills?

The remaining methods in the Forest class complete the tree model. First, createTree() uses the treeImage bitmap data to create four planes and adds them as children. A random scale on the y axis is applied to offer some slight differentiation to our identical trees, and the tree is placed in a random position on the x and z axes.

```
for (var i:uint = 0; i < PLANES_IN_TREE; i++) {
  tree.addChild(createTreePlane(treeImage, i));
}
tree.scaleY = 1+Math.random()*.8;
tree.x = Math.random()*TREE_DISPERSAL-TREE_DISPERSAL/2;
tree.z = Math.random()*TREE_DISPERSAL-TREE_DISPERSAL/2;
```

The createTreePlane() method adds the treeImage bitmap data to a new Bitmap, which it centers within a parent sprite to allow for easier rotation around the center y axis. This rotation is determined by the current index of the plane.

```
treePlane.rotationY = index*(180/PLANES_IN_TREE);
```

If you plug in some numbers, you will see that the first index will have a rotation of 0, the second 45, the third 90, and the fourth 135. Since the planes extend on both positive and negative sides of the y axis, this covers all 360 degrees around the "trunk" (0/180, 45/315, 90/270, and 135/225).

Finally, the onSpriteEnterFrame() handler rotates the populated forest on the y axis every frame, spinning the trees about the view. The result can be a little sluggish due to the amount of transparency and blur we have applied, but you can begin to see how rotated planes can be combined to create more complex models with some optimization. By being creative with how planes are rotated and positioned and by applying optimizations based on the effect, you can take advantage of this built-in feature for some original effects not possible before without a 3D engine chugging away behind the scenes.

Transforming objects

You have seen how easy it is to set positions and rotations in 3D space and how to alter the distortion of the 3D to 2D mapping using the values in PerspectiveProjection. You could be satisfied with these additions to ActionScript and the Flash Player and go forth to create a number of 3D effects. If you want to dig deeper, though, ActionScript provides a number of utility classes and methods to enable more complex 3D exploration.

The flash.geom package includes three new classes that can be used for ActionScript 3D: Vector3D, Matrix3D, and Utils3D. One of the great things about these classes is that a lot of the math previously needed to create 3D in Flash has been encapsulated within these classes, making it all the easier to create a simple 3D engine. We will not cover everything about these classes, as that goes beyond the scope of this chapter and book, but I will point out some of the methods of both Vector3D and Matrix3D that might prove useful as you create image effects.

Vector3D

A Vector3D instance represents a point in 3D space with x, y, and z coordinates. Vector3D also supports a fourth property, w, for additional data, such as angle of rotation, which is used for quaternion calculations (I know, it's an imposing word, but in this context you can think of quaternions as 4×4 matrices that can be used for representing 3D transformations; we'll discuss this a little bit more in the coming section on the Matrix3D class). To create a new Vector3D instance, you need only call its constructor and optionally pass its coordinates.

```
var point:Vector3D = new Vector3D(0, 10, 100);
```

Strictly speaking, vectors are objects that have both magnitude (length) and direction. A force, such as gravitational pull, is often represented as a vector with its magnitude determining the amount of force and the direction determining, well, the direction of the force. This vector can then act on other vectors, such as the velocity of a projectile, to determine a new vector. A Vector3D instance can be used both to represent a point in 3D space as well as a directional vector in 3D space.

There are a number of methods that the Vector3D class provides to simplify their use within your 3D scenes. Let's take a look at the more common ones.

Performing simple vector math

Here are several Vector3D methods for performing simple vector operations, such as addition, subtraction, and testing equality.

- `incrementBy(a:Vector3D):void`: Use this to add the values of each component in the specified vector to the values of each component in the vector on which this method is called. This could be used to set the new position of a vector point based on a translation vector. For instance, if you have a point at (0, 5, 0) and you want to move this by a translation of (10, 0, 0), calling `incrementBy()` would set the vector position to (10, 5, 0).
- `add(a:Vector3D):Vector3D`: This adds the values of each component in one vector to the values of each component in another vector, resulting in a new Vector3D instance (it does not affect either original vector).
- `decrementBy(a:Vector3D):void`: This one subtracts the values of each component in the specified vector from the values of each component in the vector on which this method is called.
- `subtract(a:Vector3D):Vector3D`: With this method, you can subtract the values of each component in the specified vector from the values of each component in the vector on which this method is called, resulting in a new Vector3D instance (it does not affect either original vector).
- `equals(toCompare:Vector3D, allFour:Boolean = false):Boolean`: This method tests the equality of two vectors by comparing their x, y, and z values and returning `true` if all three are equal. If `allFour` is `true`, the `w` property is compared as well (we'll talk about `w` and its use a little later in the chapter).

- nearEquals(toCompare:Vector3D, tolerance:Number, allFour:Boolean = false): Boolean: Use this method to test the equality of two vectors by comparing their x, y, and z values and returning true if all three are equal or within the tolerance range. If allFour is true, the w property is compared as well. For instance, if tolerance is set to 1, then as long as each of the properties is equal to or less than 1 apart, true is returned.

The following example, with the output shown in Figure 6-11, demonstrates how to add and subtract vectors and how to represent these vectors on the screen:

```
package {

  import flash.display.Sprite;
  import flash.geom.Vector3D;
  import flash.geom.Point;

  [SWF(width=550, height=400, backgroundColor=0xFFFFFF)]

  public class SimpleVector3DTest extends Sprite {

    public function SimpleVector3DTest() {
      x = stage.stageWidth/2;
      y = stage.stageHeight/2;

      var center:Vector3D = new Vector3D(0, 0, 20);
      drawVector(center, 0x000000);

      var vector0:Vector3D = new Vector3D(50, 50, 50);
      var vector1:Vector3D = new Vector3D(100, 100, 100);
      var vector2:Vector3D = vector0.add(vector1);

      drawVector(vector0, 0xFF0000);
      drawVector(vector1, 0x0000FF);
      drawVector(vector2, 0xFF00FF);

      vector0 = new Vector3D(-50, -50, 150);
      vector2 = vector0.subtract(vector1);

      drawVector(vector0, 0x00FF00);
      drawVector(vector2, 0x00FFFF);
    }

    private function drawVector(vector:Vector3D, color:uint):void {
      var point:Point = local3DToGlobal(vector);
      point = globalToLocal(point);
      trace(vector, point);

      graphics.beginFill(color);
      graphics.drawCircle(point.x, point.y, 20*vector.z/100);
      graphics.endFill();
```

```
        }
      }
    }
```

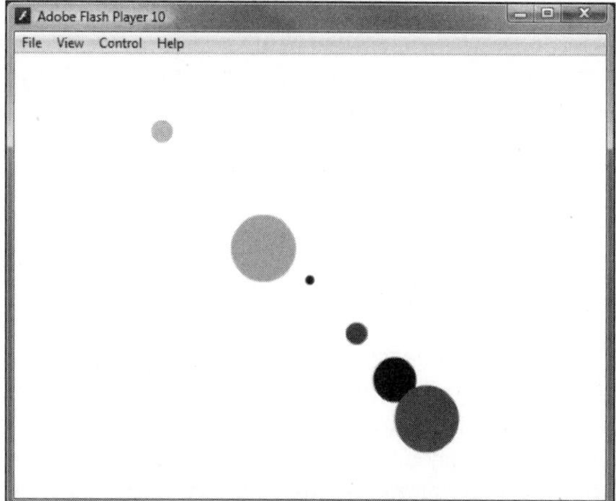

Figure 6-11. 3D vector positions represented by dots, showing the results of basic vector math

The first lines in the constructor position this sprite in the middle of the stage so that this can serve as the center point in our 3D display without any fuss with projections. I then create a vector at the center of the screen but at a positive z of 20. This z position is simply to allow for the method of scaling that I employ in the `drawVector()` method to render the points, which is not true 3D depth scaling, since vector points themselves do not have any size to represent. The way I have the radius of a circle determined in `drawVector()` by the z position requires that the z value is a positive number; otherwise, the scale would be 0 or negative.

```
graphics.drawCircle(point.x, point.y, 20*vector.z/100);
```

After the center vector is created, it is passed to the `drawVector()` method. The method converts the vector into a 2D coordinate in the global coordinate space using the new `local3DToGlobal()` method of DisplayObject, which works similarly to the old `localToGlobal()` but takes a 3D vector from another display object's 3D coordinate space and converts it into a 2D point. This can then be converted back into the sprite's coordinate space through `globalToLocal()`.

```
var point:Point = local3DToGlobal(vector);
point = globalToLocal(point);
```

At that point, I have a 2D coordinate that can be used in the `drawCircle()` call to draw our 3D vector point on the 2D display.

The rest of the class constructor creates a number of vectors to demonstrate how the `add()` and `subtract()` methods affect vectors. The first two vectors represent points that are positive in all three axes. Adding these together produces a new vector that is the sum of each component of the two other vectors, so vector2 will hold the coordinate (150, 150, 150). These three are all sent to the drawVector() method so they may be drawn to the screen.

```
var vector0:Vector3D = new Vector3D(50, 50, 50);
var vector1:Vector3D = new Vector3D(100, 100, 100);
var vector2:Vector3D = vector0.add(vector1);
```

The next vector that is created is in the negative x and y quadrants (though still with a positive z so it can have a positive scale when drawn). The original vector 1 (100, 100, 100) is subtracted from this vector to give us a new vector2 coordinate of (–150, –150, 50). These two new vectors are also sent to the drawVector() method for representation on the screen.

```
vector0 = new Vector3D(-50, -50, 150);
vector2 = vector0.subtract(vector1);
```

Vectors are useful when working with 3D points and rendering your own 3D in ActionScript, but they are also useful not just for points but when representing directional forces. You will see in the section on Matrix3D that there is a way to take the 4×4 matrix that makes up all of the transforms of a display object and break it into component vectors: one for translation, one for rotation, and one for scaling. You can then use these handy Vector3D operations to move a display object in a certain direction. Consider the following code (and just trust in the Matrix3D operations for now):

```
var windForce:Vector3D = new Vector3D(10, 0, 20);
var matrix:Matrix3D = displayObject.transform.matrix3D;
var vectors:Vector.<Vector3D> = matrix.decompose();
vectors[0].incrementBy(windForce);
matrix.recompose(vectors);
```

When decomposing a Matrix3D instance, the first component of the vectors array, vectors[0] in this example, holds the current translation transformation of the display object. We can call incrementBy() on this vector to apply our force and then put this back into our matrix. This applies the translation independent of the other transformations of our display object.

Measuring vectors

More complex operations provided by Vector3D include those that measure distance and angle between vectors.

- distance(a:Vector3D, b:Vector3D):Number: This static method returns the distance between two vectors as a scalar value.
- normalize():Number: This converts the Vector3D instance to a unit vector. A unit vector is a vector with a magnitude or length of 1. Unit vectors are important for certain calculations like dot products (discussed in a moment), and any vector can be converted to a unit vector by dividing each of its components by its magnitude. The normalize() method does just that for us and returns the original magnitude of the vector before it was normalized.

A vector's magnitude, or length, is its distance from its origin. This is probably most easily understood in a 2D coordinate system. Consider a vector point at (0, 4). Finding its magnitude requires a simple application of the Pythagorean theorem with the magnitude determined by the square root of its x coordinate squared plus its y coordinate squared, or more simply put in ActionScript:

```
magnitude = Math.sqrt(x*x + y*y);
```

Plugging in the point (0, 4), you will see its magnitude is 4, meaning it is a distance of 4 units away from the origin, which makes sense. Something a little less obvious would be a point like (3, 5), which would have a magnitude of the square root of 34, or around 5.83.

For 3D points, you just add the z coordinate into the equation, so a Vector3D's magnitude in ActionScript is:

```
magnitude = Math.sqrt(x*x + y*y + z*z);
```

Magnitude and direction are what define a vector, so even though you might think of a Vector3D instance as simply a coordinate in space, it is that coordinate's relation to the origin that is important, determining its magnitude and its direction in the coordinate system.

- `angleBetween(a:Vector3D, b:Vector3D):Number`: This static method of Vector3D returns the angle in radians between two vectors.
- `crossProduct(a:Vector3D):Vector3D`: This method returns a new vector that is perpendicular to the specified vector and the vector on which this method is invoked. The vector result of two vectors' cross product can be used to determine the normal of a plane (the direction the plane is facing) to help calculate the lighting of polygons. This vector can also be used to determine whether a plane is facing toward or away from the viewer, and thus whether it should be rendered.
- `dotProduct(a:Vector3D):Number`: This returns the angle between two unit vectors and, in combination with the cross product, can be used for lighting and backface culling.

Let's explore a few of these methods in a more complex example that shows how to calculate how an angle of a polygon face in relation to a light source can affect that polygon's color. To do that, we also need to be able to draw polygons in the first place using our vector points.

Drawing polygons

When rendering in 3D, you generally are working with 3D points that are grouped into planar polygon faces (meaning the points exist on a single plane in order to draw a flat surface). To draw the polygons, we need to go through each defined grouping of points, convert the 3D coordinates into 2D, and then draw the faces using the drawing API. In addition, you can do some more complex operations like lighting the polygons based on their relative angle to light sources, determining whether or not to render based on whether the faces are pointing toward or away from the view, and clipping polygons that intersect with the view plane.

In this next example, we will look at two things: first, how exactly to run through a collection of 3D vector points and draw polygons for these defined groups, and secondly, how to alter the color of these polygons to simulate a light source hitting the faces. The first problem is pretty easy thanks to the new Vector3D class and the new `local3DToGlobal()` method of DisplayObject. The lighting is a more complex problem that involves some higher level linear algebra, but it is still made easier with Vector3D. Let's look at how.

The class that follows draws three polygons on the screen and fills each with what is ostensibly the same color. To simulate a light source, the color is darkened based on each polygon's relative angle to the light, which is pointing straight down the positive z axis. The result is shown in Figure 6-12. Have a look at the code, relax and take breaths, and we'll step through the important pieces:

```
package {

  import flash.display.Sprite;
  import flash.geom.Vector3D;
  import flash.geom.Point;

  [SWF(width=600, height=600, backgroundColor=0xFFFFFF)]

  public class DrawingPolygons extends Sprite {

    private static const LIGHT_DIRECTION:Vector3D =➥
new Vector3D(0, 0, 1);
    private static const FACE_COLOR:uint = 0x9900FF;

    public function DrawingPolygons() {
      x = stage.stageWidth/2;
      y = stage.stageHeight/2;
      createPolygons();
    }

    private function createPolygons():void {
      var vectors:Vector.<Vector3D> = new Vector.<Vector3D>();
        vectors.push(new Vector3D(-250, -250, 0));
        vectors.push(new Vector3D(-100, -250, 0));
        vectors.push(new Vector3D(-100, -100, 0));
        vectors.push(new Vector3D(-250, -100, 0));
      drawPolygon(vectors);

      vectors = new Vector.<Vector3D>();
        vectors.push(new Vector3D(-50, -75, -50));
        vectors.push(new Vector3D(50, -75, 50));
        vectors.push(new Vector3D(50, 75, 50));
        vectors.push(new Vector3D(-50, 75, -50));
      drawPolygon(vectors);

      vectors = new Vector.<Vector3D>();
        vectors.push(new Vector3D(100, 160, 50));
```

```
      vectors.push(new Vector3D(250, 160, 50));
      vectors.push(new Vector3D(250, 180, -50));
      vectors.push(new Vector3D(100, 180, -50));
    drawPolygon(vectors);
  }

  private function drawPolygon(vectors:Vector.<Vector3D>):void {
    var color:uint = getFaceColor(vectors);
    var points:Vector.<Point> = getPoints2D(vectors);
    graphics.beginFill(color);
    graphics.moveTo(points[0].x, points[0].y);
    for (var i:uint = 1; i < points.length; i++) {
      graphics.lineTo(points[i].x, points[i].y);
    }
    graphics.lineTo(points[0].x, points[0].y);
    graphics.endFill();
  }

  private function getPoints2D(
    vectors:Vector.<Vector3D>
  ):Vector.<Point> {
    var points:Vector.<Point> = new Vector.<Point>;
    var point:Point;
    for each (var vector:Vector3D in vectors) {
      point = local3DToGlobal(vector);
      points.push(globalToLocal(point));
    }
    return points;
  }

  private function getFaceColor(vectors:Vector.<Vector3D>):uint {
    var U:Vector3D = getEdge(vectors[1], vectors[0]);
    var V:Vector3D = getEdge(vectors[1], vectors[2]);
    var crossProduct:Vector3D = U.crossProduct(V);
    var angle:Number = Vector3D.angleBetween(crossProduct,➥
LIGHT_DIRECTION);
    var brightness:Number = angle/Math.PI;
    return darkenColor(FACE_COLOR, brightness);
  }

  private function darkenColor(color:uint, percent:Number):uint {
    var red:uint = color >> 16 & 0xFF;
    var green:uint = color >> 8 & 0xFF;
    var blue:uint = color & 0xFF;
    red *= percent;
    green *= percent;
    blue *= percent;
    return red << 16 | green << 8 | blue;
  }
```

```
        private function getEdge(v1:Vector3D, v2:Vector3D):Vector3D {
          var x:Number = v1.x-v2.x;
          var y:Number = v1.y-v2.y;
          var z:Number = v1.z-v2.z;
          var vector:Vector3D = new Vector3D(x, y, z);
          vector.normalize();
          return vector;
        }

      }

    }
```

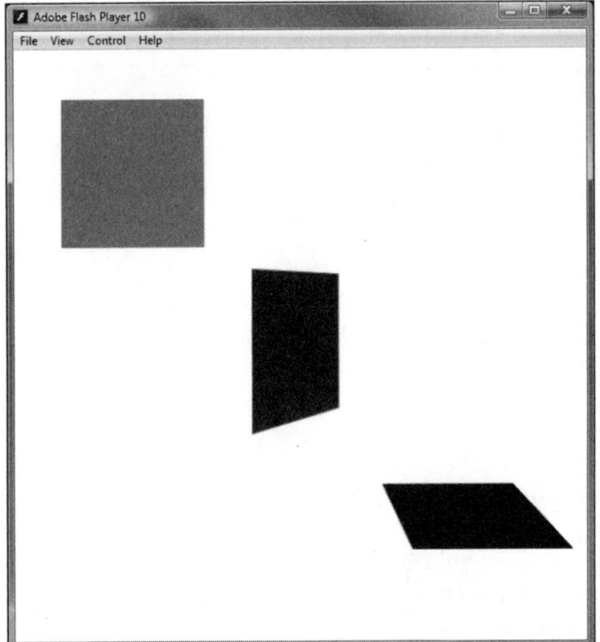

Figure 6-12. Three polygons rendered with different values of color brightness based on each polygon's orientation relative to the simulated light source's direction

OK, admittedly the getFaceColor() method might appear a little daunting, but the rest of the code mostly contains logic you've seen before. In the constructor, after positioning the sprite in the middle of the stage, the createPolygons() method is called. This method constructs three different groupings of Vector3D instances. Each of these represents a different polygon to be rendered. For each grouping, the drawPolygon() method is called and passed the vector containing the 3D points.

```
var vectors:Vector.<Vector3D> = new Vector.<Vector3D>();
  vectors.push(new Vector3D(-250, -250, 0));
  vectors.push(new Vector3D(-100, -250, 0));
```

```
    vectors.push(new Vector3D(-100, -100, 0));
    vectors.push(new Vector3D(-250, -100, 0));
  drawPolygon(vectors);
```

In the drawPolygon() method, getFaceColor() is called to get the proper color for the polygon based on its relative angle to the light. We'll put this aside for a moment to first look at how the polygon is drawn to the screen. You will see that getPoints2D() is called and passed the 3D vectors.

```
var points:Vector.<Point> = getPoints2D(vectors);
```

This method will return the 2D coordinates for all of the 3D points in the vector using the same local3DToGlobal() technique you saw in the last example.

```
for each (var vector:Vector3D in vectors) {
  point = local3DToGlobal(vector);
  points.push(globalToLocal(point));
}
```

With these 2D points, the drawing can be used to render the shapes to the screen, starting at the first point in the polygon, drawing lines to all the other points, and then closing the shape back at the first point.

```
graphics.moveTo(points[0].x, points[0].y);
for (var i:uint = 1; i < points.length; i++) {
  graphics.lineTo(points[i].x, points[i].y);
}
graphics.lineTo(points[0].x, points[0].y);
```

Now, how about getting that face color? If you take a look at the getFaceColor() method, the first things that occur are two calls to getEdge(), each passing two vector points to the method and each getting back a single vector.

```
var U:Vector3D = getEdge(vectors[1], vectors[0]);
var V:Vector3D = getEdge(vectors[1], vectors[2]);
```

What exactly are these two new vector points, U and V? Well, to determine the angle of a polygon face, you need two vectors that represent two sides of the polygon. The polygons in this example are planar, so I only need two sides, since any two sides will give me the orientation of the polygon. To get a side vector, I use two vector points and subtract each of the component parts of one vector from the component parts of the other.

```
var x:Number = v1.x-v2.x;
var y:Number = v1.y-v2.y;
var z:Number = v1.z-v2.z;
return new Vector3D(x, y, z);
```

Once I have the two edges, I find the cross product of these two vectors.

```
var crossProduct:Vector3D = U.crossProduct(V);
```

This gives me the normal of the polygon (that's just what crossProduct() does—returns a new vector perpendicular to the two vectors). The normal of a polygon shows the orientation of the polygon in 3D space. With the normal calculated, I can find the angle between it and the light source using Vector3D's angleBetween().

```
      var angle:Number = Vector3D.angleBetween(crossProduct,➥
LIGHT_DIRECTION);
      var brightness:Number = angle/Math.PI;
```

Since angleBetween will return a number between 0 and pi, I divide by pi to get a percentage between 0 and 1, which I will pass to the darkenColor() method to reduce the brightness of the face color based on the percentage. When a polygon is facing the light direction directly, the angle will be pi radians (half of a circle, since the vector of the normal and the vector of the light would be pointing in exact opposite directions), so the brightness will be set to 1. For polygons that do not face the light source directly, the brightness of their face color will be reduced.

This reduction of brightness is handled in the darkenColor() method.

```
var red:uint = color >> 16 & 0xFF;
var green:uint = color >> 8 & 0xFF;
var blue:uint = color & 0xFF;
red *= percent;
green *= percent;
blue *= percent;
return red << 16 | green << 8 | blue;
```

In darkenColor(), each of the component parts of the color is broken out using bitwise operations. Each channel is then multiplied by the percentage. The recomposited color with the new brightness in each channel is returned out of the method.

This is not the simplest of techniques but also is not overly complex considering it involves placing points in 3D space, drawing polygons for collections of points, and then lighting these based on their orientation. Much of the math has been taken out of our hands and is being graciously handled by the Vector3D class. And this class handles just simple vectors. For more complex transformations, we will want to look into matrices, and wouldn't you know that ActionScript is one step ahead of us?

Matrix3D

We have discussed matrices in the past chapters in the context of color transforms and convolutions. Now, we are in the context of 3D, and ActionScript offers the Matrix3D class to handle the complex transformations of display objects and points in 3D space. The beauty of a matrix is that, through a single entity, we can manipulate the translation, rotation, and scale of an object, and we can precalculate multiple transformations in the matrix that are cumulative before applying them to an object. Matrices also make it easy to copy transforms from one object to another or to remove transformations altogether.

The Matrix3D class goes even further by providing a number of valuable and useful methods that perform complex computations behind the scenes to do things like rotate an object to point toward another coordinate or move an object a certain distance in 3D space toward a specified coordinate. We won't go through all the methods in this section but will instead break down some of the more common and useful methods of the class.

Creating a matrix

All display objects have a `transform` property that holds a Transform instance. All Transform instances have a `matrix3D` property, but this is `null` by default unless you assign a new Matrix3D instance to it. Assigning a new Matrix3D instance is handled automatically with display objects if you alter their z position or rotate them in 3D space. At that point, you can access the Matrix3D instance that holds the transformation values of the display object in the following manner:

```
var matrix3D:Matrix3D = displayObject.transform.matrix3D;
```

A new Matrix3D object can be assigned as easily as this:

```
displayObject.transform.matrix3D = new Matrix3D();
```

The constructor takes an optional parameter, which is a vector of numbers. This vector must contain a total of 16 numbers, which specify a 4×4 matrix. The components in the 4×4 matrix represent the following transformation properties:

```
| scaleX       0       0  tX |
|      0  scaleY       0  tY |
|      0       0  scaleZ  tZ |
|      0       0       0  tW |
```

When a new Matrix3D instance is created, an identity matrix is created (no transformation), so the initial values of the 4×4 matrix are as follows:

```
| 1  0  0  0 |
| 0  1  0  0 |
| 0  0  1  0 |
| 0  0  0  1 |
```

This represented as a vector array, as it is in ActionScript, becomes this:

```
[1, 0, 0, 0, 0, 1, 0, 0, 0, 0, 1, 0, 0, 0, 0, 1]
```

You don't really need to know how these components of the matrix work and how the matrix calculations are handled in order to work with the Matrix3D class, though, nor do you need to explicitly set the values of the individual components (although you certainly can, and the constructor allows for just that). That's the joy of working with encapsulation. For instance, say you wanted to transform and rotate a display object on several axes in 3D space. This could be handled with the following lines:

```
var matrix:Matrix3D = new Matrix3D();
matrix.appendTranslation(100, 0, 200);
matrix.appendRotation(45, Vector3D.X_AXIS);
matrix.appendRotation(30, Vector3D.Z_AXIS);
displayObject.transform.matrix3D = matrix;
```

Here, we have moved the display object to 100 on the x axis and 200 on the z axis, and rotated the object 45 degrees on the parent x axis and 30 degrees on the parent z axis.

Exploring matrix methods

A lot of methods are available for the Matrix3D object. Here are some of the most useful. This list is by no means exhaustive but will serve you well as you progress through this chapter. Please see the ActionScript documentation for the complete list of available methods.

Ordering transformations Use the following methods to apply transformations to Matrix3D instances in an explicit order:

- `append(lhs:Matrix3D):void`: This method multiplies the specified matrix by the current matrix and assigns the result to the current matrix. This combines the two matrix transformations into a single transform that can be applied to an object. The parameter, `lhs`, stands for left-hand side and gives you insight into how the multiplication of the two matrices is handled. With multiplication of scalar values, like 4 * 5, it doesn't matter which order the numbers are in: 4 * 5 is the same as 5 * 4. This is known as the commutative property in multiplication. Matrix multiplication is not commutative as it is with scalar values, which basically means (A * B) != (B * A). Matrix multiplication depends on the order of the matrices in the operation. When calling the `append()` method of Matrix3D, the equation to determine the new matrix values is

  ```
  resultMatrix = lhs * currentMatrix
  ```

  You would use `append()` to combine different transformations into a single matrix, which can then be applied to an object.

- `prepend(rhs:Matrix3D):void`: Multiply the current matrix by the specified matrix and assign the result to the current matrix with this method. This works like the `append()` method, except in this case the argument is the right-hand side of the multiplication operation.

  ```
  resultMatrix = currentMatrix * rhs
  ```

- `appendTranslation(x:Number, y:Number, z:Number):void`: This method appends a translation along the x, y, and z axes to the current matrix. When a transformation is appended, it is performed by the matrix after other transformations are applied. Remember, since transformations are cumulative, the order in which they are performed is important.

- `prependTranslation(x:Number, y:Number, z:Number):void`: Prepend a translation along the x, y, and z axes to the current matrix with this method. When a translation is prepended, it is performed by the matrix before other transformations are applied.

- `appendRotation(degrees:Number, axis:Vector3D, pivotPoint:Vector3D = null):void`: Use this method to append a rotation along a specified axis around a specified pivot point. Just as with `appendTranslation()`, `appendRotation()` results in the matrix applying the rotation after other transformations have been applied. The axis of rotation can be any directional Vector3D instance, though the most common are stored as constants of Vector3D, X_AXIS, Y_AXIS, and Z_AXIS. The optional pivot point parameter allows you to specify a point around which the rotation occurs.

- prependRotation(degrees:Number, axis:Vector3D, pivotPoint:Vector3D = null):void: This method prepends a rotation along a specified axis around a specified pivot point. Because the rotation is prepended, it is performed by the matrix before other transformations are applied. Other than that, this works the same as appendRotation().
- appendScale(xScale:Number, yScale:Number, zScale:Number):void: Use this method to append an incremental scaling transformation. Each parameter determines a percentage of the current scale on each of the axes to apply, so that 1 produces no scale change upon the specified axes; 0.5 results in a reduction by 50 percent; and so on. Because the scaling is appended, it is performed by the matrix after other transformations are applied, just as with appendTranslation() and appendRotation().
- prependScale(xScale:Number, yScale:Number, zScale:Number):void: This method prepends an incremental scaling transformation. Just as with the other prepend methods, this is performed by the matrix before other transformations are applied.

To make it clear what exactly the order of translations can mean and how prepending or appending transformations can affect the final matrix, let's take a look at the following code. Its output can be seen in Figure 6-13.

```
package {

  import flash.display.Shape;
  import flash.display.Sprite;
  import flash.geom.Matrix3D;
  import flash.geom.Vector3D;

  [SWF(width=400, height=400, backgroundColor=0xFFFFFF)]

  public class AppendPrependTest extends Sprite {

    public function AppendPrependTest() {
      var shape0:Shape = createShape(0xFF0000);
      var matrix0:Matrix3D = new Matrix3D();
      matrix0.appendTranslation(250, 100, 100);
      matrix0.appendRotation(45, Vector3D.Z_AXIS);
      shape0.transform.matrix3D = matrix0;

      var shape1:Shape = createShape(0x00FF00);
      var matrix1:Matrix3D = new Matrix3D();
      matrix1.appendRotation(45, Vector3D.Z_AXIS);
      matrix1.appendTranslation(250, 100, 100);
      shape1.transform.matrix3D = matrix1;
```

```
      var matrix2:Matrix3D = new Matrix3D();
      matrix2.appendRotation(45, Vector3D.Y_AXIS);
      var matrix3:Matrix3D = matrix2.clone();
      matrix2.prepend(matrix0);
      matrix3.append(matrix0);

      var shape2:Shape = createShape(0x0000FF);
      shape2.transform.matrix3D = matrix2;

      var shape3:Shape = createShape(0xFF00FF);
      shape3.transform.matrix3D = matrix3;
    }

    private function createShape(color:uint):Shape {
      var shape:Shape = new Shape();
      shape.graphics.beginFill(color);
      shape.graphics.drawRect(-100, -100, 200, 200);
      shape.graphics.endFill();
      addChild(shape);
      return shape;
    }

  }

}
```

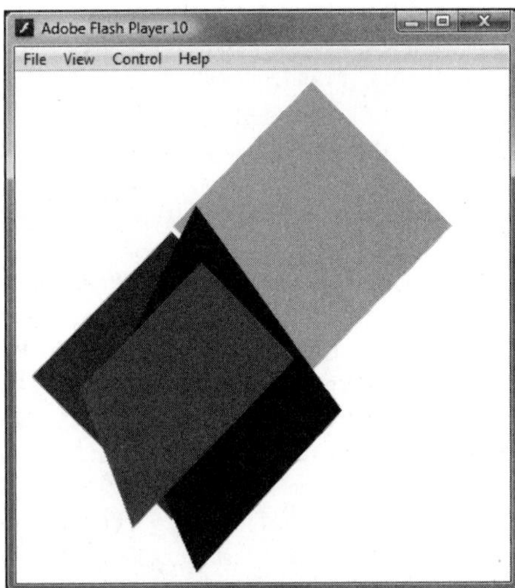

Figure 6-13. Transformations applied to multiple rectangles demonstrating how different ordering of the same transformations can affect the outcome

In this class, I create four rectangular shapes. The first two shapes (red and green, respectively) both contain identical rotation and translation transformations. However, for the red shape, the translation to (250, 100, 100) is applied before the 45-degree rotation on the z axis.

```
var shape0:Shape = createShape(0xFF0000);
var matrix0:Matrix3D = new Matrix3D();
matrix0.appendTranslation(250, 100, 100);
matrix0.appendRotation(45, Vector3D.Z_AXIS);
shape0.transform.matrix3D = matrix0;
```

For the green shape, the z axis rotation is applied before the object is translated by (250, 100, 100). Because the rotation of the object affects the direction of its axes, the translation places the green shape in a different location than the red shape.

```
var shape1:Shape = createShape(0x00FF00);
var matrix1:Matrix3D = new Matrix3D();
matrix1.appendRotation(45, Vector3D.Z_AXIS);
matrix1.appendTranslation(250, 100, 100);
shape1.transform.matrix3D = matrix1;
```

In the next block in the code, I create a new matrix that contains a rotation transformation of 45 degrees around the y axis. This matrix is then cloned so that I can affect each matrix independently and apply the first to one shape and the clone to another (it is important to note that you cannot assign the same Matrix3D instance to two different display objects anyway as it will throw a runtime exception).

```
var matrix2:Matrix3D = new Matrix3D();
matrix2.appendRotation(45, Vector3D.Y_AXIS);
var matrix3:Matrix3D = matrix2.clone();
matrix2.prepend(matrix0);
matrix3.append(matrix0);
```

I multiply the same matrix, `matrix0`, to each, but for `matrix2`, I use `prepend()`, and for `matrix3`, I use `append()`, which changes the order of the matrices in the operation. You can see from the output that this places the blue and purple shapes at two different locations. This is because the blue shape first gets translated by (250, 100, 100) and then gets the z axis rotation and the y axis rotation applied. The purple shape is rotated first on the y axis and then gets translated by (250, 100, 100) and rotated on the z axis.

So you see that although the distinction might appear small in the methods, the results of how you call them and in what order can greatly affect the resulting matrix that you apply to your display objects.

Applying transformations independently The following methods allow you to apply transformations to Matrix3D instances independent of previous transformations:

- `decompose(orientationStyle:String = "eulerAngles"):Vector.<Vector3D>`: Retrieve the matrix's translation, rotation, and scale settings as three separate vectors of Vector3D instances with this method. The first vector holds translation values, the second rotation, and the third scaling. By decomposing a matrix into vector components, you can affect an individual type of transform (for instance, just the rotation) independent of the other transformations and then use `recompose()` to apply the modified component vectors back to the original matrix.

- The orientationStyle parameter determines how rotation transformations are applied. This can be set to EULER_ANGLES, AXIS_ANGLE, or QUATERNION, all constants of flash.geom.Orientation3D.

> *When objects are rotated in 3D space, these rotations can be applied in a number of ways to produce different results, because rotation on one axis can affect the rotation on another axis, so order and method of rotation can greatly affect the outcome.*
>
> *Euler angle rotation rotates on each axis individually, rotating first on the x axis, then the y, and then the z. The decompose() and recompose() methods of Matrix3D use this method of rotation by default. When setting rotationX, rotationY, or rotationZ on a display object, Euler rotation is used, as only a single axis rotation needs to be updated. Using Euler angle rotation for multiple axes simultaneously can sometimes lead to a phenomenon called gimbal lock, where two axes rotating independently become aligned. Further rotations go wonky and fun ensues. You can use one of the other rotation methods to avoid this.*
>
> *Axis-angle rotation uses an axis represented by a unit vector defining an orientation in 3D space and an angle representing the amount of rotation about this unit vector axis. The orientation of the axis vector determines the way the object rotated is facing. The angle is used to determine the upward direction for the object. The appendRotation() and prependRotation() methods we looked at previously use axis-angle rotation behind the scenes.*
>
> *The third method of rotation, quaternion rotation, uses a 4×4 matrix to determine orientation and angle of rotation. It is for quaternion computation that the Vector3D class supports a fourth, w, property, since, as we discussed way back in Chapter 2, matrix multiplication requires the same number of rows in one matrix (a 4×4, the quaternion matrix) as columns in another (a 1×4 matrix, the vector with x, y, z, and w). Using quaternions, the shortest amount of rotation needed to transform from one orientation to another can be calculated, and gimbal lock is prevented. When using the interpolation methods, which we will cover shortly, quaternion calculations are used.*

- recompose(components:Vector.<Vector3D>, orientationStyle:String = "eulerAngles"):Boolean: This method takes three vectors, with the first holding translation settings, the second rotation, and the third scaling, and creates a new matrix for the Matrix3D instance based on these values. This method usually works hand in hand with the decompose() method to reconstruct a matrix after first decomposing it and altering its individual transformations.

When might you use the combination of decompose() and recompose()? Some methods, like interpolateTo(), which we will cover shortly, use these behind the scenes so that a single transformation, like the rotation or position, might be altered without having to account for the other current transformations. As you saw in the last example, if you translate an object that has been rotated, it might not appear in the end position that was desired.

Consider the scenario that you want to scale a shape on an axis, but that scaling transformation might be affected by the object's current rotation or position. In that situation, you could decompose the current matrix, apply the desired scaling to just the scale component vector, and then recompose the new matrix, which the following class does:

```
package {

  import flash.display.Shape;
  import flash.display.Sprite;
  import flash.geom.Matrix3D;
  import flash.geom.Vector3D;

  [SWF(width=700, height=400, backgroundColor=0xFFFFFF)]

  public class DecomposeRecomposeTest extends Sprite {

    public function DecomposeRecomposeTest() {
      var shape0:Shape = createShape(0xFF0000);
      var matrix0:Matrix3D = new Matrix3D();
      matrix0.appendTranslation(250, 200, 100);
      matrix0.appendRotation(45, Vector3D.Y_AXIS);
      shape0.transform.matrix3D = matrix0;

      var shape1:Shape = createShape(0x00FF00);
      shape1.transform.matrix3D = matrix0.clone();

      shape0.transform.matrix3D.appendScale(2, 1, 1);

      var vectors:Vector.<Vector3D> =➥
shape1.transform.matrix3D.decompose();
      vectors[2] = new Vector3D(2, 1, 1);
      shape1.transform.matrix3D.recompose(vectors);
    }

    private function createShape(color:uint):Shape {
      var shape:Shape = new Shape();
      shape.graphics.beginFill(color);
      shape.graphics.drawRect(-50, -50, 100, 100);
      shape.graphics.endFill();
      addChild(shape);
      return shape;
    }

  }

}
```

The output of this class is shown in Figure 6-14.

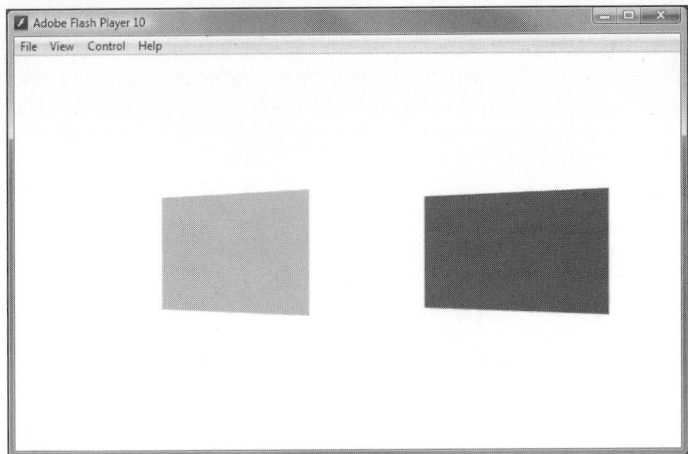

Figure 6-14. Scaling applied to a decomposed matrix so that the transformation is independent of the other current transformations. The rectangle on the right had the scaling appended to its current transformation, resulting in a scaling affected by the previous rotation and translation.

For the first rectangle, the scaling of 200 percent on the x axis is simply appended to the current matrix. This results in the scaling being relative to its parent's registration point, which alters the final position of the shape. For the second rectangle, the scaling is applied only to the scale vector component of the shape's matrix so that it is unaffected by the current rotation or position. This altered vector is then recomposed into the shape's final matrix.

Interpolating between matrices Interpolation is the method of calculating intermediate data points between two existing data points. Using interpolation, you can transform from one Matrix3D transformation to another—or to any value in between—over time. The following methods of Matrix3D make this a simple process.

- `interpolate(thisMat:Matrix3D, toMat:Matrix3D, percent:Number):Matrix3D`: This static method creates a new matrix based on two matrices and a percent of interpolation between the two. The method determines how one matrix (`thisMat` in the parameters) can be transformed into another (`toMat`). Think of this as enabling a matrix tween. Using this method, you can tween between the transformations of one display object in 3D space to another by interpolating a little each frame, starting with a percent close to 0, which will be weighted more to `thisMat`, and moving toward 1, which will be weighted more to `toMat`.
- `interpolateTo(toMat:Matrix3D, percent:Number):void`: This method is the same as `interpolate()`, but instead of being a static method, this one is called on a Matrix3D instance to interpolate it closer to the matrix specified in the argument.

> *Note that although the Adobe ActionScript documentation states these methods interpolate scale as well as position and orientation, it appears as if matrices always have their scale reset to (1, 1, 1) when interpolated by these methods.*

Although the interpolation methods are most useful for animating between two transformations, you can also use the methods to construct seemingly solid objects by creating a dense collection of shapes that are interpolated forms between two end positions (plus, it is much easier to capture in a screenshot than an animation over time!). The following class creates two rectangles and two matrices to set their positions. A loop is then run through to draw intermediate shapes between the two end shapes. The result can be seen in Figure 6-15 with the left image illustrating 10 interpolated shapes and the right image illustrating 100 shapes.

```
package {

  import flash.display.Shape;
  import flash.display.Sprite;
  import flash.geom.Matrix3D;
  import flash.geom.Vector3D;

  [SWF(width=550, height=400, backgroundColor=0xFFFFFF)]

  public class InterpolateTest extends Sprite {

    private static const TOTAL_INTERPOLATED_SHAPES:uint = 100;

    public function InterpolateTest() {
      rotationX = 30;

      var startColor:uint = 0xFF0000;
      var endColor:uint = 0xFFCC00;

      var startShape:Shape = createShape(startColor);
      var startMatrix:Matrix3D = new Matrix3D();
      startMatrix.appendRotation(-90, Vector3D.X_AXIS);
      startMatrix.appendRotation(-45, Vector3D.Y_AXIS);
      startMatrix.appendTranslation(275, 250, -100);
      startShape.transform.matrix3D = startMatrix;

      var endShape:Shape = createShape(endColor);
      var endMatrix:Matrix3D = startMatrix.clone();
      endMatrix.appendTranslation(0, -200, 0);
      endShape.transform.matrix3D = endMatrix;

      var shape:Shape;
      for (var i:uint = 0; i < TOTAL_INTERPOLATED_SHAPES; i++) {
        shape = createShape(getColor(startColor, endColor, i));
        shape.transform.matrix3D = Matrix3D.interpolate(
          startMatrix,
          endMatrix,
          getPercent(i)
        );
      }

      addChild(endShape);
    }
```

```
        private function getColor(
          startColor:uint,
          endColor:uint,
          index:uint
        ):uint {
          var percent:Number = getPercent(index);
          var startRed:uint = startColor >> 16 & 0xFF;
          var startGreen:uint = startColor >> 8 & 0xFF;
          var startBlue:uint = startColor & 0xFF;
          var endRed:uint = endColor >> 16 & 0xFF;
          var endGreen:uint = endColor >> 8 & 0xFF;
          var endBlue:uint = endColor & 0xFF;
          var red:uint = (endRed - startRed)*percent + startRed;
          var green:uint = (endGreen - startGreen)*percent + startGreen;
          var blue:uint = (endBlue - startBlue)*percent + startBlue;
          return red << 16 | green << 8 | blue;
        }

        private function getPercent(index:uint):Number {
          return (index+1)/(TOTAL_INTERPOLATED_SHAPES+1);
        }

        private function createShape(color:uint):Shape {
          var shape:Shape = new Shape();
          shape.graphics.beginFill(color);
          shape.graphics.drawRect(-100, -100, 200, 200);
          shape.graphics.endFill();
          addChild(shape);
          return shape;
        }

      }

    }
```

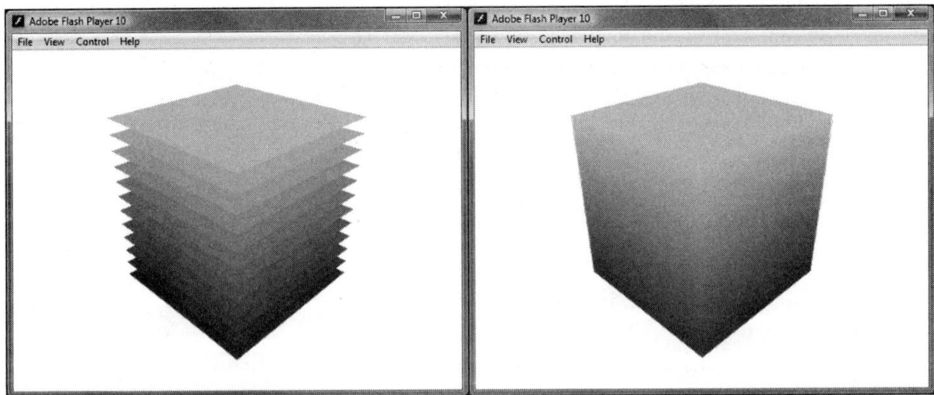

Figure 6-15. A dense interpolation between two shapes, more easily seen on the left, can produce a 3D extrusion, as shown on the right.

The two matrices are created in the constructor just as in previous examples. Note how the end matrix is simply a clone of the start matrix with an additional transformation applied to move it up on the y axis.

```
var endMatrix:Matrix3D = startMatrix.clone();
endMatrix.appendTranslation(0, -200, 0);
endShape.transform.matrix3D = endMatrix;
```

A loop is then set up to create all of the interpolated shapes. A getColor() method is used to find the intermediate color between the start and end colors. This is done by breaking each color down into the component channels using some bitwise operations so that the intermediate brightness in each channel can be calculated. The channel values can then be combined into a final composite color.

After the intermediate shape is drawn, the transformation of the shape is determined by calling the static interpolate() method of Matrix3D and passing the start and end matrices and the percent we wish to interpolate.

```
shape.transform.matrix3D = Matrix3D.interpolate(
  startMatrix,
  endMatrix,
  getPercent(i)
);
```

The method takes care of finding the new matrix that lies between the two end matrices at the specified percent. After seeing how we have to find something like an intermediate color, isn't nice to know that Matrix3D does all the work for intermediate matrices?

Orienting toward other objects Pointing a vector at a specific point is a common need in 3D. The pointAt() method simplifies this process:

- pointAt(pos:Vector3D, at:Vector3D = null, up:Vector3D = null):void: This method rotates a matrix so that its orientation is facing the specified position (pos). The at parameter is a vector defining the direction of the matrix that should be pointing toward the desired position. For instance, if we think of this in terms of display objects, the direction of a triangle shape that should point toward another object might be the right side of the shape. In that case, the at vector would be (1, 0, 0). The default for this is the negative z axis, or (0, 0, –1), which is the axis and orientation that is pointing toward the viewer. This vector is useful if you have something like a bitmap image of a human face that you want pointed toward another object.

  The up parameter is another direction vector that defines the upward direction of the matrix. When an object is rotated in 3D space to orient toward another object, it is important to know not only the point of the object that should be facing the target but also the orientation for the rest of the object. If that's not clear to you, consider a weathervane. The arrow will point in the direction of the wind, but the rest of the weathervane could be rotated any which way in 3D space. To get the rooster in the weathervane sitting upright and not standing on his head, an additional vector is needed to specify the upward direction of the weathervane. This is where the up parameter comes in.

In the following class, I create a ball that can be moved around in 3D space using the arrow keys (holding down shift moves the ball on the z axis as opposed to the y axis). The red arrow in the middle will point at the ball no matter its position using Matrix3D's pointAt() method, as shown in Figure 6-16.

```
package {

  import flash.display.Shape;
  import flash.display.Sprite;
  import flash.events.KeyboardEvent;
  import flash.geom.Matrix3D;
  import flash.geom.Vector3D;
  import flash.ui.Keyboard;

  [SWF(width=800, height=600, backgroundColor=0x000000)]

  public class PointAtTest extends Sprite {

    private static const MOVE_RATE:uint = 15;

    protected var _ball:Shape;
    protected var _pointer:Shape;

    public function PointAtTest() {
      createPointer();
      createBall();
      updatePointer();
      stage.addEventListener(KeyboardEvent.KEY_DOWN, onStageKeyDown);
    }

    private function createBall():void {
      _ball = new Shape();
      _ball.graphics.beginFill(0xFFFFFF);
      _ball.graphics.drawCircle(0, 0, 20);
      _ball.graphics.endFill();
      _ball.x = stage.stageWidth/2 + 100;
      _ball.y = stage.stageHeight/2 - 100;
      addChild(_ball);
    }

    private function createPointer():void {
      _pointer = new Shape();
      _pointer.graphics.beginFill(0xFF0000);
      _pointer.graphics.moveTo(-40, -40);
      _pointer.graphics.lineTo(40, 0);
      _pointer.graphics.lineTo(-40, 40);
      _pointer.graphics.lineTo(0, 0);
      _pointer.graphics.lineTo(-40, -40);
```

```
      _pointer.graphics.endFill();
      _pointer.x = stage.stageWidth/2;
      _pointer.y = stage.stageHeight/2;
      _pointer.z = 0;
      addChild(_pointer);
    }

    protected function updatePointer():void {
      var ballPosition:Vector3D =➥
new Vector3D(_ball.x, _ball.y, _ball.z);
      _pointer.transform.matrix3D.pointAt(
        ballPosition,
        Vector3D.X_AXIS,
        new Vector3D(0, -1, 0)
      );
    }

    private function onStageKeyDown(event:KeyboardEvent):void {
      switch (event.keyCode) {
        case Keyboard.UP:
          if (event.shiftKey) {
            _ball.z -= MOVE_RATE;
          } else {
            _ball.y -= MOVE_RATE;
          }
          break;
        case Keyboard.DOWN:
          if (event.shiftKey) {
            _ball.z += MOVE_RATE;
          } else {
            _ball.y += MOVE_RATE;
          }
          break;
        case Keyboard.RIGHT:
          _ball.x += MOVE_RATE;
          break;
        case Keyboard.LEFT:
          _ball.x -= MOVE_RATE;
          break;
      }
      updatePointer();
      event.updateAfterEvent();
    }

  }

}
```

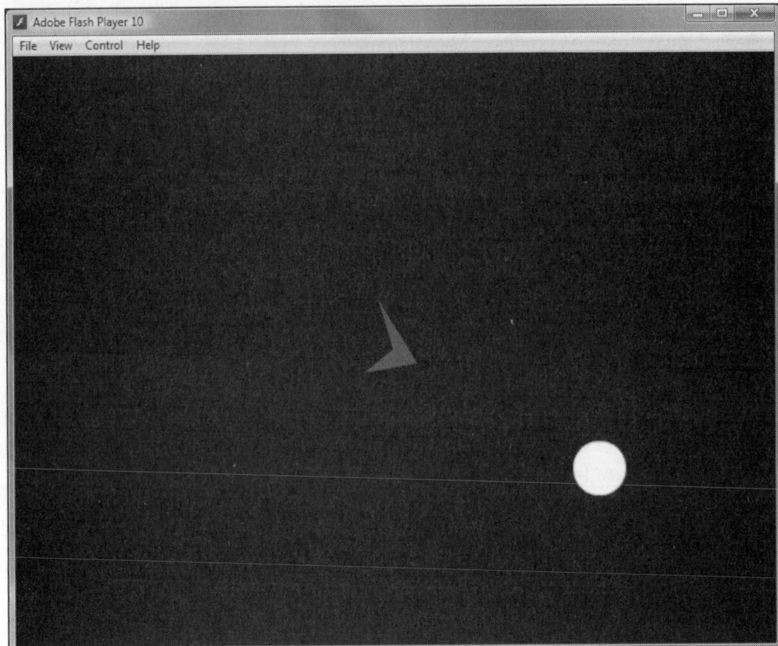

Figure 6-16. The arrow automatically orients itself based on the position of the ball.

In the constructor for this class, I call methods to create the ball and the pointer arrow and update the pointer so that it is pointing at the ball's initial position. An event handler is set up on the stage for when a key is pressed. If you look at both the `createBall()` and `createPointer()` methods, they simply draw and position the objects. The line of interest is in `createPointer()` where the z position is set.

```
_pointer.z = 0;
```

This is done to automatically create a Matrix3D instance for the pointer (alternatively, I could have explicitly created a Matrix3D instance, but this is so much easier) so that when I access the matrix in `updatePointer()` I do not get a null pointer exception.

The `onStageKeyDown()` handler will be invoked after a key press. The `UP` and `DOWN` cases handle movement both on the z and y axes, depending on whether the shift key is currently pressed.

```
if (event.shiftKey) {
  _ball.z += MOVE_RATE;
} else {
  _ball.y += MOVE_RATE;
}
```

Once the x, y, or z position of the ball is updated, `updatePointer()` is invoked. This method creates a new Vector3D instance holding the current x, y, and z coordinates of the ball. The vector is passed as the first argument to the pointer Matrix3D's `pointAt()` method.

```
var ballPosition:Vector3D = new Vector3D(_ball.x, _ball.y, _ball.z);
_pointer.transform.matrix3D.pointAt(
  ballPosition,
  Vector3D.X_AXIS,
  new Vector3D(0, -1, 0)
);
```

The point of the pointer is the right side of the shape, so the positive X_AXIS constant is passed as the at argument so the right side of the shape will be oriented towards the ball. The up parameter is specified as the negative y axis, (0, –1, 0). What you pass in really depends on what you consider to be the up position of your graphic. You could alter this example to use the z axis instead and that would work equally well.

This example shows how easy it is to direct one shape to point at another. Consider a game that required one sprite to point at and fire at another sprite. This can be easily accomplished using pointAt(). Add a little bit of animation, and you have a slick 3D effect with very little work. The example AnimatedPointAtTest.swf takes this example one step further by pulling in interpolation to add this animation.

```
package {

  import flash.events.Event;
  import flash.geom.Matrix3D;
  import flash.geom.Vector3D;

  [SWF(width=800, height=600, backgroundColor=0x000000)]

  public class AnimatedPointAtTest extends PointAtTest {

    private static const INTERPOLATION_RATE:Number = 0.05;

    private var _matrix:Matrix3D;

    public function AnimatedPointAtTest() {
      super();
      addEventListener(Event.ENTER_FRAME, onSpriteEnterFrame);
    }

    override protected function updatePointer():void {
      var ballPosition:Vector3D = new Vector3D(_ball.x, _ball.y, _ball.z);
      var pointerTransform:Matrix3D =➥
_pointer.transform.matrix3D.clone();
      _matrix = pointerTransform.clone();
      pointerTransform.pointAt(
        ballPosition,
        Vector3D.X_AXIS,
        new Vector3D(0, -1, 0)
      );
      _matrix.interpolateTo(pointerTransform, INTERPOLATION_RATE);
```

```
        }

        private function onSpriteEnterFrame(event:Event):void {
          if (_matrix) {
            _pointer.transform.matrix3D = _matrix;
            updatePointer();
          }
        }

      }

    }
```

In the overridden updatePointer() method, I take the current matrix transform of the pointer and clone it. This clone is then cloned a second time so that I have two matrices that are independent of the pointer. I can then transform one of these matrices so that it is oriented toward the ball and interpolate between the original transform and the new transform by a small percent.

```
_matrix.interpolateTo(pointerTransform, INTERPOLATION_RATE);
```

In the ENTER_FRAME handler, this new matrix transformation is applied back to the pointer and updatePointer() is called yet again. This will continue every frame, moving the pointer all the more closely in its orientation towards the ball. The Matrix3D class handles all the fun math of rotation on multiple axes, and we get to reap the benefits!

Managing depth

One thing you have seen is that, when rendering display objects in 3D space, the Flash Player does not do any depth swapping of objects based on their positions on the z axis, which means that objects that are closer to the viewer based on the z might still be rendered below objects farther away on the z axis but at a higher depth in the display list. We can handle this depth management ourselves by looking at the z positions of multiple display objects and swapping depths based on these positions.

Things can get a little tricky, though, when you are dealing with transformed coordinate spaces. How exactly do you find the z position relative to the viewer in order to properly set depths? The answer is by using the Transform class's getRelativeMatrix3D() method, which returns a Matrix3D instance that represents a display object's current transform relative to another display object's coordinate space. With this method, we can find the z of an object or object relative to the viewer and sort depths appropriately.

For instance, if you have an object that is being set in 3D space within one sprite, you can determine its transformation relative to the root by retrieving a transform matrix with the following line of code.

```
var matrix:Matrix3D = sprite.transform.getRelativeMatrix3D(root);
```

With this matrix, you can look at something like z position and set depths based on this value. The following example demonstrates this process by creating a carousel view of multiple rectangles. These rectangles are rotated around a center point and always oriented to face the viewer. Doing this without depth management would mean that certain rectangles, when farther away on the z axis, would still be rendered in front of rectangles nearer on the z axis. With depth management, the order in the display list matches the depth on the z axis.

```
package {

  import flash.display.Shape;
  import flash.display.Sprite;
  import flash.events.Event;
  import flash.geom.Matrix3D;

  [SWF(width=600, height=400, backgroundColor=0x000000)]

  public class ManagingDepth extends Sprite {

    private static const RADIUS:uint = 200;
    private static const TOTAL_RECTS:uint = 20;
    private static const ANGLE_BETWEEN:Number =➥
360/TOTAL_RECTS * Math.PI/180;

    private var _rectangleHolder:Sprite;
    private var _rectangles:Array;

    public function ManagingDepth() {
      x = stage.stageWidth/2;
      y = stage.stageHeight/2;
      rotationX = 10;
      createRectangles();
      addEventListener(Event.ENTER_FRAME, onSpriteEnterFrame);
    }

    private function createRectangles():void {
      _rectangleHolder = new Sprite();
      _rectangles = [];
      var rectangle:Shape;
      for (var i:uint = 0; i < TOTAL_RECTS; i++) {
        rectangle = createRectangle(i);
        _rectangleHolder.addChild(rectangle);
        _rectangles.push({shape:rectangle, z:0});
      }
      addChild(_rectangleHolder);
    }

    private function createRectangle(index:uint):Shape {
      var rectangle:Shape = new Shape();
      rectangle.graphics.beginFill(Math.random()*0xFFFFFF);
      rectangle.graphics.drawRect(-20, -40, 40, 80);
      rectangle.graphics.endFill();
      rectangle.x = Math.cos(ANGLE_BETWEEN*index)*RADIUS;
      rectangle.z = Math.sin(ANGLE_BETWEEN*index)*RADIUS;
```

```
      return rectangle;
    }

    private function setDepths():void {
      var matrix:Matrix3D;
      for each (var rectangle:Object in _rectangles) {
        matrix = rectangle.shape.transform.getRelativeMatrix3D(root);
        rectangle.z = matrix.position.z;
      }
      _rectangles.sortOn("z", Array.NUMERIC | Array.DESCENDING);
      for each (rectangle in _rectangles) {
        _rectangleHolder.addChild(rectangle.shape);
      }
    }

    private function onSpriteEnterFrame(event:Event):void {
      _rectangleHolder.rotationY += 1;
      for each (var rectangle:Object in _rectangles) {
        rectangle.shape.rotationY -= 1;
      }
      setDepths();
    }

  }

}
```

This class can be found in this chapter's files as `ManagingDepth.as`, and its output is shown in Figure 6-17.

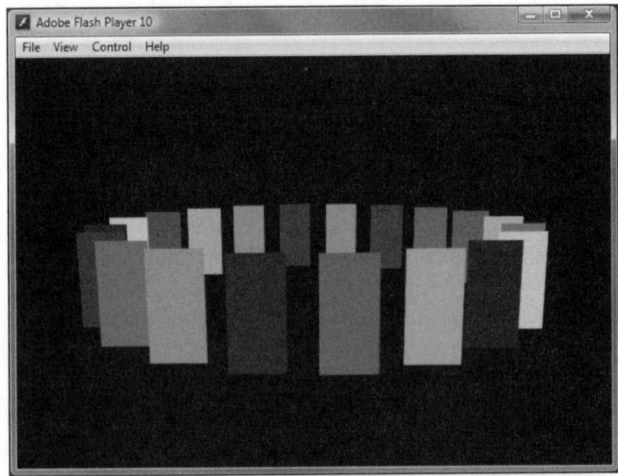

Figure 6-17. A carousel of rectangle shapes with their depths managed to place objects at higher z positions at lower depths in the display lists

The constructor of this class positions the sprite and rotates it by 10 degrees on the x axis so that the view will be looking slightly down at the rectangles. The createRectangles() method is called to create our shapes and an ENTER_FRAME event listener is set up to update the rotation of our shapes each frame.

The createRectangles() method creates a sprite, _rectangleHolder, to hold all of the rectangle shapes. It is this sprite that will be rotated on its y axis each frame. An array, _rectangles, is also initialized to hold references to the created shapes to be used for the sorting of depths. A loop is then run through to create all of the rectangle shapes and add them as children to _rectangleHolder. A reference is also pushed into _rectangles, but this reference is held in an Object instance that has both a shape and z property.

```
_rectangles.push({shape:rectangle, z:0});
```

I need to set the z position each frame once the z position of each shape is found relative to the root (and thus the viewer). Then I can swap the depths of the rectangle shape as well based on this calculated z.

The createRectangle() method simply draws a rectangle shape and positions it on both the x and z axes using standard trigonometry and our constants at the top of the class. The y position of all rectangles is left at 0.

```
rectangle.x = Math.cos(ANGLE_BETWEEN*index)*RADIUS;
rectangle.z = Math.sin(ANGLE_BETWEEN*index)*RADIUS;
```

In the ENTER_FRAME handler, _rectangleHolder is rotated on the y axis. Each shape is rotated in the opposite direction so that it counters its parent's rotation and always remains facing the viewer.

```
_rectangleHolder.rotationY += 1;
for each (var rectangle:Object in _rectangles) {
  rectangle.shape.rotationY -= 1;
}
```

Finally, each frame, the setDepths() method is called. This method runs through all of the rectangles and finds the z position of each relative to the root coordinate system. Since I haven't altered the root matrix, this is also the z position that is relative to the viewer.

```
for each (var rectangle:Object in _rectangles) {
  matrix = rectangle.shape.transform.getRelativeMatrix3D(root);
  rectangle.z = matrix.position.z;
}
```

With the z values all set based on the current positions of the shapes, the _rectangles array can be sorted by this value and all of the children can be added in the sorted order to the display list.

```
_rectangles.sortOn("z", Array.NUMERIC | Array.DESCENDING);
for each (rectangle in _rectangles) {
  _rectangleHolder.addChild(rectangle.shape);
}
```

It might strike you as odd that addChild() is called for children that already exist in _rectangleHolder, but when addChild() is invoked, the child is removed from its current parent and added at the highest depth in the new parent. In this case, the parent is the same, but the result is that all of the children get removed and subsequently added back at the proper depth order to the _rectangleHolder.

And there you have depth management of display objects! It would be nice if this was handled natively by the Flash Player, but it really is just a small amount of code that must be added to your movies when you are working with 3D display objects in order to really create the proper illusion of 3D. The Flash Player does so much for us—what are a few lines of code between friends?

Drawing with bitmaps

Back in the good old days of Chapter 1, you may recall we looked briefly into the drawTriangles() method of the drawing API. In that example, we distorted a bitmap using the UV mapping that is enabled through this method. Well, as mentioned at the time, drawTriangles() really is a method intended for use when rendering 3D through ActionScript, and I think I would be remiss and this chapter would be incomplete without inclusion of an example showcasing this. Plus, it's really cool.

Recalling drawing triangles

We already covered the drawTriangles() method, but it would probably serve you well to do a quick review (for more in-depth coverage, flip back to Chapter 1; the forests will thank us). The following is the signature of the method.

```
drawTriangles(
  vertices:Vector.<Number>,
  indices:Vector.<int>=null,
  uvtData:Vector.<Number>=null,
  culling:String="none"
):void
```

When drawTriangles() is called, it will use the last fill specified, whether that was a solid or gradient color, bitmap data, or a shader, to fill the triangles. The vertices for the triangles are defined using the first parameter of this method. If no further parameters are passed, every three vertices are considered the set of vertices that make up a different triangle. However, when defining a 3D mesh, often a single vertex might be shared by multiple triangles. In that case, you need to pass a value for the second parameter, which defines how the sides (or triangles or polygons) are composed of the vertices.

For instance, let's imagine we have two triangles that share two points. That would mean that a total of four vertices could be used to define the two triangles.

```
var vertices:Vector.<Number> = new Vector.<Number>();
vertices.push(0, -100, 0);
vertices.push(100, 0, 0);
vertices.push(0, 100, 0);
vertices.push(-100, 0, 0);
```

To use these four vertices to define two triangles, we might use the following code to populate the indices vector:

```
var indices:Vector.<int> = new Vector.<int>();
indices.push(0, 2, 1);
indices.push(0, 3, 2);
```

In this case, the triangles share the first and third indices (0 and 2).

The third parameter specifies the portion of an image that corresponds with a vertex, which is the vertex's UV or UVT data. Basically, an image will always be a rectangle, so you can specify any position along its width using a number between 0 (the left side) and 1 (the right side). This is the U value for a vertex. The V value is a position along the height of an image, with 0 representing the top and 1 representing the bottom. The T value, if used, specifies an amount of perspective distortion to apply to the image drawn into the triangle.

Finally, the fourth parameter controls whether a triangle should be drawn or not if it is facing away from the viewer. I have fallen in love with this parameter, I am not ashamed to admit. Before `drawTriangles()` was introduced, if you built any sort of 3D rendering engine, you were forced to calculate the orientation of all triangles to determine whether they were facing towards or away from the viewer, and choosing to render them or not render them based on that orientation. This is all handled behind the scenes now with `drawTriangles()`. The type of backface culling you apply depends on how you have defined your triangle sides. The default setting of `NONE` means that no culling will be applied. A setting of `POSITIVE` or `NEGATIVE` will not render triangles that are facing away from the viewer. As we step through the next example, we will look at when you would want to set one or the other and what each specifically means.

Rendering a mesh with drawTriangles()

Dynamically rendering a textured 3D object in the Flash Player used to require lots of math to determine the current transform of multiple vertices, complex calculations for depth sorting, backface culling and lighting, and lots of drawing API calls to draw segments of images into different polygons. All I can say is that we developers were all thankful for open source libraries.

Now, though, things have been greatly simplified with just a few new classes and a handful of new commands, as you will find in this next example. With the functionality of Vector3D, Matrix3D, and literally a couple of other new methods, we developers can now render simple textured 3D models with little fuss.

Of course, there's still that little fuss, like defining all the points in a 3D mesh (or writing an importer for a format like COLLADA), and so to make things easier, I have split up this example into a few classes. This should help to make things clearer and allow you to more easily reuse the code to explore further.

Before diving into that code, though, let's take a quick look at the output. Figure 6-18 shows our finished animated model, which is a textured pyramid that rotates about the y axis. The example can be found in this chapter's files as `DrawTrianglesTest.swf`, and the corresponding class files that produce the output are `DrawTrianglesTest.as`, `Mesh3D.as`, and `PyramidMesh.as`.

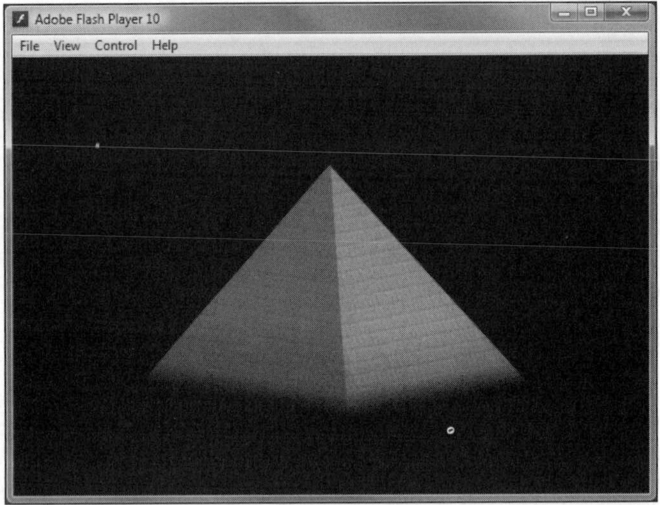

Figure 6-18. A pyramid mesh with a bitmap applied using the drawTriangles() method

Let's start with the abstract base class Mesh3D. This class holds the values for the vertices, indices and UVT data that will be passed to the `drawTriangles()` method. Its only functionality beyond that is an `applyTransform()` method that applies a matrix transformation to the vectors of the mesh and converts these vectors into 2D points.

```
package {

  import flash.display.DisplayObject;
  import flash.geom.Matrix3D;
  import flash.geom.Point;
  import flash.geom.Vector3D;

  public class Mesh3D {

    private var _vertices:Vector.<Number>;
    private var _container3D:DisplayObject;
```

```
    protected var _vectors:Vector.<Vector3D>;
    protected var _sides:Vector.<int>;
    protected var _uvtData:Vector.<Number>;

    public function Mesh3D(container:DisplayObject) {
      _container3D = container;
      createMesh();
    }

    protected function createMesh():void {}

    private function getPoint2D(vector:Vector3D):Point {
      var point:Point = _container3D.local3DToGlobal(vector);
      return _container3D.globalToLocal(point);
    }

    public function applyTransform(matrix:Matrix3D):void {
      _vertices = new Vector.<Number>();
      var vertex:Point;
      var transformedVector:Vector3D;
      for each (var vector:Vector3D in _vectors) {
        transformedVector = matrix.deltaTransformVector(vector);
        vertex = getPoint2D(transformedVector);
        _vertices.push(vertex.x, vertex.y);
      }
    }

    public function get vertices():Vector.<Number> {
      return _vertices;
    }

    public function get sides():Vector.<int> {
      return _sides;
    }

    public function get uvtData():Vector.<Number> {
      return _uvtData;
    }

  }

}
```

The constructor for this class takes a DisplayObject instance that will be used to transform the 3D vectors into 2D coordinates, which requires a display object's coordinate space and screen position (the calculations can be handled without this, but using a display object simplifies things, which I'm always in favor of!). Then createMesh() is called, which in this base class is an empty method that will be overridden by the child class.

The three implicit getters at the bottom of the class return the three values that can be used in a call to drawTriangles(). vertices will return the transformed 2D coordinates of each 3D vector; sides will return the indices of all the vectors that create a side (I find this name more intuitive than "indices," as is used in the drawTriangles() signature), and uvtData will return the UVT data for each vector.

The major functionality of this class is found in the applyTransform() method. The way this class is set up, a mesh's vectors are never permanently altered when a transform is passed in. Instead, the applyTransform() takes a matrix transformation and determines new vectors based on this matrix. These transformed vectors are then converted into 2D coordinates. The original 3D vectors are unchanged. That means it will be the responsibility of another class to manage the current transform of our model.

So let's step through the applyTransform() method to see how this is all handled. You can see that the first thing done is a new vector of numbers is created.

```
_vertices = new Vector.<Number>();
```

This property will hold the converted 2D points of our 3D vectors. Next, each 3D vector is iterated through in a loop. The first line of that loop utilizes a new method you haven't seen yet.

```
transformedVector = matrix.deltaTransformVector(vector);
```

The matrix is the Matrix3D instance passed to the applyTransform() method. Matrix3D has this terrific little method, deltaTransformVector(), which takes a Vector3D instance and returns a new Vector3D instance that has had the transformation applied. Basically, this applyTransform() method, vector by vector, applies the matrix transformation to our 3D mesh.

With a transformed vector, you can find the 2D coordinate needed to represent it on screen using the same technique demonstrated earlier, namely converting from a local 3D coordinate system to the 2D root coordinate system. This 2D point can then be converted back into the 2D coordinate space of our container and pushed into the _vertices vector.

```
var point:Point = _container3D.local3DToGlobal(vector);
return _container3D.globalToLocal(point);
```

The reason for including the container in the constructor for this class is to make this conversion easier. You can, of course, convert from 3D to 2D without these methods, but I like the simplicity these methods offer.

Now, to render a mesh, vertices and sides need to be defined. For that, a concrete child class of Mesh3D is created. Keeping these values in a second class means we can create any variety of different meshes and keep the underlying functionality for transforming and converting the 3D points in the base class. All a child class needs are the vertices, sides, and UVT data. In this example, that is handled in PyramidMesh.as.

```
package {

  import flash.display.DisplayObject;
  import flash.geom.Vector3D;

  public class PyramidMesh extends Mesh3D {

    public function PyramidMesh(container:DisplayObject) {
      super(container);
    }

    override protected function createMesh():void {
      _vectors = new Vector.<Vector3D>();
      _vectors.push(new Vector3D(0, -100, 0));
      _vectors.push(new Vector3D(130, 100, 130));
      _vectors.push(new Vector3D(130, 100, -130));
      _vectors.push(new Vector3D(-130, 100, -130));
      _vectors.push(new Vector3D(-130, 100, 130));

      _sides = new Vector.<int>();
      _sides.push(0, 1, 2);
      _sides.push(0, 2, 3);
      _sides.push(0, 3, 4);
      _sides.push(0, 4, 1);

      _uvtData = new Vector.<Number>();
      _uvtData.push(0.5, 0.5);
      _uvtData.push(0, 1);
      _uvtData.push(0, 0);
      _uvtData.push(1, 0);
      _uvtData.push(1, 1);
    }

  }

}
```

This class is so straightforward I didn't need to bold anything! In the overridden createMesh() method, the three vectors of data are created. The _vectors vector ("Roger, Roger. What's your vector, Victor?") holds the five points that make up the pyramid. The first vector (or vertex) is the top of the pyramid and the remaining four are the pyramid's base. Figure 6-19 shows where these vectors lie in a 3D coordinate system.

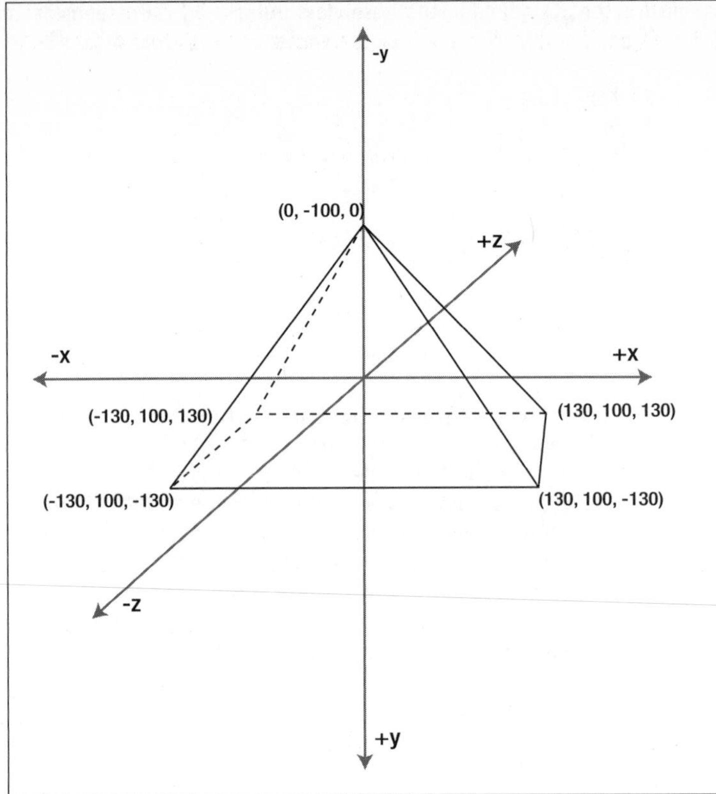

Figure 6-19. The vertices for the pyramid mesh and where they lie within 3D space

The `_sides` vector defines the four sides of the pyramid; I'm leaving off the bottom since it won't be rendered in this example and any optimization is a good optimization with 3D. Figure 6-20 shows how these sides are defined. This will be important to know when we discuss backface culling.

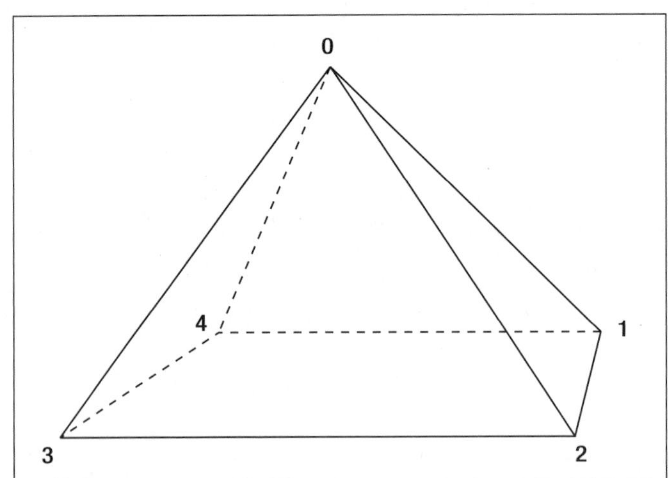

Figure 6-20. The sides of the mesh defined by a series of three vertices

The final vector, _uvtData, holds the positions in a 2D bitmap where each vertex should pull its data. The bitmap loaded for the pyramid is shown in Figure 6-21.

Figure 6-21.
The pyramid texture that is applied to the mesh

You can see that the top of the pyramid is in the exact center, so the UV position of the first vertex, which is at the top of the pyramid, is (0.5, 0.5). The other vertices' UV data lies at each corner of the bitmap.

The last piece of the puzzle is DrawTrianglesTest, the document class that creates an instance of the mesh and draws it to the screen.

```
package {

  import flash.display.TriangleCulling;
  import flash.events.Event;
  import flash.geom.Matrix3D;
  import flash.geom.Vector3D;

  [SWF(width=600, height=400, backgroundColor=0x000000)]

  public class DrawTrianglesTest extends AbstractImageLoader {

    private var _model:Mesh3D;
    private var _transform:Matrix3D;

    public function DrawTrianglesTest() {
      x = stage.stageWidth/2;
      y = stage.stageHeight/2;
      _model = new PyramidMesh(this);
      _transform = new Matrix3D();
      super("../../assets/bricks.png");
    }
```

```
        override protected function runPostImageLoad():void {
          render();
          addEventListener(Event.ENTER_FRAME, onSpriteEnterFrame);
        }

        private function render():void {
          _model.applyTransform(_transform);
          graphics.clear();
          graphics.beginBitmapFill(_loadedBitmap.bitmapData);
          graphics.drawTriangles(
            _model.vertices,
            _model.sides,
            _model.uvtData,
            TriangleCulling.NEGATIVE
          );
          graphics.endFill();
        }

        private function onSpriteEnterFrame(event:Event):void {
          _transform.appendRotation(2, Vector3D.Y_AXIS);
          render();
        }

      }

    }
```

Yes, that is indeed all that is left in order to transform and render a textured 3D model. In not one place was there complex 3D math in the code, and there was no slicing and dicing of bitmaps to be applied to polygons. Pretty considerate of those Flash Player programmers, no? I think I need to add a few more names to my Christmas card list. Let's take a look at what this class does.

In the DrawTrianglesTest constructor, the sprite is centered on the stage and is passed as the coordinate system container for the new pyramid mesh. A matrix transformation is created that will hold the current transformation of the mesh. The last line of the constructor loads our bitmap (yes, once again, AbstractImageLoader serves us well). If you are running the file yourself, make sure that the `bricks.png` exists in the specified relative directory.

```
_model = new PyramidMesh(this);
_transform = new Matrix3D();
super("../../assets/bricks.png");
```

Once the bitmap is loaded, `runPostImageLoad()` is called. This renders the mesh for the first time by calling `render()` and sets up an `ENTER_FRAME` handler to update the transformation each frame. In that handler, each time the transformation is updated to rotate a little bit more on the y axis, `render()` is called as well.

```
_transform.appendRotation(2, Vector3D.Y_AXIS);
render();
```

All remaining functionality is found in the `render()` method, and there's not much to it. First, the current transformation is passed to the mesh so that its 2D points can be updated.

```
_model.applyTransform(_transform);
```

Then I can clear the last rendering and draw a new rendering by using the loaded bitmap and the `drawTriangles()` method, just grabbing the properties from our mesh.

```
graphics.beginBitmapFill(_loadedBitmap.bitmapData);
graphics.drawTriangles(
  _model.vertices,
  _model.sides,
  _model.uvtData,
  TriangleCulling.NEGATIVE
);
```

The only other item to note is the fourth parameter of `drawTriangles()`. I pass in `NEGATIVE` for this because of the way I defined the sides in the mesh. If you look back at Figure 6-20, you should see that when an external side of the pyramid is facing the user, its vertices will be laid out on screen in a counterclockwise fashion. Sides facing away from the viewer will have vertices laid out on screen in a clockwise fashion. Now, I could have defined the polygon sides facing the viewer in a clockwise fashion and that would have been just as valid. So how does the Flash Player know which side of the polygon is the front and which is the back in order to choose which ones to render? Yep, the answer is the triangle culling setting.

If you have defined the sides in a counterclockwise fashion, you will want the `NEGATIVE` setting, which means that polygons that have their normal pointing towards the negative z axis will be rendered and those pointing on the positive z axis will not be rendered. If you have defined your sides in a clockwise fashion, you would use `POSITIVE`. If you have thrown your hands in the air like you just don't care, you probably don't want any culling and should pass `NONE`. If you do care, it doesn't matter whether you define your sides in a clockwise or counterclockwise fashion as long as you are consistent and use the correct culling parameter.

Try playing around with other meshes and different images. The new methods in ActionScript really do simplify the whole process of rendering simple 3D, taking away the possibly frustrating complexity and making it a joy to work with.

Summary

Who said 3D was hard? OK, that might have been me a year ago. Now, however, the Flash Player offers a variety of new features and functionality that make it a breeze to incorporate 3D in a number of ways into your animations, games, and applications.

In this chapter, we've looked at how to use the new properties of DisplayObject to position and rotate objects in 3D space, how to simulate 3D models using rotated planes, how to create extrusions of objects, and how to alter the way a display object is rendered in 2D by altering the perspective. We've broken down the Vector3D and Matrix3D classes and explored how to use these to manage depth of display objects, to create complex transformations, and to define and render 3D models made up of polygons. We even looked at how to use various mathematical methods to create the illusion of light hitting rotated polygons.

This was the final chapter for exploring the general areas of image manipulation that ActionScript enables. We've stepped through the drawing API, bitmap filters, blend modes, bitmap data, shaders, and 3D. In the next chapter, we will look at a number of utilities and classes that use many of the techniques presented in this and the preceding chapters that will ease the development of more complex effects. With these classes in hand, we can move to the remaining chapters of the book in which we get to create some spectacular effects and get to see all this book learnin' paying off.

Chapter 7

USING AN ANIMATION AND EFFECTS LIBRARY

I have a little confession to make. I was frustrated by several of the ActionScript examples presented in the earlier chapters. Now, this was neither because of the content of the examples nor the difficulty level of the code or the final result. It was because there was a lot of code that could have been simplified with a couple of libraries that I have become very dependent on in the last several years to make life easier for me, libraries that I created first for ActionScript 2.0 and very quickly ported to ActionScript 3.0 because of their constant use.

For instance, several times in the previous chapters we needed to desaturate an image and so duplicated code. Some animation was overly simplified or left out altogether due to the added complexity it would have introduced. The number of lines of code could have been reduced greatly by using a simple utility method.

You see, I had a little dilemma when I started writing the first half of this book. I obviously didn't want to present a book on image effects and immediately present a library that handled a lot of it for you. I considered whether inclusion of such a library, even late in the book, was beneficial at all. And yet, to create complex effects, the use of such a library to handle the simple tasks becomes almost a necessity. So I resolved to code from scratch for the first half of this book, making sure your foundation knowledge was solid. If you close this book now and need to desaturate an image, I'm confident you could do so (I hope you are, too!).

But for the later parts of this book, I decided that in order for us to really explore some more complex effects, we would take advantage of the same libraries I use in my day-to-day work. The code itself is all open source, and I have made it available under an MIT license. It is included in this chapter's files (the SWCs are included in all the remaining chapters) and links are provided for download as well.

The best thing about the libraries, though, is that they are very simple. You don't need to know a lot to use them or build on them. In fact, I only need a chapter to walk you through them, and then we can take advantage of all that they provide throughout the rest of the book. That would be this chapter, of course.

Introducing aeon animation

I have been using virtually the same animation library for about five years. In fact, I presented a scaled down version of the library in *Object-Oriented ActionScript for Flash 8* from friends of ED back in 2005 (ISBN: 978-1-59059-619-7) and updated it for *Object-Oriented ActionScript 3.0* (ISBN: 978-1-59059-845-0). Today, I call the system aeon (pronounced like "eon" with a long "E"), and updates to it can be found at `http://code.google.com/p/aeon-animation/` along with its full documentation.

Now, there are some great animation libraries for ActionScript 3.0 out there. Some examples you should check out are the Boostworthy Animation System (found at `http://www.boostworthy.com`), KitchenSync (at `http://code.google.com/p/kitchensynclib/`) and the classic Tweener (at `http://code.google.com/p/tweener/`). Some of the features of these systems are truly impressive and are worth exploring. There are also the animation classes that are included with Flash CS4 in the fl.motion and fl.transitions packages and those included in the Flex framework within the mx.effects package. Lots of options to choose from.

What I love about aeon, though, other than its obvious familiarity, is its simplicity. Most of the time when animating, I need to interpolate between values of a single property. Sometimes, I have to interpolate between multiple properties and synch these across multiple objects. Other times, I need to construct sequences of these interpolations. aeon handles these tasks and little else. However, I can use these small features to build more complex effects when needed. We'll look at how this all works, and the library in general, in this section.

Tweening values

The aeon library classes are all built around a single abstract base class, aeon.Animation, which extends EventDispatcher. Animations built with aeon and extending Animation are time based and are not dependent on frame rate or a Timer. Basically, this base class creates a static sprite that broadcasts an `ENTER_FRAME` event. Child classes of Animation can subscribe to this event and can update their values in its handler. When the handler is invoked, the time since the last update is calculated, and the values are updated accordingly. This means that the classes will not be updating values between frames using a Timer but will only update based on the time passed since the last screen update.

Animations have three methods to note. `start()` begins an animation. `stop()` stops it. Simple? `die()` is a destructor that cleans up code for an animation no longer in use. There is also a `running` property that returns whether the animation currently is running or not.

Handling animation events

Animations can follow an assign-and-forget model, where once the animation begins it just plays out to completion and you've no concern about when it completes. Many times, however, you will need to know in your code when an animation not only completes but when it is updated or even when it begins. All three of those events are available for Animation classes and can be found in aeon.events.AnimationEvent. The three supported event types are found as constants: `START`, `END`, and `CHANGE`.

There are no additional properties for this event class beyond those inherited from Event, but you can access the animation that dispatched the event through the `target` property. In some of the examples that follow, I will show how to use the AnimationEvent class with animations.

Coding single animations

The most common Animation child class used is aeon.animators.Tweener. This class takes a target object, start and end values for an animation, the time for the animation, and an optional easing function. The following is the constructor's signature:

```
Tweener(
  target:Object,
  startValue:Object,
  endValue:Object,
  time:Number,
  easeFunction:Function=null
)
```

If you have ever used any sort of animation library, such parameters might look familiar to you; they consist of the common requirements of what to animate, the start and end values of the animation, and the time the animation should take. Here's how these parameters break down:

- target: This object will have its properties altered during the course of the animation. This can be any object that contains the properties defined in the startValue and endValue parameters. If null is passed as the target, the properties defined in startValue and endValue will still be interpolated but will not be automatically assigned to any object. This allows for values to be tweened and retrieved as the Tweener animates by listeners to the Tweener's events.
- startValue: This object contains the starting values of the animation mapped to property names. A property value can be the string "*" (or the constant Tweener.CURRENT_VALUE), which will use the current value of the object's property at the start of the animation.
- endValue: This specifies the ending values of the animation mapped to property names in an object. These properties must match those defined in startValue.
- time: This is the duration in milliseconds for the animation.
- easeFunction: This function is used to interpolate the values between start and end values. The easing functions, as they are in many if not all of the animation systems, are based on Robert Penner's classic easing functions introduced back in ActionScript 1.0 and are all found in the aeon.easing package. However, if you are using Flash, you can also use the functions found in fl.motion.easing, or if you are using Flex, you can use the ones in mx.effects.easing. By default, Linear.easeNone is used.

The Tweener class has three properties to add to Animation that are useful for tweens. currentValue holds the value of the properties at the current update; lastValue holds the values from the last update, and percentComplete returns the percentage of the animation's duration that has completed.

Now, let's consider animating a sprite's x position. This could be accomplished with the following lines of ActionScript:

```
var tweener:Tweener = new Tweener(
  sprite,
  {x:5},
  {x:50},
  1000,
  Cubic.easeOut
);
tweener.start();
```

You could combine this into a single line if you do not need a reference to the tweener.

```
new Tweener(sprite, {x:5}, {x:50}, 1000, Cubic.easeOut).start();
```

Because the start and end values of the tween are passed as objects, you can tween multiple values of the same object.

```
new Tweener(sprite, {x:5, alpha:1}, {x:50, alpha:0}, 1000).start();
```

If you need to be informed of when an animation has started, has ended, or is updated, you can add event listeners to the tweener before you start it.

```
var tweener:Tweener = new Tweener(sprite, {x:5}, {x:50}, 1000);
tweener.addEventListener(AnimationEvent.END, onTweenEnd);
tweener.start();
```

One interesting feature of Tweener is the ability to use the class to interpolate values that you can then apply to a use other than altering an object's properties. You can do this by passing null as the target and adding a listener for the tweener's CHANGE event.

```
var startColor:Object = {r:0xFF, g:0x00, b:0x00};
var endColor:Object = {r:0xFF, g:0xCC, b:0x66};
var tweener:Tweener = new Tweener(null, startColor, endColor, 1000);
tweener.addEventListener(AnimationEvent.CHANGE, onTweenChange);
tweener.start();
```

In this code, a tweener is set up to interpolate individual color channels. The onTweenChange() handler could then use the interpolated values each update to construct the composite color to apply to an object or display in some other manner.

The last feature to note with Tweener is the ability to pass in certain strings to be interpreted on the start of an animation. If you pass in an asterisk, "*", as a starting value for a property, the current property value of the object is used. If you pass in a string beginning with "+" or "-" followed by a number as an end value of a property, the number is added to or subtracted from, respectively, the starting value. These special strings are often used together and are very useful when running a sequence of animations. For instance, the following code tweens an object from its current x position to a new position 100 pixels to the right:

```
new Tweener(sprite, {x:"*"}, {x:"+100"}, 1000).start();
```

Using complex animators

There are five more animation classes found with Tweener in the aeon.animators package, Scaler, Mover, Transformer3D, ColorTransformer, and FilterAnimator, and each has specific capabilities. The first, Scaler, alters the width and height of an object. You can configure how it does this though. For instance, to alter the width and height by pixels, you could use the following lines of ActionScript:

```
var startValue:Object = {x:100, y:100};
var endValue:Object = {x:200, y:200};
var scaler:Scaler = new Scaler(
  sprite,
  startValue,
  endValue,
  Scaler.PIXEL,
  1000
);
scaler.start();
```

This will start the sprite at 100×100 and scale it to 200×200. Note the use of x and y for the properties to note the axes to scale on.

> *The Scaler class is set up to work in only two dimensions. Another class, Transformer3D, can be used for 3D transformations. We'll look at that shortly.*

This example could be simplified by passing just numbers as the start and end values, since they are the same. Scaler will then assign the value to each axis.

```
new Scaler(sprite, 100, 200, Scaler.PIXEL, 1000).start();
```

If, instead, you wanted to scale by percent, you could use the following code:

```
new Scaler(sprite, 1, 2, Scaler.PERCENT, 1000).start();
```

This would double the size of the sprite during the animation.

The remaining feature to note about Scaler is that if it finds a `setSize()` method defined on the object it is scaling, it will call that method instead of explicitly setting the width and height.

Along with Tweener and Scaler, the aeon.animators package also contains a Mover class that will tween both x and y values for an object. The added feature available through Mover is the ability to apply a blur to tweened objects based on the amount of distance traveled by the object between updates.

The default is not to blur, and a simple call to move an object would look like the following:

```
new Mover(
  sprite,
  new Point(0, 0),
  new Point(500, 50),
  500,
  Quad.easeOut
).start();
```

If you wanted to add a blur, you would pass a value of `true` as an additional parameter. You could then set the blur amount and blur quality as well (which both default to 1).

```
new Mover(
  sprite,
  new Point(0, 0),
  new Point(500, 50),
  500,
  Quad.easeOut,
  true,
  5,
  2
).start();
```

To handle 3D transformations, aeon offers Transformer3D. This class takes advantage of Matrix3D (which you should know well from last chapter) to animate the transform of an object using the `interpolate()` method. All you need do with Transformer3D is pass in two matrices, the time for the animation, and any easing to apply. The following spins the sprite on the y axis using a Bounce easing out:

```
var startMatrix:Matrix3D = new Matrix3D();
var endMatrix:Matrix3D = new Matrix3D();
endMatrix.appendRotation(180, Vector3D.Y_AXIS);
new Transformer3D(
  sprite,
  startMatrix,
  endMatrix,
  500,
  Bounce.easeOut
).start();
```

If you wish to animate color transformations using aeon, you would turn to the ColorTransformer class. Much like Transformer3D, this class handles transforming between two complex objects, but in the case of ColorTransformer, the objects to interpolate are ColorTransform instances. As an example, the following code would animate a display object's color from pure white to no transform at all over 800 milliseconds:

```
var startTransform:ColorTransform =➥
  new ColorTransform(0, 0, 0, 1, 255, 255, 255);
var endTransform:ColorTransform = new ColorTransform();
new ColorTransformer(
  sprite,
  startTransform,
  endTransform,
  800
).start();
```

The final class found in aeon.animators is FilterAnimator. This class can be used if you ever need to animate the effects of one of the BitmapFilter child classes, like BlurFilter or GlowFilter. Animating filters requires reassigning the filter to the display object each time its values change, and it is this additional logic that FilterAnimator handles for you. The constructor for this class differs slightly from the other animators and looks like this:

```
public function FilterAnimator(
  target:DisplayObject,
  filter:BitmapFilter,
  startTransform:Object,
  endTransform:Object,
  filterIndex:int=-1,
  time:Number=1000,
  easeFunction:Function=null
)
```

Notice that the second parameter is the filter you wish to animate. The startTransform and endTransform parameters, much like with Tweener, can hold any number of properties that can be found in the bitmap filter. The final parameter to mention here is the filterIndex parameter. This lets the animator know where in the display object's filters array the bitmap filter can be found, if already present. If the filter has not yet been applied to the display object, –1 should be passed, which is also the default value if you pass nothing. Therefore, to animate both the blurX and blurY properties of a new BlurFilter instance, you would construct an animator in the following manner:

```
new FilterAnimator(
  sprite,
  new BlurFilter(),
  {blurX: 20, blurY:20},
  {blurX:0, blurY:0},
  -1,
  500
).start();
```

If, instead, the blur filter had already been applied to the display object and was located at the 0 index in its filters array, the code would be the following:

```
var filterIndex:int = 0;
var blurFilter:BlurFilter = sprite.filters[filterIndex] as BlurFilter;
new FilterAnimator(
  sprite,
  blurFilter,
  {blurX: 20, blurY:20},
  {blurX:0, blurY:0},
  filterIndex,
  500
).start();
```

It's interesting to note that all of the additional complex animators, Scaler, Mover, Transformer3D, ColorTransformer, and FilterAnimator, take advantage of Tweener to interpolate values. That class really makes it easy to create more complex animations. When Flash Player 10 was released, Transformer3D took five minutes to create, and I had 3D tweens zooming about my player in no time.

Creating composite animations

Sometimes, you want to group animations of multiple objects together into a single animation, or perhaps you wish to use different times or easing functions for multiple properties of the same object. In those cases, you could use the aeon.AnimationComposite class to bundle those animations up for you.

This class, which extends Animation as well, takes a single parameter: an array of Animation child class instances. All animations are then started simultaneously when the composite's start() method is called. The composite itself does not dispatch CHANGE events (you must subscribe to one of the nested animations to receive this), but it does dispatch the END event when the final animation in the managed list completes.

```
var animations:Array = [
  new Tweener(sprite1, {x:0}, {x:500}, 1000),
  new Tweener(sprite2, {x:0}, {x:500}, 1000, Quad.easeOut),
  new Mover(sprite3, new Point(0, 100), new Point(500, 100), 300)
];
var composite:AnimationComposite = new AnimationComposite(animations);
composite.start();
```

This block tweens three sprites across the stage, the first with no easing, the second with a quadratic ease out, and the third by using the Mover class. Composite animations really become powerful when combined with the next class we will look at, AnimationSequence.

Sequencing multiple animations

The class aeon.AnimationSequence works similarly to AnimationComposite, except instead of playing all animations simultaneously, the animations are played sequentially with each animation in the list beginning when the previous one ends and dispatches its END event.

Consider the following, which animates a sprite to a new position, then fades it out:

```
var animations:Array = [
  new Mover(sprite, new Point(0, 100), new Point(500, 100), 300),
  new Tweener(sprite, {alpha:1}, {alpha:0}, 1000)
];
var sequence:AnimationSequence = new AnimationSequence(animations);
sequence.start();
```

Since both AnimationSequence and AnimationComposite take arrays of Animation instances, and both are Animation subclasses themselves, you can create nested animations of composites and sequences quite easily. For instance, in the following code, I tween two clips to the same position at the same time, move one down, then the other up, then fade out both simultaneously:

```
new AnimationSequence(
  [
  new AnimationComposite(
    [
    new Mover(sprite1, new Point(50, 100), new Point(275, 200), 500),
    new Mover(sprite2, new Point(500, 100), new Point(275, 200), 500)
    ]
  ),
  new Tweener(sprite1, {y:"*"}, {y:"-50"}, 500, Quart.easeOut),
  new Tweener(sprite2, {y:"*"}, {y:"+50"}, 500, Quart.easeOut),
  new AnimationComposite(
    [
    new Tweener(sprite1, {alpha:1}, {alpha:0}, 1000),
    new Tweener(sprite2, {alpha:1}, {alpha:0}, 1000)
    ]
  )
  ]
).start();
```

With the nesting allowed by AnimationSequence and AnimationComposite, you can create some extremely complex animations, kick them off with a single call, and then be notified of their completion.

Holding and looping animations

Sometimes, an animation can be enhanced by a lack of animation, a hold of the current values before new values are tweened. For this purpose, you can use aeon.AnimationHold, which accepts a duration in milliseconds in its constructor and nothing else. Of course, this is most useful within a sequence, as in the following where a sprite is tweened into position, holds for a second, and then fades:

```
new AnimationSequence(
  [
  new Mover(sprite, new Point(50, 100), new Point(275, 200), 500),
  new AnimationHold(1000),
  new Tweener(sprite, {alpha:1}, {alpha:0}, 1000)
  ]
).start();
```

At other times, you may wish to repeat an animation, for a number of loops or even indefinitely. You can use aeon.AnimationLoop for this task. This class's constructor accepts an animation to loop and the number of loops to perform. If you do not pass the number of loops to the constructor, the animation will loop indefinitely.

As an example, the following code tweens the alpha value on a sprite back and forth from 0 to 1 and then from 1 to 0 indefinitely:

```
new AnimationLoop(
  new AnimationSequence(
    [
    new Tweener(sprite, {alpha:1}, {alpha:0}, 1000),
    new Tweener(sprite, {alpha:0}, {alpha:1}, 1000)
    ]
  )
).start();
```

The nested AnimationSequence is looped by the AnimationLoop. The sequence plays, and when it finishes the AnimationLoop begins the sequence again. Since no second parameter was passed in, the loop will continue indefinitely until `stop()` is called.

Running an animation

The following class, which you will find in this chapter's files as `AeonTest.as`, runs an animation sequence when a sprite is clicked, transforming the sprite in 3D space, holding the animation, and then zipping the sprite off stage with a bit of blur. You can see the finished result in Figure 7-1, though since the feature being explored is animation, a static screenshot doesn't really do it justice! Better to open the file `AeonTest.swf` and click the cards to see the action. The class follows, with the animation lines in bold:

```
package {

  import aeon.AnimationHold;
  import aeon.AnimationSequence;
  import aeon.animators.Transformer3D;
  import aeon.animators.Mover;
  import aeon.easing.*;

  import flash.display.Sprite;
  import flash.events.MouseEvent;
  import flash.geom.Matrix3D;
  import flash.geom.Point;
  import flash.geom.Vector3D;

  [SWF(width=800, height=600, backgroundColor=0x454545)]

  public class AeonTest extends Sprite {

    private const NUM_CARDS:uint = 5;
    private const CARD_WIDTH:uint = 120;
    private const CARD_HEIGHT:uint = 200;
    private const CARD_GUTTER:uint = 20;

    public function AeonTest() {
      drawCards();
    }

    private function drawCards():void {
      var totalCardWidth:Number =➥
(NUM_CARDS*CARD_WIDTH + CARD_GUTTER*(NUM_CARDS-1));
      var x:Number = (stage.stageWidth - totalCardWidth)/2 +➥
CARD_WIDTH/2;
      var y:Number = stage.stageHeight/2;
      for (var i:uint=0; i < NUM_CARDS; i++) {
        drawCard(x, y);
        x += (CARD_WIDTH + CARD_GUTTER);
      }
    }

    private function drawCard(x:Number, y:Number):void {
      var sprite:Sprite = new Sprite();
      with (sprite.graphics) {
        beginFill(Math.random()*0xFFFFFF);
        drawRect(
          -CARD_WIDTH/2,
          -CARD_HEIGHT/2,
          CARD_WIDTH,
          CARD_HEIGHT
        );
```

```
        endFill();
      }
      sprite.x = x;
      sprite.y = y;
      sprite.z = z;
      addChild(sprite);
      sprite.addEventListener(MouseEvent.CLICK, onCardClick);
    }

    private function onCardClick(event:MouseEvent):void {
      var card:Sprite = event.target as Sprite;
      addChild(card);
      var x:Number = stage.stageWidth/2;
      var y:Number = stage.stageHeight*3/5;
      var startMatrix:Matrix3D = card.transform.matrix3D;
      var endMatrix:Matrix3D = new Matrix3D();
      endMatrix.appendRotation(180, Vector3D.Y_AXIS);
      endMatrix.appendTranslation(x, y, -300);
      new AnimationSequence(
        [
        new Transformer3D(
          card,
          startMatrix,
          endMatrix,
          1000,
          Cubic.easeInOut
        ),
        new AnimationHold(1000),
        new Mover(
          card,
          new Point(x, y),
          new Point(x, -300),
          600,
          Quart.easeOut,
          true,
          10
        )
        ]
      ).start();
    }

  }

}
```

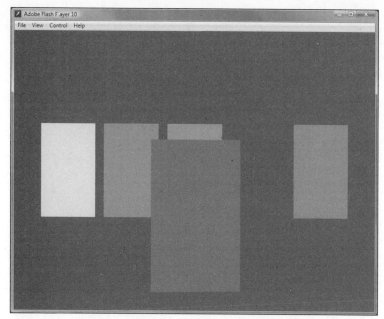

Figure 7-1. A collection of rectangles representing cards that, when clicked, run a sequence of animations including 3D transformation and motion blur

Most of the code in this class is for drawing and placing the cards. When a card is clicked, the `onCardClick()` handler is invoked. This adds the card to the top of the display list so that it appears above all the other cards. A new 3D matrix is created that will result in the card flipping over 180 degrees on the y axis and being translated to the bottom center of the stage. The animation sequence is then set up to handle this 3D transformation, the 1-second hold, and the move off stage. The `true` parameter in the Mover constructor enables the motion blur, and 10 is passed for the amount of blur to apply.

I use the aeon library all the time in both my work and play to handle animations of varying complexity. We will use it in several examples as we move through the latter part of this book to easily animate the effects we create without having to worry about the underlying mechanics of the animations.

Introducing aether effects

The aeon library is handy for animating properties, and by combining animations, you can create some really interesting effects, but these effects are pretty much designed for animation between two static states of a display object. Oftentimes, effects I create are built up from image manipulations that do not have multiple states, and for that, I turn to another library, which I have named aether (like "aeon," it's pronounced with a long "E" sound). This I have also made available as open source under an MIT license. Updates and documentation can be found at `http://code.google.com/p/aether-effects/`.

aether grew from some playing I did with creating bitmap filters that could be applied to video. It was very easy to apply an adjustment like desaturation to a video, but I wanted an extensible architecture that would make it easy to apply such effects not only to video but to any bitmap. And, like with aeon, I wanted a way to create more complex composite effects that combined simpler effects into a greater whole. The result of my play was aether.

As an example, before we dive headlong into the library, the following code produces the bottom image seen in Figure 7-2 from the top image:

```
new CompositeEffect(
  [
  new PosterizeEffect(),
  new BlurEffect(2, 2),
  new LevelsEffect(0, 100, 160),
  new SaturationEffect(.2),
  new CompositeEffect(
    [
    new FindEdgesEffect(),
    new SaturationEffect(0),
    new LevelsEffect(50, 127, 200)
    ], bitmapData, BlendMode.SCREEN
  )
  ]
).apply(bitmapData);
```

Figure 7-2. A composite image effect applied to the top image's data, resulting in the bottom image

We will be breaking down how effects work and how to create your own through the rest of this chapter, but this code basically creates a single composite effect that it applies to some bitmap data. First, the image is posterized and blurred. Some levels are applied to increase the amount of white in the image, which is then desaturated. The nested composite effect is applied to a fresh, unfiltered version of the image. This image has edge detection applied, is completely desaturated, and then has its contrast increased through a levels application. The result of this nested composite is then applied using the `SCREEN` blend mode to the image filtered by the previous effects.

By aggregating multiple effects and applying blend modes to the composites, a phenomenal number of static effects can be created. Add some animation using aeon, which of course is designed to work hand in hand with aether, and the possibilities are nearly endless. We will be exploring some of these possibilities in the chapters that follow, so it is important we break down just what makes aether tick and how you can take advantage of it.

Exploring the utilities

aether is made up of three packages of classes: effects, textures, and utils. We will break each down in the remaining sections of this chapter. The first one we will explore is the utils package, which collects a number of useful commands you can utilize not only with effects created using aether but also with general bitmap manipulation code that doesn't otherwise take advantage of the aether library.

Simplifying bitmap calls

One class in aether.utils that I use all the time is ImageUtil, which provides condensed method calls for common BitmapData methods. Call me a lazy typist, but if I can get away with less typing as I code, I'm a happy little developer. For instance, a normal call to `BitmapData.copyPixels()` where the whole of an image needs to be copied requires the following code:

```
destination.copyPixels(source, source.rect, new Point());
```

Since the rectangle and the point parameters do not change in this case, the ImageUtil class contains a static `copyPixels()` method that handles this.

```
ImageUtil.copyPixels(source, destination);
```

Similarly, calling BitmapData's `applyFilter()`, if you are applying the filter to the whole of the image, usually requires the following line:

```
source.applyFilter(source, source.rect, new Point(), filter);
```

With ImageUtil, you could instead call the following:

```
ImageUtil.applyFilter(source, filter);
```

ImageUtil also contains a condensed copyChannel() method. The following two lines of code are equivalent. Which would you rather type?

```
dest.copyChannel(source, source.rect, new Point(), channel, channel);
ImageUtil.copyChannel(source, dest, channel);
```

There are two other methods available in the ImageUtil class. The first, getChannelData(), creates a new BitmapData instance that is a grayscale representation of a single channel of a source image. We used this technique in Chapter 3's PosterizeTest so that we could apply adjustments and filters to a single channel's data in an image. ImageUtil accomplishes this with the following code:

```
static public function getChannelData(
  bitmapData:BitmapData,
  channel:uint
):BitmapData {
  var clone:BitmapData =➥
new BitmapData(bitmapData.width, bitmapData.height);
  clone.copyChannel(
    bitmapData,
    bitmapData.rect,
    new Point(),
    channel,
    BitmapDataChannel.RED
  );
  clone.copyChannel(
    bitmapData,
    bitmapData.rect,
    new Point(),
    channel,
    BitmapDataChannel.GREEN
  );
  clone.copyChannel(
    bitmapData,
    bitmapData.rect,
    new Point(),
    channel,
    BitmapDataChannel.BLUE
  );
  return clone;
}
```

How much easier is it to use the following code to do the same?

```
var image:BitmapData = ImageUtil.getChannelData(
  source,
  BitmapDataChannel.RED
);
```

The final method is getBitmapData(), which accepts a display object and returns a new BitmapData instance with the visual data from the display object. This would normally be accomplished with the following lines of code:

```
var bitmapData:BitmapData = new BitmapData(
  source.width,
  source.height,
  true,
  0x00000000
);
bitmapData.draw(source);
```

You can do the same with ImageUtil with the following code:

```
var bitmapData:BitmapData = ImageUtil.getBitmapData(source);
```

If you have a look at that method in ImageUtil, it actually just calls another class in the aether.utils package, ScreenCapture. This class has a drawFromObject() method that is exactly what ImageUtil.getBitmapData() calls, but even more usefully, it has a capture() method that allows you to pass a region of a display object to capture. If you do not pass a region, you capture the whole object, as in the following code, which captures the full stage:

```
var data:BitmapData = ScreenCapture.capture(stage);
```

If you only want to capture the top-left corner of the stage, though, you could use the following snippet. The second parameter specifies whether you wish the bitmap data returned to hold transparency or not.

```
var region:Rectangle = new Rectangle(0, 0, 100, 100);
var data:BitmapData = ScreenCapture.capture(stage, true, region);
```

Making adjustments

The Adjustments class is named after the handy, oft-used Image ➤ Adjustments menu found in Photoshop that contains much of the same functionality and so much more. The static methods of this class handle the common image adjustments like adjusting brightness, contrast, and saturation or effects like inverting, posterizing, or applying threshold or levels. Most of these techniques we explored in Chapters 2–4. You can, of course, continue to use these techniques as presented in earlier examples, or you can take advantage of the shorthand found in aether.utils.Adjustments.

As an example, in Chapter 4's GradientMapTest, I used the following method:

```
private function desaturate(bitmapData:BitmapData):void {
  var matrix:Array = [
    0.3, 0.59, 0.11, 0, 0,
    0.3, 0.59, 0.11, 0, 0,
    0.3, 0.59, 0.11, 0, 0,
    0,   0,    0,    1, 0
  ];
```

```
    bitmapData.applyFilter(
      bitmapData,
      bitmapData.rect,
      new Point(),
      new ColorMatrixFilter(matrix)
    );
  }
```

With Adjustments, you can leave this method behind and use the following code:

```
Adjustments.desaturate(bitmapData);
```

You could even pass a percentage to desaturate, with the default being 1, or full desaturation.

```
Adjustments.desaturate(bitmapData, 0.5);
```

`desaturate()` is actually just internally calling Adjustment's `saturate()` method, which can desaturate an image if the value passed is less than 1. If you pass values greater than 1, you can increase an image's color saturation.

```
Adjustments.saturate(bitmapData, 2);
```

Many other methods were presented in their full glory in earlier chapters. In Chapter 4, we also examined how to set levels, apply threshold, or posterize an image. In Chapter 3, we examined inverting an image. The following four lines show how to accomplish all these actions with Adjustments:

```
Adjustments.setLevels(bitmapData, 0, 100, 150);
Adjustments.threshold(bitmapData, 100);
Adjustments.posterize(bitmapData, 4);
Adjustments.invert(bitmapData);
```

Again, these are not hiding anything new that we have not broken down in earlier chapters. They are merely encapsulating that functionality within this utilities class.

There are a couple of new methods we haven't explored, though, so we'll take a quick look at this new code. First, `adjustBrightness()` calls the `setLevels()` command to alter the brightness levels of an image. There are many ways to alter brightness, but with the following code, I found I could very closely match the output of Photoshop's brightness adjustment:

```
static public function adjustBrightness(
  bitmapData:BitmapData,
  amount:Number
):void {
  if (amount < 0) {
    var bottom:uint = -amount;
    setLevels(bitmapData, bottom, bottom + (255-bottom)/2, 255);
  } else {
```

```
        var top:uint = 255-amount;
        setLevels(bitmapData, 0, top/2, top);
      }
    }
```

In addition to passing an image to adjust, a second parameter specifying the amount of adjustment is required. If the number is less than 0, the image will be darkened by increasing the black point through the `setLevels()` method. So if –50 is passed, the black point passed to `setLevels()` would be 50; the white point would be 255, and the medium gray point would be 152.5. If the amount passed to `adjustBrightness()` is 50, `setLevels()` would be called with 0, 102.5, and 205 as the black, medium gray, and white points, respectively.

Another new method that Adjustments introduces is `adjustContrast()`. This uses the ColorMatrixFilter to set a contrast level for an image.

```
static public function adjustContrast(
  bitmapData:BitmapData,
  amount:Number
):void {
  amount += 1;
  var filter:ColorMatrixFilter = new ColorMatrixFilter([
    amount,      0,      0, 0, (128 * (1 - amount)),
         0, amount,      0, 0, (128 * (1 - amount)),
         0,      0, amount, 0, (128 * (1 - amount)),
         0,      0,      0, 1,                    1
  ]);
  ImageUtil.applyFilter(bitmapData, filter);
}
```

`adjustContrast()` takes a number that should be in the range –1 to 1 (although you can pass values greater than 1 to really blow out the image). If –1 is passed, the resulting 4×4 matrix would look like the following:

```
| 0  0  0  0  128 |
| 0  0  0  0  128 |
| 0  0  0  0  128 |
| 0  0  0  1    1 |
```

This would produce an image that was completely medium gray. A value of 0 would result in an identity matrix that wouldn't alter the image. A value less than 0 but greater than –1 would reduce contrast in the image, which we can see by passing –0.5 as the amount.

```
| 0.5  0    0    0  64 |
| 0    0.5  0    0  64 |
| 0    0    0.5  0  64 |
| 0    0    0    1   1 |
```

Figure 7-3. The top image has its contrast reduced by 50 percent to produce the bottom image.

Figure 7-4. The top image has its contrast doubled to produce the bottom image.

This matrix would reduce the brightness in each channel by half and add the same value of 64 to each channel, bringing them closer together in brightness value and thus reducing contrast between channels. Figure 7-3 shows an image with an adjusted image beneath it using a 0.5 setting.

If you pass a value of 1 to `adjustContrast()`, the 4×4 matrix would have the following values:

```
| 2  0  0  0  -128 |
| 0  2  0  0  -128 |
| 0  0  2  0  -128 |
| 0  0  0  1     1 |
```

This doubles the brightness value of each channel and then subtracts 128 from each so the image isn't completely blown out with brightness values over 255. Since a black pixel value (0) multiplied by 2 is still black, and any pixel value under 64 will result in a black pixel as well, this adjustment increases the contrast between the higher brightness values and the darker, increasing the overall contrast of the image. Figure 7-4 shows the same initial image as the previous example but, this time, with the image on the bottom increased in contrast by 2.

The final method to note within Adjustments that we have not covered previously is the `setChannelLevels()`. This works similarly to `setLevels()`, which we looked at in Chapter 4, but instead of passing the same levels for each channel, this method allows you to pass different levels for each. For instance, if you only want to adjust the contrast of the red channel, you could use the following code:

```
setChannelLevels(
  bitmapData,
  [50, 128, 205],
  [0, 128, 255],
  [0, 128, 255]
);
```

The second parameter accepts an array containing three values for the black, medium gray, and white point for the red channel; the third parameter accepts a similar array for the green channel; and the fourth parameter does the same for the blue channel.

With the aether.utils classes like Adjustments and ImageUtil, you can greatly simplify your code when creating image effects, and the remaining classes we will look at in the aether library take advantage of these utilities classes to a great extent. I hope you will be able to as well.

Drawing textures

Another group of classes in aether is devoted to drawing tileable textures that can be used with the drawing API or copied into bitmap data. I find these are most useful for backgrounds or for texturing interface items.

All textures in aether implement the ITexture interface, which merely requires an implementation of a `draw()` method that accepts no parameters and returns a BitmapData instance. This means that a texture can basically be anything that draws an image into bitmap data. The simplest example of this is aether.textures.patterns.SolidPattern, which contains the following code:

```
package aether.textures.patterns {

  import aether.textures.ITexture;

  import flash.display.BitmapData;

  public class SolidPattern implements ITexture {

    private var _color:uint;

    public function SolidPattern(color:uint) {
      _color = color;
    }

    public function draw():BitmapData {
      return new BitmapData(1, 1, true, _color);
    }

  }

}
```

The texture here is just a solid color, which is useful when creating composite textures. The constructor takes a color to use and the `draw()` method returns a 1×1 pixel image that can be tiled.

Of course, textures can be much more complex. The following class, which you can find as `MarblePyramid`.as in this chapter's files, resurrects the 3D pyramid from the last chapter but, instead of loading in an image, generates a marble texture to apply to the polygon mesh (the rest of the code remains the same). The result is shown in Figure 7-5.

```
package {

  import aether.textures.natural.MarbleTexture;

  import flash.display.Bitmap;
  import flash.display.BitmapData;
```

```
import flash.display.Sprite;
import flash.display.TriangleCulling;
import flash.events.Event;
import flash.geom.Matrix;
import flash.geom.Matrix3D;
import flash.geom.Rectangle;
import flash.geom.Vector3D;

[SWF(width=600, height=400, backgroundColor=0x000000)]

public class MarblePyramid extends Sprite {

  private var _marble:BitmapData;
  private var _model:Mesh3D;
  private var _transform:Matrix3D;

  public function MarblePyramid() {
    x = stage.stageWidth/2;
    y = stage.stageHeight/2;
    _model = new PyramidMesh(this);
    _transform = new Matrix3D();
    createMarble();
    render();
    addEventListener(Event.ENTER_FRAME, onSpriteEnterFrame);
  }

  private function createMarble():void {
    _marble = new MarbleTexture(512, 512, 0x227766).draw();
    var lighting:BitmapData = new BitmapData(
      900,
      900,
      true,
      0x00000000
    );
    lighting.fillRect(new Rectangle(450, 0, 450, 450), 0x44000000);
    lighting.fillRect(new Rectangle(0, 450, 450, 450), 0x44000000);
    lighting.fillRect(new Rectangle(450, 450, 450, 450), 0x88000000);
    var matrix:Matrix = new Matrix();
    matrix.translate(-450, -450);
    matrix.rotate(Math.PI*.25);
    matrix.translate(255, 255);
    _marble.draw(lighting, matrix);
    lighting.dispose();
  }

  private function render():void {
    _model.applyTransform(_transform);
    graphics.clear();
    graphics.beginBitmapFill(_marble);
```

```
          graphics.drawTriangles(
            _model.vertices,
            _model.sides,
            _model.uvtData,
            TriangleCulling.NEGATIVE
          );
          graphics.endFill();
        }

        private function onSpriteEnterFrame(event:Event):void {
          _transform.appendRotation(2, Vector3D.Y_AXIS);
          render();
        }

      }

    }
```

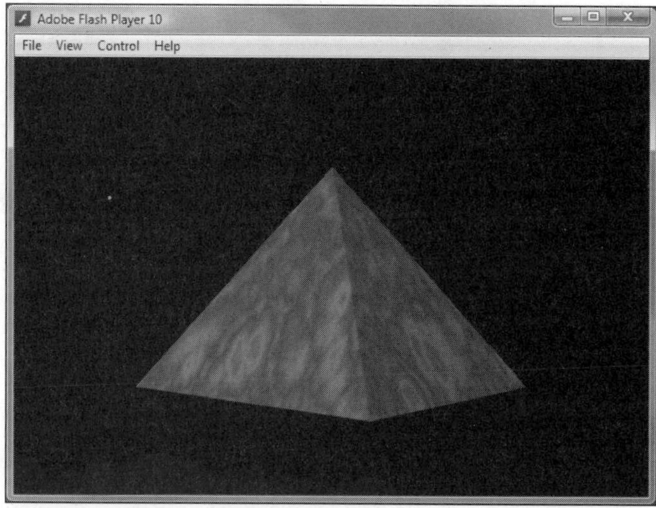

Figure 7-5. The 3D pyramid mesh with a procedural marble texture applied

Here, the createMarble() method has some additional lines that draw black overlays over each segment of the marble image in order to simulate baked-in lighting, but the marble texture itself is all generated by the following line:

```
_marble = new MarbleTexture(512, 512, 0x227766).draw();
```

The constructor for MarbleTexture takes the width and height of the texture to draw and the desired base color. If you have a look at the MarbleTexture class, you will see it creates the texture with a combination of generated Perlin noise, a gradient map, and blend modes, all techniques we have explored in the previous chapters. With textures, you can combine those techniques into usable images.

Other tileable textures already available through ITexture implementations in aether include stone, stars, bark, checkers, and tiles, some of which are demonstrated in Figure 7-6.

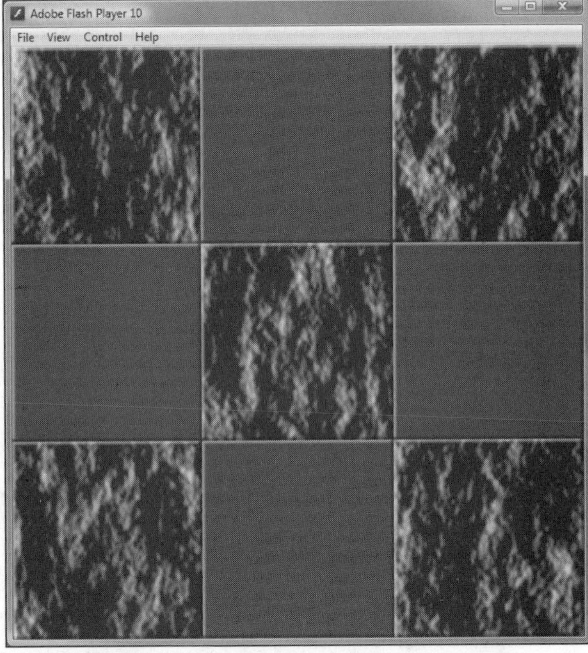

Figure 7-6. Textures generated using the classes within aether.textures

In addition, there is a handy GraphicsDataPattern that lets you pass in drawing commands that will then be translated into a tileable image, and PixelPattern takes a multidimensional array defining individual pixel colors in a rectangular matrix. These patterns can easily produce a texture like that shown in Figure 7-7.

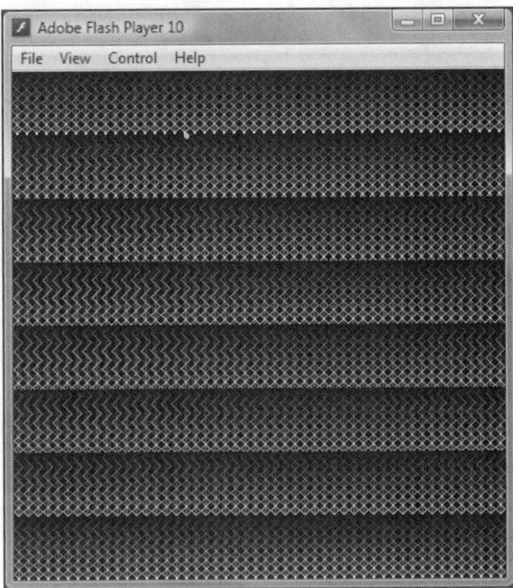

Figure 7-7. A tileable composite texture using PixelPattern and GraphicsDataPattern

Creating bitmap effects

The final feature of aether is its biggest feature, the reason the library was created in the first place. The aether.effects package contains a single class, ImageEffect, and through this class, many a complex effect can be created.

The class itself is deceptively simple, containing only the following code:

```
package aether.effects {

  import aether.utils.ImageUtil;

  import flash.display.BitmapData;
  import flash.display.BlendMode;
  import flash.geom.ColorTransform;

  public class ImageEffect {

    protected var _blendMode:String;
    protected var _alpha:Number;

    protected function init(
      blendMode:String=null,
      alpha:Number=1
    ):void {
      _blendMode = blendMode;
      _alpha = alpha;
    }

    protected function applyEffect(bitmapData:BitmapData):void {}

    public function apply(bitmapData:BitmapData):void {
      var clone:BitmapData = new BitmapData(
        bitmapData.width,
        bitmapData.height,
        true,
        0x00000000);
      ImageUtil.copyPixels(bitmapData, clone);
      if ((!_blendMode || _blendMode == BlendMode.NORMAL)➥
&& _alpha == 1){
        applyEffect(clone);
      } else {
        var overlay:BitmapData = clone.clone();
        applyEffect(overlay);
        clone.draw(
          overlay,
          null,
          new ColorTransform(1, 1, 1, _alpha),
          _blendMode
        );
      }
```

```
          ImageUtil.copyPixels(clone, bitmapData);
        }

      }

    }
```

An image effect has a blend mode and an alpha that is passed to a protected init() method. This is used in the single public method of the class, apply(). apply() first clones the image passed to the method. The conditional that follows checks to see if there is a blend mode or alpha that is to be applied. If there isn't, the protected method applyEffect() can be called to affect the cloned image.

```
if ((!_blendMode || _blendMode == BlendMode.NORMAL) && _alpha == 1){
  applyEffect(clone);
```

If there is a blend mode or alpha to apply for the effect, the cloned image is cloned once more, and it is this clone, overlay, that is passed to applyEffect().

```
var overlay:BitmapData = clone.clone();
applyEffect(overlay);
```

This overlay is then drawn into the initial clone using the blend mode and/or alpha.

```
clone.draw(
  overlay,
  null,
  new ColorTransform(1, 1, 1, _alpha, 0, 0, 0, 0),
  _blendMode
);
```

The clone can then be copied into the original bitmap data. This apply() method is what allows for multiple effects to be applied to a single image with different blend modes and alphas. Child classes of ImageEffect need only override the applyEffect() method to generate a new effect.

Applying an effect

As an example of a child class implementation of ImageEffect, let's look at aether.effects.PosterizeEffect, which contains the following code:

```
package aether.effects.adjustments {

  import aether.effects.ImageEffect;
  import aether.utils.Adjustments;

  import flash.display.BitmapData;

  public class PosterizeEffect extends ImageEffect {

    private var _levels:uint;
```

```
    public function PosterizeEffect(
      levels:uint=2,
      blendMode:String=null,
      alpha:Number=1
    ) {
      init(blendMode, alpha);
      _levels = levels;
    }

    override protected function applyEffect(
      bitmapData:BitmapData
    ):void {
      Adjustments.posterize(bitmapData, _levels);
    }

  }

}
```

To apply this to an image would only require the following line of code:

```
new PosterizeEffect().apply(bitmapData);
```

Recall when I mentioned that one of the reasons I liked these libraries was their simplicity to use and extend? I'm not sure there is a better example. The PosterizeEffect requires a constructor, a single property, and a single method override that simply calls a utility method. That gives me an effect that enables me to posterize an image and then apply it as an overlay to the original image using a blend mode, as the following code demonstrates:

Figure 7-8. The posterization effect can be applied as an overlay to the original image using a blend mode.

```
new PosterizeEffect(2, BlendMode.MULTIPLY, 0.5).apply(bitmapData);
```

The result of applying this to an image is shown in Figure 7-8.

Combining effects

If you are familiar with design patterns, you will have recognized that the aeon.AnimationComposite from earlier this chapter was an example of the Composite pattern, which basically allows for a group of objects to be treated like single instances of an object. See, the AnimationComposite doesn't care if one of its managed animations is a Tweener defining a single object's property animation or another AnimationComposite with more nested animations. If you use the class in your code, you don't need to be concerned whether an animation you are starting is a single animation or a group. All you need to know is that it is an animation and can be initiated with a call to the `start()` method.

```
animation.start();
```

Is `animation` in this context a Tweener instance or an AnimationComposite? It doesn't really matter because of polymorphism and aeon's implementation of the Composite design pattern.

> *"Poly-what-what?" Polymorphism is the ability for multiple objects to be interacted with in similar ways even though they may have different implementations. Often, this is because multiple objects implement the same interface, like `IEventDispatcher`. For any class that implements `IEventDispatcher`, you know you can call `addEventListener()` on an instance, even though how each class implements that method might be different. Another way you can get polymorphic behavior is through inheritance, as with the Animation class. Both Tweener and AnimationComposite inherit from Animation, so both have a `start()` method. How each might override that `start()` method isn't relevant to the code that might be calling it.*
>
> *For more on polymorphism and object-oriented programming in ActionScript, you might want to pick up Object-Oriented ActionScript 3.0, also available from friends of ED and, yes, yours truly.*

Turns out, I have a bit of a Composite pattern fetish. It's OK; I'm in a good place with it. I really love the pattern and use it in multiple areas of my code, including aether. The class aether.effects.common.CompositeEffect allows you to group multiple effects together and apply the composite effect with a single blend mode or alpha.

Creating a composite effect is as simple as the following code, which saturates and posterizes an image:

```
new CompositeEffect(
  [
  new SaturationEffect(2),
  new PosterizeEffect()
  ]
).apply(bitmapData);
```

CompositeEffect accepts as its first parameter an array of ImageEffect instances. It then accepts three additional parameters: a bitmap to affect other than the one passed to the `apply()` method, the blend mode, and the alpha value.

So why is there an extra bitmap to affect? This is most useful for nesting effects, as was used in this earlier example.

```
new CompositeEffect(
  [
  new PosterizeEffect(),
  new BlurEffect(2, 2),
  new LevelsEffect(0, 100, 160),
  new SaturationEffect(.2),
  new CompositeEffect(
    [
```

```
      new FindEdgesEffect(),
      new SaturationEffect(0),
      new LevelsEffect(50, 127, 200)
      ], bitmapData, BlendMode.SCREEN
    )
    ]
  ).apply(bitmapData);
```

The outer CompositeEffect instance runs linearly through its effects, first posterizing the image and then blurring it, setting levels, and desaturating it. When the nested CompositeEffect instance gets called, the image is already heavily manipulated. The nested composite, though, has also been directly passed a reference to the original bitmap data. Because of this, it is this original copy that is manipulated and then applied using the SCREEN mode to the other manipulated image.

Using shaders

A whole package in the aether library is devoted to shaders, aether.effects.shaders. The base class, ShaderEffect, basically takes care of loading the `.pbj` file if it has not been compiled in and instantiating the Shader class using the loaded or embedded bytecode. The code for loading and instantiating is very similar to the code used in the examples in Chapter 5.

As you will recall as well from Chapter 5, the pixel manipulation logic used by shaders is written into the original Pixel Bender `.pbk` file. As such, there's not too much a child class of ShaderEffect needs do other than store parameter values and pass them to the shader, as the following class, IsolateColorEffect, demonstrates:

```
package aether.effects.shaders {

  import aether.utils.MathUtil;

  public class IsolateColorEffect extends ShaderEffect {

    public static var shaderClass:String = "IsolateColorKernel";
    public static var shaderFile:String = "isolateColor.pbj";

    private var _red:uint;
    private var _green:uint;
    private var _blue:uint;
    private var _threshold:uint;
    private var _hideNonIsolated:uint;

    public function IsolateColorEffect(
      color:uint=0xFF0000,
      threshold:uint=10,
      hideNonIsolated:Boolean=false,
      blendMode:String=null,
      alpha:Number=1
    ) {
```

```
      _shaderClass = shaderClass;
      _shaderFile = shaderFile;
      this.color = color;
      this.threshold = threshold;
      this.hideNonIsolated = hideNonIsolated;
      init(blendMode, alpha);
    }

    override protected function configureShader(data:Object):void {
      data.color.value = [_red, _green, _blue];
      data.hueThreshold.value = [_threshold];
      data.hideNonIsolated.value = [_hideNonIsolated];
    }

    public function set color(color:uint):void {
      color = MathUtil.clamp(color, 0, 0xFFFFFF);
      _red = color >> 16 & 0xFF;
      _green = color >> 8 & 0xFF;
      _blue = color & 0xFF;
    }

    public function set threshold(threshold:uint):void {
      _threshold = MathUtil.clamp(threshold, 0, 360);
    }

    public function set hideNonIsolated(hide:Boolean):void {
      _hideNonIsolated = hide ? 1 : 0;
    }

  }

}
```

The constructor of the method takes the three parameters that the shader expects, `color`, `threshold`, and `hideNonIsolated`, plus the two common to all image effects, `blendMode` and `alpha`, which it passes to the `init()` method. We'll discuss the other two properties in the constructor, `_shaderClass`, and `_shaderFile` in a moment.

The class also contains three setters for the same shader parameters, converting the values into the forms expected by the shader and enforcing limits. These setters are what enable shaders to be animated by altering their parameters over time.

The only other method is the overridden `configureShader()`, which is where the setting of the shader's parameters occurs, using the `data` object and setting the values as arrays into the `value` property of each parameter, as you might remember from Chapter 5.

These few steps are all that are needed to create a new ShaderEffect child class (after you have a Pixel Bender shader to use, of course!).

So what exactly are _shaderClass and _shaderFile? Well, the shader bytecode will either be embedded in the SWF or need to be loaded, and you need a way to inform the ShaderEffect base class how to instantiate a shader. This is where these values come in, in combination with two static properties of ShaderEffect.

```
public static var shaderFilePath:String = "/pixelBender/";
public static var shaderClassPath:String = "";
```

If you are loading .pbj files, you do not need to do anything but keep the .pbj files in a pixelBender subdirectory relative to where your SWF is stored, as long as you do not change the name of the file. If you do change the name of the file, you can set the constant for the class to inform it of the new name.

```
IsolateColorEffect.shaderFile = "isolateColor_v2.pbj";
```

If you do not wish to store the .pbjs in the default directory, you can let the base class know which directory to find the files in (all .pbjs will need to be stored in this directory).

```
ShaderEffect.shaderFilePath = "../assets/";
```

If instead of loading a shader at runtime you wish to embed the bytecode, you would use the standard embed tag to do so.

```
[Embed(source='isolateColor.pbj', mimeType='application/octet-stream')]
public static const IsolateColorKernel:Class;
```

If you wish to change the name of the class as you embed it from the default for the class, you can inform the class through the constant.

```
IsolateColorEffect.shaderClass = "IsolateColorShader";
```

The shaderClassPath static property of ShaderEffect will always have to be explicitly set when embedding the shader bytecode. For instance, if your main document class is MyApplication, not within any packages, the embedded shader bytecode will actually be found with flash.utils.getDefinitionByName() (which ShaderEffect uses) by the string "MyApplication_IsolateColorKernel". So for this example, you would use the following code to let ShaderEffect know where to find the embedded classes:

```
ShaderEffect.shaderClassPath = "MyApplication";
```

This requires all embedded shader bytecode to be embedded in the same class, just as all loaded .pbj files must be in the same directory. But this does ensure a common location for all shaders, and only requires the setting of these values one time.

With that all said, creating a child class of ShaderEffect is quick, painless, and requires little logic, and the ShaderEffect class gives you the option of loading or embedding the shaders with all of the logic encapsulated. In the next and final section of this chapter, we will create an animated composite effect using aether, aeon, and shaders to tie everything together, so you can see how seamless integrating a shader really is.

Creating an image effect

There has been a lot in this chapter about what exactly the aeon and aether ActionScript libraries can accomplish. It's time to pull all of the pieces together and create an effect that would be much more difficult to achieve without these libraries, and yet with their help takes only about 100 lines of code.

The final output of the class we will make in this example can be found in this chapter's files as `Planet.swf`. If you test the SWF, you will see an animated version of Figure 7-9.

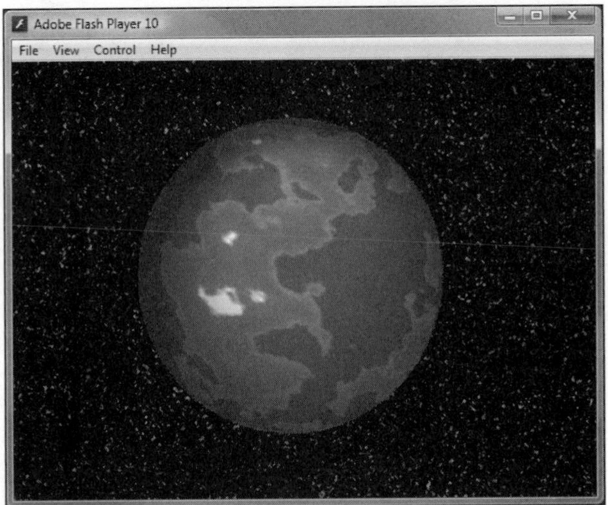

Figure 7-9. An animated composite effect using textures generated at runtime and a shader

This is all completely generated dynamically and animated using the aeon and aether libraries and a custom shader. Let's look at how:

1. Create a new ActionScript project in Flex Builder or a new Flash document and ActionScript file for Flash. Save your main document class as `Planet.as`. Remember to see the appendix if creating ActionScript projects in these environments is not something you are familiar with. You will need to import both `aether.swc` and `aeon.swc` as libraries for your application. This is covered in the appendix as well, since this will be a step common in a lot of the examples for the rest of the book.
2. In your ActionScript file, let's start with the following code:

```
package {

  import flash.display.Sprite;

  [SWF(width=550, height=400, backgroundColor=0x000000)]

  public class Planet extends Sprite {
```

```
        private const IMAGE_WIDTH:uint = 360;
        private const IMAGE_HEIGHT:uint = 288;
        private const PLANET_RADIUS:uint = IMAGE_HEIGHT/2;

        public function Planet() {
        }

    }

}
```

Here, we create a 550×400 pixel movie with a black background. Three constants are declared for the dimensions of the texture we will use for the planet and the planet's radius, which is half of the smaller dimension.

3. The first image we will create is of the stars behind the planet. There is a texture in aether that does just that, the aptly named StarsTexture. Add this code to the class to see what it gives us.

```
public function Planet() {
  var stars:BitmapData = new StarsTexture(
    stage.stageWidth,
    stage.stageHeight,
    0).draw();
  addChild(new Bitmap(stars));
}
```

You will need to import both `flash.display.Bitmap` and `aether.textures.natural.StarsTexture` for this code. The StarsTexture constructor takes a width and height for the texture as well as a density setting. If you test the movie at this point, you should see a lovely star field that is randomly generated using BitmapData covering the stage, as shown in Figure 7-10.

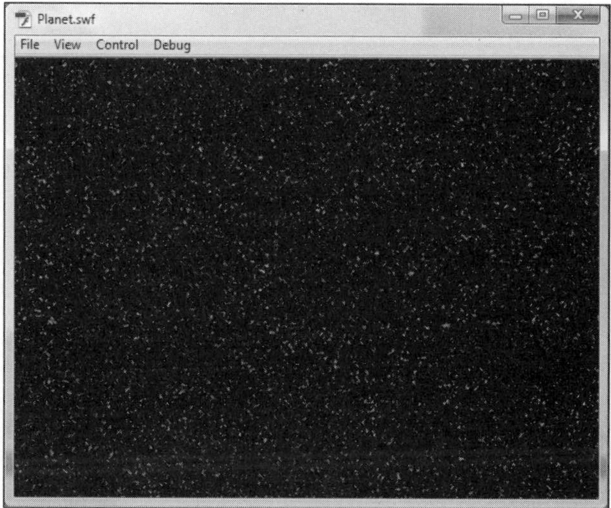

Figure 7-10. The generated star field

4. The next step is to create the planet texture. There is an aether texture for this as well, and we can try it out with the following new lines:

```
public function Planet() {
  var stars:BitmapData = new StarsTexture(
    stage.stageWidth,
    stage.stageHeight,
    0).draw();
  addChild(new Bitmap(stars));

  var planet:BitmapData = new BitmapData(
    IMAGE_WIDTH,
    IMAGE_HEIGHT,
    true,
    0x00000000
  );

  new TextureEffect(
    new EarthTexture(IMAGE_WIDTH, IMAGE_HEIGHT)
  ).apply(planet);
}
```

For this code you will need to import `flash.display.BitmapData` as well as `aether.effects.texture.TextureEffect` and `aether.textures.natural.EarthTexture`. In the first new line, we create a transparent BitmapData instance. We then apply a TextureEffect, which basically allows you to use any ITexture to draw into your bitmap data. This is necessary since the Earth texture by default is not transparent, and we need it to be. By using a TextureEffect, we can draw the Earth texture into bitmap data set up for transparency.

> *The goal of this example is to explore multiple effects within the aether library, so here, we generate an image for the planet as opposed to using an image. You could, if you wanted, load or embed an actual image of the Earth into your application to use instead. Just make sure you size it for the effect using IMAGE_WIDTH and IMAGE_HEIGHT as you draw it into the planet BitmapData instance.*

EarthTexture is a fun texture to play with, since you can pass any colors in, as well as ratios for how the colors are distributed and levels to define the contrast of the land and sea masses, all of which allows for a lot of configuration. The texture uses Perlin noise to create the initial image, applies levels to separate the landmasses from the oceans, and then applies a gradient map to color the planetary texture.

We won't see any result with these lines, since we haven't added the bitmap data to the display list. We can do this next.

5. In order to see the texture we have just created, we will need to add it to a Bitmap instance. The following bold lines take care of that:

```
public function Planet() {
  var stars:BitmapData = new StarsTexture(
    stage.stageWidth,
```

```
    stage.stageHeight,
    0).draw();
  addChild(new Bitmap(stars));

  var planet:BitmapData = new BitmapData(
    IMAGE_WIDTH,
    IMAGE_HEIGHT,
    true,
    0x00000000
  );

  new TextureEffect(
    new EarthTexture(IMAGE_WIDTH, IMAGE_HEIGHT)
  ).apply(planet);

  var bitmap:Bitmap = new Bitmap(planet);
  bitmap.x = 210;
  bitmap.y = 0;
  bitmap.rotation = 30;
  addChild(bitmap);
}
```

Be sure that you import flash.display.Bitmap in order for this to compile.

After adding the Earth texture as the data for a new Bitmap instance, we position and rotate the bitmap and then add it to the stage. The rotation will make the planet appear as if it is revolving on a rotated axis when all we will do is translate the bitmap data on the x axis. If you test your movie now, you should see a result similar to Figure 7-11.

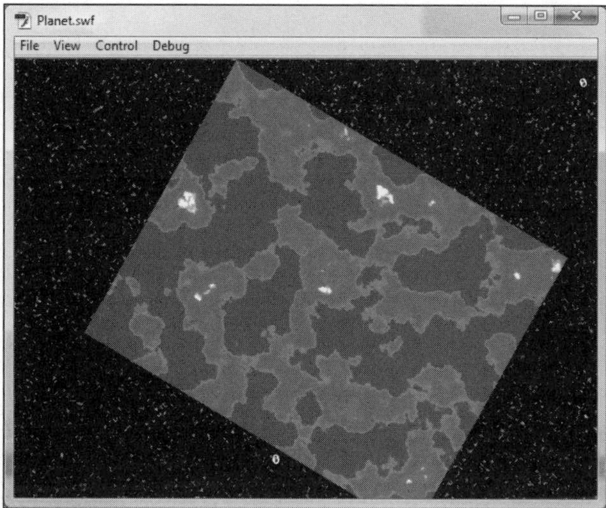

Figure 7-11. The flat planet texture is rotated within a Bitmap over the star field.

We will use a shader designed to wrap a texture around a sphere, but first, we will take care of creating some faux 3D lightning for our planet through a radial gradient.

6. Create a whole new method in this class for drawing the gradient overlay. The following code shows the entirety of the method:

```
private function getGradientOverlayShape():Shape {
  var shape:Shape = new Shape();
  var matrix:Matrix = new Matrix();
  matrix.createGradientBox(IMAGE_HEIGHT, IMAGE_HEIGHT, Math.PI/4, 18);
  var colors:Array = [0xFFFFFF, 0xFFFFFF, 0, 0];
  var alphas:Array = [.1, 0, 0, .6];
  var ratios:Array = [0, 60, 120, 255];
  shape.graphics.beginGradientFill(
    GradientType.RADIAL,
    colors, alphas,
    ratios,
    matrix,
    null,
    null,
    -0.7
  );
  shape.graphics.drawCircle(
    PLANET_RADIUS,
    PLANET_RADIUS,
    PLANET_RADIUS
  );
  shape.graphics.endFill();
  return shape;
}
```

Compiling this code requires you to import `flash.display.GradientType`, `flash.display.Shape`, and `flash.geom.Matrix`.

We have drawn shapes in previous chapters and have created gradient fills, so little of this should surprise (unless you are an easily excitable individual, which could be the case). The gradient goes through four color values, from white to white to black to black, with different opacities for each. The white will be at the center of the gradient, creating a hotspot on the sphere, with the black appearing at the edges to give the illusion of depth. The `createGradientBox()` method rotates the gradient by 45 degrees and translates it by 18 pixels. This will keep the hotspot from being in the dead center of the planet as if the light source were hitting it straight on.

The only other line to call out is the last parameter passed to `beginGradientFill()`. –0.7 is passed to shift the radial gradient's focal point away from the center of the gradient. This will help with the 3D illusion as well.

With the gradient drawn, we can apply that to our planet along with the shader that will wrap the texture around the sphere.

7. Add the following bold lines to the constructor in the class:

```
public function Planet() {
  var stars:BitmapData = new StarsTexture(
    stage.stageWidth,
    stage.stageHeight,
    0).draw();
  addChild(new Bitmap(stars));

  var planet:BitmapData = new BitmapData(
    IMAGE_WIDTH,
    IMAGE_HEIGHT,
    true,
    0x00000000
  );
  var gradientOverlay:BitmapData = planet.clone();
  gradientOverlay.draw(getGradientOverlayShape());

  new TextureEffect(
    new EarthTexture(IMAGE_WIDTH, IMAGE_HEIGHT)
  ).apply(planet);

  var savedPlanetData:BitmapData = planet.clone();

  ShaderEffect.shaderFilePath = "../../assets/";
  var shaderEffect:WrapToSphereEffect = new WrapToSphereEffect(
    PLANET_RADIUS,
    IMAGE_WIDTH,
    IMAGE_HEIGHT
  );

  new CompositeEffect(
    [
    shaderEffect,
    new OverlayImageEffect(gradientOverlay)
    ]
  ).apply(planet);

  var bitmap:Bitmap = new Bitmap(planet);
  bitmap.x = 210;
  bitmap.y = 0;
  bitmap.rotation = 30;
  addChild(bitmap);
}
```

There are three new classes that must be imported for this code to compile: `aether.effects.shaders.ShaderEffect`, `aether.effects.common.CompositeEffect`, and `aether.effects.common.OverlayImageEffect`.

Immediately after creating the planet bitmap, before drawing anything into it, we duplicate it for the gradient overlay, since this overlay will be the same size. We then draw into the bitmap data using the getGradientOverlayShape() we added in the last step.

Next, before we apply the shader and the overlay to the planet, we save a clone of its unaltered data into the savedPlanetData variable. It is this data that we will translate during the animation, so we will need it undistorted and only spherize it after it has been translated.

With that data saved, we can apply the effects to the planet texture. First, we set the path to the .pbj file as being two directories up and in an assets folder. If you have placed the wrapToSphere.pbj file found in this chapter's files in another directory, update this path accordingly. The shader is instantiated in the next line. The WrapToSphereEffect takes the radius of the sphere that it will wrap the texture to and the width and height of the texture to wrap.

The CompositeEffect is then used to apply both the shader and the gradient overlay to the planet texture. The shader wraps the texture about the sphere using the radius specified in the effect constructor. The gradient overlay is drawn onto the image by using the OverlayImageEffect.

If you test your movie now, you should see something like Figure 7-9. It's a lovely static image of a planet taken from space, but to really go for the wow, we need to crack open aeon and get it animating.

8. The following bold lines are all we need to set the world spinning:

```
public function Planet() {
  var stars:BitmapData = new StarsTexture(
    stage.stageWidth,
    stage.stageHeight,
    0).draw();
  addChild(new Bitmap(stars));

  var planet:BitmapData = new BitmapData(
    IMAGE_WIDTH,
    IMAGE_HEIGHT,
    true,
    0x00000000
  );
  var gradientOverlay:BitmapData = planet.clone();
  gradientOverlay.draw(getGradientOverlayShape());

  new TextureEffect(
    new EarthTexture(IMAGE_WIDTH, IMAGE_HEIGHT)
  ).apply(planet);

  var savedPlanetData:BitmapData = planet.clone();

  ShaderEffect.shaderFilePath = "../../assets/";
  var shaderEffect:WrapToSphereEffect = new WrapToSphereEffect(
    PLANET_RADIUS,
```

```
    IMAGE_WIDTH,
    IMAGE_HEIGHT
  );

  new CompositeEffect(
    [
    shaderEffect,
    new OverlayImageEffect(gradientOverlay)
    ]
  ).apply(planet);

  var bitmap:Bitmap = new Bitmap(planet);
  bitmap.x = 210;
  bitmap.y = 0;
  bitmap.rotation = 30;
  addChild(bitmap);

  var tweener:Tweener = new Tweener(
    null,
    {x:0},
    {x:IMAGE_WIDTH},
    30000
  );
  new AnimationLoop(tweener, -1,
    function (event:AnimationEvent):void {
      var copy:BitmapData = savedPlanetData.clone();
      new CompositeEffect(
        [
        new TranslateEffect(
          (event.target as Tweener).currentValue.x,
          0,
          true
        ),
        shaderEffect,
        new OverlayImageEffect(gradientOverlay)
        ]
      ).apply(copy);
      ImageUtil.copyPixels(copy, planet);
    }
  ).start();
}
```

First, you must import the classes aeon.animators.Tweener, aeon.events.AnimationEvent, aether.effects.transformations.TranslateEffect, and aether.utils.ImageUtil. After that, test the movie, because you're done! "Ooh" and "ahh" over the power you wield to create planets.

Now, let's have a look at that code. In the first new line, a Tweener instance is created to tween from 0 to 360 over 30 seconds. This will cover the full width of the image. An animation loop is set up in the next line, and it will loop that tweener indefinitely because of the –1 parameter passed. Since the first parameter passed to the Tweener constructor is null, though, the tweener is really doing nothing but interpolating those values. We need to do something with those values.

It turns out that AnimationLoop provides two additional parameters to be passed in its constructor: one being a function to call as the loop updates and the other being a function to call when the managed animation completes each loop. Here, we take advantage of the one to call as the animation updates.

In that function, we copy the planet bitmap data we saved earlier into `savedPlanetData`. With this copy, we apply an effect that will translate the texture on the x axis by the current value found in the tweener, something between 0 and 360. The TranslateEffect takes care of wrapping the texture around, since `true` is passed as the third parameter (the second parameter is the translation on the y axis, which we leave at 0). After the translation, we can reapply the shader that creates the spherical texture and the gradient overlay to the copy. Finally, this copy can be copied back into the planet bitmap data so that it will appear in the bitmap on stage.

There are a lot of possibilities for taking this effect further. You could add a hint of an atmosphere and clouds or modify EarthTexture so that you can concentrate formations or colors in certain areas, like putting icecaps on the poles. That star field in back looks like it might be ripe for some Perlin-generated nebula. For less than 100 lines of ActionScript, though, we can forgive a little the lack of atmosphere. Perhaps the planet's still early in its development. Or maybe it's just a beautifully clear day.

I hope, at the very least, it is clear enough to see the value that these libraries can add, and we will take advantage of them even more through the remaining chapters of this book.

Summary

I have a lot of fun playing with image effects, both in my work and when I am just experimenting. The aeon and aether libraries are a big part of what makes it fun, as they take care of lower level, and sometimes tedious, tasks and make it easy to build and combine multiple effects into increasingly complex compositions. Through this chapter, we have explored how, and we will continue to use these libraries when they will be useful in the coming examples.

This chapter marks the completion of what is conceptually, if not literally, the first half of this book. We have gone through each aspect of the ActionScript language that allows you to load, create, and manipulate images including the drawing API, filters, shaders, and BitmapData. In this chapter, we took a good look at animation and effects libraries that we can use with the ActionScript knowledge gained from earlier chapters to really create stunning effects. From here on out, that is just what we will do—investigate general areas of Flash development that you can enhance with a little creative application of some fantastic image effects.

Chapter 8

ELEMENTAL ANIMATION EFFECTS

If a picture is worth a thousand words, what exactly is an animated picture that updates itself at 30 frames per second worth? "A lot" is the answer, as those who have made their living with Flash animation, motion graphic design, and web sites that do more than present data in a static manner will attest. There are a lot of reasons to use Flash as a development platform, but one of the first and still one of its most compelling is that Flash can present its content in an exciting, dynamic way through animation.

I have always been a bit of an animation fanatic, taking in any animated feature that comes out in the cinema, hitting animation festivals, and enjoying the multitude of offerings online. The thing is—and perhaps one of the reasons I find animation so fascinating and enjoyable to watch—I find it exceedingly difficult to do in the traditional way. I have done frame-by-frame animation, at least on the computer, and even though I have produced some work I am very proud of, I am still in awe of those who produce quality work that is a joy to behold day-in, day-out at a pace that puts me to shame.

So I cheat. There, I said it. But, then again, I cheat because the programs encourage me to do it! The first time I discovered tweens in Flash, tweens that worked out all of the intermediate states between keyframes, I had a smile on my face that would have made the Cheshire Cat blush. What a perfect tool to help an animator!

Of course, soon after that I discovered ActionScript, and suddenly, there was a great big toolbox that could be used to help in the creation of animation. One of the first applications I created back in 2001 was a biped animation tool (still to be found at `http://www.27bobs.com/Bones/baseAnimator.html` and shown in Figure 8-1) that allowed users of the Flash IDE to create animations for bone structures that could then be skinned through the Flash Library. This was soon followed by a face animation tool that provided similar functionality for faces, as shown in Figure 8-2 (`http://www.27bobs.com/Bones/FaceAnimator/preloadFaceAnimator.html`).

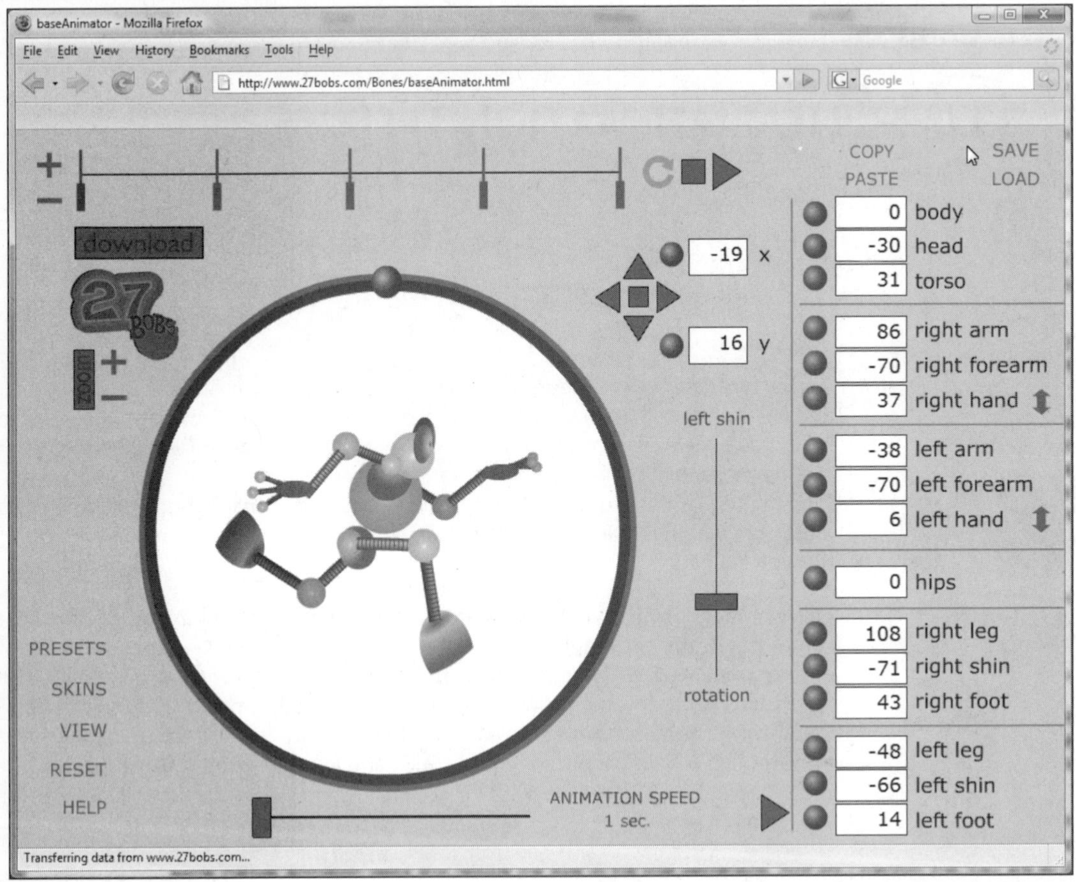

Figure 8-1. The Biped Animator allows for the animation of bone structures, which can then be skinned through the Flash Library.

Figure 8-2. The Face Animator allows for animation of facial rigs, which can then be skinned through the Flash Library.

Great 2D animation will continue to be produced by skilled animators drawing sequences of cells, but through ActionScript and the image manipulation knowledge presented in the first part of this book, we can help to enhance these primary animations with secondary effects. Effects created through ActionScript will help reduce file size for final animations as well as free up an animator to concentrate on the primary action of an animation.

In this chapter, we will look at four separate effects inspired by the four classical elements in nature: air, fire, earth, and water. Each of these effects could be transplanted easily into a game or an animation to enhance the experience, relieve some manual animation tasks, and reduce the size of the final deliverable. And did I mention that they are all pretty fun to look at?

Playing with fire

Prometheus went through all that work stealing fire from the gods, so it only seems right we should start there when creating effects based on the elements. The illusion of fire depends on the movement of the flames more than anything else, and nothing helps simulate the natural movement of flames more than animated Perlin noise. Using that noise to displace an image that contains the colors commonly seen in flames (that is, in the red to yellow range) is all you need to build a fairly realistic effect, without the need for a sequence of images or a particle system.

> *A particle system is a feature in some computer graphics languages or applications (often built in to mid- to high-level 3D programs) that allows you to create certain effects involving usually large numbers of multiple objects that have properties like orientation, direction, velocity, and duration of life, as well as their visual representation. These objects, known as particles, are generated through another object known as the emitter, which defines the origin of each particle, and these particles can often be affected by additional external forces that act on their direction and velocity like gravity or wind simulations. Particle systems are a great way to create natural effects like fire, smoke, explosions, and precipitation and can also be used to create collections of objects like hair or grass.*
>
> *One ActionScript 3.0 particle system that is available as open source under an MIT license is Flint, found at `http://flintparticles.org`. This robust library allows you to create any number of configurable effects using an extensible architecture you could use or shape for many needs, and is certainly worth checking out, especially if you desire to embed particle effects within an ActionScript 3D scene.*

The great thing about this effect is that it can be used with any object for the source of the flames, and it is easily configurable to use different colors, rate of motion, and height of flame. Figure 8-3 shows the finished effect, but of course to get the full effect, you must view the animated file, found as `BurningLetters.swf` in this chapter's files.

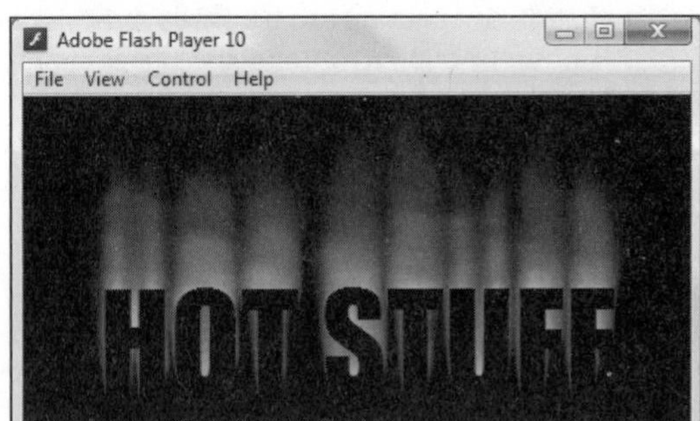

Figure 8-3. Setting letters aflame with a gradient glow filter and some animated Perlin noise

Let's step through how this effect can be achieved:

1. Start with a new document in Flash named `BurningLetters.fla` or an ActionScript project in Flex Builder saved as BurningLetters. The main ActionScript class should be named `BurningLetters.as`. Remember, for more information about setting up projects in these environments, please see the appendix.
2. For this project, we will be using the aether library, so import the `aether.swc` into your FLA or Flex Builder project from this chapter's files. Again, more info on this process can be found in the appendix.
3. Start your BurningLetters class with the following code:

```
package {

  import flash.display.Bitmap;
  import flash.display.BitmapData;
  import flash.display.Sprite;

  [SWF(width=420, height=200, backgroundColor=0x000000)]

  public class BurningLetters extends Sprite {

    private var _flame:BitmapData;

    public function BurningLetters() {
      makeFlame();
      makeFields();
      makeNoise();
    }

    private function makeFlame():void {
      _flame = new BitmapData(
        stage.stageWidth,
        stage.stageHeight,
        true,
        0x00000000
      );
      addChild(new Bitmap(_flame));
    }

    private function makeFields():void {
    }

    private function makeNoise():void {
    }

  }

}
```

Here, in the constructor for our class, we call three custom methods, makeFlame(), makeFields(), and makeNoise(). The latter two currently are empty, but in makeFlame(), we create a new BitmapData instance the size of the stage with fully transparent pixels and wrap this within a Bitmap instance that is added to the stage. It is into this BitmapData instance that we will draw our flickering flames each frame of the movie.

4. The next step in creating our fire effect is to create the object that will be used as the source of the flames. In this example, it will be a textfield, so in the makeFields() method, we create the necessary objects. Add the following bold lines to the class:

```
package {

  import flash.display.Bitmap;
  import flash.display.BitmapData;
  import flash.display.Sprite;
  import flash.filters.GradientGlowFilter;
  import flash.text.TextField;
  import flash.text.TextFieldAutoSize;
  import flash.text.TextFormat;

  [SWF(width=420, height=200, backgroundColor=0x000000)]

  public class BurningLetters extends Sprite {

    private var _blackField:TextField;
    private var _flame:BitmapData;

    public function BurningLetters() {
      makeFlame();
      makeFields();
      makeNoise();
    }

    private function makeFlame():void {
      _flame = new BitmapData(
        stage.stageWidth,
        stage.stageHeight,
        true,
        0x00000000
      );
      addChild(new Bitmap(_flame));
    }

    private function makeFields():void {
      var field:TextField = createField();
      field.filters = [
```

```
        new GradientGlowFilter(
          0,
          45,
          [0xFF0000, 0xFFFF00],
          [1, 1],
          [50, 255],
          15,
          15
        )
      ];
      _blackField = createField();
    }

    private function createField():TextField {
      var field:TextField = new TextField();
      field.autoSize = TextFieldAutoSize.LEFT;
      field.selectable = false;
      field.defaultTextFormat = new TextFormat("Impact", 80);
      field.text = "HOT STUFF";
      field.x = (stage.stageWidth - field.width)/2;
      field.y = stage.stageHeight - field.height;
      addChild(field);
      return field;
    }

    private function makeNoise():void {
    }

  }

}
```

The makeFields() method here creates two different textfields, both through calls to the new createField() method. If you look at createField() first, you will see that a nonselectable TextField instance is created, added to the display list, and placed at the bottom of the stage. The font face used is Impact, so if you do not have this installed on your system, be sure to specify a face that you have available.

Why do we create two fields of the same size with the same text at the same position? Look back to the makeFields() method, and you will see that the first field added has a GradientGlowFilter applied using a red to yellow gradient. This filtered textfield with fiery colors is what will be displaced to create the flame. The second field added in the final line of makeFields() and saved into the property _blackField will be visible on top of the distorted flaming text and itself will not be distorted. To have both the distorted and nondistorted text in the final effect it is easiest simply to create two separate fields.

If you compile this application now, nothing much will be visible; you'll see only the hint of the gradient-colored field behind the black field, as shown in Figure 8-4.

However, if you comment out the final line in makeFields() where _blackField is created, you should see the coloring of the fiery field, as shown in Figure 8-5.

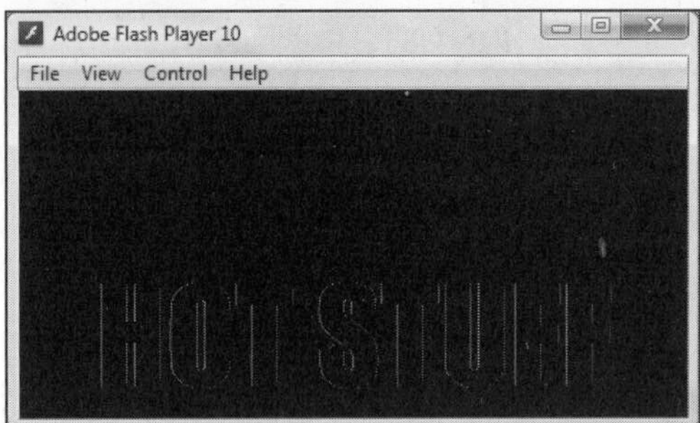

Figure 8-4. The black textfield obscuring the gradient colored textfield below it

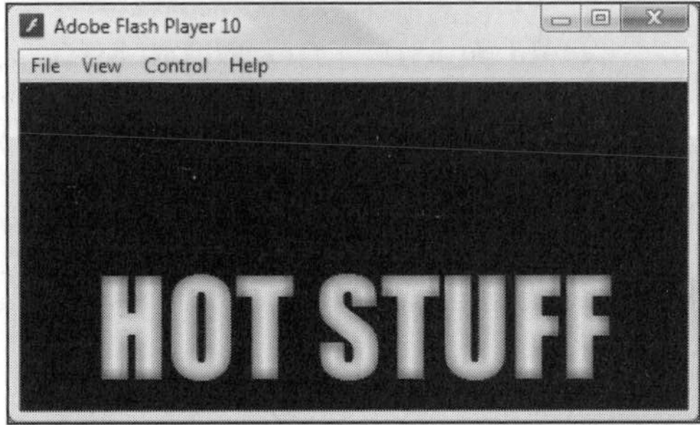

Figure 8-5. The gradient colored textfield that will be used to create the flame effect

5. At this point, we have a black textfield on top of a fiery colored textfield. The task now is to distort the fiery field in a manner that calls to mind a flame. For that, we turn to Perlin noise. The noise itself will create patches of light and dark that will work perfectly for a displacement map to distort the text, and the noise texture itself can be offset a little each frame, creating the motion needed to simulate the movement of fire.

   Add the following bold lines to your class, which initialize the properties needed to create consistent noise frame to frame, instantiates the BitmapData where the noise will be applied, and calls the method that will generate the noise itself. (Note that some of the methods have been truncated to save space, but their code remains unchanged.)

```
package {

  import flash.display.Bitmap;
  import flash.display.BitmapData;
  import flash.display.BitmapDataChannel;
  import flash.display.Sprite;
  import flash.filters.GradientGlowFilter;
  import flash.geom.Point;
  import flash.text.TextField;
  import flash.text.TextFieldAutoSize;
  import flash.text.TextFormat;

  [SWF(width=420, height=200, backgroundColor=0x000000)]
```

```
public class BurningLetters extends Sprite {

  private static const FLICKER_RATE:Number = 10;

  private var _blackField:TextField;
  private var _flame:BitmapData;
  private var _perlinNoise:BitmapData;
  private var _perlinOffsets:Array;
  private var _perlinSeed:int;

  public function BurningLetters() {
    makeFlame();
    makeFields();
    makeNoise();
  }

  private function makeFlame():void {
    // this method body is unchanged
  }

  private function makeFields():void {
    // this method body is unchanged
  }

  private function createField():TextField {
    // this method body is unchanged
  }

  private function makeNoise():void {
    _perlinNoise = _flame.clone();
    _perlinSeed = int(new Date());
    _perlinOffsets = [new Point(), new Point()];
  }

  private function applyNoise():void {
    _perlinNoise.perlinNoise(
      50,
      30,
      2,
      _perlinSeed,
      false,
      true,
      BitmapDataChannel.RED,
      true,
      _perlinOffsets
    );
    (_perlinOffsets[0] as Point).y += FLICKER_RATE;
    (_perlinOffsets[1] as Point).y += FLICKER_RATE/2;
  }

 }

}
```

The bitmap data used for the Perlin noise, instantiated in the first line of makeNoise(), is simply a clone of the initially empty _flame bitmap data, since we want them to be the same size to make a perfectly sized distortion map. The random seed property, _perlinSeed, needs to remain consistent for each call to perlinNoise() to create the same noise image each frame, so we save this into its own property. _perlinOffsets holds the offset positions for both octaves that we will be generating in the perlinNoise() call. It is by altering these offsets each frame that we will create animated flame.

The makeNoise() method itself does little but assign values to our properties. The applyNoise() method is what actually generates the noise using these values (although currently this method is not yet called by any other method, it will be). The call to perlinNoise() within this method creates a fractal noise image of two octaves (the third parameter determines this). The red channel is used for the noise and the result is set to grayscale, but these values aren't really important since the noise will only be used as an 8-bit displacement map anyway. You should, however, note that the componentX parameter is set at 50 pixels, and the componentY is set at 30, which creates noise that is longer on the horizontal axis. These are numbers that I felt worked well for this example, but they could be altered to create larger or smaller flames.

The final lines in applyNoise() adjust the offsets each time the method is called by the FLICKER_RATE, set as a constant at the top of the class. The second octave is moved at a slower rate than the first octave, but again, the numbers here are simply ones I felt worked well in this instance. I've always liked, at the very least, moving octaves at different rates, as I feel this gives a more natural effect.

6. The final piece in our class is to distort the fiery text using the Perlin noise and continue to do so each frame. This is all accomplished in the following code, which completes the example:

```
package {

  import aether.utils.ImageUtil;

  import flash.display.Bitmap;
  import flash.display.BitmapData;
  import flash.display.BitmapDataChannel;
  import flash.display.Sprite;
  import flash.events.Event;
  import flash.filters.BlurFilter;
  import flash.filters.DisplacementMapFilter;
  import flash.filters.DisplacementMapFilterMode;
  import flash.filters.GradientGlowFilter;
  import flash.geom.ColorTransform;
  import flash.geom.Point;
  import flash.text.TextField;
  import flash.text.TextFieldAutoSize;
  import flash.text.TextFormat;

  [SWF(width=420, height=200, backgroundColor=0x000000)]
```

```
public class BurningLetters extends Sprite {

  private static const FLICKER_RATE:Number = 10;

  private var _blackField:TextField;
  private var _flame:BitmapData;
  private var _perlinNoise:BitmapData;
  private var _perlinOffsets:Array;
  private var _perlinSeed:int;

  public function BurningLetters() {
    makeFlame();
    makeFields();
    makeNoise();
    addEventListener(Event.ENTER_FRAME, onSpriteEnterFrame);
  }

  private function makeFlame():void {
    // this method body is unchanged
  }

  private function makeFields():void {
    // this method body is unchanged
  }

  private function createField():TextField {
    // this method body is unchanged
  }

  private function makeNoise():void {
    // this method body is unchanged
  }

  private function applyNoise():void {
    // this method body is unchanged
  }

  private function drawFlame():void {
    _flame.draw(
      stage,
      null,
      new ColorTransform(.9, .9, .9, .7)
    );
    ImageUtil.applyFilter(
      _flame,
      new BlurFilter(3, 5)
    );
    _flame.scroll(0, -4);
    applyNoise();
```

```
        ImageUtil.applyFilter(
          _flame,
          new DisplacementMapFilter(
            _perlinNoise,
            new Point(),
            BitmapDataChannel.RED,
            BitmapDataChannel.RED,
            1,
            10,
            DisplacementMapFilterMode.CLAMP
          )
        );
      }

      private function onSpriteEnterFrame(event:Event):void {
        _blackField.visible = false;
        drawFlame();
        _blackField.visible = true;
      }

    }

  }
```

One last line was added to the constructor to set up a listener for the ENTER_FRAME event. This listener, onSpriteEnterFrame(), sets the visibility of the black textfield to false (we'll look at why in a moment), draws the flame, and turns the visibility of the field back on.

All the pyrotechnics, as it were, lie in the new drawFlame() method. The first thing that occurs is that the whole of the stage, with all of its visible items (which is why we set the visibility of _blackField to false in onSpriteEnterFrame()), is drawn into the _flame bitmap data, but as it is drawn, a color transform is applied so that the pixels drawn are at an opacity of 70 percent and are darkened slightly in each channel. This reduces the opacity and brightness of the previously drawn flame as new flame is added, which results in the flame tapering out as it animates up. If you remove the color transform from this line, you will see something like Figure 8-6, which shows how playing with the numbers of the color transform will affect the height of the flames.

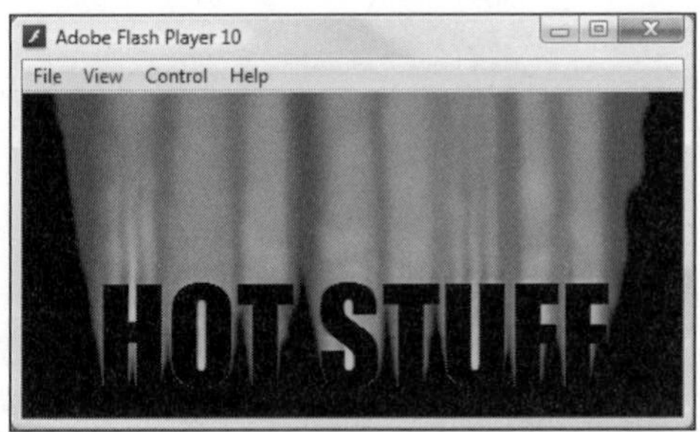

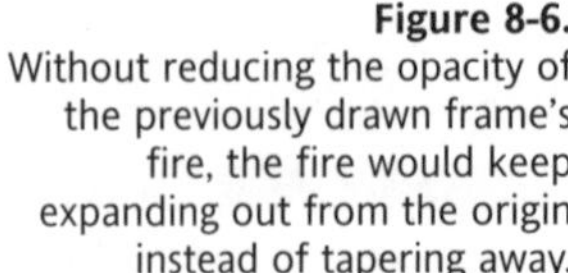

Figure 8-6.
Without reducing the opacity of the previously drawn frame's fire, the fire would keep expanding out from the origin instead of tapering away.

After the stage is drawn into `_flame`, the pixels are blurred, more vertically than horizontally to match the movement of the flames. `scroll()` is then called to move the pixels up on the stage. It is this scrolling that really gives the flames their vertical motion (try removing the line to see the effect).

The next line in `drawFlame()` is a call to `applyNoise()`, which generates new Perlin noise with new offsets that can be used to displace the flame image. This displacement occurs in the final line of `drawFlame()`, which uses the red channel from `_perlinNoise` to distort the `_flame` pixels. Note that the displacement is set to be much more pronounced on the y axis (10) than on the x axis (1). Again, this is to create more of a vertical feel for the flames and limit the distortion of the text on the horizontal axis.

You should be able to compile and test your movie at this time to see the results!

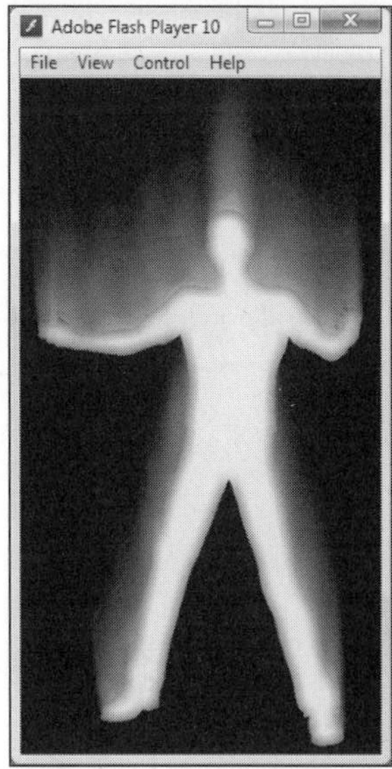

Figure 8-7. The same effect applied to another object, in this case the silhouette of a man

The great thing about this technique is that it can be applied to any image very easily, even animated images, as you will see in Chapter 10. Figure 8-7 shows the effect applied to a silhouette of a man, this time not covering up the flame with a blackened image (I'm imagining a superhero here, not a man in need of a fire department). The code for this can be found in this chapter's files as `BurningMan.as`.

One important note about this effect, and about many that would redraw large regions of pixels each frame and then displace them with an equally large bitmap, generate multioctave noise or apply multiple filters, is that you must always be conscious of performance in the Flash Player. Some ways you can help with performance of this effect, ways that may be applicable to other animated effects as well, follow:

1. *Keep the region you are redrawing and manipulating only as large as you need it, testing whether a slight and acceptable reduction in size will improve performance when necessary.*
2. *Reduce the number of octaves in the `perlinNoise()` call, only using multiple levels if it is necessary for a better effect (I found that in BurningMan I did not need the two octaves).*
3. *Apply filters, like the BlurFilter in this example, only when necessary and when their exclusion noticeably changes the effect.*
4. *Keep the quality setting on filters that use it to `LOW`, unless absolutely necessary for the effect.*

Turning to stone

Since the spinning Earth was demonstrated at the end of the last chapter I was initially a bit stuck for a stone/earth/rock effect, especially since stone itself is not a terribly animated substance, with no offense intended to The Thing, Concrete, or any talking gargoyles out there. A rockslide, perhaps? Meteor shower? In the end, I decided it would be good to explore how to create a stone-like texture at runtime, and I even went and animated it as a final flourish. The result is shown in Figures 8-8 and 8-9, with the animated version found as MedusaStare.swf in this chapter's files.

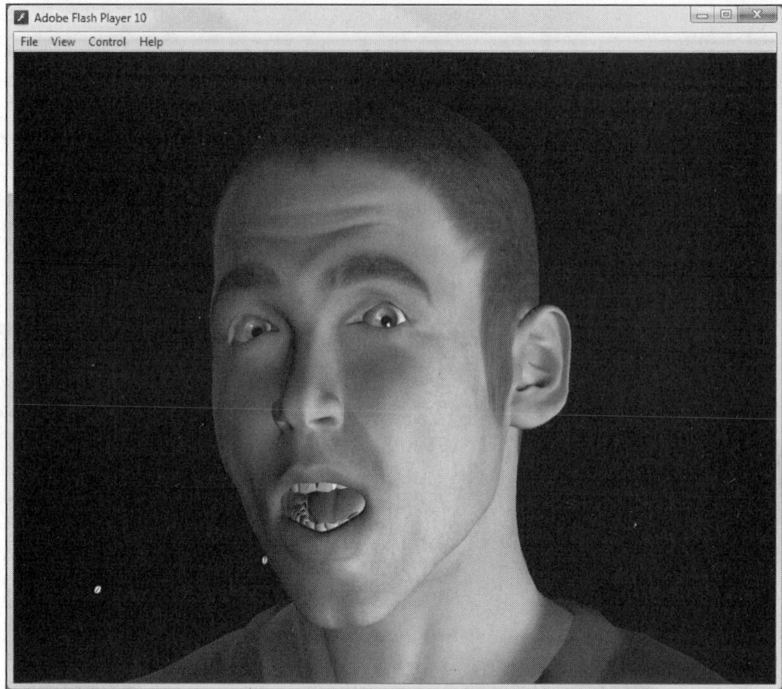

Figure 8-8. The loaded bitmap, full color in the actual file, before the stone texture is generated and applied

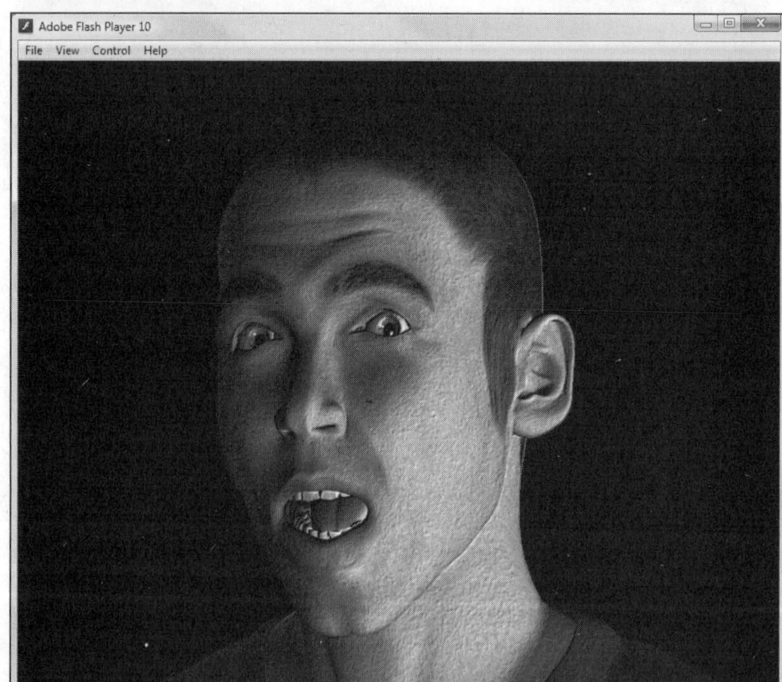

Figure 8-9. The stone-textured head using a procedural texture applied to the loaded bitmap

As you might have guessed from the name of the file, the animation consists of turning a figure to stone, but the animation in this case is a standard fade from one image to another. So why not simply import two images and be done with it? Well, obviously images take time to create and then time to load or space in the final SWF file. Imagine a game where there are multiple textures for a single object that can be used in multiple scenarios, or, as demonstrated by MedusaStare, multiple objects that turn to different textures. Using a technique similar to one we will break down in this example, you do not need to create and import all of these copies to support all these scenarios. You merely need the initial image for which you can generate and apply different textures at runtime.

1. Start with a new document in Flash named `MedusaStare.fla` or an ActionScript project in Flex Builder saved as MedusaStare. The main ActionScript class should be named `MedusaStare.as`. Once again, the appendix has all the details on setting up projects in these environments.
2. For this project, we will be using the both the aether and aeon libraries, so import `aether.swc` and `aeon.swc` into your FLA or Flex Builder project from this chapter's files.
3. Start your MedusaStare class with the following code:

```
package {

  import aether.utils.Adjustments;
  import aether.utils.ImageUtil;

  import flash.display.Bitmap;
  import flash.display.BitmapData;
  import flash.display.BitmapDataChannel;
  import flash.filters.BlurFilter;

  [SWF(width=800, height=640, backgroundColor=0x000000)]

  public class MedusaStare extends AbstractImageLoader {

    public function MedusaStare() {
      super("../../assets/fear.png");
    }

    override protected function runPostImageLoad():void {
      addChild(_loadedBitmap);
      makeStone();
    }

    private function makeStone():void {
      var map:BitmapData = new BitmapData(
        stage.stageWidth,
        stage.stageHeight,
        true,
        0x00000000
      );
```

```
        var stone:BitmapData = map.clone();
        map.draw(_loadedBitmap);
        Adjustments.desaturate(map);
        stone.noise(
          int(new Date()),
          100,
          150,
          BitmapDataChannel.RED,
          true
        );
        ImageUtil.applyFilter(stone, new BlurFilter(2, 2));

        var bitmap:Bitmap = new Bitmap(stone);
        addChild(bitmap);
      }

  }

}
```

This example extends AbstractImageLoader, a class we've used in numerous earlier chapters that simply loads in an image that we can then manipulate. You can find this class in this chapter's files as well.

In the constructor for this class, we pass the path to the image to load to the super class's constructor. If you place the `fear.png` image, which you can also find with this chapter's files, in a different relative directory, be sure to update the path accordingly.

Once the image is loaded, `runPostImageLoad()` is called by the super class. This adds the image to the stage and calls the `makeStone()` method.

We will be building up the `makeStone()` method in the next several steps. At this point, we create a transparent BitmapData instance that is the same size as the stage and save this into a `map` variable. We will use this to displace the stone texture we create. This transparent image is cloned and saved into the `stone` variable as well.

`map` then gets the loaded bitmap image drawn into it using the `draw()` method. This is fully desaturated using the `Adjustments.desaturate()` call available in the aether library.

In the lines that follow, we set `map` aside briefly to work on the stone texture. First, we fill the bitmap data with grayscale noise that is between the brightness levels of 100 and 150, which results in very limited contrast. Once again, the channel we choose is unimportant, since we make the noise grayscale anyway. A blur filter is then applied to the noise to soften the overall effect.

In the final lines of the method, the data is passed to a Bitmap instance, which is added to the stage, so you can compile and see the current state of the effect, as shown in Figure 8-10.

Figure 8-10. The noise texture that is the basis for the stone effect

4. We have the start of a stone texture and a map to displace it using the loaded image. The next step is to apply this displacement. Add the following bold lines to accomplish this:

```
package {

  import aether.utils.Adjustments;
  import aether.utils.ImageUtil;

  import flash.display.Bitmap;
  import flash.display.BitmapData;
  import flash.display.BitmapDataChannel;
  import flash.display.BlendMode;
  import flash.filters.BlurFilter;
  import flash.filters.DisplacementMapFilter;
  import flash.geom.Point;

  [SWF(width=800, height=640, backgroundColor=0x000000)]

  public class MedusaStare extends AbstractImageLoader {

    public function MedusaStare() {
      super("../../assets/fear.png");
    }
```

```
        override protected function runPostImageLoad():void {
          addChild(_loadedBitmap);
          makeStone();
        }

        private function makeStone():void {
          var map:BitmapData = new BitmapData(
            stage.stageWidth,
            stage.stageHeight,
            true,
            0x00000000
          );
          var stone:BitmapData = map.clone();
          map.draw(_loadedBitmap);
          Adjustments.desaturate(map);
          stone.noise(
            int(new Date()),
            100,
            150,
            BitmapDataChannel.RED,
            true
          );
          ImageUtil.applyFilter(stone, new BlurFilter(2, 2));
          ImageUtil.applyFilter(
            stone,
            new DisplacementMapFilter(
              map,
              new Point(),
              BitmapDataChannel.RED,
              BitmapDataChannel.RED,
              150,
              150
            )
          );
          Adjustments.adjustContrast(map, -0.2);
          stone.draw(map, null, null, BlendMode.OVERLAY);

          var bitmap:Bitmap = new Bitmap(stone);
          addChild(bitmap);
        }

      }

    }
```

The first new line in makeStone() applies the displacement map to the stone texture using a high scale value of 150 on both the x and y axes in order to create very visible distortion. To overlay the grayscale map to the distorted image in order to define the highlight and shadow areas of the head, we reduce the contrast of the map and apply it using the OVERLAY blend mode to the stone texture. The result of this is shown in Figure 8-11.

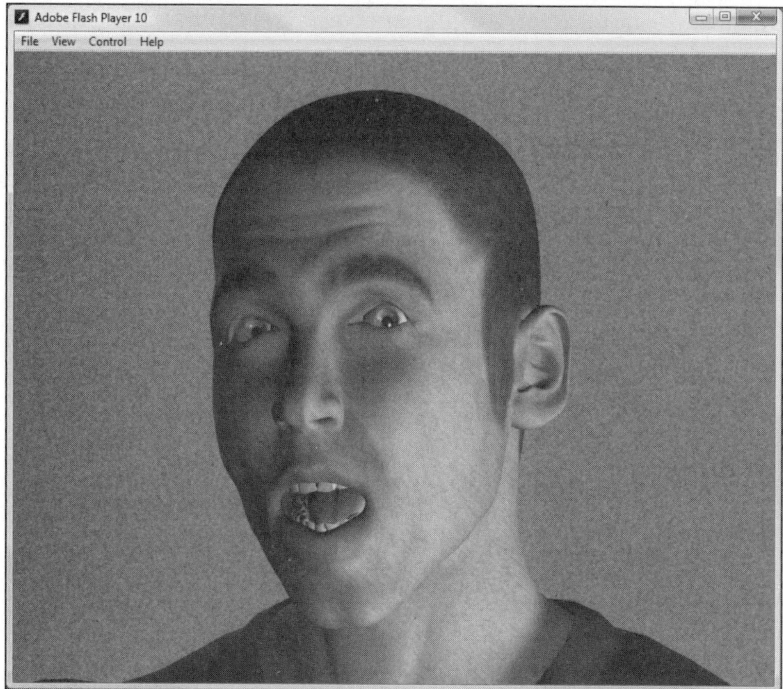

Figure 8-11. The distorted stone texture with the grayscale image applied in OVERLAY mode to define the light and shadow

5. To really create the tactile effect of stone, we must make it seem as if light is hitting a three-dimensional surface. We can accomplish this with an embossing effect. Embossing, if you recall from Chapter 2, can be achieved using the ConvolutionFilter. It so happens that there is a ConvolutionEffect in aether that allows you to easily apply this type of an effect by simply passing in a matrix, and there is a subclass EmbossEffect that makes it even easier by prebuilding the matrix and letting you simply specify the level of the effect. Although the process is encapsulated in these classes, it is the exact same technique as we previously covered in Chapter 2.

```
package {

  import aeon.animators.Tweener;

  import aether.effects.convolution.EmbossEffect;
  import aether.utils.Adjustments;
  import aether.utils.ImageUtil;
```

```
import flash.display.Bitmap;
import flash.display.BitmapData;
import flash.display.BitmapDataChannel;
import flash.display.BlendMode;
import flash.filters.BlurFilter;
import flash.filters.DisplacementMapFilter;
import flash.geom.Point;

[SWF(width=800, height=640, backgroundColor=0x000000)]

public class MedusaStare extends AbstractImageLoader {

  public function MedusaStare() {
    super("../../assets/fear.png");
  }

  override protected function runPostImageLoad():void {
    addChild(_loadedBitmap);
    makeStone();
  }

  private function makeStone():void {
    var map:BitmapData = new BitmapData(
      stage.stageWidth,
      stage.stageHeight,
      true,
      0x00000000
    );
    var stone:BitmapData = map.clone();
    map.draw(_loadedBitmap);
    Adjustments.desaturate(map);
    stone.noise(
      int(new Date()),
      100,
      150,
      BitmapDataChannel.RED,
      true
    );
    ImageUtil.applyFilter(stone, new BlurFilter(2, 2));
    ImageUtil.applyFilter(
      stone,
      new DisplacementMapFilter(
        map,
        new Point(),
        BitmapDataChannel.RED,
        BitmapDataChannel.RED,
        150,
        150
```

```
            )
        );
        Adjustments.adjustContrast(map, -0.2);
        stone.draw(map, null, null, BlendMode.OVERLAY);
        new EmbossEffect(1).apply(stone);
        Adjustments.setLevels(map, 0, 75, 150);
        stone.draw(map, null, null, BlendMode.MULTIPLY);
        ImageUtil.copyChannel(map, stone, BitmapDataChannel.ALPHA);

        var bitmap:Bitmap = new Bitmap(stone);
        bitmap.alpha = 0;
        addChild(bitmap);
        new Tweener(bitmap, {alpha:0}, {alpha:.9}, 5000).start();
      }

    }

}
```

A new EmbossEffect is applied to the stone texture to simulate light hitting the surface. The EmbossEffect class applies a matrix using the ConvolutionFilter to the image passed in the apply() call. The matrix in the EmbossEffect class looks like this:

```
var matrix:Array = [
  -amount, -1,      0,
       -1,  1,      1,
        0,  1, amount
];
```

You may recognize this matrix from Chapter 2, where we covered embossing techniques, with the only difference being the amount of embossing here is configurable. The result of applying this matrix to the stone texture is the illusion of light hitting the texture from the upper left.

After the embossing is applied to the stone, the levels on the grayscale map are adjusted to brighten the overall image (anything that originally had a brightness of 150 or more will be pure white, with all levels below that being evenly distributed across a range of 255). This brightened image can then be drawn onto the stone image using the MULTIPLY blend mode, creating a little more shadow but not too much more shadow since the image was first considerably brightened.

The stone texture, at this point, covers the whole of the stage, so we finish up by copying the alpha channel from the map, which you will recall was drawn from the original loaded image that contained an alpha channel, into the stone texture.

At this point, we can use the Tweener class to tween the opacity of the stone texture from 0 to 1 over the course of 5 seconds, completing the effect of the stone metamorphosis. Now where's Perseus when you need him?

Waving the flag

Earlier in this chapter, we used animated Perlin noise to distort a flame-colored image to simulate fire. By applying slightly less distortion without blur, you can use Perlin noise to help simulate other natural motion like an ocean's rolling waves or, as you will see in this example, the flapping of a flag, or any cloth, in the wind, as shown in Figure 8-12.

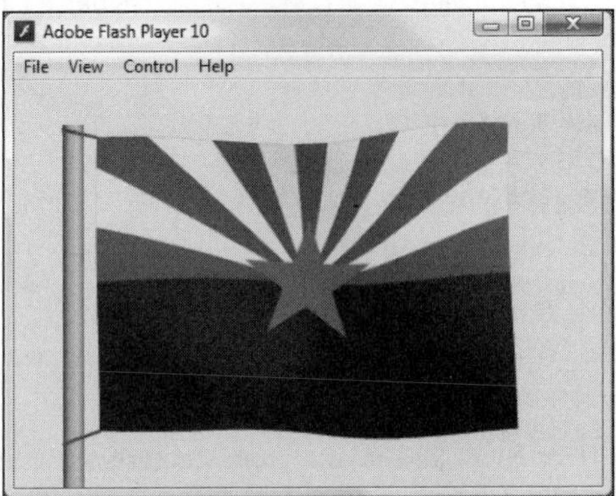

Figure 8-12. The Arizona state flag blowing in the breeze using some Perlin noise as a displacement map

Such an effect, when solved accurately, requires an implementation of 3D cloth dynamics, but with just a little displacement, we can achieve a similar slick effect with considerably less code (and no 3D engine!).

1. Start with a new document in Flash named `FlagWaving.fla` or an ActionScript project in Flex Builder saved as FlagWaving. The main ActionScript class should be named `FlagWaving.as`. You should be well versed by this point on how to set up your projects, but if not, please see the appendix.
2. For this project, we will be using the aether library, so import `aether.swc` into your FLA or Flex Builder project from this chapter's files.
3. Start your FlagWaving class with the following code, which will load in the flag bitmap and draw it to the stage:

```
package {

  import flash.display.BitmapData;
  import flash.display.GradientType;
  import flash.display.Shape;
  import flash.geom.Matrix;
  import flash.geom.Point;

  [SWF(width=420, height=280, backgroundColor=0xBEEBF0)]

  public class FlagWaving extends AbstractImageLoader {
```

```
private var _flag:BitmapData;

public function FlagWaving() {
  super("../../assets/flag.png");
}

override protected function runPostImageLoad():void {
  makeFlag();
}

private function makeFlag():void {
  var stageWidth:Number = stage.stageWidth;
  var stageHeight:Number = stage.stageHeight;

  var bitmapData:BitmapData = _loadedBitmap.bitmapData;
  var bitmapWidth:Number = bitmapData.width;
  var bitmapHeight:Number = bitmapData.height;

  var poleWidth:Number = 15;
  var poleHeight:Number = 250;
  var poleX:Number = 35;
  var poleY:Number = stageHeight - poleHeight;

  var matrix:Matrix = new Matrix();
  matrix.createGradientBox(poleWidth, poleHeight);
  var pole:Shape = new Shape();
  pole.graphics.beginGradientFill(
    GradientType.LINEAR,
    [0x333333, 0x999999, 0xCCCCCC, 0xAAAAAA, 0x666666],
    [1, 1, 1, 1, 1],
    [0, 50, 160, 200, 255],
    matrix
  );
  pole.graphics.drawRect(0, 0, poleWidth, poleHeight);
  pole.graphics.endFill();
  pole.x = poleX;
  pole.y = poleY;
  addChild(pole);

  var point:Point = new Point(
    (stageWidth - bitmapWidth)/2,
    (stageHeight - bitmapHeight)/2
  );

  var cord:Shape = new Shape();
  cord.graphics.lineStyle(2, 0x333333);
  cord.graphics.moveTo(poleX, poleY+3);
  cord.graphics.lineTo(point.x, point.y);
```

```
        cord.graphics.moveTo(point.x, point.y + bitmapHeight);
        cord.graphics.lineTo(poleX, poleY + bitmapHeight+20);

        _flag = new BitmapData(
          stageWidth,
          stageHeight,
          true,
          0x00000000
        );
        _flag.draw(cord);
        _flag.copyPixels(bitmapData, bitmapData.rect, point);
        _loadedBitmap.bitmapData = _flag;
        addChild(_loadedBitmap);
      }

  }

}
```

FlagWaving once again extends AbstractImageLoader to handle the loading of the flag.png. Make sure you keep this image in the specified relative directory or alter the path as needed.

Once the image loads and runPostImageLoad() is invoked, the method makeFlag() is called. This fairly lengthy method works to produce the flag, the flag pole, and the cords that attach the flag to the pole. The first several groupings of lines initialize the variables we will use within the method. After that, the flag pole is drawn using the drawing API and a gradient-filled shape. This shape is added to the stage and will be at the bottom of the display list, under all other elements.

The cord for the flag is also drawn using the drawing API and a number of lines. This shape, however, is not added to the stage but is instead drawn into a new BitmapData instance along with the loaded flag image, referenced here in the variable bitmapData.

```
_flag = new BitmapData(
  stageWidth,
  stageHeight,
  true,
  0x00000000
);
_flag.draw(cord);
_flag.copyPixels(bitmapData, bitmapData.rect, point);
```

This puts both the cord and flag into the same bitmap data so that both can be distorted using the Perlin noise. This composite bitmap data consisting of the flag and cord is used as the bitmap data for the _loadedBitmap Bitmap, which is added to the stage in the final line of the method. Figure 8-13, which shows the pole and the undistorted flag and cord, illustrates the result of this makeFlag() method, if you view your movie at this point.

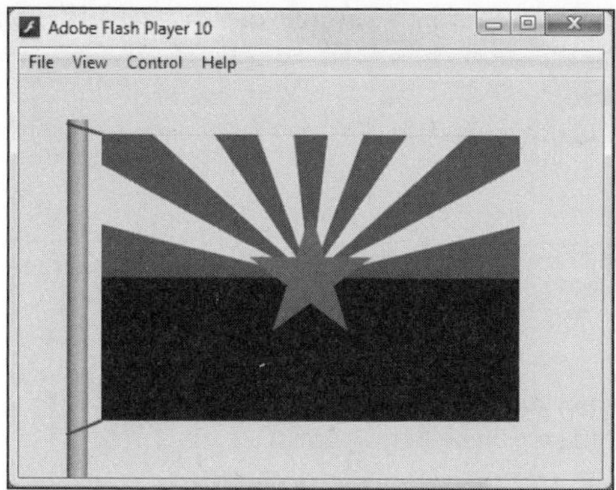

Figure 8-13. The undistorted flag image with the pole and the cords drawn using the drawing API

4. Now, we will create the Perlin noise animation that will distort the flag each frame, simulating the wind effect in a similar way to how we achieved the fire animation in this chapter's first example. Add the following bold lines to your class:

```
package {

  import aether.utils.ImageUtil;

  import flash.display.BitmapData;
  import flash.display.BitmapDataChannel;
  import flash.display.GradientType;
  import flash.display.Shape;
  import flash.events.Event;
  import flash.filters.DisplacementMapFilter;
  import flash.filters.DisplacementMapFilterMode;
  import flash.geom.Matrix;
  import flash.geom.Point;

  [SWF(width=420, height=280, backgroundColor=0xBEEBF0)]

  public class FlagWaving extends AbstractImageLoader {

    private static const WIND_RATE:Number = 30;

    private var _flag:BitmapData;
    private var _perlinNoise:BitmapData;
    private var _perlinOffsets:Array;
    private var _perlinSeed:int;

    public function FlagWaving() {
      super("../../assets/flag.png");
    }
```

```
override protected function runPostImageLoad():void {
  makeFlag();
  makeNoise();
  addEventListener(Event.ENTER_FRAME, onSpriteEnterFrame);
}

private function makeFlag():void {
  // this method body is unchanged
}

private function makeNoise():void {
  _perlinNoise = new BitmapData(
    stage.stageWidth,
    stage.stageHeight
  );
  _perlinSeed = int(new Date());
  _perlinOffsets = [new Point()];
}

private function applyNoise():void {
  _perlinNoise.perlinNoise(
    200,
    200,
    1,
    _perlinSeed,
    false,
    true,
    BitmapDataChannel.RED,
    true,
    _perlinOffsets
  );
  (_perlinOffsets[0] as Point).x -= WIND_RATE;
}

private function waveFlag():void {
  applyNoise();
  var flag:BitmapData = _flag.clone();
  ImageUtil.applyFilter(
    flag,
    new DisplacementMapFilter(
      _perlinNoise,
      new Point(),
      BitmapDataChannel.RED,
      BitmapDataChannel.RED,
      40,
      60
    )
  );
  _loadedBitmap.bitmapData = flag;
}
```

```
    private function onSpriteEnterFrame(event:Event):void {
      waveFlag();
    }

  }

}
```

Much of this new code is the same technique as explored in more detail in the fire example. In the constructor we call a new makeNoise() method, which instantiates the _perlinNoise bitmap data and initializes the Perlin noise variables we will need to keep consistent for each call to perlinNoise(). We then set up a listener for the ENTER_FRAME event, so we can update the view each frame in order to create the animation.

The listener, onSpriteEnterFrame(), simply calls the new waveFlag() method, which itself calls out to the applyNoise() method. applyNoise() is where the call to perlinNoise() is made each frame, updating the noise with a new offset value based on the WIND_RATE constant. It is the offsetting of the noise each frame that creates the illusion of wind motion. Note that, for this effect, we only use a single octave of Perlin noise.

Back in waveFlag(), after the call to applyNoise() is made, we first clone the original, undistorted _flag bitmap data and then apply the displacement map filter, distorting a little more on the y axis than the x axis. This distorted bitmap data is then passed to the bitmap currently in the display list so that it may be rendered. The result of this is shown in Figure 8-14.

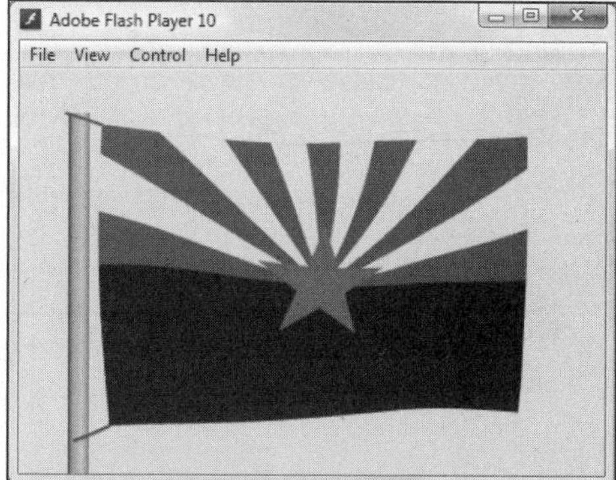

Figure 8-14. The flag image is distorted using a displacement map but so are the cords; plus there is little indication of depth.

There are a few issues with the effect at this point. First, the cords when they are distorted do not remain in contact with the pole. Second, although the flag distorts, there is little indication of depth since the lighting remains consistent across the surface. We will tackle the cord issue first in the next step.

5. In order to distort the flag and the portion of the cords that is attached to the flag, but not the portion of the cords that is attached to the pole, we need to create a

gradient that will gradually lessen the displacement effect on the left side of the image. We know that any value in the displacement map that is medium gray will not result in a distortion, so the solution is to draw a tight gradient into the Perlin noise image that will fade the noise image to a medium gray on its left side. In this way, the flag can continue to be distorted while the cord won't be, with a nice gradual reduction in the displacement to make it appear seamless and natural. The following bold lines achieve this:

```
package {

  // imports remain unchanged

  [SWF(width=420, height=280, backgroundColor=0xBEEBF0)]

  public class FlagWaving extends AbstractImageLoader {

    private static const WIND_RATE:Number = 30;

    private var _gradient:BitmapData;
    private var _flag:BitmapData;
    private var _perlinNoise:BitmapData;
    private var _perlinOffsets:Array;
    private var _perlinSeed:int;

    public function FlagWaving() {
      super("../../assets/flag.png");
    }

    override protected function runPostImageLoad():void {
      makeFlag();
      makeGradientOverlay();
      makeNoise();
      addEventListener(Event.ENTER_FRAME, onSpriteEnterFrame);
    }

    private function makeFlag():void {
      // method body is unchanged
    }

    private function makeGradientOverlay():void {
      var width:Number = stage.stageWidth;
      var height:Number = stage.stageHeight;
      var matrix:Matrix = new Matrix();
      matrix.createGradientBox(width, height);
      var shape:Shape = new Shape();
      shape.graphics.beginGradientFill(
        GradientType.LINEAR,
        [0x7F7F7F, 0x7F7F7F],
        [1, 0],
        [20, 80],
```

```
        matrix
      );
      shape.graphics.drawRect(0, 0, width, height);
      shape.graphics.endFill();
      _gradient = new BitmapData(width, height, true, 0x00000000);
      _gradient.draw(shape);
    }

    private function makeNoise():void {
      // method body is unchanged
    }

    private function applyNoise():void {
      // method body is unchanged
    }

    private function waveFlag():void {
      applyNoise();
      var flag:BitmapData = _flag.clone();
      _perlinNoise.copyPixels(
        _gradient,
        _gradient.rect,
        new Point(),
        _perlinNoise,
        new Point(),
        true
      );
      ImageUtil.applyFilter(
        flag,
        new DisplacementMapFilter(
          _perlinNoise,
          new Point(),
          BitmapDataChannel.RED,
          BitmapDataChannel.RED,
          40,
          60
        )
      );
      _loadedBitmap.bitmapData = flag;
    }

    private function onSpriteEnterFrame(event:Event):void {
      waveFlag();
    }

  }

}
```

Since the gradient will remain unchanged, we can draw it once from the constructor and use the same image each frame. The makeGradientOverlay() draws the gradient, which is a simple linear gradient consisting of the same medium gray color drawn from full opacity to full transparency.

Each frame, when waveFlag() is called, this gradient is drawn into the generated Perlin noise image to lessen the black-and-white contrast on the left side of the image. When this noise is applied as a displacement map to the flag, the result is that the flag is distorted, but the left side of the two cords remains stuck to the pole, as shown in Figure 8-15.

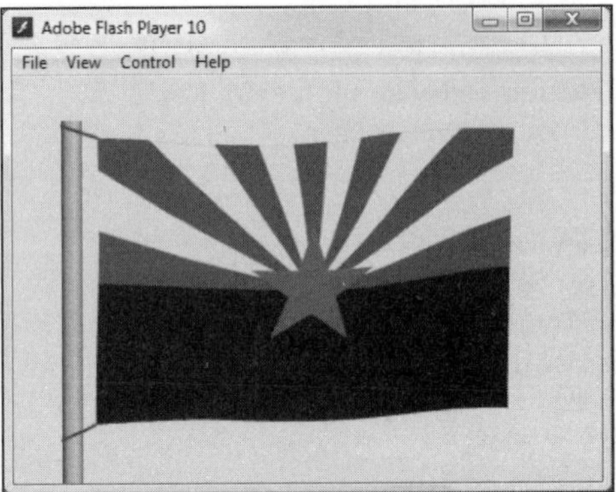

Figure 8-15. By drawing a gradient onto the displacement map, the distortion effect is limited to the flag and the right side of the cords.

6. The effect is nearly complete, but what is missing is some simulated lighting to suggest depth to the waving flag. This can be easily added using the current displacement map, with its light and dark regions already being used to displace the flag, as an overlay. Add the following bold lines to the class to finish the effect:

```
package {

  import aether.utils.ImageUtil;

  import flash.display.BitmapData;
  import flash.display.BitmapDataChannel;
  import flash.display.BlendMode;
  import flash.display.GradientType;
  import flash.display.Shape;
  import flash.events.Event;
  import flash.filters.DisplacementMapFilter;
  import flash.filters.DisplacementMapFilterMode;
  import flash.geom.ColorTransform;
  import flash.geom.Matrix;
  import flash.geom.Point;

  [SWF(width=420, height=280, backgroundColor=0xBEEBF0)]
```

```
public class FlagWaving extends AbstractImageLoader {

  // constants and properties remain unchanged

  public function FlagWaving() {
    super("../../assets/flag.png");
  }

  override protected function runPostImageLoad():void {
    // method body is unchanged
  }

  private function makeFlag():void {
    // method body is unchanged
  }

  private function makeGradientOverlay():void {
    // method body is unchanged
  }

  private function makeNoise():void {
    // method body is unchanged
  }

  private function applyNoise():void {
    // method body is unchanged
  }

  private function waveFlag():void {
    applyNoise();
    var flag:BitmapData = _flag.clone();
    _perlinNoise.copyPixels(
      _gradient,
      _gradient.rect,
      new Point(),
      _perlinNoise,
      new Point(),
      true
    );
    ImageUtil.applyFilter(
      flag,
      new DisplacementMapFilter(
        _perlinNoise,
        new Point(),
        BitmapDataChannel.RED,
        BitmapDataChannel.RED,
        40,
        60
      )
    );
```

```
        ImageUtil.copyChannel(
          flag,
          _perlinNoise,
          BitmapDataChannel.ALPHA
        );
        flag.draw(
          _perlinNoise,
          null,
          new ColorTransform(1, 1, 1, 0.5),
          BlendMode.HARDLIGHT
        );
        _loadedBitmap.bitmapData = flag;
      }

      private function onSpriteEnterFrame(event:Event):void {
        waveFlag();
      }

    }

  }
```

The first new line in waveFlag() copies the alpha channel from the flag into the _perlinNoise bitmap data so that the overlay will have the same alpha as the flag and so will only be visible on the opaque pixels. Once the alpha channel is copied, we can call draw() to copy the _perlinNoise data into the flag, setting it at 50 percent opacity with a HARDLIGHT blend mode, which will brighten or darken the flag's colors based on the light and dark regions in the overlay. The result is a flag with apparent depth as it waves in the wind!

Bringing rain

There's a lot of fun to be had simulating water effects in ActionScript, from producing ripples in images, to applying distortions to simulate light refracting through water or generating caustics, to creating pooling liquids that interact with each other. One area that I feel could help tremendously when building animations is the simple generation of precipitation effects that do not require the overhead of a particle system. That way, just as with the fire effect earlier, work could be concentrated on the primary animation while background animation could all be procedurally generated.

The technique I present here involves the animation of multiple planes of precipitation, to help simulate depth and multiple independent particles. It is adaptable for different types of weather effects, as shown in Figures 8-16 and 8-17, demonstrating rain and snow fall.

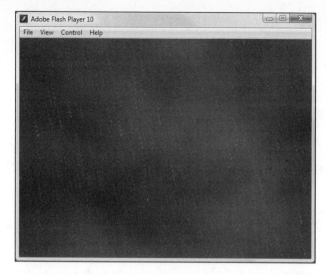

Figure 8-16.
A rainstorm produced by planes of rain droplets procedurally drawn and then animated at separate speeds

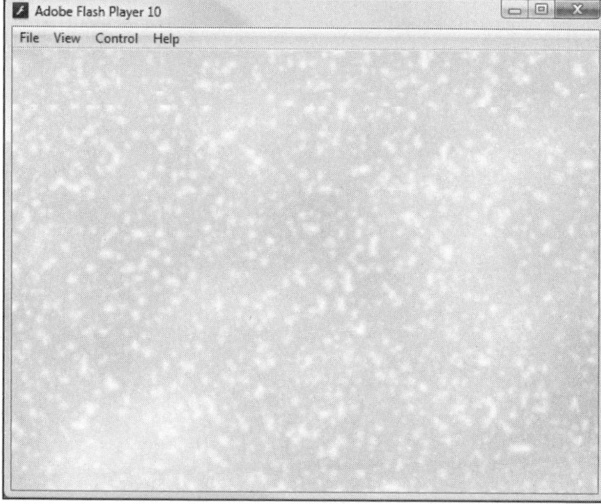

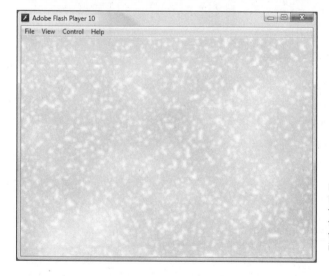

Figure 8-17.
Multiple planes of snow flakes procedurally drawn and then animated independently to create the illusion of independent particles

In this example, we will break down how to produce the rain effect. Don't forget your umbrella!

1. Start with a new document in Flash named `Rainstorm.fla` or an ActionScript project in Flex Builder saved as Rainstorm. The main ActionScript class should be named `Rainstorm.as`.
2. For this project, we will be using the aether library as well, so import `aether.swc` into your FLA or Flex Builder project from this chapter's files.

3. Start your Rainstorm class with the following code:

```
package {

  import aether.utils.Adjustments;

  import flash.display.Bitmap;
  import flash.display.BitmapData;
  import flash.display.BitmapDataChannel;
  import flash.display.Sprite;

  [SWF(width=550, height=400, backgroundColor=0x000000)]

  public class Rainstorm extends Sprite {

    public function Rainstorm() {
      makeSky();
    }

    private function makeSky():void {
      var sky:BitmapData = new BitmapData(
        stage.stageWidth,
        stage.stageHeight
      );
      sky.perlinNoise(
        250,
        200,
        3,
        Math.random(),
        false,
        true,
        BitmapDataChannel.RED,
        true
      );
      Adjustments.adjustContrast(sky, -0.8);
      Adjustments.adjustBrightness(sky, -100);
      addChild(new Bitmap(sky));
    }


  }

}
```

We start off nice and easy in this last example by calling a `makeSky()` method from our constructor that draws grayscale Perlin noise of three octaves and then lowers its contrast and darkens it before adding it to a Bitmap instance and the stage. The result is a dark and stormy night sky, as shown in Figure 8-18. Snoopy would be proud.

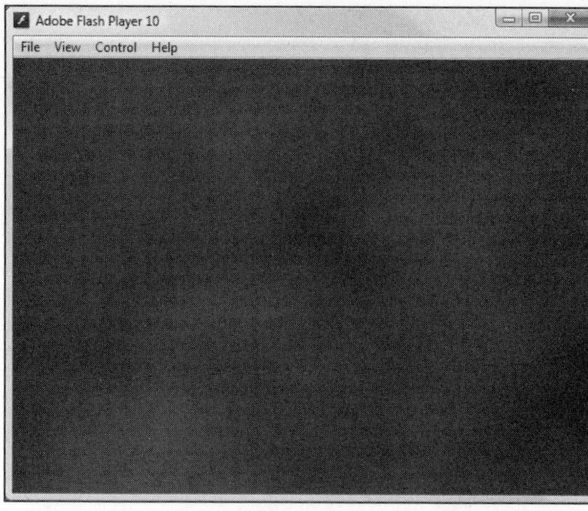

Figure 8-18. Perlin noise and some brightness and contrast adjustment used to create a dark and stormy night sky

4. In this step, we create the two planes we will use for the rain effect. By creating two planes and animating them at different rates and at slightly different directional vectors, we create an effect with a believable illusion of depth and randomization.

```
package {

  import aether.utils.Adjustments;
  import aether.utils.ImageUtil;

  import flash.display.Bitmap;
  import flash.display.BitmapData;
  import flash.display.BitmapDataChannel;
  import flash.display.BlendMode;
  import flash.display.Sprite;
  import flash.filters.BlurFilter;

  [SWF(width=550, height=400, backgroundColor=0x000000)]

  public class Rainstorm extends Sprite {

    private var _rainData0:BitmapData;
    private var _rainData1:BitmapData;
    private var _rainBitmap0:Bitmap;
    private var _rainBitmap1:Bitmap;

    public function Rainstorm() {
      makeSky();
      makeRainPlanes();
    }

    private function makeSky():void {
      // this method body is unchanged
    }
```

```
    private function makeRainPlanes():void {
      _rainData0 = getRainTexture(0.4);
      _rainBitmap0 = new Bitmap(_rainData0.clone());
      _rainBitmap0.blendMode = BlendMode.SCREEN;
      addChild(_rainBitmap0);
      _rainData1 = getRainTexture(0.5);
      _rainBitmap1 = new Bitmap(_rainData1.clone());
      _rainBitmap1.blendMode = BlendMode.SCREEN;
      addChild(_rainBitmap1);
    }

    private function getRainTexture(density:Number):BitmapData {
      var noise:BitmapData = new BitmapData(
        stage.stageWidth,
        stage.stageHeight
      );
      var perlin:BitmapData = noise.clone();
      noise.noise(
        int(new Date()),
        0,
        255,
        BitmapDataChannel.RED,
        true
      );
      ImageUtil.applyFilter(noise, new BlurFilter(2, 2));
      var black:uint = 240 - 127*density;
      var mid:uint = (240 - black)/2 + black;
      Adjustments.setLevels(noise, black, mid, 240);
      perlin.perlinNoise(
        50,
        50,
        2,
        Math.random(),
        false,
        true,
        BitmapDataChannel.RED,
        true
      );
      noise.draw(perlin, null, null, BlendMode.MULTIPLY);
      perlin.dispose();
      ImageUtil.applyFilter(noise, new BlurFilter(1, 2));
      return noise;
    }

  }

}
```

We will be creating two separate planes for the rainfall, and for these, we declare four separate properties: two for the bitmap data (`_rainData0` and `_rainData1`) and two for the bitmaps that will be displayed (`_rainBitmap0` and `_rainBitmap1`).

In the new makeRainPlanes() method that is called from the constructor, the two BitmapData instances are created using the getRainTexture() method and passing in two different densities. The density controls how many droplets will appear in the plane, with higher numbers producing more droplets. We'll look at that method next, but after the bitmap data is created, a clone is passed to a Bitmap constructor, and the resulting bitmap is added to the stage after setting its blend mode to SCREEN so that only the light rain droplets are visible. We clone this to keep the bitmap data independent of the bitmap so that we can perform additional manipulations on the rendered copy that won't affect the original bitmap data.

To create a rain plane, the getRainTexture() method is called. The technique used here to create the droplets is the same technique employed by the aether StarsTexture that we used last chapter to create the star field. Basically, we generate noise within some bitmap data, blur it slightly so that there are more intermediate shades of gray, and then adjust the levels to darken the overall image and increase its contrast. The density passed to the method determines how dark to make the image, which affects how many white spots are visible. For instance, the density of 0.4 results in the following when plugged into the method:

```
var black:uint = 240 - 127*0.4;
var mid:uint = (240 - 89)/2 + 89;
Adjustments.setLevels(noise, 89, 164, 240);
```

The result of this levels adjustment is a considerably darker image overall, with anything that was originally over a brightness level of 240 becoming pure white. This produces bright spots over a generally black background.

Once the levels of the noise have been adjusted, we generate some Perlin noise and then apply this as an overlay using the MULTIPLY blend mode to the dotted white noise to create more levels of light and dark. Finally, the dotted white noise is blurred slightly on the y axis to slightly elongate the droplets and then the bitmap data is returned from the method. The result of the two planes added to the stage is shown in Figure 8-19. You can see how this could be easily applied as a star field effect as well.

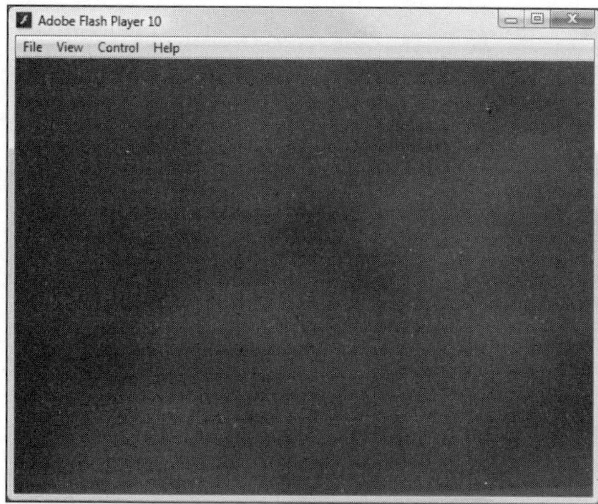

Figure 8-19.
The two planes of rain droplets are generated and added to the stage. When not in motion, the effect is like a star field.

At this point, we are nearly finished, having created the textures we need for the rain. All that is left is to animate these each frame.

5. To animate the planes, we simply need to apply the aether TranslateEffect, which handles wrapping the bitmap data as it scrolls by copying the necessary regions from one side of the image to the other as it scrolls out of the rectangle. To add a little bit more visual interest, instead of just copying over the previous rendering of the rain, we overlay the new data using a blend mode of SCREEN so that you can still see the previous rendering, creating streaks of rain. Add the bold lines that follow to your class to achieve this effect:

```
package {

  import aether.effects.transformations.TranslateEffect;
  import aether.utils.Adjustments;
  import aether.utils.ImageUtil;

  import flash.display.Bitmap;
  import flash.display.BitmapData;
  import flash.display.BitmapDataChannel;
  import flash.display.BlendMode;
  import flash.display.Sprite;
  import flash.events.Event;
  import flash.filters.BlurFilter;

  [SWF(width=550, height=400, backgroundColor=0x000000)]

  public class Rainstorm extends Sprite {

    private var _rainData0:BitmapData;
    private var _rainData1:BitmapData;
    private var _rainBitmap0:Bitmap;
    private var _rainBitmap1:Bitmap;
    private var _blackRect:BitmapData;

    public function Rainstorm() {
      makeSky();
      makeRainPlanes();
      _blackRect = new BitmapData(stage.stageWidth, stage.stageHeight,➥
true, 0x44000000);
      addEventListener(Event.ENTER_FRAME, onSpriteEnterFrame);
    }

    private function makeSky():void {
      // this method body is unchanged
    }

    private function makeRainPlanes():void {
      // this method body is unchanged
    }

    private function getRainTexture(density:Number):BitmapData {
      // this method body is unchanged
    }
```

```
    private function onSpriteEnterFrame(event:Event):void {
      new TranslateEffect(1, 6, true).apply(_rainData0);
      _rainBitmap0.bitmapData.draw(_blackRect);
      _rainBitmap0.bitmapData.draw(
        _rainData0,
        null,
        null,
        BlendMode.SCREEN
      );
      new TranslateEffect(2, 8, true).apply(_rainData1);
      _rainBitmap1.bitmapData.draw(_blackRect);
      _rainBitmap1.bitmapData.draw(
        _rainData1,
        null,
        null,
        BlendMode.SCREEN
      );
    }

  }

}
```

In the constructor, before we set up the listener for the ENTER_FRAME event that will handle redrawing the images to create the animation, we instantiate a new BitmapData instance that is the size of our stage with black pixels set at a low opacity. What are these used for exactly? Well, if you look at onSpriteEnterFrame(), where the animation occurs, the original bitmap data is first translated into a new position, creating the illusion of movement. Before drawing this into our rendered bitmaps on the stage, though, we first draw the black rectangle into these bitmaps so that the previous frame's rain will be darkened before the new rain is drawn. This is what creates slight streaks in the rain as it falls. Try removing these lines, and you will see the result of not drawing the black plane over the previous rendering, which is shown in Figure 8-20. This effect is interesting as well, but as a rainstorm, it's pretty Biblical in its intensity!

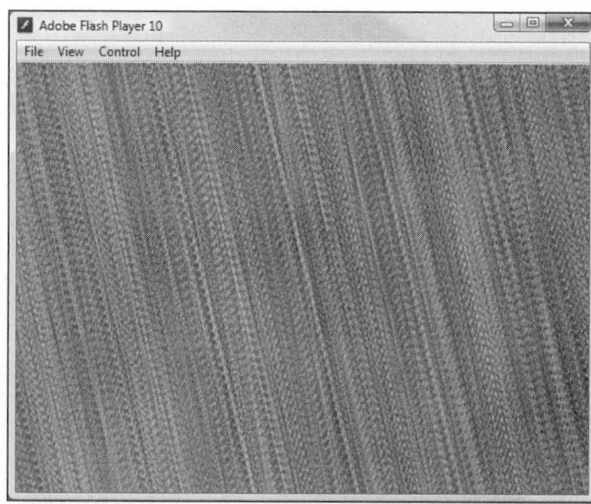

Figure 8-20.
When previous renderings of the rain are not reduced in opacity, the results are long, continuous streaks of rain.

You can create other precipitation effects with this multiple planes technique, including a snowfall, as demonstrated in the `Snowfall.swf` available in this chapter's files. The major difference in the Snowfall class is that the planes do not use noise to generate the particles, but instead use BitmapData's `pixelDissolve()` method to create scattered white pixels on a transparent image that are then scaled up and blurred. The movement uses the aether TranslateEffect as the Rainstorm example did, but instead of advancing the planes in a single direction, the `Math.sin()` method is used to create some back-and-forth movement.

Summary

There is no doubt that animation is a skill requiring diligence, patience, and loads of talent, but procedural image manipulation can help out with some of the secondary effects tasks that are often needed and thus free up the animator to concentrate on the primary, and more important, animation. In this chapter, we've looked at several techniques for creating natural effects and used the four classical elements in nature as the inspiration for the examples. For fire, we explored how Perlin noise could be used to distort any image to set it on fire. For earth, we generated a stone texture using methods that could be applied to any object. For air, we took the Perlin noise distortion technique further and demonstrated how we could limit the distortion to certain regions of an image using a gradient overlay, producing the animation for a flag blowing in the wind. Finally, for water, we used multiple planes of generated textures to simulate precipitation without the need for a particle engine.

Not only were these interesting effects with practical applications, but they also took advantage of a whole host of classes and methods we explored in the earlier chapters of this book. We used the drawing API to create lines and gradient shapes; we used filters and blend modes extensively on the images, and nearly everything was based around manipulation of BitmapData instances, using the methods we covered in depth in Chapters 3 and 4. Hopefully, you can begin to see how complex effects can be achieved through the creative combination of these graphics classes and methods. We will take this even further in the next chapter where we look at how we can apply our image effect knowledge to text as well. Obviously, you can now set a word on fire, turn it to stone, flap it in the wind, or soak it in a storm, but there is still so much more we can do to those malleable little letters!

Chapter 9

TEXT EFFECTS

The World Wide Web began as a way to exchange textual data. Today, it is used for everything from a business and social networking facilitator to a game and media entertainment destination to a means of completing your collection of knitted toaster cozies in the shape of farm animals (or is that just me?). But even as the Web has evolved and offered support for additional media types like images, audio, and video, its main form of content has remained, and probably will remain for years and years to come, text.

When considering text within the Flash Player in the context of a book on image manipulation, it's important to understand that whether we are dealing with text or a static image or a video, what we have at the smallest level is a pixel containing color information. For text, collections of pixels make up letters and symbols, then words and sentences, and then possibly lyrics to a Flaming Lips song or a recipe for Bundt cake, but in the end, it is all pixels. As such, everything we have covered thus far on image manipulation is as applicable to text as it is with the static images we have generally been dealing with. In fact, several of the examples previously presented obviously took advantage of the dynamic text capabilities of ActionScript and the Flash Player, such as the scrolling 3D text or the text extrusion, both demonstrated in Chapter 6.

In this chapter, we will be looking at effects that could certainly be applied to nontext images but are really tailored for textual data and, more specifically, textual data that could be presented as titles in an animation, a game, or a presentation (as opposed to large chunks of fascinating paragraph data like you are reading now). These effects can help transform text dynamically generated at runtime into something a little more exciting and interesting than what is available when only using vector fonts in the Flash Player without the need to create and load in custom images into your SWFs. This will help to keep the size of your files down and limit the amount of time needed to prepare external files for use in your applications.

Since rendered text in the player simply becomes pixels on the screen, it is possible to use ActionScript to create text, or allow a user to input text, and then transform that text into a manipulated image with a little more punch and visual interest. So, enough words! Or, rather, enough nonmanipulated words! Let's do some pixel twisting and explore just what is possible when you stop seeing text as text and start reading between the pixels.

Distressing text

The last time I sat down and put together a version of my personal web site, found at `http://www.27Bobs.com`, the drawing API had just been released in the latest version of the Flash Player. I can't believe it's been that long. I should consider it a good thing that my work and life have kept me away from updating it since, but even though it is older now than children entering kindergarten, there is one aspect I was always pleased with. Inspired by this new-fangled drawing API that Flash offered, I wanted to create a site that was a bit messier than what was the norm by treating it like a chalkboard or sketchpad with a lot of scribbles, all dynamically drawn and animated. The result is shown in Figure 9-1 (I can always hope I have updated it by the time this book hits the shelves, but I am realistic about that possibility!).

For the font on the site, I chose one I felt had a hand-drawn quality to complete the effect. The result is nice, but today, you can go so much further with creating a site with an organic, natural feel to combat the crispness, gradients, and reflective surfaces of Web 2.0. Of course, you can do this in HTML or in Flash from 2003 if you imported enough images and included fonts containing exorbitant amounts of vector data. Or you could look to BitmapData in ActionScript and what it offers to take images and fonts and dirty them up at runtime.

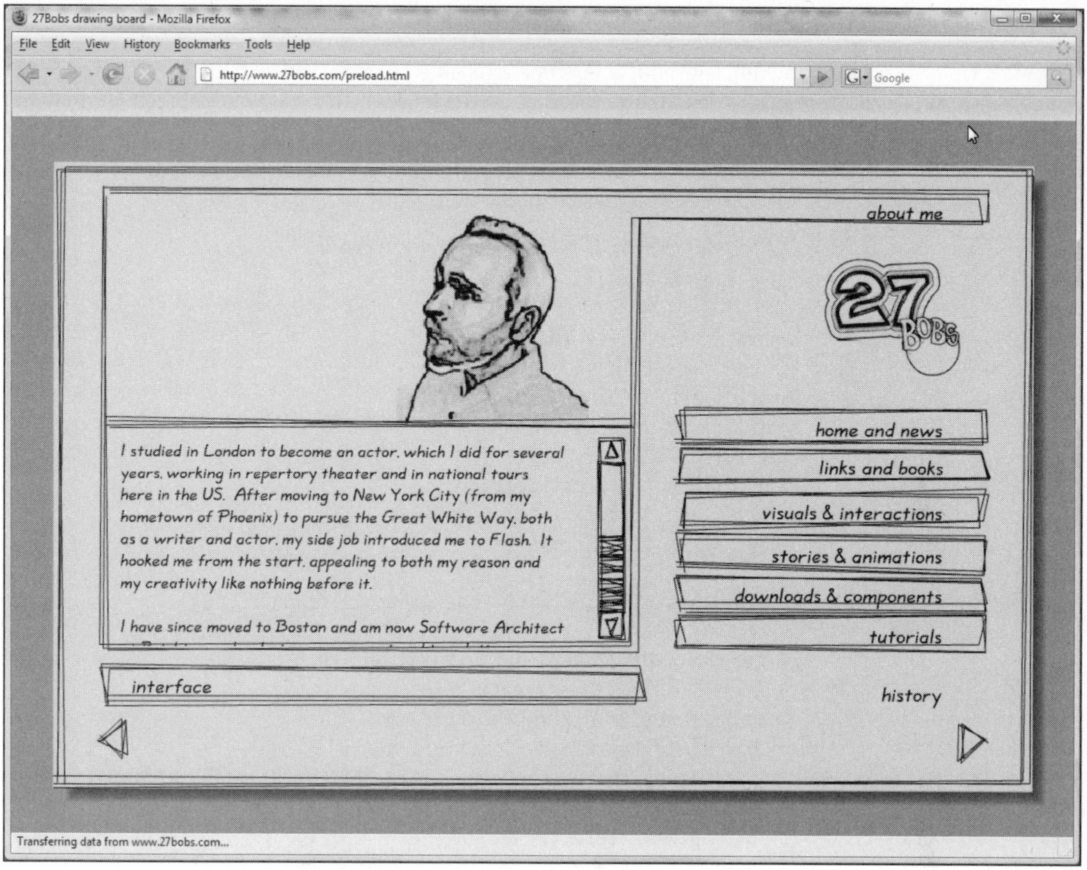

Figure 9-1. The 27Bobs web site with its sketchy interface

Distressing text—taking a clean, crisp vector font and running it through a grinder—can be done in a number of ways. The effect we will walk through in this section is just one way to handle it, but one you could tweak and expand to create any number of variations. The end result of this next example can be seen in Figure 9-2, with the original textfield and the poor, abused copy that has seen better days right below it.

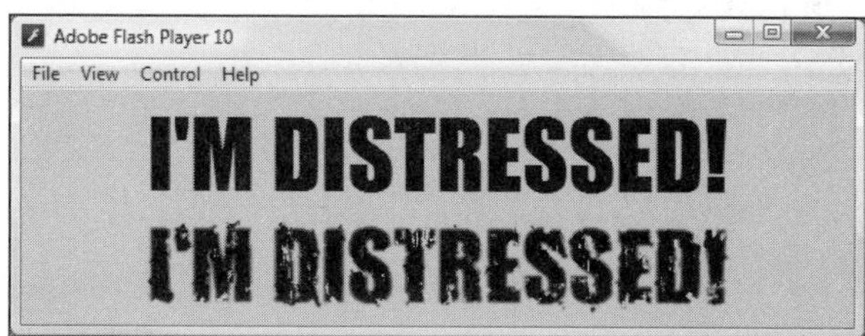

Figure 9-2. Dynamic text on top with its distressed sibling below it

Let's step through exactly how this is done:

1. Start with a new document in Flash named `DistressedText.fla` or an ActionScript project in Flex Builder saved as DistressedText. The main ActionScript class should be named `DistressedText.as`.
2. This example uses the aether library, so import `aether.swc` into your FLA or Flex Builder project from this chapter's files.
3. Start your DistressedText class with the following code:

```
package {

  import aether.utils.ImageUtil;

  import flash.display.Bitmap;
  import flash.display.BitmapData;
  import flash.display.Sprite;
  import flash.text.TextField;
  import flash.text.TextFieldAutoSize;
  import flash.text.TextFormat;

  [SWF(width=550, height=150, backgroundColor=0xCCCCCC)]

  public class DistressedText extends Sprite {

    public function DistressedText() {
      var field:TextField = createField();
      var bitmapData:BitmapData = ImageUtil.getBitmapData(field);
      var bitmap:Bitmap = new Bitmap(bitmapData);
      bitmap.x = field.x;
      bitmap.y = stage.stageHeight - bitmap.height;
      addChild(bitmap);
    }

    private function createField():TextField {
      var field:TextField = new TextField();
      field.selectable = false;
      field.defaultTextFormat = new TextFormat("Impact", 60);
      field.autoSize = TextFieldAutoSize.LEFT;
      field.text = "I'M DISTRESSED!";
      field.x = (stage.stageWidth - field.width)/2;
      addChild(field);
      return field;
    }

  }

}
```

Here, in our constructor, we call the custom `createField()` method to instantiate and add a textfield to the stage. This field uses the font Impact, so if you do not have this font installed, be sure to specify another, preferably thick, font in the `TextFormat`.

The field created is passed to aether's `ImageUtil.getBitmapData()`, which draws the pixels for the textfield into a BitmapData instance. This data is passed to a Bitmap instance and added to the stage below the original textfield. The result of this, with a textfield and a bitmap on the stage, is shown in Figure 9-3.

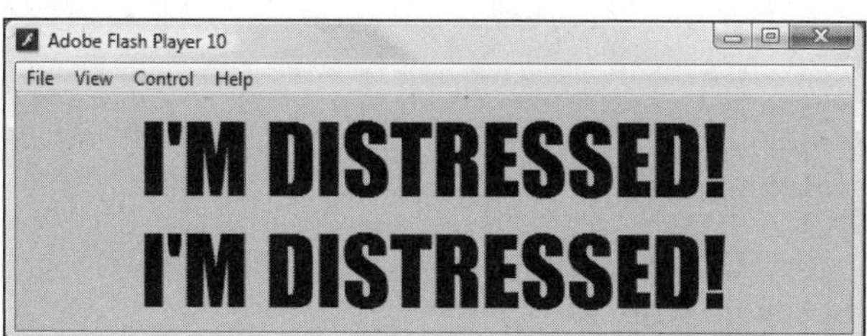

Figure 9-3.
Dynamic text on top with a bitmap copy rendered below it

4. The next bit of code begins the process of distorting the pixels of the text stored in the bitmap data. Add the bold lines to your class.

```
package {

  import aether.utils.Adjustments;
  import aether.utils.ImageUtil;

  import flash.display.Bitmap;
  import flash.display.BitmapData;
  import flash.display.BitmapDataChannel;
  import flash.display.Sprite;
  import flash.filters.DisplacementMapFilter;
  import flash.filters.DisplacementMapFilterMode;
  import flash.geom.Point;
  import flash.text.TextField;
  import flash.text.TextFieldAutoSize;
  import flash.text.TextFormat;

  [SWF(width=550, height=150, backgroundColor=0xCCCCCC)]

  public class DistressedText extends Sprite {

    public function DistressedText() {
      var field:TextField = createField();
      var bitmapData:BitmapData = ImageUtil.getBitmapData(field);
      distressImage(bitmapData, 5);
```

```
    var bitmap:Bitmap = new Bitmap(bitmapData);
    bitmap.x = field.x;
    bitmap.y = stage.stageHeight - bitmap.height;
    addChild(bitmap);
  }

  private function createField():TextField {
    var field:TextField = new TextField();
    field.selectable = false;
    field.defaultTextFormat = new TextFormat("Impact", 60);
    field.autoSize = TextFieldAutoSize.LEFT;
    field.text = "I'M DISTRESSED!";
    field.x = (stage.stageWidth - field.width)/2;
    addChild(field);
    return field;
  }

  private function distressImage(
    bitmapData:BitmapData,
    amount:Number
  ):void {
    var perlin:BitmapData = ➥
new BitmapData(bitmapData.width, bitmapData.height);
    perlin.perlinNoise(
      10,
      10,
      5,
      Math.random(),
      true,
      true,
      BitmapDataChannel.RED,
      true
    );
    Adjustments.setLevels(perlin, 0, 50, 100);
    var displaceX:Number = amount;
    var displaceY:Number = amount*3;
    ImageUtil.applyFilter(
      bitmapData,
      new DisplacementMapFilter(
        perlin,
        new Point(),
        BitmapDataChannel.RED,
        BitmapDataChannel.RED,
        displaceX,
        displaceY,
        DisplacementMapFilterMode.WRAP
      )
    );
```

```
    }

  }

}
```

We have now added a `distressImage()` method that first creates a new BitmapData instance the same size as the image passed to the method. Within this new bitmap data, we draw some Perlin noise of 5 octaves with a high frequency (remember, the 10 for `baseX` and `baseY` controls this). The levels are adjusted on the noise so that contrast and the overall brightness are increased.

```
Adjustments.setLevels(perlin, 0, 50, 100);
```

This noise data is then used as a displacement map on the image passed in. Here, we use an image containing text, but you could do the same for any image. Note that the displacement on the y axis is three times greater than that on the x axis. This is done because letters can be distorted more vertically and still remain legible, whereas horizontal distortion can cause problems in readability. The amount we displace is directly dependent on the `amount` passed to the method.

```
distressImage(bitmapData, 5);
```

A greater `amount` passed in will result in more displacement being applied to the bitmap.

At this point, we have pretty good distortion, as shown in Figure 9-4, but there is still another step we can do to enhance the effect.

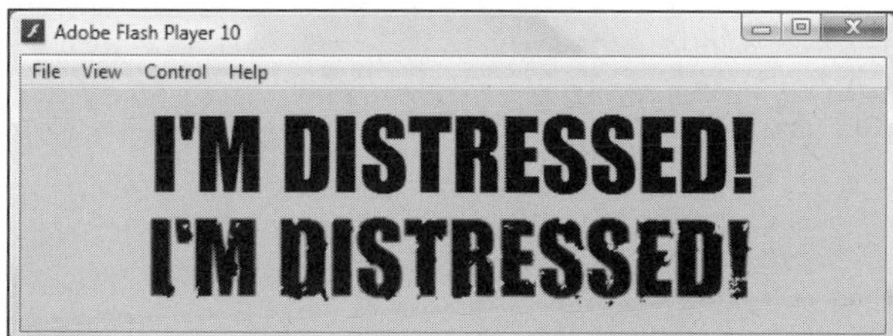

Figure 9-4.
Dynamic text on top with a bitmap below it with some slight distress applied

5. To add a little bit more distress to our text, add the following lines of bold code:

```
package {

  import aether.utils.Adjustments;
  import aether.utils.ImageUtil;

  import flash.display.Bitmap;
  import flash.display.BitmapData;
```

```
import flash.display.BitmapDataChannel;
import flash.display.BlendMode;
import flash.display.Sprite;
import flash.filters.BlurFilter;
import flash.filters.DisplacementMapFilter;
import flash.filters.DisplacementMapFilterMode;
import flash.geom.ColorTransform;
import flash.geom.Point;
import flash.text.TextField;
import flash.text.TextFieldAutoSize;
import flash.text.TextFormat;

[SWF(width=550, height=150, backgroundColor=0xCCCCCC)]

public class DistressedText extends Sprite {

  public function DistressedText() {
    // this method body is unchanged
  }

  private function createField():TextField {
    // this method body is unchanged
  }

  private function distressImage(
    bitmapData:BitmapData,
    amount:Number
  ):void {
    var perlin:BitmapData = ➥
new BitmapData(bitmapData.width, bitmapData.height);
    perlin.perlinNoise(
      10,
      10,
      5,
      Math.random(),
      true,
      true,
      BitmapDataChannel.RED
    );
    Adjustments.setLevels(perlin, 0, 50, 100);
    var displaceX:Number = amount;
    var displaceY:Number = amount*3;
    ImageUtil.applyFilter(
      bitmapData,
      new DisplacementMapFilter(
        perlin,
        new Point(),
        BitmapDataChannel.RED,
        BitmapDataChannel.RED,
```

```
        displaceX,
        displaceY,
        DisplacementMapFilterMode.WRAP
      )
    );

    var noise:BitmapData = ➥
new BitmapData(bitmapData.width, bitmapData.height);
    noise.noise(Math.random(), 0, 255, BitmapDataChannel.RED, true);
    ImageUtil.applyFilter(
      noise,
      new BlurFilter(displaceX, displaceY)
    );
    Adjustments.setLevels(noise, 100, 102, 105);
    var alpha:BitmapData = ImageUtil.getChannelData(
      bitmapData,
      BitmapDataChannel.ALPHA
    );
    alpha.draw(
      noise,
      null,
      new ColorTransform(
        1,
        1,
        1,
        Math.min(1, amount*.2)
      ),
      BlendMode.MULTIPLY
    );
    bitmapData.copyChannel(
      alpha,
      alpha.rect,
      new Point(),
      BitmapDataChannel.RED,
      BitmapDataChannel.ALPHA
    );
  }

}

}
```

In these final lines, we once more create a new BitmapData instance to match the size of the one passed to the method. Within this, we generate some basic grayscale noise (not of the fancy Perlin variety). A blur is applied to this noise, once again blurring more on the y axis than the x axis, and then the levels are adjusted on this noise as well to increase the contrast between the black and white. This is similar to the methods we used to create the rain images in the last chapter.

What is done with this noise? It is used to add some extra opacity variance in the final image, and to do that we need to apply it to the alpha of the distressed image, but at a reduced level. One way to accomplish this is to first retrieve the grayscale representation of the alpha channel of the current distressed image.

```
var alpha:BitmapData = ImageUtil.getChannelData(
  bitmapData,
  BitmapDataChannel.ALPHA
);
```

As discussed in Chapter 7, getChannelData() creates a new image using the data from the requested channel of the specified bitmap in all three color channels of a new BitmapData instance. This produces a grayscale image showing the data from the specified channel of the original image, in this particular case the alpha channel.

We can then draw the noise into this new image but use a ColorTransform instance to reduce its strength by altering the noise's alpha as it is copied.

```
alpha.draw(
  noise,
  null,
  new ColorTransform(
    1,
    1,
    1,
    Math.min(1, amount*.2)
  ),
  BlendMode.MULTIPLY
);
```

Once again, we use the distress amount to control how much this noise affects the alpha. The MULTIPLY blend mode is used so only the darker pixels are applied to the alpha. The result of this is that opacity will only be removed from the distressed image, not added.

At this point, the modified alpha image can be copied back into the alpha channel of the distressed image.

```
bitmapData.copyChannel(
  alpha,
  alpha.rect,
  new Point(),
  BitmapDataChannel.RED,
  BitmapDataChannel.ALPHA
);
```

The red channel is the one copied over, but either of the other two color channels could also be used, since each channel contains the same data in a grayscale image.

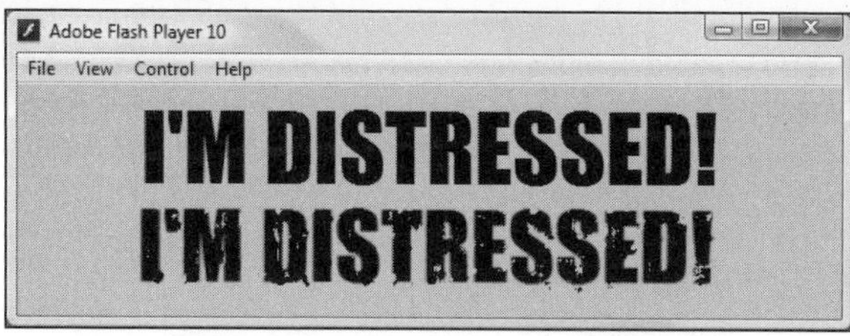

Figure 9-5. Dynamic text on top with a decent amount of distress applied, but the pixels are shifted up and to the left

The resulting effect, as shown in Figure 9-5, is good for the amount of distress we are setting, but there is an issue that will arise when using larger settings. Because of the way displacement maps work, the text will always be shifted up and to the left. The distortion will be obvious on and below the text, but unfortunately, the lack of distortion will be apparent above the text, as shown in Figure 9-6, when a setting of 15 is applied (I've made the textfield itself invisible for this example).

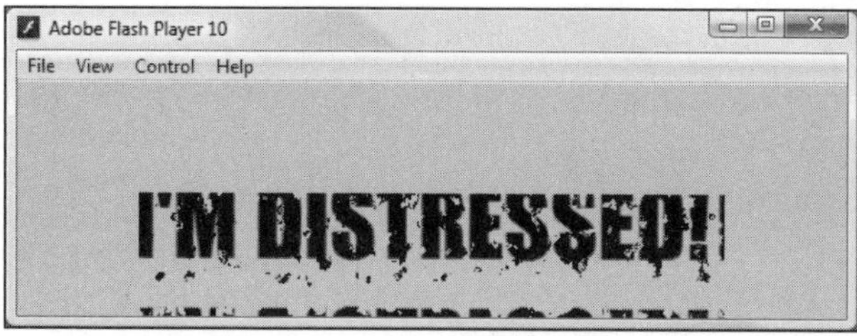

Figure 9-6. A large amount of displacement for the distress effect reveals the limitations.

As you can see, the wrapping of the pixels also becomes an issue. So how do we solve this? Well, if displacement shifts pixels up and to the left, the simple solution is to rotate the bitmap 180 degrees and apply the same displacement to the rotated image. This will shift the pixels back toward their original positions and display a nice amount of distress both above and below the image (once the image is rotated back, of course). We'll take care of this in the next step.

6. Add the following bold lines to complete the class and our example:

```
package {

  import aether.utils.Adjustments;
  import aether.utils.ImageUtil;

  import flash.display.Bitmap;
  import flash.display.BitmapData;
  import flash.display.BitmapDataChannel;
  import flash.display.BlendMode;
  import flash.display.Sprite;
  import flash.filters.BlurFilter;
  import flash.filters.DisplacementMapFilter;
  import flash.filters.DisplacementMapFilterMode;
  import flash.geom.ColorTransform;
  import flash.geom.Matrix;
  import flash.geom.Point;
```

```
  import flash.text.TextField;
  import flash.text.TextFieldAutoSize;
  import flash.text.TextFormat;

  [SWF(width=550, height=150, backgroundColor=0xCCCCCC)]

  public class DistressedText extends Sprite {

    public function DistressedText() {
      var field:TextField = createField();
      var bitmapData:BitmapData = ImageUtil.getBitmapData(field);
      distressImage(bitmapData, 5);
      rotateImage(bitmapData);
      distressImage(bitmapData, 5);
      rotateImage(bitmapData);
      var bitmap:Bitmap = new Bitmap(bitmapData);
      bitmap.x = field.x;
      bitmap.y = stage.stageHeight - bitmap.height;
      addChild(bitmap);
    }

    private function createField():TextField {
      // this method body is unchanged
    }

    private function rotateImage(bitmapData:BitmapData):void {
      var width:Number = bitmapData.width;
      var height:Number = bitmapData.height;
      var matrix:Matrix = new Matrix();
      matrix.rotate(Math.PI);
      matrix.translate(width, height);
      var rotated:BitmapData = ➥
new BitmapData(width, height, true, 0x00000000);
      rotated.draw(bitmapData, matrix);
      bitmapData.copyPixels(rotated, rotated.rect, new Point());
    }

    private function distressImage(
      bitmapData:BitmapData,
      amount:Number
    ):void {
      // this method body is unchanged
    }

  }

}
```

After the image is first distressed in its original position, it is rotated by 180 degrees (`Math.PI` radians), distressed a second time, and then rotated back to its original rotation. At this point, you can compile the movie to see the distressing result.

This method of distressing an image would work equally well for other kinds of images, too (though perhaps you would tweak the lines where the effect is greater on the vertical axis and make this either consistent or configurable). Plus the amount setting allows you to go from subtle effects to a much more pronounced distortion, as shown in Figure 9-7, where our text gets a distress setting of 15. Gritty never looked so pretty!

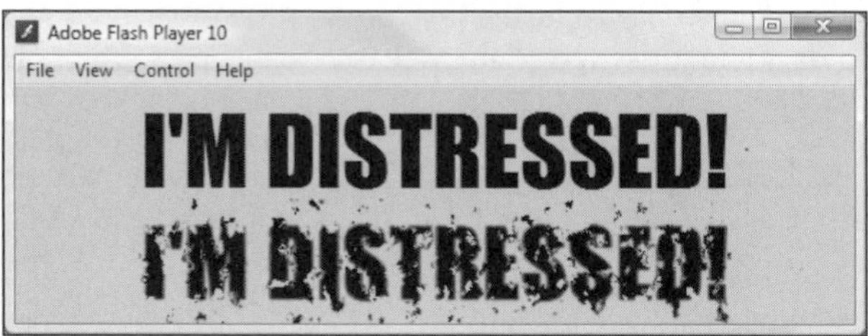

Figure 9-7. A large amount of displacement can now be applied with the result of the distress appearing on all sides of the bitmap without apparent shifting of the letter positions.

Creating custom bevels

In Chapter 2, we looked at the BevelFilter and GradientBevelFilter as ways to apply a bevel to a display object such as a shape or textfield. These are great for simple bevels, but the filters don't offer the ability to create more complex or custom beveled surfaces like a double bevel or a pillow emboss. Thankfully, BitmapData can step in to help us out in creating these types of effects, working hand in hand—if filters had hands, of course—with the bevel bitmap filters to produce some unique effects that can still be applied to dynamic text, saving you from having to load in images for titles when something more than a vector font or standard filter effects are desired.

Have a look at Figure 9-8, which shows three different types of interesting bevels applied to three fields, or rather what originally were fields but have since entered triumphantly into the realm of bitmap data.

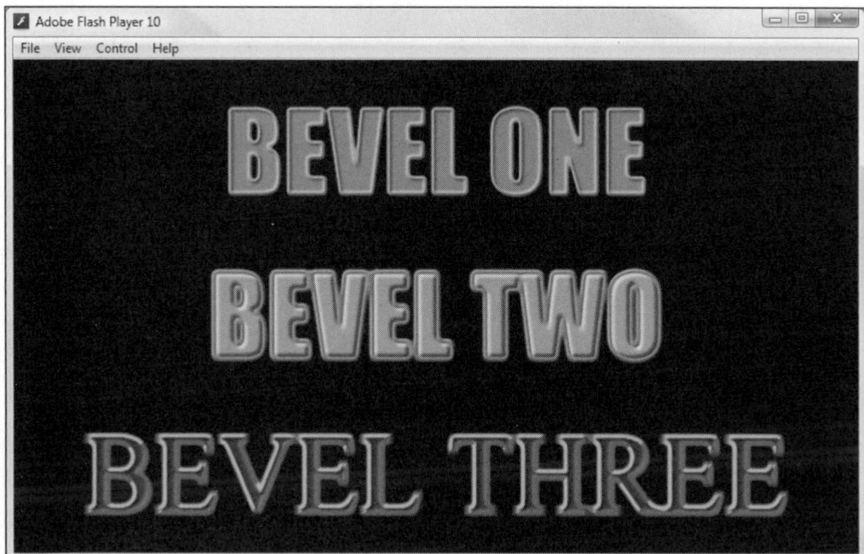

Figure 9-8. Three-layered bevel effects for dynamic textfields using blurred copies with threshold applied to create thicker and thinner layers

The technique we will walk through in this next example will produce these beveled fields. With it, you can produce any number of additional beveled effects with just some slight tweaking of numbers. The basic method is to make duplicates of a field that can be increased and decreased in thickness. Each duplicate can then have different colors or filters applied to create a stacked, complex effect.

I love techniques like this, which open the door to further exploration and discovery. I was taught it back in my Photoshop days and it has served me well, so I gladly pass it on now to you.

1. Start with a new document in Flash named `BeveledText.fla` or an ActionScript project in Flex Builder saved as BeveledText. The main ActionScript class should be named `BeveledText.as`.
2. This example uses the aether library as well, so import `aether.swc` into your FLA or Flex Builder project from this chapter's files.
3. Start your BeveledText class with the following code:

```
package {

  import aether.utils.ImageUtil;

  import flash.display.Bitmap;
  import flash.display.BitmapData;
  import flash.display.BitmapDataChannel;
  import flash.display.Sprite;
  import flash.text.TextField;
  import flash.text.TextFieldAutoSize;
  import flash.text.TextFormat;

  [SWF(width=800, height=450, backgroundColor=0x000000)]

  public class BeveledText extends Sprite {

    public function BeveledText() {
      var field:TextField = createField(
        "BEVEL ONE",
        new TextFormat("Impact", 100)
      );
      var bitmapData:BitmapData = ImageUtil.getBitmapData(field);
      bevelImageOne(bitmapData);
      var bitmap:Bitmap = new Bitmap(bitmapData);
      bitmap.x = (stage.stageWidth - bitmap.width)/2;
      bitmap.y = 20;
      addChild(bitmap);
    }

    private function createField(
      text:String,
      format:TextFormat
    ):TextField {
```

```
      var field:TextField = new TextField();
      field.defaultTextFormat = format;
      field.autoSize = TextFieldAutoSize.LEFT;
      field.text = text;
      return field;
    }

    private function bevelImageOne(source:BitmapData):void {
    }

  }

}
```

This code does not differ much from how the last example on distressed text began. The constructor simply creates a new textfield through a call to a `createField()` method, captures the field's pixel data, and adds this to the stage via a Bitmap instance. The only significant change is that the `createField()` method in this class takes a TextFormat instance as well, which is applied to the textfield. Also, you may note that `field` itself is never added to the stage, just the bitmap.

The text format used here specifies black text, which in itself won't be visible on a black background. That's OK, since it is not the text that we will add to the stage but a filtered bitmap image that will have color applied. In the constructor, a call has been made to the empty `bevelImageOne()` method. This is where we will begin manipulating the bitmap data to add our custom bevel. Let's do that now.

4. Add these bold lines to your class as a start to our beveling effect. These will create a thickened copy of our bitmap data that we can further manipulate:

```
package {

  import aether.utils.Adjustments;
  import aether.utils.ImageUtil;

  import flash.display.Bitmap;
  import flash.display.BitmapData;
  import flash.display.BitmapDataChannel;
  import flash.display.Sprite;
  import flash.filters.BlurFilter;
  import flash.geom.Point;
  import flash.text.TextField;
  import flash.text.TextFieldAutoSize;
  import flash.text.TextFormat;

  [SWF(width=800, height=450, backgroundColor=0x000000)]

  public class BeveledText extends Sprite {

    public function BeveledText() {
      // this method body is unchanged
    }
```

```
private function createField(
  text:String,
  format:TextFormat
):TextField {
  // this method body is unchanged
}

private function bevelImageOne(source:BitmapData):void {
  var destination:BitmapData = new BitmapData(
    source.width,
    source.height,
    true,
    0x00000000
  );
  addBevel(
    source,
    destination,
    0xFFFF9900,
    5,
    90
  );
  ImageUtil.copyPixels(destination, source);
}

private function addBevel(
  source:BitmapData,
  destination:BitmapData,
  fillColor:uint,
  blurAmount:Number,
  threshold:uint
):void {
  var alpha:BitmapData = ImageUtil.getChannelData(
    source,
    BitmapDataChannel.ALPHA
  );
  ImageUtil.applyFilter(
    alpha,
    new BlurFilter(blurAmount, blurAmount)
  );
  Adjustments.setLevels(
    alpha,
    threshold-20,
    threshold,
    threshold+20
  );
  ImageUtil.applyFilter(
    alpha,
    new BlurFilter(1.5, 1.5)
  );
```

```
      var bevel:BitmapData = source.clone();
      bevel.fillRect(bevel.rect, fillColor);
      bevel.copyChannel(
        alpha,
        alpha.rect,
        new Point(),
        BitmapDataChannel.RED,
        BitmapDataChannel.ALPHA
      );
      destination.draw(bevel);
    }

  }

}
```

If you look first at bevelImageOne(), you can see that a duplicate of the original bitmap data is made and saved into the destination variable. The custom addBevel() is then called, passing in the original source, the destination, a color that will be used as a base color for the destination, and two additional parameters for blurAmount and threshold.

These last parameters are better understood if we move into the addBevel() method, which we will be able to reuse for all of our beveled duplicates. The first thing that is done in that method is that we once more use the getChannelData(), just as we did in the last example, to create a grayscale image using the data from one channel of another image. In this case, the grayscale image produced uses the alpha channel from the source.

```
var alpha:BitmapData = ImageUtil.getChannelData(
  source,
  BitmapDataChannel.ALPHA
);
```

This grayscale duplicate is blurred by the blurAmount setting passed to the method. Its levels are adjusted to increase the contrast between the black and white pixels in the image. The adjusted image is blurred slightly again to remove any jaggies.

```
ImageUtil.applyFilter(
  alpha,
  new BlurFilter(blurAmount, blurAmount)
);
Adjustments.setLevels(
  alpha,
  threshold-20,
  threshold,
  threshold+20
);
ImageUtil.applyFilter(
  alpha,
  new BlurFilter(1.5, 1.5)
);
```

The threshold setting that the setLevels() call uses determines how much white vs. black will be visible in the adjusted image. A lower threshold, for instance the 90 setting we use here, means that any pixel that has a brightness of 110 or more (90 + 20) will be made white. A higher threshold will result in more black. Basically, then, by blurring the image then applying a low threshold, we can create thicker copies of our fonts (similar to using the Filter ➤ Other ➤ Minimum setting in Photoshop), while a higher threshold will decrease the thickness (corresponding to Photoshop's Filter ➤ Other ➤ Maximum setting). The more you blur the grayscale image with the blurAmount setting, the more gray pixels you will have to play with using the threshold setting.

Finishing up the addBevel() method, the next lines duplicate the alpha image, just so we have the same size image, and then fill it with the fillColor passed to addBevel().

```
var bevel:BitmapData = source.clone();
bevel.fillRect(bevel.rect, fillColor);
```

This will give us a solid-colored rectangle of the desired color. We use the data from the alpha image to apply opacity to this colored rectangle in order to reveal the color only in the minimized or maximized text, and it is this that is drawn into the destination bitmap.

```
bevel.copyChannel(
  alpha,
  alpha.rect,
  new Point(),
  BitmapDataChannel.RED,
  BitmapDataChannel.ALPHA
);
destination.draw(bevel);
```

If you test the application at this point, you should see something like Figure 9-9. We have created a thicker copy of our text, and the same addBevel() method could be used to create thinner copies as well. Now we can play.

Figure 9-9. A thicker version of the dynamic textfield is created and filled with the desired color.

5. There is nothing wrong with using the BevelFilter to create bevels. It is simple, intuitive, and produces a pleasing result with the right settings. We can take advantage of this filter in conjunction with our expansion or contraction of the opaque pixels of the text to create multiple bevels for a field. To do this, we'll enhance the addBevel() method to take in an additional parameter, the bevel filter to apply. This is handled with the following bold lines:

```
package {

  import aether.utils.Adjustments;
  import aether.utils.ImageUtil;

  import flash.display.Bitmap;
  import flash.display.BitmapData;
  import flash.display.BitmapDataChannel;
  import flash.display.Sprite;
  import flash.filters.BevelFilter;
  import flash.filters.BlurFilter;
  import flash.geom.Point;
  import flash.text.TextField;
  import flash.text.TextFieldAutoSize;
  import flash.text.TextFormat;

  [SWF(width=800, height=450, backgroundColor=0x000000)]

  public class BeveledText extends Sprite {

    public function BeveledText() {
      // this method body is unchanged
    }

    private function createField(
      text:String,
      format:TextFormat
    ):TextField {
      // this method body is unchanged
    }

    private function bevelImageOne(source:BitmapData):void {
      var destination:BitmapData = new BitmapData(
        source.width,
        source.height,
        true,
        0x00000000
      );
      addBevel(
        source,
        destination,
        0xFFFF9900,
        5,
        90,
        new BevelFilter(
          3, 45, 0xFFFFFF, 0.4,
          0x000000, 0.4, 2, 2
        )
      );
      ImageUtil.copyPixels(destination, source);
    }
```

```
    private function addBevel(
      source:BitmapData,
      destination:BitmapData,
      fillColor:uint,
      blurAmount:Number,
      threshold:uint,
      bevelFilter:BevelFilter
    ):void {
      var alpha:BitmapData = ImageUtil.getChannelData(
        source,
        BitmapDataChannel.ALPHA
      );
      ImageUtil.applyFilter(
        alpha,
        new BlurFilter(blurAmount, blurAmount)
      );
      Adjustments.setLevels(
        alpha,
        threshold-20,
        threshold,
        threshold+20
      );
      ImageUtil.applyFilter(
        alpha,
        new BlurFilter(1.5, 1.5)
      );
      var bevel:BitmapData = source.clone();
      bevel.fillRect(bevel.rect, fillColor);
      bevel.copyChannel(
        alpha,
        alpha.rect,
        new Point(),
        BitmapDataChannel.RED,
        BitmapDataChannel.ALPHA
      );
      ImageUtil.applyFilter(bevel, bevelFilter);
      destination.draw(bevel);
    }

  }

}
```

Now addBevel(), in addition to creating thinner or thicker letters, will apply an individual bevel. The one we pass in the preceding code adds a standard inner bevel with a 45-degree angle and a depth of 3. The result, which is fairly subtle, is shown in Figure 9-10.

Figure 9-10.
A slight inner bevel is applied to the image of the thickened textfield.

6. By adding a second, thinner copy of the field on top of this thicker copy, we can create multiple levels of a beveled surface. Add the following lines to create a second layer to our beveled text:

```
package {

  // imports remain unchanged

  [SWF(width=800, height=450, backgroundColor=0x000000)]

  public class BeveledText extends Sprite {

    public function BeveledText() {
      // this method body is unchanged
    }

    private function createField(
      text:String,
      format:TextFormat
    ):TextField {
      // this method body is unchanged
    }

    private function bevelImageOne(source:BitmapData):void {
      var destination:BitmapData = new BitmapData(
        source.width,
        source.height,
        true,
        0x00000000
      );
      addBevel(
        source,
        destination,
        0xFFFF9900,
        5,
        90,
        new BevelFilter(
          3, 45, 0xFFFFFF, 0.4,
          0x000000, 0.4, 2, 2
        )
      );
```

```
      addBevel(
        source,
        destination,
        0xFFCC7700,
        5,
        210,
        new BevelFilter(
          2, 45, 0x000000, 0.8,
          0xFFFFFF, 0.8, 3, 3
        )
      );
      ImageUtil.copyPixels(destination, source);
    }

    private function addBevel(
      source:BitmapData,
      destination:BitmapData,
      fillColor:uint,
      blurAmount:Number,
      threshold:uint,
      bevelFilter:BevelFilter
    ):void {
      // this method body is unchanged
    }

  }

}
```

Here, we simply draw another beveled image onto the first beveled image layer. For this call to addBevel(), we pass the same blur amount but set the threshold to be much higher, which will result in thinner letters. The color for the layer is set to be a slightly darker orange, and the bevel we apply reverses the highlight and shadow colors with the result that it looks as if the light is hitting the letters from the bottom right (we also could have changed the angle instead of the bevel colors). With the darker, thinner letters receiving light from the opposite direction than the thicker, lighter letters, the illusion is one of an inset surface with a raised, rounded beveled edge, as shown in Figure 9-11.

Figure 9-11. A second, thinner layer is added to the thicker layer with the bevel lighting reversed, creating an inner bevel effect.

7. At this point, we can just play with adding different fields and more beveled layers. This next bit of code adds a second bitmap with three layers:

```
package {

  import aether.utils.Adjustments;
  import aether.utils.ImageUtil;

  import flash.display.Bitmap;
  import flash.display.BitmapData;
  import flash.display.BitmapDataChannel;
  import flash.display.Sprite;
  import flash.filters.BevelFilter;
  import flash.filters.BitmapFilterQuality;
  import flash.filters.BitmapFilterType;
  import flash.filters.BlurFilter;
  import flash.geom.Point;
  import flash.text.TextField;
  import flash.text.TextFieldAutoSize;
  import flash.text.TextFormat;

  [SWF(width=800, height=450, backgroundColor=0x000000)]

  public class BeveledText extends Sprite {

    public function BeveledText() {
      var field:TextField = createField(
        "BEVEL ONE",
        new TextFormat("Impact", 100)
      );
      var bitmapData:BitmapData = ImageUtil.getBitmapData(field);
      bevelImageOne(bitmapData);
      var bitmap:Bitmap = new Bitmap(bitmapData);
      bitmap.x = (stage.stageWidth - bitmap.width)/2;
      bitmap.y = 20;
      addChild(bitmap);

      field = createField(
        "BEVEL TWO",
        new TextFormat("Impact", 100)
      );
      bitmapData = ImageUtil.getBitmapData(field);
      bevelImageTwo(bitmapData);
      bitmap = new Bitmap(bitmapData);
      bitmap.x = (stage.stageWidth - bitmap.width)/2;
      bitmap.y = stage.stageHeight/3 + 20;
      addChild(bitmap);
    }

    private function createField(
      text:String,
      format:TextFormat
    ):TextField {
```

```
  // method body is unchanged
}

private function bevelImageOne(source:BitmapData):void {
  // method body is unchanged
}

private function bevelImageTwo(source:BitmapData):void {
  var destination:BitmapData = new BitmapData(
    source.width,
    source.height,
    true,
    0x00000000
  );
  addBevel(
    source,
    destination,
    0xFF5484b4,
    8,
    50,
    new BevelFilter(
      2, 45, 0xFFFFFF, 0.8,
      0x000000, 0.8, 2, 2
    )
  );
  addBevel(
    source,
    destination,
    0xFFFFFFFF,
    6,
    200,
    new BevelFilter(
      2, 225, 0xFFFFFF, 0.5,
      0x000000, 0.5, 1.5, 1.5, 1,
      BitmapFilterQuality.HIGH, BitmapFilterType.OUTER, true
    )
  );
  addBevel(
    source,
    destination,
    0xFF6AA6E3,
    6,
    200,
    new BevelFilter(
      4, 45, 0xFFFFFF, 0.7,
      0x000000, 0.7, 2, 2
    )
  );
  ImageUtil.copyPixels(destination, source);
}
```

```
    private function addBevel(
      source:BitmapData,
      destination:BitmapData,
      fillColor:uint,
      blurAmount:Number,
      threshold:uint,
      bevelFilter:BevelFilter
    ):void {
      // method body is unchanged
    }

  }

}
```

With this second image, three layers are created, with the first being thickest with a standard, soft inner bevel applied and the other two layers set to the same size. Why the same size? Well, if you look at the bevel applied to the second layer, you will see that its type is set to OUTER with knockout set to true.

```
new BevelFilter(
  2, 225, 0xFFFFFF, 0.5,
  0x000000, 0.5, 1.5, 1.5, 1,
  BitmapFilterQuality.HIGH, BitmapFilterType.OUTER, true
)
```

This layer is being used only to create an outer bevel for the thinner text but does not itself have a fill. The fill, and an additional inner bevel, is being provided by the third layer. The result of this three-level layering is a pillow emboss, as shown in Figure 9-12.

Figure 9-12.
A pillow emboss effect is created from two layered images derived from the same textfield.

8. As a final example, we'll create a more chiseled bevel with the following bold code, which will complete our class:

```
package {

  // imports remain unchanged

  [SWF(width=800, height=450, backgroundColor=0x000000)]

  public class BeveledText extends Sprite {

    public function BeveledText() {
      var field:TextField = createField(
        "BEVEL ONE",
        new TextFormat("Impact", 100)
      );
```

```
    var bitmapData:BitmapData = ImageUtil.getBitmapData(field);
    bevelImageOne(bitmapData);
    var bitmap:Bitmap = new Bitmap(bitmapData);
    bitmap.x = (stage.stageWidth - bitmap.width)/2;
    bitmap.y = 20;
    addChild(bitmap);

    field = createField(
      "BEVEL TWO",
      new TextFormat("Impact", 100)
    );
    bitmapData = ImageUtil.getBitmapData(field);
    bevelImageTwo(bitmapData);
    bitmap = new Bitmap(bitmapData);
    bitmap.x = (stage.stageWidth - bitmap.width)/2;
    bitmap.y = stage.stageHeight/3 + 20;
    addChild(bitmap);

    field = createField(
      "BEVEL THREE",
      new TextFormat("Times New Roman", 100)
    );
    bitmapData = ImageUtil.getBitmapData(field);
    bevelImageThree(bitmapData);
    bitmap = new Bitmap(bitmapData);
    bitmap.x = (stage.stageWidth - bitmap.width)/2;
    bitmap.y = stage.stageHeight*2/3 + 20;
    addChild(bitmap);
  }

  private function createField(
    text:String,
    format:TextFormat
  ):TextField {
    // this method body is unchanged
  }

  private function bevelImageOne(source:BitmapData):void {
    // this method body is unchanged
  }

  private function bevelImageTwo(source:BitmapData):void {
    // this method body is unchanged
  }

  private function bevelImageThree(source:BitmapData):void {
    var destination:BitmapData = new BitmapData(
      source.width,
      source.height,
```

```
        true,
        0x00000000
      );
      addBevel(
        source,
        destination,
        0xFF56B77D,
        10,
        30,
        new BevelFilter(
          3, 45, 0xFFFFFF, 0.4,
          0x000000, 0.4, 2, 2,
          80, BitmapFilterQuality.HIGH
        )
      );
      addBevel(
        source,
        destination,
        0xFF142B1D,
        4,
        140,
        new BevelFilter(
          3, 45, 0x000000, 0.8,
          0xFFFFFF, 0.4, 2, 2,
          1, BitmapFilterQuality.HIGH
        )
      );
      ImageUtil.copyPixels(destination, source);
    }

    private function addBevel(
      source:BitmapData,
      destination:BitmapData,
      fillColor:uint,
      blurAmount:Number,
      threshold:uint,
      bevelFilter:BevelFilter
    ):void {
      // this method body is unchanged
    }

  }

}
```

For this third image, the strength is set to 80 for the thicker layer, which produces a chiseled bevel effect. Note that the quality has been set to HIGH, as I generally feel this produces a nicer result with this type of bevel. Using a similar technique as with the first field, the thinner bevel has its highlight and shadow colors reversed to create an inset in the letters. The result of this is shown in Figure 9-13.

Figure 9-13. A chiseled look is given to an image derived from a textfield using the layered bevel technique.

This method of layering different thicknesses of beveled shapes can produce any number of unique beveling effects, but you don't have to stop there. If you generalize the `addBevel()` method to simply expand or contract the opaque pixels in a shape and then apply any number of bitmap filters, from glows to shadows to even shaders, the combinations would be nearly endless. In fact, that's just what I did in the file `StackedText.as` in this chapter's files. The result, which does not use any beveling filters but instead uses a mix of blurs, glows, and drop shadows, is shown in Figure 9-14.

Figure 9-14. Instead of just using bevels, these images had blurs, glows, and drop shadows applied to the layers to create these effects.

More play would result in more effects. That's a great reason to play.

Building a text animation engine

Back in 2003, I was a contributing author to the friends of ED book *Flash MX Components Most Wanted* (ISBN: 978-1-59059-178-9). The component I offered was called

PuppetStrings:transitions, one in an intended series of components (a series that ended in two and a half, I should add) dealing with the manipulation of text.

The transitions component, shown in Figure 9-15, offered an interface in which you could specify animations that would be applied individually to every letter in a dynamic textfield located in your SWF.

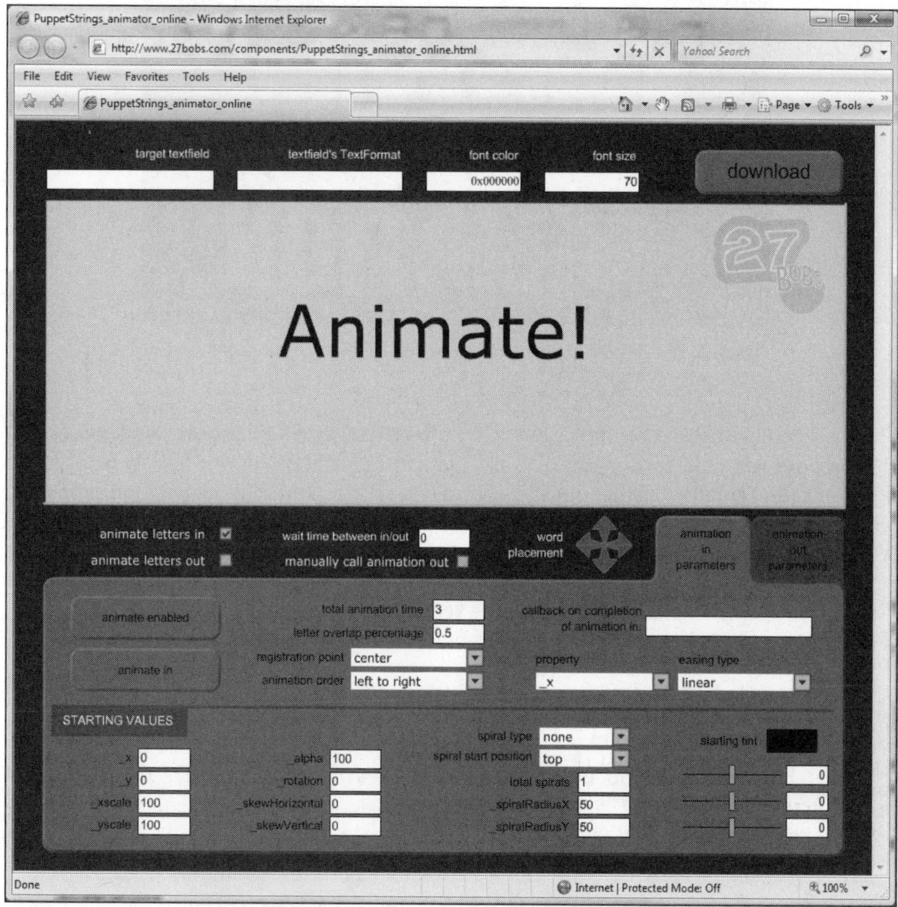

Figure 9-15. The PuppetStrings:transitions component interface that aided in animation of individual letters in a dynamic textfield

These animations could vary from position translations, to altering opacity, to more complex operations like skewing and spiraling in. Back in the days of Flash MX, this required creating nested movie clips and instantiating dynamic textfields within these with an embedded font in which to place each individual letter. It was a pain, which is why I found the component so useful, since it handled all the grunt work for me. Today, however, this can all be taken care of in a single, small method using BitmapData. I love today.

For a look at the finished effect we will be creating, open `TextAnimationEngine.swf` from this chapter's files. A looping animation has been set up that animates in the letters of a single field using 3D matrix transformations, bitmap filters, and alpha and scale animations. Three captures of the same animation are shown in Figure 9-16.

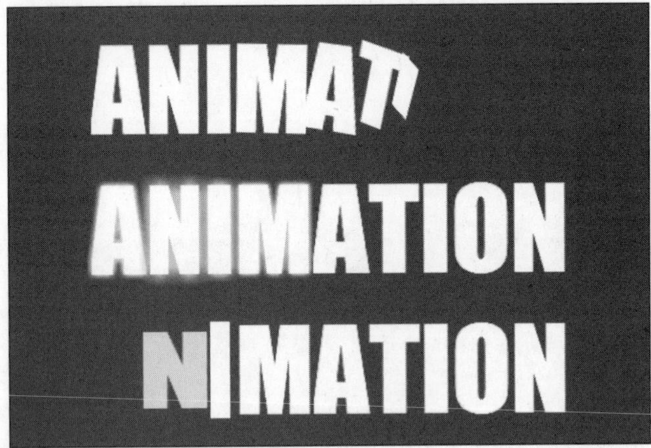

Figure 9-16. Three frames in an animation of letters from a textfield, which were drawn into BitmapData instances

Once again, like the last example, this is an effect that offers countless permutations. In the class we will walk through next, I use the aeon animation library heavily in order to complete the animated effect, but it is not reliant on this library at all and could be used with any other library or homegrown solution. The basic technique is in how the individual letters of a word are broken up and positioned so that each may be animated separately. How you then animate those letters is up to you, and because this is so open-ended it is not even primarily an animation effect. The technique would also allow you to easily apply different position offsets or colors or even bitmap filters to individual letters in a field.

For now, though, let's look at how this might be used for animation. Like most examples involving text, it all starts off with a textfield:

1. Start with a new document in Flash named `TextAnimationEngine.fla` or an ActionScript project in Flex Builder saved as TextAnimationEngine. The main ActionScript class should be named `TextAnimationEngine.as`.
2. This example uses both the aeon and aether libraries, so import both SWCs into your FLA or your Flex Builder project from this chapter's files.
3. Start your TextAnimationEngine class with the following code:

```
package {

  import aeon.AnimationSequence;

  import flash.display.Sprite;
  import flash.text.TextField;
  import flash.text.TextFieldAutoSize;
  import flash.text.TextFormat;
```

```
  [SWF(width=600, height=400, backgroundColor=0x333333)]

  public class TextAnimationEngine extends Sprite {

    public function TextAnimationEngine() {
      var field:TextField = createField();
      var letters:Vector.<Sprite> = createLetterBitmaps(field);
      animateLetters(letters);
    }

    private function createField():TextField {
      var field:TextField = new TextField();
      field.defaultTextFormat = ➥
new TextFormat("Impact", 100, 0xFFFFFF);
      field.autoSize = TextFieldAutoSize.LEFT;
      field.text = "ANIMATION";
      field.x = (stage.stageWidth - field.width)/2;
      field.y = (stage.stageHeight - field.height)/2;
      return field;
    }

    private function createLetterBitmaps(
      field:TextField
    ):Vector.<Sprite> {
    }

    private function animateLetters(letters:Vector.<Sprite>):void {
    }

  }

}
```

This code won't compile as is, since we need to provide a return value from the `createLetterBitmaps()` method, but before we do that, let's have a look at exactly what this code will do.

Just as in the previous examples in this chapter, we begin by creating and positioning a textfield using a custom `createField()` method. Note that the field isn't actually ever added to the stage. The remaining two lines in the constructor call two methods that at the present time are empty. The first, `createLetterBitmaps()`, will take care of creating individual Bitmap instances for each letter in the field and placing these into a vector. The vector, you may notice, is actually of Sprite instances, and the reason for this is that we will need to nest the bitmaps within sprites in order to alter their registration points, as you will see in the next step. Once this vector is created here in the constructor, though, another method, `animateLetters()` is called that will eventually initiate the animation.

There's not much to look at right now, so let's take care of breaking the textfield apart into individual letter bitmaps so that we can manipulate each one individually.

4. Add the following bold lines to your class to place each letter into its own bitmap:

```
package {

  import aeon.AnimationSequence;

  import aether.utils.ImageUtil;

  import flash.display.Bitmap;
  import flash.display.BitmapData;
  import flash.display.Sprite;
  import flash.text.TextField;
  import flash.text.TextFieldAutoSize;
  import flash.text.TextFormat;

  [SWF(width=600, height=400, backgroundColor=0x333333)]

  public class TextAnimationEngine extends Sprite {

    public function TextAnimationEngine() {
      // this method body is unchanged
    }

    private function createField():TextField {
      // this method body is unchanged
    }

    private function createLetterBitmaps(
      field:TextField
    ):Vector.<Sprite> {
      var bitmapData:BitmapData = ImageUtil.getBitmapData(field);
      var letters:Vector.<Sprite> = new Vector.<Sprite>();
      var text:String = field.text;
      var numLetters:uint = field.text.length;
      var halfHeight:Number = field.height/2;
      var startX:Number = field.x;
      var y:Number = field.y + halfHeight;
      var letterData:BitmapData;
      var x:Number;
      var bitmap:Bitmap;
      var sprite:Sprite;
      var bitmapWidth:Number;
      for (var i:uint = 0; i < numLetters; i++) {
        sprite = new Sprite();
        field.text = text.charAt(i);
        letterData = ImageUtil.getBitmapData(field);
        bitmap = new Bitmap(letterData);
        bitmapWidth = bitmap.width;
        bitmap.x = -bitmapWidth/2;
        bitmap.y = -halfHeight;
```

```
        field.text = text.substr(0, i+1);
        x = startX + field.width - bitmapWidth;
        sprite.x = x + bitmapWidth/2;
        sprite.y = y;
        sprite.addChild(bitmap);
        addChild(sprite);
        letters.push(sprite);
      }
      return letters;
    }

  }

}
```

The first half of this method sets up variables that will be used in the second half, which is a loop that iterates through each letter in the field. The first thing that happens in the method is that pixel data of the textfield is drawn into a new BitmapData instance. The vector of Sprite instances is initialized next before several values are saved into variables, including the text in the field, the number of letters in that text, and half of the height of the field, which will be used to position the letter bitmaps with a center registration point. Two further variables are then set up:

```
var startX:Number = field.x;
var y:Number = field.y + halfHeight;
```

`startX` holds the position of the first letter in the field. This will be used for each subsequent letter as a starting position to determine its placement. The variable y will be used to set the y position of each letter, which is the vertical middle of the field. This will allow 3D or scale transformations of the letters to be from a center registration point.

The remaining properties declared outside the loop are not initialized with values but will have values assigned within the loop.

As for the loop itself, it runs through each letter in the field, as you would expect. For each letter, a new Sprite instance is created in which the bitmap image will be placed. The field itself is assigned a single letter so that we can capture the pixel data from just that letter. This data is passed to a new Bitmap instance and positioned so that its registration point will be centered on the bitmap.

```
field.text = text.charAt(i);
letterData = ImageUtil.getBitmapData(field);
bitmap = new Bitmap(letterData);
bitmapWidth = bitmap.width;
bitmap.x = -bitmapWidth/2;
bitmap.y = -halfHeight;
```

The field is then given the substring of letters from the start up to the letter position for the current iteration of the loop. This allows us to determine the x position for the current letter based on the bitmap's width and the width of the field. Using this data, we can position the sprite so that the letter drawn will be placed at the same position as the original letter, with the registration point centered for the bitmap.

```
field.text = text.substr(0, i+1);
x = startX + field.width - bitmapWidth;
sprite.x = x + bitmapWidth/2;
sprite.y = y;
```

All that remains in the function is adding the sprite to the stage and pushing the letter bitmap into the `letters` vector (perhaps as an alternative and a further generalization of this method, the sprites themselves would not be added to the stage, but would rely on the caller to do so if it was desired). Once the loop completes, the `letters` vector is returned out of the method.

If you compile your movie at this point, what you should see are your letters added to the stage looking like nothing more than a textfield, as shown in Figure 9-17.

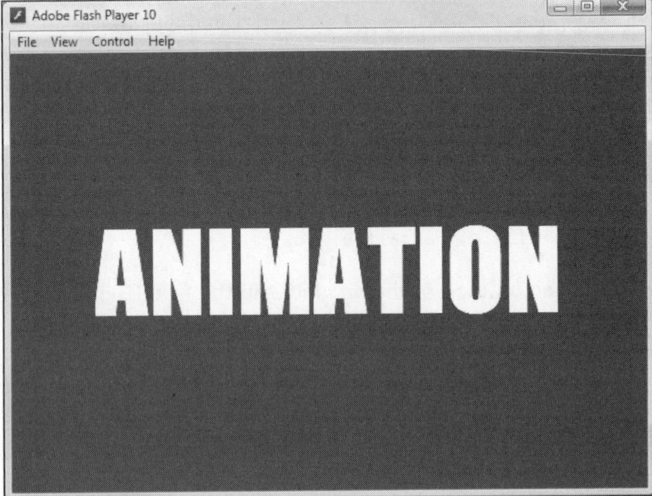

Figure 9-17. Letters drawn as bitmap images from the data in a dynamic textfield, positioned and ready for animation

Of course, at this point, you may as well have just placed the textfield if we were going to stop here. However, now that the letters are all broken up into individual display objects, we can begin work on animating them.

5. The following code begins filling in the `animateLetters()` method invoked in the constructor. Add the following bold lines to your class:

```
package {

  import aeon.AnimationComposite;
  import aeon.AnimationHold;
  import aeon.AnimationSequence;
  import aeon.animators.Transformer3D;
  import aeon.animators.Tweener;
  import aeon.easing.Quad;
```

```
import aether.utils.ImageUtil;

import flash.display.Bitmap;
import flash.display.BitmapData;
import flash.display.Sprite;
import flash.geom.Matrix3D;
import flash.geom.Vector3D;
import flash.text.TextField;
import flash.text.TextFieldAutoSize;
import flash.text.TextFormat;

[SWF(width=600, height=400, backgroundColor=0x333333)]

public class TextAnimationEngine extends Sprite {

  private var _animations:Vector.<AnimationSequence>;

  public function TextAnimationEngine() {
    // this method body is unchanged
  }

  private function createField():TextField {
    // this method body is unchanged
  }

  private function createLetterBitmaps(
    field:TextField
  ):Vector.<Sprite> {
    // this method body is unchanged
  }

  private function animateLetters(letters:Vector.<Sprite>):void {
    _animations = new Vector.<AnimationSequence>();
    var endMatrix:Matrix3D;
    var startMatrix:Matrix3D;
    var animation:AnimationSequence;
    for (var i:uint = 0; i < letters.length; i++) {
      letters[i].z = 0;
      letters[i].alpha = 0;
      endMatrix = letters[i].transform.matrix3D;
      startMatrix = endMatrix.clone();
      startMatrix.prependRotation(120, Vector3D.Y_AXIS);
      startMatrix.prependRotation(90, Vector3D.Z_AXIS);
      startMatrix.appendTranslation(-50, 0, 0);
      animation = new AnimationSequence(
        [
        new AnimationHold((i+1)*150),
        new AnimationComposite(
```

```
                [
                new Tweener(letters[i], {alpha:0}, {alpha:1}, 100),
                new Transformer3D(
                  letters[i],
                  startMatrix,
                  endMatrix,
                  800,
                  Quad.easeOut
                )
                ]
              )
              ]
            )
            _animations.push(animation);
            animation.start()
          }
        }

      }

    }
```

animateLetters() sets up a loop to iterate through each sprite in the letters vector. Each letter is given a z value of 0 so that its matrix3D property is initialized and its opacity is set to 0 so that it is initially invisible.

```
letters[i].z = 0;
letters[i].alpha = 0;
```

To create a 3D animation for each letter, we will use aeon's Transformer3D animator, previously discussed in Chapter 7. For this animator, we need to pass a start and end 3D matrix. The end matrix will simply be the current matrix for an untransformed letter. The start matrix takes the end position then prepends two rotations, one about the y axis and one about the z axis, and a –50 x translation is appended.

```
endMatrix = letters[i].transform.matrix3D;
startMatrix = endMatrix.clone();
startMatrix.prependRotation(120, Vector3D.Y_AXIS);
startMatrix.prependRotation(90, Vector3D.Z_AXIS);
startMatrix.appendTranslation(-50, 0, 0);
```

At this point, the animation can be initialized. For this, an AnimationSequence is set up so that there will be a delay between the start time of each letter, followed by a composite animation of the alpha fading up to full opacity and the 3D transformation.

```
animation = new AnimationSequence(
  [
  new AnimationHold((i+1)*150),
  new AnimationComposite(
```

```
      [
      new Tweener(letters[i], {alpha:0}, {alpha:1}, 100),
      new Transformer3D(
        letters[i],
        startMatrix,
        endMatrix,
        800,
        Quad.easeOut
      )
      ]
    )
    ]
  )
```

This animation sequence is pushed into the _animations vector so that its reference is saved and won't be garbage collected, and the animation is kicked off with a call to the start() method.

```
_animations.push(animation);
animation.start()
```

If you compile now, you will see a single 3D animation of the letters. We can add a bit more interest by adding more animations to the sequence.

6. The next bold lines add a glow filter animation to the letters:

```
package {

  import aeon.AnimationComposite;
  import aeon.AnimationHold;
  import aeon.AnimationSequence;
  import aeon.animators.FilterAnimator;
  import aeon.animators.Transformer3D;
  import aeon.animators.Tweener;
  import aeon.easing.Quad;

  import aether.utils.ImageUtil;

  import flash.display.Bitmap;
  import flash.display.BitmapData;
  import flash.display.Sprite;
  import flash.filters.GlowFilter;
  import flash.geom.Matrix3D;
  import flash.geom.Vector3D;
  import flash.text.TextField;
  import flash.text.TextFieldAutoSize;
  import flash.text.TextFormat;

  [SWF(width=600, height=400, backgroundColor=0x333333)]

  public class TextAnimationEngine extends Sprite {
```

```
private var _animations:Vector.<AnimationSequence>;

public function TextAnimationEngine() {
  // this method body is unchanged
}

private function createField():TextField {
  // this method body is unchanged
}

private function createLetterBitmaps(
  field:TextField
):Vector.<Sprite> {
  // this method body is unchanged
}

private function animateLetters(letters:Vector.<Sprite>):void {
  _animations = new Vector.<AnimationSequence>();
  var endMatrix:Matrix3D;
  var startMatrix:Matrix3D;
  var animation:AnimationSequence;
  for (var i:uint = 0; i < letters.length; i++) {
    letters[i].z = 0;
    letters[i].alpha = 0;
    endMatrix = letters[i].transform.matrix3D;
    startMatrix = endMatrix.clone();
    startMatrix.prependRotation(120, Vector3D.Y_AXIS);
    startMatrix.prependRotation(90, Vector3D.Z_AXIS);
    startMatrix.appendTranslation(-50, 0, 0);
    animation = new AnimationSequence(
      [
      new AnimationHold((i+1)*150),
      new AnimationComposite(
        [
        new Tweener(letters[i], {alpha:0}, {alpha:1}, 100),
        new Transformer3D(
          letters[i],
          startMatrix,
          endMatrix,
          800,
          Quad.easeOut
        )
        ]
      ),
      new AnimationHold(800),
      new FilterAnimator(
        letters[i],
        new GlowFilter(0x66FF66),
```

```
              {blurX:0, blurY:0},
              {blurX:20, blurY:20},
              -1,
              400
            ),
            new FilterAnimator(
              letters[i],
              new GlowFilter(0x66FF66),
              {blurX:20, blurY:20},
              {blurX:0, blurY:0},
              -1,
              400
            )
            ]
          )
          _animations.push(animation);
          animation.start()
        }
      }

    }

  }
```

After the Transformer3D animation, the animation sequence for each letter is held for 800 milliseconds before continuing with an animation of the GlowFilter using aeon's FilterAnimator, which animates up from a blurX and blurY of 0 to 20, followed by an animation down of the same properties.

This produces a fairly pleasing animation of the glow around the letters after they animate in. We can add to this further by now animating the letters out.

7. To remove the letters using another animation in the sequence, add the following bold lines to your class:

```
package {

  import aeon.AnimationComposite;
  import aeon.AnimationHold;
  import aeon.AnimationSequence;
  import aeon.animators.FilterAnimator;
  import aeon.animators.Transformer3D;
  import aeon.animators.Tweener;
  import aeon.easing.Back;
  import aeon.easing.Quad;

  import aether.utils.ImageUtil;

  import flash.display.Bitmap;
  import flash.display.BitmapData;
```

```
import flash.display.Sprite;
import flash.filters.GlowFilter;
import flash.geom.Matrix3D;
import flash.geom.Vector3D;
import flash.text.TextField;
import flash.text.TextFieldAutoSize;
import flash.text.TextFormat;

[SWF(width=600, height=400, backgroundColor=0x333333)]

public class TextAnimationEngine extends Sprite {

  private var _animations:Vector.<AnimationSequence>;

  public function TextAnimationEngine() {
    // this method body is unchanged
  }

  private function createField():TextField {
    // this method body is unchanged
  }

  private function createLetterBitmaps(
    field:TextField
  ):Vector.<Sprite> {
    // this method body is unchanged
  }

  private function animateLetters(letters:Vector.<Sprite>):void {
    _animations = new Vector.<AnimationSequence>();
    var endMatrix:Matrix3D;
    var startMatrix:Matrix3D;
    var animation:AnimationSequence;
    for (var i:uint = 0; i < letters.length; i++) {
      letters[i].z = 0;
      letters[i].alpha = 0;
      endMatrix = letters[i].transform.matrix3D;
      startMatrix = endMatrix.clone();
      startMatrix.prependRotation(120, Vector3D.Y_AXIS);
      startMatrix.prependRotation(90, Vector3D.Z_AXIS);
      startMatrix.appendTranslation(-50, 0, 0);
      animation = new AnimationSequence(
        [
        new AnimationHold((i+1)*150),
        new AnimationComposite(
          [
          new Tweener(letters[i], {alpha:0}, {alpha:1}, 100),
```

```
            new Transformer3D(
              letters[i],
              startMatrix,
              endMatrix,
              800,
              Quad.easeOut
            )
            ]
          ),
          new AnimationHold(800),
          new FilterAnimator(
            letters[i],
            new GlowFilter(0x66FF66),
            {blurX:0, blurY:0},
            {blurX:20, blurY:20},
            -1,
            400
          ),
          new FilterAnimator(
            letters[i],
            new GlowFilter(0x66FF66),
            {blurX:20, blurY:20},
            {blurX:0, blurY:0},
            -1,
            400
          ),
          new AnimationHold(800),
          new Tweener(
            letters[i],
            {scaleX:1, scaleY:1, alpha:1},
            {scaleX:3, scaleY:0, alpha:0},
            400,
            Back.easeIn
          )
          ]
        )
        _animations.push(animation);
        animation.start()
      }
    }

  }

}
```

Here, we hold each letter once again for 800 milliseconds before proceeding with a scale and alpha animation for the letter. The animation will transform the letter from full opacity to full transparency and from a scale of 100 percent on both axes to 300 percent on the x axis and 0 percent on the y.

This completes a single animation of the letters and a fairly complex one at that. But to demonstrate how it could go even further, let's loop the animation to replay infinitely.

8. The following bold lines establish a loop for the animation sequence. Add them to your class to complete the example:

```
package {

  import aeon.AnimationComposite;
  import aeon.AnimationHold;
  import aeon.AnimationLoop;
  import aeon.AnimationSequence;
  import aeon.animators.FilterAnimator;
  import aeon.animators.Transformer3D;
  import aeon.animators.Tweener;
  import aeon.easing.Back;
  import aeon.easing.Quad;

  import aether.utils.ImageUtil;

  import flash.display.Bitmap;
  import flash.display.BitmapData;
  import flash.display.Sprite;
  import flash.filters.GlowFilter;
  import flash.geom.Matrix3D;
  import flash.geom.Vector3D;
  import flash.text.TextField;
  import flash.text.TextFieldAutoSize;
  import flash.text.TextFormat;

  [SWF(width=600, height=400, backgroundColor=0x333333)]

  public class TextAnimationEngine extends Sprite {

    private var _animations:Vector.<AnimationSequence>;

    public function TextAnimationEngine() {
      // this method body is unchanged
    }

    private function createField():TextField {
      // this method body is unchanged
    }

    private function createLetterBitmaps(
      field:TextField
    ):Vector.<Sprite> {
```

```
    // this method body is unchanged
  }

  private function animateLetters(letters:Vector.<Sprite>):void {
    _animations = new Vector.<AnimationSequence>();
    var endMatrix:Matrix3D;
    var startMatrix:Matrix3D;
    var animation:AnimationSequence;
    for (var i:uint = 0; i < letters.length; i++) {
      letters[i].z = 0;
      letters[i].alpha = 0;
      endMatrix = letters[i].transform.matrix3D;
      startMatrix = endMatrix.clone();
      startMatrix.prependRotation(120, Vector3D.Y_AXIS);
      startMatrix.prependRotation(90, Vector3D.Z_AXIS);
      startMatrix.appendTranslation(-50, 0, 0);
      animation = new AnimationSequence(
        [
        new AnimationHold((i+1)*150),
        new AnimationLoop(
          new AnimationSequence(
            [
            new AnimationComposite(
              [
              new Tweener(letters[i], {alpha:0}, {alpha:1}, 100),
              new Transformer3D(
                letters[i],
                startMatrix,
                endMatrix,
                800,
                Quad.easeOut
              )
              ]
            ),
            new AnimationHold(800),
            new FilterAnimator(
              letters[i],
              new GlowFilter(0x66FF66),
              {blurX:0, blurY:0},
              {blurX:20, blurY:20},
              -1,
              400
            ),
            new FilterAnimator(
              letters[i],
              new GlowFilter(0x66FF66),
              {blurX:20, blurY:20},
              {blurX:0, blurY:0},
              -1,
```

```
                        400
                      ),
                      new AnimationHold(800),
                      new Tweener(
                        letters[i],
                        {scaleX:1, scaleY:1, alpha:1},
                        {scaleX:3, scaleY:0, alpha:0},
                        400,
                        Back.easeIn
                      ),
                      new AnimationHold(2000),
                      new Tweener(
                        letters[i],
                        {scaleX:1, scaleY:1},
                        {scaleX:1, scaleY:1},
                        0
                      )
                      ]
                    )
                  )
                  ]
                )
                _animations.push(animation);
                animation.start()
              }
            }

          }

        }
```

The final bit of code added to this class nests the main animation sequence after the initial hold to offset the start time for each letter, within another AnimationSequence instance that is managed by an AnimationLoop. In order to effectively create the loop, we have to set each letter back to a scale of 100 percent before the next loop begins, which we do at the end of the sequence after a delay of 2 seconds. The result of all this is an infinitely looping complex letter animation all created from an initial textfield.

Although the latter half of this example was more of an exploration of how you might animate a textfield using aeon, you could fill the `animateLetters()` with any code you wanted to animate the letters. The technique to walk away with is how you might extract the pixel information from each letter in a field in order to perform individual operations on each, whether for a static or an animated effect. As an example, with only some slight tweaking, I combined the methods from the distress example with the letter pixel extraction from this animation example to produce Figure 9-18, which can be found as

GrowingDistress.swf in this chapter's files. Because each letter's data can be manipulated separately, I was able to increase the amount of distress for each character in the word.

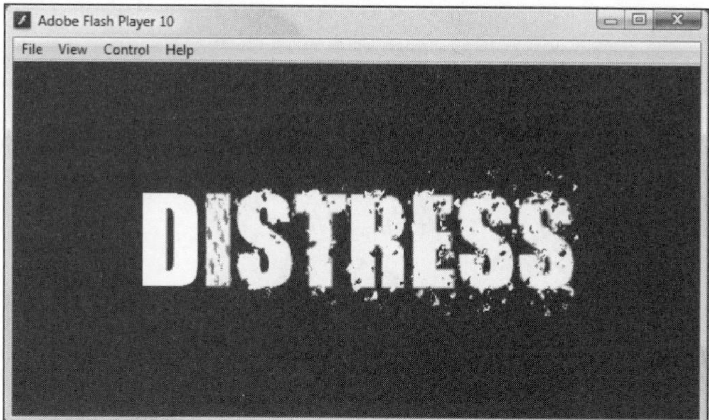

Figure 9-18. The same technique used to capture individual letter data is applied to a distressed field with settings increased for each letter.

Getting individual pixel data from an image opens the doors to many effects. In a similar way, getting access to the data from each letter in a field while keeping the relative position of each is a powerful tool for constructing some great text effects.

Summary

Flash is fantastic at presenting data in graphical forms, but text is how the majority of information is shared in web applications. Even with Flash animations and games produced for entertainment, of course, you will find titles, instructions, and credits presented in text. So why not combine Flash's graphical capabilities with its text-rendering capabilities and create some unique and eye-catching text effects, without having to rely on external images, when required to add some visual interest to text?

In this chapter, we looked at three extensible techniques. The first two dealt with distressing and beveling text using methods that are equally applicable to nontext images and shapes as well. These both took advantage of BitmapData and the bitmap filters to capture the pixel data from a dynamic textfield and manipulate it. The third technique demonstrated how you can capture the pixel data from each letter in a textfield in order to perform individual manipulation, such as performing animation. All of these techniques are ones that can be experimented with further and enhanced to create any number of terrific text effects.

In the next chapter, we will continue on our journey of image manipulation by exploring how we can apply the bitmap operations and techniques discussed up to this point in the book to a little something called video. There's no reason that textfields should have all the fun.

Chapter 10

VIDEO EFFECTS

"Video killed the radio star," the Buggles sang back at the dawn of MTV, and what a prophetic lyric that was. Of course, video had been around for quite a while before MTV launched (for the kids out there, the "M" used to stand for "music"; I don't know what it stands for these days). But there wasn't any major delivery mechanism for music videos other than sporadic programs like *American Bandstand* or *Saturday Night Live*. With cable television and the appearance of channels with dedicated programming like MTV, music videos became a primary way that a pop culture was introduced to and seduced by bands and singers.

In a similar way, video has been available on the Web for a while now, at least in the relatively short history of the medium, but video contains a lot of data and so consumes a lot of bandwidth. It was expensive to store and deliver. Client machines could not be relied on for playback. So although video was available, its appearances were sporadic, and it couldn't be used as a primary way of delivering information.

However, with the increase of broadband networks globally, with the competition of content delivery networks helping to drive down the cost of storage and delivery, and with the march of time and technology, video has more and more become a viable solution for disseminating data on the Internet. It has become an integral part of the online presences and businesses of media companies that already deal with video in other forms (e.g., music labels, movie studios) as well as media companies that can enhance their reach with its addition, like newspaper organizations. It is also being used heavily by nonmedia companies to deliver information, internal training, and entertainment to enhance user experiences. And, of course, there is the staggeringly large amount of user-generated video that ranges from personal to instructional to fanatical to a whole slew of cat videos I could consider an entirely new subgenre of media.

The Flash Player has been able to play back video for several versions now, and, in the context of this book, video in the player is really nothing more than pixel data that changes each frame. What this means is that everything we've explored up to this point on bitmap manipulation can be applied to video as well. The only differences are in how video is brought into the player for playback and in the extra consideration needed for performance when applying repetitive bitmap effects to a video, which can already tax some client machines just through general playback.

In this chapter, we will look not only at how to bring video into the Flash Player but at what sort of effects we can apply at runtime to videos and for what purposes. Once more, we will leverage the aether image effects library in order to speed and ease our development (it was for video effects, after all, that the library was conceived) as we explore dynamic filters that could be used for applying post effects, transitioning between clips, and generally enhancing video experiences.

There's a lot to do and fun to be had with video in Flash, so quiet on the set! Roll camera! And action!

Applying runtime filters

A frame of video is simply a grid of pixel data. Just as with any graphic object in the Flash Player, we can use ActionScript to draw its contents into a BitmapData instance in order to manipulate it. As long as the manipulations performed are optimized enough for reapplication each frame as the video plays, you are free to perform any number of runtime filters on the video data. These could include such standard effects as applying blurs, tinting, or adding contrast. They could even be more creative filters like creating a kaleidoscope or painterly effect. Effects like these could be used for cleaning up video for which the original source is not available, enabling transitions between multiple clips or just creating special effects for, well, special effect.

Of course, before you can manipulate video data, you first need to get that data into the player. In the next section, we will look at how.

> *There's a lot to the subject of video playback in the Flash Player, from loading progressive video over HTTP, to loading streaming content over RTMP via the Flash Media Server, to setting buffering logic to ensure smooth playback no matter the method of loading. There are topics like listening and responding to errors, events, embedded metadata, and cue points; monitoring load to enable seeking to later points of a progressive video; and dynamically switching streams based on bandwidth or screen size. In fact, entire books have been written on the subject of Flash video, such as friends of ED's* Foundation Flash CS3 Video *by Tom Green and Adam Thomas (ISBN: 978-1-59059-956-3). The comprehensive subject is not a topic for a single section in a single chapter of a book.*
>
> *What this next section instead contains is the basic knowledge you will need to load and play back video in the Flash Player for the purpose of testing the image manipulation for video that is the true topic of the chapter. For more detailed information on the subject of video in the Flash Player, please refer to Adobe's documentation.*

Building a video loader

Loading and displaying video in the Flash Player is handled by three separate classes in ActionScript all working together: NetConnection, NetStream, and Video. NetConnection handles connection of the Flash Player to the local file system or a web server, or to the Flash Media Server (FMS) if you are streaming video. NetStream manages loading and interaction with the video data using the connection managed by NetConnection. Video is the simplest of the bunch, being a DisplayObject child class that is used to display the video data managed by NetStream, much like how Bitmap is used to display pixel data from a BitmapData instance.

Generally, in your code, you will set up loading of video in the following manner, whether you are using progressive or streaming playback:

1. Create a NetConnection instance, and set up a listener for its status. Connect to `null` for a connection to a local file system or web server, or connect using a path to an FMS application instance for streaming playback.
2. In the NetConnection status handler, if the connection is successful, create a new NetStream instance that uses the NetConnection instance as its connection. Set up a handler for the stream's status event as well.

3. Create a new Video instance, and attach the NetStream instance. This will display any data loaded in the stream through the Video instance, which should be added to the stage.

4. Make a call to `NetStream.play()` to begin loading or streaming in video data. As the data loads in, it will appear in the Video instance.

Because the examples we will work on through the rest of the chapter only require simple loading and playback of video, we will first create a class that encapsulates all of these steps in order to simplify our examples later on. The goal is to then be able to create and load a progressive video by simply calling

```
var videoLoader:VideoLoader = new VideoLoader(320, 240, "video.flv");
addChild(videoLoader);
```

That's a pleasant way of loading a video, isn't it? It's not really that hard to do, and in the following steps, we will explore how to accomplish it:

1. Create a new ActionScript file, in Flash or through a new ActionScript project named VideoFilters in Flex Builder, saved as `VideoLoader.as`.

2. Begin the VideoLoader class with the following code:

```
package {

  import flash.events.NetStatusEvent;
  import flash.events.SecurityErrorEvent;
  import flash.media.Video;
  import flash.net.NetConnection;

  public class VideoLoader extends Video {

    private var _netConnection:NetConnection;
    private var _streamPath:String;

    public function VideoLoader(
      width:Number=320,
      height:Number=240,
      path:String=null
    ) {
      this.width = width;
      this.height = height;
      if (path != null) {
        load(path);
      }
    }

    private function onNetStatus(event:NetStatusEvent):void {
    }

    private function onSecurityError(event:SecurityErrorEvent):void {
      trace(event);
```

```
    }

    public function load(path:String):void {
      _streamPath = path;
      _netConnection = new NetConnection();
      _netConnection.addEventListener(➥
NetStatusEvent.NET_STATUS, onNetStatus);
      _netConnection.addEventListener(➥
SecurityErrorEvent.SECURITY_ERROR, onSecurityError);
      _netConnection.connect(null);
    }

  }

}
```

VideoLoader extends Video and will encapsulate all of the functionality for connecting via NetConnection and loading through NetStream. At this point in the class, the constructor sets its width and height based on arguments, and if a path to a video file is passed to the constructor as well, the `load()` method is called to kick off the connection.

The `load()` method saves the path to the video file and then creates a new NetConnection instance and sets up its listeners. The `onNetStatus` handler will be called for any number of events, from the initial acceptance or rejection to a closing of the connection to an error due to a bad connection path. Security errors are handled in the separate `onSecurityError` handler. Right now, all we do within this handler is trace out the event, though in a more robust class you might choose to handle this error in a more useful way to external classes.

Note that the `connect()` method call that is made on the connection is passed the parameter `null`. This is necessary when you are not connecting to an FMS instance but are instead going to progressively load videos over HTTP. This, in most circumstances, will connect and allow you to continue, though I have encountered an instance where a remote SWF loaded into a local SWF for testing was not allowed to connect, since the Flash Player determined that `null` was local and threw a security error.

Once the net connection connects, or is rejected, a NetStatusEvent will be dispatched and handled by our `onNetStatus`. Let's fill that in now to act on the necessary events in our examples.

3. Add the following bold code to your class:

```
package {

  import flash.events.NetStatusEvent;
  import flash.events.SecurityErrorEvent;
  import flash.media.Video;
  import flash.net.NetConnection;
  import flash.net.NetStream;
```

```
  public class VideoLoader extends Video {

    private var _netConnection:NetConnection;
    private var _netStream:NetStream;
    private var _streamPath:String;

    public function VideoLoader(
      width:Number=320,
      height:Number=240,
      path:String=null
    ) {
      // this method body is unchanged
    }

    private function connectStream():void {
      _netStream = new NetStream(_netConnection);
      _netStream.addEventListener(➥
NetStatusEvent.NET_STATUS, onNetStatus);
      attachNetStream(_netStream);
      _netStream.play(_streamPath);
    }

    private function onNetStatus(event:NetStatusEvent):void {
      switch (event.info.code) {
        case "NetConnection.Connect.Success":
            connectStream();
            break;
        case "NetStream.Play.StreamNotFound":
            trace("Stream not found: " + _streamPath);
            break;
      }
    }

    private function onSecurityError(event:SecurityErrorEvent):void {
      trace(event);
    }

    public function load(path:String):void {
      // this method body is unchanged
    }

  }

}
```

In this simple class, for NetConnection we are only really worried about the NetStatus event that contains the info code of "NetConnection.Connect.Success", which lets us know that the connection was successful (we'll discuss the other case in a moment). If that event is received, we call connectStream() to begin loading the video.

In connectStream(), a NetStream instance is created and passed the successful connection in the constructor. A listener is set up for the stream NET_STATUS event as well using the same handler as the net connection, so events for both the stream and the connection will be handled by the same onNetStatus() method. This is the reason there is a case on onNetStatus() for "NetStream.Play.StreamNotFound", which will be dispatched by the net stream if the path to the video is invalid.

Back in createStream(), before calling play() to load the video through the net stream, attachNetStream() is first invoked in order to set the display for the net stream's data, which is this VideoLoader instance. VideoLoader, remember, extends Video, where the attachNetStream() method is defined.

Once play() is called, the video will start to load and be displayed through this VideoLoader instance. In order for our dynamic filters to work, though, we will need to let external classes know when the video is updating. This will be handled in the following new code.

4. Add the bold code that follows to the VideoLoader class to enable the dispatch of update events as the video is rendered:

```
package {

  import flash.events.Event;
  import flash.events.NetStatusEvent;
  import flash.events.SecurityErrorEvent;
  import flash.media.Video;
  import flash.net.NetConnection;
  import flash.net.NetStream;

  public class VideoLoader extends Video {

    private var _netConnection:NetConnection;
    private var _netStream:NetStream;
    private var _streamPath:String;

    public function VideoLoader(
      width:Number=320,
      height:Number=240,
      path:String=null
    ) {
      // this method body is unchanged
    }

    private function connectStream():void {
      // this method body is unchanged
    }
```

```
    private function startProgressEvent(start:Boolean):void {
      if (start) {
        addEventListener(Event.ENTER_FRAME, onEnterFrame);
      } else {
        removeEventListener(Event.ENTER_FRAME, onEnterFrame);
      }
    }

    private function onEnterFrame(event:Event):void {
      dispatchEvent(new Event(Event.RENDER));
    }

    private function onNetStatus(event:NetStatusEvent):void {
      switch (event.info.code) {
        case "NetConnection.Connect.Success":
            connectStream();
            break;
        case "NetStream.Play.StreamNotFound":
            trace("Stream not found: " + _streamPath);
            break;
        case "NetStream.Play.Start":
            startProgressEvent(true);
            break;
        case "NetStream.Play.Stop":
            startProgressEvent(false);
            dispatchEvent(new Event(Event.COMPLETE));
            break;
      }
    }

    private function onSecurityError(event:SecurityErrorEvent):void {
      trace(event);
    }

    public function load(path:String):void {
      // this method body is unchanged
    }

  }

}
```

Two more cases have now been added to onNetStatus(), one for when playback of video begins ("NetStream.Play.Start") and one for video completion ("NetStream.Play.Stop"). When the video starts, the method startProgressEvent() is called and passed a true parameter. This will set up an ENTER_FRAME listener so that a RENDER event is dispatched each frame as the video plays. When the video completes, the same method is passed a `false` parameter, which removes the listener. A `COMPLETE` event is also fired at this time.

This last step is to handle custom events for NetStream. This class will throw exceptions if we do not, so even though we will not use the events, we need to include the code.

5. Complete the VideoLoader class with the following bold lines of ActionScript:

```
package {

  // imports remain unchanged

  public class VideoLoader extends Video {

    private var _netConnection:NetConnection;
    private var _netStream:NetStream;
    private var _streamPath:String;

    public function VideoLoader(
      width:Number=320,
      height:Number=240,
      path:String=null
    ) {
      // this method body is unchanged
    }

    private function connectStream():void {
      _netStream = new NetStream(_netConnection);
      _netStream.addEventListener(➥
NetStatusEvent.NET_STATUS, onNetStatus);
      _netStream.client = this;
      attachNetStream(_netStream);
      _netStream.play(_streamPath);
    }

    private function startProgressEvent(start:Boolean):void {
      // this method body is unchanged
    }

    private function onEnterFrame(event:Event):void {
      dispatchEvent(new Event(Event.RENDER));
    }

    private function onNetStatus(event:NetStatusEvent):void {
      // this method body is unchanged
    }

    private function onSecurityError(event:SecurityErrorEvent):void {
      trace(event);
    }
```

```
    public function onMetaData(info:Object):void {}
    public function onCuePoint(info:Object):void {}
    public function onImageData(info:Object):void {}
    public function onPlayStatus(info:Object):void {}
    public function onTextData(info:Object):void {}
    public function onXMPData(info:Object):void {}

    public function load(path:String):void {
      // this method body is unchanged
    }

  }

}
```

NetStream has a client property that should be passed an object that contains handlers for the NetStream custom events (these events are not standard Event instances, but simply Object instances). We can pass this VideoLoader instance as the client as long as the handler for the events are defined, which is done with the preceding bold code. These handlers include onMetaData, which receives width and height info for the video, and onCuePoint, which will be fired if the video loaded contains any embedded cue point data. We will not be filling in these handlers, as they are not needed in our examples.

The class is complete at this point and will serve its purpose for our examples. A more robust version would include better handling for the events and errors as well as methods to control the net stream, such as pause() and resume(). But for simply loading and playing back a video, we're all set! We'll test out this class by using it in our first example.

If you are using Flash, the Components library includes an fl.video.FLVPlayback component that handles loading and playing back of videos, which also includes playback controls (it wraps fl.video.VideoPlayer, which does not include the controls). For Flex users, the Flex framework includes the mx.controls.VideoDisplay class, which does a similar job of encapsulating the interaction with NetConnection and NetStream, simplifying the process of loading and playing a video.

Filtering video frames

With VideoLoader built, we can load in a video and begin filtering its pixel data. Bringing the data into Flash, you will see, is now a piece of cake. Pick your flavor (I'm partial to German chocolate myself).

1. Start with a new document in Flash named VideoFilters.fla. If you are using Flex Builder and created the VideoFilters project for the VideoLoader class, the project should already be set up as VideoFilters. The main ActionScript class in either Flash or Flex Builder should be named VideoFilters.as.
2. This example, like all of the examples in this chapter, uses aether, so import aether.swc into your FLA or Flex Builder project from this chapter's files.

3. Start your VideoFilters class with the following code:

```
package {

  import flash.display.Sprite;

  [SWF(width=400, height=450, backgroundColor=0x666666)]

  public class VideoFilters extends Sprite {

    public var _video:VideoLoader;

    public function VideoFilters() {
      _video = new VideoLoader(400, 225, "../../assets/road.flv");
      addChild(_video);
    }

  }

}
```

How's that for simple? VideoLoader takes care of all of the interaction with loading and playback. This class just needs to give it a size, tell it where to find the video, and add it to the stage. If you test the movie at this point, you should see *The Road, a documentary*, load and play, as shown in Figure 10-1. A special thanks to Brandon Aaskov and the rest of Danny Glover's Super Action Adventure Force Brigade Squad for use of the video.

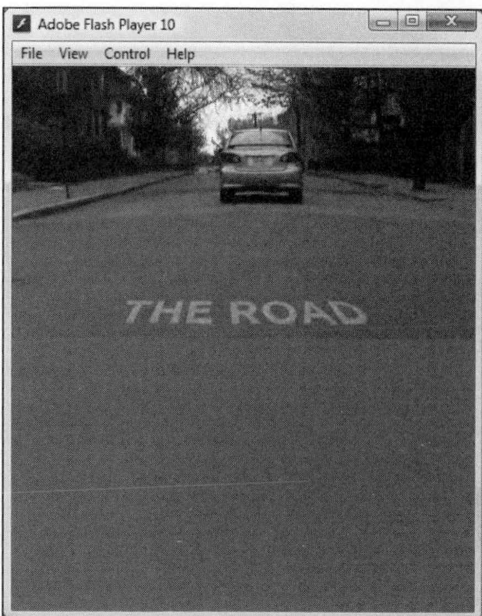

Figure 10-1. A video loaded into the Flash Player

With the pixel data available, we can now twist it around however we want.

4. Add the bold lines that follow to your class. These will copy the pixels from the video into a new BitmapData instance.

```
package {

  import flash.display.Bitmap;
  import flash.display.BitmapData;
  import flash.display.Sprite;
  import flash.events.Event;
  import flash.geom.Matrix;

  [SWF(width=400, height=450, backgroundColor=0x666666)]

  public class VideoFilters extends Sprite {

    public var _video:VideoLoader;
    public var _filteredScreen:Bitmap;
```

```
        public function VideoFilters() {
          _video = new VideoLoader(400, 225, "../../assets/road.flv");
          _video.addEventListener(Event.RENDER, onVideoRender);
          addChild(_video);
          _filteredScreen = new Bitmap();
          _filteredScreen.y = _video.height;
          addChild(_filteredScreen);
        }

        private function onVideoRender(event:Event):void {
          var bitmapData:BitmapData = ➥
    new BitmapData(_video.width, _video.height);
          var matrix:Matrix = new Matrix();
          matrix.scale(_video.scaleX, _video.scaleY);
          bitmapData.draw(_video, matrix);
          _filteredScreen.bitmapData = bitmapData;
        }

      }

    }
```

Figure 10-2. A video on top with a bitmap copy rendered below it, updated each frame as the video plays

In the constructor, we set up an event listener for the RENDER event dispatched by VideoLoader while video is playing. We will use this event to update our bitmap data with new pixel data each frame. The Bitmap instance we will use to display that data is also created in the constructor and positioned below the video.

onVideoRender() handles the RENDER event from VideoLoader. In it, we create a new BitmapData instance in which we draw the current video frame. A matrix is used in case the video loaded into the player has been scaled, in which case the original frame size would be drawn. Using the matrix ensures that we copy the video at its current size. This copied data is then passed to the Bitmap instance on the stage.

If you test your movie now, you should see something like Figure 10-2, with what appears to be two copies of the video. Instead, what we have is the video on top with its bitmap copy below it, a bitmap just ripe for some manipulation.

At this point of the exercise, we will be taking advantage of some of the effects available in aether. In the next section, we will create a new effect to apply, but there are many effects already available in the aether library that will allow us to play and very quickly to see what sort of manipulations can be done to the video.

5. First, let's try the old Vaseline-on-the-camera-lens trick that used to be done in order to create a soft, dreamy effect (or to hide an aging star's wrinkles before there was Botox). This can be achieved by blurring a copy of the video that is then screened over the original video. The following bold lines take care of this:

```
package {

  import aether.effects.filters.BlurEffect;

  import flash.display.Bitmap;
  import flash.display.BitmapData;
  import flash.display.BlendMode;
  import flash.display.Sprite;
  import flash.events.Event;
  import flash.geom.Matrix;

  [SWF(width=400, height=450, backgroundColor=0x666666)]

  public class VideoFilters extends Sprite {

    public var _video:VideoLoader;
    public var _filteredScreen:Bitmap;

    public function VideoFilters() {
      // this method body is unchanged
    }

    private function onVideoRender(event:Event):void {
      var bitmapData:BitmapData = ➥
new BitmapData(_video.width, _video.height);
      var matrix:Matrix = new Matrix();
      matrix.scale(_video.scaleX, _video.scaleY);
      bitmapData.draw(_video, matrix);
      new BlurEffect(5, 5, 1, BlendMode.SCREEN).apply(bitmapData);
      _filteredScreen.bitmapData = bitmapData;
    }

  }

}
```

One new import and one new line of code are all it takes! The result can be seen in Figure 10-3, though it is a subtle effect. If you recall from Chapter 7, all ImageEffects in aether have an apply() method to which you pass the BitmapData instance to affect. The BlurEffect() accepts the amount of blur on the x and y axes as the first two parameters and the quality level of the blur. All ImageEffects take as their last two parameters the blend mode to use, if any, (NORMAL is the default) and the alpha to use in the final blend (1 is the default there). Here, we apply a standard blur in SCREEN mode.

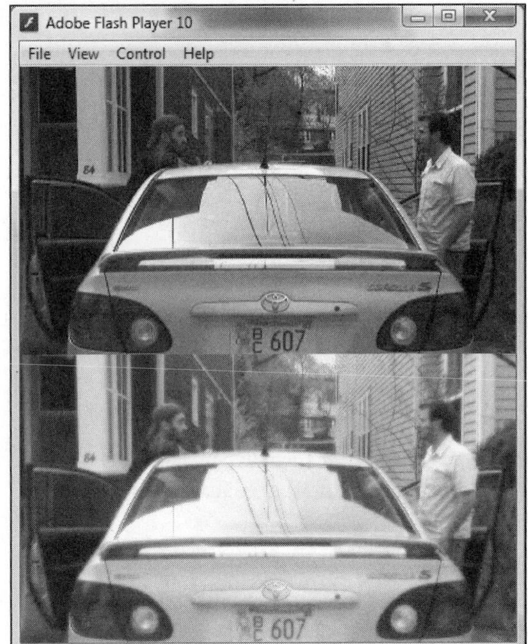

Figure 10-3.
A blurred copy of the video is screened over the original image to create the effect on the bottom.

Let's try a few additional effects.

6. Alter the onVideoRender() method to replace the BlurEffect. Be sure to import aether.effects.transformations.GridEffect in order to compile.

```
    private function onVideoRender(event:Event):void {
      var bitmapData:BitmapData = ➥
new BitmapData(_video.width, _video.height);
      var matrix:Matrix = new Matrix();
      matrix.scale(_video.scaleX, _video.scaleY);
      bitmapData.draw(_video, matrix);
      new GridEffect(3, 3).apply(bitmapData);
      _filteredScreen.bitmapData = bitmapData;
    }
```

The GridEffect, as you might expect, produces a grid of copies in the specified number of columns and rows, as shown in Figure 10-4. How Brady Bunch.

Figure 10-4.
The video is drawn into a grid of copies.

7. We'll try out a couple more for fun. First, import the following classes at the top of your class:

```
import aether.effects.adjustments.LevelsEffect;
import aether.effects.common.CompositeEffect;
import aether.effects.filters.ColorMatrixEffect;
import aether.effects.texture.NoiseEffect;
```

Now, once more, alter onVideoRender() as specified in bold:

```
    private function onVideoRender(event:Event):void {
      var bitmapData:BitmapData = ➥
new BitmapData(_video.width, _video.height);
      var matrix:Matrix = new Matrix();
      matrix.scale(_video.scaleX, _video.scaleY);
      bitmapData.draw(_video, matrix);
      new CompositeEffect(
        [
        new LevelsEffect(50, 127, 200),
        new ColorMatrixEffect(ColorMatrixEffect.SEPIA),
        new NoiseEffect(0.2, BlendMode.MULTIPLY, 0.3)
        ]
      ).apply(bitmapData);
      _filteredScreen.bitmapData = bitmapData;
    }
```

This is a much more complex effect and yet it runs just as well as the previous example, though of course, you would have to assess how the performance scaled with larger video at higher bitrates. In this effect within the CompositeEffect, to which we pass an array of ImageEffects, we first apply a levels adjustment to increase contrast. The three arguments for LevelEffect are the black, medium gray, and white points for the levels. The adjustment is followed by a tinting of the image with a sepia tone. Finally, noise is added at a small amount (0.2) and then set to `MULTIPLY` in the final composite at a reduced alpha (0.3).

The result of this effect is an aged film, as shown in Figure 10-5, though not as apparent in a grayscale screenshot.

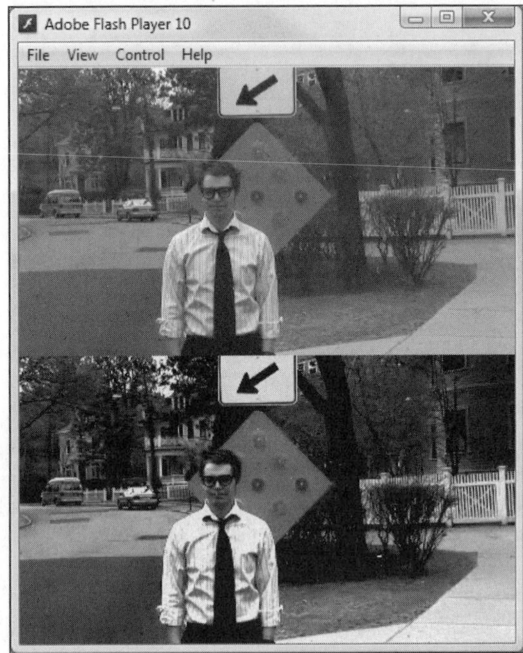

Figure 10-5. A composite effect including a levels adjustment, tinting, and noise is applied to the video.

Now that you see how easy it is to apply an image effect, let's see about how easy it is to create our own as well.

Extending ImageEffect for new filters

To extend ImageEffect, you simply have to provide a constructor and an override for the protected `applyEffect()` method. Any bitmap manipulation performed needs to occur in `applyEffect()`, which can be as simple or as complex as necessary in order to create the desired result. In this next example, we will reproduce the pointillism painting effect that we created at the beginning of Chapter 4 when we looked at BitmapData's `pixelDissolve()` method.

If you recall from Chapter 4, the pointillism effect involved saturating the image, applying `pixelDissolve()`, and then blurring the result. aether already includes a SaturationEffect and a BlurEffect, so what we will do here is create a DissolveEffect that takes care of applying `pixelDissolve()` to an image. Then we can add a PointillismEffect that combines all three of these individual effects (saturation, dissolve, and blur) to create the final effect. By breaking the dissolve out into its own effect, we allow for greater modularity of the effects so that they can be reused easily.

1. Create a new ActionScript file, either in Flash or through the VideoFilters ActionScript project in Flex Builder, saved as `DissolveEffect.as`.
2. The following code is the entirety of the DissolveEffect class:

```
package {

  import aether.effects.ImageEffect;

  import flash.display.BitmapData;
  import flash.geom.Point;

  public class DissolveEffect extends ImageEffect {

    private var _amount:Number;
    private var _color:uint;

    public function DissolveEffect(
      amount:Number=.5,
      color:uint=0xFFFFFFFF,
      blendMode:String=null,
      alpha:Number=1
    ) {
      init(blendMode, alpha);
      _amount = amount;
      _color = color;
    }

    override protected function applyEffect(
      bitmapData:BitmapData
    ):void {
      var numPixels:uint = ➥
(bitmapData.width*bitmapData.height)*_amount;
      bitmapData.pixelDissolve(
        bitmapData,
        bitmapData.rect,
        new Point(),
```

```
                0,
                numPixels,
                _color
            );
        }

    }

}
```

Once again, to extend ImageEffect and gain the advantages of the super class, which include being able to create composite, blended effects easily and apply them in a single line of code, you need to provide a constructor and an override for the applyEffect() method. The constructor should take at the very least the blend mode and alpha to apply to the final effect, which are then passed in a call to the super class's init() method.

```
init(blendMode, alpha);
```

The constructor should also take any additional parameters that would be useful to make the effect configurable. In this case, the amount is the percent of pixels that should dissolve, and the color is the color to use for those dissolved pixels. These are saved into properties of the instance.

```
_amount = amount;
_color = color;
```

The applyEffect() method is where all the work is done to manipulate the bitmap data. For a pixel dissolve effect, the work is relatively minor, calling pixelDissolve() on the data and passing the number of pixels to dissolve based on the amount and the color.

3. Return to VideoFilters.as, and alter the onVideoRender() method with the following bold code, which applies our new DissolveEffect:

```
    private function onVideoRender(event:Event):void {
      var bitmapData:BitmapData = ➥
new BitmapData(_video.width, _video.height);
      var matrix:Matrix = new Matrix();
      matrix.scale(_video.scaleX, _video.scaleY);
      bitmapData.draw(_video, matrix);
      new DissolveEffect().apply(bitmapData);
      _filteredScreen.bitmapData = bitmapData;
    }
```

See? There's nothing to plugging your own effects into aether! If you compile the SWF now, you should see something like Figure 10-6, which shows half of the video's pixels dissolved to white.

Figure 10-6.
An effect using pixelDissolve() is applied to the video.

Of course, what we were looking to do was create the pointillism effect, so next, we will add a new class that combines the three other effects needed to achieve this.

4. Create a new ActionScript file, either in Flash or through the VideoFilters ActionScript project in Flex Builder, saved as `PointillismEffect.as`.
5. The following code is the entirety of the PointillismEffect class:

```
package {

  import aether.effects.ImageEffect;
  import aether.effects.adjustments.SaturationEffect;
  import aether.effects.common.CompositeEffect;
  import aether.effects.filters.BlurEffect;

  import flash.display.BitmapData;

  public class PointillismEffect extends ImageEffect {

    private var _saturation:Number;
    private var _lightColor:uint;
    private var _lightAmount:Number;
    private var _blurAmount:Number;
```

```
    public function PointillismEffect(
      saturation:Number=2.2,
      lightColor:uint=0xFFFFFFFA,
      lightAmount:Number=.33,
      blurAmount:Number=5,
      blendMode:String=null,
      alpha:Number=1
    ) {
      init(blendMode, alpha);
      _saturation = saturation;
      _lightColor = lightColor;
      _lightAmount = lightAmount;
      _blurAmount = blurAmount;
    }

    override protected function applyEffect(
      bitmapData:BitmapData
    ):void {
      new CompositeEffect(
        [
        new SaturationEffect(_saturation),
        new DissolveEffect(_lightAmount, _lightColor),
        new BlurEffect(_blurAmount, _blurAmount)
        ]
      ).apply(bitmapData);
    }

  }

}
```

The constructor here takes a couple more arguments than DissolveEffect, but that is because it is allowing for each of the three subeffects to be configurable. The applyEffect() method merely instantiates a CompositeEffect of the three necessary operations: saturating, dissolving, and blurring. Of course, you don't have to reuse the aether effects in this case if you simply have code within this method that takes care of these three operations, but the reuse of the simpler subeffects is what makes it a breeze to construct new effects in aether.

6. Now, return once again to VideoFilters.as, and alter the onVideoRender() method with the following bold code, which applies this PointillismEffect and completes our class and exercise:

```
    private function onVideoRender(event:Event):void {
      var bitmapData:BitmapData = ➥
new BitmapData(_video.width, _video.height);
      var matrix:Matrix = new Matrix();
      matrix.scale(_video.scaleX, _video.scaleY);
      bitmapData.draw(_video, matrix);
      new PointillismEffect().apply(bitmapData);
      _filteredScreen.bitmapData = bitmapData;
    }
```

If you compile now, you should see something like Figure 10-7, with the three effects of saturating, dissolving, and blurring all combined into a final, composite effect, without a drop of paint spilled!

Figure 10-7. A pointillism painting effect is applied to the video using subeffects for saturation, dissolving, and blurring.

This exercise should demonstrate how easy it is to pull video into the Flash Player and apply runtime effects to its frames as it plays back. These effects can be used to enhance the video, such as adjusting its levels to brighten, darken, or add contrast. You could apply effects to transition between multiple clips, from fading one clip out as another one fades in, fading in and out of black, or blurring from one clip to another. The manipulations could also be used as special effects, like tinting to grayscale or sepia tones, adding noise to dirty up the video, or posterizing the frame images.

Of course, as with all bitmap effects, you must be conscious of the processing involved and build effects with that always in mind, and this is especially true—if not more so—with video, since this processing will occur every frame. The larger the video and the higher the encoding rate, the more difficult it is to apply effects and not have it adversely affect performance.

But when the video allows for the effects, there's a lot of fun to be had and a lot of use to be found. In the next section, we will take this a step further and see how a Pixel Bender shader can be used in a similar way to create some interesting post effects not possible through ActionScript alone.

Isolating colors for effect

Back in Chapter 5, we looked at the new Pixel Bender Toolkit and how to use it to create shaders for the Flash Player. A shader embedded or loaded into a SWF can be applied as a BitmapFilter through ActionScript, which means that, just as in the previous example, we can apply a shader to a video's pixel data that has been copied into a new BitmapData instance, or, since Video is a DisplayObject, you could also simply add the shader to the Video instance's filters' array.

One effect that is difficult to achieve using just the methods of BitmapData is the isolation of a certain color range in an image. This could be used for chroma keying or for special effect, as demonstrated with the color palette in movies like *Sin City* or *The Spirit*. In Chapter 4, we explored using the `threshold()` method to isolate colors in order to perform chroma keying, but the process requires several applications of the method and its results are far from perfect. What you really need to be able to do in order to successfully isolate a hue in an image is perform tests on each individual pixel, tests of more complexity than the `threshold()` method allows. This is exactly what a shader does.

Creating a color isolation shader

Obviously, before we can apply such a shader in a SWF, we need to create the kernel in the Pixel Bender Toolkit. We'll return to that application now to author our color isolation shader.

1. Launch the Adobe Pixel Bender Toolkit. Select File ➤ Load Image from the menu, and load in the `YellowFlowers.png` that is in the default images directory for Pixel Bender.
2. Select File ➤ New Kernel Filter from the menu. Alter the default code that appears to the following, though feel free to adjust the namespace and vendor. I promise not to be offended. Much.

```
<languageVersion: 1.0;>

kernel IsolateColor
<
  namespace:      "com.bobs27";
  vendor:         "Todd Yard";
  version:        1;
  description:    "Isolates hue in image.";
>
{

  input image4 source;
  output pixel4 result;

  void
  evaluatePixel()
```

```
  {
    float4 px = sampleNearest(source, outCoord());
    result = px;
  }

}
```

Here, we have just expanded the variable names from `src` and `dst` to `source` and `result` and then split up the lines in `evaluatePixel()` so that the sampled pixel is saved into a px variable, which we will perform further operations on.

In order to be able to isolate a color, we need to know which color to isolate. Also, when a color is isolated, what happens to the other pixels in the image? I thought a nice configurable property might be one that indicates whether to hide all nonisolated pixels by setting their alphas to 0 or to completely desaturate the nonisolated pixels. To make these values configurable, we need to add parameters to our kernel.

3. Add the following bold lines to the code:

```
<languageVersion: 1.0;>

kernel IsolateColor
<
  namespace:       "com.bobs27";
  vendor:          "Todd Yard";
  version:         1;
  description:     "Isolates hue in image.";
>
{

  parameter int3 color
  <
    minValue:        int3(0, 0, 0);
    maxValue:        int3(255, 255, 255);
    defaultValue:    int3(255, 0, 0);
    description:     "The color to isolate.";
  >;

  parameter int hideNonIsolated
  <
    minValue:        int(0);
    maxValue:        int(1);
    defaultValue:    int(0);
    description:     ➥
"Whether alpha of 0 should be applied to non-isolated pixels.";
  >;

  input image4 source;
  output pixel4 result;
```

```
  void
  evaluatePixel()
  {
    float4 px = sampleNearest(source, outCoord());
    result = px;
  }

}
```

For color, we will expect a vector of three integers with each component between 0 and 255 representing a single color channel. hideNonIsolated should really be a Boolean, but since that is unsupported by Pixel Bender for the Flash Player, we make this an integer that can either be 0 or 1.

With our parameters set, we can add the code that finds the hue of the color to isolate.

4. The following bold code determines the hue of the color to isolate based on its RGB values:

```
<languageVersion: 1.0;>

kernel IsolateColor
<
  namespace:      "com.bobs27";
  vendor:         "Todd Yard";
  version:        1;
  description:    "Isolates hue in image.";
>
{

  // parameters and variables are unchanged

  void
  evaluatePixel()
  {
    float4 px = sampleNearest(source, outCoord());

    int hue = 0;
    int r = color.r;
    int g = color.g;
    int b = color.b;
    if (r == g && g == b) {
      hue = 0;
    } else if (r >= g && g >= b) {
      hue = 60 * (g - b)/(r - b);
    } else if (g >= r && r >= b) {
      hue = 60 + 60*(g - r)/(g - b);
    } else if (g >= b && b >= r) {
      hue = 120 + 60*(b - r)/(g - r);
    } else if (b >= g && g >= r) {
```

```
      hue = 180 + 60*(b - g)/(b - r);
    } else if (b >= r && r >= g){
      hue = 240 + 60*(r - g)/(b - g);
    } else if (r >= b && b >= g) {
      hue = 300 + 60*(r - b)/(r - g);
    }
    float isolateHue = float(hue);

    result = px;
  }

}
```

No, it's not a pretty block of code, but it is the group of equations needed to convert RGB to a hue value between 0 and 360. Basically, each conditional looks to see which channel has the greatest value and finds the hue in the visible color spectrum based on that and the other two channels' values.

After the conditional is run, the hue integer value is stored as a float in the isolateHue variable. We will need it to be a float for the coming calculations.

With the isolated color's hue determined, we can now do the same for the sampled pixel's hue. This is where having subroutines in separate functions would be fantastic, but we deal with the limitations we have. Prepare to copy and paste.

5. Add the following bold lines to determine the hue of the currently sampled pixel:

```
<languageVersion: 1.0;>

kernel IsolateColor
<
  namespace:      "com.bobs27";
  vendor:         "Todd Yard";
  version:        1;
  description:    "Isolates hue in image.";
>
{

  // parameters and variables are unchanged

  void
  evaluatePixel()
  {
    float4 px = sampleNearest(source, outCoord());

    int hue = 0;
    int r = color.r;
    int g = color.g;
    int b = color.b;
    if (r == g && g == b) {
      hue = 0;
    } else if (r >= g && g >= b) {
```

```
      hue = 60 * (g - b)/(r - b);
    } else if (g >= r && r >= b) {
      hue = 60 + 60*(g - r)/(g - b);
    } else if (g >= b && b >= r) {
      hue = 120 + 60*(b - r)/(g - r);
    } else if (b >= g && g >= r) {
      hue = 180 + 60*(b - g)/(b - r);
    } else if (b >= r && r >= g){
      hue = 240 + 60*(r - g)/(b - g);
    } else if (r >= b && b >= g) {
      hue = 300 + 60*(r - b)/(r - g);
    }
    float isolateHue = float(hue);

    hue = 0;
    r = int(px.r * 255.0);
    g = int(px.g * 255.0);
    b = int(px.b * 255.0);
    if (r == g && g == b) {
      hue = 0;
    } else if (r >= g && g >= b) {
      hue = 60 * (g - b)/(r - b);
    } else if (g >= r && r >= b) {
      hue = 60 + 60*(g - r)/(g - b);
    } else if (g >= b && b >= r) {
      hue = 120 + 60*(b - r)/(g - r);
    } else if (b >= g && g >= r) {
      hue = 180 + 60*(b - g)/(b - r);
    } else if (b >= r && r >= g){
      hue = 240 + 60*(r - g)/(b - g);
    } else if (r >= b && b >= g) {
      hue = 300 + 60*(r - b)/(r - g);
    }
    float pixelHue = float(hue);

    result = px;
  }

}
```

Yes, it's the exact same code, but this time using the RGB values from the sampled pixel. Notice that, since these values will initially be between 0 and 1 for each color channel, we need to multiply them by 255 and convert them to an int to store them within the r, g, and b variables.

```
r = int(px.r * 255.0);
g = int(px.g * 255.0);
b = int(px.b * 255.0);
```

We now have the color to isolate and the color of the sampled pixel.

6. Add the following bold code to hide or desaturate pixels that are not of the hue being isolated. Note that the huge chunk of code used to determine the hues and the code declaring the parameters should still be in your code but is removed from this listing to save space.

```
<languageVersion: 1.0;>

kernel IsolateColor
<
  namespace:      "com.bobs27";
  vendor:         "Todd Yard";
  version:        1;
  description:    "Isolates hue in image.";
>
{

  // color and hideNonIsolated declarations are unchanged

  const float3 grayValues = float3(0.3, 0.59, 0.11);

  input image4 source;
  output pixel4 result;

  void
  evaluatePixel()
  {
    float4 px = sampleNearest(source, outCoord());

    // code to determine hues remains unchanged

    if (pixelHue != isolateHue) {
      if (hideNonIsolated == 1) {
        px.a = 0.0;
      } else {
        float distanceToDesaturatedValues = dot(px.rgb, grayValues);
        px.rgb = float3(distanceToDesaturatedValues);
      }
    }

    result = px;
  }

}
```

The conditional we have set up checks to see if the isolated hue matches the sampled hue. If it doesn't, we will either hide or desaturate the pixel (pixels that pass the test are left unchanged). Setting the alpha to 0 is easy (though the value must be a float, which is why 0.0 is used). For desaturation, we use the same technique we used in Chapter 5, finding the distance between the sampled colors and the grayscale color and setting the RGB values to this in each channel. With all three channels having an equal brightness, we have a grayscale pixel.

You can test your filter now by clicking the Run button, and you should see something like Figure 10-8 (though in full color for you), with the exact pixel color specified isolated in the final image. If you set `hideNonIsolated` to 1, you should see the pixels hidden where they don't match.

Figure 10-8. A single hue is isolated in the image with all other pixels desaturated, an effect more obvious in full color.

At this point, what we have done is little different (and a heck of lot more work) than simply using the `BitmapData.threshold()` method in ActionScript. To make this a more useful filter, we need to allow a hue range in which the sampled hue could fall in order to still be isolated. For instance, if the pixel being evaluated had a hue of 201 and the hue to isolate was 200, does this fall into the desired range?

Similar to that, a range for luminosity would be useful as well. If we were looking to isolate red and the pixel being evaluated had an RGB value of 0x010000, this would be considered a valid red pixel, but to the human eye it just appears black. Should that be excluded from the isolation?

To take care of these issues, we will add two more parameters to set these ranges, or thresholds, within which a pixel can pass the test.

7. Add the following bold code to complete the kernel code:

```
<languageVersion: 1.0;>

kernel IsolateColor
<
  namespace:      "com.bobs27";
  vendor:         "Todd Yard";
  version:        1;
  description:    "Isolates hue in image.";
>
{

  parameter int3 color
  <
    minValue:       int3(0, 0, 0);
    maxValue:       int3(255, 255, 255);
    defaultValue:   int3(255, 0, 0);
    description:    "The color to isolate.";
  >;

  parameter int hueThreshold
  <
    minValue:       int(0);
    maxValue:       int(360);
    defaultValue:   int(10);
    description:    "The amount off-hue to allow.";
  >;

  parameter int luminanceThreshold
  <
    minValue:       int(0);
    maxValue:       int(255);
    defaultValue:   int(100);
    description:    "The amount off-luminance to allow.";
  >;

  parameter int hideNonIsolated
  <
    minValue:       int(0);
    maxValue:       int(1);
    defaultValue:   int(0);
    description:    ➥
"Whether alpha of 0 should be applied to non-isolated pixels.";
  >;

  const float3 grayValues = float3(0.3, 0.59, 0.11);
```

```
  input image4 source;
  output pixel4 result;

  void
  evaluatePixel()
  {
    float4 px = sampleNearest(source, outCoord());

    // code to determine hues remains unchanged

    if (pixelHue - float(hueThreshold) < 0.0 &&
        isolateHue + float(hueThreshold) > 360.0
    ) {
      pixelHue = 360.0 - float(hueThreshold);
    } else if (pixelHue + float(hueThreshold) > 360.0 &&
               isolateHue - float(hueThreshold) < 0.0
    ) {
      pixelHue = float(hueThreshold) - 360.0;
    }

    float pixelLuminance = px.r * 0.3 +
                           px.g * 0.59 +
                           px.b * 0.11;
    float isolateLuminance = float(color.r)/255.0 * 0.3 +
                             float(color.g)/255.0 * 0.59 +
                             float(color.b)/255.0 * 0.11;

    if (abs(pixelHue - isolateHue) > float(hueThreshold) ||
        abs(pixelLuminance - isolateLuminance) > ➥
float(luminanceThreshold)/255.0
    ) {
      if (hideNonIsolated == 1) {
        px.a = 0.0;
      } else {
        float distanceToDesaturatedValues = dot(px.rgb, grayValues);
        float3 fullDesaturate = float3(distanceToDesaturatedValues);
        px.rgb = mix(px.rgb, fullDesaturate, 1.0);
      }
    }

    result = px;
  }

}
```

For the hueThreshold parameter, we allow an integer value between 0 and 360. The range is set at 0 to 255 for the luminanceThreshold parameter.

hueThreshold is first used in evaluatePixel() after the hue of both the isolated color and the sampled pixel are determined. There is a conditional set up to take care of the cases when a hue is near 0 or 360. For instance, if the sampled hue was 2 and the hue to isolate was 360, this would be a valid pixel to isolate as long as the hueThreshold was 2 or more. That case is handled by the following lines:

```
if (pixelHue - float(hueThreshold) < 0.0 &&
    isolateHue + float(hueThreshold) > 360.0
) {
  pixelHue = 360.0 - float(hueThreshold);
```

Here, the sampled hue would be adjusted to be 358, which makes it easier to test against. The hue itself is not used to recolor the pixel, so it doesn't matter that we are altering it in this way. This is simply to place the value within a range that will pass the test if it is valid.

The second part of the conditional checks the opposite direction, such as when the hue sampled is 355 and the hue to isolate is 0. If the hueThreshold is 5 or more, this sampled pixel should pass, and this is handled with the following lines:

```
} else if (pixelHue + float(hueThreshold) > 360.0 &&
           isolateHue - float(hueThreshold) < 0.0
) {
  pixelHue = float(hueThreshold) - 360.0;
```

In this case, the sampled hue would become 5 and so would fall within the hue threshold.

With those adjustments made, we can calculate the luminosity of the isolated color and the sampled pixel. There is a standard equation for that, too, and we used it back in Chapter 5 as well:

```
float pixelLuminance = px.r * 0.3 +
                       px.g * 0.59 +
                       px.b * 0.11;
float isolateLuminance = float(color.r)/255.0 * 0.3 +
                         float(color.g)/255.0 * 0.59 +
                         float(color.b)/255.0 * 0.11;
```

Note that, for the isolated color passed in, we first convert the integers that are between 0 and 255 to instead be floats between 0 and 1. This is just to keep the two luminance values in the same range, but we could also have gone in the other direction and made both sets of values between 0 and 255.

The final new line of code now uses these new parameters and luminance values to determine which pixels pass the test.

```
    if (abs(pixelHue - isolateHue) > float(hueThreshold) ||
        abs(pixelLuminance - isolateLuminance) > ➥
float(luminanceThreshold)/255.0
```

As long as the hue and luminance are within the specified thresholds, the pixel will be left alone. If not, then the pixel will either be hidden or desaturated.

If you test your filter now, you should see that you are able to set better ranges of pixels to isolate, as shown in Figure 10-9, although, once again, this is more obvious in the full color file.

Figure 10-9. Hue and luminosity ranges are used to isolate pixels in the image.

Of course, for Flash, there is one step left here within the toolkit.

8. Save the kernel, and select File ➤ Export Filter for Flash Player to save the `.pbj` file as `isolateColor.pbj`.

You can close the Pixel Bender Toolkit and return to your ActionScript editor. We have completed the shader and now can bring it into the Flash Player to do some pretty cool filtering tricks.

Extending ShaderEffect

You can use the shader in ActionScript as it is written, or perhaps utilizing the ShaderProxy class used back in Chapter 5. However, aether has a ShaderEffect class that takes care of loading or instantiating embedded shader bytecode for you. It also extends ImageEffect, which means you can include it in composite effects with no additional work. Let's take advantage of this by extending ShaderEffect for our new color isolation filter.

1. Create a new ActionScript file, either in Flash or through a new ActionScript project named LadyInRed in Flex Builder, and save the file as `IsolateColorEffect.as`.
2. Since there is only a little code needed to extend ShaderClass, and this only to store the configurable parameters and pass them to the shader, let's cover it all in one block. The following is the entirety of the IsolateColorEffect class:

```
package {

  import aether.effects.shaders.ShaderEffect;
  import aether.utils.MathUtil;

  public class IsolateColorEffect extends ShaderEffect {

    public static var shaderClass:String = "IsolateColorKernel";
    public static var shaderFile:String = "isolateColor.pbj";

    private var _red:uint;
    private var _green:uint;
    private var _blue:uint;
    private var _hueThreshold:uint;
    private var _luminanceThreshold:uint;
    private var _hideNonIsolated:uint;

    public function IsolateColorEffect(
      color:uint=0xFF0000,
      hueThreshold:uint=10,
      luminanceThreshold:uint=60,
      hideNonIsolated:Boolean=false,
      blendMode:String=null,
      alpha:Number=1
    ) {
      _shaderClass = shaderClass;
      _shaderFile = shaderFile;
      this.color = color;
      this.hueThreshold = hueThreshold;
      this.luminanceThreshold = luminanceThreshold;
      this.hideNonIsolated = hideNonIsolated;
      init(blendMode, alpha);
    }

    override protected function configureShader(data:Object):void {
      data.color.value = [_red, _green, _blue];
      data.hueThreshold.value = [_hueThreshold];
      data.luminanceThreshold.value = [_luminanceThreshold];
      data.hideNonIsolated.value = [_hideNonIsolated];
    }
```

```
    public function set color(color:uint):void {
      color = MathUtil.clamp(color, 0, 0xFFFFFF);
      _red = color >> 16 & 0xFF;
      _green = color >> 8 & 0xFF;
      _blue = color & 0xFF;
    }

    public function set hueThreshold(threshold:uint):void {
      _hueThreshold = MathUtil.clamp(threshold, 0, 360);
    }

    public function set luminanceThreshold(threshold:uint):void {
      _luminanceThreshold = MathUtil.clamp(threshold, 0, 255);
    }

    public function set hideNonIsolated(hide:Boolean):void {
      _hideNonIsolated = hide ? 1 : 0;
    }

  }

}
```

Just as with the DissolveEffect we created in the last example, the constructor for a shader effect takes the configurable parameters and the standard blend mode and alpha values. Each parameter is passed to the implicit setter method, which takes care of ensuring the value is kept within the allowed range. For instance, the hueThreshold must be between 0 and 360. aether's `MathUtil.clamp()` uses `min()` and `max()` to keep the first parameter within the range of the second and third parameters.

```
public function set hueThreshold(threshold:uint):void {
  _hueThreshold = MathUtil.clamp(threshold, 0, 360);
}
```

A similar operation is performed for the `luminanceThreshold`. hideNonIsolated stores either 0 or 1.

```
_hideNonIsolated = hide ? 1 : 0;
```

The `color` setter ensures the value is between 0x000000 and 0xFFFFFF but then also splits the color up into three separate values, one for each channel, which is how the shader expects the color to be passed.

```
color = MathUtil.clamp(color, 0, 0xFFFFFF);
_red = color >> 16 & 0xFF;
_green = color >> 8 & 0xFF;
_blue = color & 0xFF;
```

The overridden `configureShader()` method is where parameter values are passed to the shader in the required form. If you recall from Chapter 5, parameters are always arrays assigned to the value property of the ShaderParameter.

```
data.color.value = [_red, _green, _blue];
data.hueThreshold.value = [_hueThreshold];
data.luminanceThreshold.value = [_luminanceThreshold];
data.hideNonIsolated.value = [_hideNonIsolated];
```

The only other lines to note are the static properties defined at the top of the class.

```
public static var shaderClass:String = "IsolateColorKernel";
public static var shaderFile:String = "isolateColor.pbj";
```

It is these that allow for either loading or embedding of the kernel bytecode. We talked about these in Chapter 7 when discussing the aether library, but basically the shaderClass is the name of the class that the embedded bytecode should be assigned to. The `shaderFile` is the name of the `.pbj` file if the shader is instead to be loaded. These are the default names, but since the variables are public, they can be altered if the application requires it.

This class, in combination with the aether library of course, is all we need to get our shader into the Flash Player. In the next section, we will apply it for effects.

Highlighting a color for comic book noir

Frank Miller's *Sin City* comic had a distinct visual style with a limited color palette (very noir and cheaper to produce!) that Robert Rodriguez, with Frank Miller credited as codirector, successfully recreated for the movie version. Frank Miller then went on to write and direct *The Spirit*, which used similar effects.

We can produce the same sort of effect with images or video in Flash using the `isolateColor` shader we just completed. In this next example, we will take the still image in Figure 10-10, which was produced purposely with greens to enable easy color isolation, and run it through our effects gamut to produce a comic book noir image à la *Sin City*. The same could be applied to video, but using a single image simplifies the tutorial.

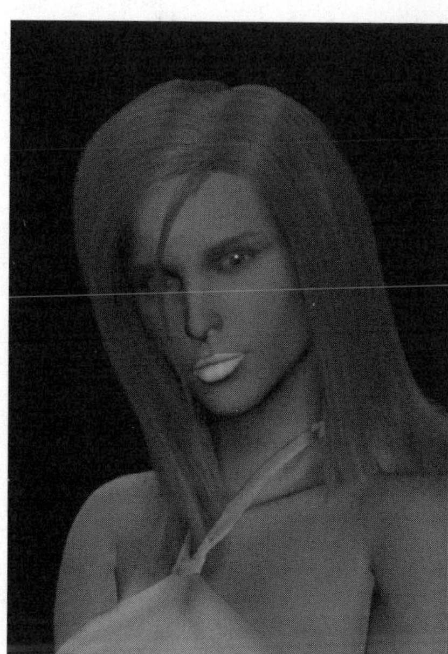

Figure 10-10. A render of a woman with distinct green regions that can be easily isolated

1. Start with a new document in Flash named `LadyInRed.fla`. If you are using Flex Builder and created the LadyInRed project for the IsolateColorEffect class, the project should already be set up as LadyInRed. The main ActionScript class should be named `LadyInRed.as`.
2. This example uses aether as well, so import `aether.swc` into your FLA or Flex Builder project from this chapter's files.
3. The LadyInRed class will extend the AbstractImageLoader class we have used in past examples, so be sure to include this file from this chapter's files in the same directory as `LadyInRed.as`.

4. Start your LadyInRed class with the following code:

```
package {

  import aether.effects.shaders.ShaderEffect;
  import aether.utils.ImageUtil;

  import flash.display.Bitmap;
  import flash.display.BitmapData;
  import flash.events.Event;

  [SWF(width=920, height=630, backgroundColor=0xFFFFFF)]

  public class LadyInRed extends AbstractImageLoader {

    private var _shaderEffect:IsolateColorEffect;

    public function LadyInRed() {
      super("../../assets/ladyInRed.jpg");
    }

    override protected function runPostImageLoad():void {
      ShaderEffect.shaderFilePath = "../../assets/";
      _shaderEffect = new IsolateColorEffect(0x00FF00, 20, 120, true);
      _shaderEffect.addEventListener(Event.COMPLETE, onShaderReady);
    }

    private function onShaderReady(event:Event):void {
      _shaderEffect.removeEventListener(Event.COMPLETE, onShaderReady);
      addChild(_loadedBitmap);
      var bitmapData:BitmapData = ➥
ImageUtil.getBitmapData(_loadedBitmap);
      _shaderEffect.apply(bitmapData);
      var bitmap:Bitmap = new Bitmap(bitmapData);
      bitmap.x = bitmap.width;
      addChild(bitmap);
    }

  }

}
```

This class uses the AbstractImageLoader once more to handle loading in the image. When `runPostImageLoader()` is invoked the path to the `.pbj` file is set (so if you do not have the `isolateColor.pbj` file two directories up from the SWF in an assets directory, update this path accordingly). Then, a new IsolateColorEffect, which we created in the last section, is instantiated with the color of green passed for isolation. 20 is passed as the hue threshold, and 120 is passed as the luminance threshold. The fourth value, true, specifies that any nonisolated color should be hidden.

```
_shaderEffect = new IsolateColorEffect(0x00FF00, 20, 120, true);
```

Since the shader is being loaded, we need to set up a listener for when the shader is ready. This is done through a COMPLETE event listener added to the shader.

When the handler for that event is called, we first remove the listener and then add the loaded bitmap to the stage. The two lines that follow grab the pixel data from the bitmap and apply our color isolation filter.

```
var bitmapData:BitmapData = ImageUtil.getBitmapData(_loadedBitmap);
_shaderEffect.apply(bitmapData);
```

This should remove all but the green pixels from the image, which is then added to the stage to the right of the original image. If you test your movie now, you will see just the green pixels isolated, as shown in Figure 10-11.

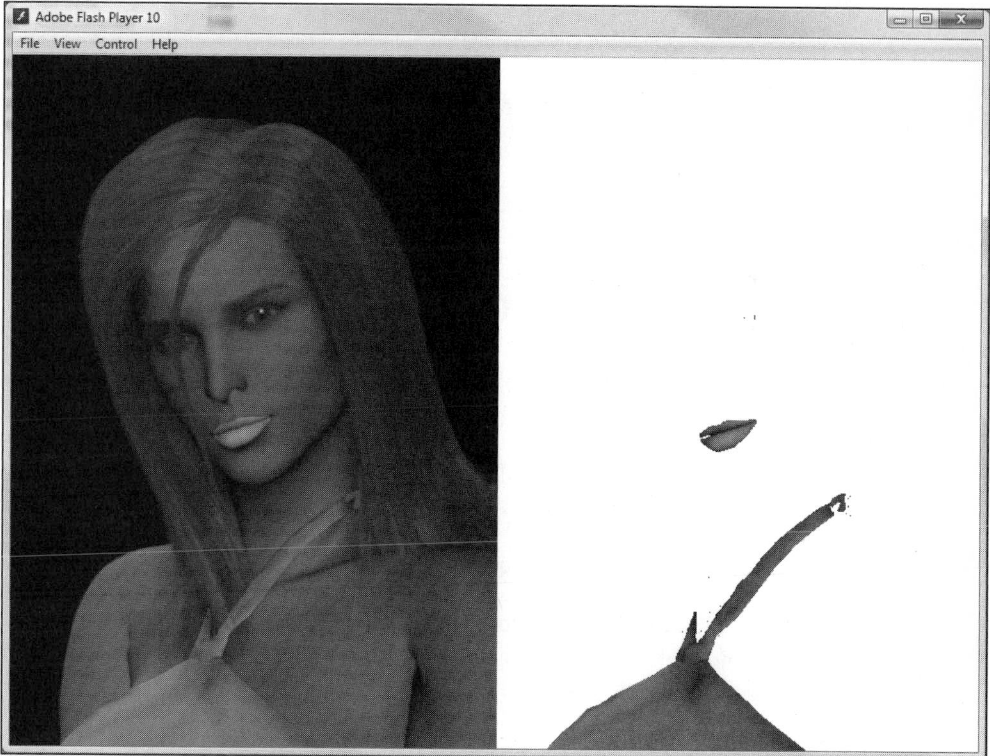

Figure 10-11. The green pixels from the image on the left are isolated in the image on the right.

Now that we've confirmed the shader works as needed, we can enhance the effect by doing several things to create our comic book noir image. We will need to reduce the colors in the rest of the image to black and white, change the green color to red, and then apply a levels adjustment to the final composite in order to limit the range of each color by increasing the overall contrast. This can all be accomplished through a well-constructed composite effect.

5. Add the following bold lines to your class, replacing the previous call to apply() on the shader effect. This will complete the class and the effect.

```
package {

  import aether.effects.adjustments.GradientMapEffect;
  import aether.effects.adjustments.LevelsEffect;
  import aether.effects.adjustments.SaturationEffect;
  import aether.effects.common.CompositeEffect;
  import aether.effects.shaders.ShaderEffect;
  import aether.utils.ImageUtil;

  import flash.display.Bitmap;
  import flash.display.BitmapData;
  import flash.events.Event;

  [SWF(width=920, height=630, backgroundColor=0xFFFFFF)]

  public class LadyInRed extends AbstractImageLoader {

    private var _shaderEffect:IsolateColorEffect;

    public function LadyInRed() {
      super("../../assets/ladyInRed.jpg");
    }

    override protected function runPostImageLoad():void {
      ShaderEffect.shaderFilePath = "../../assets/";
      _shaderEffect = new IsolateColorEffect(0x00FF00, 20, 120, true);
      _shaderEffect.addEventListener(Event.COMPLETE, onShaderReady);
    }

    private function onShaderReady(event:Event):void {
      _shaderEffect.removeEventListener(Event.COMPLETE, onShaderReady);
      addChild(_loadedBitmap);
      var bitmapData:BitmapData = ➥
ImageUtil.getBitmapData(_loadedBitmap);
      new CompositeEffect(
        [
        new SaturationEffect(0),
        new CompositeEffect(
          [
          _shaderEffect,
          new GradientMapEffect([0, 0xFF0000], [0, 255])
          ],
```

```
            bitmapData
          ),
          new LevelsEffect(60, 62, 64)
          ]
        ).apply(bitmapData);
        var bitmap:Bitmap = new Bitmap(bitmapData);
        bitmap.x = bitmap.width;
        addChild(bitmap);
      }

  }

}
```

The first thing that is done in the composite effect is the color in the image is desaturated completely. The nested composite effect, however, uses the original bitmap data (the second argument of CompositeEffect) and so can still isolate the green pixels before remapping these to reds using a gradient map. The final composite gets a levels adjustment, which results in an extremely high contrast between the lights and darks of the image, as shown in Figure 10-12, the final image.

Figure 10-12. A composite effect using color isolation, tinting, and levels adjustment is applied to the image on the right.

Although this effect was performed on a still image, the same could be applied to a video as well. Using this same technique of isolating pixels in an image based on color, though, we can do more than just alter colors, as will be demonstrated in the next example.

Building dynamic post effects

As a final example this chapter, we will use the color isolation filter to aid us in limiting an effect to a region in a video frame. This can be used to apply post effects, like glows, to a video or more complex effects, like smoke and fire. Of course, these could be applied to the video source itself through programs like After Effects or Combustion, but if you do not have access to the original, precompression file or if the effect needs to be dynamic—for instance, an effect that only appears through user interaction—then this is a useful technique that can be applied.

In this example, we will add fire to a video using the method already explored in Chapter 8. We will use the color isolation filter that we created and worked with in the last example, applying it each frame of the video as we did in the first example this chapter on video filters. In fact, there is nothing new in this example that you have not worked through previously. This is the point when effects really do become a combination of the smaller techniques you will use over and over. The trick is seeing of what smaller techniques a larger effect is composed.

Have a look at `Alien.swf` in this chapter's files. You will see the alien's eyes begin to emit fire, just as the burning letters did in Chapter 8. Figure 10-13 shows a single frame from the movie. Don't worry. No aliens or cameramen were harmed in the making of this effect.

Figure 10-13. An alien render with its green eyes isolated to apply a fire effect at runtime

Here is how you can accomplish this effect:

1. Start with a new document in Flash named `Alien.fla` or an ActionScript project in Flex Builder saved as Alien. The main ActionScript class should be named `Alien.as`.

2. This example used aether, so import `aether.swc` into your FLA or Flex Builder project from this chapter's files.
3. This example also uses the IsolateColorEffect that we created for the last example. Be sure this file is included in the same directory as `Alien.as`.
4. This example also uses the VideoLoader that we created for the chapter's first example VideoFilters. Be sure this file is included in the same directory as `Alien.as`.
5. Start your Alien class with the following code:

```
package {

  import aether.effects.shaders.ShaderEffect;

  import flash.display.Bitmap;
  import flash.display.BitmapData;
  import flash.display.Sprite;
  import flash.events.Event;
  import flash.geom.Matrix;

  [SWF(width=490, height=370, backgroundColor=0x000000)]

  public class Alien extends Sprite {

    private var _video:VideoLoader;
    private var _filteredScreen:Bitmap;
    private var _shaderEffect:IsolateColorEffect;

    public function Alien() {
      ShaderEffect.shaderFilePath = "../../assets/";
      _shaderEffect = new IsolateColorEffect(0x00FF00, 5, 50, true);
      _shaderEffect.addEventListener(Event.COMPLETE, onShaderReady);
    }

    private function onShaderReady(event:Event):void {
      _shaderEffect.removeEventListener(Event.COMPLETE, onShaderReady);
      addVideo();
      _filteredScreen = new Bitmap();
      addChild(_filteredScreen);
    }

    private function onVideoRender(event:Event):void {
      var bitmapData:BitmapData = ➥
new BitmapData(_video.width, _video.height);
      var matrix:Matrix = new Matrix();
      matrix.scale(_video.scaleX, _video.scaleY);
      bitmapData.draw(_video, matrix);
      _shaderEffect.apply(bitmapData);
      _filteredScreen.bitmapData = bitmapData;
    }
```

```
    private function addVideo():void {
      _video = new VideoLoader(490, 370, "../../assets/alien.flv");
      addChild(_video);
      _video.addEventListener(Event.RENDER, onVideoRender);
    }

  }

}
```

We won't be breaking this class down line by line, since we did so in the previous examples. Just as in LadyInRed, the shader is loaded with a listener set up for the COMPLETE event. Once this is fired and the shader is ready, a VideoLoader instance is added to the stage in the addVideo() method with a relative path to an FLV file (make sure this is two directories up in an assets directory, as it is in this chapter's files, or alter the path accordingly). A RENDER event listener is set up so that we can draw new bitmap data each frame as the video plays.

onVideoRender() is the handler for this event, and just as in the VideoFilters example, we draw the video's pixel data into a new BitmapData instance. The shader is applied to this data, which will isolate the greens in the image, and this data is passed to the _filteredScreen bitmap, which was added in onShaderReady(), layered on top of the video image.

If you test now, you shouldn't see anything more than the alien video with no visible effects. The reason for this is that the eyes are being isolated but are being drawn on top of the original video. If you comment out the line where the video is added to the stage, you will see the eyes in isolation, as in Figure 10-14. It's almost like a *Scooby Doo* cartoon where the lights have all turned off leaving just eyes floating about the television screen. And that's my second *Scooby Doo* reference in this book—heaven help me.

Figure 10-14. The isolated eyes from the video using the custom shader

In Chapter 8, when we completed the burning letters example, I mentioned that the same effect could be applied to any isolated object and demonstrated this with the burning man. Well, we can use the exact same technique for some burning eyes. All we need to do is draw our moving, displaced flame on the isolated eyes each time the video frame renders.

6. The following bold code completes our Alien class, adding glowing green flame to our sour-looking ET:

```
package {

  import aether.effects.shaders.ShaderEffect;
  import aether.utils.ImageUtil;

  import flash.display.Bitmap;
  import flash.display.BitmapData;
  import flash.display.BitmapDataChannel;
  import flash.display.Sprite;
  import flash.events.Event;
  import flash.filters.DisplacementMapFilter;
  import flash.filters.DisplacementMapFilterMode;
  import flash.geom.ColorTransform;
  import flash.geom.Matrix;
  import flash.geom.Point;

  [SWF(width=490, height=370, backgroundColor=0x000000)]

  public class Alien extends Sprite {

    private static const FLICKER_RATE:Number = 10;

    private var _flame:BitmapData;
    private var _perlinNoise:BitmapData;
    private var _perlinOffsets:Array;
    private var _perlinSeed:int;
    private var _video:VideoLoader;
    private var _filteredScreen:Bitmap;
    private var _shaderEffect:IsolateColorEffect;

    public function Alien() {
      ShaderEffect.shaderFilePath = "../../assets/";
      _shaderEffect = new IsolateColorEffect(0x00FF00, 5, 50, true);
      _shaderEffect.addEventListener(Event.COMPLETE, onShaderReady);
    }

    private function onShaderReady(event:Event):void {
      _shaderEffect.removeEventListener(Event.COMPLETE, onShaderReady);
      addVideo();
      makeFlame();
      makeNoise();
```

```
      _filteredScreen = new Bitmap();
      addChild(_filteredScreen);
    }

    private function onVideoRender(event:Event):void {
      var bitmapData:BitmapData = ➥
new BitmapData(_video.width, _video.height);
      var matrix:Matrix = new Matrix();
      matrix.scale(_video.scaleX, _video.scaleY);
      bitmapData.draw(_video, matrix);
      _shaderEffect.apply(bitmapData);
      _filteredScreen.bitmapData = bitmapData;
      drawFlame();
    }

    private function addVideo():void {
      _video = new VideoLoader(490, 370, "../../assets/alien.flv");
      addChild(_video);
      _video.addEventListener(Event.RENDER, onVideoRender);
    }

    private function makeFlame():void {
      _flame = new BitmapData(
        stage.stageWidth,
        stage.stageHeight,
        true,
        0x00000000
      );
      addChild(new Bitmap(_flame));
    }

    private function makeNoise():void {
      _perlinNoise = _flame.clone();
      _perlinSeed = int(new Date());
      _perlinOffsets = [new Point()];
    }

    private function applyNoise():void {
      _perlinNoise.perlinNoise(
        20,
        20,
        1,
        _perlinSeed,
        false,
        true,
        BitmapDataChannel.RED,
        true,
        _perlinOffsets
      );
```

```
            (_perlinOffsets[0] as Point).y += FLICKER_RATE;
          }

          private function drawFlame():void {
            _flame.scroll(0, -3);
            _flame.draw(
              _filteredScreen,
              null,
              new ColorTransform(1, 1, 1, .1)
            );
            applyNoise();
            ImageUtil.applyFilter(
              _flame,
              new DisplacementMapFilter(
                _perlinNoise,
                new Point(),
                BitmapDataChannel.RED,
                BitmapDataChannel.RED,
                2,
                8,
                DisplacementMapFilterMode.CLAMP
              )
            );
          }

        }

      }
```

You can compare this code with that in Chapter 8 and see that very little of it has changed. In fact, makeFlame(), makeNoise(), and applyNoise() are exactly the same as the methods found in BurningLetters.as except for the amount of displacement and the number of octaves (here, only one octave is used to ease processing). drawFlame() differs only slightly more with only the _filteredScreen data being drawn into flame as opposed to the whole stage, and here no blur is applied, again to help limit the amount of processing needed.

Because this technique for creating fire was explored more in depth in Chapter 8, I won't break it down once again here. The important things to understand are that, each frame, the video is drawn into a BitmapData instance and that this instance's data has its green color isolated using our shader. With the pixels isolated, we can displace them and scroll them vertically each frame, creating a fire effect that emanates solely from the isolated pixels.

Isolating colors is a great way to create your own runtime chroma keying, to reduce and alter the palettes of your video, and to limit the range of certain effects within the frame. Of course, the shader we created would work equally well with still images, as you saw with the lady in red. In fact, I think perhaps our alien—let's call him Toby—I think perhaps Toby was upset that we spent so much time on the lady, and that's why he's fuming. It certainly gives new meaning to "Smoke Gets in Your Eyes."

Summary

In 1877, Eadweard Muybridge took a sequence of images of a horse galloping to settle a bet about whether all four hooves of a horse are ever off the ground simultaneously (they are). When these images are viewed rapidly in a sequence, you get an animation of a horse running. This chapter has been about reversing this process, taking the individual frames of a video loaded into the Flash Player and acting on each one as an individual image. If you stop thinking about video only as video, but instead also as a sequence of bitmap images, you can begin to see the possibilities available for video manipulation.

In this chapter, we looked at how you can extract pixel data from a video as it plays and draw this into bitmap data. This bitmap data can be rendered on the stage to appear like video but can then have any bitmap effects applied that you could apply to a still image. We looked at ImageEffect in aether and how this could be leveraged and extended to create complex composite effects and how the child class ShaderEffect could be used with new Pixel Bender shaders to enable effects not possible through ActionScript alone.

Video is more and more becoming an integral part of the online presences of many companies. The Flash Player has long been at the forefront of providing the means for many to get their video on the Web. As a Flash, Flex, or ActionScript developer, you should understand this technology and how it may be included in your work, not only just to play video but to bend it to suit your needs and enhance a user's experience.

In all of this discussion of video, not once has sound been mentioned. I feel bad. Let's dedicate all of the next chapter to sound to make up for it.

Chapter 11

SOUND VISUALIZATION EFFECTS

I am entranced by sound visualizers, those blurs of shapes, colors, and animations that can be seen in Windows Media Player and iTunes. There is something so captivating about the often organic visuals immediately reacting to the highs and lows of the music, responding to it in much the same way as humans on a dance floor, that I can sit and watch song after song just to see how each is interpreted. I don't know whether the visualizers are the computer age's version of the classical sirens that lured sailors to crash upon the rocks, but I do know I should probably never sail a ship while my MP3s play on my laptop just in case.

Building a sound visualizer in ActionScript is one of those techniques that you initially might think is quite difficult. After all, it involves loading in a sound, analyzing its data in real time as it plays, and creating visual effects based on a bunch of numbers that represent the sound. However, loading and playing back a sound through ActionScript in its simplest form is fairly straightforward, requiring less work than loading video and only slightly more than loading a static image. Analyzing the sound data is all handled for you behind the scenes; thank you very much, Flash Player. The work then comes in how you choose to take a collection of numbers and create something with visual interest.

Ah, did I say "work"? Actually, I find that transforming the numeric representation of a sound into an image is one of the more playful aspects of programming in ActionScript. The goal of a sound visualization is to engage and entertain the user, dynamically providing graphics for a media type that is completely without visuals, usually to take advantage of screen real estate that would otherwise be left empty. Sound visualizers bridge the gap between utilitarian image effects and pure eye candy and, as such, are as open to complete interpretation and creative freedom as you can get in Flash.

In this chapter, we will walk through all the steps required for creating a sound visualizer in ActionScript, from loading and playing the sound to different techniques of representing the numbers with pixels on the screen. There are so many possibilities for visualizing sound, permutations both major and minor, that you should consider this chapter an introduction to what you might achieve with just a little knowledge and a lot of play.

Loading and playing sound

In past chapters, we have looked at loading static images into the Flash Player through the Loader class, Pixel Bender bytecode through the URLLoader class, and video files through NetConnection and NetStream. Loading sound files progressively over HTTP requires the use of additional specialized classes, Sound and SoundChannel.

The Sound class is used to load and play a sound file. When a sound plays back, it does so through a single channel, represented by an instance of the SoundChannel class. It is through this instance that you can stop playback, set volume, and receive notification on when the sound is complete.

> *Just as we discussed last chapter with video, there is a lot to loading and playing sounds in the Flash Player that cannot be covered in depth in a book on ActionScript image effects, such as streaming audio over RTMP, reading metadata, allowing for buffering, and dynamic sound generation. Even much discussion on controlling basic sound properties, like volume and pan, must remain a topic for another book if we want to get to actually creating visual effects with the sound. Please refer to Adobe's ActionScript 3.0 documentation for further information on the sound classes and sound functionality in general in the Flash Player. I can also recommend friends of ED's* Foundation ActionScript 3.0 with Flash CS3 and Flex *(ISBN: 978-1-59059-815-3), which contains an excellent chapter on audio in ActionScript.*

In this next tutorial, we will build a class that works similarly to the VideoLoader class, which handled all of the code for loading and playing video in the last chapter. The new class, SoundController, will contain the bare bones code needed for us to load and play back a sound, dispatching notifications on when the sound changes so that a visual display can be updated. This class will help simplify the later examples when we build our visualizations.

1. Create a new ActionScript file, either in Flash or through a new ActionScript project named SoundTest in Flex Builder, saved as `SoundController.as`.

2. Begin the SoundController class with the following code. This is all we need to load and play a sound, though we will add additional methods in later tutorials to allow for creating visualizations:

```
package {

  import flash.display.Sprite;
  import flash.events.Event;
  import flash.events.EventDispatcher;
  import flash.events.IOErrorEvent;
  import flash.media.Sound;
  import flash.media.SoundChannel;
  import flash.net.URLRequest;

  public class SoundController extends EventDispatcher {

    private var _sound:Sound;
    private var _soundChannel:SoundChannel;

    public function SoundController(file:String=null) {
      if (file) {
        load(file);
      }
    }

    private function onSoundComplete(event:Event):void {
      dispatchEvent(event);
    }

    private function onLoadError(event:Event):void {
      dispatchEvent(event);
    }

    public function load(file:String):void {
      _sound = new Sound();
      _sound.addEventListener(IOErrorEvent.IO_ERROR, onLoadError);
      try {
        _sound.load(new URLRequest(file));
        _soundChannel = _sound.play();
```

```
          _soundChannel.addEventListener(Event.SOUND_COMPLETE, ➥
onSoundComplete);
        } catch (e:Error) {
          trace(e.getStackTrace());
        }
      }

    }

  }
```

Much like in VideoLoader, we allow for a file to be passed to the class's constructor. If the file parameter is not null, then `load()` is immediately called. This `load()` method creates a new Sound instance and sets up a listener for a loading error. Then, within a `try . . . catch` block to catch any security errors, the sound file is loaded using a `URLRequest` in the Sound instance's `load()` method.

Loading the sound does not initiate playback; it merely begins the loading of the bytes. To start playback, the Sound instance's `play()` method is invoked, which returns the SoundChannel instance used for that sound. It is on this SoundChannel instance that we can set up a listener for the sound's completion.

For both the `onLoadError()` and `onSoundComplete()` handlers, we merely redispatch the event to be handled by an external class. We will expand on `onSoundComplete()` in the next tutorial as we build our first visualizer.

This is all that is needed to simply load in and play a sound file. Let's continue with a main application class that will use this SoundController to play back a sound.

3. Start with a new document in Flash named `SoundTest.fla`. If you are using Flex Builder and created the SoundTest project for the SoundController class, the project should already be set up as SoundTest. The main ActionScript class in either Flash or Flex Builder should be named `SoundTest.as`.

4. Enter the following code for the SoundTest class:

```
package {

  import flash.display.Sprite;

  [SWF(width=400, height=300, backgroundColor=0x000000)]

  public class SoundTest extends Sprite {

    private var _soundController:SoundController;

    public function SoundTest() {
      _soundController = ➥
new SoundController("../../assets/AlienInTheCaverns.mp3");
```

```
      }
    }
  }
```

Yes, it's that easy. If you compile this now, you should hear the track load and play within the Flash Player (if you don't, check to see whether the IOErrorEvent is fired, which would mean the path to the track is incorrect for the way you have set up your project).

> *A special, great big thanks to Sean Neville (`http://www.seanneville.com`) for the use of several of his original compositions throughout this chapter—Sean is one of those amazing individuals who can create pieces like this for a living and can also build amazing software like Flex, which he helped to produce while at Macromedia and Adobe.*

You can see how easy it is to get sound into the Flash Player. Now, we need to extract data about the sound in order to build visuals that react to the sound as it plays.

Visualizing sound data

We have discussed in previous chapters how images in an electronic form are just a collection of data, pixels that hold bits of information that can be represented as ones and zeros. Sound in an electronic form is much the same. We know that a sound, at some point when loaded into the Flash Player, is just some numeric data that needs to be interpreted. If we can get at the underlying data, we can build visualizations off of it.

Accessing sound data

ActionScript provides a means to get at the raw sound data through the SoundMixer class. This class allows for global control over sound in the Flash Player, and its static `computeSpectrum()` method can return data about the sounds currently playing, placing the result in a ByteArray that you pass to the method. A call to `computeSpectrum()` would look like the following:

```
var data:ByteArray = new ByteArray();
SoundMixer.computeSpectrum(data);
```

In this case, the `data` variable would be populated with the numeric data representing the currently playing sounds in the Flash Player. That means all of the sounds. There is no passing of individual sound channels to the `computeSpectrum()` method, so the data returned is for all sound channels currently playing.

Just what is in this data, though? When a ByteArray is populated with values through a call to computeSpectrum(), it will always contain 512 numeric values. These values will be normalized between –1 and 1, with the first 256 values representing the left channel's data and the last 256 values representing the right channel's data. By default, the 256 values for each channel will define the raw sound wave, with amplitude of the sound represented by the value in each index and frequency determined by the length of each waveform. If you drew vertical lines with the numbers in the first 256 indices of the byte array, as we will do in our next tutorial, you would get an image of a sound wave like that shown in Figure 11-1.

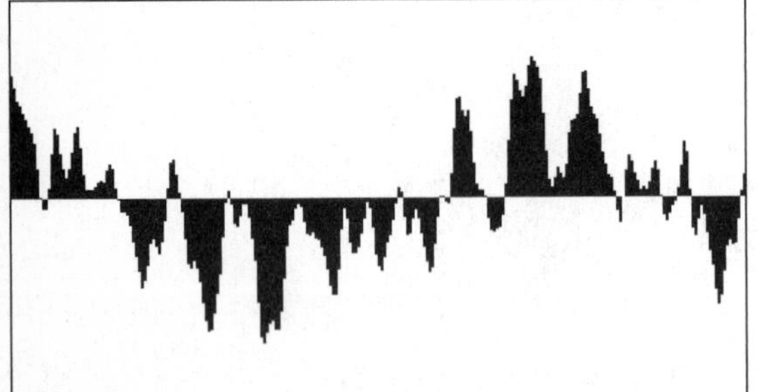

Figure 11-1. An example of sound wave data that you can access through ActionScript

We won't dive in depth into the physics of sound (and I'm not the guy to be writing that chapter anyway), but the beauty of SoundMixer and computeSpectrum() is that you don't need in-depth knowledge in order to create a visualization. You just need to understand that each index will hold a value between –1 and 1. In the grand scheme of things, that's a pretty easy thing to have to understand.

There is another way to represent the sound in that byte array, though, and that is through a frequency spectrum. In a frequency spectrum, each index in the byte array would hold the value for a different frequency, from lower frequencies to higher frequencies (so the 0 index would hold the value for the lowest frequency, and the 255 index would hold the highest frequency). Each frequency value would be between 0 and 1. If you drew vertical lines for each of the first 256 values in a frequency spectrum, as we will in a coming tutorial, you would get an image like Figure 11-2.

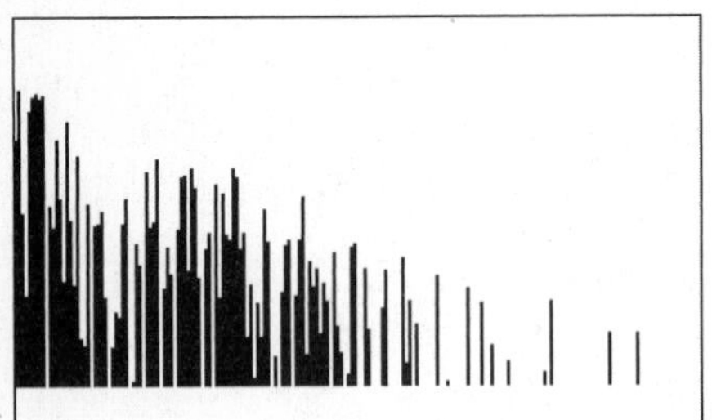

Figure 11-2. An example of a frequency spectrum visualized with the drawing API, with lower frequencies on the left and higher frequencies on the right

Using a frequency spectrum, you can more easily determine the types of sound playing at a given moment. For instance, if you have a thumping base, chances are that the byte array will contain higher values in its lower numbers. A cymbal crash would produce higher frequencies, and so the indices near the end of the 256 values would hold higher values. Sound visualizers can then act on the different frequencies in different ways.

Getting a frequency spectrum simply requires passing a second parameter, true, to the computeSpectrum() method.

```
var data:ByteArray = new ByteArray();
SoundMixer.computeSpectrum(data, true);
```

This second parameter tells SoundMixer to perform a Fourier transformation on the data so that the byte array will contain the frequency spectrum, as opposed to the raw sound wave. A Fourier transform is an operation that transforms one complex function into another function that expresses the frequencies present in the original. Fortunately, you don't need to understand the algorithm involved in order to use it, for which we all should be grateful. The transformation from raw sound wave to frequency spectrum is handled completely behind the scenes.

Finally, computeSpectrum() takes a third, optional parameter, stretchFactor. This alters the resolution of the sound samples. By default, this value is 0, and the sound is sampled at 44.1 KHz. Each higher integer will halve the sampling rate, so a value of 1 will sample the sound at 22.05 KHz; 2 will sample at 11.025 KHz, and so on. For music, you can generally leave this at the default 0 value, though for other types of sound, such as the spoken word, you could reduce the sampling rate.

So now you know how to get the currently playing sound data and store it in a byte array, with each index holding values between –1 and 1 for a raw sound wave or between 0 and 1 for a frequency spectrum. Here comes the fun part where we can act on that data.

Displaying the waveform

Before we can produce visuals based on data from the current sounds in the Flash Player, we will have to make some additions to SoundController that will allow us to access the data.

1. Return to SoundController.as, and add the following bold lines of code:

```
package {

  import flash.display.Sprite;
  import flash.events.Event;
  import flash.events.EventDispatcher;
  import flash.events.IOErrorEvent;
  import flash.media.Sound;
  import flash.media.SoundChannel;
  import flash.media.SoundMixer;
  import flash.net.URLRequest;
  import flash.utils.ByteArray;

  public class SoundController extends EventDispatcher {

    private var _sound:Sound;
    private var _soundChannel:SoundChannel;

    public function SoundController(file:String=null) {
      // this method body is unchanged
    }

    private function onSoundComplete(event:Event):void {
      dispatchEvent(event);
    }

    private function onLoadError(event:Event):void {
      dispatchEvent(event);
    }

    public function load(file:String):void {
```

```
      // this method body is unchanged
    }

    public function getSoundSpectrum(
      fftMode:Boolean=true,
      stretchFactor:int=0
    ):ByteArray {
      var spectrumData:ByteArray = new ByteArray();
      SoundMixer.computeSpectrum(spectrumData, fftMode, stretchFactor);
      return spectrumData;
    }

  }

}
```

Although the getSoundSpectrum() method is not necessary in this class, since SoundMixer does not act on specific sound channels and its static methods are available everywhere, including it here makes accessing and using the data a little easier for external classes. You can see that, by default, we pass true to the computeSpectrum() method since this is more common when creating visualizations, and otherwise, this getSoundSpectrum() simply handles creation of the byte array and passes on the parameters to computeSpectrum().

One last enhancement we can make is to set up an event for when the sound is playing so that visual displays can update. We can handle this by using a Sprite to add an ENTER_FRAME event listener and then dispatching a CHANGE event in the ENTER_FRAME handler while the sound is playing. We will use a Sprite instead of a Timer so that updates will only occur when the stage needs to rerender.

2. Complete the SoundController class with the following bold lines of code:

```
package {

  // imports remain unchanged

  public class SoundController extends EventDispatcher {

    private var _timerSprite:Sprite;
    private var _playing:Boolean;
    private var _sound:Sound;
    private var _soundChannel:SoundChannel;

    public function SoundController(file:String=null) {
      _timerSprite = new Sprite();
      _timerSprite.addEventListener(Event.ENTER_FRAME, ➥
onSpriteEnterFrame);
      if (file) {
        load(file);
      }
    }
```

```
    private function onSpriteEnterFrame(event:Event):void {
      if (_playing) {
        dispatchEvent(new Event(Event.CHANGE));
      }
    }

    private function onSoundComplete(event:Event):void {
      _playing = false;
      dispatchEvent(event);
    }

    private function onLoadError(event:Event):void {
      dispatchEvent(event);
    }

    public function load(file:String):void {
      _playing = false;
      _sound = new Sound();
      _sound.addEventListener(IOErrorEvent.IO_ERROR, onLoadError);
      try {
        _sound.load(new URLRequest(file));
        _soundChannel = _sound.play();
        _soundChannel.addEventListener(Event.SOUND_COMPLETE, ➥
onSoundComplete);
        _playing = true;
      } catch (e:Error) {
        trace(e.getStackTrace());
      }
    }

    public function getSoundSpectrum(
      fftMode:Boolean=true,
      stretchFactor:int=0
    ):ByteArray {
      var spectrumData:ByteArray = new ByteArray();
      SoundMixer.computeSpectrum(spectrumData, fftMode, stretchFactor);
      return spectrumData;
    }

  }

}
```

A Sprite instance is created in the constructor, and a listener is set up for the ENTER_FRAME event it dispatches. In the onSpriteEnterFrame() handler, we dispatch a CHANGE event if the new _playing property is true. This property is set to true when the sound is first loaded and then set to false when the onSoundComplete() handler is invoked.

This code will allow for an external class to load a sound and listen for a CHANGE event. A handler for this event can then call getSoundSpectrum() in order to update a visual display with the sound data. All the plumbing is in place, so what are we waiting for?

3. Start with a new document in Flash named SoundWave.fla or an ActionScript project in Flex Builder saved as SoundWave. The main ActionScript class should be named SoundWave.as.

4. If you are using Flash, make sure the SoundController.as file is in the same directory as SoundWave.as. If you are working within a new project in Flex Builder, make sure that the SoundController class is accessible by either adding its directory as a source directory or copying the file into your project's source.

5. The following code is the entirety of the code for the SoundWave class:

```
package {

  import flash.display.Sprite;
  import flash.events.Event;
  import flash.utils.ByteArray;

  [SWF(width=400, height=300, backgroundColor=0x000000)]

  public class SoundWave extends Sprite {

    private const WAVE_WIDTH:uint = 300;
    private const WAVE_HEIGHT:uint = 100;
    private const WAVE_COLOR:uint = 0xFFFFFF;

    private var _soundController:SoundController;

    public function SoundWave() {
      _soundController = ➥
new SoundController("../../assets/AlienInTheCaverns.mp3");
      _soundController.addEventListener(Event.CHANGE, onSoundChange);
    }

    private function updateGraph():void {
      var spectrumData:ByteArray = ➥
_soundController.getSoundSpectrum(false);
      graphics.clear();
      graphics.beginFill(WAVE_COLOR);
      var ratio:Number = WAVE_WIDTH/512;
      var x:Number = (stage.stageWidth-WAVE_WIDTH)/2;
      var y:Number = stage.stageHeight/2;
      var i:int = -1;
      var value:Number;
      while (++i < 512) {
        value = Math.ceil(WAVE_HEIGHT*spectrumData.readFloat());
        graphics.drawRect(x+i*ratio, y, 1, -value);
```

```
      }
    }

    private function onSoundChange(event:Event):void {
      updateGraph();
    }

  }

}
```

In the constructor for this class, we create a new SoundController and pass it a path to a file to load, just as we did in SoundTest. In addition, we add a listener for the CHANGE event we added to SoundController in the preceding step. When this event fires, onSoundChange() will be invoked, which in turn calls updateGraph().

updateGraph() contains all the code to draw the sound wave playing. First, we access the data using the getSoundSpectrum() method we just added to SoundController.

```
var spectrumData:ByteArray = _soundController.getSoundSpectrum(false);
```

We pass false as a parameter, since we are looking to display the raw sound wave in this example, not the frequency spectrum. Then, after some drawing API code to clear the previous drawing and set a fill color to draw with, several variables are set up.

```
var ratio:Number = WAVE_WIDTH/512;
var x:Number = (stage.stageWidth-WAVE_WIDTH)/2;
var y:Number = stage.stageHeight/2;
var i:int = -1;
```

ratio is the amount we will have to scale the drawing to fit its 512 values onto the stage to match the value set for WAVE_LENGTH. We could have made the stage at least 512 pixels wide and not worried about this, but it is good to know the technique for scaling the visualization to fit whatever space you have.

x and y will determine the initial position on the stage from which the graph will be drawn, just to make it centered.

The variable i will hold the byte position in the byte array that we are currently reading. Accessing a byte array is a little different than accessing a normal array. Generally, you will read the data in order using the read() methods provided, and so we need to keep track of the current position as we loop through. Keeping this in a variable will make the loop run faster than if we accessed the position of the byte array in every loop iteration.

Let's take a look at the loop to better understand this.

```
while (++i < 512) {
  value = Math.ceil(WAVE_HEIGHT*spectrumData.readFloat());
  graphics.drawRect(x+i*ratio, y, 1, -value);
}
```

Since there are a known 512 entries in the byte array, we can set up a while loop to quickly iterate over them all in the fastest manner possible. Within each iteration, the readFloat() method is used to access the next value in the byte array. This automatically updates the position in the byte array, so in the next iteration, the next index will be accessed.

The value returned from readFloat() will be between –1 and 1. This is multiplied by the desired WAVE_HEIGHT (here, 100 pixels) to give us a value between –100 and 100. We can then draw a rectangle with a single pixel width at the current x and y position, with a value that is made negative (or made positive if already negative) for the height.

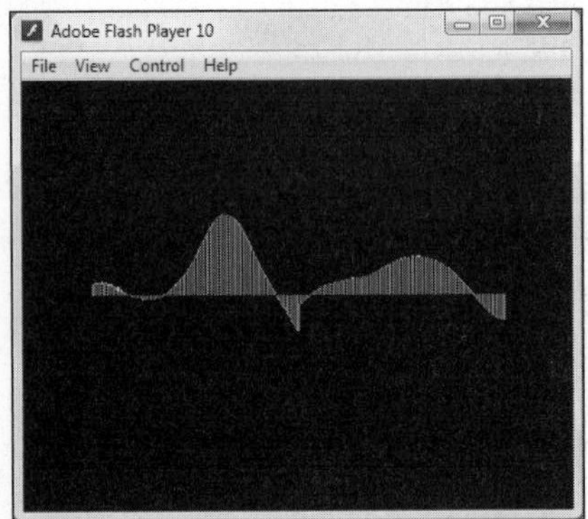

Figure 11-3. A simple sound visualization displaying the raw sound wave with the left and right channels separated over 512 values

Why invert the height value in this way? Well, remember that a rectangle is drawn using the drawing API in a positive direction on the screen y axis, which is down to you and me. In order to make positive values from the byte array be drawn up on the screen, as we would normally consider a positive value in a column chart, we need to draw it on the negative y axis. So a positive value of 100 will result in a rectangle that is drawn with a –100 height from the graph's origin y axis.

The result of all of this is our first, simple sound visualization, showing the raw sound wave with the left side of the wave displaying the left channel and the right side of the wave displaying the right channel, as shown in Figure 11-3.

This is what the sound waves look like that the Flash Player is processing. The next step is to transform this into frequency information for a different type of display.

Displaying the frequencies

To visualize the sound information in the Flash Player based on low, medium, and high frequencies, we need to pass a value of true as the second parameter to a call to computeSpectrum(). This will perform a Fourier transformation on the sound wave, creating a byte array of frequency information that we can then display.

1. Start with a new document in Flash named SoundSpectrum.fla or an ActionScript project in Flex Builder saved as SoundSpectrum. The main ActionScript class should be named SoundSpectrum.as.
2. If you are using Flash, make sure the SoundController.as file is in the same directory as SoundSpectrum.as. If you are working within a new project in Flex Builder, make sure that the SoundController class is accessible by either adding its directory as a source directory or copying the file into your project's source.
3. The following code is the entirety of the code for the SoundSpectrum class:

```
package {

  import flash.display.Sprite;
  import flash.events.Event;
```

```
  import flash.utils.ByteArray;

  [SWF(width=400, height=300, backgroundColor=0x000000)]

  public class SoundSpectrum extends Sprite {

    private const WAVE_WIDTH:uint = 300;
    private const WAVE_HEIGHT:uint = 200;
    private const WAVE_COLOR:uint = 0xFFFFFF;

    private var _soundController:SoundController;

    public function SoundSpectrum() {
      _soundController = ➥
new SoundController("../../assets/AlienInTheCaverns.mp3");
      _soundController.addEventListener(Event.CHANGE, onSoundChange);
    }

    private function updateGraph():void {
      var spectrumData:ByteArray = _soundController.getSoundSpectrum();
      graphics.clear();
      graphics.beginFill(WAVE_COLOR);
      var ratio:Number = WAVE_WIDTH/512;
      var x:Number = (stage.stageWidth-WAVE_WIDTH)/2;
      var y:Number = stage.stageHeight*4/5;
      var value:Number;
      var i:int = -1;
      while (++i < 512) {
        value = Math.ceil(WAVE_HEIGHT*spectrumData.readFloat());
        graphics.drawRect(x+i*ratio, y, 1, -value);
      }
    }

    private function onSoundChange(event:Event):void {
      updateGraph();
    }

  }

}
```

The majority of this code remains unchanged from the last example. The most important item to note is that in the call to `getSoundSpectrum()` no parameters are passed, which results in the frequency spectrum being returned instead of the sound wave.

```
var spectrumData:ByteArray = _soundController.getSoundSpectrum();
```

Because the values will now be between 0 and 1, the y position of the graph, which won't display anything on the negative axis, is adjusted to be near the bottom of the stage.

```
var y:Number = stage.stageHeight*4/5;
```

Inside the loop that reads the bytes and draws the graph, we are using the same code as in SoundWave, with a 1-pixel column being drawn for each frequency value, made negative so that it can be drawn going up on the screen. The result of this is illustrated in Figure 11-4, which shows that the music playing is heavier on the lower frequencies in each channel.

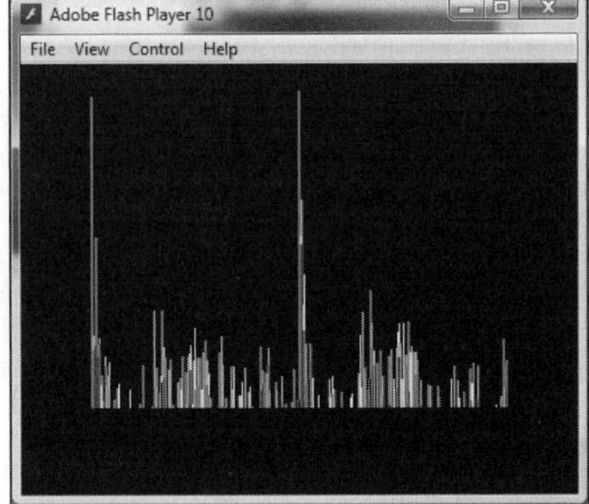

Figure 11-4. The frequency spectrum for a sound displayed, with data in both channels showing more activity in the lower frequencies

Remember, the first 256 values in the byte array contain data for the left channel with the last 256 values holding data for the right. Sometimes, it's helpful to view the graph with these values combined so that you can see the low frequencies in one place and the high frequencies in another. You might see code that only uses 256 values so that only a single channel is represented in order to accomplish this. We can make a slight alteration to updateGraph() so that the values are interspersed, with the lowest frequency for both left and right channels drawn side by side, then the next highest, and so on, all the way to the highest frequency.

4. Update the updateGraph() method with the following bold code:

```
private function updateGraph():void {
  var spectrumData:ByteArray = _soundController.getSoundSpectrum();
  graphics.clear();
  graphics.beginFill(WAVE_COLOR);
  var ratio:Number = WAVE_WIDTH/512;
  var x:Number = (stage.stageWidth-WAVE_WIDTH)/2;
  var y:Number = stage.stageHeight*4/5;
  var value:Number;
  var position:uint;
  var i:int = -1;
  while (++i < 512) {
    value = Math.ceil(WAVE_HEIGHT*spectrumData.readFloat());
    if (i < 256) {
      position = i*2;
```

```
      } else {
        position = (i%256)*2+1;
      }
      graphics.drawRect(x+position*ratio, y, 1, -value);
    }
  }
```

For values in the left channel, they are drawn in even slots in our graph (i*2). For those values in the right channel, the equation (i%256)*2+1 results in the values being drawn into the odd slots. For example, the value found at byte position 256 will have a position of 1; 257 will have a position of 3, and so on. With this code, frequencies in both channels are kept together, producing the result shown in Figure 11-5.

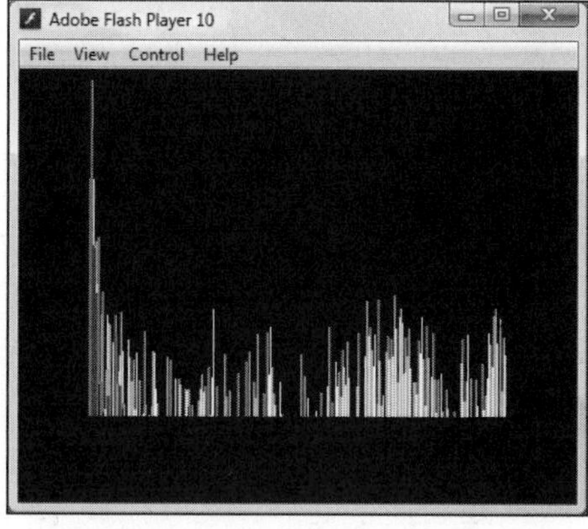

Figure 11-5.
The frequency spectrum display redistributed so that left and right channels are interspersed

You can hopefully now see that loading and playing the sound then accessing its data for display, whether as a sound wave or frequency spectrum, is not a difficult task in itself. The challenge comes in displaying something more than white bands of data. Ready for that challenge?

Rounding the waveform

In both of the last tutorials, we drew the graphs of the sound data in a straight line across the stage. Another way to easily represent this data in a manner that will lend itself to multiple effects is to draw the lines radiating out from the center of the stage. All it takes is a little trigonometry to create a nice foundation for innumerable effects.

1. Start with a new document in Flash named CircularSoundWave.fla or an ActionScript project in Flex Builder saved as CircularSoundWave. The main ActionScript class should be named CircularSoundWave.as.
2. If you are using Flash, make sure the SoundController.as file is in the same directory as CircularSoundWave.as. If you are working within a new project in Flex Builder, make sure that the SoundController class is accessible by either adding its directory as a source directory or copying the file into your project's source.

3. This example uses the aether library, so import the `aether.swc` into this project from this chapter's source files.

4. Enter the following code as the start of the CircularSoundWave class:

```
package {

  import flash.display.Sprite;
  import flash.events.Event;
  import flash.utils.ByteArray;

  [SWF(width=400, height=300, backgroundColor=0x000000)]

  public class CircularSoundWave extends Sprite {

    private const WAVE_RADIUS:uint = 150;

    private var _soundController:SoundController;
    private var _centerSprite:Sprite;

    public function CircularSoundWave() {
      makeCenterSprite();
      _soundController = ➥
new SoundController("../../assets/IrishRock.mp3");
      _soundController.addEventListener(Event.CHANGE, onSoundChange);
    }

    private function makeCenterSprite():void {
      _centerSprite = new Sprite();
      _centerSprite.x = stage.stageWidth/2;
      _centerSprite.y = stage.stageHeight/2;
      addChild(_centerSprite);
    }

    private function updateCenterSprite():void {
      var spectrumData:ByteArray = ➥
_soundController.getSoundSpectrum(false);
      _centerSprite.graphics.clear();
      _centerSprite.graphics.lineStyle(1, 0xFFFFFF);
      var x:Number;
      var y:Number;
      var value:Number;
      var angle:Number;
      var i:int = -1;
      while (++i < 512) {
        value = Math.ceil(WAVE_RADIUS*spectrumData.readFloat());
        angle = i/512*Math.PI*2;
        x = Math.cos(angle)*value;
        y = Math.sin(angle)*value;
        _centerSprite.graphics.moveTo(0, 0);
```

```
        _centerSprite.graphics.lineTo(x, y);
      }
    }

    private function onSoundChange(event:Event):void {
      updateCenterSprite();
    }

  }

}
```

It's a simple start. In the constructor for this class, a makeCenterSprite() method is called to create and center a sprite on the stage. It is within this sprite that all of the drawing will occur. Using a sprite centered on the stage makes it easy to center the effect without worrying about offsets in the drawing code.

As to that drawing code found in updateCenterSprite(), which is called every frame by the onSoundChange() handler, once again we step through all 512 bytes found in the sound's computed byte array. Notice that here we are using the sound wave, not the frequency spectrum, which is determined by the false parameter passed to getSoundSpectrum().

```
var spectrumData:ByteArray = _soundController.getSoundSpectrum(false);
```

The reason for this is that a sound wave with any sort of amplitude (representing volume) will consistently have values distributed out among the 512 values, obviously in a wave-like form that modulates between –1 and 1. In contrast, frequency spectrums will often have values sporadically placed, with some sounds, especially musical tracks, having more information in the lower frequencies with few values other than 0 for the higher frequencies, as you can see in Figure 11-5. Creating a consistent visual effect can therefore be difficult using the full range of these values (you might often see an effect based mainly on the lower frequencies for this reason). Using the raw sound wave, though, can often produce more consistent results.

In this class, we take this raw sound wave, and within the loop, multiply each value by the maximum radius.

```
value = Math.ceil(WAVE_RADIUS*spectrumData.readFloat());
```

This will result in a value between –150 and 150, which will be the length of each line drawn. To get the direction, we calculate the angle based on the current position in the byte array.

```
angle = i/512*Math.PI*2;
```

i/512 will result in a number between 0 and 1. Multiplying this by 2 PI radians (which is 360 degrees) means that each index position will be an incremental angle on a 360-degree circle. We can then use standard trigonometry to take the length of the line and the angle in order to determine the x and y position to draw to.

```
x = Math.cos(angle)*value;
y = Math.sin(angle)*value;
```

These can be plugged into the drawing API commands to draw a line for each index position radiating out from the center of our stage. The result of this is shown in Figure 11-6.

Figure 11-6. A sound wave represented with levels radiating from a central point

The first thing we can do to jazz up the effect is to apply a filter. The GradientGlowFilter is a great way to get multiple colors into an image, so let's begin with that.

5. Add the following bold lines to the CircularSoundWave class:

```
package {

  import flash.display.Sprite;
  import flash.events.Event;
  import flash.filters.BitmapFilterQuality;
  import flash.filters.BitmapFilterType;
  import flash.filters.GradientGlowFilter;
  import flash.utils.ByteArray;

  [SWF(width=400, height=300, backgroundColor=0x000000)]

  public class CircularSoundWave extends Sprite {

    private const WAVE_RADIUS:uint = 150;
    private const WAVE_COLORS:Array = [0x6666FF, 0xFFFFFF, 0x9966FF];

    private var _soundController:SoundController;
    private var _centerSprite:Sprite;

    public function CircularSoundWave() {
      // this method body is unchanged
    }

    private function makeCenterSprite():void {
      _centerSprite = new Sprite();
      _centerSprite.x = stage.stageWidth/2;
      _centerSprite.y = stage.stageHeight/2;
```

```
        addChild(_centerSprite);
        _centerSprite.filters = [
          new GradientGlowFilter(
            5,
            45,
            WAVE_COLORS,
            [0, 1],
            [0, 180, 255],
            10,
            10,
            1,
            BitmapFilterQuality.MEDIUM,
            BitmapFilterType.FULL,
            true
          )
        ];
      }

      private function updateCenterSprite():void {
        // this method body is unchanged
      }

      private function onSoundChange(event:Event):void {
        updateCenterSprite();
      }

    }

  }
```

The result of this new code is shown in Figure 11-7.

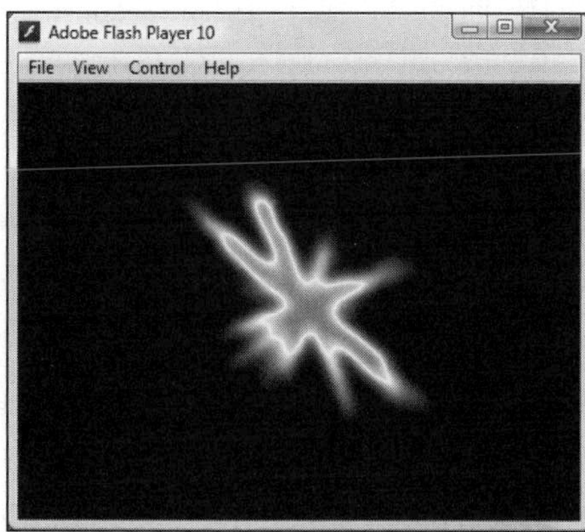

Figure 11-7.
A gradient glow filter is added to the previous example to alter the look of the effect.

Now we're getting somewhere. Already we've gone from a ball of spikes to an organic little glowing blob, which has to be higher up on the food chain. All it took was an application of GradientGlowFilter, which draws the new `WAVE_COLORS` onto the spikes, the blur giving a nice rounding to the spikes' jagginess. With the colors defined in the gradient, you could even animate over sets of colors to alter the gradient over time to add another level to the effect.

We won't add the color animation at this time, but what I do want to add is a little more interest to the background, which is looking pretty barren. This can be achieved by simply copying the graphics on the stage into a new BitmapData instance and scaling it up, similar to the way we created fire in Chapter 8 by duplicating the foreground image and translating and distorting it.

6. Add the following bold code to complete the CircularSoundWave class:

```
package {

  import aether.utils.ImageUtil;

  import flash.display.Bitmap;
  import flash.display.BitmapData;
  import flash.display.Sprite;
  import flash.events.Event;
  import flash.filters.BitmapFilterQuality;
  import flash.filters.BitmapFilterType;
  import flash.filters.GradientGlowFilter;
  import flash.geom.ColorTransform;
  import flash.geom.Matrix;
  import flash.utils.ByteArray;

  [SWF(width=400, height=300, backgroundColor=0x000000)]

  public class CircularSoundWave extends Sprite {

    private const WAVE_RADIUS:uint = 150;
    private const WAVE_COLORS:Array = [0x6666FF, 0xFFFFFF, 0x9966FF];

    private var _soundController:SoundController;
    private var _centerSprite:Sprite;
    private var _backgroundData:BitmapData;

    public function CircularSoundWave() {
      makeBackground();
      makeCenterSprite();
      _soundController = ➥
new SoundController("../../assets/IrishRock.mp3");
      _soundController.addEventListener(Event.CHANGE, onSoundChange);
    }

    private function makeBackground():void {
      _backgroundData = new BitmapData(
        stage.stageWidth,
        stage.stageHeight,
```

```
        false,
        0xFF000000
      );
      var background:Bitmap = new Bitmap(_backgroundData);
      addChild(background);
    }

    private function makeCenterSprite():void {
      // this method body is unchanged
    }

    private function updateBackground():void {
      var capture:BitmapData = ImageUtil.getBitmapData(this);
      var scale:Number = 1.3;
      var matrix:Matrix = new Matrix();
      matrix.scale(scale, scale);
      matrix.translate((width-width*scale)/2, (height-height*scale)/2);
      _backgroundData.draw(
        capture,
        matrix,
        new ColorTransform(.8, .6, .7, .3)
      );
    }

    private function updateCenterSprite():void {
      // this method body is unchanged
    }

    private function onSoundChange(event:Event):void {
      updateBackground();
      updateCenterSprite();
    }

  }

}
```

A call to makeBackground() has been added to the constructor. This method creates a new BitmapData instance the size of the stage and adds it to the display list. Then, whenever the screen is updated during sound playback, updateBackground() is called to capture the current view of the stage. This capture is scaled up by 30 percent and translated based on this scale to keep it centered on the drawn graphic.

```
var scale:Number = 1.3;
var matrix:Matrix = new Matrix();
matrix.scale(scale, scale);
matrix.translate((width-width*scale)/2, (height-height*scale)/2);
```

The scaled image is then drawn into the background bitmap data, with a color transform applied to set it at a lower alpha with darker colors moving towards a reddish purple.

```
_backgroundData.draw(
  capture,
  matrix,
  new ColorTransform(.8, .6, .7, .3)
);
```

The result of this small addition can be seen in the completed effect, shown in Figure 11-8.

Figure 11-8. The view of the stage is drawn onto the background and scaled up to add more visual interest.

Drawing the sound data in a circular pattern opens the door to many effects, since it concentrates the data in a central area that can then be easily transformed. Using the raw sound wave as opposed to the frequency spectrum helps to produce a more consistent effect with an even distribution of visual data. We will take this even further in the next example.

Evolving effects for visualization

With this next effect I wanted to experiment with drawing the circular wave form that we played with in the last example onto spinning 3D planes, like those we used for the tree model back in Chapter 6. As often happens when playing and experimenting, the initial idea didn't pan out, but I stumbled on some happy accidents that produced a better result than what I was initially striving for.

It all starts off innocently enough, with much of the same code we ended up with in the CircularWaveForm example.

1. Start with a new document in Flash named `MothFlowers.fla` or an ActionScript project in Flex Builder saved as MothFlowers. The main ActionScript class should be named `MothFlowers.as`.
2. If you are using Flash, make sure the `SoundController.as` file is in the same directory as `MothFlowers.as`. If you are working within a new project in Flex Builder,

make sure that the SoundController class is accessible by either adding its directory as a source directory or copying the file into your project's source.

3. This example uses the aether library, so import the `aether.swc` file into this project from this chapter's source files.

4. Enter the following code as the start of the MothFlowers class:

```
package {

  import flash.display.Bitmap;
  import flash.display.BitmapData;
  import flash.display.Shape;
  import flash.display.Sprite;
  import flash.events.Event;
  import flash.filters.BitmapFilterQuality;
  import flash.filters.BitmapFilterType;
  import flash.filters.GradientGlowFilter;
  import flash.utils.ByteArray;

  [SWF(width=400, height=300, backgroundColor=0x000000)]

  public class MothFlowers extends Sprite {

    private const WAVE_RADIUS:uint = 250;
    private const WAVE_COLORS:Array = [0xFFFF66, 0xFFFFFF, 0x666699];

    private var _soundController:SoundController;
    private var _drawingPlane:Sprite;
    private var _drawingShape:Shape;
    private var _background:Bitmap;
    private var _backgroundShape:Shape;

    public function MothFlowers() {
      makeBackground();
      makeDrawingPlane();
      _soundController = ➥
new SoundController("../../assets/SunriseStay.mp3");
      _soundController.addEventListener(Event.CHANGE, onSoundChange);
    }

    private function makeBackground():void {
      _backgroundShape = new Shape();
      _backgroundShape.graphics.beginFill(0);
      _backgroundShape.graphics.drawRect(0, 0, stage.stageWidth, ➥
stage.stageHeight);
      _backgroundShape.graphics.endFill();
      addChild(_backgroundShape);
      _background = new Bitmap();
      addChild(_background);
    }
```

```
    private function makeDrawingPlane():void {
      _drawingPlane = new Sprite();
      _drawingShape = new Shape();
      _drawingShape.x = stage.stageWidth/2;
      _drawingShape.y = stage.stageHeight/2;
      _drawingPlane.addChild(_drawingShape);
      _drawingPlane.filters = [
        new GradientGlowFilter(
          5,
          45,
          WAVE_COLORS,
          [0, 1, 1],
          [0, 180, 255],
          2,
          2,
          1,
          BitmapFilterQuality.MEDIUM,
          BitmapFilterType.FULL,
          true
        )
      ];
    }

    private function updateDrawingShape():void {
      var spectrumData:ByteArray = ➥
_soundController.getSoundSpectrum(false);
      _drawingShape.graphics.clear();
      _drawingShape.graphics.lineStyle(1, 0xFFFFFF);
      var x:Number;
      var y:Number;
      var i:int = -1;
      var value:Number;
      var angle:Number;
      while (++i < 512) {
        value = Math.ceil(WAVE_RADIUS*spectrumData.readFloat());
        angle = i/512*Math.PI*2;
        x = Math.cos(angle)*value;
        y = Math.sin(angle)*value;
        _drawingShape.graphics.moveTo(0, 0);
        _drawingShape.graphics.lineTo(x, y);
      }
    }

    private function onSoundChange(event:Event):void {
      updateDrawingShape();
    }

  }

}
```

As I said, much of this code is the same, or at least startlingly similar to, the previous example, so we won't dwell too long on it. In the constructor, we call makeBackground() to add a black rectangle on the bottom of the display list and a bitmap on top of it.

```
addChild(_backgroundShape);
_background = new Bitmap();
addChild(_background);
```

These will be the only children added to the display list in this class. The black rectangle will be used as the initial stage background (without a shape on the stage when we initially attempt to draw the stage contents into bitmap data we would get an exception thrown) and also to draw into our effect at a later stage in order to fade its graphics to black. The _background bitmap will contain all of the other graphics that we create in our visualization, but for now, it is empty.

Next in the constructor, createDrawingPlane() is called. This creates a shape in which we will draw our sound data, putting it in the center of the stage and applying the same GradientGlowFilter as in the last tutorial. The shape itself is placed inside another sprite that will be positioned at (0, 0) on the stage.

```
_drawingPlane.addChild(_drawingShape);
```

This is done to more easily allow for capturing of the _drawingShape's graphic data. Since we will be drawing circular spikes out from the shape's (0, 0) origin, the graphics will be in both positive and negative coordinates. When drawing with BitmapData, though, it is easier to capture data in the positive quadrants. The solution here is to nest _drawingShape within _drawingPlane. We can then capture the data from _drawingPlane, and all of _drawingShape's data will be within its positive space, as Figure 11-9 should help demonstrate.

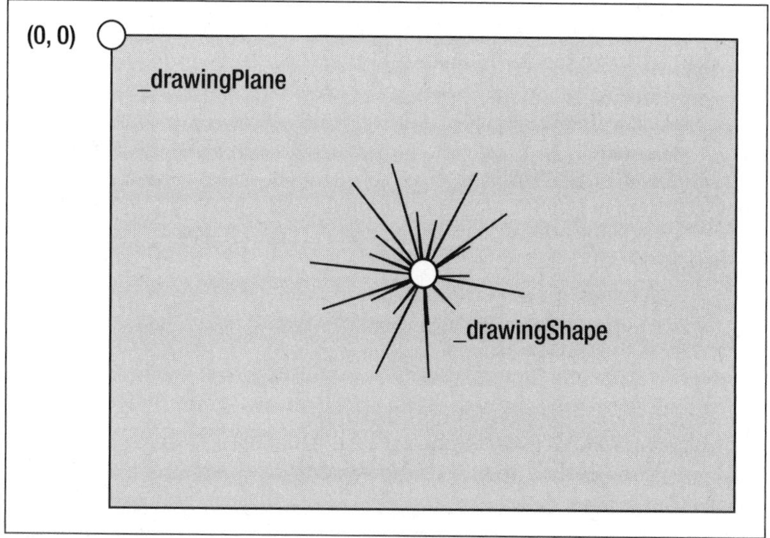

Figure 11-9. Nesting _drawingShape within _drawingPlane will allow for easy capture of its bitmap data, since the pixels will all fall within the postive rectangular region of the _drawingPlane.

As the loaded sound plays, onSoundChange() will be invoked, which will call updateDrawingPlane(). This method has exactly the same body as the updateCenterSprite() in the last tutorial, drawing spikes out from the center of _drawingShape based on the sound's wave form.

There's nothing to test at this point since _drawingShape and _drawingPlane aren't on the display list. All you will see is a lovely black rectangle. To see the graphic data, we first need to create the bitmap data into which the graphics in _drawingShape will be drawn.

5. Add the following bold lines of code to the class. These create the three rotated planes onto which we will draw the shape data:

```
package {

  // imports remain unchanged

  [SWF(width=400, height=300, backgroundColor=0x000000)]

  public class MothFlowers extends Sprite {

    private const WAVE_RADIUS:uint = 250;
    private const WAVE_COLORS:Array = [0xFFFF66, 0xFFFFFF, 0x666699];

    private var _soundController:SoundController;
    private var _planes:Vector.<Bitmap>;
    private var _planesHolder:Sprite;
    private var _drawingPlane:Sprite;
    private var _drawingShape:Shape;
    private var _background:Bitmap;
    private var _backgroundShape:Shape;

    public function MothFlowers() {
      makeBackground();
      makeDrawingPlane();
      makePlanes();
      _soundController = ➥
new SoundController("../../assets/SunriseStay.mp3");
      _soundController.addEventListener(Event.CHANGE, onSoundChange);
    }

    private function makeBackground():void {
      // this method body is unchanged
    }

    private function makeDrawingPlane():void {
      // this method body is unchanged
    }
```

```
    private function makePlanes():void {
      _planes = new Vector.<Bitmap>();
      _planesHolder = new Sprite();
      var plane:Bitmap;
      var planeHolder:Sprite;
      var x:Number = stage.stageWidth/2;
      var y:Number = stage.stageHeight/2;
      var numPlanes:uint = 3;
      for (var i:uint = 0; i < numPlanes; i++) {
        plane = new Bitmap();
        plane.x = -x;
        plane.y = -y;
        planeHolder = new Sprite();
        planeHolder.x = x;
        planeHolder.y = y;
        planeHolder.addChild(plane);
        planeHolder.rotationY = i*(180/numPlanes);
        _planes.push(plane);
        _planesHolder.addChild(planeHolder);
      }
    }

    private function updateDrawingShape():void {
      // this method body is unchanged
    }

    private function updatePlanes():void {
      var width:Number = stage.stageWidth;
      var height:Number = stage.stageHeight;
      var capture:BitmapData = new BitmapData(
        width,
        height,
        true,
        0x00000000
      );
      capture.draw(_drawingPlane);
      for each (var bitmap:Bitmap in _planes) {
        bitmap.bitmapData = capture.clone();
      }
    }

    private function onSoundChange(event:Event):void {
      updateDrawingShape();
      updatePlanes();
    }

  }

}
```

The technique for adding the 3D planes here is very similar to what we worked through for the tree model back in Chapter 6. It all takes place within the makePlanes() method. First, we create a vector to hold references to the three bitmaps we will create and a sprite to contain these bitmaps.

```
_planes = new Vector.<Bitmap>();
_planesHolder = new Sprite();
```

The loop is set up to run through three planes. Each plane bitmap is added to another container sprite and offset by half the stage width and height. The container sprite is placed at the center of the stage.

```
plane = new Bitmap();
plane.x = -x;
plane.y = -y;
planeHolder = new Sprite();
planeHolder.x = x;
planeHolder.y = y;
planeHolder.addChild(plane);
```

When we rotate the container sprite around its y axis, the effect will be the same as if the bitmap was rotated around its own center because of how it has been offset. This rotation is done in the following line, which will rotate the first plane by 0 degrees, the second by 60, and the third by 120.

```
planeHolder.rotationY = i*(180/numPlanes);
```

The result of all of this nesting, positioning, and rotation is illustrated in Figure 11-10.

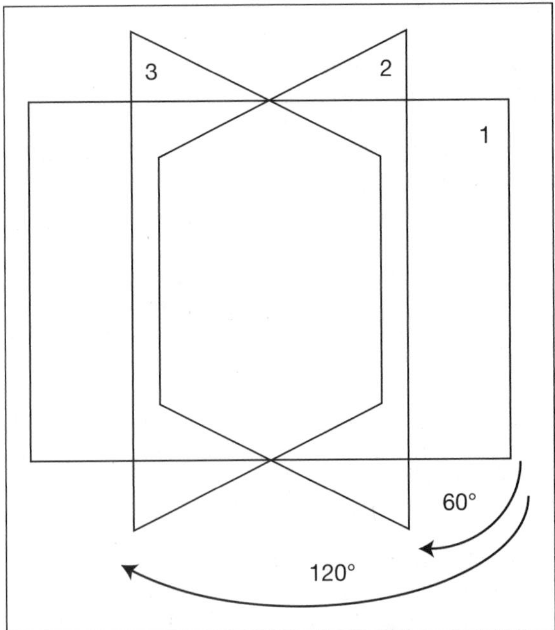

Figure 11-10. Three planes in 3D space with their nested bitmaps offset by half of the width allowing for rotation about the bitmaps' centers

When the sound changes each frame, the updatePlanes() method is called to redraw into the planes. The current graphics of the _drawingShape are drawn into bitmap data, and this data is copied into each drawing plane so that each shares the same graphics though is rotated at a different angle.

```
capture.draw(_drawingPlane);
for each (var bitmap:Bitmap in _planes) {
  bitmap.bitmapData = capture.clone();
}
```

We are getting closer to the goal of drawing sound data onto multiple rotated planes, but still there is nothing visible on the display list. In the next step, we will take the pixel data currently displayed within the rotated planes and draw it into the background bitmap that is on the display list. Then we'll have something to look at.

6. Add the following bold lines to your class to display the graphics we currently are producing:

```
package {

  import aether.utils.ImageUtil;

  import flash.display.Bitmap;
  import flash.display.BitmapData;
  import flash.display.Shape;
  import flash.display.Sprite;
  import flash.events.Event;
  import flash.filters.BitmapFilterQuality;
  import flash.filters.BitmapFilterType;
  import flash.filters.GradientGlowFilter;
  import flash.geom.ColorTransform;
  import flash.utils.ByteArray;

  [SWF(width=400, height=300, backgroundColor=0x000000)]

  public class MothFlowers extends Sprite {

    // the class properties remain the same

    public function MothFlowers() {
      // this method body is unchanged
    }

    private function makeBackground():void {
      // this method body is unchanged
    }

    private function makeDrawingPlane():void {
      // this method body is unchanged
    }
```

```
    private function makePlanes():void {
      // this method body is unchanged
    }

    private function updateDrawingShape():void {
      // this method body is unchanged
    }

    private function updatePlanes():void {
      // this method body is unchanged
    }

    private function updateBackground():void {
      var capture:BitmapData = ImageUtil.getBitmapData(_planesHolder);
      var stageCapture:BitmapData = ImageUtil.getBitmapData(this);
      stageCapture.draw(
        _backgroundShape,
        null,
        new ColorTransform(1, 1, 1, 0.3)
      );
      stageCapture.draw(capture);
      _background.bitmapData = stageCapture;
    }

    private function onSoundChange(event:Event):void {
      updateDrawingShape();
      updatePlanes();
      updateBackground();
    }

  }

}
```

If you compile and test the movie now, the result should look something like Figure 11-11.

Figure 11-11. Three 3D planes rotated about the y axis with the same visualization of the sound data drawn on each

The 3D planes are captured in a new BitmapData instance. Before this is drawn into the background, the current graphics on the stage are drawn into the stageCapture variable. On top of this image, we draw the black rectangle at a low alpha and then the new capture of the 3D planes. This leaves a little of the previous renders visible but slowly fading out as new captures are placed on top. This final composite image is placed into the background bitmap.

It was at this point, or possibly slightly after, when I started rotating the 3D planes each frame, that I saw that the 3D planes effect itself was not going to produce what I was hoping. One little line change, though, gave me something new, and a new direction in which to experiment.

7. Add the following new line to the makePlanes() method. Make sure that you include flash.display.BlendMode in your imports at the top of your class in order for this to compile.

```
private function makePlanes():void {
  _planes = new Vector.<Bitmap>();
  _planesHolder = new Sprite();
  var plane:Bitmap;
  var planeHolder:Sprite;
  var x:Number = stage.stageWidth/2;
  var y:Number = stage.stageHeight/2;
  var numPlanes:uint = 3;
  for (var i:uint = 0; i < numPlanes; i++) {
    plane = new Bitmap();
    plane.x = -x;
    plane.y = -y;
    planeHolder = new Sprite();
    planeHolder.x = x;
    planeHolder.y = y;
    planeHolder.blendMode = BlendMode.DIFFERENCE;
    planeHolder.addChild(plane);
    planeHolder.rotationY = i*(180/numPlanes);
    _planes.push(plane);
    _planesHolder.addChild(planeHolder);
  }
}
```

Remember, in order to get this to compile, make sure to add the following import at the top of the class.

```
import flash.display.BlendMode;
```

Because each plane contains the same graphical data just rotated at a different angle, the DIFFERENCE blend mode produces an interesting effect where the planes overlap and share the same colors. Basically, holes appear in the center of the composite shape, as shown in Figure 11-12.

Figure 11-12. The three rotated 3D planes from the previous step with the DIFFERENCE mode applied to each

I really liked this, and with the new shapes, I began to think of moths or butterflies. To go further toward this effect requires a mirroring of the image so that shapes on the left and right are symmetrical. Fortunately, this is a snap to do with our good friend BitmapData.

8. Add the following bold lines to updateBackground() in order to flip and copy the right side of the image to the left to create a symmetrical image. This new code requires that you import both the Matrix and Rectangle classes from the flash.geom package.

```
private function updateBackground():void {
  var capture:BitmapData = ImageUtil.getBitmapData(_planesHolder);
  var matrix:Matrix = new Matrix();
  matrix.scale(-1, 1);
  matrix.translate(width, 0);
  var rect:Rectangle = new Rectangle(0, 0, width/2, height);
  var halfData:BitmapData = capture.clone();
  capture.fillRect(rect, 0x00000000);
  capture.draw(halfData, matrix, null, null, rect);
  var stageCapture:BitmapData = ImageUtil.getBitmapData(this);
  stageCapture.draw(
    _backgroundShape,
    null,
    new ColorTransform(1, 1, 1, .3)
  );
  stageCapture.draw(capture);
  _background.bitmapData = stageCapture;
}
```

Again, in order to compile, be sure to add the following imports at the top of your class.

```
import flash.geom.Matrix;
import flash.geom.Rectangle;
```

Before drawing the 3D planes into the background bitmap, we first create a new matrix that will result in the image being flipped on the y axis. This is achieved by setting the scale on the x axis to –1 and then translating the whole image over to the right by its width. Remember that when you scale an image, it is around its origin at (0,0), so when the image is scaled by –1, it will be in negative quadrants, requiring the translation back into positive quadrants, as demonstrated in Figure 11-13.

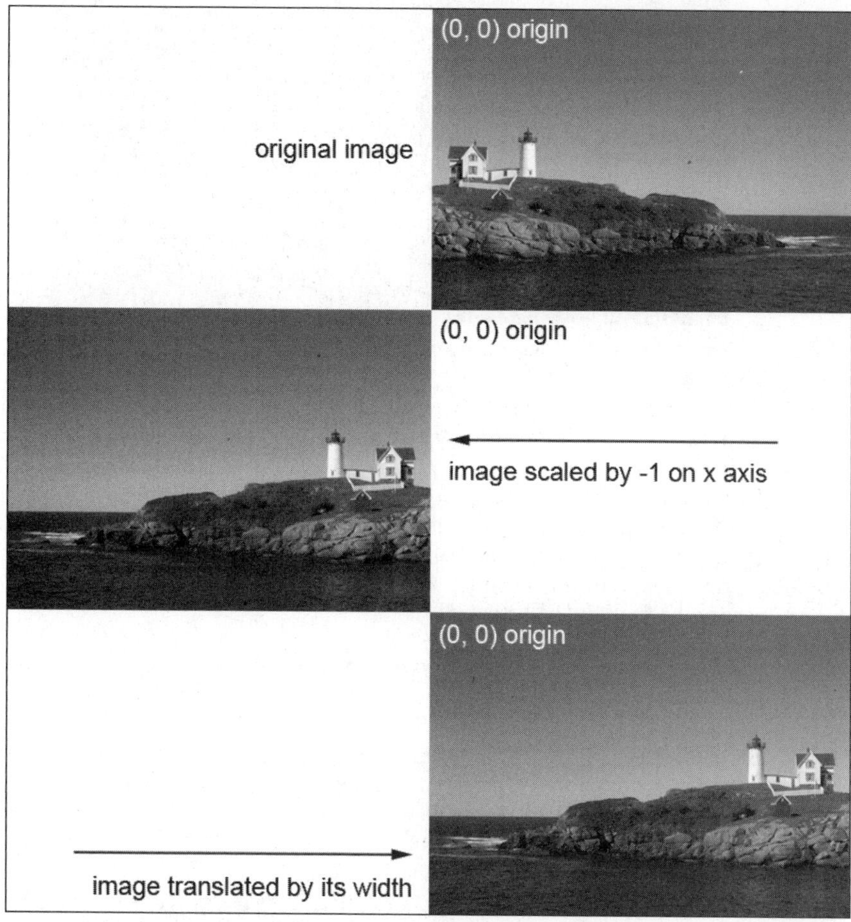

Figure 11-13. A symmetrical image is made by copying and flipping half of the stage's display.

After the matrix is set up, a rectangle is initialized that is half the width of the image. The capture of the 3D planes is cloned so that we can fill half of it with black and then copy in the clone into the same rectangle, using the matrix to flip the copy. It is this symmetrical image that is drawn into the background.

You can test your movie now to see the pretty moths. Or flowers. I couldn't decide, which resulted in the current name of the class. But whatever they are, I find them fascinating to look at. A few variations can be seen in Figure 11-14.

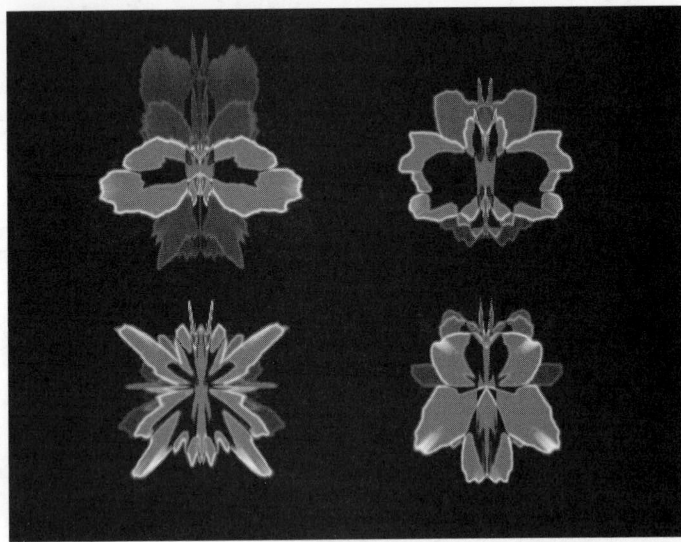

Figure 11-14. Four separate frames produced by this visualization

I hope this tutorial has shown you how you can play with and evolve effects with a lot of experimentation and utilization of BitmapData. This book really is all about giving you the knowledge you need of the underlying graphics classes in ActionScript, making you comfortable with their use, so that you are free to take advantage of the possibilities no matter the programmatic situation. This particular effect grew out of the initial sound wave, which became the circular wave representation. This effect rotated in 3D and made symmetrical produced this final moth/flower effect. At each step, the question was "What can I do with this?" as opposed to "How do I do this?"

Starting at a different point would obviously evolve effects in a whole different direction. Provided with this chapter's files is another example of a sound visualization, which started from a different path. The result can be seen in Figure 11-15 and can be found as `Pinwheel.as` in this chapter's files. This effect draws a different colored bar for each frequency value in the sound spectrum and then uses an aether effect to mirror and duplicate a section of this visualization around a central point. The image created is then tilted in 3D space and revolved around this central point as the sound plays.

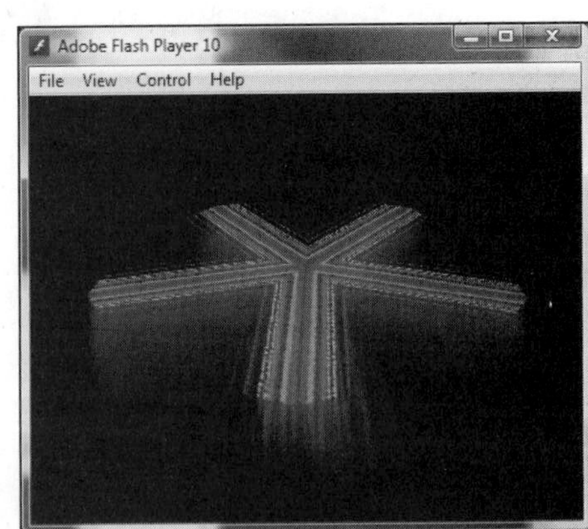

Figure 11-15. A visualization using the aether KaleidoscopeEffect and a 3D rotation and animation

Summary

There's not much more freedom to be had producing image effects than when creating sound visualizations. You have a blank canvas and 512 different kinds of paint with which to create. In this chapter, I have demonstrated a couple of ways of using this paint, this sound data, but the possibilities are nearly limitless. Not only can you draw shapes and images from scratch as we did here, using many of the additional methods we didn't take advantage of, but you could also use the sound's values to manipulate images that have been loaded in or trigger previously drawn animations. The visualizations can change more over time, not based on the sound data itself but rather on the duration the user has been engaged, using different color palettes or altering variables that drive the effects. Visualizations can morph over time into new visualizations or react to both the sound and user interaction.

This chapter wasn't about sound as much as it was about how to play with a sound's data to create visual effects. Still, we covered the basics of loading and playing back a sound in the Flash Player as well as how to retrieve its data in order to display it in an interesting and dynamic manner. We then went on to create a couple of cool effects for that data using the classes and methods we've been exploring throughout the book, relying heavily on BitmapData and the drawing API, with some filters and blend modes thrown in for good measure. The last example even sprinkled in a little 3D.

We're nearly at the end of our journey through the pixelated world of the Flash Player. After looking at the graphic classes in the ActionScript language through the first part of the book, we explored effects for animations, text, video, and sound through this second part. Although these effects might have been fun to create, the whole purpose was to produce something not for ourselves, the developers, but rather for the end user. That user's got a mouse and is not afraid to use it, so in the next and final chapter, we will look into effects driven by user interaction.

Chapter 12

INTERACTIVE EFFECTS

Every effect presented in the second part of this book so far has been completely independent of decisions made and actions taken by the user. That was very selfish of me. Of course, the end result was always intended to benefit the user, whether it was producing a smaller file size or creating a better overall visual appeal and experience, but one element that was missing is one of the greatest arguments for delivering your applications in Flash in the first place, as opposed to making a static movie that a user could download and enjoy, and that is the ability to interact with and have the application respond to user input.

When walking through the graphics features of ActionScript in the first part of this book, we did take advantage of perhaps the most common way for a user to input information in a Flash application, and that is through the mouse. If you recall way back in the bygone days of Chapter 1, we used mouse clicks and movements to explore the drawing API, creating simple drawing tools that responded to user input. We continued utilizing mouse input while exploring BitmapData (for example, the coloring book application using `floodFill()`), shaders (for example, setting the level of desaturation using the mouse position), and 3D (for example, extruding text toward the mouse position).

Another common form of input is, of course, through the keyboard. Although we didn't utilize this nearly as much as mouse input, it did pop up in Chapter 1 when we altered a line's width by the arrows keys and in Chapter 6 when the arrows keys were used to translate the position of a 3D object.

There are three additional forms of input that are readily available for use by the Flash Player, two of which will be the primary focus of this final chapter. First, as opposed to generating images from scratch or loading predefined images as we have done previously, you can load local images specified by the user into your application for processing. This feature is new to Flash Player 10 and is a fantastic addition to the capabilities of the player. In prior versions, the security sandbox of the player prevented this action and to process a user's image required the uploading of the file to a server (probably the one hosting the SWF) and then downloading it into the application. This made it more difficult, or at least more frustrating, to create an application that could work with user-defined images. This restriction, though, is no longer in place. Prohibition has been lifted. Drink up.

Another way to capture user input is through a webcam. Just as we did with video files in Chapter 10, you can draw webcam frames into BitmapData instances and manipulate them as you would any other bitmap data. You can also analyze the data each frame and respond to changes in the images, like tracking motion and using it to control objects within your application.

One final form of input is the user's microphone. Your application can listen to changes in activity or volume and respond to these events. Unfortunately, you cannot gain much more useful information from sound input in this way; the spectrum data that you can access in loaded sound files isn't available with user-generated sound. As such, the use of sound input for image effects is a bit limited, and this is a form of input we won't be exploring within this chapter.

What we will be looking at is how we can use the mouse, keyboard, webcam, and user images within a Flash application to help dynamically generate our image effects. Not only will we be exploring two new forms of input, but we will also be pulling in and applying a lot of knowledge presented through the rest of book, including use of the drawing API, shaders, and, of course, a healthy portion of BitmapData.

I started this book with a comment on how fun I find it to create image effects, from fire blazing to smoking aliens to funky sound visualizations. This last chapter embraces that fun with two effects that are visual toys in the real world, a kaleidoscope and a funhouse mirror. Hopefully, this book can leave you both with knowledge and a smile.

Using image and mouse input

If you have worked through this book in a linear order, you are no stranger to using mouse input when creating visual effects. The difference in this next tutorial is in how we get the initial image into the player for manipulation. Instead of generating the image or loading in a predetermined image, this next application will allow the user to select a local image to manipulate.

ActionScript 3.0 has two classes you will need to use in order to load a local image file, FileReference and FileFilter. You use FileFilter simply to limit the types of files that can be selected in the operating system's file browse dialog. For images, you would filter based on the image types that the Flash Player can load, `.jpg`, `.png`, and `.gif`. FileReference will perform the rest of the work. It is through a FileReference instance that you will open a browse dialog, initiate the load of the image data, and access that data once loaded.

In this next tutorial, after we load the user's selected image, we will use the drawing API and BitmapData to cut up and transform the image, creating a kaleidoscope effect. A kaleidoscope in the real world is a tube of mirrors that reflects internal beads or liquid that changes position as the tube is rotated, creating symmetrical patterns. We can create a similar digital effect by mirroring slices of the image and rotating the mirrored slices about a central point. By changing the portion of the image copied into the slice based on mouse activity, we can re-create the kaleidoscope experience of turning the tube to alter the view.

Loading a local image

The first thing we need to do before we can create a kaleidoscope effect with an image is get the image into the Flash Player in the first place. ActionScript 3.0 offers a FileReference class that handles such functionality.

1. Start with a new document in Flash named `Kaleidoscope.fla` or an ActionScript project in Flex Builder saved as Kaleidoscope. The main ActionScript class should be named `Kaleidoscope.as`.
2. This example uses the aether library, so import `aether.swc` into your FLA or Flex Builder project from this chapter's files.
3. Start your Kaleidoscope class with the following code, which handles prompting the user with the file browse dialog once the stage is clicked:

```
package {

  import flash.display.Sprite;
  import flash.events.Event;
  import flash.events.MouseEvent;
  import flash.net.FileFilter;
  import flash.net.FileReference;
```

```
  [SWF(width=500, height=500, backgroundColor=0xCCCCCC)]

  public class Kaleidoscope extends Sprite {

    private var _file:FileReference;

    public function Kaleidoscope() {
      stage.addEventListener(MouseEvent.CLICK, onStageClick);
    }

    private function onStageClick(event:MouseEvent):void {
      _file = new FileReference();
      _file.addEventListener(Event.SELECT, onFileSelect);
      _file.browse(
        [new FileFilter("Images", "*.jpg;*.jpeg;*.gif;*.png")]
      );
    }

    private function onFileSelect(event:Event):void {
      stage.removeEventListener(MouseEvent.CLICK, onStageClick);
    }

  }

}
```

In the Flash Player, you can only open the operating system's file browse dialog as the direct result of user interaction. If you try to open the dialog outside of the event flow begun by a user action, such as at the load of the application or within an `ENTER_FRAME` handler, you will get an error. For this reason, the constructor in this class simply sets up a listener for when the stage is clicked.

When that event occurs, the `onStageClick()` handler is invoked. This creates a new FileReference instance. Through this instance, we can cause the operating system's file browse dialog to open, which we do with a call to `browse()`.

`browse()` takes an array of FileFilter instances. These instances dictate which types of files can be seen and selected in the browse dialog. When a new FileFilter is instantiated, you pass to it two strings. The first is the description of the file types as it will appear in the Files of type drop-down list in the browse dialog on a Windows system (it is not used on a Mac). The second string is a list of the extensions allowed, each extension separated by a comma. In this example, any image type that the Flash Player can load is allowed:

```
new FileFilter("Images", "*.jpg;*.jpeg;*.gif;*.png")
```

Once the dialog is opened, there are two possible outcomes. The user can either find and select a file or click the close or cancel button to exit the dialog without a selection. A FileReference instance will dispatch events in each case, `Event.SELECT` for the file selection and `Event.CANCEL` if the dialog is exited without a selection.

For this example, we really are only worried about whether a file is selected. If the dialog is exited, nothing will happen, and the user can bring the dialog back with another click of the stage. If the selection occurs, though, this will be handled in the `onFileSelect()` handler, which we set up before calling `browse()`.

If you compile now, you should be able to call up a browse dialog, like the one shown in Figure 12-1. Nothing else is set to happen. Not a very fun application at this point unless you thrill at the browse dialog. Our next addition will take a successful file selection and load in the bytes for the file so that they may be processed.

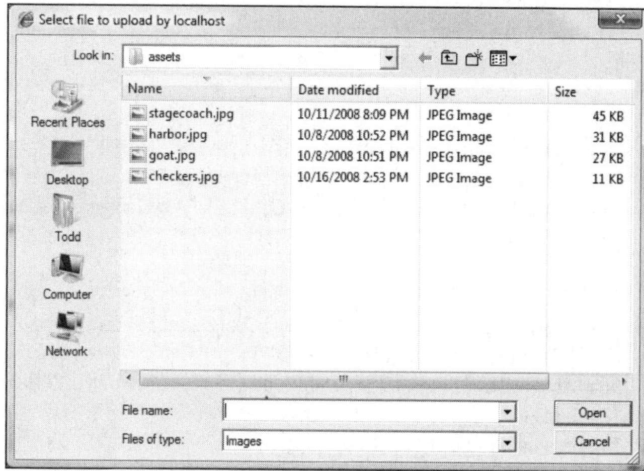

Figure 12-1. The Windows file browse dialog that is opened through FileReferece in the Flash Player

4. Add the following bold lines to your Kaleidoscope class:

```
package {

  import flash.display.Bitmap;
  import flash.display.Loader;
  import flash.display.LoaderInfo;
  import flash.display.Sprite;
  import flash.events.Event;
  import flash.events.MouseEvent;
  import flash.net.FileFilter;
  import flash.net.FileReference;
```

```
[SWF(width=500, height=500, backgroundColor=0xCCCCCC)]

public class Kaleidoscope extends Sprite {

  private var _file:FileReference;
  private var _kaleidoscope:Bitmap;

  public function Kaleidoscope() {
    stage.addEventListener(MouseEvent.CLICK, onStageClick);
  }

  private function onStageClick(event:MouseEvent):void {
    _file = new FileReference();
    _file.addEventListener(Event.SELECT, onFileSelect);
    _file.browse(
      [new FileFilter("Images", "*.jpg;*.jpeg;*.gif;*.png")]
    );
  }

  private function onFileSelect(event:Event):void {
    stage.removeEventListener(MouseEvent.CLICK, onStageClick);
    _file.addEventListener(Event.COMPLETE, onImageLoadComplete);
    _file.load();
  }

  private function onImageLoadComplete(event:Event):void {
    var loader:Loader = new Loader();
    loader.contentLoaderInfo.addEventListener(Event.COMPLETE, ➥
onLocalFileRead);
    loader.loadBytes(_file.data);
  }

  private function onLocalFileRead(event:Event):void {
    var loaderInfo:LoaderInfo = event.target as LoaderInfo;
    _kaleidoscope = loaderInfo.content as Bitmap;
    addChild(_kaleidoscope);
  }

}

}
```

Now, in the onFileSelect() handler, we remove the MOUSE_DOWN handler, since we will allow only one file to be selected. Then, once again through the powerful FileReference instance, we call its load() method to load in the data that was selected in the browse dialog. This will load the bytes from the selected image into the memory of the Flash Player. To be informed of when this load is complete, we set up a listener for the handily named COMPLETE event.

```
_file.addEventListener(Event.COMPLETE, onImageLoadComplete);
_file.load();
```

onImageLoadComplete() is what will be called when this event occurs. Up until this point, I believe things are pretty straightforward with the FileReference class and loading in local data. "Up until this point," I said. Now, even though the data for the image is loaded into memory once the COMPLETE event is fired, it is just a collection of bytes. You need to throw those bytes into a new Loader instance to transform them into a Bitmap instance that you can then manipulate.

Thankfully, this process is relatively painless and simply requires that you create a new Loader instance, set up a listener through its LoaderInfo for when the reading of the bytes is complete, and then call the loadBytes() method of Loader, passing in the bytes stored in the FileReference instance.

```
      var loader:Loader = new Loader();
      loader.contentLoaderInfo.addEventListener(Event.COMPLETE, ➥
onLocalFileRead);
      loader.loadBytes(_file.data);
```

Once this data is read in our example, the onLocalFileRead() handler will be invoked. At this point, we deal with the Loader data in the same way as when loading images from a remote location. We can access the Bitmap instance through the LoaderInfo's content property.

```
var loaderInfo:LoaderInfo = event.target as LoaderInfo;
_kaleidoscope = loaderInfo.content as Bitmap;
```

This bitmap can then be added to the stage. If you compile your movie now, you should be able to click the stage to select a file in the browse dialog and load the image into the movie. Figure 12-2 shows the result if you load hydrant.jpg from this chapter's files. You will notice that the image is cropped in the player since its height is 602 pixels, but we will deal with that in the next steps.

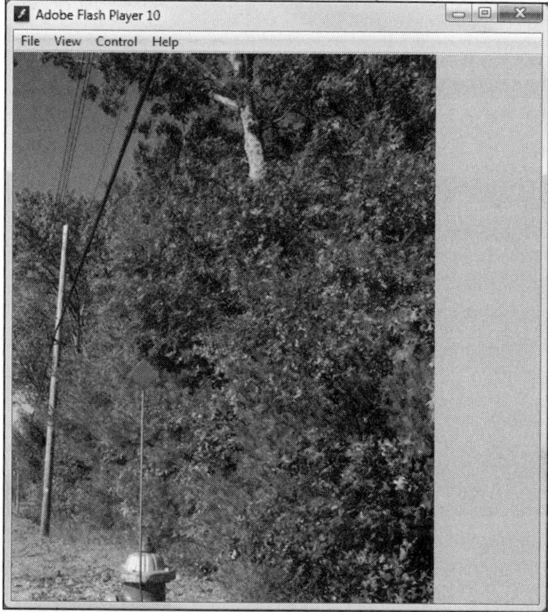

Figure 12-2.
The hydrant.jpg file loaded into the Flash Player through FileReference

Creating a kaleidoscope

Now that the bitmap has been loaded and is accessible in the Flash Player, we can slice it up and turn it into a kaleidoscopic image.

1. Add the following bold lines to your Kaleidoscope class:

```
package {

  import flash.display.Bitmap;
  import flash.display.BitmapData;
  import flash.display.Loader;
  import flash.display.LoaderInfo;
  import flash.display.Sprite;
  import flash.events.Event;
  import flash.events.MouseEvent;
  import flash.geom.Matrix;
  import flash.net.FileFilter;
  import flash.net.FileReference;

  [SWF(width=500, height=500, backgroundColor=0xCCCCCC)]

  public class Kaleidoscope extends Sprite {

    private var _file:FileReference;
    private var _originalImage:BitmapData;
    private var _kaleidoscope:Bitmap;

    public function Kaleidoscope() {
      stage.addEventListener(MouseEvent.CLICK, onStageClick);
    }

    private function onStageClick(event:MouseEvent):void {
      // this method body is unchanged
    }

    private function onFileSelect(event:Event):void {
      // this method body is unchanged
    }

    private function onImageLoadComplete(event:Event):void {
      // this method body is unchanged
    }
```

```
    private function onLocalFileRead(event:Event):void {
      var loaderInfo:LoaderInfo = event.target as LoaderInfo;
      _kaleidoscope = loaderInfo.content as Bitmap;
      addChild(_kaleidoscope);
      var width:Number = stage.stageWidth;
      var height:Number = stage.stageHeight;
      _originalImage = new BitmapData(width, height);
      var bitmapData:BitmapData = _kaleidoscope.bitmapData;
      var matrix:Matrix = new Matrix();
      matrix.scale(width/bitmapData.width, height/bitmapData.height);
      _originalImage.draw(bitmapData, matrix);
      _kaleidoscope.bitmapData = _originalImage.clone();
    }

  }

}
```

To create the kaleidoscope, we need a square image that is the size of our virtual tube, which in this example will be the width and height of our square stage. We could crop the loaded image to be this size, but I chose in this case to scale the image to the proportions needed. To do this, we first create a BitmapData instance of the preferred size.

```
var width:Number = stage.stageWidth;
var height:Number = stage.stageHeight;
_originalImage = new BitmapData(width, height);
```

A matrix is then created that will scale the loaded image to match this desired size.

```
var matrix:Matrix = new Matrix();
matrix.scale(width/bitmapData.width, height/bitmapData.height);
```

This matrix is used to draw the loaded image into our new BitmapData instance. This instance is saved as `_originalImage` so that we can copy it each time we need to regenerate the kaleidoscope image. To keep the original image intact without further distortion, it is a clone that we put into the `_kaleidoscope` bitmap.

```
_originalImage.draw(bitmapData, matrix);
_kaleidoscope.bitmapData = _originalImage.clone();
```

We have now loaded the image, copied it into a new BitmapData instance at the desired size, and drawn its clone into our bitmap. The result is shown in Figure 12-3, with the `hydrant.jpg` image scaled to match the dimensions of the stage so that it is no longer cropped. In fact, it is squashed and widened to match the dimensions of the player. Now comes the part where we slice up this image into the wedges needed for the kaleidoscope effect.

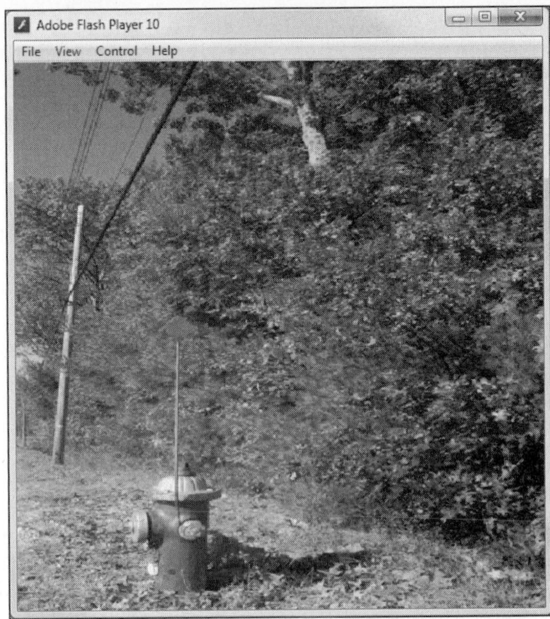

Figure 12-3. The local hydrant image scaled to match the dimensions of the player

2. Add the following bold lines to your Kaleidoscope class in order to copy, reflect, and rotate slices around a central position in order to create the visual of a kaleidoscope:

```
package {

  import aether.utils.ImageUtil;
  import aether.utils.MathUtil;

  import flash.display.Bitmap;
  import flash.display.BitmapData;
  import flash.display.Loader;
  import flash.display.LoaderInfo;
  import flash.display.Shape;
  import flash.display.Sprite;
  import flash.events.Event;
  import flash.events.MouseEvent;
  import flash.geom.Matrix;
  import flash.geom.Point;
  import flash.net.FileFilter;
  import flash.net.FileReference;

  [SWF(width=500, height=500, backgroundColor=0xCCCCCC)]
```

```
public class Kaleidoscope extends Sprite {

  private static const NUM_SEGMENTS:uint = 8;

  private var _file:FileReference;
  private var _originalImage:BitmapData;
  private var _kaleidoscope:Bitmap;

  public function Kaleidoscope() {
    stage.addEventListener(MouseEvent.CLICK, onStageClick);
  }

  private function drawKaleidoscope():void {
    var width:Number = _originalImage.width;
    var height:Number = _originalImage.height;
    var radius:Number = Math.min(width, height)/2;
    var segmentAngle:Number = 360/NUM_SEGMENTS;
    var theta:Number = MathUtil.degreesToRadians(segmentAngle);
    var x:Number = Math.cos(theta)*radius;
    var y:Number = Math.sin(theta)*radius;
    var matrix:Matrix = new Matrix();
    matrix.translate(-width/2, -height/2);
    var shape:Shape = new Shape();
    shape.graphics.beginBitmapFill(_originalImage, matrix, false);
    shape.graphics.lineTo(radius, 0);
    shape.graphics.lineTo(x, y);
    shape.graphics.lineTo(0, 0);
    shape.graphics.endFill();
    var segment:BitmapData = ImageUtil.getBitmapData(shape);
    var sprite:Sprite = new Sprite();
    var center:Point = new Point(width/2, height/2);
    for (var i:uint; i < NUM_SEGMENTS; i++) {
      sprite.addChild(drawSegment(i, segment, center, segmentAngle));
    }
    _kaleidoscope.bitmapData.dispose();
    _kaleidoscope.bitmapData = ImageUtil.getBitmapData(sprite);
    segment.dispose();
  }

  private function drawSegment(
    index:uint,
    segment:BitmapData,
    center:Point,
    angle:Number
  ):Bitmap {
    var bitmap:Bitmap = new Bitmap(segment);
    if (index % 2 > 0) {
      bitmap.scaleY = -1;
      bitmap.rotation = (index+1)*angle;
```

```
        } else {
          bitmap.rotation = index*angle;
        }
        bitmap.x = center.x;
        bitmap.y = center.y;
        return bitmap;
      }

      private function onStageClick(event:MouseEvent):void {
        // this method body is unchanged
      }

      private function onFileSelect(event:Event):void {
        // this method body is unchanged
      }

      private function onImageLoadComplete(event:Event):void {
        // this method body is unchanged
      }

      private function onLocalFileRead(event:Event):void {
        var loaderInfo:LoaderInfo = event.target as LoaderInfo;
        _kaleidoscope = loaderInfo.content as Bitmap;
        addChild(_kaleidoscope);
        var width:Number = stage.stageWidth;
        var height:Number = stage.stageHeight;
        _originalImage = new BitmapData(width, height);
        var bitmapData:BitmapData = _kaleidoscope.bitmapData;
        var matrix:Matrix = new Matrix();
        matrix.scale(width/bitmapData.width, height/bitmapData.height);
        _originalImage.draw(bitmapData, matrix);
        _kaleidoscope.bitmapData = _originalImage.clone();
        drawKaleidoscope();
      }

    }

  }
```

This is a pretty big chunk of code to add in one step, but we will walk through each piece so that you can be confident about what's going on. Before that point, though, go ahead and compile your application and load in an image to apply the effect to. Selecting the `hydrant.jpg` will produce a result like that shown in Figure 12-4.

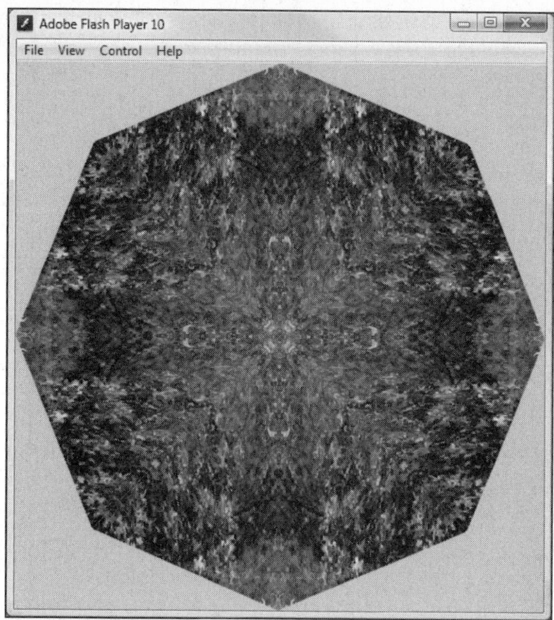

Figure 12-4. The local hydrant image sliced up and rotated into a kaleidoscope effect

So what exactly is going on in this code? After we load and process the image in `onLocalFileRead()`, we call a new `drawKaleidoscope()` method. Jumping into that method, you can see that the first thing we do is to set a number of variables we need to draw a segment of the kaleidoscope. After the width and height are placed into local variables for quicker access, the radius of the tube is determined based on half of the smaller dimension of the image. In this example, we altered the image so that the width and height are the same, but if the dimensions were not equal, these lines would ensure that the smaller dimension was used, with it divided in half for the radius of the virtual tube. This allows you to use an image for the effect that is already square, as we did here after distorting the image, or to use an image that is wider or taller in one dimension. The effect will work in either case because of these lines.

```
var width:Number = _originalImage.width;
var height:Number = _originalImage.height;
var radius:Number = Math.min(width, height)/2;
```

We then need to calculate the amount of the image that will be drawn into a slice. For this, we divide the number of desired segments into 360, or the number of degrees in a full circle. Therefore, for eight segments, the slices will be 45-degree wedges of the whole; for six segments, the slices would be 60 degrees, and so on. Using degrees will be helpful for rotating display objects, but for rotating bitmap data we need radians, so aether's `MathUtil.degreesToRadians()` handles this conversion for us (the equation is simply to multiply the degrees by pi/180).

```
var segmentAngle:Number = 360/NUM_SEGMENTS;
var theta:Number = MathUtil.degreesToRadians(segmentAngle);
```

With the angle of a slice calculated, we are almost ready to draw the image into a shape. First, however, we need to find the final x and y coordinates on the triangle we will use for the slice. Consider Figure 12-5.

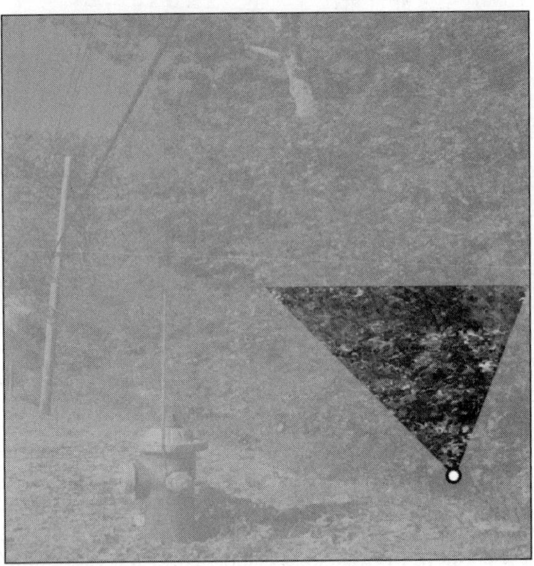

Figure 12-5. The portion of the image drawn into a triangle, with the coordinate to calculate represented by the white dot

The slice of the image we will use for the kaleidoscope is drawn darker than the rest of the image for demonstration purposes. The center of the image is a known location. The right side of the image is also a known location, based on the radius of our tube. The point remaining to be calculated is the third point of the triangle, shown with a white dot in the screenshot. Since we know the angle within the slice, the third point can be calculated using standard trigonometric equations.

```
var x:Number = Math.cos(theta)*radius;
var y:Number = Math.sin(theta)*radius;
```

Next comes the block of code for actually drawing the slice of the image. To do this, we use the drawing API's `beginBitmapFill()`, first creating a transform matrix so that the slice is drawn from the center of the image by translating the image so that its top-left pixel is the center of the image.

```
var matrix:Matrix = new Matrix();
matrix.translate(-width/2, -height/2);
```

This matrix is used in the beginBitmapFill() call to draw the image into a triangular shape.

```
var shape:Shape = new Shape();
shape.graphics.beginBitmapFill(_originalImage, matrix, false);
shape.graphics.lineTo(radius, 0);
shape.graphics.lineTo(x, y);
shape.graphics.lineTo(0, 0);
shape.graphics.endFill();
```

At this point, we have drawn a segment of the image into a shape. We put this shape into a BitmapData instance so that it can easily be used with multiple Bitmap instances, which we can rotate around a central point. That duplication is handled within a for loop that runs through the desired number of segments, calling a drawSegment() method, which we will look at next.

```
var segment:BitmapData = ImageUtil.getBitmapData(_shape);
var sprite:Sprite = new Sprite();
var center:Point = new Point(width/2, height/2);
for (var i:uint; i < NUM_SEGMENTS; i++) {
  sprite.addChild(drawSegment(i, segment, center, segmentAngle));
}
```

Let's take a moment to look at the drawSegment() method that is called from within the loop. This is passed the index of the slice, the slice of bitmap data itself, the center of the image to rotate around, and the angle of each segment. Within the method, we create a Bitmap instance with the image data and then flip it on the y axis if its index is odd to create the mirrored effect for every other slice. This bitmap copy is rotated based on its index in the full circle, with the mirrored slices offset by one to account for the scaling on the y axis.

```
var bitmap:Bitmap = new Bitmap(segment);
if (index % 2 > 0) {
  bitmap.scaleY = -1;
  bitmap.rotation = (index+1)*angle;
} else {
  bitmap.rotation = index*angle;
}
```

Calling this method for each segment will result in the desired number of segments all positioned and rotated around a central point with every other segment mirrored on the y axis. Each of these segments is added to a single sprite, which is drawn into a new BitmapData instance that is added to the _kaleidoscope bitmap, but not before the previous bitmap data is disposed. After the new data is added, we can also dispose of the segment bitmap data as it is no longer needed.

```
_kaleidoscope.bitmapData.dispose();
_kaleidoscope.bitmapData = ImageUtil.getBitmapData(sprite);
segment.dispose();
```

That's the extent of the code needed to draw the kaleidoscope effect one time. It's a pretty little effect but not too exciting at the present moment, since the angle at which the image is sliced can never be changed. It will always be the lower-right quadrant of the image that is drawn and rotated. To truly make a kaleidoscopic effect, we need to allow the slice of the image displayed to be changed, and better yet, we need to allow the user to do it at runtime.

Rotating the view

The last piece of the kaleidoscope effect to complete is the ability to alter the rotation of the image based on mouse input. To do this, we will take the position of the mouse when the user clicks the stage and watch the change of position until the mouse is released. By comparing the start position with the changed position of the mouse, we can rotate the view in the kaleidoscope.

1. We can complete the effect here in a single step. Add the following bold lines to the Kaleidoscope class:

```
package {

  // imports remain unchanged

  [SWF(width=500, height=500, backgroundColor=0xCCCCCC)]

  public class Kaleidoscope extends Sprite {

    private static const NUM_SEGMENTS:uint = 8;

    private var _file:FileReference;
    private var _originalImage:BitmapData;
    private var _kaleidoscope:Bitmap;
    private var _startAngle:Number;
    private var _angle:Number;
    private var _center:Point;

    public function Kaleidoscope() {
      stage.addEventListener(MouseEvent.CLICK, onStageClick);
    }

    private function drawKaleidoscope():void {
      var width:Number = _originalImage.width;
      var height:Number = _originalImage.height;
      var radius:Number = Math.min(width, height)/2;
      var segmentAngle:Number = 360/NUM_SEGMENTS;
      var theta:Number = MathUtil.degreesToRadians(segmentAngle);
      var x:Number = Math.cos(theta)*radius;
      var y:Number = Math.sin(theta)*radius;
      var matrix:Matrix = new Matrix();
      matrix.translate(-width/2, -height/2);
      matrix.rotate(_angle);
      var shape:Shape = new Shape();
```

```
    shape.graphics.beginBitmapFill(_originalImage, matrix, false);
    shape.graphics.lineTo(radius, 0);
    shape.graphics.lineTo(x, y);
    shape.graphics.lineTo(0, 0);
    shape.graphics.endFill();
    var segment:BitmapData = ImageUtil.getBitmapData(shape);
    var sprite:Sprite = new Sprite();
    var center:Point = new Point(width/2, height/2);
    for (var i:uint; i < NUM_SEGMENTS; i++) {
      sprite.addChild(drawSegment(i, segment, center, segmentAngle));
    }
    _kaleidoscope.bitmapData.dispose();
    _kaleidoscope.bitmapData = ImageUtil.getBitmapData(sprite);
    segment.dispose();
  }

  private function drawSegment(
    index:uint,
    segment:BitmapData,
    center:Point,
    angle:Number
  ):Bitmap {
    // this method body is unchanged
  }

  private function onStageClick(event:MouseEvent):void {
    // this method body is unchanged
  }

  private function onFileSelect(event:Event):void {
    // this method body is unchanged
  }

  private function onImageLoadComplete(event:Event):void {
    // this method body is unchanged
  }

  private function onLocalFileRead(event:Event):void {
    var loaderInfo:LoaderInfo = event.target as LoaderInfo;
    _kaleidoscope = loaderInfo.content as Bitmap;
    addChild(_kaleidoscope);
    var width:Number = stage.stageWidth;
    var height:Number = stage.stageHeight;
    _originalImage = new BitmapData(width, height);
    var bitmapData:BitmapData = _kaleidoscope.bitmapData;
    var matrix:Matrix = new Matrix();
    matrix.scale(width/bitmapData.width, height/bitmapData.height);
    _originalImage.draw(bitmapData, matrix);
    _kaleidoscope.bitmapData = _originalImage.clone();
```

```
      _angle = 0;
      _center = new Point(stage.stageWidth/2, stage.stageHeight/2);
      drawKaleidoscope();
      stage.addEventListener(MouseEvent.MOUSE_DOWN, onStageMouseDown);
    }

    private function onStageMouseDown(event:MouseEvent):void {
      var position:Point = new Point(
        stage.mouseX-_center.x,
        stage.mouseY-_center.y
      );
      _startAngle = _angle - Math.atan2(position.y, position.x);
      stage.addEventListener(MouseEvent.MOUSE_UP, onStageMouseUp);
      stage.addEventListener(MouseEvent.MOUSE_MOVE, onStageMouseMove);
    }

    private function onStageMouseUp(event:MouseEvent):void {
      stage.removeEventListener(MouseEvent.MOUSE_UP, onStageMouseUp);
      stage.removeEventListener(MouseEvent.MOUSE_MOVE, ➥
onStageMouseMove);
    }

    private function onStageMouseMove(event:MouseEvent):void {
      var position:Point = new Point(
        stage.mouseX-_center.x,
        stage.mouseY-_center.y
      );
      _angle = _startAngle + Math.atan2(position.y, position.x);
      drawKaleidoscope();
    }

  }

}
```

Here the _angle property has been added to hold the desired angle at which to slice the image and draw it into a kaleidoscope segment. Using this angle, we can rotate the image as we draw it into a slice to alter the view.

```
matrix.rotate(_angle);
```

This line in drawKaleidoscope() rotates the matrix that is used when drawing the image into the triangle shape. Initially, this value is 0, so the image is not rotated at all when first drawn. However, this value can be changed when the user clicks and drags. This is first handled in the onStageMouseDown() handler, which determines the angle of the mouse in relation to the center of the image, subtracting this from the current angle of the kaleidoscope and saving this into the _startAngle property.

```
      var position:Point = new Point(stage.mouseX-_center.x, ➥
stage.mouseY-_center.y);
      _startAngle = _angle - Math.atan2(position.y, position.x);
```

This handler also takes care of setting up listeners for when the mouse moves and is released. Once the mouse is released, onStageMouseUp() is called, and the listeners are removed. Updating the kaleidoscope view occurs in the onStageMouseMove() handler, which determines the new angle of the mouse in relation to the image center and adds this change to the start angle.

```
    var position:Point = new Point(stage.mouseX-_center.x, ➥
stage.mouseY-_center.y);
    _angle = _startAngle + Math.atan2(position.y, position.x);
```

A call to drawKaleidoscope() after the _angle property is updated with the new value causes the kaleidoscope to be redrawn at the new angle.

Go ahead and compile your application at this point. You should be able to click the stage to select and load an image. Once the image is loaded, click and drag to rotate the kaleidoscope and alter the view. Rotating the hydrant image to reveal the sky produces a result like the one shown in Figure 12-6. Try different images, and change the number of segments to see how that changes the overall effect.

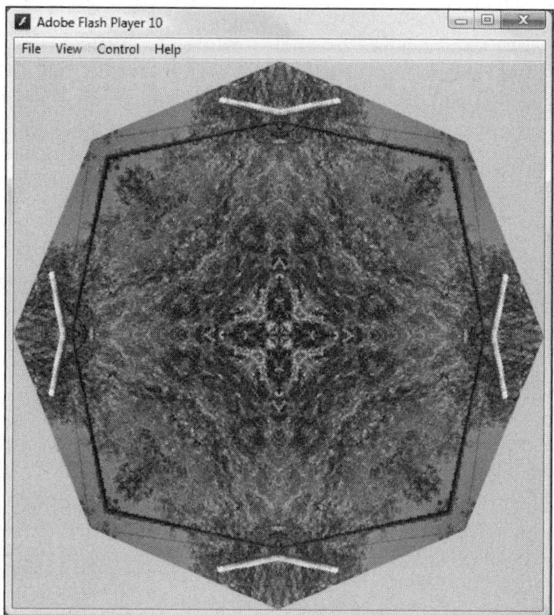

Figure 12-6. The user can rotate the view of the kaleidoscope with the mouse.

I wanted to walk through what it takes to create the effect of a kaleidoscope, since doing so uses a lot of the techniques previously discussed and so demonstrates how different pieces of functionality can fit together. But you might be interested in knowing that aether offers a KaleidoscopeEffect within its library, which you can apply to an image in one line of code:

```
new KaleidoscopeEffect(segments, angle).apply(bitmapData);
```

To demonstrate this, and to show how you could animate the effect by altering the `_angle` value over an interval, I've included in this chapter's files an AetherKaleidoscope class for you to take a look at.

However the kaleidoscope is created, though, the purpose of this tutorial was user interactivity. We created an application that allowed the user to load in a local file and then responded to mouse movement to alter the view of the effect. In the next and final tutorial in this book, we look at two additional kinds of user input, the webcam and keyboard.

Using webcam and keyboard input

Pulling data into a Flash application via a user's webcam is surprisingly easy and, unsurprisingly, is very fun to play with. Obviously, such video is useful for web conferencing applications but can also be creatively applied in refreshingly original ways, such as the viral ad campaign for Mentos (`http://www.mentoskisscam.com`) where the movie responded to the user's proximity to the camera to advance its images and simulate a kiss.

In this next tutorial, we'll create a toy more than a utilitarian tool, but in it, we will look at the basic steps needed to pull in a user's webcam data and manipulate it. In addition, we will once more step into the world of Pixel Bender, creating a shader we can use to distort the webcam images not unlike a funhouse mirror. Since this chapter's about user input and interactivity, we'll take advantage of keyboard input as well in the final application to alter the settings of our shader.

After nearly 12 chapters of concepts and code, it's about time we bent reality a bit. Remember, there is no spoon.

Coding a distortion shader

The shader we will create in this next section definitely has a lot of bark but only a little bite. It may seem like a lot of code, but this is because of duplicate code necessary to allow for distortions on both the x and y axes (ah, to be able to separate code out into subroutine functions!). As such, we will only step through the code needed to distort an image on the y axis, and then I will present the code in full that handles both the x and y axes.

In Figure 12-7, you can see the distortion shader we will create applied to our old familiar goat, with the image on the left being the unfiltered image and the image on the right receiving the distortion. There are many ways you could choose to distort an image in this way by bloating or pinching its pixels. The method I chose was to transfer one of Robert Penner's easing functions, `Quad.easeInOut()`, into the world of Pixel Bender. The resulting shader allows you to set the start and end pixels on each axis between which the effect will be applied. The pixels in between these points will start stretched on either end, compress together, and then stretch once more in the middle, as visible on the distorted checkerboard's y axis in Figure 12-8.

Figure 12-7.
A funhouse mirror distortion applied on both the x and y axes to the image on the right

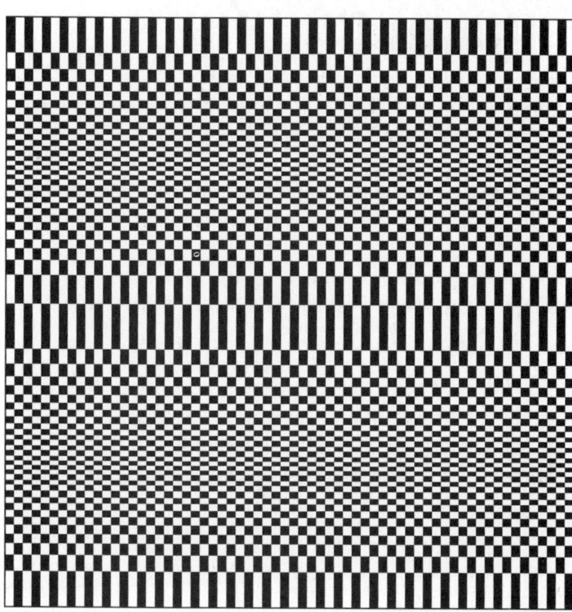

Figure 12-8.
A checkerboard distorted on the y axis with a ratio of 0.5

The "middle" is actually defined by a ratio between the start and end positions of the effect. A ratio value of 0.5 will weigh the effect evenly to both ends. A ratio 0.25 will place the stretched central position at 25 percent between the start and end, as shown in Figure 12-9.

Figure 12-9. The same checkerboard image distorted on the y axis with a ratio of 0.25

A final parameter will determine the amount of distortion to apply. A value of 0.0 will not apply any distortion, whereas a value of 1.0 will apply the full distortion. This will allow the completed shader to be applied to the x axis, the y axis, or both, with variable distortion levels on each.

That's all very nice conceptually, but how is it done exactly? It all begins with step 1, of course.

1. Open up the Pixel Bender Toolkit, and select File ➤ New Kernel Filter. When the default kernel code appears, let's jump right in and set up the variables we will use in the shader. Remember that we will at this time only be looking at distortions on the y axis.

```
<languageVersion : 1.0;>

kernel FunhouseMirror
<   namespace : "com.bobs27";
    vendor : "Todd Yard";
    version : 1;
    description : "Distorts image like a warped funhouse mirror.";
>
{
    input image4 source;
    output pixel4 result;

    parameter int warpBeginY
    <
```

```
        minValue:       0;
        maxValue:       1024;
        defaultValue:   0;
        description:    "The start of the image warp on the y axis.";
    >;

    parameter int warpEndY
    <
        minValue:       0;
        maxValue:       1024;
        defaultValue:   512;
        description:    "The end of the image warp on the y axis.";
    >;

    parameter float warpRatioY
    <
        minValue:       0.0;
        maxValue:       1.0;
        defaultValue:   0.5;
        description:    "The percent of the curved warp distortion➥
weighted towards the beginning on the y axis.";
    >;

    parameter float distortionY
    <
        minValue:       0.0;
        maxValue:       1.0;
        defaultValue:   0.5;
        description:    "The amount of distortion to apply ➥
on the y axis.";
    >;

    void
    evaluatePixel()
    {
        result = sampleNearest(source, outCoord());
    }

}
```

In addition to the input and output parameters, renamed `source` and `result`, respectively, this kernel code sets up four parameters to calculate distortion on the y axis. `warpBeginY` and `warpEndY` determine the start and end pixels in between (and including) which the effect will be applied. `warpRatioY` is the percentage between the beginning and end where the middle stretch of the distortion will be seen. Finally, `distortionY` is the amount of effect that will be applied.

We've got the parameters. Now we need to do something with them like, perhaps, distort an image.

2. Add the following bold lines to the evaluatePixel() method:

```
void
evaluatePixel()
{
    float2 coord = outCoord();

    if (distortionY > 0.0) {
        int y = int(coord.y);
        if (y >= warpBeginY && y <= warpEndY) {
        }
    }

    result = sampleNearest(source, coord);
}
```

After saving the coordinate of the pixel being evaluated into the coord variable, we check whether the distortion on the y axis is set greater than 0. There's no point doing any further processing if there is no distortion to apply. In that case, the final line of the function is run, which samples the pixel at the evaluated coordinate position.

If, however, there is distortion to be applied, we take the float stored in coord.y and assign this to an int variable, y. If this value is between the specified beginning and ending positions of the effect, further processing is required.

3. And on to the further processing. Add the following bold lines to the evaluatePixel() function:

```
void
evaluatePixel()
{
    float2 coord = outCoord();
    int firstHalf;

    if (distortionY > 0.0) {
        int y = int(coord.y);
        if (y >= warpBeginY && y <= warpEndY) {
            float tY = float(y - warpBeginY);
            float fullWarpY = float(warpEndY - warpBeginY);
            if (tY/fullWarpY <= warpRatioY) {
                fullWarpY *= warpRatioY;
                firstHalf = 1;
            } else {
                fullWarpY = fullWarpY*(1.0-warpRatioY);
                tY = float(warpEndY - y);
                firstHalf = 0;
            }
        }
    }
```

```
    result = sampleNearest(source, coord);
}
```

tY as a variable will hold our transformed y position, the position that we will use in the original image to draw at the evaluated coordinate. The first value assigned to this is the beginning of the effect subtracted from the coordinate position.

```
float tY = float(y - warpBeginY);
```

So if the effect starts at 50 and the pixel being evaluated is at 70, then tY will be 20, which we will use to determine how far into the effect the pixel lies. Next, we determine the full range of the effect by subtracting the beginning position from the end.

```
float fullWarpY = float(warpEndY - warpBeginY);
```

Knowing the full range will allow us to determine the percentage along that range that is currently being evaluated. Using these values, we can see whether tY lies before or after the warpRatioY position, which splits the effect into two halves.

```
if (tY/fullWarpY <= warpRatioY) {
```

Consider once more that the start position is 50 and tY is 20. If the end position is 100 and warpRatioY is 0.5, then 20 / (100 – 50) is less than 0.5, so the pixel would be determined to be in the first half of the effect. In that case, the following block is run:

```
fullWarpY *= warpRatioY;
firstHalf = 1;
```

Since the effect is split between two halves, we need to find the range of just the first half. This is easily determined by multiplying the full range by the ratio. A full range of 50 with a ratio of 0.5 would then use 25 as the range for each half of the effect. In the second line of code, the firstHalf variable is set; we will need this in a few lines to know on which side of the middle of the effect we are on. Since we are not allowed Boolean values, 1 in this case will be used to represent true.

If tY is determined to be in the second half of the effect, then the following code is run:

```
fullWarpY = fullWarpY*(1.0-warpRatioY);
tY = float(warpEndY - y);
firstHalf = 0;
```

The range used for the second half of the effect is the ratio subtracted by 1 and multiplied by the full range. This means that for a warpRatioY of 0.25, the range for the second half of the effect would be 75 percent of the full range. tY, in this case, needs to be recalculated to find its distance from the end of the effect. Of course, the final line sets the firstHalf variable to 0, or false.

Almost there! The next several lines use Robert Penner's Quad.easeInOut() equation to find values between 0 and the range of each half of the effect.

4. Add the following bold lines to the kernel:

```
void
evaluatePixel()
{
    float2 coord = outCoord();
    int firstHalf;

    if (distortionY > 0.0) {
        int y = int(coord.y);
        if (y >= warpBeginY && y <= warpEndY) {
            float tY = float(y - warpBeginY);
            float fullWarpY = float(warpEndY - warpBeginY);
            if (tY/fullWarpY <= warpRatioY) {
                fullWarpY *= warpRatioY;
                firstHalf = 1;
            } else {
                fullWarpY = fullWarpY*(1.0-warpRatioY);
                tY = float(warpEndY - y);
                firstHalf = 0;
            }
            tY /= (fullWarpY/2.0);
            if (tY < 1.0) {
                tY = (fullWarpY/2.0)*tY*tY;
            } else {
                tY = -(fullWarpY/2.0)*((--tY)*(tY - 2.0) - 1.0);
            }
        }
    }

    result = sampleNearest(source, coord);
}
```

I'm not too proud, and I'm no mathematician, so I have no problem admitting when numbers have me licked. I have been using Robert Penner's easing equations (found at `http://www.robertpenner.com/easing/`) almost as long as I've been using Flash, and I still couldn't tell you exactly what is going on. What I do know is that the equations calculate values between a start and end position, and that is precisely what I was looking for to produce this effect. `tY` here is a value between 0 and the full range of half of the effect, a value held in `fullWarpY`. The equations will return a number that is very small at the outset (easing in to the full value) and very close to the full range as it nears the end of the range (easing out as it nears the full value). The result will be pixels that are stretched at the beginning and end of the range and compressed or pinched in the middle.

With `tY` now calculated using these equations, we can use the transformed value to set the coordinate to sample from the original image.

5. The following bold lines will complete the code needed for distortion on the y axis of an image:

```
void
evaluatePixel()
{
    float2 coord = outCoord();
    int firstHalf;

    if (distortionY > 0.0) {
        int y = int(coord.y);
        if (y >= warpBeginY && y <= warpEndY) {
            float tY = float(y - warpBeginY);
            float fullWarpY = float(warpEndY - warpBeginY);
            if (tY/fullWarpY <= warpRatioY) {
                fullWarpY *= warpRatioY;
                firstHalf = 1;
            } else {
                fullWarpY = fullWarpY*(1.0-warpRatioY);
                tY = float(warpEndY - y);
                firstHalf = 0;
            }
            tY /= (fullWarpY/2.0);
            if (tY < 1.0) {
                tY = (fullWarpY/2.0)*tY*tY;
            } else {
                tY = -(fullWarpY/2.0)*((--tY)*(tY - 2.0) - 1.0);
            }
            if (firstHalf == 1) {
                tY += float(warpBeginY);
            } else {
                tY = float(warpEndY) - tY;
            }
            coord.y = mix(coord.y, tY, distortionY);
        }
    }

    result = sampleNearest(source, coord);
}
```

Here is where we use the firstHalf variable we set in the earlier conditional. For those values in the first half of the effect, we add the transformed value to the start of the effect. Remember that tY will hold some value between 0 and the range of the half warp, so the result here will be a value between the start of the effect and the middle determined by the warpRatioY.

For the second half of the effect, we subtract the tY variable from the end of the effect. The final new line sets the y coordinate based on the desired amount of distortion. A full distortion where `distortionY` is equal to 1 will use the `tY` value. Anything less will be interpolated between `tY` and the original coordinate position.

If you load in an image and run the filter, you should see something like Figure 12-10. This chapter's files include the `checkerboard.png` image that shows the effect very clearly.

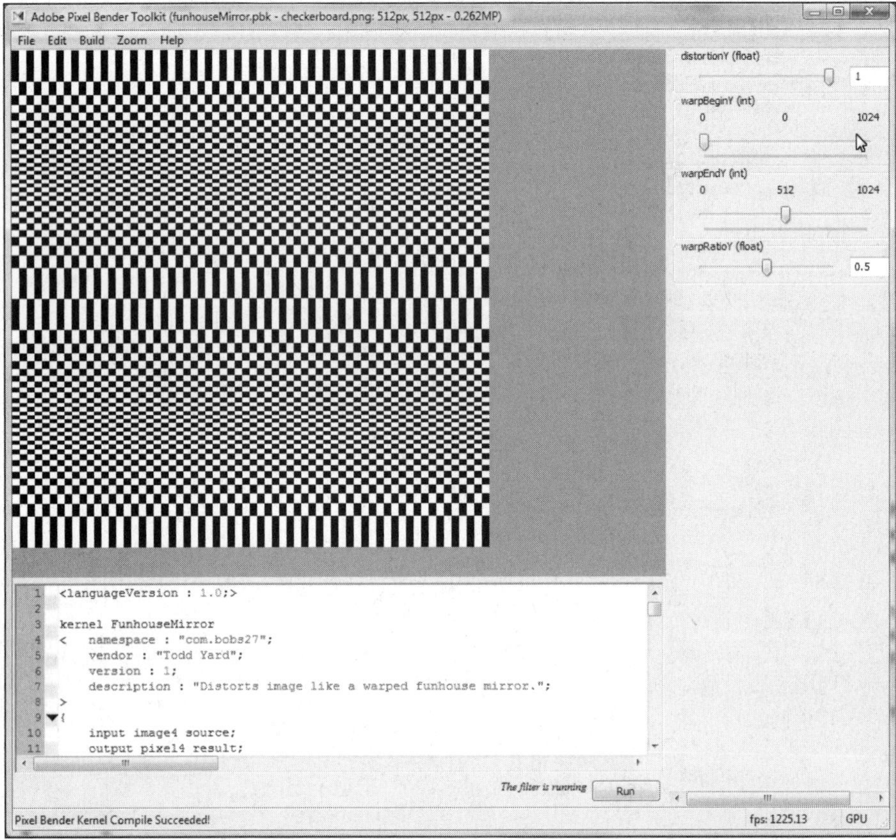

Figure 12-10. The funhouse mirror kernel applied to a checkerboard image, distorting it on the y axis

6. Adding the ability to distort on the x axis as well simply requires duplication of the code, looking to the x coordinate instead of the y. The following is the entire listing for the kernel, with logic for distorting both axes. If you are in a copy and paste mood, have at it with the code you already wrote for the y axis distortion. Otherwise, you can find the completed kernel in this chapter's files.

```
<languageVersion : 1.0;>

kernel FunhouseMirror
<   namespace : "com.bobs27";
    vendor : "Todd Yard";
```

```
    version : 1;
    description : "Distorts image like a warped funhouse mirror.";
>
{
    input image4 source;
    output pixel4 result;

    parameter int warpBeginX
    <
        minValue:       0;
        maxValue:       1024;
        defaultValue:   0;
        description:    "The start of the image warp on the x axis.";
    >;

    parameter int warpEndX
    <
        minValue:       0;
        maxValue:       1024;
        defaultValue:   512;
        description:    "The end of the image warp on the x axis.";
    >;

    parameter float warpRatioX
    <
        minValue:       0.0;
        maxValue:       1.0;
        defaultValue:   0.5;
        description:    "The percent of the curved warp distortion➥
weighted towards the beginning on the x axis.";
    >;

    parameter float distortionX
    <
        minValue:       0.0;
        maxValue:       1.0;
        defaultValue:   0.5;
        description:    "The amount of distortion to apply ➥
on the x axis.";
    >;

    parameter int warpBeginY
    <
        minValue:       0;
        maxValue:       1024;
        defaultValue:   0;
        description:    "The start of the image warp on the y axis.";
    >;
```

```
    parameter int warpEndY
    <
        minValue:       0;
        maxValue:       1024;
        defaultValue:   512;
        description:    "The end of the image warp on the y axis.";
    >;

    parameter float warpRatioY
    <
        minValue:       0.0;
        maxValue:       1.0;
        defaultValue:   0.5;
        description:    "The percent of the curved warp distortion➥
weighted towards the beginning on the y axis.";
    >;

    parameter float distortionY
    <
        minValue:       0.0;
        maxValue:       1.0;
        defaultValue:   0.5;
        description:    "The amount of distortion to apply ➥
on the y axis.";
    >;

    void
    evaluatePixel()
    {
        float2 coord = outCoord();
        int firstHalf;

        if (distortionX > 0.0) {
            int x = int(coord.x);
            if (x >= warpBeginX && x <= warpEndX) {
                float tX = float(x - warpBeginX);
                float fullWarpX = float(warpEndX - warpBeginX);
                if (tX/fullWarpX <= warpRatioX) {
                    fullWarpX *= warpRatioX;
                    firstHalf = 1;
                } else {
                    fullWarpX = fullWarpX*(1.0-warpRatioX);
                    tX = float(warpEndX - x);
                    firstHalf = 0;
                }
                tX /= (fullWarpX/2.0);
                if (tX < 1.0) {
                    tX = (fullWarpX/2.0)*tX*tX;
```

```
                } else {
                    tX = -(fullWarpX/2.0)*((--tX)*(tX - 2.0) - 1.0);
                }
                if (firstHalf == 1) {
                    tX += float(warpBeginX);
                } else {
                    tX = float(warpEndX) - tX;
                }
                coord.x = mix(coord.x, tX, distortionX);
            }
        }

        if (distortionY > 0.0) {
            int y = int(coord.y);
            if (y >= warpBeginY && y <= warpEndY) {
                float tY = float(y - warpBeginY);
                float fullWarpY = float(warpEndY - warpBeginY);
                if (tY/fullWarpY <= warpRatioY) {
                    fullWarpY *= warpRatioY;
                    firstHalf = 1;
                } else {
                    fullWarpY = fullWarpY*(1.0-warpRatioY);
                    tY = float(warpEndY - y);
                    firstHalf = 0;
                }
                tY /= (fullWarpY/2.0);
                if (tY < 1.0) {
                    tY = (fullWarpY/2.0)*tY*tY;
                } else {
                    tY = -(fullWarpY/2.0)*((--tY)*(tY - 2.0) - 1.0);
                }
                if (firstHalf == 1) {
                    tY += float(warpBeginY);
                } else {
                    tY = float(warpEndY) - tY;
                }
                coord.y = mix(coord.y, tY, distortionY);
            }
        }

        result = sampleNearest(source, coord);
    }
}
```

Running this with the checkerboard image will produce a result like Figure 12-11.

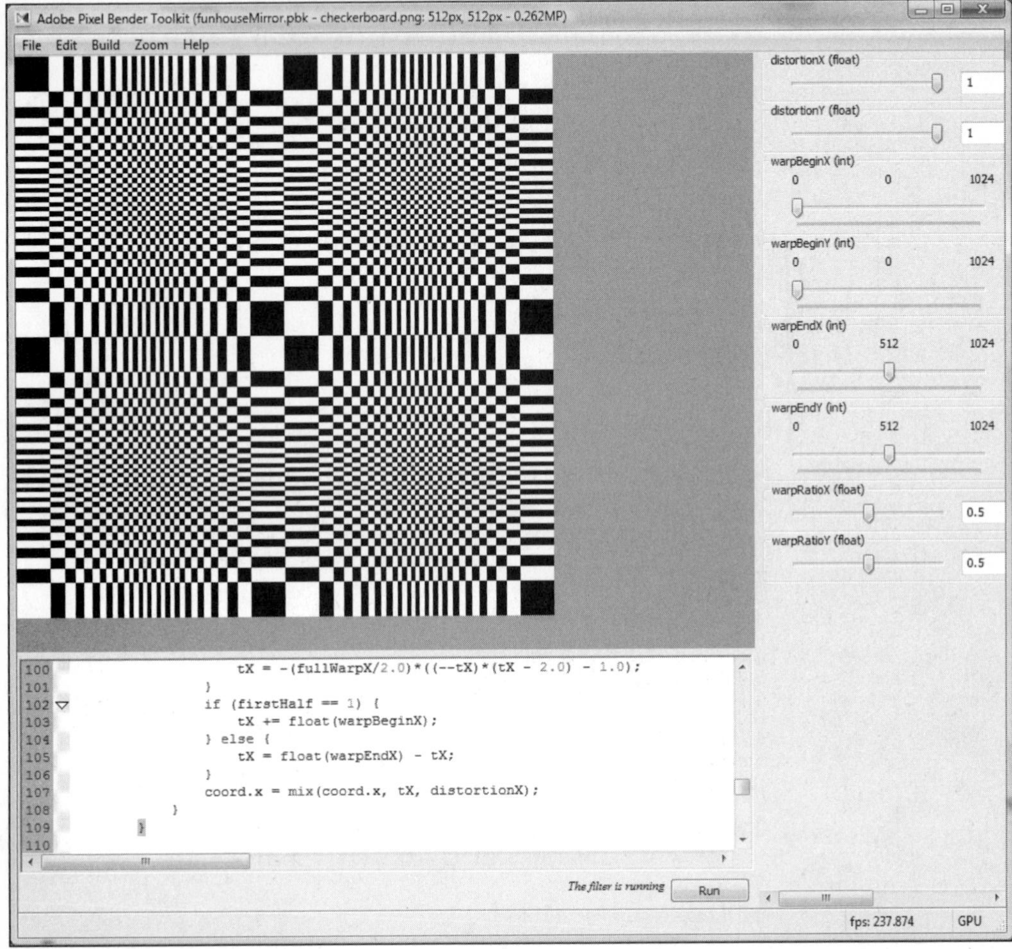

Figure 12-11. The completed funhouse mirror kernel distorting the checkerboard image on both the x and y axes

7. As a final, all-important step, we need to export the bytecode for the Flash Player. Save the kernel if you have not already done so as funhouseMirror.pbk. Then select File ➤ Export Filter for Flash Player to export the bytecode as funhouseMirror.pbj.

That's it! To see the effect applied to an image other than the checkerboard, simply use File ➤ Load Image 1 to load in another image to test. Figure 12-12 shows the effect applied to the ladyInRed.jpg from the Chapter 11.

Now it's time to bid a fond farewell to the Pixel Bender Toolkit and return to your ActionScript editor of choice. We have our bytecode ready. It's time to do some distorting!

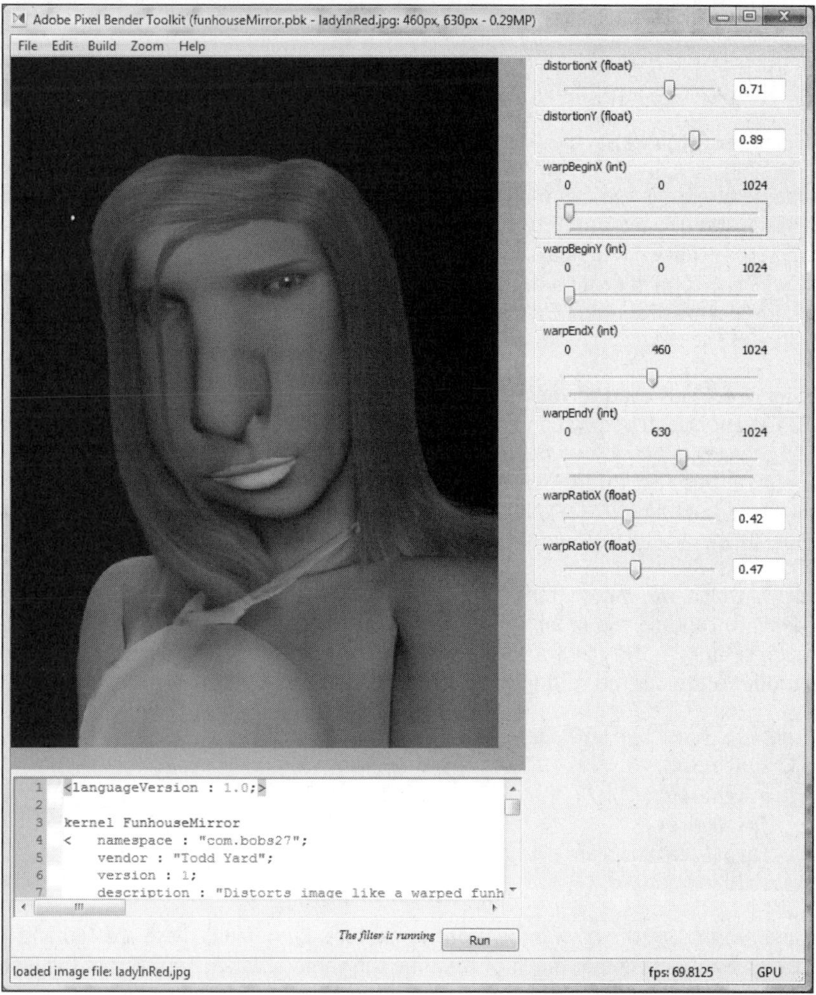

Figure 12-12. The funhouse mirror effect applied to an image from the previous chapter

Distorting user video

Creating the shader was the more difficult aspect of this tutorial. We've already pulled Pixel Bender bytecode into the Flash Player a number of times previously, and the technique hasn't changed in the last couple of chapters. We will go ahead and reuse the handy ShaderProxy that we put together in Chapter 5 to make it a snap to load and interact with the shader. The two methods of input we will incorporate are keyboard input, which we've used several times in previous examples, and webcam input, which just requires a few calls through the Camera class.

Working with the Camera class

The Camera class in ActionScript is used solely for capturing user webcam data. It's a simple class that offers a single static method to retrieve a reference to a user webcam.

```
getCamera(name:String = null):Camera
```

The name parameter is the name of the camera to reference. The available names can be found in the static names property of Camera, though generally, you can leave the parameter blank to retrieve the default camera. The remaining methods for Camera are mostly for use when streaming camera data through Flash Media Server and aren't needed when using the webcam as input for your application. The two exceptions are setMotionLevel() and setMode().

setMotionLevel() is used to specify the amount of motion required in order to have the ACTIVITY event dispatched by Camera. You can set up a handler for this event and respond to these changes in activity, so being able to set the baseline for the motion level can be very useful. In this next tutorial, we won't be responding specifically to changes in activity but will instead use an ENTER_FRAME handler to constantly update the view based on camera input, so we won't be using this method here.

setMode(), which we will be taking advantage of, is used to specify the desired pixel dimensions to capture and at what frame rate. I wrote "desired" since this relies on capture mode settings in the camera itself, so what you get is what Flash considers the closest native mode to the desired settings. The signature of setMode() looks like this:

```
public function setMode(
  width:int,
  height:int,
  fps:Number,
  favorArea:Boolean = true
):void
```

width and height are the pixel dimensions to capture. By default, these are 160 and 120, respectively. Considering that much of the time the camera data is sent across the wire to the Flash Media Server, the low settings make sense. When using the camera input locally, as we will be doing in this tutorial, you can up these numbers at least a little bit to get better picture quality.

fps (frames per second) is the frame rate the Flash Player should try to capture data at. This is 15 frames per second by default, which is generally a good number. However, if you are using a larger frame size, as we will be, or need to manage bandwidth when streaming the video out, you can lower the number.

The final parameter, favorArea, tells Flash what to sacrifice between the dimensions and the frame rate if the camera does not have settings that match the desired numbers. The default value of true will result in the Flash Player trying to closely match the dimensions, favoring that over frame rate. A value of false will result in the frame rate being matched more closely at the expense of the dimensions not being as closely met.

Displaying camera input

Once you have the camera set up and capturing data, you need a place to view that data. Just as with videos loaded through the NetStream class, camera data is displayed within a Video instance that can be added to the stage. All it takes is instantiating a Video, attaching camera input to it, and adding it to the display list, as the following lines demonstrate:

```
var camera:Camera = Camera.getCamera();
var video:Video = new Video();
video.attachCamera(camera);
addChild(video);
```

Of course, you don't need to add the video to the display list. You could, of course, keep the video off of the display list and draw its data into a BitmapData instance, just as we did with videos in Chapter 10. But for simply displaying user webcam input in your application, those lines are all you need.

Applying a shader to webcam data

We've covered all the basics you need to know about Camera in order to use it. So let's use it.

1. Start with a new document in Flash named `FunhouseMirror.fla` or an ActionScript project in Flex Builder saved as FunhouseMirror. The main ActionScript class should be named `FunhouseMirror.as`.
2. This example uses the ShaderProxy class created in Chapter 5. Either copy the class from your own Chapter 5 projects or import the `ShaderProxy.as` file included with this chapter's files into your project. For Flash users, just make sure the `ShaderProxy.as` file is in the same directory as `FunhouseMirror.as`.
3. Start your FunhouseMirror class with the following code:

```
package {

  import flash.display.Sprite;
  import flash.events.Event;

  [SWF(width=640, height=480, backgroundColor=0x666666, frameRate=12)]

  public class FunhouseMirror extends Sprite {

    private static const MIRROR_WIDTH:uint = 640;
    private static const MIRROR_HEIGHT:uint = 480;

    private var _shaderProxy:ShaderProxy;

    public function FunhouseMirror() {
      _shaderProxy = ➥
new ShaderProxy("../../assets/funhouseMirror.pbj");
      if (_shaderProxy.shader == null) {
        _shaderProxy.addEventListener(Event.COMPLETE, onShaderLoaded);
```

```
      } else {
        createMirror();
      }
    }

    private function createMirror():void {
    }

    private function onShaderLoaded(event:Event):void {
      _shaderProxy.removeEventListener(Event.COMPLETE, onShaderLoaded);
      _shaderProxy.warpEndX = MIRROR_WIDTH;
      _shaderProxy.warpEndY = MIRROR_HEIGHT;
      createMirror();
    }

  }

}
```

We'll start off simply here. We take advantage of the ShaderProxy class written earlier to handle the loading and readying of our shader bytecode. This application expects the `.pbj` file to be two directories up from the SWF in an `assets` directory, so if your setup differs, be sure to update the path.

Once the shader is ready to go, the onShaderLoaded() handler will be called. In it, we set the end positions of the horizontal and vertical distortions based on the width and height of the mirror we will be creating (which happens to be the width and height of the stage).

```
_shaderProxy.warpEndX = MIRROR_WIDTH;
_shaderProxy.warpEndY = MIRROR_HEIGHT;
```

`createMirror()` is then called. This is where we will set up the camera. And that's just what we will do next.

4. Add the following bold lines to your class:

```
package {

  import flash.display.Shader;
  import flash.display.Sprite;
  import flash.events.Event;
  import flash.filters.ShaderFilter;
  import flash.media.Camera;
  import flash.media.Video;

  [SWF(width=640, height=480, backgroundColor=0x666666, frameRate=12)]

  public class FunhouseMirror extends Sprite {

    private static const MIRROR_WIDTH:uint = 640;
    private static const MIRROR_HEIGHT:uint = 480;

    private var _shaderProxy:ShaderProxy;
```

```
    private var _video:Video;

    public function FunhouseMirror() {
      // this method body is unchanged
    }

    private function createMirror():void {
      var camera:Camera = Camera.getCamera();
      if (camera != null) {
        camera.setMode(MIRROR_WIDTH, MIRROR_HEIGHT, stage.frameRate);
        _video = new Video(MIRROR_WIDTH, MIRROR_HEIGHT);
        _video.attachCamera(camera);
        _video.filters = [new ShaderFilter(_shaderProxy.shader)];
        addChild(_video);
      }
    }

    private function onShaderLoaded(event:Event):void {
      // this method body is unchanged
    }

  }

}
```

Since it is possible the user will not have a camera, we need to test for null after attempting to access it through Camera.getCamera(). If a camera reference is returned, we can proceed with setting its mode to match our pixel dimensions and movie frame rate. Since the webcam input here isn't being streamed out, just used locally, we can use a larger capture size, but you probably wouldn't want to try to send that much data across the wire. Also, even though everything is local, that is an awful lot of pixel data to update each frame through our shader, so that is an additional consideration. I felt this size worked fine for this example, but optimizing for your intended audience, even offering choices of dimensions or dynamically determining the ideal size, is always a good idea.

With the camera ready, we can create a Video instance of the same size and attach the camera input to it. Our shader is applied through the filters property found on Video (a DisplayObject child class) and a ShaderFilter instance.

```
_video.filters = [new ShaderFilter(_shaderProxy.shader)];
```

If you can recall way back from Chapter 5, the shader property of ShaderProxy will return a reference to the actual Shader instance. It is this that needs to be passed in the ShaderFilter constructor.

The camera is receiving input; the video is displaying it, and the shader is processing it. All that remains is to add the video to the display list at the end of the method. If you test your movie now, you should see a distorted image of yourself. A distorted image of me is shown in Figure 12-13.

Figure 12-13. Yours truly seen through the funhouse mirror

It's like a screen test for a new PlasticMan movie. But we can go further by giving the user the ability to alter the distortion. PlasticMan would've wanted it that way.

5. The final lines of code added here in bold use keyboard input to change the settings for our shader. Add these to your class, save, compile, and enjoy:

```
package {

  import flash.display.Shader;
  import flash.display.Sprite;
  import flash.events.Event;
  import flash.events.KeyboardEvent;
  import flash.filters.ShaderFilter;
  import flash.media.Camera;
  import flash.media.Video;
  import flash.ui.Keyboard;

  [SWF(width=640, height=480, backgroundColor=0x666666, frameRate=12)]

  public class FunhouseMirror extends Sprite {

    private static const MIRROR_WIDTH:uint = 640;
    private static const MIRROR_HEIGHT:uint = 480;

    private var _shaderProxy:ShaderProxy;
    private var _video:Video;
```

```
public function FunhouseMirror() {
  // this method body is unchanged
}

private function createMirror():void {
  var camera:Camera = Camera.getCamera();
  if (camera != null) {
    camera.setMode(MIRROR_WIDTH, MIRROR_HEIGHT, stage.frameRate);
    _video = new Video(MIRROR_WIDTH, MIRROR_HEIGHT);
    _video.attachCamera(camera);
    _video.filters = [new ShaderFilter(_shaderProxy.shader)];
    addChild(_video);
    stage.addEventListener(KeyboardEvent.KEY_DOWN, onStageKeyDown);
  }
}

private function onStageKeyDown(event:KeyboardEvent):void {
  var rate:Number = .05;
  var rX:Number = _shaderProxy.warpRatioX;
  var rY:Number = _shaderProxy.warpRatioY;
  var dX:Number = _shaderProxy.distortionX;
  var dY:Number = _shaderProxy.distortionY;
  switch (event.keyCode) {
    case Keyboard.UP:
      if (event.shiftKey) {
        _shaderProxy.distortionY = Math.min(1, dY + rate);
      } else {
        _shaderProxy.warpRatioY = Math.max(0, rY - rate);
      }
      break;
    case Keyboard.DOWN:
      if (event.shiftKey) {
        _shaderProxy.distortionY = Math.max(0, dY - rate);
      } else {
        _shaderProxy.warpRatioY = Math.min(1, rY + rate);
      }
      break;
    case Keyboard.RIGHT:
      if (event.shiftKey) {
        _shaderProxy.distortionX = Math.min(1, dX + rate);
      } else {
        _shaderProxy.warpRatioX = Math.min(1, rX + rate);
      }
      break;
    case Keyboard.LEFT:
      if (event.shiftKey) {
        _shaderProxy.distortionX = Math.max(0, dX - rate);
      } else {
        _shaderProxy.warpRatioX = Math.max(0, rX - rate);
      }
```

```
          break;
        default:
          return;
      }
      _video.filters = [new ShaderFilter(_shaderProxy.shader)];
    }

    private function onShaderLoaded(event:Event):void {
      // this method body is unchanged
    }

  }

}
```

Once we have set up the camera and video in the createMirror() method, we add a listener for when a key is pressed. This event is handled by the onStageKeyDown() method, which uses a switch statement to look for four possible cases, whether the key pressed was any of the four arrow keys. The default for the switch exits out of the function so that the shader is not reapplied, since none of the properties were altered.

Let's take a look at one particular case, and that is when the up arrow is pressed.

```
switch (event.keyCode) {
  case Keyboard.UP:
    if (event.shiftKey) {
      _shaderProxy.distortionY = Math.min(1, dY + rate);
    } else {
      _shaderProxy.warpRatioY = Math.max(0, rY - rate);
    }
    break;
```

The code for the key pressed will be found in the keyCode property of the KeyboardEvent passed to the method. If the code is that for the up arrow, this case is entered. The conditional checks whether the shift key is currently pressed. We use this to toggle the action taken by the arrow key. When the shift key is pressed, clicking the up arrow increases the amount of distortion on the y axis, making sure it does not exceed 1. If the shift key is not depressed, clicking the up arrow changes the warpRatioY value, ensuring that it is never less than 0.

This same logic is used in all four cases to allow the user to change the amount of distortion on the x and y axes when the shift key is depressed and to change the ratio positions on the two axes when the shift key is not depressed. Once the values in _shaderProxy have been set (which in turn sets the internal shader properties), the filter can be reapplied to the video.

```
_video.filters = [new ShaderFilter(_shaderProxy.shader)];
```

And that, ladies and gentlemen, is that. If you compile your movie now, you can use the arrow keys to alter the distortion to get all kinds of crazy results. Figure 12-14 shows four different captures I took with different settings of my own. I think I've got a new headshot.

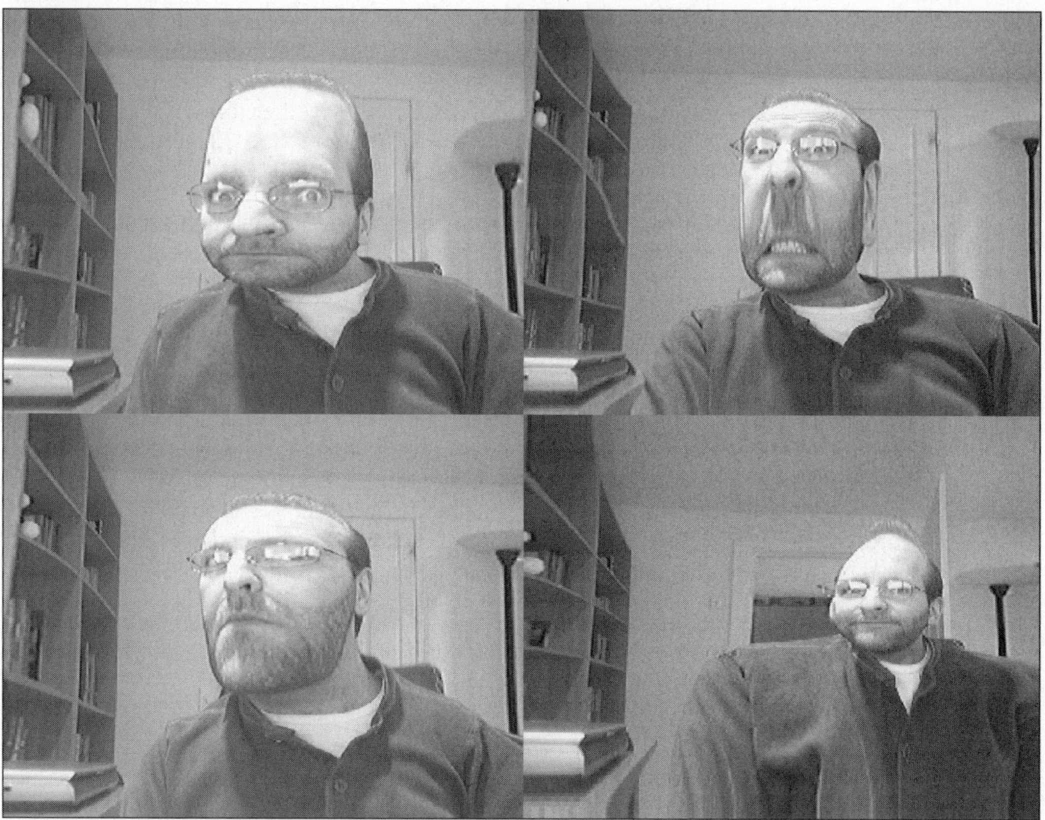

Figure 12-14. Four different distortions made possible by changes to the shader at runtime through keyboard input

In this tutorial, we've once again stepped through the wardrobe into the magical realm of Pixel Bender in order to create a shader that could be used to distort an image. The image, though, as opposed to being a bitmap file loaded into the Flash Player as we have done previously, was brought in through a user webcam. This is a powerful input device you can easily take advantage of in your applications with just a few lines of code, offering video for web conferencing, processing the input to control objects on screen, or creating visual toys as we did in this tutorial. Once the camera input is in the Flash Player, it is just pixels in memory, just as any other type of image we have dealt with through this book, open to the same manipulations. Using these pixels in combination with keyboard input, we created an amusement that entertains as the user interacts.

Summary

This chapter has been about combining visual effects with user input and interactivity. Visual effects in the Flash Player certainly don't have to be static and irrespective of user activity and, in fact, can greatly benefit from the methods of input provided through ActionScript and the Flash Player.

The two tutorials presented took advantage of webcam and bitmap file input to create imagery and offered ways to alter the effects at runtime through mouse and keyboard input from the user. The effects themselves used a combination of filters, shaders, the drawing API, and lots of BitmapData instances, rolling together many of the techniques we've spent chapters honing through the rest of the book (no 3D here, but we don't always need the kitchen sink!).

I think these two tutorials are a great way to finish our exploration of the graphical capabilities of the Flash Player. First, the effects are composed of different pieces that all work together to create the final effect, as you will find most image effects are. By understanding each individual component that goes into an effect, you can build more interesting, more original, more complex results by rearranging these components. The chapters through the first part of this book were focused on these individual components, and these later chapters were about putting all those components together.

Second, these tutorials presented visual effects that were primarily visual toys. Although you could certainly find applications for each, even if it was to attract and engage users, that wasn't the focus of the exercises. I wanted to have fun here in the final chapter and present effects that were entertaining for the user, just as creating image effects can be, and in my opinion should be, entertaining for the developer.

So I hope you do find it enjoyable pushing pixels about like Play-Doh on the screen, and I hope this book can serve you well as a reference, starting-off point, or inspiration as you create your own effects.

Appendix

DEVELOPING WITHIN FLASH AND FLEX BUILDER

This book assumes basic knowledge of either Flash or Flex Builder for creating and compiling movies or applications in those development environments. If you have never worked in these applications, please consult the Adobe documentation for detailed instructions. This appendix can help serve as a refresher on how to create and compile a project, particularly as applied to this book's files, for easy testing within either Flash CS4 or Flex Builder 3.

Working in Flash CS4

Creating an ActionScript project in Flash CS4 or working with this book's prepared files is a fairly straightforward process. To compile a SWF in Flash using an ActionScript document class merely requires an FLA and the associated ActionScript file.

Working with chapter files in Flash

If you download the chapter files for this book and extract them from the zipped file, you will find the directory structure, which is shown in Figure A-1, consistent from chapter to chapter.

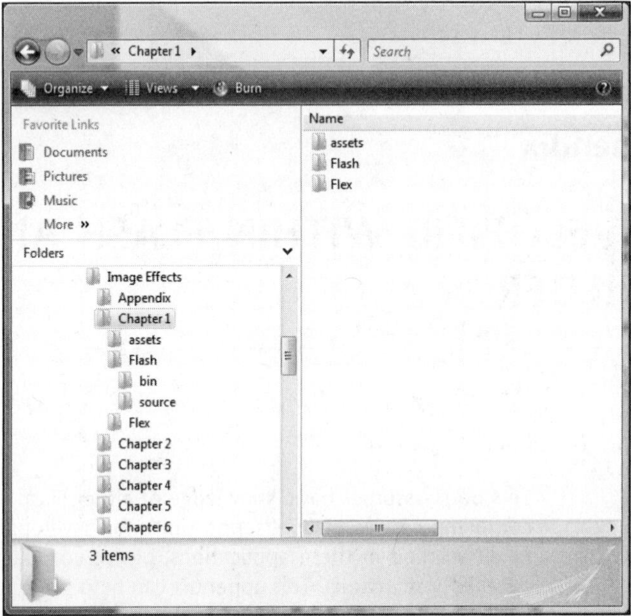

Figure A-1. The directory structure for a single chapter's files shown in Windows Explorer

In each chapter, you should find a `Flash`, `Flex`, and `assets` directory, with a few chapters also containing a `source` directory with Pixel Bender `.pbk` files. To use the prepared chapter files in Flash CS4, open the `Flash` directory, and you will find all of the FLAs discussed in the chapter, plus a `bin` and `source` directory, as shown in Figure A-2.

To compile and test any of the chapter files, simply open one of the FLA files and compile (Control ➤ Test Movie). The ActionScript classes used by the FLA will be found in the `Flash/source` directory, and this is configured in the ActionScript Settings dialog. If you go to the Flash tab in the File ➤ Publish Settings dialog and click the Settings button, you should see a Source path tab, as shown in Figure A-3.

Name	Date modified	Type	Size
ShapesMadeEasy.fla	12/23/2008 12:04 AM	Flash Document	61 KB
RenderingTriangles.fla	12/23/2008 1:07 AM	Flash Document	87 KB
PreservingPathData.fla	12/23/2008 12:29 AM	Flash Document	73 KB
FillingShapesWithBitmaps.fla	12/23/2008 12:07 AM	Flash Document	67 KB
DrawTrianglesVerticesTest.fla	12/23/2008 12:55 AM	Flash Document	80 KB
DrawTrianglesUVTTest.fla	12/23/2008 1:07 AM	Flash Document	87 KB
DrawTrianglesIndicesTest.fla	12/23/2008 12:57 AM	Flash Document	80 KB
DrawTrianglesCullingTest.fla	12/23/2008 1:08 AM	Flash Document	82 KB
DrawingStraightLines.fla	12/22/2008 11:33 PM	Flash Document	31 KB
DrawingSolidFills.fla	12/22/2008 11:40 PM	Flash Document	64 KB
DrawingGradientLines.fla	12/23/2008 12:04 AM	Flash Document	64 KB
DrawingGradientFills.fla	12/22/2008 11:54 PM	Flash Document	66 KB
DrawingCurves.fla	12/22/2008 11:37 PM	Flash Document	61 KB
DrawingBitmapStrokes.fla	12/23/2008 12:25 AM	Flash Document	38 KB
CopyingGraphics.fla	12/23/2008 12:15 AM	Flash Document	69 KB
ChangingPointsOnAPath.fla	12/23/2008 12:55 AM	Flash Document	76 KB
source	12/22/2008 11:32 PM	File Folder	
bin	12/20/2008 2:07 AM	File Folder	

Figure A-2.
The Flash directory within a chapter's files, containing all FLA files and source and bin subdirectories

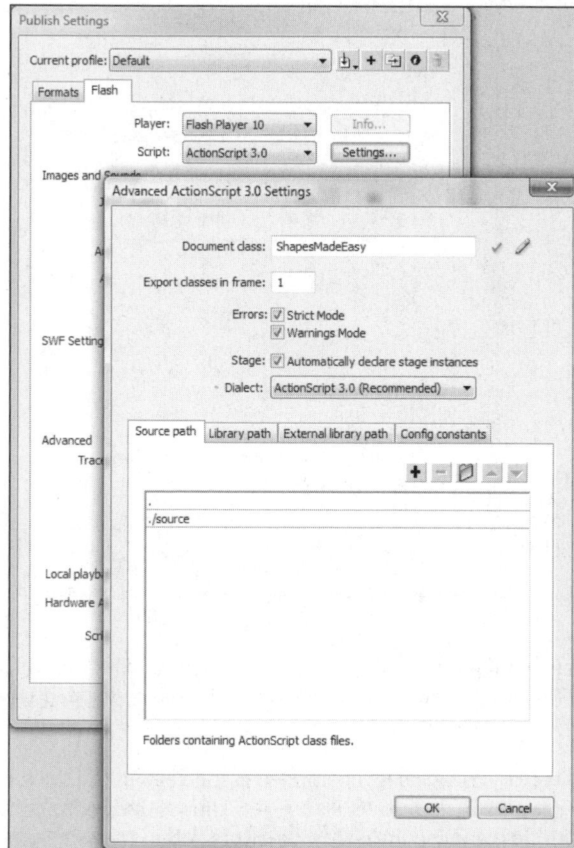

Figure A-3.
The Advanced ActionScript 3.0 Settings dialog that allows you to configure the source path

The Flash document files in the chapter files have all been configured to look for source files in a source directory located in the same directory as the FLA and is where all of the ActionScript files for the chapters are located.

For Chapters 7–12 that use SWC libraries, these are configured in the same Settings dialog but under the Library path tab, as shown in Figure A-4.

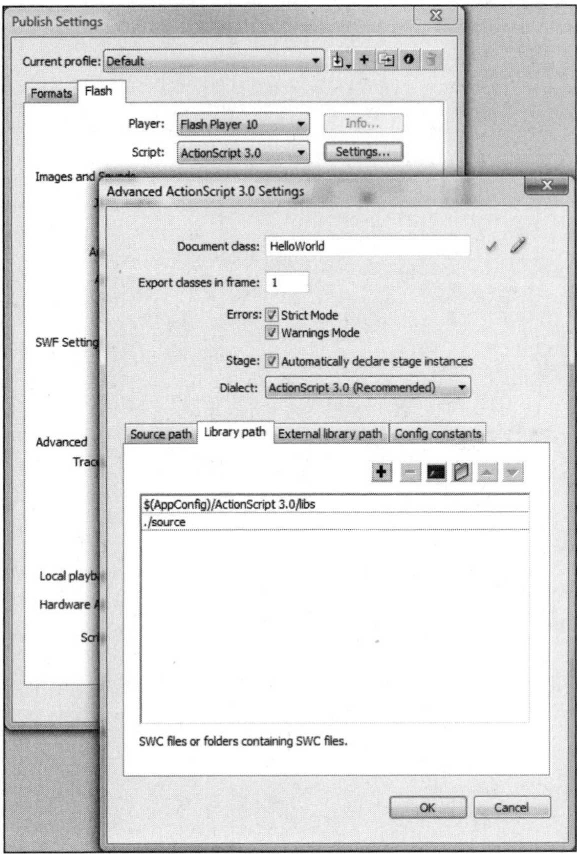

Figure A-4.
The Library path settings that can be used to specify paths to SWCs

As you can see, the path has been configured here as well to be a source directory within the same directory as the FLA. This source directory is where the SWCs are located when used by the chapters.

When a SWF is compiled, the directory to which it is compiled is specified in the same File ➤ Publish Settings dialog under the Formats tab. As Figure A-5 shows, the SWFs for the chapter files are all configured to be compiled into a bin directory within the same directory as the FLA. In this bin directory, you will find all of the SWFs for the chapter examples.

Figure A-5.
The SWF is specified to be output to a bin subdirectory.

All of the assets loaded at runtime are located in the same directory for both the Flex and Flash projects. This `assets` directory, located at the top level in the same directory as the `Flash` and `Flex` directories, contains the images and Pixel Bender bytecode loaded by the SWFs at runtime. In the classes that include a path to the assets, the path will always be defined relative to the SWF. For instance, one such path looks like this:

```
"../../assets/footprints.jpg"
```

The `footprints.jpg` is being looked for two directories up from the SWF (located in `Flash/bin`) in the `assets` directory. If you extract the files in the same directory structure, you should not need to update these paths. However, if you alter the directory structure then you may need to update the paths accordingly.

Creating a Flash project from scratch

Please first read the preceding section, so you may better understand the directory structure of the chapter files. If you are working through the examples in the chapters and wish to create all of the files from scratch, you will need to follow these general steps to use the

ActionScript classes as they are. If you do not wish to keep the same directory structure, be sure that you update any paths to loaded assets accordingly.

1. Create a new directory that you will use for an entire chapter or for the entire book.
2. Within this directory, copy the `assets` folder from the chapter files. This will hold all of the images and Pixel Bender shaders you will need to load at runtime.
3. In the same directory as the `assets` folder, create a `Flash` directory. All of your Flash files will be stored here.
4. Within the `Flash` directory, create a `bin` and a `source` directory. The `bin` directory will hold all of your SWFs. The `source` directory will hold all of your ActionScript and any SWCs you will need to reference. At this point, your directory structure should look like Figure A-6.

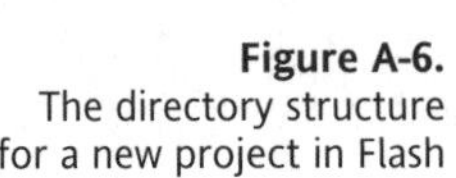

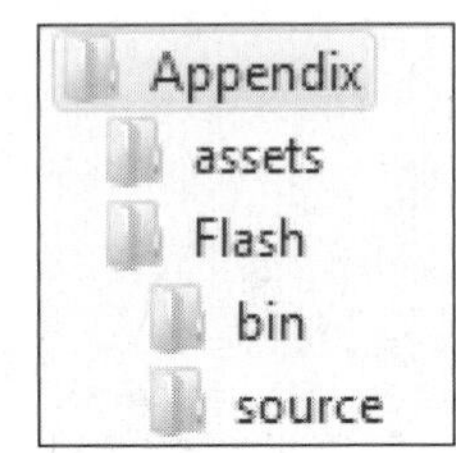

Figure A-6. The directory structure for a new project in Flash

Figure A-7. The bin subdirectory specified for the SWF output

5. We will create a HelloWorld application to test this directory structure. In Flash, create a new ActionScript file, and save it as `HelloWorld.as` into your `Flash/source` directory. Type the following code:

```
package {

  import flash.display.Sprite;

  public class HelloWorld extends Sprite {

    public function HelloWorld() {
      trace("Hello, World!");
    }

  }

}
```

6. Now, create a new ActionScript 3.0 FLA saved into the `Flash` directory as `HelloWorld.fla`. In the File ➤ Publish Settings dialog, go to the Formats tab, and enter `bin/HelloWorld.swf` into the Flash File input, as shown in Figure A-7. (Note that I have also deselected the HTML setting, which is not mandatory. You can leave this selected if you wish for Flash to create the HTML file for you.)

7. Now, we need to tell Flash where it can find the ActionScript source file. In the same Publish Settings dialog, go to the Flash tab, and click the Settings button next to the Script field. In the Advanced ActionScript 3.0 Settings dialog that pops up, type **HelloWorld** as the Document class, and add an additional source path at the bottom of the dialog by clicking the plus button. This new path should be `./source`, which tells Flash that ActionScript files can be found in a `source` subdirectory in the same directory as the FLA itself. The result is shown in Figure A-8.

8. Although not needed for this example, there will be some examples in this book that require classes found in an external SWC. You can let Flash know where to find such a SWC in the same Advanced ActionScript 3.0 Settings dialog. On the Library path tab at the bottom of the dialog, you can specify the path to a SWC. In Figure A-9, I have added `./source` as the relative path to where SWCs may be found. If I place a SWC in this directory now, Flash can compile classes found in the SWC into my compiled SWF.

9. Click OK to exit the dialog, and test your movie using Control ➤ Test Movie. You should see the trace statement "Hello, World!" appear in your Output panel.

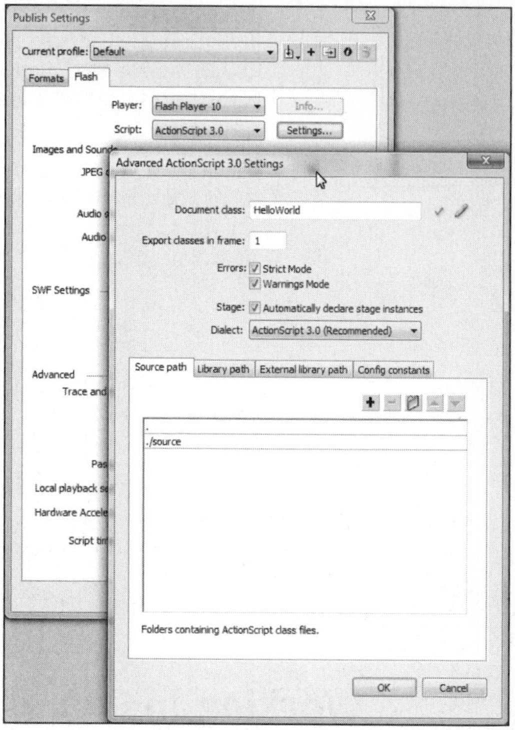

Figure A-8. The source ActionScript path specified for the FLA

Using the Flex compiler within Flash

If you are using the Flash IDE but want to take advantage of some of the nifty features of the Flex compiler, like using `Embed` metatags to embed image assets or Pixel Bender bytecode, you can set up your Flash environment to use the Flex compiler when generating SWFs. This is not necessary for working with files in this book but is a great new feature to leverage in Flash CS4.

1. Download the 3.2 (or later) milestone build from Adobe's Open Source page found at `http://opensource.adobe.com/wiki/display/flexsdk/Download+Flex+3`. Download the Adobe Flex SDK, not the Open Source Flex SDK.

2. Extract the downloaded SDK into a directory of your choice. If you have Flex Builder installed, you should place it in your `Flex Builder 3/sdks` directory.

3. If you wish to use the Flex compiler for a certain Flash document, you will need to add a path to the `flex.swc` in your

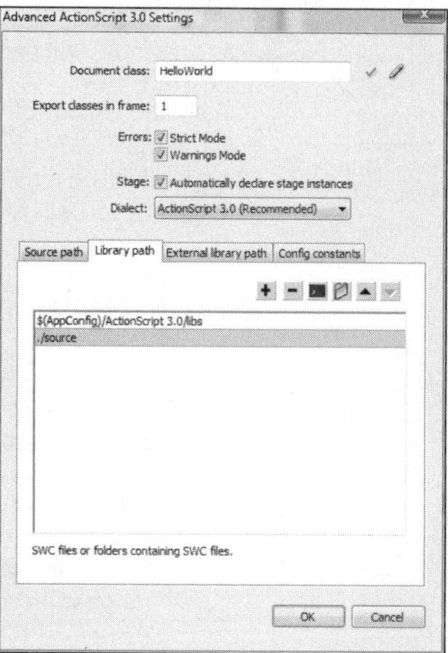

Figure A-9. The Library path for additional SWCs specified for the FLA

Library Path tab of your Advanced ActionScript 3.0 Settings dialog, as shown in step 8 in the previous section. You can do this manually by opening the dialog and using the Browse to SWC file to add the SWC (it can be found in the frameworks/libs directory of the SDK you extracted), or you can let Flash do this for you.

How does that work? If you are compiling ActionScript that contains Flex-specific metatags (like the Embed metatag), Flash will offer the dialog shown in Figure A-10 when you compile, informing you that the Flex compiler needs to be used and allowing you to browse to the SDK. To have Flash update the path to the flex.swc for you, all you need is to have it browse to the SDK using the dialog then click OK.

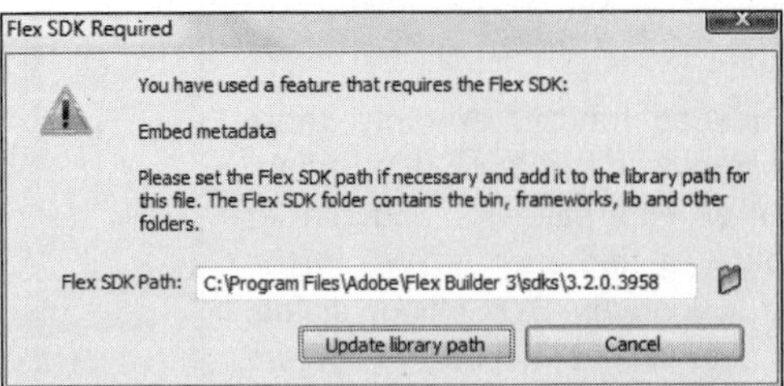

Figure A-10. The dialog in Flash CS4 allowing you to set a path to the Flex SDK in order to use its compiler

Working in Flex Builder 3

If you are using Flex Builder 3 as a development environment, be sure that you are using ActionScript projects, not Flex projects, for this book. None of the examples in this book use the Flex framework. Although you can easily adapt the examples to do so, the classes as presented will need to be set up as part of an ActionScript, not a Flex, project.

In addition, many of the examples used in this book take advantage of new features in Flash Player 10. The ActionScript classes through which these new features can be explored are not available in the Flex SDK that ships with Flex Builder 3. To compile these examples in Flex Builder 3, you will have to configure the IDE with the newer SDK that includes these classes.

Compiling for Flash Player 10

At the time of this writing, compiling a SWF in Flex Builder 3 to use the new Flash Player 10 features requires downloading a newer SDK than the one that ships with the IDE and configuring your project to use the newer SDK. The following steps walk you through this process. You can also find more information at http://opensource.adobe.com/wiki/display/flexsdk/Targeting+Flash+Player+10.

1. Download the 3.2 (or later) milestone build from Adobe's Open Source page found at http://opensource.adobe.com/wiki/display/flexsdk/Download+Flex+3. Download the Adobe Flex SDK, not the Open Source Flex SDK.
2. Extract the downloaded SDK, and place it in your Flex Builder 3/sdks directory, as shown in Figure A-11.

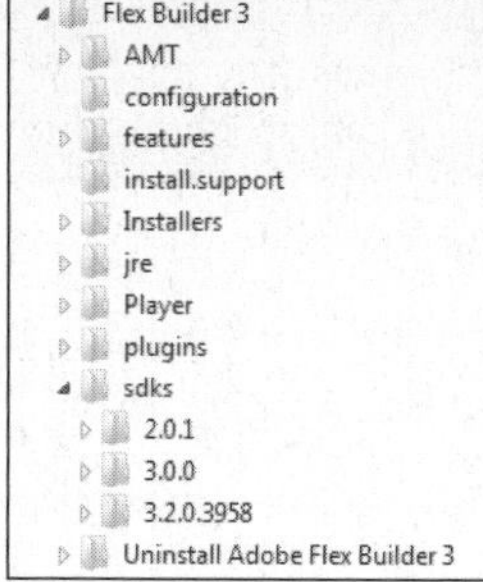

Figure A-11. The Flex Builder 3 directory structure with the additional SDK added

3. Open Flex Builder, and select Window ➤ Preferences. In the dialog that opens, go to the Flex ➤ Installed Flex SDKs screen. Click Add, and give the new SDK the name of Flex 3.2 (or whatever version you downloaded), navigating to the directory where you extracted the SDK. The result of this is shown in Figure A-12. If you want to use this SDK by default, select its check box in the list. Click OK to exit this dialog.

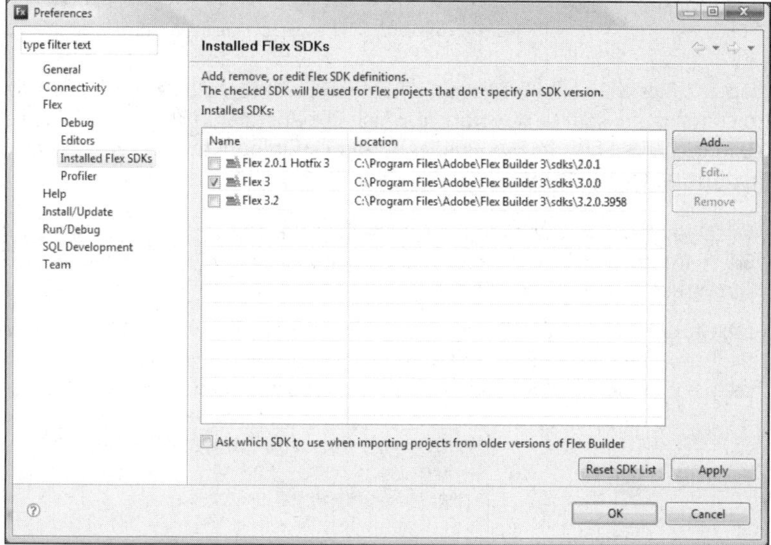

Figure A-12. The new SDK configured in Flex Builder

You are now configured for the new SDK that can be compiled to use the new Flash Player 10 features. When a new project is created you will need to specify the SDK you wish to use as well as the player version. We will cover that in the next sections.

Working with chapter files in Flex Builder

If you download this book's chapter files and extract each from its zipped file, you will find the directory structure consistent from chapter to chapter, as shown in Figure A-13.

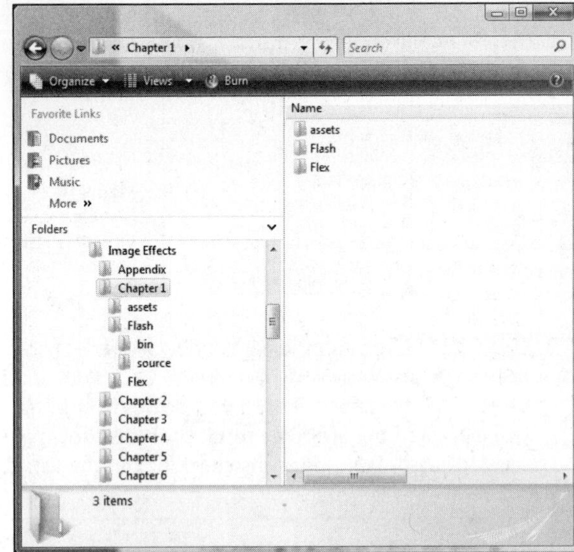

Figure A-13.
The directory structure for a single chapter's files shown in Windows Explorer

Each chapter's files will contain a `Flash`, a `Flex`, and an `assets` directory, with a few chapters also containing a `source` directory in which Pixel Bender `.pbk` files are stored. To use the prepared chapter files in Flex Builder 3, you can import the project files as they are with little fuss, as the next steps demonstrate.

1. Once you have downloaded the source for a chapter, open Flex Builder, and select File ➤ Import ➤ Other. In the dialog that appears, select General ➤ Existing Projects into Workspace, and click Next.
2. Next to the Select root directory input field, click the Browse button, and navigate to the `Flex` directory within the chapter files you downloaded. Click OK, and you should see a project selected for you in the Projects list, as shown in Figure A-14. Click Finish.

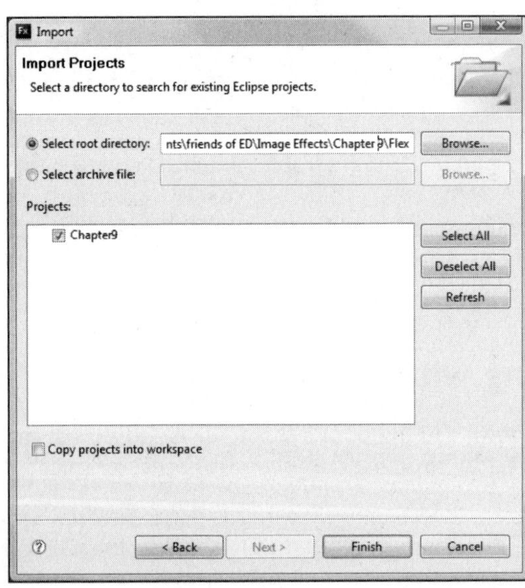

Figure A-14.
The Import dialog in Flex Builder that allows you to import an existing project into your workspace

3. At this point, the project should appear in your Flex Navigator pane. All of the main document classes that are used for examples in a chapter are found at the root of the project. You can test any of these examples by simply opening the file and running or debugging the application.

By default, all of the SWFs will be compiled into the `bin-debug` directory within the project. If a chapter uses additional SWC libraries, these will be found in the `source` directory within the project. You can see where this is configured by opening Project ➤ Properties and looking at the Library path tab on the ActionScript Build Path screen, as shown in Figure A-15. Here, `source` is indicated as a directory in which SWCs may be found.

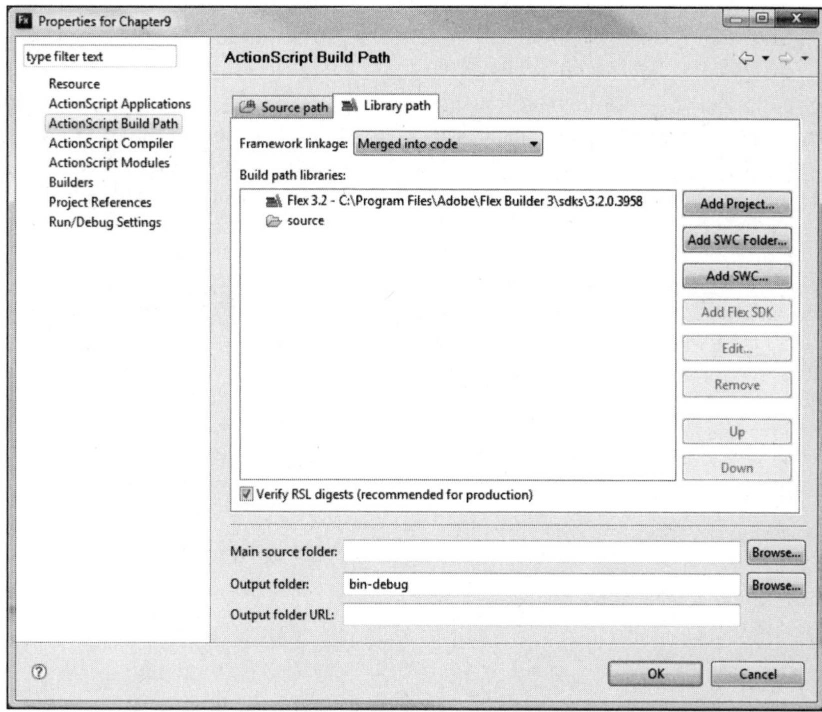

Figure A-15. A Library path to additional SWCs is specified in the Properties dialog

All of the assets loaded at runtime can be found in the same directory that is used for both the Flex and Flash projects. This `assets` directory is located at the top level in the same directory as the `Flash` and `Flex` directories, and it contains the images and Pixel Bender bytecode loaded at runtime by the SWFs. There are many classes in the chapter files that include a path to assets, and the paths will always be defined relative to the SWF. For instance, a path in one class looks like this:

```
"../../assets/footprints.jpg"
```

This `footprints.jpg` file will be looked for in the `assets` directory two directories up from the SWF (located in `Flex/bin-debug`). You should not need to update these paths if you extract the chapter files in the same directory structure. However, if you alter the directory structure, you may need to update the paths to ensure the assets can be found.

Creating a Flex Builder project from scratch

It is important that you read the preceding section so you may better understand the directory structure of the chapter files before building a project from scratch. If you would like to create project files from scratch as you work through the examples in this book's chapters, you will need to follow these general steps to use the ActionScript classes without modification. If you do not wish to keep the same directory structure, be sure that you update any paths referenced in the classes so that the loaded assets may be found.

We will step through a HelloWorld example to demonstrate how an ActionScript project can be set up to work similarly to the projects included for this book.

1. Open Flex Builder 3, and select File ➤ New ➤ ActionScript Project. Be sure to use an ActionScript project, not a Flex project.
2. In the New ActionScript Project dialog, give the project a name, and specify its directory. Under the Flex SDK version, select Use specific SDK, and in the drop-down list, select the latest SDK, as covered earlier in the "Compiling for Flash Player 10" section. (If you have already set the default SDK to be the latest SDK that you downloaded, you can use the Use default SDK radio button.) The result is shown in Figure A-16. Click Finish.

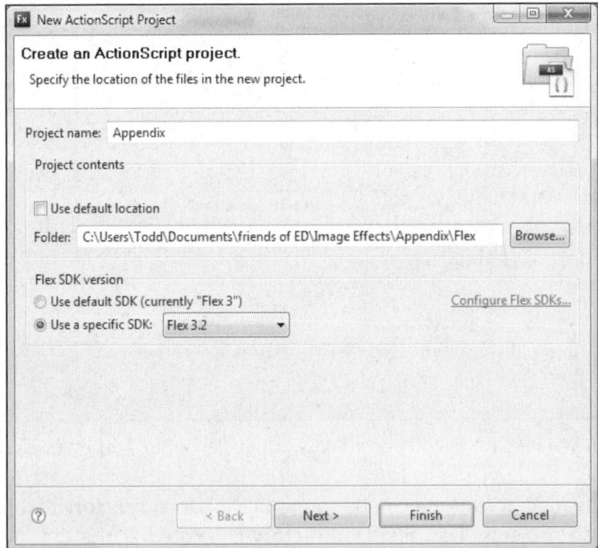

Figure A-16. A new ActionScript project is created using the newly configured SDK

3. Although this example will not use additional SWCs, we'll add a new directory here to mimic how the chapter files are created. In the Flex Navigator tree, select the project directory, and then select File ➤ New ➤ Folder. In the dialog that opens, keep the project root selected, and type **source** as the Folder name, as shown in Figure A-17. Click Finish.

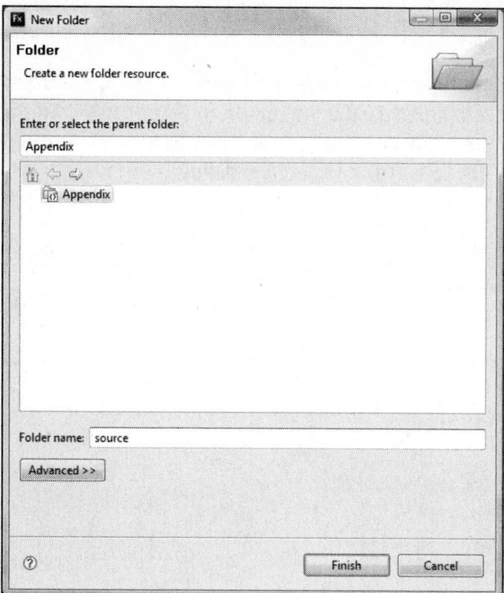

Figure A-17.
A new source folder is added to the project.

4. We will now configure the project so the compiler looks in this folder for additional SWCs. Select Project ➤ Properties, and on the Library path tab in the ActionScript Build Path screen, click Add SWC Folder, and type **source** into the pop-up that appears. Click OK, and the result should look something like Figure A-18.

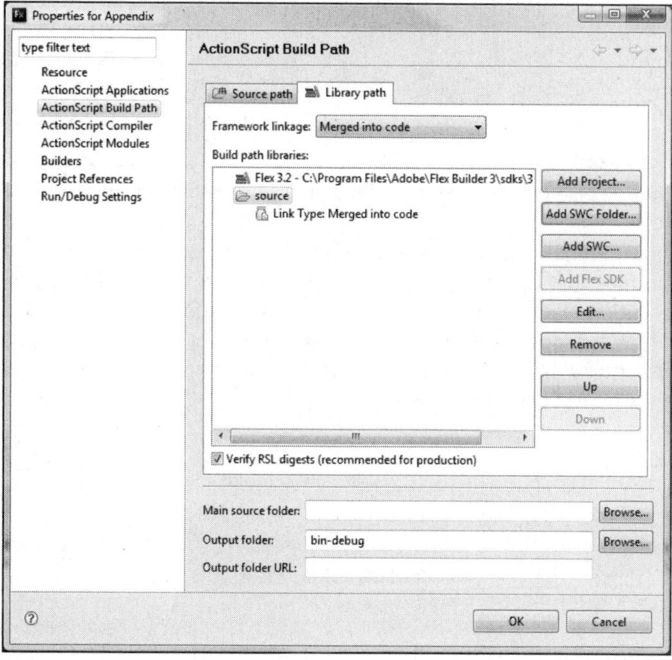

Figure A-18. A new library path is added to point to a directory where SWCs may be placed.

Now, if you put a SWC into this source directory, the compiler will be able to use classes contained in the SWC.

5. With the Properties dialog still open, go to the ActionScript Compiler screen. Update the required Flash Player version to 10.0.0, as shown in Figure A-19. This is necessary if you use any of the new features available in Flash Player 10, as many of this book's examples do. Click OK to exit the Properties dialog.

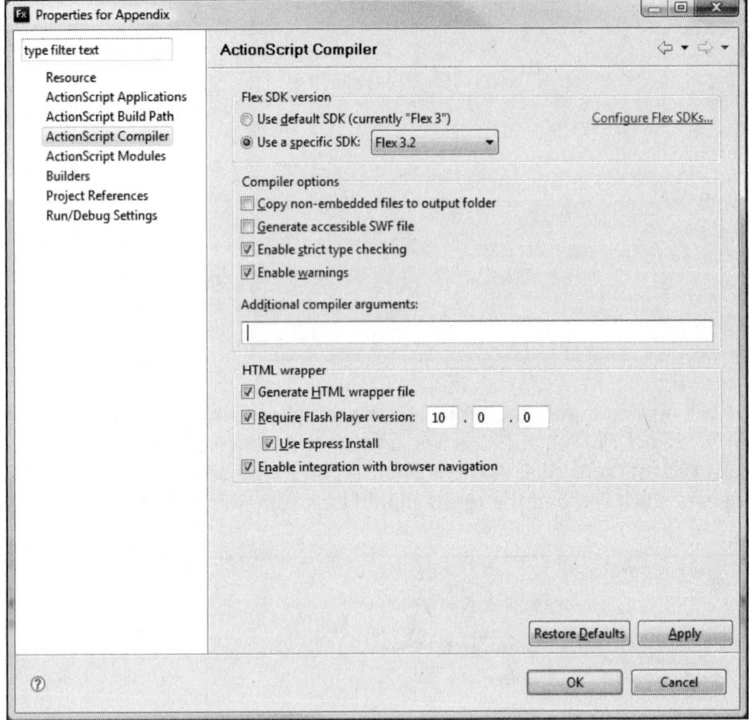

Figure A-19. The project is set to compile for and require Flash Player 10.

6. In this book's chapter files, a single ActionScript project contains many different application files that can be used as the main document class. Although a default main application class was created when we created this project, we will create a new class now for the HelloWorld example. With the root project directory selected in the Flex Navigator tree, select File ➤ New ➤ ActionScript Class. Name it **HelloWorld** and have it extend **Sprite**, as shown in Figure A-20.

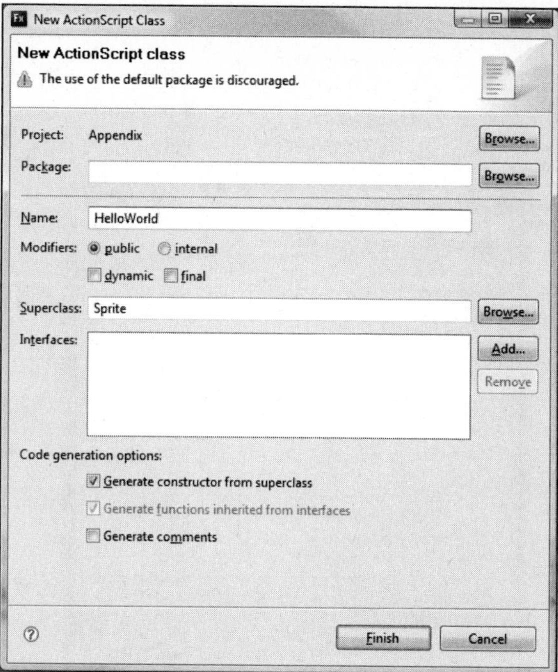

Figure A-20. A new ActionScript class is created to serve as a main application class.

7. Click Finish to create the class, and then enter the following code:

```
package {

  import flash.display.Sprite;

  public class HelloWorld extends Sprite {

    public function HelloWorld() {
      trace("Hello, World!");
    }

  }

}
```

8. Return to Project ➤ Properties, and go to the ActionScript Applications screen. Click the Add button, and select the HelloWorld class, as shown in Figure A-21. Click OK.

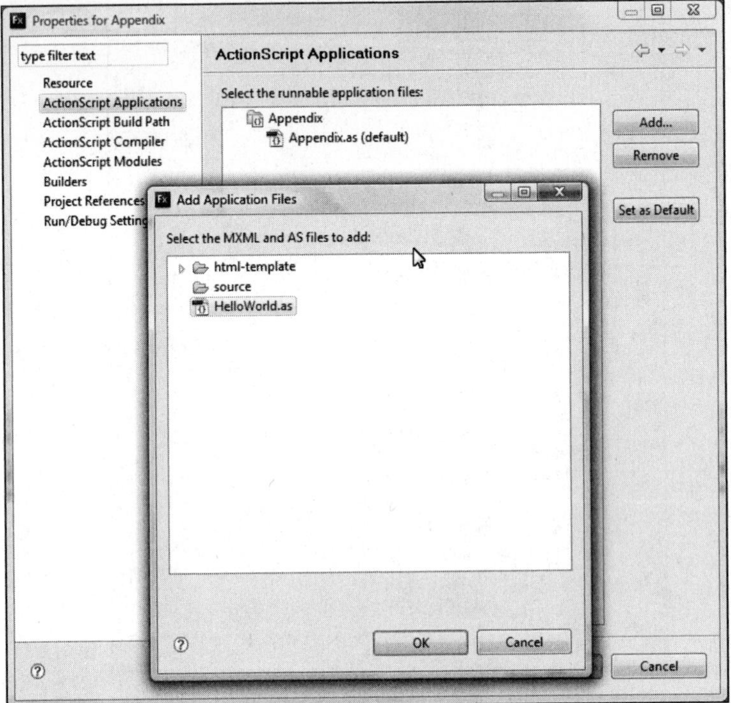

Figure A-21. The HelloWorld class is added as an application in the project.

9. With the HelloWorld application class added, you can run or debug the SWF and see the output in the Console. To run different applications within a project containing multiple applications, you simply have to select the document class to run.

INDEX

Numbers and Symbols

A

B

D

T

XYZ